Using LetterPerfect®

Robert M. Beck

que®
CORPORATION
LEADING COMPUTER KNOWLEDGE

Using LetterPerfect®

Copyright © 1991 by Que® Corporation.

Library of Congress Catalog No.: 90-63258

ISBN: 0-88022-667-6

94 93 92 91   8 7 6 5 4 3 2 1

Interpretation of the printing code: the rightmost double-digit number is the year of the book's printing; the rightmost single-digit number, the number of the book's printing. For example, a printing code of 91-1 shows that the first printing of the book occurred in 1991.

Using LetterPerfect is based on LetterPerfect 1.0.

Publisher

Lloyd J. Short

Acquisitions Editor

Terrie Lynn Solomon

Product Development Manager

Charles O. Stewart III

Managing Editor

Mary Bednarek

Editors

Lisa Hunt Tally
Diane L. Steele
C. Beth Burch
Caroline Gryta
Frances R. Huber

Technical Editor

Jim Wright

Indexer

Jeanne Clark

Production

Beth Baker
Jeff Baker
Claudia Bell
Martin Coleman
Sandy Grieshop
Betty Kish
Bob LaRoche
Sarah Leatherman

Kim Leslie
Howard Peirce
Cindy L. Phipps
Tad Ringo
Suzanne Tully
Johnna VanHoose
Mary Beth Wakefield
Lisa A. Wilson

Composed in ITC Garamond and Macmillan
by Que Corporation.

Robert M. Beck

Robert M. Beck is a former judge, now practicing law in Oklahoma City; he is also a former newspaper editor and reporter. Currently a computer consultant for small-to-medium-sized law offices, Mr. Beck's experience with LetterPerfect 1.0 began during beta testing. He was a technical editor and contributing author for Que's *Using WordPerfect 5.1*, Special Edition, and a contributing author for Que's *WordPerfect 5.1 Tips, Tricks, and Traps*, 3rd Edition. He is a regular participant on the WordPerfect Support Group's A and B forums under CIS identification number 72707,1765.

A C K N O W L E D G M E N T S ▼

One of the problems with acknowledging the people who make a book like this possible is that the total list would be longer than the longest chapter in it. However, there are certain key people without whose help this book never would have been printed. I am tremendously indebted to the following persons:

David Ewing, former Publishing Director of Que, now President of New Riders Publishing, without whose vision and support this book would never have been started.

Charles O. Stewart III, Product Development Manager, and Terrie L. Solomon, Acquisitions Editor, whose friendship, good humor, patience, guidance, and understanding kept me on track, and made the rough times bearable and the good times more enjoyable.

Production Editor Lisa Hunt Tally, whose dedication, eye for detail, and ear for English greatly enhanced the manuscript.

Stacey Beheler for her patience and help when David, Chuck, and Terrie were not available.

James L. Wright, formerly of the LetterPerfect beta testing team, whose technical editing of the manuscript and, most important, encouragement is as much responsible for the final product as my contribution. Thanks, Jim.

Don LaVange, Durk Merrell, Julie Denver, Alisa Nord, Jim Wright, Lisa Cram, Brad Blackham, Greg Hall, Jeff Hall, and all the other present and past members of the WordPerfect Corporation beta testing teams with whom it has been my good fortune to be associated since 1987.

Tony Rairden, who shares my interest and enthusiasm for WordPerfect programs, and whose advice and knowledge are always invaluable.

Joan M. Thompson, my secretary, guinea pig, and sounding board, whose insight and suggestions made this book better.

Robert and Sue Beck, my parents, who instilled in me the curiosity and thirst for knowledge that naturally led me to where I am today.

And last, but certainly not least, to Sandy, my wife, whose understanding, encouragement, and support in all things made it possible for me to begin and finish this book.

RMB

T R A D E M A R K
A C K N O W L E D G M E N T S

Que Corporation has made every attempt to supply trademark information about company names, products, and services mentioned in this book. Trademarks indicated below were derived from various sources. Que Corporation cannot attest to the accuracy of this information.

AT&T is a registered trademark of American Telephone and Telegraph Corporation.

COMPAQ is a registered trademark of COMPAQ Computer Corporation.

CompuServe Information Service is a registered trademark of CompuServe Incorporated and H&R Block, Inc.

DESQView is a trademark of Quarterdeck Software.

Genius is a registered trademark of KYE International Corporation.

Hercules is a registered trademark of Hercules Computer Technology. Hercules Graphics Card, Hercules Graphics Card Plus, Hercules InColor Card, and Hercules Ram Font are trademarks of Hercules Computer Technology.

Hewlett-Packard LaserJet Series II is a trademark of Hewlett-Packard Co.

IBM PC, IBM PC AT, IBM 8514/A, PS/2, and TopView are registered trademarks of International Business Machines Corporation. IBM PC XT is a trademark of International Business Machines Corporation.

LetterPerfect, WordPerfect, WordPerfect Office, and WordPerfect Library are registered trademarks of WordPerfect Corporation.

Microsoft is a registered trademark of Microsoft Corporation.

PostScript is a registered trademark of Adobe Systems Incorporated.

Wordstar and MultiMate are registered trademarks of MicroPro International Corporation.

CONTENTS AT A GLANCE

TABLE OF CONTENTS ▼

6 Formatting and Enhancing Text

II   Using LetterPerfect's Supplemental Features

9   Managing and Protecting Files and Directories

12   Working with the Character Feature and LRS File

III   Using LetterPerfect's Advanced Features

13   Creating and Using Macros

Introduction

L etterPerfect 1.0 has all the basic features expected of a word processing software program plus many advanced features otherwise found only in the most expensive word processing packages. The program makes editing a long, complex document as easy as writing a short memo.

LetterPerfect's impressive features include the following:

- An editing screen with a single menu bar across the top

- Complete control, for the user, of the size and appearance of type fonts for document enhancement

- Context-sensitive help that provides easy access to the appropriate help menus from anywhere in the program

- Document formatting with automatic appearance of headers and footers on selected pages

- Document annotation with automatically numbered endnotes that appear at the end of the document

- Automatic numbering of each page in the document

- An outline feature that can also automatically number paragraphs

- Pull-down menus accessible through either the keyboard or a mouse

- Fast-key access to many frequently used functions

- Mouse support for text highlighting and selecting from the regular and pull-down menus

- A spell-checking feature with a standard dictionary that contains more than 80,000 words

- A thesaurus feature with suggested alternative words provided while the document is being written or edited

- A merge feature with meaningful word codes used to automatically create documents from different source files

- A macro feature provided by the Shell 3.01 program for the 07/24/90 version of LetterPerfect for automating simple or complex editing tasks

- A built-in macro feature in the 11/01/90 version of LetterPerfect, plus a macro feature provided by the Shell 3.01 program, each of which can automate simple or complex editing tasks

- Support for 27 language modules used in foreign-language editing and for automatic hyphenation

- A graphics feature that easily integrates graphics images into a document with wrap-around text

- Complete document compatibility with WordPerfect 4.2, WordPerfect 5.0, and WordPerfect 5.1

- An easy-to-use file management feature

- Enhanced printer definitions that, depending on the capability of the printer, print more than a thousand characters as a graphic image— even when the character is not usually available with the printer

- Efficient use of conventional and expanded random-access memory (RAM)

- Toll-free customer support

Using LetterPerfect offers basic instructions on the set-up and use of the LetterPerfect program. In addition, *Using LetterPerfect* is designed to be a primary reference tool that supplements the documentation shipped with the software package by providing the following:

- Insights on the program's basic features

- Detailed information on the program's advanced features

- Shortcuts to using the program's features

- Warnings about inefficient editing techniques and potential loss of data or documents

Who Should Use This Book?

Using LetterPerfect is written and organized to meet the needs of a wide range of readers, from those who are new to word processing to experienced WordPerfect users. You can quickly master the basics of LetterPerfect 1.0 by using this book's clear instructions, complete coverage of program features, mix of step-by-step procedures with reference information, and examples of real-world applications.

How To Use This Book

Using LetterPerfect is designed for you to use as a complement to the manual and workbook that come with the software package. If you are a beginner, you will find the step-by-step information in this book helpful. As an experienced user of WordPerfect 4.2, WordPerfect 5.0, or WordPerfect 5.1 you will appreciate the comprehensive coverage and expert advice in this book. Once you become proficient with the program, you can use this book as a desktop reference.

Each chapter in this book focuses on a particular operation or set of operations with LetterPerfect 1.0. Overall, the book is applications-oriented, from the steps typical to the creation of any document (such as entering text, spell-checking, and printing) to more specialized topics (such as macros, styles, columns, tables, equations, special characters, and integration of text with graphics).

The special information boxes in the body of the text include Tips, Notes, Cautions, and Reminders. The Tips and Notes either highlight information often overlooked in the documentation or help you use LetterPerfect 1.0 more efficiently. The Cautions alert you to potential loss of data or harm to your system. The Reminders draw your attention to basic program operations.

Look for the Reminder notes in the margin that emphasize key concepts and procedures. As you become more comfortable with LetterPerfect, you can use the Cues in the margin for hints on how to use the program more efficiently.

How This Book Is Organized

Using LetterPerfect is organized to follow the natural flow of learning and using LetterPerfect. Your approach to using this book will depend on your level of experience in using WordPerfect and on how you intend to use the program.

Using LetterPerfect is divided into three parts as follows:

  I: Using LetterPerfect's Basic Features
 II: Using LetterPerfect's Supplemental Features
III: Using LetterPerfect's Advanced Features

Part I, including Chapters 1-8, describes the steps for installing, setting up, and preparing to use LetterPerfect: starting the program, running the tutorial, and completing the cycle of document preparation—planning, creating, blocking, editing, formatting, and printing.

Part II, including Chapters 9-12, explains the more advanced features of the program: file management, outlining, endnotes, spell-checking, thesaurus, creating and printing special characters, and the Language Resource file.

Part III, including Chapters 13-15, covers LetterPerfect's most advanced features: macros, simple merges and complex merge operations, and integration and placement of text and graphics images.

Following is a chapter-by-chapter breakdown of the book's contents:

Chapter 1, "Installing and Setting Up LetterPerfect and Shell," explains the installation and start-up of LetterPerfect 1.0 and Office Shell 3.01. Chapter 1 describes each step of the Installation program and the options for starting the LetterPerfect and Office Shell programs.

Chapter 2, "Preparing To Use LetterPerfect," introduces you to LetterPerfect 1.0. This chapter covers hardware and memory requirements, and shows you how to start the program on hard and floppy disk systems, run the tutorial, and exit the program. You learn about LetterPerfect's editing screen, function-key commands, pull-down menus, mouse support, cursor movement, context-sensitive help, and LetterPerfect's hidden formatting codes.

Chapter 3, "Creating a Document," shows you how to start LetterPerfect, enter text, move the cursor through a document with either the keyboard or the mouse, use the keyboard or the mouse to give commands, select menu options, cancel operations, use both document windows, print the document, and name and save a file. The chapter ends with advice on how to use word processing to improve your effectiveness as a writer.

Chapter 4, "Editing a Document," takes the composing process to the next step—revising and editing a document. After you learn the basics of retrieving a file saved to disk, you examine the methods for deleting text. This chapter also covers how to enter simple text enhancements (bold and underline), how to use search and replace as an editing tool, and how to edit hidden codes in LetterPerfect.

Chapter 5, "Working with Blocks," teaches you how to use Block to select (highlight) text that you then can move, copy, delete, append, save, or print. You learn to enhance a block of characters with the bold, underline, or italic features; then you learn to enlarge or reduce the size of characters in a block.

Chapter 6, "Formatting and Enhancing Text," demonstrates how to alter the appearance of text on the page by changing margins, indenting text, altering line spacing, using various types of tabs, and centering, justifying, and hyphenating text. This chapter also explains how to change the base font to a larger size and how to choose a particular font appearance, such as italic or superscript.

Chapter 7, "Designing Document Pages," expands the elements of formatting from the individual page to the overall document. You learn to create headers and footers, number pages, control page breaks, define and use printer forms, and establish custom settings for all your documents.

Chapter 8, "Printing and Print Options," shows you how to install a printer definition and use the options for printing a document with LetterPerfect.

Chapter 9, "Managing and Protecting Files and Directories," explains the principles of file and hard disk management. You practice using List Files to retrieve, delete, move, rename, look at, copy, and search for text strings within a document file on disk. You learn how to protect your documents using LetterPerfect's Password feature.

Chapter 10, "Working with the Outline and Endnote Features," covers the steps necessary to create outlines and automatic paragraph numbers, and explains how to incorporate endnotes into documents. This chapter presents the steps for creating, looking at, previewing, adding, deleting, moving, customizing, and editing endnotes.

Chapter 11, "Using the Speller and Thesaurus," teaches you to use the Speller and Thesaurus. You learn how to use the Speller to create custom supplemental dictionaries, if you need them, and to check the spelling in your documents. You learn to use the Thesaurus to give your writing freshness and precision.

Chapter 12, "Working with the Character Feature and LRS File," examines how to access and print the special character sets available with LetterPerfect 1.0. This chapter also discusses how to use the optional WordPerfect Language Modules with multilingual documents in LetterPerfect. You learn how to change some of the program default settings by editing the Language Resource (LRS) File.

Chapter 13, "Creating and Using Macros," provides a comprehensive introduction to the program's internal macro feature (11/01/90 version) and the macro feature supplied by Shell 3.01. This chapter teaches you how to plan, create, run, stop, and replace macros. You can copy the macro examples provided in the chapter, and you can use the examples as a basis for your own macros.

Chapter 14, "Assembling Documents with Merge," introduces the Merge feature to users who have little or no experience with Merge. You learn the basics of merge, how to perform a simple merge, how to handle special situations with merge, common uses for merge, and how to use the WordPerfect Programming Language merge commands.

Chapter 15, "Integrating Text and Graphics," explores the mechanics of integrating text and graphics with LetterPerfect 1.0. You learn how to create a box and import a graphics image. You learn to position a box on the page, wrap text accordingly, and edit the borders surrounding the images you import. The chapter also covers the Line Draw feature.

The Appendix, "LetterPerfect for WordPerfect 4.2-5.1 Users," compares LetterPerfect and other WordPerfect Corporation word processing software programs. This discussion includes how LetterPerfect handles documents created with WordPerfect 4.2, 5.0, and 5.1.

A Note on LetterPerfect Interim Releases

WordPerfect Corporation "fine-tunes" its software programs by issuing interim releases every few months. Although the version number remains unchanged, these "maintenance" releases correct problems that have been discovered in the program since the previous release. Occasionally, WordPerfect Corporation adds minor features on an interim release.

This book is based on the 11/01/90 interim release of LetterPerfect 1.0. The 11/01/90 program offers more features and flexibility than the initial 07/24/90 software. You can determine the date of your release by pressing Help (F3) and noting the date at the top right corner of the screen.

When the 11/01/90 interim version was released, WordPerfect Corporation offered users of the 07/24/90 software an upgrade to the 11/01/90 program for a nominal charge of less than $20.00. If you are using the 07/24/90 software, you should consider upgrading to the 11/01/90 program.

If you want to keep your program up-to-date through the interim releases, consider subscribing to the Software Subscription Service offered by WordPerfect Corporation. As a subscriber to this service, for a fixed annual fee you receive every software upgrade automatically. To find out more about this service, call Software Subscriptions at 1-801-222-1400.

At this writing, WordPerfect Corporation automatically sends a free copy of the interim release to any user who reports a software problem prior to the date of the release that corrects the error.

Where To Find More Help

If you cannot find a solution to a particular problem, LetterPerfect's context-sensitive Help (F3) feature may answer your question. In addition, you can turn to this text or to LetterPerfect's manual and workbook for help.

As another resource, WordPerfect Corporation provides telephone support. From within the United States, Puerto Rico, the U.S. Virgin Island, or Canada, call toll-free 1-800-541-5096. This help line is open Monday through Friday, 7 a.m. to 6 p.m. Mountain Standard Time. After-hours support, from 6 p.m. to 7 a.m. Mountain Standard Time, is available at 1-801-222-9010 (not a toll-free number). From other locations, call 1-801-226-7900 (not a toll-free number).

The people who work on the telephone support line are helpful and knowledgeable. If they cannot provide an immediate answer to your question, they will research your problem and promptly contact you with the answer.

One of the best sources of help is the WordPerfect Support Group (WPSG), an independent group not affiliated with WordPerfect Corporation. The group publishes an excellent monthly newsletter, *The WordPerfectionist*. You can subscribe to *The WordPerfectionist* for $36 a year by writing to the following address:

The WordPerfectionist
Newsletter of the WordPerfect Support Group
Lake Technology Park
P.O. Box 130
McHenry, MD 21541

The WordPerfectionist is intended for all levels of users and is filled with helpful hints, clever techniques, solid guidance, and objective reviews of books and software. In addition, you can purchase a monthly disk subscription, a communications program (TAPCIS) that you'll want to have if you join CompuServe and participate in the support group forum, WordPerfect books, and related items from the support group.

Many knowledgeable LetterPerfect and WordPerfect users—including the author—belong to the WordPerfect Support Group (WPSG) and subscribe to the newsletter; many of them participate nightly in the lively dialogue on the WPSG's special interest group on CompuServe. If you join the WPSG, you can download useful files from the WPSGA forum's many data libraries. You usually can get an answer to any LetterPerfect question, no matter how thorny or complex, within a day or two—sometimes within a few hours.

Conventions Used in This Book

The conventions used in this book are established to help you learn to use the program quickly and easily.

For function-key commands, the name of the command is presented first, followed by the keystrokes used to invoke the command. For example, Help (F3) means that you press F3 to invoke Help. For keystrokes separated by hyphens, such as Format (Shift-F8), hold down the first key (Shift in this example) and press the second key (F8 in this example) to invoke the option.

When a series of keys is separated by commas, press and release each key. To move to the top of a document, for example, press and release Home, press and release Home again, and then press the up arrow; this sequence is shown as Home, Home, up arrow. A few commands involve both hyphens and commas. For example, the key sequence for the GoTo feature which returns the cursor to its previous location, is Ctrl-Home, Ctrl-Home. This sequence means hold the Ctrl key and press the Home key, then hold the Ctrl key and press the Home key a second time.

LetterPerfect 1.0 enables you to use both keyboard and mouse to select a menu item: you can press a letter or a menu number, or you can select an item by "clicking" it with the mouse. When you are instructed to use the terms "press," "select," or "choose," you can either press a key or move the mouse pointer to an item and click on it.

In this book, the name of the menu option is presented first followed by the appropriate menu-number in parentheses—for instance, Footnote (1). The letter (the mnemonic) or number you press appears in bold. Pull-down menu options are treated in a similar manner: the Save option on the File pull-down menu. LetterPerfect's hidden codes are also shown in bold: [Tab].

When an instruction tells you to "Access the <option> pull-down menu and select <option>" you can click the right button (or left button on a left-handed mouse) to display the pull-down menu, and then select the desired option. You also can either press Alt (unless this option has been disabled through the Setup feature) or Alt-= to access the pull-down menus. Full instructions for using the pull-down menus and mouse appear in Chapters 2 and 3.

Uppercase letters are used to distinguish file names, DOS (disk operating system) commands, and macro commands such as {ON ERROR}. In most cases, the keys on the keyboard are represented as they appear on your keyboard (for example, G, Enter, Tab, Ctrl, Ins, and Backspace). Special words or phrases defined for the first time, the text you are asked to type, and macro variables appear in italics. On-screen messages appear in `digital`.

The original 07/24/90 version of LetterPerfect 1.0 does not have the built-in macro feature that was added with the 11/01/90 interim release. However, both versions of LetterPerfect can use the Shell program's macro feature; it operates in a similar, but slightly different, manner from the internal LetterPerfect macro feature.

The term "portable" computer includes all types of small microcomputer systems designated as laptop, notebook, and portable computers by the manufacturers. The term "desktop" computer includes microcomputer systems that are either in cabinets which are placed horizontally on a desk or table, or in tower cases that rise vertically from the floor. The term "network" computer system includes any type of portable or desktop computer that is connected to a network linking two or more computer systems together so that they can share files and/or resources, such as a printer.

A Final Note

WordPerfect Corporation updated LetterPerfect 1.0 just before this book went to press. Dated 11/01/90, the interim release includes new options for existing features and a few new features. Because of these changes, the menus on your screen may appear slightly different from those shown in this book.

Many factors control how LetterPerfect displays a document on your screen. Most figures in this book use an 8.5" x 11" page definition. The margins are one inch from all edges. The tab stops are one-half inch apart. The font is a 10-point Courier fixed pitch. If you create documents with other settings, the text placement and status-line information may differ from that shown in the figures.

The generic term mouse includes all devices, such as mouse, tracker ball, and light pen, capable of moving the screen pointer. All instructions in this book assume that you use a mouse with your right hand. If the mouse is set to be operated with your left hand, reverse the button sequences. For example, if an instruction says to click the right mouse button, you click the left button instead.

There are several ways to use the LetterPerfect pull-down menu system. With a mouse and the main pull-down menu bar permanently displayed on the screen, move the pointer to an option. Select the option by clicking the left mouse button. With a mouse and the main pull-down menu bar not displayed, click the right mouse button. LetterPerfect displays the pull-down menu bar. Move the pointer to an option and select it by clicking the left mouse button.

To use the pull-down menu bar from the keyboard, press either the Alt key or the Alt-= key combination. Select an option by pressing its highlighted mnemonic letter. NOTE: The single Alt key may not start the pull-down menu system on some computer systems.

LetterPerfect prevents you from selecting the pull-down menu options that do not work with blocked text. After defining a text block, you cannot select pull-down menu options enclosed in brackets.

With one exception, LetterPerfect cannot access the pull-down menus from within List Files. The mouse does work normally to select menu choices from regular List Files menus. Certain features not on these menus, such as Search, Mark Text, Block, and Text Out, are accessible only from the keyboard when List Files is active.

Robert M. Beck
Oklahoma City, OK

Part I

Using LetterPerfect's Basic Features

Includes

Installing and Setting Up LetterPerfect and Shell

Preparing To Use LetterPerfect

Creating a Document

Editing a Document

Working with Blocks

Formatting and Enhancing Text

Designing Document Pages

Printing and Print Options

1

Installing and Setting Up LetterPerfect and Shell

LetterPerfect 1.0 —the "little brother" of the all-time, best-selling word processing software program, WordPerfect 5.1—is a full-featured, entry-level word processing program. Designed to run on all types of computer systems (portable, desktops, and networks) with or without hard disk drives, LetterPerfect contains approximately 80% of the features available in WordPerfect 5.1, including WordPerfect file compatibility and printer support, font size and appearance control, spell-checking, thesaurus, graphics, macros, merge, outline, endnotes, print preview, and expanded memory support.

The LetterPerfect software package includes all of the program, auxiliary, and basic printer files required to operate the program on any type of computer system. In addition, the package includes the DOS menu shell program, Shell 3.01, from WordPerfect's Office PC and LAN 3.0 software package.

> *Reminder:* WordPerfect Corporation updated LetterPerfect 1.0 just before this book went to press. Dated 11/01/90, the interim release includes new options for existing features, and a few new features. The menus on your screen may, therefore, differ slightly from those shown in this book. Also, depending on the printer-form definition, margins, tab stops, and font you specify, the text placement and status-line information in documents you create may differ from those shown in this book's figures. You can determine the date of your release by pressing Help (F3) and noting the date at the top right corner of the screen.
>
> For more information about using the mouse and accessing the pull-down menus, refer to the Introduction.

Chapter 1 shows you how to install the 11/01/90 version of LetterPerfect 1.0 to run on portable and desktop computer systems. You also learn how to start LetterPerfect from the DOS prompt and the Shell 3.01 menu. Finally, you are shown how to change the program's default settings using the Setup feature.

The 11/01/90 Installation program offers more options and is more automatic than the program used to install the 07/24/90 software. In addition, the 11/01/90 LetterPerfect 1.0 software offers more features and flexibility of use than the 07/24/90 program. At the time of the release, WordPerfect Corporation was offering users of the 07/24/90 software an upgrade to the 11/01/90 program for a nominal charge of less than $20.00. If you are using the 07/24/90 software you should strongly consider upgrading to the 11/01/90 program.

> *Tip:* When LetterPerfect displays either a Yes/No or a No/Yes menu prompt, the first option is usually the menu's default option. You can press Enter or any other key—except for the opposite Yes or No mnemonic letter, Cancel (F1), Esc, or Exit (F7)—to select the menu's default option. However, the alternative methods for selecting the non-default option do not always work with other types of menus. To develop consistent menu-using habits, you can always press Enter to select the default option, and always select the non-default option by pressing its mnemonic letter.

Meeting LetterPerfect's Hardware Requirements

LetterPerfect runs on the portable and desktop computer systems that are compatible with the IBM PC, XT, AT, and PS/2 computers containing 8086, 80286, 80386, or 80486 microprocessing chips. The program requires Microsoft, IBM PC, or compatible DOS version 2.0 or higher, 512K of RAM (random-access memory) with 330K free, and a minimum of one 3 1/2-inch 720K or two 5 1/4-inch 360K floppy disk drives. Although the program supports monochrome video cards and monitors, displaying graphics images requires a system with either a Hercules graphics card and monochrome monitor, or a graphics video-display card and a CGA, EGA, or VGA monitor.

LetterPerfect operates satisfactorily on a computer system with a minimum hardware configuration; like any other software program it runs more efficiently and quickly on computer systems with more advanced hardware configurations.

The LetterPerfect files are compressed on the master program diskettes, called *source disks*. Compressed files cannot be used "as is"—each contains several program files that must be decompressed. You *must* use LetterPerfect 1.0's Installation program to transfer the program, utility, and printer files to the correct *target disk* or *target directory*.

Caution: When you start the 11/01/90 Installation program, it automatically checks for the system's memory configuration to make sure that DOS is using at least 20 files. If the system does not have at least 20 files, the program prompts you to add the statement FILES=20 to the CONFIG.SYS file, after which you must reboot the computer. The Installation program does not install LetterPerfect until after you start the computer with a CONFIG.SYS file that gives the system at least 20 files with which to work.

The 07/24/90 Installation program does not make the memory configuration check before transferring files to the hard disk; however, you probably will not be able to complete the program installation with less than 20 files available to the system.

Regardless of which software package you are using, check the files statement in the CONFIG.SYS file to be sure that the system has at least 20 files available prior to running the Installation program.

Depending on the type of printer you select, a complete installation of all LetterPerfect files, including those for the Shell program, requires approximately 1.8 megabytes of disk space. WordPerfect Corporation also offers two products that include programs which increase the amount of disk space to more than three megabytes:

- The files that are part of an optional WordPerfect Language Module (WLM) include thousands of additional words for the Spell and Thesaurus features and occupy approximately 740K of disk space. LetterPerfect's hyphenation feature requires either the WLM's expanded Spell dictionary or the WordPerfect 5.1 Spell dictionary to function.

- The files included in the optional Supplementary Disk sets—the printer modification program (PTR.EXE and PTR.HLP), the DrawPerfect 1.1 Font File (WP.DRS), and the expanded form file ({LP}SPC.FRM)—occupy more than one megabyte of disk space.

Installing LetterPerfect on a Hard Disk Drive

The instructions in this section are intended for a user running the Installation program from floppy disk drive A and installing the program files to a subdirectory on hard disk drive C. If you are using a system with disk drives that have different drive designations, substitute the appropriate letters for drives A and C.

Follow these steps to install LetterPerfect 1.0 and Shell 3.01 on a hard disk drive:

1. Insert the *Install/Utilities 1* diskette into the floppy disk drive A. If the drive uses 5 1/4-inch diskettes, turn the lever so that it covers the slot into which you insert the floppy diskette.

2. From the DOS C> prompt, type *A:* and press Enter.

3. Type *install* and press Enter. After a few seconds, the Installation program displays its initial information screen as shown in figure 1.1. The boxed text includes the prompt Do you want to Continue? Yes (No).

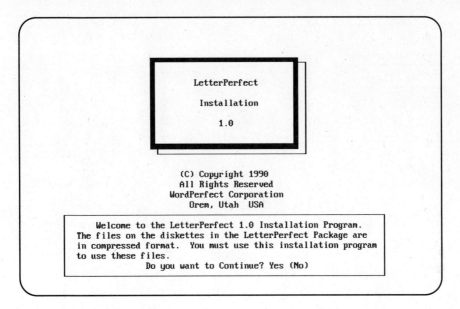

Fig. 1.1. *The initial Installation screen.*

4. Press Enter to select the **Yes** default. The program displays the screen shown in figure 1.2. The boxed text includes the prompt Do you see red, green, and blue colored boxes? Yes (No).

5. If you see three colored boxes below the menu prompt, press Enter to select the default **Yes**. If you do not see the colored boxes, select **No**.

   The program displays the menu for selecting installation to a hard disk as shown in figure 1.3

6. Press Enter to select the **Yes** default. The program displays the main *Installation* menu screen shown in figure 1.4.

Note: The main Installation menu in the 07/24/90 program does not include the **Update** (**4**), and **Copy** (**5**) options, and the Exit option is numbered **6**. If the 07/24/90 software has previously been installed on the hard disk, select the **Update** (**4**) option and respond to the menu prompts.

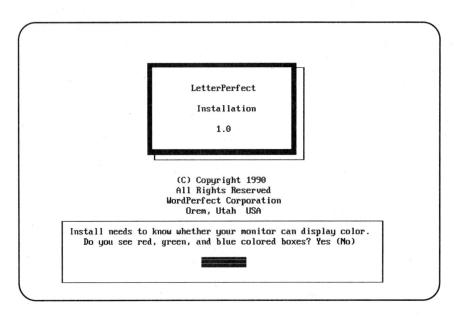

Fig. 1.2. *The color selection screen.*

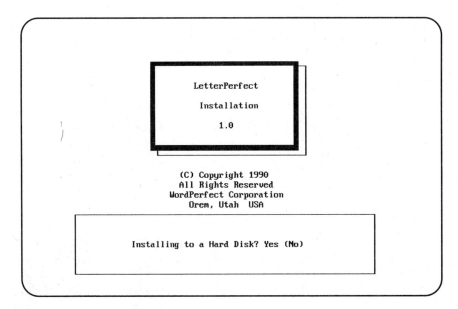

Fig. 1.3. *The hard disk selection screen.*

```
Installation

    1 - Install        First time installation of LetterPerfect.

    2 - Network        First time installation of LetterPerfect on a Network.

    3 - Printer        Install a Printer (.ALL) File.  Use this option to
                       install more printers after you have already installed
                       LetterPerfect.

    4 - Update         Update previously-installed LetterPerfect 1.0 software.

    5 - Copy Disks     Install every file from a master diskette to a
                       location you specify.  (Useful for installing all the
                       Printer (.ALL) Files.)

    6 - Exit           Exit Installation program.




Selection: 1
```

Fig. 1.4. The main Installation menu screen.

7. Select the **Install** (**1**) option if you are installing the program for the first time or if you previously have deleted the program files from your hard disk. Select the **Update** (**4**) option if you are installing the 11/01/90 program on a hard disk that contains the 07/24/90 program. Select the **Copy** (**5**) option if you want all program files automatically placed in the same central directory.

   For the purposes of these instructions, select **Install** (**1**). The program displays the instructions and prompt shown in figure 1.5.

8. Press Enter to select the default drive, A:\. Alternatively, type the drive and full path to the location of the drive and subdirectory where the Installation program can find its program files. The program displays the instructions and prompt shown in figure 1.6.

9. Press Enter to select the default drive and subdirectory, C:\LP10\. Alternatively, type the drive and full path to the location of the drive and subdirectory where you want the program to install the files.

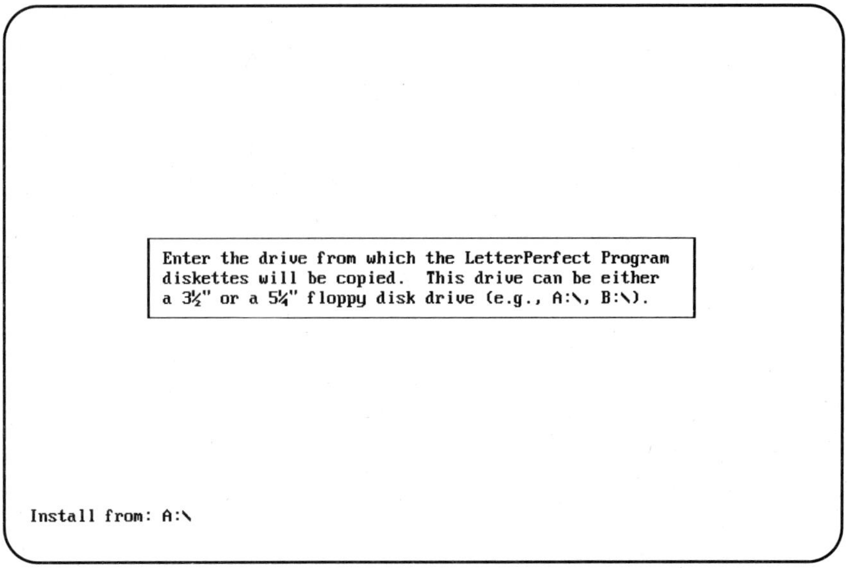

```
Enter the drive from which the LetterPerfect Program
diskettes will be copied.  This drive can be either
a 3½" or a 5¼" floppy disk drive (e.g., A:\, B:\).
```

```
Install from: A:\
```

Fig. 1.5. *The Installation source drive selection screen.*

```
Enter the location where the LetterPerfect Program
files will be copied.
```

```
Install LetterPerfect to: C:\LP10\
```

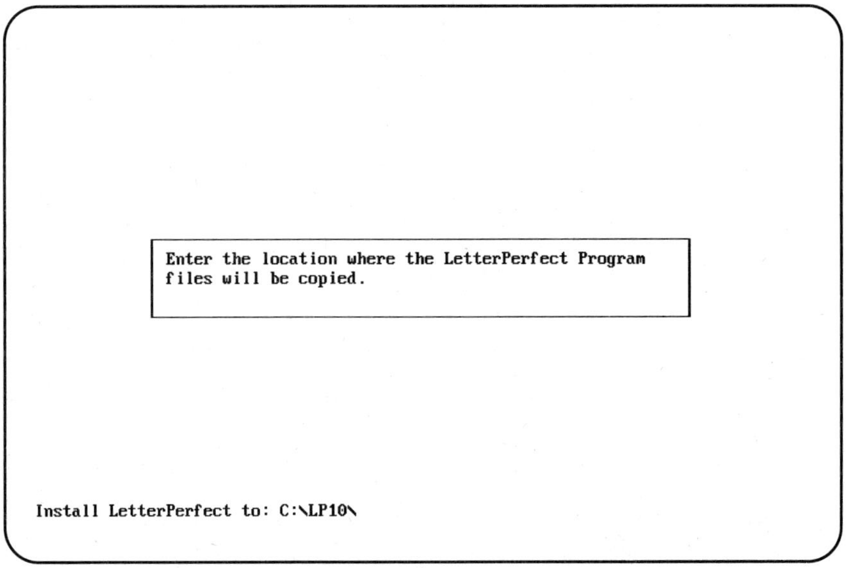

Fig. 1.6. *The Installation target drive selection screen.*

Tip: If the subdirectory does not exist, at the bottom of the screen the program displays a menu prompt: C:\LP10\ doesn't exist, create? Yes (No). Press Enter to select the default **Yes.** Select **No** if you want the program to redisplay the instructions and menu shown in figure 1.6. From the menu prompt, type the drive and full path to the location of the drive and subdirectory where you want the program to install the files.

On systems with two floppy disk drives, if you are installing LetterPerfect from the same drive in which you started the Installation program, the program displays the Auxiliary Files installation screen and menu prompt shown in figure 1.7. (The 07/24/90 Installation program displays a similar menu but lists Utility files instead of Auxiliary Files.)

If you are installing from the other floppy disk drive with the 11/01/90 program, or if you are using the 07/24/90 Installation program, you are prompted to insert the Install/Utilities 1 diskette into the correct floppy disk drive. After you insert the diskette and press Enter, the program displays the installation screen and menu prompt shown in figure 1.7.

```
Do you want to install the Auxiliary Files? Yes (No)




                   The Auxiliary Files contain a variety of utility programs
                   and the learning files.  These files are not necessary to
                   run LetterPerfect.
```

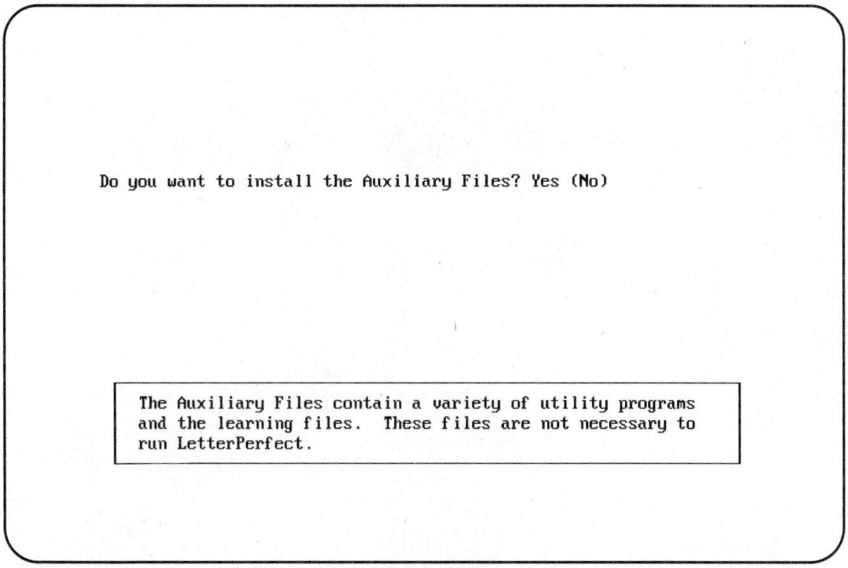

Fig. 1.7. *The Auxiliary Files installation screen.*

Table 1.1 lists the 55 LetterPerfect auxiliary files that require approximately 616K of disk space. The 07/24/90 program includes similar files that require the same amount of disk space. Strangely these auxiliary files include all of the files required to create and use either LetterPerfect (LPM) or Shell (SHM) macros. If you want to use either of these macro features, you *must* select the **Yes** option.

Table 1.1
LetterPerfect Auxiliary Files Installed
by the 11/01/90 Installation Program

General Category	Number of Files	Specific Files	Disk Space Used
Program Feature Files	2		7.63K
		LP.MRS	
		STANDARD.CRS	
Shell Program Files	6		116.64K
		SH.MRS	
		SHELL.EXE	
		SHELL.HLP	
		SHELL.NEW	
		SHELL.OVL	
		SHELLDOS.COM	
Tutor Program Files	37		180.91K
		ADDRESS.TUT	
		BEGIN.TUT	
		FILENAME.TUT	
		FLATTIRE.LRN	
		LETTER.TUT	
		LETTER1.TUT	
		LETTER_F.TUT	
		LETTER_P.TUT	
		LPBANNER.TUT	
		LPINTRO.TUT	
		LPINTRO1.TUT	
		LPLESS.TUT	
		LPLESS1.TUT	
		LPLESS2.TUT	
		LPLESS3.TUT	
		LPLESS4.TUT	
		LPLESS5.TUT	
		LPLESS6.TUT	
		LPMERGE.TUT	

General Category	Number of Files	Specific Files	Disk Space Used
		LPMERGE2.TUT	
		LPMORE.TUT	
		LPTUTORM.TUT	
		MAP.LRN	
		MEMO.LRN	
		MEMO.TUT	
		MEMOFORM.TUT	
		MUSICBOX.WKB	
		NAMES.LRN	
		PARK.TUT	
		PARK1.TUT	
		PARKMEMO.TUT	
		QUIT.TUT	
		REPORT.LRN	
		RESTART.TUT	
		TUTOR.COM	
		TUTOR.TUT	
		WORKBOOK.PRS	
Utility Program Files	7		316.63K
		C.CONVERT.EXE	
		CURSOR.COM	
		FIXBIOS.COM	
		GRAPHCNV.EXE	
		INSTALL.EXE	
		NLPSETUP.EXE	
		WPINFO.EXE	
Windows Program Information Files	3		1.25K
		LP10-286.PIF	
		LP10-386.PIF	
		WIN30-LP.PIF	

Tip: Unless you do not have the disk space, you should install the auxiliary files so that all LetterPerfect features are available. After the installation process is completed, you can recover disk space by deleting files in a specific program category. For example, if you do not want to use the tutor program, you can delete the 37 listed tutor files and recover approximately 181K of disk space.

10. For the purpose of these instructions, press Enter to select the **Yes** option. The program displays this message: `Reading In-stall/Utilities 1 master diskette...`

   After a few seconds, the program displays a message: `Installing <filename> C:\LP10\`. The <filename> portion changes to list each file as the program places it in the `C:\LP10\` subdirectory. Depending on your system's speed, the names may change so quickly that you cannot read them.

   After installing all of the files on the Install/Utility 1 diskette, the program prompts you to insert the `Program 1` diskette. The program automatically installs the auxiliary files *and*, except for the <filename>. ALL and <filename>.PRS files, all of the files listed in Table 1.2.

Table 1.2
LetterPerfect's main files installed
by the 11/01/90 Installation Program

General Category	Number of Files	Specific Files	Disk Space Used
Program Files	10		983.39K
		LP.DRS	
		LP.EXE	
		LP.FIL	
		LP{LP}.SET	
		LPHELP.FIL	
		STANDARD.VRS	
		WP.LRS	
		WP{WP}.SPW	
		WP{WP}US.LEX	
		WP{WP}US.THS	
Printer Definition Files	5		*52.00K
		<filename>.ALL	
		<filename>.PRS	
		{LP}SPC.FRM	
		PRINTER.TST	
		STANDARD.PRS	

General Category	Number of Files	Specific Files	Disk Space Used
Graphic Images Files	30		72.51K
		ARROW-22.WPG	
		BALLOONS.WPG	
		BANNER-3.WPG	
		BICYCLE.WPG	
		BKGRND-1.WPG	
		BORDER-8.WPG	
		BULB.WPG	
		BURST-1.WPG	
		BUTTRFLY.WPG	
		CALENDAR.WPG	
		CERTIF.WPG	
		CHKBOX-1.WPG	
		CLOCK.WPG	
		CNTRCT-2.WPG	
		DEVICE-2.WPG	
		DIPLOMA.WPG	
		FLOPPY-2.WPG	
		GAVEL.WPG	
		GLOBE2-M.WPG	
		HANDS-3.WPG	
		MAGNIF.WPG	
		MAILBAG.WPG	
		NEWS.WPG	
		PC-1.WPG	
		PRESNT-1.WPG	
		PRINTR-3.WPG	
		SCALE.WPG	
		STAR-5.WPG	
		TELPHONE.WPG	
		TROPHY.WPG	

*   Approximate size. The actual amount of disk space required depends on the specific printer definition you select.

Note: At this point, the 07/24/90 Installation program functions differently than the 11/01/90 program. After the 07/24/90 Installation program completes the action you selected for the Utilities file category, the program displays confirmation screens for the following program categories:

- Graphics
- Thesaurus
- Learning Files
- Shell
- LetterPerfect
- Language Resource Files
- Speller
- Help

Press Enter at each confirmation screen to select the default **Yes** option so that the program installs the files for the listed category. Select **No** to instruct the program not to install the files in each category.

11. After installing the program files, the Installation program displays informational screens and menu prompts that let you decide whether the program should modify the CONFIG.SYS and AUTOEXEC.BAT that your system automatically uses each time it begins operation. At each prompt, select **Yes** to cause the program to modify (or create, if the file does not exist) the control file listed on the screen. Your system does *not* use the modified settings until you restart the computer. If you select **No** the program skips the modification/creation action.

12. Next the Installation program displays an informational screen and menu prompt so you can designate whether the F1 key activates the Cancel or Help feature. Press Enter to select the default Cancel function. Alternatively, select **Help** (**2**) to choose the Help feature.

Tip: The Esc key always activates the Cancel feature whether the F1 key activates the Cancel or Help feature; the F3 key always activates the Help feature whether the F1 key activates the Cancel or Help feature.

13. Now LetterPerfect displays the message menu: `Do you want to select a printer? Yes (No)`. **Press Enter to select Yes** and install a printer definition. Select **No** to return to the main Installation menu. For information on installing a printer, see the "Selecting and Installing a Printer Definition File" section later in this chapter, and the "Defining and Selecting a Printer" section in Chapter 8, "Printing and Print Options."

Installing LetterPerfect on a Floppy-Disk-Drive System

The instructions in the following sections show you how to install the full LetterPerfect program files on floppy diskettes using single and dual floppy disk drives. The number and storage capacity of the floppy disk drives determine the messages displayed by the Installation program. For this reason, the screen messages, menus, and prompts that you see on your system may vary from those shown in this chapter.

The 07/24/90 and 11/01/90 Installation programs each provide options for installing the LetterPerfect program files on systems with only floppy disk drives. The exact number of diskettes and the installation sequence depend on the date of the software package, the number and capacity of floppy disk drives, and whether you select a minimal or full program installation. Table 1.3 lists the number of diskettes required to install LetterPerfect on different types of floppy disk drive systems.

LetterPerfect requires a system with at least two 5 1/4-inch 360k floppy disk drives or one 3 1/2-inch 720k floppy disk drive. A more efficient program operation requires at least one 5 1/4-inch 1.2M, or 3 1/2-inch 1.44M, floppy disk drive. The most efficient and convenient program operation requires two 5 1/4-inch 1.2M, or 3 1/2-inch 1.44M, floppy disk drives, or a combination of one of each type of drive.

Table 1.3
Number of Floppy Diskettes Required to
Install Minimal and Full LetterPerfect Program Files

Number of Disk Drives	Capacity/Size Of Disk Drives	07/24/90 Installation Program		11/01/90 Installation Program	
		Diskettes (Minimal)	Diskettes (Full)	Diskettes (Minimal)	Diskettes Full)
2	360K (5 1/4-inch)	not available	seven	not available	seven
1 or 2	720K (3 1/2-inch)	one	four	one [1]	four
1 or 2	1.2M (5 1/4-inch)	one	three	not available	two
1 or 2	1.44M (3 1/2-inch)	one	three	not available	two
1 each [2]	360K (5 1/4-inch) 1.2M (5 1/4-inch)	one	three	not available	two
1 each [2]	360K (5 1/4-inch) 720K (3 1/2-inch)	one	three	one [1]	two
1 each [2]	360K (5 1/4-inch) 1.44M (3 1/2-inch)	one	three	not available	two
1 each [2]	720K (3 1/2-inch) 1.2M (5 1/4-inch)	one	three	one [1]	two
1 each [2]	720K (3 1/2-inch) 1.44M (3 1/2-inch)	one	three	one [1]	two
1 each [3]	1.2M (5 1/4-inch) 1.44M (3 1/2-inch)	one	three	not available	two

[1] Available on systems with two floppy disk drives *only* if you tell the installation program that LetterPerfect is being installed on a system with a single 720K drive.

[2] The Installation program does not properly install the LetterPerfect program files on systems with different size floppy disk drives. See the section on "Installing LetterPerfect on Different Capacity Dual Floppy Drive Systems" later in this chapter.

[3] The Installation program properly installs the LetterPerfect program files on systems with this combination of floppy disk drives even though the program displays a message warning that it does *not* correctly install LetterPerfect.

Tip: If you do not know the storage capacity of the floppy disk drive, insert the DOS program diskette that contains the CHKDSK.COM program into the disk drive. At the A:\ prompt, type *chkdsk*, and press Enter. After a few seconds, information about your system appears on the screen. The first entry is: `<number> bytes total disk space`. The `<number>` is the maximum storage capacity of the disks used by the drive.

Here is what the numbers mean:
362496 bytes = 360K diskettes
730112 bytes = 720K diskettes
1213952 bytes = 1.2M diskettes
1457664 bytes = 1.44M diskettes

Generally, a higher capacity disk drive can read and write to lower-capacity diskettes of the same physical dimensions. For example, a 1.2M, 5 1/4-inch high-density drive can install LetterPerfect on 360K, 5 1/4-inch low-density diskettes. However, this installation method usually limits the 360K diskettes to use with a 1.2M high-density floppy disk drive.

Preparing the Floppy Disks for the Installation Process

Depending on the number of drives and the storage capacity of each drive, the Installation needs between one and seven formatted floppy diskettes available to install LetterPerfect. Refer to Table 1.3 to determine the number of floppy diskettes required to install LetterPerfect on your system.

If the floppy diskettes are not formatted, you use the DOS formatting command to format each diskette before running the Installation program. Regardless of the type of diskette used by your system, follow these steps to format each diskette:

1. Insert the program diskette that contains the DOS FORMAT.COM program into the disk drive.

2. Type *format* and press Enter.

3. Remove the DOS program diskette.

4. Make sure that the diskette to be formatted is not write-protected. For 3 1/2-inch diskettes, the hole on the left-hand side as you insert the diskette into the drive must be blocked by the plastic slide. For 5 1/4-inch diskettes, the notch on the left-hand side as you insert the diskette into the drive must *not* be covered by tape.

5. Insert an unformatted diskette into the disk drive.

6. Follow the instructions on your screen to format each diskette.

Installing the 11/01/90 Program Using a Single Floppy Disk Drive

The instructions in this section show you how to install the full LetterPerfect program files on floppy diskettes using a single 1.2M 5 1/4-inch disk drive, designated as drive A. If you install LetterPerfect on a system using a floppy disk drive with different storage capacity, the screen messages, menus, and prompts may vary from those shown in this chapter.

After formatting the floppy diskettes as described in "Preparing the Floppy Diskettes for the Installation Process" earlier in this chapter, follow these steps to install the LetterPerfect 1.0 and Shell 3.01 program files to the floppy diskettes:

1. Insert the diskette that contains the Install program into drive A. If the drive uses 5 1/4-inch diskettes, turn the lever so that it covers the slot into which you inserted the floppy diskette.

2. Type *install* and press Enter. After a few seconds, the Installation program displays its initial information screen (see fig. 1.1). The boxed text includes the prompt `Do you want to Continue? Yes (No)`.

3. Press Enter to select the **Yes** default. The program displays the screen shown in figure 1.2. The boxed text includes the prompt `Do you see red, green, and blue colored boxes? Yes (No)`.

4. If you see three colored boxes below the menu prompt, press Enter to select the default **Yes**. If you do not see the colored boxes, select **No**.

The program displays the menu for selecting installation to a hard disk as shown in figure 1.3.

5. Select the **No** option. The program displays the initial `Disk Drive Installation` menu shown in figure 1.8.

```
Disk Drive Installation


  Do you want to install on 3½" or 5¼" diskettes?
    1) 3½" Diskettes    2) 5¼" Diskettes
```

```
  Choosing the diskette size: Your LetterPerfect package contains two sizes
  of program diskettes.  The smaller diskettes are 3½"; the larger diskettes
  are 5¼".  If you have 3½" and 5¼" disk drives, choose to install on 3½"
  diskettes.  Note: LetterPerfect does not directly support running on two
  disk drive systems where the disk drives are different sizes (for example,
  one disk drive is 3½" and the other is 5¼").
```

Fig. 1.8. The initial Disk Drive Installation menu.

6. Select the physical size of the floppy diskettes to which the program will install LetterPerfect. (Except where stated differently, the following instructions are based on an installation to 5 1/4-inch diskettes.) The program displays the menu for selecting the number of disk drives shown in figure 1.9.

7. For the purposes of these instructions, select the **1** option. The program displays the confirmation menu shown in figure 1.10.

   If you select the **2** option in step 7, the program displays the storage capacity menu shown in figure 1.11. If you select either option from this menu, the program displays the confirmation menu shown in figure 1.12.

```
Disk Drive Installation


   Do you want to install on 3½" or 5¼" diskettes?        5¼" Diskettes


   Do you have one or two 5¼" disk drives?
      1) One disk drive    2) Two disk drives




   ┌────────────────────────────────────────────────────────────────────┐
   │  Choosing the number of drives: If your disk drives are the same size │
   │  (for example, two 3½" disk drives), chose option 2.  If you have 3½" │
   │  and 5¼" disk drives, you should choose option 1 to install to one (1)│
   │  disk drive rather than to two (2).                                   │
   │                                                                      │
   │                                                                      │
   │                                                                      │
   └────────────────────────────────────────────────────────────────────┘
```

Fig. 1.9. The Disk Drive Installation disk number menu.

```
Disk Drive Installation


   Do you want to install on 3½" or 5¼" diskettes?        5¼" Diskettes


   Do you have one or two 5¼" disk drives?                 1


   What is the storage capacity of your floppy diskette(s)?  High
      LetterPerfect will not run on a system with
      only one low capacity 5¼" (360K) disk drive.




                    Is this correct? Yes (No)
```

Fig. 1.10. The Disk Drive Installation confirmation menu.

```
Disk Drive Installation


  Do you want to install on 3½" or 5¼" diskettes?        5¼" Diskettes


  Do you have one or two 5¼" disk drives?                2


  What is the storage capacity of your floppy diskette(s)?
    1) Low Capacity (360K)   2) High Capacity (1.2M)


  ┌──────────────────────────────────────────────────────────────┐
  │ Choosing the diskette capacity: Choose the option that matches the capacity │
  │ (density) of the diskettes on which you will install LetterPerfect.  If │
  │ your system has two 3½" disk drives for different capacities (i.e., one │
  │ for 720K and the other for 1.44M), choose the lower capacity option.  Check │
  │ your system manual, consult your dealer, or use the DOS CHKDSK command │
  │ (see your DOS Manual) to find out your diskette capacity.  The package for │
  │ your blank diskettes should note the diskette's capacity.  If you're still │
  │ not sure what capacity you have, choose the lower capacity option. │
  └──────────────────────────────────────────────────────────────┘
```

Fig. 1.11. *The Disk Drive Installation disk storage capacity menu.*

```
Disk Drive Installation


  Do you want to install on 3½" or 5¼" diskettes?        5¼" Diskettes


  Do you have one or two 5¼" disk drives?                2


  What is the storage capacity of your floppy diskette(s)?  Low




                  Is this correct? Yes (No)
```

Fig. 1.12. *The Disk Drive Installation confirmation menu.*

8. For the purposes of these instructions, press Enter to select the **Yes** option on the menu shown in either figure 1.10 or figure 1.12. The program displays its main installation menu shown in figure 1.13. However, if you previously told the program that you are installing LetterPerfect on a system with only *one* 720K floppy disk drive, it displays the program-choice installation menu shown in figure 1.14.

```
Installation

    1 - Install       First time installation of LetterPerfect.

    2 - Network       First time installation of LetterPerfect on a Network.

    3 - Printer       Install a Printer (.ALL) File.  Use this option to
                      install more printers after you have already installed
                      LetterPerfect.

    4 - Update        Update previously-installed LetterPerfect 1.0 software.

    5 - Copy Disks    Install every file from a master diskette to a
                      location you specify.  (Useful for installing all the
                      Printer (.ALL) Files.)

    6 - Exit          Exit Installation program.




Selection: 1
```

Fig. 1.13. The main Installation menu screen.

If you select **Minimal Installation (2)** from the menu shown in figure 1.14, the program displays a message advising you that one blank diskette is required to install the program. From this point, skip the remaining steps in this section and respond to the informational messages and prompts that follow. The program automatically installs the following LetterPerfect program files: LP.EXE, LP.FIL, LP.VRS, LPSMALL.DRS, PRINTER.TST, and STANDARD.PRS.

> *Caution:* If you select the minimal option, only the program files required for basic word processing are installed. The files required to use the Spell, Thesaurus, Graphics, Shell Macro, and Help features, and to use the printer attached to your computer are *not* installed.

```
    1    Normal Installation        This option allows installation of all
                                    LetterPerfect files.

    2    Minimal Installation       Installs only necessary program files.
                                    With this option you will not be able
                                    to install the dictionary, thesaurus,
                                    utilities, graphic, or learning files.
                                    This will let you run LetterPerfect
                                    with only one diskette.




 Selection: 1
```

Fig. 1.14. The program-choice installation menu.

For the purposes of these instructions, select Normal (**1**) if you
see the menu shown in figure 1.14. The program displays the
menu shown in figure 1.13.

9. For the purposes of these instructions, select Install (**1**) from the
   menu shown in figure 1.13. The program displays an informational message that tells you the number of diskettes required to
   install the complete LetterPerfect and Shell program files.

   ```
   To install LetterPerfect,
   you need at least 2 blank
   formatted diskettes.
   Enter=continue   F7=exit
   ```

   Table 1.3 lists the disk requirements for all possible disk drive
   combinations. The suggested number of diskettes is the number
   required to install all of the LetterPerfect and Shell program files.
   If you have less than the suggested number of diskettes available
   and you plan to install less than all of the program files, you may
   have enough diskettes.

10. At this point you can press Enter to continue the installation
    process or press Exit (F7) to stop the installation process. For the
    purposes of these instructions, press Enter. The program displays
    the Install from: message and source disk prompt shown in
    figure 1.15.

```
    Enter the drive from which the LetterPerfect Program
    diskettes will be copied.  This drive can be either
    a 3½" or a 5¼" floppy disk drive (e.g., A:\, B:\).



Install from: A:\
```

Fig. 1.15. *The Install from: message and source disk prompt.*

11. At this point, you can either press Enter to select the default: A:\,
    or type *B:* and press Enter. For the purposes of these instruc-
    tions, press Enter. The program displays the Install
    LetterPerfect to: message and target disk prompt shown in
    figure 1.16.

12. At this point, you can either press Enter to select the default: A:\,
    or type *B:* and press Enter. For the purposes of these instruc-
    tions, press Enter. The program displays the LetterPerfect 1/2
    prompt shown in figure 1.17 that instructs you to label and insert
    a diskette into drive A.

13. Label a diskette as *LetterPerfect 1/2*, insert it into drive A, and
    press Enter.

> ***Caution:*** When you press Enter in step 13, the program creates a unique
> zero byte file—LP{INST}.011—on the LetterPerfect 1/2 diskette. Each
> additional diskette also receives a file with a different ending number. *Do
> not delete* or alter this file and its number. The program looks for the
> diskette's unique file name and number during the installation process. If
> the program cannot find the file name and number, it displays a message
> prompt that offers the options either to insert the correct diskette or to skip
> installation of the files for that diskette.

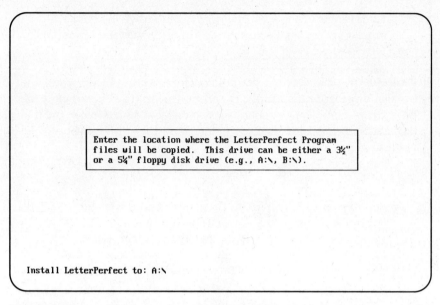

Enter the location where the LetterPerfect Program files will be copied. This drive can be either a 3½" or a 5¼" floppy disk drive (e.g., A:\, B:\).

Install LetterPerfect to: A:\

Fig. 1.16. *The Install LetterPerfect to: message and target disk prompt.*

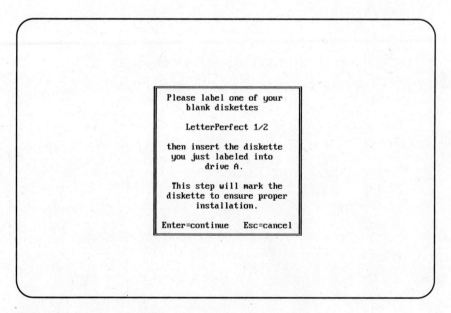

Please label one of your blank diskettes

LetterPerfect 1/2

then insert the diskette you just labeled into drive A.

This step will mark the diskette to ensure proper installation.

Enter=continue   Esc=cancel

Fig. 1.17. *The LetterPerfect 1/2 message and menu prompt.*

LetterPerfect changes the message menu shown in figure 1.17 to instruct you to label a diskette *Learning/Printer* and insert it into the disk drive.

> ***Caution:*** If your system uses a software disk-caching program, the Installation program may display the prompt to insert a diskette before the program has completed installing files on the disk. Always make sure that the light on the disk drive is not lit before you switch diskettes during the installation process.

14. Repeat step 13. If you follow these instructions while using a floppy disk drive with a storage capacity other than 1.2M, repeat step 13 for each remaining diskette the program requests you to label and insert. After you complete this procedure for the last diskette, the program displays the Auxiliary files installation message and menu prompt shown in figure 1.18.

```
Do you want to install the Auxiliary Files? Yes (No)




      ┌─────────────────────────────────────────────────────┐
      │ The Auxiliary Files contain a variety of utility programs │
      │ and the learning files.  These files are not necessary to │
      │ run LetterPerfect.                                  │
      └─────────────────────────────────────────────────────┘
```

Fig. 1.18. The Auxiliary Files installation message and menu prompt.

15. Press Enter to select the default **Yes** and have the Auxiliary programs installed. Select **No** if you do not want the Auxiliary programs installed (see Table 1.1). The program displays this

informational message in a box: `Reading Install/Utilities 1 master diskette....` After a few seconds, the program displays the following message in a box:

```
Insert into drive A
the diskette you labeled
Learning/Printer
Enter=continue    Esc=cancel
```

16. Insert the *Learning/Printer* diskette and press Enter. The program displays this message in a box: `Installing <`*program name*`> A:\`. The *<program name>* lists the name of the current program file that is being installed. Some file names may flash by faster than you can read them.

17. From this point on, the Installation program installs all of the LetterPerfect program files, and prompts you only to switch disks. At any point, if you insert the wrong source disk and press Enter, the program remains stopped until you either insert the correct source disk and press Enter, or press Esc to return to the program at the point reached in step 8. If you insert the wrong target disk, the program displays this message at the lower left corner of the screen: `Correct disk not found.` You must either insert the correct target disk and press Enter to install the program files, or press Esc to return to the program at the point reached in step 8.

18. After installing the program files, the Installation program displays informational screens and menu prompts so that you can decide whether the program should modify the CONFIG.SYS and AUTOEXEC.BAT files that your system automatically uses each time it begins operation.

    If you want the program to modify these files, insert the disk from which your system boots and select **Yes** at each prompt. The program modifies (or creates, if the file does not exist) the control file listed on the screen. Your system does *not* use the modified settings until you reboot the computer. Select **No** if you want the program to skip the modification/creation action.

19. Next the Installation program displays an informational screen and menu prompt so that you can designate whether the F1 key activates the Cancel or Help feature. Press Enter to select the default **Cancel** (**1**) function. Alternatively, select **Help** (**2**) to designate the Help feature.

> *Tip:* The Esc key also activates the Cancel feature whether the F1 key activates the Cancel or Help feature. The F3 key also activates the Help feature whether the F1 key activates the Cancel or Help feature.

20. Now the Installation program displays the message menu: Do you want to select a printer? Yes (No).

    Press Enter to select **Yes** and install a printer definition. Select **No** and the Installation program finishes the installation and returns to the DOS prompt. For information on installing a printer, see the "Selecting and Installing a Printer Definition File" section later in this chapter, and the "Defining and Selecting a Printer" section in Chapter 8, "Printing and Print Options."

Installing the 11/01/90 Program Using Dual Floppy Disk Drives

The instructions in this section show you how to install the full LetterPerfect program files on floppy diskettes using dual 1.2M 5 1/4-inch disk drives, designated as drive A and drive B. If you install LetterPerfect on a system using floppy disk drives with different storage capacities, the screen messages, menus, and prompts may vary from those shown in this chapter. If you use a system with disk drives that have different drive designations, substitute the appropriate letters for the drives on your system in place of drives A and B.

After you format the floppy diskettes as described in "Preparing the Floppy Diskettes for the Installation Process" earlier in this chapter, follow these steps to install the LetterPerfect 1.0 and Shell 3.01 program files to the floppy diskettes:

1. Insert the diskette that contains the Install program in drive A. If the drive uses 5 1/4-inch diskettes, turn the lever so that it covers the slot into which you inserted the floppy diskette.

2. Type *install* and press Enter. After a few seconds, the Installation program displays its initial information screen (see fig. 1.1). The boxed text includes the prompt Do you want to Continue? Yes (No).

3. Press Enter to select the **Yes** default. The program displays the screen shown in figure 1.2. The boxed text includes the prompt `Do you see red, green, and blue colored boxes? Yes (No)`.

4. If you see three colored boxes below the menu prompt, press Enter to select the default **Yes**. If you do not see the colored boxes, select **No**.

    The program displays the menu for selecting installation to a hard disk as shown in figure 1.3.

5. Select the **No** option. The program displays the initial `Disk Drive Installation` menu shown in figure 1.8.

6. Select the physical size of the floppy diskettes to which the program will install LetterPerfect. (Except where stated differently, the following instructions are based on an installation to 5 1/4-inch floppy diskettes.) The program displays the menu for selecting the number of disk drives shown in figure 1.9.

7. For the purposes of these instructions, select the **2** option. The program displays the storage capacity menu shown in figure 1.11.

Tip: If your system has dual floppy disk drives with different storage capacities, you can install the LetterPerfect program files to either drive. Even though the message at the bottom of the menu shown in figure 1.11 suggests that you select the drive with the least storage capacity as the target drive, you can designate the drive with the greater storage capacity as the target drive. In most situations, LetterPerfect runs more efficiently on floppy diskettes with the greatest storage capacity.

8. For the purposes of these instructions, select the **2** option. The program displays the storage capacity menu shown in figure 1.19.

9. For the purposes of these instructions, press Enter to select the **Yes** option. The program displays its main installation menu shown in figure 1.20.

10. Select **Install (1)**. The program displays an informational message that tells you the number of diskettes required to install the complete LetterPerfect and Shell program files.

    ```
    To install LetterPerfect,
    you need at least 2 blank
    formatted diskettes.
    Enter=continue    F7=exit
    ```

```
Disk Drive Installation


Do you want to install on 3½" or 5¼" diskettes?        5¼" Diskettes


Do you have one or two 5¼" disk drives?                2


What is the storage capacity of your floppy diskette(s)?  High




                              Is this correct? Yes (No)
```

Fig. 1.19. The Disk Drive Installation confirmation menu.

```
Installation

    1 - Install       First time installation of LetterPerfect.

    2 - Network       First time installation of LetterPerfect on a Network.

    3 - Printer       Install a Printer (.ALL) File.  Use this option to
                      install more printers after you have already installed
                      LetterPerfect.

    4 - Update        Update previously-installed LetterPerfect 1.0 software.

    5 - Copy Disks    Install every file from a master diskette to a
                      location you specify.  (Useful for installing all the
                      Printer (.ALL) Files.)

    6 - Exit          Exit Installation program.




Selection: 1
```

Fig. 1.20. The main Installation menu screen.

Table 1.3 lists the disk requirements for all possible disk drive combinations. The suggested number of diskettes is the number required to install all of the LetterPerfect and Shell program files.

11. At his point you can press Enter to continue the installation process; or press Exit (F7) to stop the installation process. For the purposes of these instructions, press Enter. The program displays the `Install from:` message and source disk prompt shown in figure 1.21.

```
┌─────────────────────────────────────────────────────────┐
│                                                         │
│                                                         │
│                                                         │
│                                                         │
│     ┌───────────────────────────────────────────────┐   │
│     │ Enter the drive from which the LetterPerfect Program │   │
│     │ diskettes will be copied.  This drive can be either  │   │
│     │ a 3½" or a 5¼" floppy disk drive (e.g., A:\, B:\).   │   │
│     └───────────────────────────────────────────────┘   │
│                                                         │
│                                                         │
│                                                         │
│                                                         │
│ Install from: A:\                                       │
└─────────────────────────────────────────────────────────┘
```

Fig. 1.21. The Install from: message and source disk prompt.

12. At this point, you can either press Enter to select the default: `A:\`, or type *B:* and press Enter. For the purposes of these instructions, press Enter. The program displays the `Install LetterPerfect to:` message and target disk prompt shown in figure 1.22.

```
Enter the location where the LetterPerfect Program
files will be copied.  This drive can be either a 3½"
or a 5¼" floppy disk drive (e.g., A:\, B:\).
```

```
Install LetterPerfect to: B:\
```

Fig. 1.22. The Install LetterPerfect to: message and target disk prompt.

13. At this point, you can either press Enter to select the default: A:\, or type *B:* and press Enter. For the purposes of these instructions, press Enter. The program displays the LetterPerfect 1/2 prompt shown in figure 1.23, instructing you to label and insert a diskette into drive A.

Caution: If you install the program files on a system with two floppy disk drives that have different storage capacities, instead of the LetterPerfect 1/2 menu prompt, the program displays the warning message and menu prompt shown in figure 1.24.

The warning message is *not* accurate if the installation source drive is either a high-density 1.2M or 1.44M floppy disk drive and the installation target drive is the other type of high-density drive. LetterPerfect runs correctly from either drive. In this situation, if you see the warning message, press Enter to display the LetterPerfect 1/2 prompt.

If the dual drive combination includes either a 360K or 720k floppy disk drive, the warning message is accurate. Press Esc and perform an installation for a single floppy disk drive.

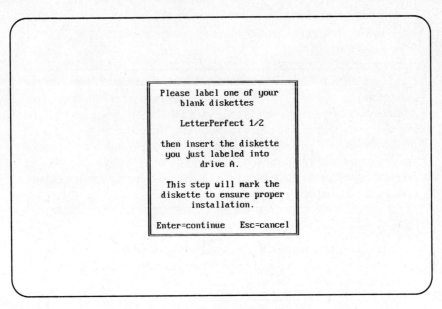

```
        Please label one of your
             blank diskettes

            LetterPerfect 1/2

        then insert the diskette
         you just labeled into
                drive A.

        This step will mark the
        diskette to ensure proper
              installation.

    Enter=continue    Esc=cancel
```

Fig. 1.23. The LetterPerfect 1/2 message and menu prompt.

```
You have chosen to install LetterPerfect to a 2 floppy drive system
with different size floppy disk drives.  You will be able to install
all files but LetterPerfect will not run correctly.

                    Press Enter to continue or Esc to cancel
```

Fig. 1.24. The installation warning message and menu prompt.

14. Label a diskette as *LetterPerfect 1/2*, insert it into drive A, and press Enter.

> *Caution:* When you press Enter in step 14, the program creates a unique zero byte file—LP{INST}.010—on the LetterPerfect 1/2 diskette. Each additional diskette also receives a file with a different ending number. *Do not delete* or alter this file and its number. The program looks for the diskette's unique file name and number during the installation process. If the program cannot find the file name and number, it displays a message prompt that offers the options either to insert the correct diskette or to skip installation of the files for that diskette.

LetterPerfect changes the message menu shown in figure 1.24 to instruct you to label a diskette *Learning/Printer* and insert it into the disk drive.

> *Caution:* If your system uses a software disk-caching program, the Installation program may display the prompt to insert a diskette before the program has completed installing files on the disk. Always make sure that the light on the disk drive is not lit before you switch diskettes during the installation process.

15. If you follow these instructions while using dual floppy disk drives with a storage capacity other than 1.2M, repeat step 13 for each of the remaining diskettes. After you complete this procedure for the final diskette, the program displays the Auxiliary files installation message and menu prompt shown in figure 1.25.

16. Press Enter to select the default **Yes** and have the Auxiliary programs installed. Select **No** if you do not want the Auxiliary programs installed (see Table 1.1). The program displays this informational message in a box: `Reading Install/Utilities 1 master diskette....` After a few seconds, the program displays the following message in a box:

    ```
    Insert into drive A
    the diskette you labeled
    Learning/Printer
    Enter=continue    Esc=cancel
    ```

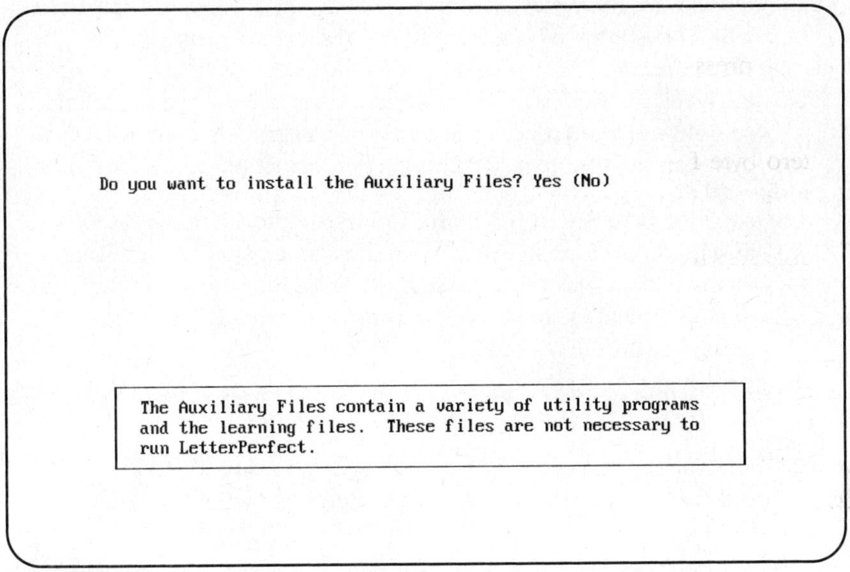

```
Do you want to install the Auxiliary Files? Yes (No)
```

```
The Auxiliary Files contain a variety of utility programs
and the learning files.  These files are not necessary to
run LetterPerfect.
```

Fig. 1.25. *The Auxiliary Files installation message and menu prompt.*

17. Insert the *Learning/Printer* diskette and press Enter. The program displays this message in a box: Installing *<program name>* A:\. The *<program name>* lists the name of the current program file that is being installed. Some file names may change faster than you can read them.

18. From this point on, the Installation program installs all of the LetterPerfect program files and prompts you only to switch disks. At any point, if you insert the wrong source disk and press Enter, the program remains stopped until you either insert the correct source disk and press Enter, or press Esc to return to the program at the point reached in step 8. If you insert the wrong target disk, the program displays this message at the lower left corner of the screen: Correct disk not found. You must either insert the correct target disk and press Enter to install the program files, or press Esc to return to the program at the point reached in step 8.

19. After installing the program files, the Installation program displays informational screens and menu prompts so that you can decide whether the program should modify the CONFIG.SYS and AUTOEXEC.BAT files that your system automatically uses each time it begins operation.

If you want the program to modify these files, insert the disk from which your system boots and select **Yes** at each prompt. The program modifies (or creates, if the file does not exist) the control file listed on the screen. Your system does *not* use the modified settings until you reboot the computer. Select **No** if you want the program to skip the modification/creation action.

20. Next the Installation program displays an informational screen and menu prompt so that you can designate whether the F1 key activates the Cancel or Help feature. Press Enter to select the default **Cancel (1)** function. Alternatively, select **Help (2)** to designate the Help feature.

> *Tip:* The Esc key also activates the Cancel feature whether the F1 key activates the Cancel or Help feature. The F3 key also activates the Help feature whether the F1 key activates the Cancel or Help feature.

21. Now the Installation program displays the message menu: `Do you want to select a printer? Yes (No)`.

    Press Enter to select **Yes** and install a printer definition. Select **No** to instruct the Installation program to finish the installation and return to the DOS prompt. For information on installing a printer, see the "Selecting and Installing a Printer Definition File" section later in this chapter, and the "Defining and Selecting a Printer" section in Chapter 8, "Printing and Print Options."

Selecting and Installing a Printer Definition File

LetterPerfect supports more than 800 printers. Theoretically, you do not need to select or install a printer definition to run LetterPerfect. However, a document may not print exactly as you formatted it on the main editing screen if you do not select and install a printer definition prior to creating the document.

The following instructions assume that you installed LetterPerfect (as described in one of the preceding sections), or selected the **Printer (3)** option from the main Installation menu (shown in fig. 1.20) and responded properly to the messages and prompts that follow, so that the list-of-printers menu (see fig. 1.26) is on the screen.

```
 1 *Acer LP-76
 2 *AEG Olympia Compact RO            Printers marked with '*' are
 3 *AEG Olympia ESW 2000              not included with shipping
 4 *AEG Olympia Laserstar 6           disks.  Select printer for
 5 *AEG Olympia Laserstar 6e          more information.
 6  AEG Olympia NP 136-24
 7 *AEG Olympia NP 136-24 (Additional)  If you do not see your printer
 8  AEG Olympia NP 136 SE             listed, press F3 for Help.
 9  AEG Olympia NP 30
10  AEG Olympia NP 80-24
11 *AEG Olympia NP 80-24 (Additional)
12  AEG Olympia NP 80 SE
13  AEG Olympia NPC 136-24
14 *AEG Olympia NPC 136-24 (Additional)
15 *AEG Olympia Startype
16 *AGFA Compugraphic 9400PS
17  Alphacom Alphapro 101
18  Alps Allegro 24
19 *Alps Allegro 24 (Additional)
20 *Alps Allegro 500
21  Alps ALQ200 (18 pin)
22  Alps ALQ200 (24 pin)

N Name Search; PgDn More Printers; PgUp Previous Screen; F3 Help; F7 Exit;
Selection: 0
```

Fig. 1.26. The list-of-printers menu.

Note: With the 11/01/90 software, if you installed the Auxiliary files and are running the Installation program installed on the target disk, the main Installation menu appears with a Supplementary (6) option as shown in figure 1.27.

Follow these steps to select and install a printer definition:

1. If your printer is listed on the screen, type its number and press Enter. If your printer is not listed on the screen, use the cursor-movement keys listed at the bottom of the screen to display additional names of printers (22 per screen) until you see the name of your printer.

```
Installation

    1 - Install         First time installation of LetterPerfect.

    2 - Network         First time installation of LetterPerfect on a Network.

    3 - Printer         Install a Printer (.ALL) File.  Use this option to
                        install more printers after you have already installed
                        LetterPerfect.

    4 - Update          Update previously-installed LetterPerfect 1.0 software.

    5 - Copy Disks      Install every file from a master diskette to a
                        location you specify.  (Useful for installing all the
                        Printer (.ALL) Files.)

    6 - Supplementary   Install selected files from the the LetterPerfect
                        Supplementary diskettes.  (Available for a nominal
                        charge directly from WordPerfect Corporation.  For
                        further information or to order call (801) 225-5000.)

    7 - Exit            Exit Installation program.

Selection: 1
```

Fig. 1.27. The 11/01/90 installed version of the main Installation menu.

Note: If an asterisk is to the left of the printer's name, the printer definition is not included with the main LetterPerfect program disks and must be ordered at an extra charge. To display the ordering information, press the number of the printer and press Enter.

If the printer you want to use is not listed, press Help (F3) and follow the instructions listed on the screen.

LetterPerfect displays a confirmation menu prompt: Select printer <printer name>? Yes (No).

2. At this point you can select the default **Yes**, or select **No**, Cancel (F1), Esc, or Exit (F7) if you do not want to install the selected printer definition.

If you select **Yes**, the program installs a file whose name ends with the extension ALL. The 07/24/90 Installation program displays a message that advises you that it is installing the printer definition. The 11/01/90 Installation program displays a message: Percentage Installed for Current Printer: <*number*>%. With either program, if the ALL printer file is installed to a system with a single floppy disk drive you will have to switch the source and target disks several times.

When the ALL file has been installed, the program displays the menu prompt: `Do you want to install another printer? No (Yes).`

3. At this point you can press Enter to select the default **No**, or select **Yes** if you want to install an additional printer definition. When you select the **No** option, the program automatically starts LetterPerfect and selects the printer as LetterPerfect's default printer; this process creates another file whose name ends with the extension PRS. When you choose the **Yes** option, you must repeat steps 1 and 2.

After the Installation program creates the PRS file, it terminates and the DOS prompt appears on screen.

Starting LetterPerfect from DOS

Depending on the amount of RAM and disk space available, you can run LetterPerfect directly under DOS or through the Shell 3.01 program. Generally, run the 07/24/90 version of LetterPerfect through Shell to provide the Macro feature (described in Chapter 13) and other options such as task switching. The primary advantage of running the 11/01/90 program through Shell is the task-switching option. Follow these steps to run LetterPerfect directly from DOS:

1. *On a hard-disk system:* change to the drive (and subdirectory, if appropriate) that contains the LetterPerfect program files. For example, on a system with a hard disk drive and LetterPerfect in the D:\LP10 subdirectory, type *D:* and press Enter; then type *CD \LP10* and press Enter.

   On a single-floppy-disk system: insert the *LetterPerfect 1* or *LetterPerfect 1/2* diskette into the disk drive.

   On a dual-floppy-disk system: insert the *LetterPerfect 1* or *LetterPerfect 1/2* diskette into the disk drive from which you want to start the program.

2. Type *LP* (plus any of the optional switches listed in Table 1.4) and press Enter.

   LetterPerfect briefly displays first its initial screen shown in figure 1.28 and then its main editing screen shown in figure 1.29.

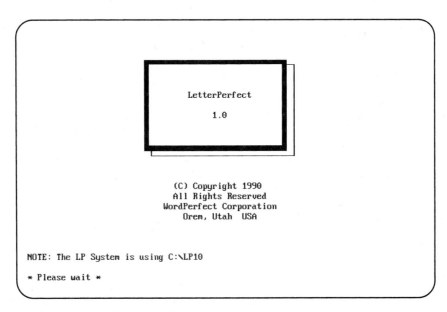

Fig. 1.28. *LetterPerfect's initial screen.*

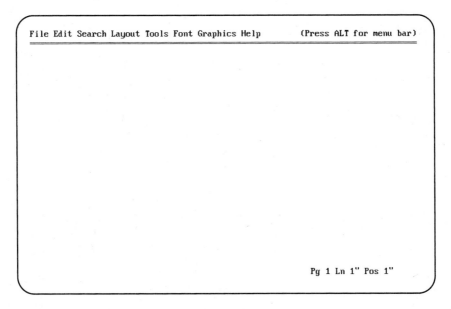

Fig. 1.29. *LetterPerfect's main editing screen.*

Table 1.4
LetterPerfect Commands and Program Switches
Note: When you use a switch, do *not* type the brackets surrounding the italicized variable names in the examples in this table.

Switch	Action
lp	This switch starts LetterPerfect.
lp/bp=*x*	If you have LetterPerfect configured to bypass DOS and print directly to hardware, this switch designates the amount of RAM in kilobytes (from 0k to 63k) you want the program to allocate for its print buffer. 0k prevents the program from printing to the hardware port.
lp/cp=<*number*>	This "code-page" switch designates the keyboard and 256-character ASCII settings used by the system's BIOS. This option makes LetterPerfect display or print using language represented by the code. LetterPerfect supports the following code pages:

437 = Standard
850 = PC Multilingual
851 = Greek
8510 = Greek Alternate
860 = Portuguese
8600 = Portuguese Alternate
8601 = Brazilian Alternate
861 = Icelandic
863 = French (Canada)
865 = Norwegian and Dutch
895 = Czechoslovakian
897 = Hungarian
899 = Russian
8990 = Russian Alternate

Table 1.4 (continued)

Switch	Action
	Note: The 11/01/90 software package enables the user to create customized code pages to redefine the characters created by ASCII values 128 through 256. See the LetterPerfect manual for more information on using this feature with the code-page switch.
lp/d-<*drive\directory*>	This switch causes LetterPerfect to put its over-flow files and temporary buffers in the specified subdirectory. If you run LetterPerfect on a system with a large amount of RAM and two floppy disk drives but no hard disk drive, using this switch with the /r switch enables you to remove the LetterPerfect 2 diskette from drive A. For example, if the RAM disk is C, start LetterPerfect with lp/d-c:/r.
lp<*filename*>	This switch starts LetterPerfect and automatically retrieves the specified file from the program's default directory to the main editing screen. If the file is not in the default directory, you must include the path name to the drive and/or subdirectory that contains the file.

Switch	Action
lp/f2	This switch may solve problems with a screen that displays more than 25 lines and 80 columns if not corrected by using the /ss switch described in this table. The /f2 switch—which enables LetterPerfect to attempt to preserve the current number of columns and rows when the program exits graphics screens or terminates itself and returns to DOS—remains in effect until the computer is restarted.
lp/ln	This switch causes LetterPerfect to prompt you for the program's license number the program starts.
lp/mono	If the system is emulating a monochrome display, this switch provides better access to the display.
lp/nb	This switch causes LetterPerfect to save/replace an existing disk file by overwriting the file. This arrangement is useful if disk space is limited. By default, when you save a file using the name of an existing file, LetterPerfect renames the existing file with a .BK! extension, saves the on-screen file with the original file name, and deletes the file with the .BK! extension. If there is a power failure during the saving operation, the original

Table 1.4 (continued)

Switch	Action
	document remains on the disk with its .BK! extension. If LetterPerfect is running with the /nb (no backup) switch, both the new document and the original are lost in this situation.
lp/ne	This switch prevents LetterPerfect from using expanded RAM available to the system.
lp/nh	This switch overcomes problems LetterPerfect has with systems that use the first version of the Phoenix BIOS (such as older model AT&T computers); it also disables LetterPerfect's capability to print directly to the hardware's printer port.
lp/nf	This "non-flash" switch is required by some systems and windowing programs (other than TopView and DESQview). Use this switch if text is displayed over the window or if the screen unexpectedly goes blank.
lp/nk	This switch prevents LetterPerfect from recognizing keyboard functions supported by an enhanced ROM BIOS. See the "Using the Keyboard" section in Chapter 2. Use this switch if the system stops working after LetterPerfect begins running.

Switch	Action
lp/nt	This switch designates the type of network to which the system is attached.
lp/pf=*<path>*	This switch causes LetterPerfect to use the specified drive and/or subdirectory for its temporary print queue files. On systems with two floppy disk drives but no hard disk drive, use this switch to redirect the print queue to drive B. On systems attached to a network, using this switch to redirect the print queue to a hard disk drive increases print speed.
lp/ps=*<path>*	This switch causes LetterPerfect to use the LP{LP}.SET file, which contains the program's starting configuration, in the specified path instead of the .SET file found with the LP.EXE file. This switch is used primarily with systems attached to a network.
lp/r	This switch speeds up LetterPerfect operation by loading the program overlay files into approximately 300k of expanded memory. Using the /r switch with the /d switch enables the program to operate without having the LetterPerfect 2 diskette in drive A. On most systems, the /r switch causes LetterPerfect to take longer to display its main editing screen but enables the program to operate more quickly from that point on.

Table 1.4 (continued)

Switch	Action
lp/sa	On a system attached to a network, this "stand-alone" switch causes LetterPerfect to run as though the system were *not* attached to the network.
lp/ss=*<rows,columns>*	This switch designates the actual number of horizontal rows and vertical columns used by the system's display if they are other than the default 25 rows and 80 columns. Designating a display size other than the actual size may cause improper program display.
lp/u=*<user name>*	On a system attached to a network, the <user name> switch is a unique three-letter code assigned to the user that causes LetterPerfect to use the LP{LP}.SET file for the user.
lp/w=*<number>,<number> or* *	This "workspace" switch limits in kilobytes the amount of conventional and expanded RAM used by LetterPerfect. The first number, which must be 43 or higher, represents conventional RAM. The second number, which can be any value, represents expanded RAM. By default, when you run LetterPerfect directly under DOS, 100% of conventional RAM and 87.5% of expanded RAM is used. By default, when you run LetterPerfect through Shell 3.01, 50% of expanded RAM is

Switch	Action
	used. If you substitute an asterisk (*) in place of the second number, LetterPerfect uses all available expanded RAM. If the program cannot locate expanded RAM, it ignores the second number.
lp/ws	This switch pauses the program at the initial program screen and displays information on the conventional and expanded memory available for use by LetterPerfect. This switch is available only with the 11/01/90 software package.
lp/x	The /x switch causes LetterPerfect to ignore the configuration designated in the LP{LP}.SET file and use the default configuration coded into the program.
lp/1	On a system with dual floppy disk drives, this switch forces LetterPerfect to act as though the system has only *one* floppy disk drive. This option is useful if you are using a portable system with the DOS on a hardware ROM chip. With this type of computer, LetterPerfect sometimes assumes that the system has a hard disk.
lp/32	By default, LetterPerfect works only with expanded RAM under the 4.0 LIM memory specification. This switch enables LetterPerfect to work with expanded RAM under the 3.2 LIM memory specification.

Tip: Whether you run LetterPerfect directly under DOS or through the Shell 3.01 program, the DOS SET command can automatically assign any of the switches listed in Table 1.4 to the LP command. For example, suppose that you run LetterPerfect from drive A on a system with dual 360K floppy disk drives, expanded RAM, and the following SET command in its AUTOEXEC.BAT file: `SET LP=LP/D-B:/R`.

When you start the program from the DOS prompt by typing LP and pressing Enter, or through Shell 3.01, LetterPerfect automatically starts with its overflow and temporary files directed to drive B and its overlay files loaded into expanded memory. With this configuration you can remove the LetterPerfect 2 disk from drive A so that both disk drives can be used for data disks. Alternatively, you can put the Speller/Help disk in drive A so that the Spell and Help features are available without switching disks.

If you type LP followed by a startup string that includes an option also in the SET command but with a different value, the value you type takes precedent over the value designated in the SET command.

Using The Shell 3.01 Program

Shell 3.01 is a menu program that enables you to start DOS software programs by pressing a single key. The Installation program automatically installed the Shell program files with the LetterPerfect program files if you answered **Yes** to the confirmation prompt for installing Shell with the 07/24/90 software package, or to the confirmation prompt for installing Auxiliary files with the 11/01/90 software package.

On most systems with 640k of conventional RAM, Shell also simulates the running of two or more programs simultaneously. This simulation is called *task switching*, which enables you to change from one program to another without terminating either program. Shell's macro feature is available for use with most programs that do not have a built-in macro feature (like the 07/24/90 version of LetterPerfect). See Chapter 13 for more information about macros.

For programs with a built-in macro feature (like the 11/01/90 version of LetterPerfect), Shell's macro feature provides a second macro option that, among other things, uses Shell's task-switching capabilities for automatically transferring information between programs.

The following sections cover the basic information about setting up and running Shell. By adapting the steps that follow, you can add other DOS programs to the Shell menu and run them through the Shell program. The LetterPerfect software package includes an informational pamphlet, *WordPerfect Shell 3.0*, that provides a more detailed discussion of the program.

Note: The examples in the following sections assume that you have installed LetterPerfect on hard disk drive C and keep document files in the default subdirectory named: C:\LP10. If you operate Shell from a system that has only floppy disk drives or one or more hard disk drives, or if you use a different subdirectory for document files, substitute the appropriate drive letters or subdirectory (or both) for your system.

Although LetterPerfect 1.0 supports a mouse, WordPerfect's Shell 3.01 program does not. As a result, the mouse *cannot* be used to select options from any Shell menu.

Starting The Shell Program

Follow these steps to run the Shell 3.01 program:

1. *On a hard disk system:* change to the drive (and subdirectory, if appropriate) that contains the SHELL.EXE program file. For example, on a system with a hard disk drive and the Shell program file in the D:\LP10 subdirectory, type *D:* and press Enter, followed by *CD \LP10* and press Enter.

   On a single floppy disk system: insert the floppy diskette that contains the SHELL.EXE program into the disk drive.

   On a dual floppy disk system: insert the floppy diskette that contains the SHELL.EXE program into the disk drive from which you want to start the program.

2. Type *shell* and press Enter.

   Shell briefly displays first its initial screen and then its main menu screen shown in figure 1.30. (The Shell menu with the 07/24/90 software package lists only LetterPerfect as a menu option.) By default, the Installation program installs the Shell program configured to run LetterPerfect without any of the switches listed in Table 1.4.

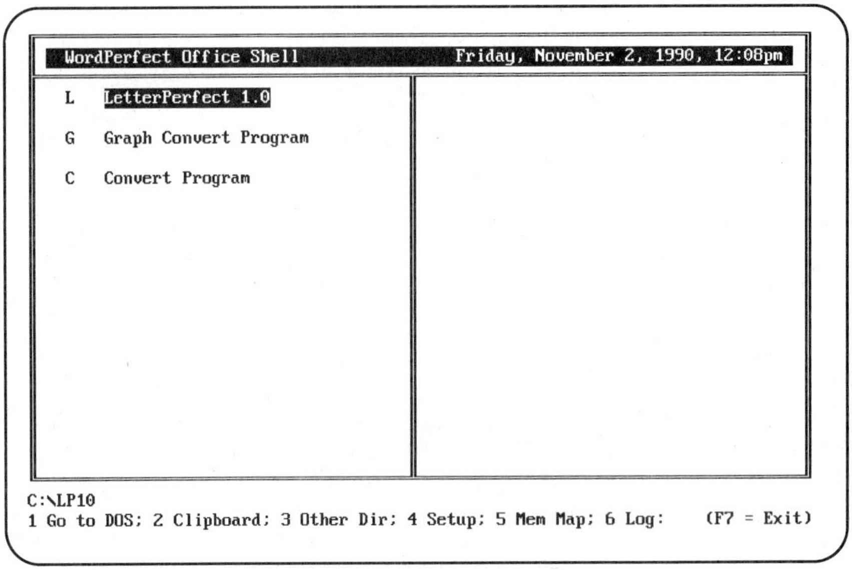

```
┌──────────────────────────────────────────────────────────────────┐
│  ██WordPerfect Office Shell██        Friday, November 2, 1990, 12:08pm │
│   L   ██LetterPerfect 1.0██       │                                │
│                                   │                                │
│   G   Graph Convert Program       │                                │
│                                   │                                │
│   C   Convert Program             │                                │
│                                   │                                │
│                                   │                                │
│                                   │                                │
│                                   │                                │
│                                   │                                │
│                                   │                                │
│                                   │                                │
│                                   │                                │
│                                   │                                │
│ C:\LP10                                                            │
│ 1 Go to DOS; 2 Clipboard; 3 Other Dir; 4 Setup; 5 Mem Map; 6 Log:    (F7 = Exit) │
└──────────────────────────────────────────────────────────────────┘
```

Fig. 1.30. *The Shell main menu screen.*

Note: If you are using a system with only floppy disk drives, insert the LetterPerfect 1 or LetterPerfect 1/2 diskette into the floppy disk drive from which LetterPerfect is started.

 3. Type *L* to start LetterPerfect.

Tip: When the menu lists two or more programs, you can use the cursor movement keys to move the cursor bar to highlight a program's name and press Enter.

Modifying Shell Menu Options

Follow these steps to change the options for LetterPerfect running under Shell on a system with a hard disk:

 1. From the main Shell menu, press Setup (4) and press Enter.

   Shell displays the Program Information screen for LetterPerfect. At the bottom of the screen, Shell displays information about the option highlighted by the cursor bar.

Tip: Like all WordPerfect software programs, you can press Help (F3) to display context-sensitive information about the program and/or the menu option highlighted by the cursor bar.

   2. Press Enter four times to move to the Default Directory field.

   3. Type *C:\LP10*.

Tip: If you type the name of a subdirectory that does not exist, Shell displays a menu prompt that requests confirmation to create the subdirectory. For example, in step 3 if you type *C:\LP10\DOCUMENT* and press Enter, the program displays a menu prompt: `C:\LP10\DOCUMENT does not exist, Create? (Y/N)`. You can either select **Y** to instruct the program to create the new subdirectory, or you can select **No**, Exit (F7), Cancel (F1) or Esc to return the cursor to the `Default directory` box. If you want the program to use a different subdirectory, type its name and press Enter. Press Cancel (F1) or Esc and press Enter to leave the box without selecting a default directory.

   4. Press Enter to move to the Program Name field.

   5. Press the right-arrow (→) key followed by left-arrow (←) key and type *C:\LP10*. If you begin typing without pressing the arrow keys, the Shell program automatically removes the *lp.exe* program command and you must retype the command.

   6. Press Enter three times to move to the Startup Options field. The Program Information screen appears as shown in figure 1.31.

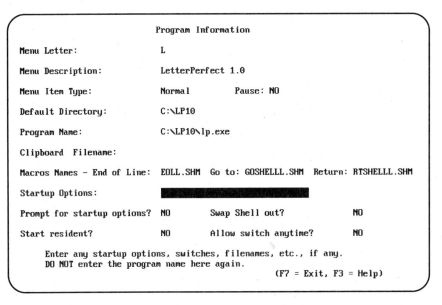

Fig. 1.31. The Shell program's Information screen with new parameters.

7. Type one or more of the switches listed in Table 1.4.

8. Press Exit (F7) twice to save the new parameters and return to the main Shell menu screen.

9. Type *L* to start LetterPerfect.

Understanding and Using LetterPerfect's Setup Feature

All software programs are subject to the capabilities and limitations of the computer hardware on which they are run.

LetterPerfect is no exception to this rule. However, the Setup feature lets you adjust LetterPerfect's default parameters to take full advantage of the computer system on which you operate the program.

LetterPerfect stores the adjustable program settings in a file named LP{LP}.SET that it places at the same location as LP.EXE, the main program file. If you accidentally delete LP{LP}.SET, the program reverts to its preset default parameters.

The following sections show you how to access and use the Setup feature and its options. Although these sections discuss the Setup options in numerical sequence, you can access the options in any sequence. When you change an option's parameters, the changes are immediately effective for the current and subsequent editing sessions.

Setting Screen Colors

On systems with color monitors, LetterPerfect offers you six color options. On desktop systems with color monitors, any of the color options is available. The one you select is a matter of personal preference. The appearance and intensity of the colors displayed depend on the type of video-display card and monitor used by your system.

The following steps show you how to adjust the color settings on a system with a color monitor:

    1. Access the **File** pull-down menu and select Se**t**up. Alternatively, press Setup (Shift-F1). LetterPerfect displays its default Setup menu screen (see fig. 1.32).

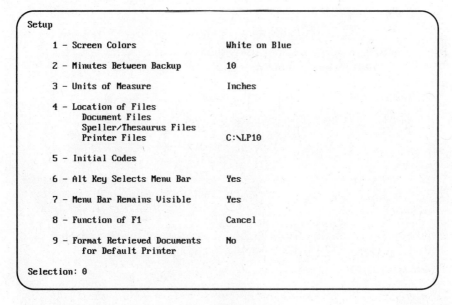

```
Setup

     1 - Screen Colors              White on Blue

     2 - Minutes Between Backup      10

     3 - Units of Measure            Inches

     4 - Location of Files
           Document Files
           Speller/Thesaurus Files
           Printer Files            C:\LP10

     5 - Initial Codes

     6 - Alt Key Selects Menu Bar    Yes

     7 - Menu Bar Remains Visible    Yes

     8 - Function of F1              Cancel

     9 - Format Retrieved Documents  No
           for Default Printer

Selection: 0
```

Fig. 1.32. *The Setup feature's default menu screen.*

2. Select **Screen Colors (1)**. LetterPerfect displays the `Screen Colors` menu shown in figure 1.33.

```
Screen Colors

    1 - White on Blue (Default)

    2 - Blue on White

    3 - LCD Display "Colors"

    4 - LCD Display "Colors" - No Intensity

    5 - Plasma Display "Colors"

    6 - Monochrome

    Note: Options 3, 4, 5 and 6 may also be useful on color screens.




Selection: 0
```

Fig. 1.33. *The Setup feature's default Screen Colors menu screen.*

3. Select the color option you want LetterPerfect to use. The program immediately begins using the color combination you choose and redisplays the Setup menu shown in figure 1.32.

4. Press Exit (F7) to return to the main editing screen.

Tip: If you run LetterPerfect on a desktop system with a monochrome monitor, the default Screen Colors option is *Monochrome*. On this type of system, LetterPerfect does *not* display the menu shown in figure 1.33. If you try to access the Screen Colors menu, LetterPerfect briefly displays a message at the bottom of the screen: `Unable to change colors for this monitor type`.

If you run LetterPerfect on a portable system, follow steps 1 through 3 and try the options for LCD and Plasma displays.

Setting the Timed Backup

The timed-backup feature automatically saves your documents as a file on disk at a set interval. By default, every 10 minutes the program creates a new backup file—LP{LP}.BK1—and puts the file on the disk drive where LetterPerfect looks for its program files. However, if you specify a directory for document files (see "Selecting Locations for Files" in a section following these instructions), the program places the backup file in that directory.

If your system loses power while the document is on screen or if you do not properly exit LetterPerfect, the most recently created backup file remains on the disk. When you restart LetterPerfect, you can retrieve LP{LP}.BK1, rename it, and resume creating or editing the document. When you properly exit LetterPerfect, the program automatically deletes LP{LP}.BK1.

Follow these steps to change the time interval that LetterPerfect uses to create a backup file:

1. Access the File pull-down menu and select Setup. Alternatively, press Setup (Shift-F1). LetterPerfect displays its default Setup menu screen (see fig. 1.32).

2. Select Minutes Between Backup (**2**).

3. Type the number of minutes that you want LetterPerfect to use for creating a backup file and press Enter.

> *Caution:* The LP{LP}.BK1 file takes up just as much disk space as your main document. This sometimes creates problems on systems with a single floppy disk drive, especially when you edit a large document. Setting the time interval for timed backup to zero minutes turns off this feature, saving disk space. Although this sometimes is useful, avoid deactivating the timed-backup feature unless you can afford the accidental loss of your document. If you do set the interval to zero, you should manually save the document to disk at frequent intervals.

4. Press Exit (F7) to return to the main editing screen.

Setting the Units of Measure

LetterPerfect uses the selected units of measure to calculate automatically how many columns and rows fit on a page. The value you designate for the unit of measure determines the units used in menu choices for margins (top, bottom, left, and right), tab settings, paper size, and the information displayed in the status line at the lower right corner of the screen. The default measurement unit is inches.

When you change units of measurement, all unit displays, including those contained in hidden codes, immediately and automatically change to reflect the new choice. (For a complete explanation of how LetterPerfect uses units of measure, see "Changing the Units of Measure" in Chapter 6.)

1. Access the File pull-down menu and select Setup. Alternatively, press Setup (Shift-F1). LetterPerfect displays its default Setup menu screen (see fig. 1.32).

2. Select Units of Measure (3). At the bottom of the screen, LetterPerfect displays the following menu:

1 Inches; **2** Centimeters; **3** Points; **4** 1200ths of an inch; **5** WP 4.2 **units: 0**

3. Select the measurement unit you want LetterPerfect to use in creating and displaying documents.

4. Press Exit (F7) to return to the main editing screen.

Selecting the Locations of Files

By default, LetterPerfect automatically looks to the same drive and directory for all of its program and document files. The Setup feature's Location of Files (4) option enables you to select different directories for some of these files.

The 07/24/90 software enables you to select only a different directory in which to save and retrieve documents. In addition to a different directory for documents, the 11/01/90 program also provides you the opportunity to designate alternative directories for the Spell and Thesaurus features, and the printer definition files.

While the files-location option is of little use on systems with a single floppy disk drive and only 640 K of RAM, the capability for different directories can be useful on systems with dual floppy disk drives, hard disk drives, or on systems attached to a network. For example, if you run LetterPerfect on a desktop system with a hard disk that also contains WordPerfect 5.1, the following steps show you how to use the files-location option to use the larger WordPerfect Spell, hyphenation, Thesaurus, and printer-definition files. The example assumes that you are using a system with a hard disk drive that has the following:

- A subdirectory named C:\LP10\DOCUMENT where you want LetterPerfect to store the documents you create

- The WordPerfect Spell, hyphenation, Thesaurus program files in a subdirectory named C:\WP51\DICTION

- The WordPerfect printer-definition files in a subdirectory named C:\WP51\PRINT

Follow these steps to change the default location of files:

1. Access the **File** pull-down menu and select **Setup**. Alternatively, press Setup (Shift-F1). LetterPerfect displays its default Setup menu screen (see fig. 1.32).

2. Select **Location of Files (4)**.

3. Type *C:\LP10\DOCUMENT* and press Enter.

4. Type *C:\WP51\DICTION* and press Enter.

5. Type *C:\WP51\PRINT* and press Enter. The Setup menu appears as shown in figure 1.34.

6. Press Exit (F7) to return to the main editing screen.

Selecting Initial Document Codes

LetterPerfect offers dozens of document formatting features such as printer page size, adjustable margins, justification, and base font. The program uses these formatting features and their default settings to define each document you create.

If the default formatting parameters are not suited to your requirements, the Setup feature's initial-document-codes option enables you to change the settings. For example, if all documents must have full justification instead of the default ragged-right margin, you can use the Initial Codes (**5**) option to change the default settings for all documents you create, as follows:

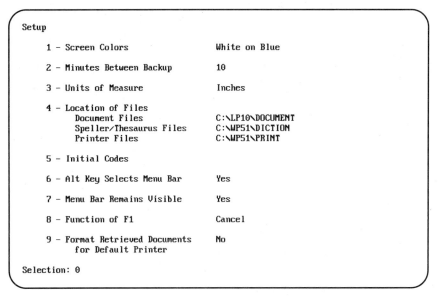

```
Setup

    1 - Screen Colors              White on Blue

    2 - Minutes Between Backup     10

    3 - Units of Measure           Inches

    4 - Location of Files
          Document Files           C:\LP10\DOCUMENT
          Speller/Thesaurus Files  C:\WP51\DICTION
          Printer Files            C:\WP51\PRINT

    5 - Initial Codes

    6 - Alt Key Selects Menu Bar   Yes

    7 - Menu Bar Remains Visible   Yes

    8 - Function of F1             Cancel

    9 - Format Retrieved Documents No
          for Default Printer

Selection: 0
```

Fig. 1.34. The Setup feature with defined alternative file locations.

1. Access the **File** pull-down menu and select Se**t**up. Alternatively, press Setup (Shift-F1). LetterPerfect displays its default Setup menu screen (see fig. 1.32).

2. Select Initial Codes (**5**). LetterPerfect displays its default initial-codes screen as shown in figure 1.35.

3. Move the cursor to highlight the **[Just:Left]** code.

4. Press Del.

5. Access the Layout pull-down menu and select Format. Alternatively, press Format (Shift-F8). LetterPerfect displays its Format menu.

6. Select Justification (**1**). At the bottom of the screen, LetterPerfect displays a menu:

   Justification: 1 Left; **2** Center; **3** Right; **4** Full: **0**

7. Select Full (**4**).

8. Press Exit (F7). The program returns to its initial-codes screen with the **[Just:Full]** code.

9. Press Exit (F7) twice to return to the main editing screen.

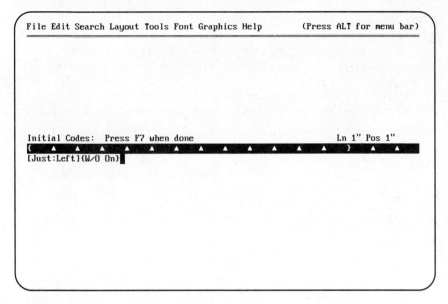

Fig. 1.35. *The Setup feature's default Initial Codes screen.*

> *Note:* When you install LetterPerfect, it automatically adds the **{W/O On}** code, a WordPerfect 5.1 document formatting code, to each document. If you retrieve the document into WordPerfect 5.1, this code activates that program's Widows/Orphans feature so that the document formats correctly. When you delete this code you do *not* turn off LetterPerfect's Widows/Orphans feature, which is permanently active.

Selecting the Method for Accessing the Pull-down Menu Bar

If you want to use LetterPerfect's pull-down menus, you must access them using either a mouse or the keyboard. By default, LetterPerfect offers two methods from the keyboard:

- press the Alt key

- hold down the Alt key while pressing the equal (=) key

Pressing the Alt key is quicker; however, you also can access some terminate-and-stay-resident (TSR) programs by pressing the Alt key. To avoid a conflict with these TSR programs, the Setup feature's Alt-key option enables you to change LetterPerfect so that only the Alt-= key combination accesses the pull-down menu.

Follow these steps to deactivate the Alt-key option for accessing the pull-down menu bar:

1. Access the **File** pull-down menu and select Setup. Alternatively, press Setup (Shift-F1). LetterPerfect displays its default Setup menu screen (see fig. 1.32).

2. Select **Alt Key Selects Menu Bar (6)**. LetterPerfect displays a menu prompt: No (Yes).

3. Select **No**.

4. Press Exit (F7) to return to the main editing screen.

> *Tip:* You can disable only the Alt-key option. The Alt-= key combination *cannot* be deactivated. When the Alt-key option can access the pull-down menu bar, LetterPerfect displays the message: (Press ALT for menu bar) at the right edge of the pull-down menu. When the Alt-key option is deactivated, the message displayed at the right edge of the pull-down menu is the following: (Press ALT= for menu bar).

Changing Display of the Pull-down Menu Bar

By default, LetterPerfect displays the pull-down menu and its separator bar across the top two rows of the main editing screen. With the default setting, LetterPerfect can display only 22 document lines at a time. The Setup feature includes an option to hide the pull-down menu bar except when you are using it, enabling LetterPerfect to display 24 document lines on the main editing screen. When the menu bar is not visible, you can access and display it by doing one of the following:

• Click the right mouse button

• Press the Alt key (unless this key has been disabled)

• Hold down the Alt key while pressing the equal (=) key

Follow these steps to hide the pull-down menu bar from the main editing screen:

1. Access the **File** pull-down menu and select **Setup**. Alternatively, press Setup (Shift-F1). LetterPerfect displays its default Setup menu screen (see, fig. 1.32).

2. Select **Menu Bar Remains Visible (7)**. LetterPerfect displays a menu prompt: No (Yes).

3. Select **No**.

4. Press Exit (F7) to return to the main editing screen.

Selecting the Function of the F1 Key

When you installed LetterPerfect, you chose the function for the F1 key—Cancel or Help. An option on the Setup feature also lets you select which function the F1 key performs. To use the option, do the following:

1. Access the **File** pull-down menu and select **Setup**. Alternatively, press Setup (Shift-F1). LetterPerfect displays its default Setup menu screen (see fig. 1.32).

2. Select **Function of F1 (8)**. At the bottom of the screen, LetterPerfect displays a menu prompt:

   1 Help; **2** Cancel: **0**

3. Choose the option you want the F1 key to perform.

4. Press Exit (F7) to return to the main editing screen.

Tip: The Esc key always activates the Cancel feature, whether the F1 key activates the Cancel or Help feature. The F3 key always activates the Help feature, whether the F1 key activates the Cancel or Help feature.

Selecting Whether LetterPerfect Automatically Reformats Documents

When LetterPerfect retrieves a document to the main editing screen, it automatically formats the document to use the printer definition with which it was created—if that definition is available on your system. This situation usually occurs when your system has more than one printer attached to it, for example, a dot-matrix printer for creating rough drafts and a laser printer for printing final documents.

Although you can use several methods to manually change the formatting of a document for printing with a different printer, the quickest and easiest way is with the Setup feature's automatic document formatting option. The following steps show you how to use this option:

1. Access the **File** pull-down menu and select Se**t**up. Alternatively, press Setup (Shift-F1). LetterPerfect displays its default Setup menu screen (see fig. 1.32).

2. Select F**o**rmat Retrieved Documents for Default Printer (**9**). LetterPerfect displays a menu prompt: No (Yes).

3. Select **Y**es.

4. Press Exit (F7) to return to the main editing screen.

While the automatic reformatting feature remains active, LetterPerfect automatically reformats each document it retrieves to use the current printer definition.

Summary

In this chapter you have learned how to do the following:

- Install the 11/01/90 LetterPerfect 1.0 and Shell 3.01 programs on a hard disk drive and on floppy diskettes

- Install a printer-definition file

- Start LetterPerfect directly from DOS using switches

- Start and configure the Shell program

- Start LetterPerfect from the Shell menu

- Use LetterPerfect's Setup feature to change the program's default parameters

In Chapter 2, "Preparing to Use LetterPerfect", you learn how to run the program on portable and desktop systems.

2

Preparing To Use
LetterPerfect

This chapter acquaints you with LetterPerfect 1.0 and prepares you for the tasks in Chapter 3: creating and printing a simple document. Beginning with a brief introduction to LetterPerfect, this chapter covers the hardware you need for operating LetterPerfect and shows you how to "boot," or start, LetterPerfect on your computer. You also learn about LetterPerfect's editing screen, the special ways LetterPerfect uses your keyboard, and the context-sensitive on-line help that comes with the program. And if you're interested in taking the LetterPerfect tutorial to get more comfortable with the program, this chapter provides a brief overview of the Tutor program and shows you how to start it.

If you need to install LetterPerfect on your system, turn to Chapter 1, which covers everything you need to know to get LetterPerfect running on systems with one or two floppy disk drives or a hard disk drive.

Reminder: WordPerfect Corporation updated LetterPerfect 1.0 just before this book went to press. Dated 11/01/90, the interim release includes new options for existing features, and a few new features. The menus on your screen may, therefore, differ slightly from those shown in this book. Also, depending on the printer-form definition, margins, tab stops, and font you specify, the text placement and status-line information in documents you create may differ from that shown in this book's figures.

For information about using the mouse and accessing the pull-down menus, refer to the Introduction.

What Is LetterPerfect?

LetterPerfect 1.0 is a lean version of WordPerfect 5.1, one of the world's most popular word processing software programs, currently enjoying nearly 50 percent of the word processing market. LetterPerfect users who also are experienced with WordPerfect have humorously referred to the program as "WordPerfect lite," "low-cal WordPerfect," and "WordPerfect slim."

The first release of LetterPerfect, dated 07/24/90, has all the basic features expected in a word processing package, as well as less complex versions of many features found in its big brother, WordPerfect 5.1. LetterPerfect is suited to your needs, whether they entail short memos or complex, lengthy documents. The program also supports the same wide range of printers as WordPerfect. LetterPerfect presents you with an editing screen that is blank except for a single menu bar at the top and a document information line at the bottom.

The features of LetterPerfect 07/24/90 include the following:

- Context-sensitive help, which lets you quickly access appropriate Help menus from anywhere in the program

- Pull-down menus, accessible through either the keyboard or a mouse, which simplify procedures for the novice or occasional user

- Mouse support, which enables you to use a mouse for selecting text and menu options from either the new pull-down menus or the regular menus

- Improved editing control, including fast-key combinations that let you access many of the program's features simply by pressing two keys

- A merge feature with meaningful codes that makes creating documents quick and easy

- Complete file compatibility with WordPerfect 5.1 documents

- On-line speller and thesaurus features

- Enhanced drivers that support hundreds of printers

- Shell macros accessed through the WordPerfect Office Shell 3.0 program included with LetterPerfect

- The efficient use of expanded memory

The second version of LetterPerfect is an interim release dated 11/01/90. This release adds new features, as well as new options for existing features, including the following:

- A simplified Installation program for installing and updating the LetterPerfect program files

- Additional start-up switches and error messages that provide more information about the way LetterPerfect interacts with your computer system

- An internal macro feature that lets you create and use macros without running LetterPerfect through the Shell program

- A revamped exit feature that protects a document from accidental loss if you try to save the document and receive a `Disk Full` error message.

- New options or methods of functioning for using menu prompts and entering units of measure

- New options or methods of functioning for the Backup, Help, Keyboard Redefinition, Language Code, Look, Printing, and Screen Rewrite features

Noting the Hardware Required To Run LetterPerfect

LetterPerfect 1.0 runs on an IBM PC or a completely compatible portable or desktop computer that has the following:

- DOS 2.0 or a later version for its main operating system

- 512K of conventional random-access memory (RAM), at least 330K of which must be available to LetterPerfect

- One 3 1/2-inch 720K floppy disk drive, one 3 1/2-inch 1.44M floppy-disk drive, one 5 1/4-inch 1.2M floppy disk drive, two 5 1/4-inch 360K disk drives, or one hard disk drive and one of the floppy disk drives just listed.

> ***Caution:*** LetterPerfect cannot be run on a computer system that has a single 5 1/4-inch 360K disk drive, unless your system has a hard disk.

A computer temporarily stores its operating programs and data in volatile RAM. The system loses everything stored in RAM if you turn off the computer or if the system loses power. A power interruption usually does not affect the original program and data files on the floppy or hard disk.

Most computers made since 1987 contain between 640K and 1M of conventional RAM. Many also have an additional 1M of either extended or expanded memory. How can you determine the amount of conventional RAM available for running LetterPerfect? The answer depends on which version of LetterPerfect you are using.

If you have the 07/24/90 version, you must use the DOS CHKDSK command to determine the amount of available RAM. Before you start LetterPerfect, type *CHKDSK* at the DOS prompt and press Enter. The computer displays information about the total RAM ("bytes total memory") and the RAM available to run LetterPerfect ("bytes free").

If you have the 11/01/90 version, then as an alternative to using CHKDSK, you can start LetterPerfect and specify the /ws switch. At the DOS prompt, type *lp/ws* and press Enter. LetterPerfect pauses on its opening screen and lists the conventional memory available to the program (see fig. 2.1) after it loads into RAM. The screen also lists the amount of expanded memory available to LetterPerfect.

The system's speed and amount of RAM control how fast the program works. LP.EXE, the primary LetterPerfect program file, uses 212K of RAM. The remaining RAM holds your document file and the code for some of the program's features.

After filling RAM, the program automatically swaps and stores information in overflow files. LetterPerfect puts these overflow files on the disk containing its program files. When LetterPerfect needs the information in these files, the program moves the data into RAM. To make room for the retrieved information, the program removes other information from RAM. LetterPerfect stores this information in the overflow files. This process slows program speed.

LetterPerfect automatically detects and uses expanded memory for storing and swapping operations. Program functions that use expanded memory are many times faster than those involving the disk drive. This arrangement lets LetterPerfect work faster, especially when you edit large documents.

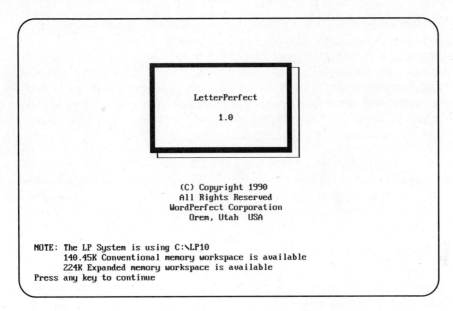

Fig. 2.1. The LetterPerfect introductory screen with memory listing.

LetterPerfect 1.0 comes on four 5 1/4-inch disks or two 3 1/2-inch disks (excluding disks for printer drivers). The disks contain compressed files that are expanded automatically by the Installation program. As shown in Chapter 1, you can install LetterPerfect 1.0 either to a hard disk or to diskettes. Like all software programs, LetterPerfect runs most efficiently—quicker and with fewer interruptions—from a hard disk drive.

Monitors and Graphics Cards

LetterPerfect supports a wide range of video systems, including Hercules Graphics, the Color Graphics Adapter (CGA), Enhanced Graphics Adapter (EGA), and Video Graphics Array (VGA). Other systems supported include the AT&T 6300, IBM 8514/A, Genius (full-page), and COMPAQ Portable III/386 with plasma display. If your monitor is not supported, call WordPerfect Corporation's main support number (1-800-541-5096) for assistance. Because WordPerfect is always adding support for new hardware, a new driver that supports your monitor may be available.

You can run LetterPerfect on a system that has a monochrome monitor without a graphics card, but if you do so, the program's View Document feature does not display graphics, font changes, or font attributes (superscript, subscript, italics, and so on). With a CGA video card and a color or monochrome monitor, the program displays graphics in View Document mode. A color monitor with this card enables you to designate different background and foreground screen colors to differentiate font attributes. EGA and VGA systems provide better resolution in graphics mode and offer more possibilities for displaying font attributes in various color combinations.

LetterPerfect also supports the Hercules Graphics Card, the Hercules Graphics Card Plus, and the Hercules InColor Card (the color version of the Hercules Graphics Card Plus). These last two cards come with the Hercules RamFont mode, which offers you WYSIWYG (*what you see is what you get*—pronounced "wizzy wig") as you work with a document on LetterPerfect's main editing screen.

RamFont mode displays on the main editing screen most changes in font size or appearance as they will print. For example, LetterPerfect displays fonts in their relative sizes (including superscript and subscript) and appearances (underlined, bolded, and italicized).

Printers

LetterPerfect supports a wide variety of printers, from dot-matrix to laser. Printer installation is covered in detail in Chapter 8. The printer drivers supplied on the printer disks are for the most part common printers. If you cannot locate a definition for your printer, follow the instructions in Chapter 8 for emulating a similar printer, or call WordPerfect Corporation for updated information on LetterPerfect's list of supported printers. Unless you have an ancient (pre-1987) printer manufactured and sold outside the United States or Europe, there should be a printer definition that lets LetterPerfect operate your printer.

The Mouse

LetterPerfect 1.0 supports a mouse, but you do not need the device to use the program. Even if you have a mouse, you may find it easier to operate the program exclusively from the keyboard. You use the mouse to perform two main activities:

- Making selections from most menus, including the pull-down menus

- Highlighting text so that you can perform a block action (such as deleting or moving) or modification (such as underlining or centering)

Before loading LetterPerfect, you must load a separate, external mouse-driving program so that LetterPerfect will recognize the mouse and you will be able to use it. Virtually every type of two- and three-button mouse is supported by LetterPerfect. For information on operating the mouse, see this chapter's section, "Using the Mouse."

Starting LetterPerfect on a Single-Floppy-Drive System

If you use LetterPerfect on a system that has one 3 1/2-inch 720K floppy drive, the main LetterPerfect program files are located on two disks labeled *LetterPerfect 1* and *LetterPerfect 2*. If you are running LetterPerfect with these two disks, at some point in the start-up process LetterPerfect displays this prompt: Insert diskette labeled "LetterPerfect 2" and press any key

If you press a key without inserting the LetterPerfect 2 disk, LetterPerfect displays this prompt:

```
Can't find correct copy of LP.FIL
Enter full path and filename (example: C:\LP\LP.FIL)
LP.FIL
```

At this point you must either insert the LetterPerfect 2 disk or terminate the start-up procedure by pressing Cancel (F1).

In the following instructions, the assumption is that when the program prompts you to insert the LetterPerfect 2 disk, you do so and press Enter.

If you are using LetterPerfect on a system that has one 3 1/2-inch 1.44M or 5 1/4-inch 1.2M floppy drive, the main LetterPerfect program files are located on a single disk labeled *LetterPerfect*.

> *Caution:* In this section, the assumption is that you have installed a copy of the DOS COMMAND.COM file on your working copy of the LetterPerfect disk. If you have not already formatted disks and made a working copy of the original LetterPerfect disks, do so according to the procedure outlined in Chapter 1.

As explained in Chapter 1, you can start LetterPerfect by using either the SHELL or LP command. To start LetterPerfect on a computer that has a single floppy drive, follow these steps:

1. Insert the working copy of your LetterPerfect program disk into the drive.

2. Turn on your computer.

3. Respond appropriately to the operating-system prompts for the date and time. (If your system retains this information or uses an AUTOEXEC.BAT file, this step may not be necessary.)

4. At the A> prompt, type *cd \lp10* and press Enter. If you want to run LetterPerfect through the Office Shell 3.01 program, follow steps 5 and 6. If you want to run LetterPerfect directly under DOS outside of the Shell program, skip step 5 and do only step 6.

5. Type *shell* and press Enter. As the Shell program loads into RAM, the program briefly displays the introductory screen shown in figure 2.2, followed by the main Shell menu shown in figure 2.3.

6. If LetterPerfect is running under Shell, select **L**. If LetterPerfect is running directly under DOS, type *lp* and press Enter. The program briefly displays the introductory screen shown in figure 2.4, unless LetterPerfect is running under the Shell and automatically starts as a resident program. After a few seconds, LetterPerfect's main editing screen appears as shown in figure 2.5.

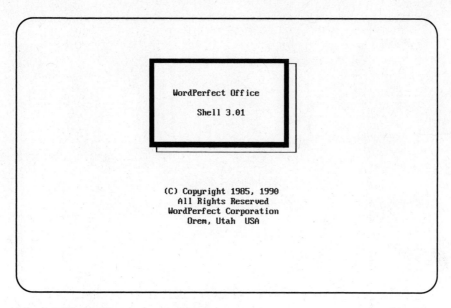

Fig. 2.2. *The Shell introductory screen.*

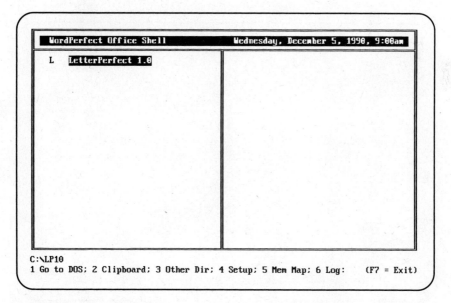

Fig. 2.3. *The main Shell menu.*

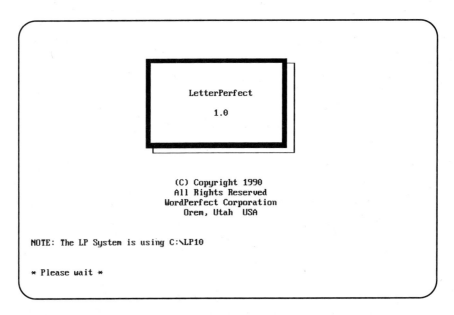

Fig. 2.4. *The LetterPerfect introductory screen.*

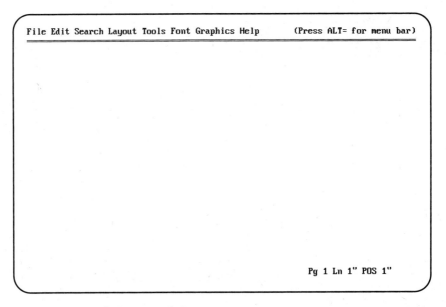

Fig. 2.5. *LetterPerfect's main editing screen.*

Regardless of the size of the floppy disk drive, on single-drive systems you may not remove the LetterPerfect 2 disk (unless you are using the Thesaurus feature). All documents are saved on the LetterPerfect 2 disk. If you need to transfer the documents to another disk, you must use either the COPY or the XCOPY command at the DOS prompt and follow the prompts displayed on the screen.

If you have created a subdirectory on your disk, LetterPerfect lets you choose it for storing document files. The section "Choosing the Location of Files" in Chapter 1 shows you how to use the Setup feature and permanently change the default storage area.

The following steps indicate how to change the default subdirectory for the current editing session:

1. Access the **File** pull-down menu and select **List Files**. Alternatively, press List Files (F5). LetterPerfect displays the following at the lower left corner of the screen: `Dir A:\`

2. Press =. LetterPerfect displays this prompt at the lower left corner of the screen: `New Directory = A:\`

3. Type *a:\<pathname>* and press Enter. LetterPerfect uses the subdirectory as the storage area for your documents.

4. If the subdirectory does not exist, LetterPerfect displays this prompt at the lower left corner of the screen: `Create A:\`*<pathname>*`? No (Yes)`

If you select **Yes**, LetterPerfect creates the subdirectory on the disk. If you select **No**, LetterPerfect cancels the subdirectory operation.

Starting LetterPerfect on a Dual-Floppy-Drive System

If you are using LetterPerfect on a system that has two 5 1/4-inch 360K floppy disk drives, the main LetterPerfect program files are located on two disks labeled *LetterPerfect 1* and *LetterPerfect 2*. If you are running LetterPerfect with two disks, at some point in the start-up process LetterPerfect displays this prompt: `Insert diskette labeled "LetterPerfect 2" and press any key`

If you press a key without inserting the LetterPerfect 2 disk, LetterPerfect displays this prompt:

```
Can't find correct copy of LP.FIL
Enter full path and filename (example: C:\LP\LP.FIL)
LP.FIL
```

At this point you must either insert the LetterPerfect 2 disk or terminate the start-up procedure by pressing Cancel (F1).

The following instructions are based on the assumption that when the program prompts you to insert the LetterPerfect 2 disk, you do so and press Enter.

> *Caution:* In this section, the assumption is that you have installed a copy of the DOS COMMAND.COM file on your working copy of the LetterPerfect disk. If you have not already formatted disks and made a working copy of the original LetterPerfect disks, do so according to the procedure outlined in Chapter 1.

As explained in Chapter 1, you can start LetterPerfect by using either the SHELL or the LP command. To start LetterPerfect on a computer that has two 360K floppy disk drives, follow these steps:

1. Insert the working copy of your LetterPerfect program disk into drive A.

2. Insert a formatted data disk into drive B.

3. Turn on the computer.

4. Respond appropriately to the operating-system prompts for the date and time. (If your system retains this information or uses an AUTOEXEC.BAT file, this step may not be necessary.)

5. At the A> prompt, type *cd \lp10* and press Enter. If you want to run LetterPerfect through the Office Shell 3.01 program, follow steps 6 and 7. If you want to run LetterPerfect directly under DOS outside of the Shell program, skip step 6 and do only step 7.

6. Type *shell* and press Enter. As the Shell program loads into RAM, it briefly displays the introductory screen shown in figure 2.2, followed by the main Shell menu shown in figure 2.3.

7. If LetterPerfect is running under Shell, select **L.** If LetterPerfect is running directly under DOS, type *lp* and press Enter. The

program briefly displays the introductory screen shown in figure 2.4 unless LetterPerfect is running under the Shell and automatically starts as a resident program. After a few seconds, LetterPerfect's main editing screen appears as shown in figure 2.5.

LetterPerfect automatically places the documents on the disk and subdirectory containing its program files. However, the program lets you choose a different default drive and subdirectory for storing these files. The section "Choosing the Location of Files" in Chapter 1 shows you how to use the Setup feature and permanently change the default storage area.

The following steps indicate how to change the default drive and subdirectory for the current editing session:

1. Access the File pull-down menu and select **List Files**. Alternatively, press List Files (F5). LetterPerfect displays the following at the lower left corner of the screen: `Dir A:\`

2. Press =. LetterPerfect displays this prompt at the lower left corner of the screen: `New Directory = A:\`

3. Type *b:* and press Enter. LetterPerfect uses the disk in drive B as the storage area for your documents. If you have created a subdirectory on the disk, type *b:\<pathname>* and press Enter. LetterPerfect uses the subdirectory on the disk in drive B as the storage area for your documents.

4. If the subdirectory does not exist, LetterPerfect displays this prompt at the lower left corner of the screen: `Create` `B:\`*<u>pathname</u>*`?` `No (Yes)`

If you select **Yes**, LetterPerfect creates the subdirectory on the disk. If you select **No**, LetterPerfect cancels the subdirectory operation.

Starting LetterPerfect on a Hard Disk System

As explained in Chapter 1, you can start LetterPerfect by using either the SHELL or the LP command. If you created an AUTOEXEC.BAT file during installation (see Chapter 1), LetterPerfect loads automatically after you turn on the computer. (Depending on the instructions in the AUTOEXEC.BAT file, you may be required to enter the current date and time.) The instructions in this chapter are based on the assumption that your system does not automatically start LetterPerfect through the AUTOEXEC.BAT file.

Make sure that the floppy drive (or drives) does not contain disks. On systems with 5 1/4-inch floppy disk drives, turn drive A's lever so that it is parallel to the disk slot. Systems with 3 1/2-inch floppy drives do not have levers. Follow these steps to start LetterPerfect:

1. Turn on your computer.

2. At the C> prompt, type *cd \lp10* and press Enter. If you want to run LetterPerfect through the Office Shell 3.01 program, follow steps 3 and 4. If you want to run LetterPerfect directly under DOS outside the Shell program, skip step 3 and do only step 4.

3. Type *shell* and press Enter. As the Shell program loads into RAM, it briefly displays the introductory screen shown in figure 2.2, followed by the main Shell menu shown in figure 2.3.

4. If LetterPerfect is running under Shell, select **L**. If LetterPerfect is running directly under DOS, type *lp* and press Enter. The program briefly displays the introductory screen shown in figure 2.4, unless LetterPerfect is running under Shell and automatically starts as a resident program. After a few seconds, LetterPerfect's main editing screen appears, as shown in figure 2.5.

LetterPerfect automatically places the documents on the disk and subdirectory containing its program files. However, the program lets you choose any available drive and subdirectory for storing these files. The section "Choosing the Location of Files" in Chapter 1 shows you how to use the Setup feature and permanently change the default storage area.

The following steps indicate how to change the default drive and subdirectory for the current editing session:

1. Access the File pull-down menu and select List Files. Alternatively, press List Files (F5). LetterPerfect displays the following at the lower left corner of the screen: Dir C:\LP10

2. Press =. LetterPerfect displays this prompt at the lower left corner of the screen: New Directory = C:\LP10

3. Type *<drive letter>:\<pathname>* and press Enter. The program uses the subdirectory on the designated disk as the storage area for your documents.

4. If the subdirectory does not exist, LetterPerfect displays this prompt at the lower left corner of the screen: `Create` *<drive letter>*:*<pathname>*? `No (Yes)`

If you select **Yes**, LetterPerfect creates the subdirectory on the disk. If you select **No**, LetterPerfect cancels the subdirectory operation.

Troubleshooting Problems with Starting LetterPerfect

If you have trouble starting LetterPerfect, always check the following things:

On all computer systems regardless of drive type:

1. Check all power cords and cables to make certain that they are connected properly.

2. Make sure that your monitor is turned on and adjusted properly.

On systems with single or dual floppy disk drives:

1. Make certain that you are starting the program from drive A.

2. Make certain that you typed the proper commands.

3. Make certain that the program and data disks are properly formatted (see Chapter 1).

4. Make certain that the program files are properly copied to the working disks.

5. Make certain that the working copy of the LetterPerfect system disk is in drive A.

6. Check drive B to make certain that you have a formatted data disk in the drive.

7. Make certain that the disks are inserted properly into the disk drives.

8. On systems with 5 1/4-inch disk drives, make certain that the lever is turned 90 degrees to the disk slot.

On systems with a hard disk drive:

1. Make certain that you are starting the program from the proper subdirectory.

2. Make certain that you typed the proper commands.

Restarting LetterPerfect

What happens if the power fails because of an electrical storm or an accidental pull of the plug while you are using LetterPerfect? Or what happens if the program stops working—a condition called "crashing," "hanging," or "freezing"—and no longer accepts any keyboard input? The latter situation forces you to press the Ctrl-Alt-Del key combination (a process called *soft*, or *warm*, rebooting) or turn off the computer and then turn it on again (a process called *hard*, or *cold*, rebooting). In either event, the result is an improper program exit from LetterPerfect. (The end of this chapter shows you how to exit the program properly.)

When you restart LetterPerfect, the program displays the following prompt: `Are other copies of LetterPerfect currently running? Y/N`

Press N in response to this prompt. If when you installed the program you chose to have LetterPerfect perform a timed backup of your document, you'll eventually (depending on the intervals you've chosen for the timed backup) get the following error message: `Old backup file exists 1 Rename 2 Delete`

At the interval you designated through the timed-backup option on the Setup menu (see Chapter 1), LetterPerfect automatically saves the document on the main editing screen as a file named LP{LP}.BK1 in the directory where the program stores your documents. LetterPerfect deletes this file when you exit from the program properly. However, if the program terminates without your using the exit procedure, LP{LP}.BK1 remains a file on the disk.

If you select **R**ename (**1**), LetterPerfect displays a prompt so that you can give the backup file a document name. After you enter the name, LetterPerfect prompts you to press Enter to complete loading the program. From the main editing screen you can then retrieve the document and resume editing it. If you select **D**elete (**2**), the program continues loading, but you lose the document as it existed on the disk when the program terminated.

Understanding LetterPerfect's Main Editing Screen

Most of the formatting and editing of a document is done on LetterPerfect's main editing screen, shown in figure 2.4. LetterPerfect automatically displays the pull-down menu bar across the top of the screen unless you change the default so that the menu bar is visible only when you press the Alt-= key combination or click the right mouse button.

LetterPerfect's blank editing screen does not display editing icons and may seem intimidating if you are familiar with word processing programs that use icons. Actually, the uncluttered screen comes about as close as possible to a blank piece of paper in a typewriter. This simple screen lets you concentrate on writing without unnecessary visual distractions, freeing you to write and see as many of your words as possible on screen. LetterPerfect's editing screen provides you with the maximum area for viewing your work.

When you begin creating a new document, the only information on the screen is found in the bottom right corner (see fig. 2.5). This status-line information tells you the position of the *cursor*—the blinking bar or box on the screen— relative to the document's edges. The cursor marks the point where you begin typing characters; inserting and deleting text; retrieving documents stored on disk; and embedding the hidden codes for formatting and text enhancements, such as bold and underline.

The Pg listing tells you the page number on which the cursor is located. In figure 2.5, the cursor is on page 1. The Ln listing indicates the cursor's vertical position relative to the top edge of the page. The Pos listing indicates the cursor's horizontal position relative to the left edge of the page.

When you save a document as a file on the disk, you give it a name that LetterPerfect then displays in the lower left corner of the screen.

By default, the U.S. version of LetterPerfect uses an 8 1/2-by-11-inch page form (sometimes called *template*). Foreign versions of the program may use a different default value. The flush-left position for the cursor is at 1 inch from the edge of the paper, and the status line reads Pos 1$dp. When the cursor moves past the right margin of the page—7 1/2 inches from the form's left edge, 1 inch from the right edge—LetterPerfect automatically moves the cursor to the beginning of the next line.

LetterPerfect offers several choices for its display measurement: inches, centi- meters, w units (1/1200 inch), and WordPerfect 4.2 units. You designate the measurement value from the Setup menu. (See Chapter 1 for information on the Setup menu.)

The Caps Lock and Num Lock keys are feature toggle switches. When you press the Caps Lock key to enter uppercase characters, Pos displays as POS. When you press the Num Lock key to enter numerals from the numeric keypad, the Pos indicator blinks on and off.

The number following the Pos indicator changes intensity or color to show you the document's font appearance or size at the cursor's present location: normal, bold, underline, italic, superscript, and subscript. See Chapters 6 and 7 for an explanation of the font appearance and size attributes. Only a color monitor displays text attributes in various colors.

Using the Keyboard

LetterPerfect uses either the function keys or the pull-down menus to carry out many operations. The keyboard for a desktop computer has its function keys in one of two places: either in two rows to the left of the character keys or in a line above the character keys. The location and arrangement of the function keys on the keyboard of a portable computer are not standardized but vary with each manufacturer and model.

This section is descriptive and intended to familiarize you with the keyboard's functions. Although it focuses on the keyboards for desktop computers, the functions discussed apply equally to keyboards for portable computers. Later chapters give you the chance to try out all these keys as you create, edit, revise, and print various documents.

When you press a key, the keyboard sends a unique electrical signal to the computer system's ROM BIOS. The ROM BIOS interprets the signal and tells the computer to take a specific action. For character and numeric keys, the action usually displays the key's character or number on the screen. For the function and other system-specific keys, the action usually moves the cursor or causes the active program to take a specific action.

There are three common types of desktop keyboards: the 84-key old-style keyboard shown in figures 2.6 and 2.7, the 101-key Enhanced Keyboard shown in figure 2.8, and intelligent keyboards with many extra keys that perform specialized functions. Older-model computers (primarily the IBM XT and compatible clones and early-model IBM ATs and compatible clones) use a ROM BIOS that recognizes only the 84 keys used on old-style keyboards, like those shown in figures 2.6 and 2.7. Newer-model computers (primarily later-model IBM ATs and compatible clones and most computers manufactured since 1988) use a ROM BIOS that requires the 101-key Enhanced Keyboard like that shown in figure 2.7. Some newer Enhanced Keyboards have 12 function keys located on the left side instead of across the top. Intelligent keyboards come in many different shapes with dozens of extra keys and special hardware or software that create capabilities exceeding those of the old-style keyboards and Enhanced Keyboards.

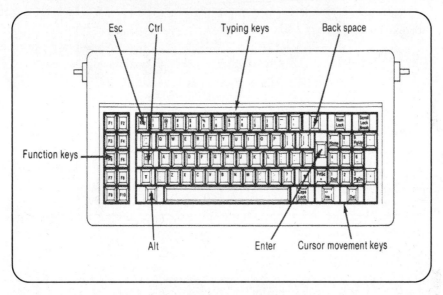

Fig. 2.6. *The original 84-key personal-computer keyboard.*

Although an old-style 84-key ROM BIOS may work with a 101-key Enhanced Keyboard, the ROM BIOS recognizes signals from only 84 keys. There are two easy ways to test for the type of ROM BIOS in your computer system.

First, while operating LetterPerfect on a computer equipped with an Enhanced Keyboard, press the F11 key. If this action activates the Reveal Codes feature, the ROM BIOS supports the Enhanced Keyboard. If this action does not activate the Reveal Codes feature, your system probably has the old-style ROM BIOS.

Second, you can run the WPINFO.EXE testing program—included with LetterPerfect 1.0—from DOS and check its description of your keyboard. If it says "Enhanced," as shown in figure 2.9, the ROM BIOS supports the 101-key enhanced format.

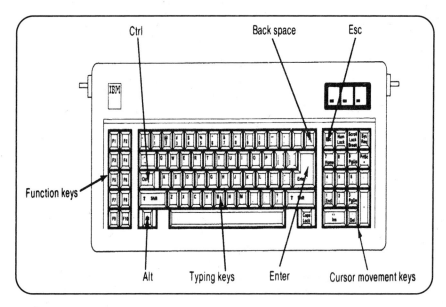

Fig. 2.7. The second 84-key personal-computer keyboard.

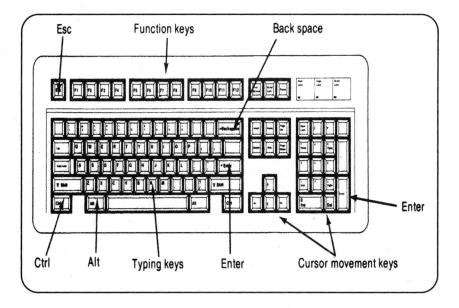

Fig. 2.8. The 101-key Enhanced Keyboard.

```
           WordPerfect Information
Machine Type . . . . . . . . . .   PS/2 Model 60
BIOS Make . . . . . . . . . . .    PHOENIX
BIOS Date . . . . . . . . . .      01/15/88
Processor Type . . . . . . . . .   Intel 80386
Math Coprocessor . . . . . . .     Present
RAM Memory . . . . . . . . . .     639K total RAM, 365K available
Expanded Memory . . . . . . .      EMS 4.0, 992K total, 992K available
Keyboard Supported . . . . . .     Enhanced
Display Type . . . . . . . . .     VGA
Display Size . . . . . . . . .     80 columns, 25 rows
File Handles Available to WP . .   20
I/O Ports . . . . . . . . . .      1 parallel, 2 serial
DOS Version . . . . . . . . .      3.31
Number of DOS Buffers . . . . .    5
Drive Types . . . . . . . . .      2 Diskette: A,B
                                   3 Fixed: C,D,E
                                   0 RAM:
                                   (No Network drives found)
WPCORP Software . . . . . . .      Repeat Performance,



        Hit a key to continue:
```

Fig. 2.9. The WPINFO information screen.

If the ROM BIOS supports only the 84-key format and you want to use all 101 keys on an Enhanced Keyboard, you have two options.

First, you can replace the old-style ROM BIOS with a new ROM BIOS that supports the Enhanced Keyboard. Depending on where you obtain the new chip and who does the actual work, the replacement cost ranges from a few dollars to approximately $75.00.

Second, you can use a software driver that works with the old-style ROM BIOS to give full support of all 101 keys on an Enhanced Keyboard. Several commercial and public-domain (free) software programs provide support for Enhanced Keyboards. One such program is ENHKBD.COM, found on many computer bulletin-board systems (BBS), including CompuServe. ENHKBD.COM is a terminate-and-stay resident (TSR) program that uses approximately 750 bytes of memory and provides full support for the Enhanced Keyboard on systems with the old-style ROM BIOS. Currently, the ENHKBD program is available on the WordPerfect Support Group Forum A, Library 9, under the name ENHKBD.ARC.

Although all computer keyboards are similar to the keyboard of a typewriter, there are some important differences. One critical but easily overlooked difference between composing with a typewriter and composing with LetterPerfect is that you do not end a text line at the right margin by pressing the Enter key. When you type text in LetterPerfect and reach the end of a line, the program automatically "wraps" the text to the next line. If you are accustomed to using a typewriter, you will find the word-wrap feature a genuine pleasure. Automatic word wrap makes it easy to create, edit, and revise your text.

If you press the Enter key before LetterPerfect has a chance to wrap the text to the next line, the program inserts a hidden hard-return code, **[HRt]**, that causes unnecessary problems if you later reformat the document by inserting or deleting characters.

LetterPerfect uses the following three main areas of the keyboard:

- The function keys—10 or 12 depending on the type of keyboard— located as shown in figures 2.6, 2.7, and 2.8

- The alphanumeric, or "typing," keys, located in the center of the keyboard (the keys most familiar to you from your experience with typewriter keyboards)

- The numeric and cursor-movement keys, located as shown in figures 2.6, 2.7, and 2.8

Using the Shift, Alt, and Control Keys

The Shift, Alt, and Control (Ctrl) keys are part of the alphanumeric keyboard. These keys are used with the function keys to activate features or insert many of LetterPerfect's hidden formatting codes.

The Shift key creates uppercase letters and other special characters, as it does on a typewriter keyboard. Pressing the Shift key with a function key starts some program features. Pressing either the Alt or Ctrl key with function keys, number keys, or letter keys also starts program features. Pressing the Alt key by itself starts the pull-down menu feature. A Setup feature option lets you turn off this feature (see Chapter 1).

When you press the Ctrl key with certain letter keys, you can activate some of LetterPerfect's features with fewer keystrokes than if you use the pull-down menu bar or the function keys. LetterPerfect calls these special Ctrl-key combinations *fast keys*.

Using the Function Keys and Fast Keys

Each function key performs four operations, depending on whether it is pressed alone or in combination with the Alt, Shift, or Ctrl key. Pressing a function key either activates a LetterPerfect feature or inserts a hidden formatting code. The keyboard template shipped with LetterPerfect (see fig. 2.10) is color-coded in the following manner:

- *Black* indicates what the key does alone. For example, pressing Help (F3) displays the opening Help screen.

- *Red* indicates what the key does when you hold down the Ctrl key and press the function key. For example, pressing Spell (Ctrl-F2) activates the Spell feature.

- *Green* indicates what the key does when you hold down the Shift key and press the function key. For example, pressing Retrieve (Shift-F10) displays a prompt that lets you enter the name of the disk file you want brought into the main editing screen.

- *Blue* indicates what the key does when you hold down the Alt key and press the function key. For example, pressing Block (Alt-F4) activates the Block feature.

LetterPerfect displays the two types of Help template on your screen. To display the template for function keys across the top of the keyboard as shown in figure 2.11, do the following:

Access the **Help** pull-down menu and select **Template**. Alternatively, press Help (F3) twice.

If you want to see the on-screen template for the function keys on the left side of the keyboard, as shown in figure 2.12, follow one of the preceding steps and then press 1. If you want to see information about fast keys, press 2 (see fig. 2.13).

> *Tip:* If you misplace the template or the tear-out command card in the back of this book, use PrtSc to print the on-screen templates shown in figures 2.11 and 2.12. Then use red, green, and blue highlighters to create a temporary function-key template.

Table 2.1 shows the action performed by each function key alone and in combination with the Shift, Ctrl, or Alt key.

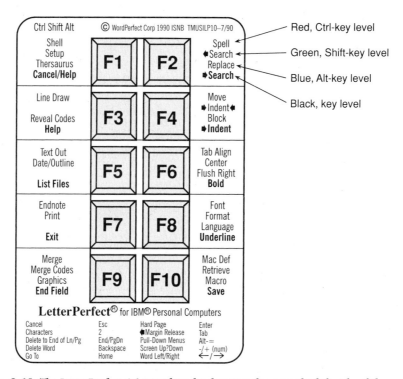

Fig. 2.10. The LetterPerfect 1.0 template for function keys on the left side of the keyboard.

When you press some of the function keys, such as Bold (F6) or Underline (F8), LetterPerfect inserts at the cursor's location a hidden code—such as that for bolding or underlining text, respectively. To turn off bolding or underlining, you may either press the appropriate key again or press the right-arrow key. Pressing other function keys causes LetterPerfect to display either a status-line or a full-screen menu for selecting an option.

In most menus, pressing Cancel (F1), Esc, or Exit (F7) enables you to leave the menu without selecting an option and returns the program to its main editing screen.

LetterPerfect's fast keys provide an alternative keyboard method for activating some of its features or inserting hidden formatting codes into the document. Fast keys are a combination of the Ctrl key plus a letter key that is a mnemonic of the feature or function accessed (see fig. 2.13). Table 2.2 lists the fast-key combinations and their function-key alternatives.

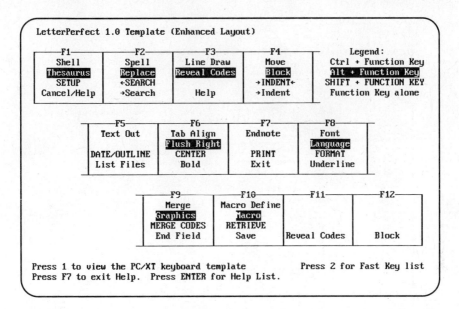

Fig. 2.11. *The on-screen Help template for function keys across the top of the keyboard.*

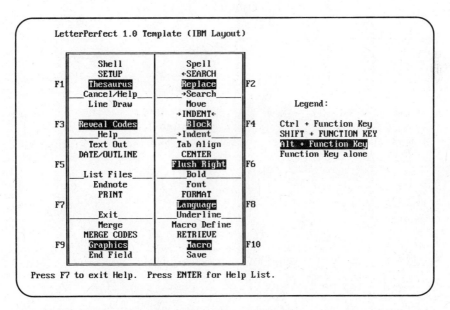

Fig. 2.12. *The on-screen Help template for function keys on the left side of the keyboard.*

```
Fast Keys

    The main interface with LetterPerfect is the pull-down menus.
    LetterPerfect also provides a set of Fast Keys which allow you to access
    some features more quickly than the pull-down method.

        Ctrl-a  Paste Block          Ctrl-m  Move (Cut)
        Ctrl-b  Bold                 Ctrl-n  Normal Text
        Ctrl-c  Center               Ctrl-p  Preview (View Document)
        Ctrl-d  Date Text            Ctrl-r  Reveal Codes
        Ctrl-e  Endnote Create       Ctrl-s  Spell
        Ctrl-f  Base Font            Ctrl-t  Thesaurus
        Ctrl-g  Graphics Create      Ctrl-u  Underline
        Ctrl-i  Italics              Ctrl-v  Characters
        Ctrl-k  Copy




    Press F7 to exit Help.  Press ENTER for Help List.
```

Fig. 2.13. *The fast-keys Help listing.*

Table 2.1
LetterPerfect's Function-Key Commands

Key	Alone	Ctrl Key	Shift Key	Alt Key
F1*	Cancel, Undelete, or Help	Go to Shell	Setup	Thesaurus
F2	Forward Search	Spell	Backward Search	Replace
F3	Help	Line Draw †	—	Reveal Codes
F4	Indent	Move	L/R indent	Block
F5	List Files	Text Out	Date/Outline	—
F6	Bold	Tab Align	Center	Flush Right
F7	Exit	Endnote	Print	—
F8	Underline	Font	Format	Language
F9	End Field	Merge	Merge Codes	Graphics
F10	Save	Macro Define‡	Retrieve	Macro‡

Key	Alone	Ctrl Key	Shift Key	Alt Key
F11§	Reveal Codes	—	—	—
F12§	Block	—	—	—

* If LetterPerfect is set up so that F1 activates the Help feature, the Esc key performs the Cancel and Undelete functions.

† In the 11/01/90 version, pressing Ctrl-F3 twice causes the program to immediately display editing changes without scrolling the cursor through the document.

‡ In the 07/24/90 version, this feature is available only when LetterPerfect is running under Shell 3.01.

§ Available only on systems with an Enhanced ROM BIOS and the Enhanced Keyboard.

Table 2.2
LetterPerfect's Fast-Key Combinations

Key Combination	Feature Activated	Function-Key Equivalent
Ctrl-a	Paste Block	Ctrl-F4, **Block (4)**
Ctrl-b	Bold	F6
Ctrl-c	Center	Shift-F
Ctrl-d	Date Text	Shift-F5, **Date Text (1)**
Ctrl-e	Endnote Create	Ctrl-F7, **Create (1)**
Ctrl-f	Base Font	Ctrl-F8, **Base Font (4)**
Ctrl-g	Graphics Create	Alt-F9, **Create (1)**
Ctrl-i	Italics	Ctrl-F8, **Italic (5**
Ctrl-k	Copy	Alt-F4 or F12, Ctrl-F4, **Copy (2)**
Ctrl-m	Move (Cut)	Alt-F4 or F12, Ctrl-F4, **Move (1)**
Ctrl-n	Normal Text	Ctrl-F8, **Normal (3)**
Ctrl-p	Preview (View Document)	Shift-F7, **View Document (3)**

Table 2.2 (continued)

Key Combination	Feature Activated	Function-Key Equivalent
Ctrl-r	Reveal Codes	Alt-F3 or F12
Ctrl-s	Spell	Ctrl-F2
Ctrl-t	Thesaurus	Alt-F1
Ctrl-u	Underline	F8
Ctrl-v	Create Characters	None

Some fast-key combinations enable you to activate or access a LetterPerfect feature in fewer keystrokes than the function keys require; some require the same number of keystrokes; others require more keystrokes. However, on portable computers the fast keys are usually quicker to use than are the function keys, because the Ctrl, Alt, and function keys are less conveniently located on the keyboard. The fast keys also require fewer keystrokes than does the pull-down menu system, unless you access the pull-down menus with a mouse.

Using the Alphanumeric Keyboard

The alphanumeric keyboard on a computer works much the same as an electric typewriter. If you are just now making the transition from typewriter to word processing, you already know certain features of the keyboard. For instance, if you press and hold down a key, the character is repeated across the screen until you release the key. You use the Shift key to uppercase letters and to access special characters above the number keys at the top of the keyboard. Shift's real power in LetterPerfect, however, is its link with the function keys, as described in the last section.

You use the Enter key to insert a *hard return*, **[HRt]**, which ends a line and moves the cursor to the beginning of the next line when the automatic word-wrap feature is not wanted. In this sense, Enter works like the Return key on a typewriter, moving the cursor down one or more lines. However, unlike the Return key on a typewriter, Enter breaks an existing text line and inserts extra blank lines between text lines.

You also press Enter to initiate some LetterPerfect commands or to make the system recognize a menu option you've selected or data you've entered in a menu.

Although the space bar appears to work the same as it does on a typewriter, the key actually functions differently. In LetterPerfect you cannot simply press the space bar to move through a line of text, as you can with a typewriter. Instead, to move the cursor horizontally through a line of text, press the right- and left-arrow keys or use the mouse.

When you press the space bar while in the default Insert mode, LetterPerfect inserts a character space, pushing ahead any text that may follow the cursor. However, if you switch to Typeover mode by pressing the Ins key on the numeric keypad, the space bar wipes out any character above the cursor, inserting a blank space in its place. The cursor continues to move forward until you release the space bar.

Another key that works differently in LetterPerfect than on a typewriter is the Backspace key, sometimes represented on the keyboard by a left-pointing arrow. When you press this key, LetterPerfect deletes text (and formatting codes if you are editing with the Reveal Codes feature active) to the left of the cursor. If you have highlighted text with the Block feature, pressing the Backspace key lets you delete all the highlighted text.

Pressing the Ctrl key in combination with the Backspace key (Ctrl-Backspace) deletes a word at the cursor. Pressing the Home key and then the Backspace key (Home, Backspace) deletes a word to the left of the cursor. (See Chapter 3 for an explanation of the many strategies LetterPerfect provides for deleting text.)

> *Tip:* To use Home with Backspace to delete the word immediately to the left of the cursor, you must press and release the Home key before you press the Backspace key. If you want to delete another word to the left of the cursor, you must repeat this procedure. Holding down the Home key while holding down the Backspace key or pressing it repeatedly erases the text to the left only one character at a time, which is what the Backspace key can do on its own.

Another key in the alphanumeric section of the keyboard is Tab, which works in part like the Tab key on a typewriter keyboard. While LetterPerfect is in Insert mode and there is a tab stop to the right of the cursor's location (the default is a tab stop every half-inch), pressing Tab inserts a hidden **[Tab]** formatting code. The cursor and any text to the right of the cursor on that line move to the spot designated by the tab setting. However, if you press Tab while LetterPerfect is in Typeover mode, the cursor moves right to the next tab setting *without* inserting a **[Tab]** code or moving text ahead of the cursor.

On some keyboards, the Esc key is located at the top left corner of the alphanumeric key section. On other keyboards, the Esc key is positioned within the numeric keypad at the right end of the keyboard. The Enhanced Keyboard has the Esc key positioned just to the left of the 12 function keys, which run across the top of the keyboard.

Esc performs the same function as the default Cancel (F1). However, if the Setup feature specifies F1 as the Help key, Esc is the only method of accessing the Cancel feature.

Using the Numeric Keypad

The keys in the numeric keypad at the far right of the keyboard perform two functions. When you press the Num Lock key and activate the Numbers feature, pressing any of the keys 0 through 9 enters a number into the document. Initially, the `Pos` indicator in the lower right corner of the screen blinks until you press a key.

When the Numbers feature is inactive, the Home, End, PgUp, PgDn, Screen Up (keyboard plus), Screen Down (keyboard minus), and arrow keys move the cursor in various ways. An Enhanced Keyboard also has a second set of keys that move the cursor; this set is located between the alphanumeric keys and the numeric keypad. Cursor movement is explained in detail in the following section.

Two other keys on the numeric keypad—Ins and Del—perform critical functions. The Ins key switches LetterPerfect between its Insert and Typeover modes. In the default Insert mode, you enter text into a document at any point without deleting the existing text. Typeover mode automatically replaces existing text with new text without your having to delete the old text first. While in Typeover mode, LetterPerfect displays the `Typeover` message in the lower left corner of the screen.

The Del key removes the character (or formatting code if you are editing with the Reveal Codes feature active) directly above the cursor. Pressing the Del key lets you remove text that you've highlighted with the Block feature.

Moving the Cursor

A number of keys or key combinations in LetterPerfect let you move the cursor with precision within your file. These keys are the following:

- Home (in combination with other keys)
- End
- PgUp
- PgDn
- Screen Up (keyboard plus key)
- Screen Down (keyboard minus key)
- GoTo (Ctrl-Home)
- Arrow keys

Moving the cursor with precision, especially with respect to LetterPerfect's hidden formatting codes, is important when you edit the document. Mastering the different cursor-movement kcy combinations allows you to move the cursor quickly through the document. Another way to move the cursor through the document quickly is with the mouse, a method explained later in this chapter.

Table 2.3 summarizes the cursor-movement keys, many of which you'll explore and use in the chapters to come. Remember: The cursor moves through preexisting text or blank character spaces inserted by the space bar; only Tab, Enter, and the space bar move the cursor on a blank screen. Once you've begun your document, you can use the keys shown in table 2.3 to move the cursor.

Table 2.3
The Cursor-Movement Keys

Key Combination	Cursor Movement
Left ($\leftarrow$) or right ($\rightarrow$) arrow	One character space to the left or right
Up ($\uparrow$) or down ($\downarrow$) arrow	Up or down one line
Ctrl-$\leftarrow$ or Ctrl-$\rightarrow$	Beginning of the preceding or next word
Home, $\leftarrow$	Left edge of the screen or the beginning of the line

Table 2.3 (continued)

Key Combination	Cursor Movement
Home, →	Right edge of the screen or the end of the line
Home, Home, ←	Beginning of the line, just after any hidden codes
Home, Home, Home, ←	Beginning of the line, before any hidden codes
Home, Home, → (or End)	Far right of the line
Home, ↑ (or Screen Up [keyboard minus key])	Top of the current screen
Home, ↓ (or Screen Down [keyboard plus key])	Bottom of the current screen
Ctrl-Home, ↑	Top of the current page
Ctrl-Home, ↓	Bottom of the current page
PgUp	Top of the preceding page
PgDn	Top of the next page
Home, Home, ↑	Top of the file
Home, Home, ↓	Bottom of the file
Ctrl-Home, n	Page number n
Ctrl-Home, x	Next occurrence of the character represented by x that occurs within the next 2,000 characters
Ctrl-Home, Ctrl-Home	Original cursor location before the last major cursor movement

Note: Ctrl-Home is known as the GoTo command.

Using Pull-Down Menus

The three major advantages of LetterPerfect's pull-down menu system are these:

- Menus grouped according to major categories of functions. This grouping makes it easier for the occasional or new user to become familiar and productive with LetterPerfect.

- Easier access to LetterPerfect's functions on portable computers whose function, Ctrl, and Alt keys are not as conveniently placed as those on keyboards used with desktop computers.

- Easy access and selection of options with a mouse.

With LetterPerfect you have the option of keeping the pull-down menu bar visible at all times or only when wanted. See Chapter 1 for information on using the Setup feature to customize LetterPerfect.

The menu bar lists eight main-menu categories (see fig. 2.5). LetterPerfect uses pull-down menus as a gateway for the regular menu system displayed by the function-key sequence or fast-key combinations.

Although logically organized, the pull-down menu system usually requires more keystrokes than the function-key system for accessing menus from the keyboard. The reason is that you must press either Alt or Alt-= to activate the pull-down menu system before selecting a menu option.

For example, if you want to print a document, you can use the regular function-key sequence of Print (Shift-F7)—two keys—to access the Print/Options screen. Using the pull-down menu system, press Alt or Alt-=, choose the **File** option (the document you want to print), and select **P**rint from the pull-down menu—for a total of three or four keystrokes. Of course, if you are proficient with a mouse, using this device to display menus and selecting options can be much quicker than using the keyboard, especially on portable computers.

However, as noted in the section "Using the Function Keys and Fast Keys," the quickest method for accessing LetterPerfect features (especially on portable computers) is frequently the fast-key combinations.

Because you can select so many options with either the function keys or the new pull-down menus, this book includes instructions for all three methods. For the sake of consistency, instructions in this book first list the pull-down menu method, followed by the function-key method, and, if available, the fast-key combination. You should try each method for each feature and decide which works best for a given feature on your particular system.

For example, on many systems the easiest and quickest way to access the Help, Bold, and Underline features is by pressing the single function key—F1 or F3, F6, and F8, respectively. However, on these same systems the easiest and quickest way to access the italic font and view a document is by pressing the fast-key combinations—Ctrl-i and Ctrl-p, respectively.

There are four methods of accessing the pull-down menu system:

- Moving the mouse pointer to the pull-down menu bar (if it is permanently displayed at the top of the screen)

- Clicking the right mouse button

- Pressing the Alt key

- Holding down Alt and pressing the = key (if the Alt-key method is turned off)

Whenever this book instructs you to access the pull-down menu system, you may use whichever of the four methods you find most convenient on your system.

> *Tip:* Pressing Alt by itself seems a convenient way to access the pull-down menu system. However, using Alt can be inconvenient if you also use the function-key system, because LetterPerfect uses Alt in combination with the function keys to start many of its features. If you press the Alt key and release it before pressing the function key, LetterPerfect automatically activates the pull-down menu system. In addition, some programs (DESQView, for example) use the Alt key by itself as their activation key. In either event, after LetterPerfect activates the pull-down menu system, you must press Cancel (F1) or Esc to return the program to the main editing screen.

Fortunately, you can turn off the Alt-key-only method by accessing the **File** pull-down menu and selecting Se**t**up—or, alternatively, by pressing Setup (Shift-F1)—and changing the **A**lt Key Selects Menu Bar (**6**) setting to **N**o. After you disable the Alt-key-only option, Alt-= continues to access the pull-down menu system.

After activating the pull-down menu system, you can select its options with the mouse (see the next section, "Using the Mouse") or from the keyboard. To make selections from the keyboard, press the option's mnemonic letter. The mnemonic letter, usually but not always the first letter of the command, appears as a highlighted character on systems with a monochrome display, and in a different color on systems with a color monitor.

> *Caution:* Although this fact is not documented in the LetterPerfect manual, you can select an option while in the pull-down menu system by pressing a number that corresponds to its numerical sequence on the menu. For example, pressing S or 3 from the main bar displays the Search pull-down menu. Then pressing either G or 4 activates the GoTo feature. This numeric-selection capability causes problems for users who mistype and press a number above the letters on the top row. For example, if you are trying to select the Edit option from the main bar and press either the 3 or 4 above it, LetterPerfect displays either the Search or Layout pull-down menu, respectively, instead of the Edit pull-down menu you expected.

As an alternative to pressing a mnemonic letter, you can select an option by using cursor-movement keys to move the cursor bar to highlight the option and pressing Enter. Finally, many menu options display the function-key system or fast-key alternatives that you can press to select the option.

A menu item enclosed in brackets usually indicates that some other step needs to be taken before that item can be used. For example, on the Edit pull-down menu, the Copy command appears in brackets if text has not been previously blocked. After you use the Block feature to highlight text, the Copy command becomes available to the pull-down menu system. The instructions in this chapter are based on the assumption that if a block is required to activate a pull-down menu option, you blocked the text before accessing the pull-down menu.

LetterPerfect lets you back out of the pull-down menus one level at a time by pressing Esc, Cancel (F1), or the space bar. To back out of all the menus at once, press Exit (F7). If you are using the mouse, you can click the right button to exit the menu. If the mouse pointer is outside the pull-down menu area, clicking the right button of the mouse exits the system.

Using the Mouse

If you are proficient with a mouse, you may find it easier to access the pull-down menu system with that device than with the keyboard. You can easily choose items from pull-down menus by moving the mouse pointer to an option and *clicking* (quickly pressing and releasing) the mouse buttons. Initially, moving the mouse displays the mouse pointer (a block cursor) on the screen. Moving the mouse causes the mouse pointer to move on the screen; this action lets you select menu options and block text. Pressing any key makes the mouse pointer disappear.

Although you can position the mouse pointer in blank areas of the screen that contain neither text nor codes, clicking on a blank area places the mouse pointer at the last text character or code. LetterPerfect and Shell macros do not record cursor movements made with the mouse pointer. However, if you use the mouse to activate the pull-down menu system and select menu options, the commands are stored in the macro as normal keystrokes.

A mouse has either two or three buttons. Regardless of the number of buttons, you can perform any of the following actions with them:

- Press and quickly release a button. This process is called *clicking*, as mentioned earlier.

- Press and quickly release the button twice. This process is called *double-clicking*.

- Press and hold down a button while moving the mouse pointer. This process is called *dragging*.

- Press and release two (or more) buttons at the same time.

The following explains the operation of the left mouse button (or the right button on a mouse set up for left-handed users):

With the editing screen:

- Clicking positions the cursor.

- Clicking on a screen prompt (for example, clicking on the equal sign in `Type = to change default Dir`) is the same as pressing the specified key itself.

- Clicking or dragging in the Reveal Codes portion of the screen does nothing.

- Dragging activates the Block feature, just as if you had pressed Block (Alt-F4 or F12). Position the mouse pointer, press the left button, and hold it down as you drag the mouse over the text you want to block. Once you have highlighted the text, you can perform many editing operations, including bolding, underlining, and deleting.

- Dragging at the top or bottom edge of the screen scrolls the document.

With pull-down menus:

- Clicking on any of the eight menu-bar items displays the pull-down menu for that item.

- Clicking on a menu option selects that item.

- Dragging across the pull-down menu bar displays the pull-down menu for each of the eight options.

- Dragging down a pull-down menu highlights each choice as you move onto it. Releasing the mouse button chooses the highlighted selection.

With other menus:

- Clicking selects menu choices.

- When a prompt line for entering values appears, clicking positions the cursor on the line.

With lists:

- Double-clicking on a default value is the same as pressing Enter. For example, after choosing List Files from the File pull-down menu, you can either double-click on `Dir C:\LP10\*.*` or press Enter to accept the default file filter.

- Double-clicking on a file name in List Files causes the file to be displayed, as if you had highlighted the file and selected Look (**6**).

The following explains the right mouse button (or the left button on a mouse set up for left-handed users):

With the editing screen:

- If the menu bar is not permanently visible, clicking makes it appear and places the mouse pointer on the word *File* on the menu bar.

- If the menu bar is permanently visible, clicking places the mouse pointer on the word *File* on the menu bar.

- Dragging above, below, to the left of, or to the right of the visible screen scrolls the text (assuming that there is something to scroll to).

With pull-down menus and lists:

- Clicking is the same as pressing Exit (F7).

With other menus:

- Clicking is the same as pressing Exit (F7).

The following explains the effect of pressing two buttons at once and the function of a three-button mouse's middle button:

- On a two-button mouse, holding down one button while clicking the other button is the same as pressing Cancel (F1).

- On a three-button mouse, clicking the middle button is the same as pressing Cancel (F1).

Understanding LetterPerfect's Hidden Formatting Codes

Fundamental to understanding LetterPerfect's document structure is the program's use of hidden formatting codes. Often when you press a key, LetterPerfect inserts a hidden formatting code into the text. These codes give LetterPerfect the information it needs to create your documents.

Some hidden codes contain information about the location of tab spaces, margin settings, line spacing, hard returns, indents, font size and appearance changes, headers or footers, and endnotes. Other hidden codes are used to activate and deactivate a feature, such as center justification. Some hidden codes come in pairs, such as the codes for bold, underline, italic, and font attributes.

The first code in a pair turns on the feature. The second code in a pair turns off the feature. Typical examples include the paired codes for bolding text, as shown in figure 2.14.

The paired codes for bolded (**[BOLD]** and **[bold]**), underlined (**[UND]** and **[und]**), and italicized (**[ITALC]** and **[italc]**) text mark the beginning and end of each different format change. The first **[HRt]** (hard return) marks the end of a line, which also is the end of a paragraph. The second **[HRt]** code on a line by itself inserts a blank line between the paragraphs. The **[SRt]** (soft return) codes mark the end of a line within the paragraph where LetterPerfect wraps the line to the beginning of the next line. The **[Tab]** code indents the beginning of a new paragraph.

LetterPerfect's invisible formatting codes may seem perplexing to novice users. At this point, don't worry too much about hidden codes. Just remember how these codes become a part of the document and how they appear when displayed with LetterPerfect's Reveal Codes feature. When you know how to search for hidden codes, navigate the Reveal Codes screen, and edit by using the Reveal Codes feature, you will appreciate how LetterPerfect stays out of your way, letting you concentrate on writing.

```
 File Edit Search Layout Tools Font Graphics Help        (Press ALT= for menu bar)

 Note that paired codes for bolding ([BOLD] and [bold]) surround
 the title.  Also note the [HRt] (hard return) codes, which
 indicate each time the Enter key was pressed; the [SRt] (soft
 return) codes, which indicate the word wrap; and the [Tab] code
 inserted when the Tab key was pressed to indent the first
 paragraph.

 Don't worry too much about LetterPerfect's hidden codes just yet.
 It's enough for now to know something about the concept of hidden
                                            Pg 1 Ln 1.67" Pos 1"
 [     ▲     ▲     ▲     ▲     ▲     ▲     ▲     ▲     ▲     ▲     ]
 the title.  Also note the [BOLD][HRt][bold] (hard return) codes, which[SRt]
 indicate each time the Enter key was pressed; the [BOLD][SRt][bold] (soft[SRt]
 return) codes, which indicate the word wrap; and the [BOLD][Tab][bold] code[SRt]

 inserted when the Tab key was pressed to indent the first[SRt]
 paragraph.[HRt]
 [HRt]
 Don't worry too much about LetterPerfect's hidden codes just yet. [SRt]
 It's enough for now to know something about the concept of hidden[SRt]
 codes, how these codes become a part of your document, and how[SRt]

 Press Reveal Codes to restore screen
```

Fig. 2.14. *Hidden codes displayed by the Reveal Codes feature.*

In Chapter 3, when you are actively involved in editing a document, you will see the full range of LetterPerfect's hidden codes. You learn strategies for examining, searching for, inserting, and editing codes. You also learn how to avoid problems with codes.

Using the Help Feature

At almost any time, you can get information on LetterPerfect's features by doing one of the following:

- Accessing the **Help** pull-down menu and selecting the **Help** option.

- Pressing Help (F3). You must use this method to access LetterPerfect's context-sensitive help while the program displays its feature menus.

When you activate the Help feature from the main editing screen, LetterPerfect displays its main Help menu, shown in figure 2.15.

Fig. 2.15. *The opening Help screen.*

If you are using LetterPerfect on a floppy disk drive system, the LPHELP.FIL file required by the Help feature is located on the LetterPerfect 1 disk. If LetterPerfect displays an error message indicating that it cannot find the Help files, insert the LetterPerfect 1 disk into a disk drive, close the drive door, and type the drive letter (*a*, for example). The Help feature now functions properly.

The main Help screen presents an alphabetical list of LetterPerfect's features. For information on a specific LetterPerfect feature, use the techniques discussed earlier in this chapter to move the cursor bar until it highlights the feature.

> **Tip:** You also can use the **Name Search** feature to move the cursor bar. Press **N** and begin typing the feature's name. When the cursor bar highlights the feature's name, press Enter.

When the cursor bar highlights the feature, select **Help for Function (1)** or press Enter. Alternatively, after LetterPerfect displays the main Help screen, you can press either the feature's function-key combination—except for Cancel (F1),

Exit (F7), or Esc—or the fast-key combination. LetterPerfect displays information about the feature.

To exit from any informational screen and return to the main Help screen, press Enter. To exit the Help feature completely, press Cancel (F1), Esc, Exit (F7), or the space bar.

LetterPerfect's context-sensitive help lets you summon appropriate help from anywhere in the program, not just from the main editing screen. For example, if you are using the Setup feature and need additional information about an option, press Help (F3). LetterPerfect displays the main Help screen for Setup, the first of several screens concerning the Setup feature. Read about the feature; then press Enter or the space bar to return to where you were.

When using the Help feature, you must press Enter, the space bar, or Exit (F7) to leave. Pressing any other key simply brings up another Help screen.

LetterPerfect's Help feature includes an option not found in any other program from WordPerfect Corporation—the ability to invoke the feature from the main Help screen. When the cursor bar highlights the feature's name on the alphabetical list, select **P**erform Function (**2**), and LetterPerfect automatically activates the feature. For example, if you highlight Backward Search and use the perform-function option, LetterPerfect automatically returns the program to the main editing screen, with the Backward Search feature active.

Taking the Tutorial

WordPerfect Corporation provides LetterPerfect with a simple, self-paced tutorial, Tutor, which you can work through from beginning to end in approximately two and a half hours. You don't have to complete the lessons in any particular order, nor do you have to finish a lesson to exit from the tutorial. Completion time for most of the lessons ranges from 12 to 20 minutes.

The tutorial begins with an introduction that explains the LetterPerfect screen and the use of the keyboard. The introduction is followed by seven lessons. Because these lessons build on one another, you should probably complete them in sequence.

Regardless of whether you are running the Tutor program on a system with one or more floppy disk drives or a hard disk drive, the TUTOR.COM program and its lesson files must be in the same directory as the LetterPerfect program files. To use it, at the DOS prompt type *tutor* and press Enter. After displaying an opening screen, the program starts LetterPerfect and takes you to the main tutorial selection menu.

To run a lesson, use the up arrow or down arrow to move the cursor bar to highlight the lesson; then press Enter. Tutor lets you complete each lesson at your own pace. If you need to stop the lesson without completing it, press Exit (F3). As you complete each lesson, LetterPerfect places a check mark by its name on the main menu.

Summary

This chapter has briefly introduced LetterPerfect 1.0 and the hardware necessary to run the program. In particular, you learned the following:

- The procedure for starting, or "booting," LetterPerfect

- The function of the status line

- The use of the Enter key in LetterPerfect

- The use of function keys in LetterPerfect

- The purpose of hidden codes

- Different ways to move the cursor

- The function of the mouse

- LetterPerfect's context-sensitive on-line Help feature

- The LetterPerfect Tutor

In the next two chapters, you'll have an opportunity to apply many of the concepts that you've learned in this preparatory chapter. Chapters 3 and 4 discuss creating, editing, saving, retrieving, and printing a simple document.

3

Creating a Document

In Chapter 2 you learned the fundamentals of LetterPerfect: starting the program; reading the information on the editing screen; using the keyboard, fast keys, and mouse; accessing the pull-down and pop-out menus; exiting the program; and using the on-line tutorial. This chapter shows you how to create memos, brief notes, letters, reports—in short, any kind of document—with LetterPerfect.

In this chapter, you learn in much more detail how to use your computer and LetterPerfect to compose the documents you need. After an introduction to writing with a word processor, you look at procedures for the following:

- Entering text

- Moving the cursor through a document

- Using function keys, fast keys, or the mouse to give commands

- Invoking features by number or letter from menus or with the mouse

- Using the Cancel function or the mouse to back out of a menu or cancel a prompt

- Printing a document

- Naming and saving a document

> *Reminder:* WordPerfect Corporation updated LetterPerfect 1.0 just before this book went to press. Dated 11/01/90, the interim release includes new options for existing features, and a few new features. The menus on your screen may, therefore, differ slightly from those shown in this book. Also, depending on the printer-form definition, margins, tab stops, and font you specify, the text placement and status-line information in documents you create may differ from that shown in this book's figures.
>
> For information about using the mouse and accessing the pull-down menus, refer to the Introduction.

Writing with a Word Processor

Reminder: Research reveals that word processing makes people more enthusiastic about writing.

Unfortunately, writing is seldom easy, even for experienced writers. For many people, however, a good word processing program makes writing easier. Researchers observing what happens when people learn to write with word processors have discovered an encouraging fact: people who once dreaded composing documents develop a more positive attitude about writing after they learn to use a word processing program.

Composing with a word processor is different from writing in longhand or at the typewriter. Ann Berthoff, a professor of composition theory, writes that "composing—putting things together—is a continuum, a process that continues without any sharp breaks."[1]

Researchers tell us that short-term memory lasts about five seconds—all the more reason to have a tool that enables you to record your ideas quickly. LetterPerfect is ideally suited to the writing process, allowing you to "put things together" as well as to take them apart with ease at any stage of the writing process.

Reminder: The "fluid" medium of word processing enables you to record your thoughts almost as fast as they occur.

LetterPerfect lets you put words on-screen as fast as you can type them, so you are freed from the frustration of not being able to record thoughts almost as fast as they occur. Although the program cannot think or plan for you, it simplifies the rearrangement, deletion, or embellishment of your words on-screen—making the self-expression process far easier than in longhand or at the typewriter.

Unlike a typewriter, LetterPerfect gives you great freedom to alter what you write. You use the mouse or keyboard to tell LetterPerfect to do something with the text. You can use the program across the full range of writing tasks—to create, format, revise, edit, save, retrieve, and print documents.

Reminder:
Revising a
document is
easier with
LetterPerfect
than on a
typewriter.

The program keeps your words on-screen in the computer's temporary memory (also called random-access memory, or RAM) until you tell the program to save the information as a disk file—either on the system's hard disk or on a floppy disk—or print a hard copy. As explained in Chapter 5, LetterPerfect lets you save text in *blocks* (words, sentences, or paragraphs) for later retrieval and consideration. You can easily insert or delete text as a single letter, word, sentence, paragraph, or many pages. You can also move up and down through a document to see what you have written.

With LetterPerfect's many formatting features, you can change the look of the text on the page, as you see in later chapters. You can change margins, indent text, vary line spacing, control word spacing, create headers and footers, center text, and so on. In this chapter, though, you focus on the built-in settings that most LetterPerfect users are assumed to use (at least initially). Later you learn how to modify these defaults to meet your needs.

LetterPerfect's ease of editing lets you concentrate on getting your thoughts on the screen as words. By freeing you from much of the drudgery of writing, LetterPerfect gives you more time to be creative or to rethink your work. If poor handwriting or the tedium of recopying your work was once an obstacle to writing, the program may give you new enthusiasm for drafting, reworking, and polishing your text.

Understanding LetterPerfect's Built-In Settings

Before you even put fingers to keys and begin typing, LetterPerfect has been at work for you. Recall from your experience with a typewriter that you must set margins, line spacing, and tabs, for example, before you begin composing. With LetterPerfect, you don't have to make any formatting decisions before you begin unless the preset values do not suit you.

Reminder:
LetterPerfect
comes with a
number of
default set-
tings—for
margins, page
numbers, tabs, a
base font or
basic character
style, line
spacing, and
other features.

You should be familiar with LetterPerfect's screen and basic document default settings before you begin writing. Later chapters, especially those devoted to formatting and printing, explore the many ways you can alter the look of a document. For now, though, assume that the default settings are acceptable.

Table 3.1 lists just a few of LetterPerfect's many built-in settings. To change any of these settings, see Chapter 1. (Don't worry if terms like *base font* and *form size* are unfamiliar to you at this time. You will learn about them in later chapters.)

Table 3.1
Some of LetterPerfect's Built-In Settings

Setting	*Preset Value*
Margins	1-inch top, bottom, left, and right
Tabs	Every 0.5 inch relative to the left margin
Base font	Uses default for the active printer
Line spacing	Single-spaced
Page numbering	Off
Justification	Left (ragged right margins)
Hyphenation	Permanently active but requires special hyphenation files not included with program for automatic operation
Center page (top to bottom)	Off
Form size	Letter-size paper (8 1/2 by 11 inches)
Date format	Month (word), day, year (all four digits); example: July 4, 1989
Automatic file backup	Every 10 minutes
File name displayed on status line	On (displayed when you save or retrieve a document)
Pull-down menu bar	Visible
Location of document files	Subdirectory with the LP.EXE program
Location of Speller/ Thesaurus files	Subdirectory with the LP.EXE program (available only with program dated 11/01/90 or later)
Location of Printer Files	Subdirectory with the LP.EXE program (available only with program dated 11/01/90 or later)

Setting	Preset Value
Keys to access pull-down menu bar	Alt or Alt-=
Function of F1 key	Cancel
Function of F3 key	Help
Screen colors	White on blue (only on systems using color monitors)

Entering Text

LetterPerfect's uncluttered editing screen resembles a blank sheet of paper inserted into a typewriter. Unlike some other word processors, LetterPerfect doesn't require a file name before it lets you enter an editing screen and begin typing. Unless you want to save your work to disk, you don't ever have to give the text a file name.

Reminder: LetterPerfect doesn't require that you name a file before you enter an editing screen and begin typing.

If you haven't started LetterPerfect and you want to follow the examples in this chapter, see the steps for starting LetterPerfect in Chapter 2.

LetterPerfect's default "clean" editing screen lets you see a maximum of 80 characters per line and 23 lines per screen (24 lines if the pull-down menu bar is not displayed). With some exceptions, what you see on-screen is what prints. In word processing jargon, LetterPerfect's editing screen comes close to "what you see is what you get," or "WYSIWYG" (pronounced "wizzy wig"). The Hercules graphics cards mentioned in Chapter 2 produce an editing screen even closer to true WYSIWYG by displaying text in different type sizes and in appearance attributes such as italic, bold, and underline.

If you have LetterPerfect running and want to get started right away, type the following paragraph. You don't need to press Enter at the end of each line. LetterPerfect "wraps" the text to the next line as your words reach the right margin.

Think of a place that you either have visited or can clearly visualize, a place for which you have strong feelings. Write a personal description of it, attempting to re-create for your reader the experience of seeing or entering the place about which you've chosen to write.

Reminder:

Unlike a typewriter, LetterPerfect does not require that you press Enter to end a line; text wraps automatically to the next line.

After you type a few words, look at the Pos indicator on the status line. This value increases as you type and as the cursor moves horizontally across the line to the right. Unlike a typewriter, LetterPerfect does not require that you press Enter to end a line. Instead, if LetterPerfect cannot fit a word on a line, it inserts a **[SRt]** formatting code called a *soft return*. This code—which can be seen only when you view the document by using the Reveal Codes (Alt-F3 or F11) feature—ends the line and "wraps" the word to the next line. This feature is often referred to as *word wrap*.

Inserting Blank Lines

To end a paragraph or insert blank lines in the text, press the Enter key (sometimes called the Return key). If you're following the preceding example, when you come to the end of the last sentence, press Enter twice and type this second paragraph:

Details are essential in picturing whatever is described. Try to think of rich and suggestive words and phrases that will evoke emotional responses in your readers. Appeal to the senses. Use concrete nouns and active verbs.

Your screen should look like the one in figure 3.1. When you press Enter the first time, LetterPerfect inserts a *hard-return* formatting code—which is displayed as **[HRt]** and can be seen only when you view the document by using the Reveal Codes feature (access the **E**dit pull-down menu and select **R**eveal Codes; alternatively, press Alt-F3, F11, or Ctrl-r). When you press Enter the second time, LetterPerfect inserts another hard-return code, creating a blank line in the text.

Moving the Cursor with the Mouse

LetterPerfect lets you move the cursor through a document in one of two ways: with the mouse or with the keys on the numeric keypad (and separate cursor keys on Enhanced Keyboards). This section explains how to use the mouse to move the cursor. To learn how to use the keyboard to move the cursor, see the next section, "Moving the Cursor with the Keyboard."

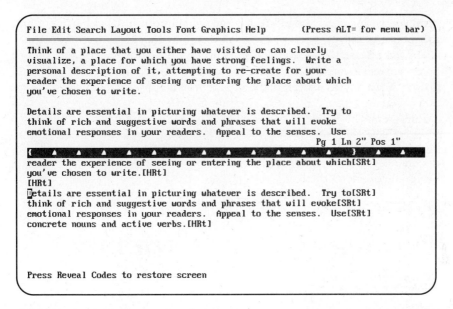

Fig. 3.1. *A blank line inserted with the Enter key.*

You can position the cursor anywhere on the screen with the mouse by placing the mouse pointer at a specific spot and clicking the left button. *Dragging* the mouse—pressing a mouse button while moving the mouse pointer across the screen—lets you scroll the screen up, down, left, or right to see additional text. You cannot move the cursor beyond the last character at the bottom of the document. If you position the mouse pointer beyond the bottom of the document and click the left button, the cursor immediately moves to the right of the last character or formatting code in the document.

To move one character left, move the mouse pointer one space left and click the left button. To move one character right, move the mouse pointer one space right and click the left button.

To move from word to word with the mouse, position the mouse pointer anywhere in the appropriate word and click the left button to relocate the cursor.

To move the cursor up or down a line, position the mouse pointer on the line you want to move to and click the left button.

To scroll up line by line through a document, place the mouse pointer anywhere in the top line and press and hold down the right button. To scroll down line by line through a document, place the mouse pointer at the bottom of the screen and press and hold down the right button. You may have to move the mouse slightly upward or downward to start the scrolling, which stops when you release the mouse button or when the cursor reaches the top or bottom of the document. If you want to block text as you scroll, press and hold down the left button instead of the right button before you move the mouse.

You can scroll left or right to see text not visible on-screen by placing the mouse pointer on a text line at the right or left edge of the screen, pressing the right button and moving the mouse slightly in the direction you want to scroll the document. The scrolling stops when you release the mouse button or reach the beginning or end of the line.

Moving the Cursor with the Keyboard

The location of the cursor-movement keys depends on the type of computer you are using. On desktop computers with an old-style keyboard, a single set of cursor-movement keys is located on the right side of the keyboard on the numeric keypad (you use these keys with the activated Num Lock key to type numbers). A desktop computer with an Enhanced Keyboard (101 or more keys) has two sets of cursor-movement keys: one set is located on the right side of the keyboard on the numeric keypad; the second set is located between the character keys and the numeric keypad. The location of the cursor-movement keys on portable (sometimes called "laptop") computers depends on the brand and model.

LetterPerfect provides various ways to move the cursor through the text, or to "scroll" a document. To understand the document-scrolling concept, imagine that your on-screen document is a continuous sheet of paper that you can roll up or down. You can view only 23 lines of the document at a time, however, depending on your monitor (some monitors let you view more than 23 lines). The sections that follow explain the various ways to move the cursor around in the document.

Moving from Character to Character

The smallest increment in which LetterPerfect lets you move the cursor is from character to character. This method is useful when you want to make small editing changes or position the cursor with respect to LetterPerfect's hidden codes. However, this method is the slowest for moving through large portions of text.

To move from character to character, use the following keys:

- Press and release the left arrow to move one character left.
- Press and release the right arrow to move one character right.

Using the passage typed in the "Inserting Blank Lines" section earlier in this chapter, move the cursor a few characters into the last word: *verbs*. Watch the cursor's movement as you press and release either the left or right arrow several times.

If you hold down the arrow key, the cursor continues to move across the line. If you hold down the left arrow, for instance, until the cursor reaches the left margin of a line, the cursor automatically moves up to the right margin or the end of the next line above. Similarly, if you hold down the right arrow until the cursor reaches the right margin or end of the line, the cursor automatically moves down to the left margin at the beginning of the next line.

For the purposes of cursor movement, LetterPerfect treats a hidden formatting code, such as **[HRt]**, like an individual text character: the entire code is considered one unit as the cursor moves past it. When you press the left or right arrow in a document that contains hidden formatting codes, on the main editing screen the cursor does not appear to move as it encounters each hidden code. Activating the Reveal Codes feature (access the **E**dit pull-down menu and select **R**eveal Codes; alternatively, press Alt-F3, F11, or Ctrl-r) lets you see the cursor move through these formatting codes.

Reminder: You cannot move the cursor past the last character or hidden formatting code at the end of the document.

In LetterPerfect, you can not move the cursor past the document's last character or hidden code by using the arrow keys. Only the Enter key or the space bar lets you move the cursor past the document's last character or hidden code at the bottom of the document.

Moving from Word to Word

In LetterPerfect, a *word* is any group of characters followed by a punctuation character, space, tab, indent, align code, center code, flush-right code, or hard-return code. Use the following key combinations to move from word to word:

Reminder: Press Ctrl-left arrow or Ctrl-right arrow to move from word to word in a document.

- Press Ctrl-right arrow to move from anywhere in a word to the first character in the next word to the right.

- Press Ctrl-left arrow to move to the first character of the word to the left of the cursor's location.

Note: There is an important difference between Ctrl-right arrow and Ctrl-left arrow: when the cursor is located under any character other than the first character in a word and you press Ctrl-left arrow, the cursor moves to the first character of *that* word, not to the beginning of the preceding word.

Moving from Line to Line

Reminder:
Press the up arrow or down arrow to move vertically from line to line.

LetterPerfect lets you move the cursor vertically from line to line, up and down the document. Use the following key combinations to move from line to line:

- Press the up arrow to move the cursor up a line.

- Press the down arrow to move the cursor down a line.

These keys repeat the movement if you hold them down. You can move up or down several lines at a time by pressing and holding down the up or down arrow. You can move one line at a time by pressing and releasing the up or down arrow.

Moving to the End of the Line or the Edge of the Screen

Occasionally, you may need to move the cursor from some position within a line to the end of the line or the edge of the screen. On most screens, you can see 80 characters of text. If LetterPerfect is set to use 1-inch left and right margins with a base font size equivalent to 10 pitch, the lines extend from the left edge of the screen 65 characters across, making all the text visible. If you expand the margins or change to a smaller font, the lines extend beyond the right or left edges of the screen and are not completely visible. Use the following key combinations to move to the end of the line or the edge of the screen:

- Press Home, left arrow to move the cursor to the beginning of the line or the left edge of the screen, whichever comes first.

- Press Home, right arrow to move the cursor to the end of the line or the right edge of the screen, whichever comes first. Pressing the End key also moves the cursor to the end of the line.

If you change margins and text "runs off" the screen, do the following:

- Press Home, Home, left arrow to move the cursor to the beginning of the line, just right of any hidden formatting codes.

- Press Home, Home, Home, left arrow to move the cursor to the beginning of the line before all hidden formatting codes.

- Press Home, Home, right arrow to move to the far right of the line. (You also can press the End key.)

Reminder:
Press Home, Home, left arrow or right arrow to move the cursor to the first or last character of a line.

The cursor's position with respect to hidden codes becomes important when you delete, enter, or examine hidden codes. The "Editing in Reveal Codes" section in Chapter 4 explains how to edit documents that contain hidden formatting codes.

Using the passage typed in the "Inserting Blank Lines" section earlier in this chapter, move the cursor to *can* in the middle of the first line of the first paragraph. Then perform these steps:

1. Press Home, right arrow. The cursor moves to the end of the line or the edge of the screen.

2. Press Home, left arrow. The cursor moves to the beginning of the line, under the *T* of *Think*.

You also can use the End key to move the cursor to the end of a line. With the cursor anywhere in a line, press End. The cursor moves to the line's end.

Moving to the Top or Bottom of the Screen

LetterPerfect offers several methods for moving the cursor up and down the screen, 23 lines at a time (24 lines if the pull-down menu bar is not displayed):

- Press the Screen Up key on the numeric keypad (the keypad minus sign) to move the cursor to the first line at the top of the screen.

- Press Home, up arrow to move the cursor to the first line at the top of the screen.

- Press the Screen Down key on the numeric keypad (the keypad plus sign) to move the cursor to the last line on the screen.

- Press Home, down arrow to move the cursor to the last line on the screen.

Note: On some keyboards that have separate cursor and numeric keypads, you must press Shift-Screen Up and Shift-Screen Down.

When the cursor is on the top line of a screen, each time you press Screen Up (–) the cursor moves 23 lines (24 lines if the pull-down menu bar is not displayed) toward the top of the document. When the cursor is on the bottom line of a screen, each time you press Screen Down (+) the cursor moves 23 lines toward the bottom of the document (24 lines if the pull-down menu bar is not displayed).

Moving to the Top of the Preceding Page

When you press PgUp, LetterPerfect moves the cursor to the first character or hidden formatting code on the first line of the preceding page. To review the flow of the text, move quickly to the first line of the preceding page and scroll the text. Press PgUp and the up arrow to check page breaks.

Moving to the Top of the Next Page

When you press PgDn, LetterPerfect moves the cursor to the first character or hidden formatting code on the first line of the next page of the document. Press PgDn and the up arrow to check page breaks.

Moving the Cursor with GoTo

With LetterPerfect's GoTo command, you can move the cursor in great "leaps" through a document. In a large document, the GoTo feature is one of the quickest methods for moving through the document. For example, use GoTo to move the cursor to any of the following points:

- The top or bottom of a page

- A particular page number

- The next occurrence of a particular character

- The starting point of the cursor after you have moved the cursor
  with an earlier GoTo command (if certain conditions are met)

To move the cursor to the first character on the first line of the current page,
activate the GoTo feature (access the **S**earch pull-down menu and select **G**o To;
alternatively, press Ctrl-Home) and press the up arrow. To move the cursor to
the first character on the last line of the current page, activate the GoTo feature
as just described and press the down arrow.

You cannot use GoTo to move the cursor to the right of its location. To move
the cursor quickly to a particular character within approximately 2,000
characters to the right of the cursor's location, activate GoTo as described in the
preceding paragraph and type the character. Activating GoTo and pressing
Enter moves the cursor to the first line following the current paragraph.

The GoTo-character method does not work if the character you type after
activating GoTo is not found within approximately 2,000 characters of the
cursor's location. When the character is not found, LetterPerfect sounds a tone
on the computer's speaker, and the cursor does not move. If you attempt to use
this method and the search fails, you *cannot* use the GoTo (Ctrl-Home) feature—explained shortly—to return the cursor to a previous location.

One of the most common uses of the GoTo feature is to move the cursor to a
specific page in a long document. The only drawback to this method of moving
around your document is that you have to know the specific page number to
which you want to move the cursor. Follow these steps to use this method:

Reminder: Use the GoTo feature to move the cursor to a specific page within the document.

1. Activate the GoTo feature by accessing the **S**earch pull-down
   menu and selecting **G**o To. Alternatively, press Ctrl-Home.

2. Type the page number.

3. Press Enter.

Cue: Hold down the Ctrl key and press the Home key twice to return the cursor quickly to its previous position.

The GoTo feature also moves the cursor to its original location when you use any of these features:

- Arrow keys
- Block
- End
- GoTo
- Home, arrow keys
- Page Up
- Page Down

- Replace Backward
- Replace Forward
- Screen Up
- Screen Down
- Spell Check
- Word Left
- Word Right

To use the cursor-return feature, hold down the Ctrl key while pressing the Home key twice. LetterPerfect returns the cursor to the position it occupied before you used any of the features listed above. However, if after you use one of those features LetterPerfect performs a search that results in a not-found condition, activating the cursor-return feature does not return the cursor to its original location.

> *Tip:* You can use the return-cursor feature with the pull-down menu bar by accessing the **S**earch pull-down menu, selecting **G**o To, and pressing the Ctrl-Home key combination. However, using this method takes much longer than holding down the Ctrl key and pressing the Home key twice.

Moving to the Top or Bottom of a Document

You can quickly move the cursor to the top or bottom of a document, a useful feature for documents longer than one page. The following actions move the cursor in these particular ways:

- Press Home, Home, up arrow to move the cursor to the beginning of a document's first line, after any hidden formatting codes but before the first character.

- Press Home, Home, Home, up arrow to move the cursor to the beginning of a document's first line, before any hidden formatting codes and the first character.

- Press Home, Home, down arrow to move the cursor to the end of a document.

Moving to the Next Paragraph

On newer-model desktop and portable (laptop) computer systems with an enhanced ROM BIOS, LetterPerfect offers two additional cursor-movement features: the capability to move up or down one paragraph. If your computer system was made after 1987 and has an Enhanced Keyboard or is a portable (laptop), the system probably has an enhanced ROM BIOS.

To move the cursor to the first character in the paragraph immediately above the cursor's location, press Ctrl-up arrow. To move the cursor to the first character in the paragraph immediately below the cursor's location, press Ctrl-down arrow.

Using Alternative Cursor-Movement Keys

LetterPerfect offers a set of cursor-movement key combinations that may be more convenient to use on portable (laptop) computers than the primary cursor-movement keys. Table 3.2 lists the primary keys and combination substitutes. You can use the alternative key combinations in any of the cursor-movement methods described in this book.

Table 3.2
LetterPerfect's Substitute Cursor-Movement Keys

Primary Cursor-Movement Key	Substitute Key Combination
Home	Ctrl-h
Enter (Return)	Ctrl-j
Up arrow	Ctrl-w
Right arrow	Ctrl-x
Left arrow	Ctrl-y
Down arrow	Ctrl-z

Inserting Text

Reminder: To add a word, phrase, or sentence to a document, position the cursor where you want to insert the text and then begin typing.

One of the boons of word processing is the freedom to add text to what is already written. If you are using a typewriter, you must retype the entire paragraph to add a sentence in the middle of that paragraph. Not so with LetterPerfect. To add a word, phrase, or sentence to a document, position the cursor where you want to insert the text and then begin typing. What you type is inserted to the *left* of the cursor's beginning location. With LetterPerfect's Block feature, explained in Chapter 5, you can move or copy text anywhere in a document. If you store blocks of *boilerplate* (frequently used text, sometimes called *universal text*) as separate files on disk, you can insert the blocks into a document.

The following exercise shows how easy it is to add a sentence to an existing paragraph, using LetterPerfect. Before starting, check to see whether the Typeover prompt appears on the status line at the left edge of the screen. If the prompt appears, press Ins to switch to Insert mode (explained in the next section).

Using the example you created earlier in this chapter, move the cursor to the beginning of the second sentence in the first paragraph. With the cursor under the *W* in *Write*, type this sentence:

> *It can be a room, a natural setting, an interesting building, the house in which you grew up, King Tut's tomb--any place that interests you and that you think you can make engrossing to read about.*

As you enter new text, the existing text is pushed ahead of the cursor. The text reformats when you press the down arrow once (see fig. 3.2).

Using Typeover

The Ins key on your keyboard works like a toggle switch, allowing you to switch LetterPerfect between its default Insert ("push ahead") mode and its Typeover mode. When you press the Ins key, the program switches to Typeover mode, and the new text *overwrites* existing text. Typeover mode is most useful when you are making one-for-one replacements, such as changing *adn* to *and*. (Chapter 4 explains the use of Typeover mode during editing.)

```
File Edit Search Layout Tools Font Graphics Help      (Press ALT= for menu bar)

Think of a place that you either have visited or can clearly
visualize, a place for which you have strong feelings.  It can be
a room, a natural setting, an interesting building, the house in
which you grew up, King Tut's tomb--any place that interests you
and that you think you can make engrossing to read about.  Write
a personal description of it, attempting to re-create for your
reader the experience of seeing or entering the place about which
you've chosen to write.

Details are essential in picturing whatever is described.  Try to
think of rich and suggestive words and phrases that will evoke
emotional responses in your readers.  Appeal to the senses.  Use
concrete nouns and active verbs.




                                              Pg 1 Ln 1.67" Pos 6.9"
```

Fig. 3.2. *A new sentence inserted in the middle of a paragraph.*

Using Cancel (F1) or Esc

LetterPerfect offers two Cancel keys: the F1 and Esc keys. The Esc key always functions as the Cancel feature, but the F1 key can function as either the Cancel feature or the Help feature. For the purposes of this book, all the references to the Cancel feature apply equally to pressing either the F1 or the Esc key. See Chapter 1 for instructions on how to designate which function the F1 key performs.

For example, if you activate the Block feature and then decide that you do not need to use it, you can turn Block off by pressing either Block, Cancel (F1), or Esc. You can use Cancel (F1) or Esc to get out of any screen menu or prompt.

The Cancel feature also is known as the *undelete* or *undo* feature because it lets you restore up to the last three text or hidden-code deletions. Chapter 4 explains the role of the Cancel feature in document editing.

If you have a three-button mouse, press the middle button to cancel a command or back out of a menu. With a two-button mouse, press the right button to cancel a command or get out of the pull-down menu system. If you are several levels deep in the pull-down menu system and want to back up one level, press and hold down the left button, press the right button, and then release both buttons. Some mouse-driver software for a two-button mouse requires pressing both the left and right buttons to cancel a command.

Printing a Document

Reminder: If you do not want to save a document, you still can print it from the screen without saving it to disk first.

Unlike WordPerfect 5.1, which offers various printing options, LetterPerfect has a single printing option. Although you do not have to save the document as a disk file before printing it, LetterPerfect requires that the document be on-screen for printing either the full document or selected pages in it. Printing in this manner is called *screen printing* because the document is stored in the computer system's temporary video memory area during the printing process.

Note: The steps that follow are based on the assumption that you have installed your printer properly. See Chapters 1 and 8 for information on installing, selecting, and customizing printer drivers.

To print the document, follow these steps:

1. Access the File pull-down menu (see fig. 3.3) and select **P**rint. Alternatively, press Print (Shift-F7). The Print menu appears as shown in figure 3.4.

2. Select **Full Document (1)**. LetterPerfect momentarily flashes `* Please Wait *` on the status line and then displays the Print: Control Printer menu (see fig. 3.5), which keeps you informed of the document's printing status.

   If the printer is properly configured and connected, printing begins almost immediately, unless LetterPerfect has to download one or more soft type fonts for the document. Regardless of the type of computer system, printing a document requires all of LetterPerfect's program and memory resources. As a result, you cannot use any of the program's other features until the entire document has been sent to the printer.

   When the program completes the print job, it displays a prompt instructing you to press any key to continue.

3. Press any key, and LetterPerfect returns to its Printer Control menu.

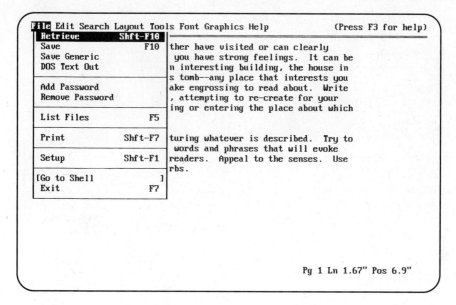

```
File Edit Search Layout Tools Font Graphics Help        (Press F3 for help)
┌─────────────────────────┐
│ Retrieve       Shft-F10 │
│ Save            F10      ther have visited or can clearly
│ Save Generic             you have strong feelings.  It can be
│ DOS Text Out            n interesting building, the house in
│                         s tomb--any place that interests you
│ Add Password            ake engrossing to read about.  Write
│ Remove Password         , attempting to re-create for your
│                         ing or entering the place about which
│ List Files      F5      
│
│ Print          Shft-F7  turing whatever is described.  Try to
│                          words and phrases that will evoke
│ Setup          Shft-F1  readers.  Appeal to the senses.  Use
│                         rbs.
│ [Go to Shell         ]  
│ Exit            F7      
└─────────────────────────┘



                                       Pg 1 Ln 1.67" Pos 6.9"
```

Fig. 3.3. *The File pull-down menu.*

```
Print

      1 - Full Document
      2 - Multiple Pages
      3 - View Document
      4 - Initialize Printer


Options

      5 - Select Printer        Laser
      6 - Binding Offset        0"
      7 - Number of Copies      1
      8 - Graphics Quality      Medium
      9 - Text Quality          High






Selection: 0
```

Fig. 3.4. *The Print menu.*

```
Print: Control Printer


Port:        LPT 1                       Page Number:  1
Status:      Printing                    Current Copy: 1 of 1
Message:     None
Paper:       Standard 8.5" x 11"
Location:    Continuous feed
Action:      None











1 Cancel Job; 2 Go (start printer); 3 Stop: 0
```

Fig. 3.5. *The Print: Control Printer menu.*

To print a single page from the document, follow these steps:

1. Access the **File** pull-down menu and select **Print** (see fig. 3.3). Alternatively, press Print (Shift-F7). The Print menu appears as shown in figure 3.4.

2. Select **Multiple Pages (2)**. LetterPerfect displays the Pages: prompt on the status line.

3. Enter the number of the page or pages that you want LetterPerfect to print. For example, type the number *2* to have LetterPerfect print page 2.

   LetterPerfect displays the Print: Printer Control menu (see fig. 3.5), which informs you of the printing status. When the program completes the print job, it displays a prompt instructing you to press any key to continue.

4. Press any key, and LetterPerfect returns to its Printer Control menu.

LetterPerfect also lets you designate several pages for printing during a single print operation. The procedure is identical to that described for printing a single page, except that you enter more than one page number in step 3. Table 3.3 lists the types of page combinations you can enter to print multiple pages during a single print operation.

Table 3.3
Designations for Printing Multiple Pages

Pages to Print	*Method for Designating Pages*
First page to a specific page	Type a hyphen and the number of the last page to be printed. Example: *-8*.
Consecutive pages	Type the beginning page number, a hyphen, and the last page number. Example: *3-9*.
Nonconsecutive pages	Type each page number followed by a comma. Example: *3,8,10,14*.
Specific page to the document's end	Type the beginning page number followed by a hyphen. Example: *5-*.
All even pages	Type the letter *e* without any page number. Example: *e*.
Consecutive even pages	Type the letter *e*, a comma, the beginning page number, a hyphen, and the ending page number. Example: *e,4-10*. **Note:** If you omit an ending page number, LetterPerfect prints all even-numbered pages beginning with the designated first page and continuing to the last even-numbered page in the document.
All odd pages	Type the letter *o* without any page number. Example: *o*.
Consecutive odd pages	Type the letter *o*, a comma, the beginning page number, a hyphen, and the ending page number. Example: *o,7-15*. **Note:** If you omit an ending page number, LetterPerfect prints all odd-numbered pages beginning with the designated first page and continuing to the last odd-numbered page in the document.

Table 3.3 (continued)

Pages to Print	Method for Designating Pages
Labels	LetterPerfect considers each individual label on a sheet as a separate page. The same commands and page combinations are available to print labels, with two exceptions: the program recognizes a maximum of only two multiple-page commands, and you must precede the *e* and *o* commands with an *l* (for example: *le,4-12*). If you enter more than two multiple-page print commands separated by commas, LetterPerfect prints the labels required by the first two commands and ignores the remaining commands.

Tip: You can select one or more of the page combinations listed in table 3.3 to print during a single print operation by separating each of the categories with a comma. However, LetterPerfect limits you to a maximum of 30 characters, including separators, for designating the pages. For example, to print pages 3 through 5, 7, even-numbered pages from 10 through 20, odd-numbered pages from 23 through 27, and all pages from 30 to the end of the document, type the following in step 3:

3-5,7,e,10-20,o,23-27,30-

Saving a Document to Disk

During the composition process, it is best to save a copy of the document periodically to the system's hard disk drive or on a floppy disk. LetterPerfect offers two methods of saving a file:

- The Save feature, which lets you save a copy of the on-screen document to disk. With Save, the document remains on-screen for additional work.

- The Exit feature, which lets you save a copy of the document to disk and allows you to exit the program. To keep the document on-screen, press Cancel when the `Exit LP?` prompt appears.

Use Exit to clear the screen without saving the document. This method is handy when you decide to discard what you have written.

The first time you save a document, LetterPerfect prompts you for a file name. Suppose that you created the short document shown in figure 3.2 and now want to save the file. With the document on-screen, follow these steps:

1. Access the **F**ile pull-down menu and select **S**ave. Alternatively, press Save (F10).

   The prompt `Document to be saved:` appears on the status line.

2. Type a file name for the document. In this example, you can type *describe.doc* or some other unique file name. A file name consists of two parts: a *root name* (or *primary file name*) and an optional *suffix* (or *extension*). The root name can have one to eight characters. You can use the root name to describe the file's contents. The suffix can have one to three characters. If you use a suffix, separate it from the root name by a period (.). The optional suffix can be omitted. When you name a file, observe your operating-system (MS-DOS or PC DOS) guidelines for naming files.

3. Press Enter. A prompt on the status line indicates that LetterPerfect is saving the file to the current drive and directory. To save the file to a different drive or directory, type the drive and directory information before you type the file name. After you name and save a file, the file name is displayed on the status line in the left corner of the screen.

LetterPerfect responds a bit differently when you save a file that you saved before. When you issue the Save command, LetterPerfect displays the file name on the status line. To save the file under the same name, press Enter. LetterPerfect prompts you to confirm the replacement of the file on disk. If you select **Y**es, the program replaces the document in the disk file with the document on the screen. If you select **N**o, you can rename the file and save it under a different name. If you want to save the document under a different name, move the cursor to the old file name and change it. You can change any information following the `Document to be saved:` prompt.

Reminder: You can save a document under a different name.

Clearing the Screen and Exiting LetterPerfect

LetterPerfect's Exit feature has many different functions. Use the Exit feature to do any of the following:

- Save the document and clear the screen so that you can start work on a new document.

- Save the document and exit LetterPerfect.

- Clear the screen without saving the document.

- Exit LetterPerfect without saving the document.

Use the following steps to save the document and clear the screen:

1. Access the **File** pull-down menu and select **Exit**. Alternatively, press Exit (F7).

2. In response to the `Save Document?` prompt, select **Yes**.

3. Type the file name under which you want to save the document and press Enter, or accept the current file name by pressing Enter. In response to the `Replace?` prompt, select **Yes**.

4. In response to the `Exit LP?` prompt, select **No**.

The following procedure saves the document and exits you from LetterPerfect:

1. Access the **File** pull-down menu and select **Exit**. Alternatively, press Exit (F7).

2. In response to the `Save Document?` prompt, select **Yes**.

3. Type the file name under which you want to save the document and press Enter, or accept the current file name by pressing Enter. In response to the `Replace?` prompt, select **Yes**.

4. In response to the `Exit LP?` prompt, select **Yes**.

Use the following steps to clear the screen without saving the document:

1. Access the **File** pull-down menu and select **Exit**. Alternatively, press Exit (F7).

2. In response to the `Save Document?` prompt, select **No**.

3. In response to the `Exit LP?` prompt, select **No**.

Do the following to exit LetterPerfect without saving the document:

1. Access the **File** pull-down menu and select **Exit**. Alternatively, press Exit (F7).

2. In response to the `Save Document?` prompt, select **No**.

3. In response to the `Exit LP?` prompt, select **Yes**.

Summary

In this chapter, you learned a great deal about using a word processor to help you write. You read about how you can do the following with LetterPerfect:

- Move the cursor around the document by using either the mouse or the keyboard

- Type, save, and print a document

- Print multiple pages of a document

Chapter 4 discusses techniques for editing a document

---

[1] Ann Berthoff, *Forming, Thinking, Writing: The Composing Imagination* (Montclair, NJ: Boynton/Cook, Publishers, Inc., 1982), p. 11.

4

Editing a Document

I n earlier chapters you learned how to enter text, move the cursor, make menu choices, print and save a document, and exit LetterPerfect. This chapter presents the basics of editing a document and introduces the fun and excitement of using LetterPerfect's powerful editing tools.

In this chapter, you learn how to do the following:

- Retrieve a file

- Edit text and revise extensively

- Delete (erase) a single character, word, line, sentence, paragraph, and page

- Undelete (unerase) what you recently deleted

- Overwrite text in typewriter style

- Enhance text by using **bold** typeface or <u>underlining</u>

- Edit in Reveal Codes for greater format control

- Use LetterPerfect's powerful Search and Replace features

Reminder: WordPerfect Corporation updated LetterPerfect 1.0 just before this book went to press. Dated 11/01/90, the interim release includes new options for existing features, and a few new features. The menus on your screen may, therefore, differ slightly from those shown in this book. Also, depending on the printer-form definition, margins, tab stops, and font you specify, the text placement and status-line information in documents you create may differ from that shown in this book's figures.

For information about using the mouse and accessing the pull-down menus, refer to the Introduction.

Retrieving a Document

LetterPerfect 1.0 automatically retrieves documents in WordPerfect 4.2, 5.0, or 5.1 format; in generic word processing format; or in DOS (ASCII) format and converts a document in any of these formats into WordPerfect 5.1 format. LetterPerfect saves documents in either WordPerfect 5.1 or DOS text or generic word processing formats. Although LetterPerfect 1.0 can retrieve and edit a document in any of these formats, formatting codes not recognized by the program are ignored.

WordPerfect 4.2 can neither retrieve nor edit a document saved in WordPerfect 5.1 format. A document saved by LetterPerfect in its normal format cannot be read by WordPerfect 4.2 unless that document is saved in either the generic word processing format or the DOS format by the use of the Text Out feature.

LetterPerfect includes a document-conversion program—CONVERT.EXE— that lets you change documents created with other word processors, such as WordStar or MultiMate, to WordPerfect 5.1 format. To use the conversion program, do the following:

1. At the DOS prompt, type *convert*. At the top of the screen, LetterPerfect displays the prompt `Name of Input File?`

2. Type the name of the document file (including the path name if the document is in a subdirectory different from that containing the conversion program) and press Enter. At the top of the screen, LetterPerfect displays the prompt `Name of Output File?`

3. Type the name you want given to the document file created by the conversion program and press Enter. LetterPerfect displays a list of conversion formats, as shown in figure 4.1.

4. Type the number of the conversion you want and press Enter. LetterPerfect displays the prompt Enter name of CRS File or press ENTER and default will be used. If the CRS (conversion resource) file exists, it contains information that the Convert program uses to format the document into WordPerfect 5.1 format.

5. If a CRS file exists for your printer, type the file's name and press Enter. If a CRS file does not exist, press Enter. The Convert program creates a new document file in the WordPerfect 5.1 format recognized by LetterPerfect.

```
Name of Input File? report.txt
Name of Output File? report.doc


0 EXIT
1 WordPerfect to another format
2 Revisable-Form-Text (IBM DCA Format) to WordPerfect
3 Final-Form-Text (IBM DCA Format) to WordPerfect
4 Navy DIF Standard to WordPerfect
5 WordStar 3.3 to WordPerfect
6 MultiMate Advantage II to WordPerfect
7 Seven-Bit Transfer Format to WordPerfect
8 WordPerfect 4.2 to WordPerfect 5.1
9 Mail Merge to WordPerfect Secondary Merge
A Spreadsheet DIF to WordPerfect Secondary Merge
B Word 4.0 to WordPerfect
C DisplayWrite to WordPerfect

Enter number of Conversion desired
```

Fig. 4.1. The conversion formats available with the Convert program.

Using List Files To Retrieve a File

The simplest way to retrieve a document is to use the List Files feature. The feature's options are discussed in detail in Chapter 10. To use the List Files feature to retrieve a document, follow these steps:

1. Access the File pull-down menu (see fig. 4.2) and select List Files. Alternatively, press List Files (F5).

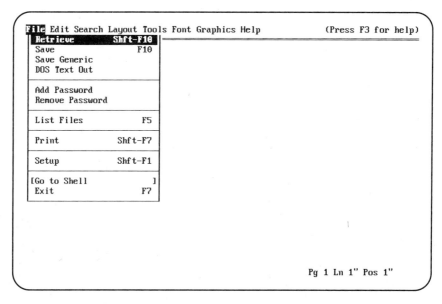

```
File Edit Search Layout Tools Font Graphics Help          (Press F3 for help)
┌─────────────────────────┐
│ Retrieve        Shft-F10 │═══════════════════════════════════════
│ Save                 F10 │
│ Save Generic             │
│ DOS Text Out             │
│                          │
│ Add Password             │
│ Remove Password          │
│                          │
│ List Files            F5 │
│                          │
│ Print            Shft-F7 │
│                          │
│ Setup            Shft-F1 │
│                          │
│ [Go to Shell          ] │
│ Exit                  F7 │
└─────────────────────────┘


                                          Pg 1 Ln 1" Pos 1"
```

Fig. 4.2. The File pull-down menu.

A prompt appears in the lower left corner of the screen, listing the current drive, default subdirectory, and file specification. The default file specification is *.*, which displays all files in the default subdirectory. If you press List Files (F5) at this point, LetterPerfect lists the files last displayed with the List Files feature. This display may be different from the default subdirectory.

2. Press Enter. The editing screen is replaced by the List Files screen (see fig. 4.3).

3. If you see the name of the document you want to retrieve, use the mouse or the arrow keys to highlight the file name. If you don't see the name of the document you want to retrieve, do the following:

   a. Select Name Search (**N**) from the menu at the bottom of the screen. Alternatively, press Search (**F2**).

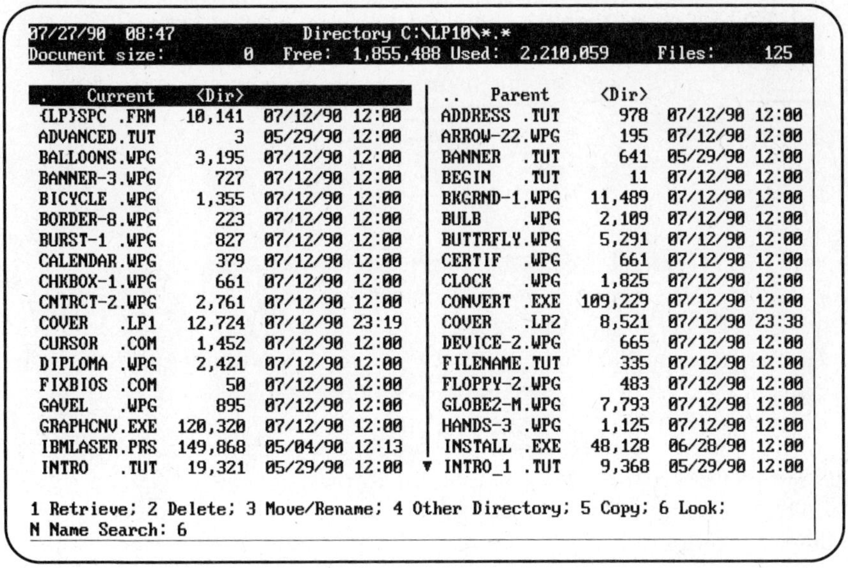

```
07/27/90  08:47                 Directory C:\LP10\*.*
Document size:        0   Free: 1,855,488 Used: 2,210,059      Files:     125

.     Current   <Dir>                 ..     Parent    <Dir>
{LP}SPC .FRM   10,141  07/12/90 12:00  ADDRESS .TUT      978  07/12/90 12:00
ADVANCED.TUT        3  05/29/90 12:00  ARROW-22.WPG      195  07/12/90 12:00
BALLOONS.WPG    3,195  07/12/90 12:00  BANNER  .TUT      641  05/29/90 12:00
BANNER-3.WPG      727  07/12/90 12:00  BEGIN   .TUT       11  07/12/90 12:00
BICYCLE .WPG    1,355  07/12/90 12:00  BKGRND-1.WPG   11,489  07/12/90 12:00
BORDER-8.WPG      223  07/12/90 12:00  BULB    .WPG    2,109  07/12/90 12:00
BURST-1 .WPG      827  07/12/90 12:00  BUTTRFLY.WPG    5,291  07/12/90 12:00
CALENDAR.WPG      379  07/12/90 12:00  CERTIF  .WPG      661  07/12/90 12:00
CHKBOX-1.WPG      661  07/12/90 12:00  CLOCK   .WPG    1,825  07/12/90 12:00
CNTRCT-2.WPG    2,761  07/12/90 12:00  CONVERT .EXE  109,229  07/12/90 12:00
COVER   .LP1   12,724  07/12/90 23:19  COVER   .LP2    8,521  07/12/90 23:38
CURSOR  .COM    1,452  07/12/90 12:00  DEVICE-2.WPG      665  07/12/90 12:00
DIPLOMA .WPG    2,421  07/12/90 12:00  FILENAME.TUT      335  07/12/90 12:00
FIXBIOS .COM       50  07/12/90 12:00  FLOPPY-2.WPG      483  07/12/90 12:00
GAVEL   .WPG      895  07/12/90 12:00  GLOBE2-M.WPG    7,793  07/12/90 12:00
GRAPHCNV.EXE  120,320  07/12/90 12:00  HANDS-3 .WPG    1,125  07/12/90 12:00
IBMLASER.PRS  149,868  05/04/90 12:13  INSTALL .EXE   48,128  06/28/90 12:00
INTRO   .TUT   19,321  05/29/90 12:00 ▼ INTRO_1 .TUT   9,368  05/29/90 12:00

1 Retrieve; 2 Delete; 3 Move/Rename; 4 Other Directory; 5 Copy; 6 Look;
N Name Search: 6
```

Fig. 4.3. *The List Files screen.*

    b.   Type the first few letters of the document name. The highlight moves to the name of the document for which you are looking.

    c.   Press Enter to end the Name Search operation.

If you think you've found the document you want but are not sure, the Look (6) option lets you view the contents of the file before you retrieve it. Because Look is List Files' default option, pressing Enter displays the file's contents. You can scroll through the text of the document by using the arrow, Screen Up (keyboard plus sign on the numeric keypad) or PgUp, Screen Down (keyboard minus sign on the numeric keypad) or PgDn, and Home (in conjunction with arrow) keys. You also can look at the next or previous document in the list by choosing Next (1) or Prev (2). Press Exit (F7) or Enter to return to the List Files screen.

Beginning with the 11/01/90 interim release, the Look feature does not display the contents of LetterPerfect's temporary program files, such as LP}LP{.BV1 and LP}LP{.TV1. If you attempt to use the Look feature on one of these files, the list of files remains on the screen. If you select the Next Doc (1) and Prev

Doc (**2**) options while using the Look feature, LetterPerfect ignores the temporary files and shows the next displayable file in sequence. If there is not a displayable file in sequence, the list of files is displayed.

4. When you are sure that you have the right file name, choose **Retrieve (1)**.

Reminder: To retrieve files in a format not supported by LetterPerfect, first use the Convert utility to change the file's format.

LetterPerfect is careful about what files are retrieved. If you try to retrieve a document whose format is not supported by the program, LetterPerfect displays the `ERROR: Incompatible file format` message. To retrieve files in a format not supported by LetterPerfect, use the Convert utility to change the document's format as described at the beginning of this section.

If the document you need is not in LetterPerfect's default subdirectory, the List Files feature offers two methods for displaying a list of files in other subdirectories and on other drives. From the main editing screen, use the following procedure to display lists of files in other subdirectories and on other drives:

1. Access the File pull-down menu and select **List Files**. Alternatively, press List Files (F5). LetterPerfect displays a prompt at the lower left corner of the screen, similar to the following: `Dir C:\LP10\DOCUMENT\*.*`

   The `C:\` is the current default drive letter. The `LP10\DOCUMENT\` is the current default subdirectory. The `*.*` designates all files in the subdirectory. If you replace either `*` with a file name or extension, LetterPerfect limits the list of files it displays to the file or files matching the modified file designation. This combination of drive letter, subdirectory name, and file designation is called the *path* or *path name*.

2. If you want to change the default directory used by LetterPerfect, move the mouse pointer to the = at the bottom right of the screen and click the left button. Alternatively, press the equal sign. If you click the right mouse button, LetterPerfect displays a list of files for the current subdirectory.

   If you do not want to change LetterPerfect's default directory, omit this step and go to step 3.

3. Press a cursor-movement key to position the cursor on the portion of the path name you want to change. If typing a completely different path name is easier, do *not* press a cursor-movement key but begin typing the new path name.

4. Press Enter to display a list of the files in the new subdirectory.

If the document you need is not in the subdirectory displayed by the List Files feature, use the following procedure to display lists of files in other subdirectories and on other drives:

1. Move the cursor bar to highlight the `. Current <Dir>` subdirectory listing.

2. Press Enter. LetterPerfect displays the full path name of the subdirectory currently displayed.

3. Press a cursor-movement key to position the cursor on the portion of the path name you want to change. If typing a completely different path name is easier, do *not* press a cursor-movement key but begin typing the new path name.

4. Press Enter to display a list of the files in the new subdirectory.

Alternatively, you can use the other-directory option of the List Files feature to display a list of files in a different subdirectory. To use the other-directory option, which permanently changes the default subdirectory used by LetterPerfect, follow these steps:

1. Choose **Other Directory (4)** and type the name of the new directory.

2. Press Enter twice to access the directory.

If you are unsure of the name of the directory you want to change, perform the following steps:

1. Access the **File** pull-down menu and select List Files. Alternatively, press List Files (F5).

2. Press Enter.

3. Move the cursor bar to highlight a file name followed by `<Dir>` instead of by the size of the file. This is a subdirectory. In addition to using the cursor-movement keys and mouse to move the cursor, you can do one of the following:

Reminder: If you're not sure which directory you want, access the List Files screen, highlight a subdirectory name, and press Enter.

- Select **N**ame Search to find subdirectories, but remember to include a backslash (\) before typing any letters.

- Press Search (F2) and type the name of the subdirectory.

4. Press Enter twice.

LetterPerfect lists the files in the new subdirectory. You can use these procedures to list files in any subdirectory on any disk available to your computer system.

Using the Retrieve Feature

If you know the name of the document you want, do the following to retrieve the file:

1. Access the **F**ile pull-down menu and select **R**etrieve. Alternatively, press Retrieve (Shift-F10).

   The `Document to be retrieved:` prompt appears in the lower left corner of the screen.

Reminder: If the document you want is in a directory different from the current directory, type the complete path name.

2. Type the name of the document. If the document is not in the current default subdirectory, be sure to include its full path name, such as *c:\lp10\notes\report.txt*.

3. Press Enter.

LetterPerfect brings the document onto the main editing screen and places the cursor at the left edge on the first line after any hidden formatting codes. If LetterPerfect displays the message `ERROR: File not found`, check to be sure that the disk drive and subdirectory are correct in the path name and that the file name is correct.

Using Retrieve To Combine Documents

You may want to combine portions of several documents to create one large document. Doctors, attorneys, and other report writers often have standard paragraphs inserted into many documents. Journalists, authors, and thesis writers often want to use previously written material. LetterPerfect is a powerful editing tool that allows you to combine two or more documents into a single document.

Whenever you retrieve a document, LetterPerfect adds the text at the cursor's location. If the screen is blank, you don't have to worry about combining. But if a document is already on-screen, the new document is inserted at the cursor position. For example, if the cursor is in the middle of the current document, the retrieved document is inserted into the middle of the current document. To combine documents, place the cursor where you want the new document inserted; then retrieve a document by using one of the methods described in the preceding sections. If you use either **Retrieve** from the **File** pull-down menu or Retrieve (Shift-F10), the new document is retrieved immediately. If you use either **List Files** from the **File** pull-down menu or List Files (F5) while a document is currently on-screen, LetterPerfect asks you to confirm the retrieval with the following prompt: `Retrieve into current document? No (Yes)`

Select **Yes** to retrieve the document or **No** to cancel the retrieval.

> *Tip:* Save the current document before retrieving additional text. That way, if you make a mistake, you can just erase the screen and start over by retrieving the document you just saved.

Revising and Editing Text

LetterPerfect serves two general groups of people. The first consists of writers, journalists, doctors, lawyers, and other professionals who compose original material. The second consists of typists or secretaries who must transcribe and proofread someone else's thoughts from either a recording or a manuscript.

Members of the first group may need to rewrite their prose extensively or revise it substantially. The second group may verify spelling, correct punctuation and grammar, and format the final document for an appealing presentation.

In some instances, one person may do all the creating, revising, correcting, and formatting. In other instances, several people may be involved. Regardless of the circumstances, LetterPerfect is a powerful tool for performing these tasks.

Substantive Changes (Revision)

After you create a document, you may need to revise it. Revision goes deeper than checking spelling and punctuation and formatting the document for attractive presentation. Revision requires polishing the thoughts behind the presentation.

LetterPerfect makes editing so simple that users tend to polish the page and not the thought. Because the revising and editing processes use some of the same tools (for example, deleting and moving text), one function is easily confused with the other. The following suggestions show how you can use LetterPerfect's editing environment to its fullest:

- Use LetterPerfect's large blank screen to write thoughts quickly. Chapter 10 shows how to organize the document with LetterPerfect's outlining capabilities.

- Use the editing capabilities (described later in this chapter) to eliminate unwanted text and to add new ideas or thoughts.

- Use the powerful Block feature (explained in Chapter 5) to rear-range text.

- Use LetterPerfect's Thesaurus to find the "perfect" word; use the Speller to find misspellings. These features are explained in Chapter 11.

- Use the editing screen or a printed copy of the document for additional revisions.

Surface Changes (Editing)

LetterPerfect's editing capabilities are a powerful subset of its feature-rich big brother, WordPerfect 5.1, and include all the basic features needed to edit the document's contents and enhance its appearance.

The editing process is comparable to polishing a gemstone. After the initial cut has been made, changes to the surface make a rock a treasure. Similarly, you can polish a document by using a two-stage editing process.

First, you handle rough editing, such as correcting typographical errors by deleting or adding letters and words. In this stage, LetterPerfect helps you by proofreading for spelling errors and double words.

Second, you polish the document by putting it into its final format—how it looks when printed. Most formatting can be done through the Format, Font, and hot-key formatting features discussed in detail in the next three chapters.

Deleting Text

With LetterPerfect, deleting text is easy. You can delete single letters, entire words, whole sentences, complete paragraphs, or full pages with the mouse or with only a few keystrokes.

Deleting Text with the Mouse

A benefit of using a mouse with LetterPerfect is the device's capability to block text quickly. You can block text more quickly with the mouse than with the Block (Alt-F4 or F12) command (for more information on using the Block command, see Chapter 5).

As shown in the following section, although the pull-down menu bar offers a method of block-deleting a sentence or paragraph, the method is cumbersome compared to using the mouse. Also, the method's options are limited to **Move**, **Copy**, and **Delete**. If you block text with a mouse, you can perform a **Move** (Cut), **Copy**, or **Delete** operation directly from the Edit pull-down menu. LetterPerfect also lets you perform any other operation that can normally be done on blocked text.

To delete text by using the mouse, complete the following steps:

1. Click the left mouse button at either the upper left or the lower right of the block (character, word, sentence, or paragraph) you want to delete.

2. Drag the mouse to the opposite corner of the block you are defining (the area is highlighted as you move the mouse).

3. Access the **Edit** pull-down menu and select **Delete** (or press Del or Backspace). LetterPerfect displays the prompt `Delete Block?`

4. Select **Yes** to delete the highlighted text or **No** to cancel the deletion operation.

You also can use the Select Sentence or Select Paragraph commands as described in the following section.

There is one limitation to using the mouse to block text: the block will not include any formatting codes on the document's first line before the first character *unless* the cursor is located to the left of these codes before you begin the block operation.

Deleting Text with the Keyboard

The following sections show you how to use the keyboard to delete various amounts of text.

Deleting a Single Character

LetterPerfect lets you delete single characters by using any of three methods:

- Press the Backspace key to delete the character to the left of the cursor.

- Press the Del key to delete the character at the cursor.

- Press the space bar in Typeover mode (press Ins) to delete the character at the cursor and leave a space.

Deleting a Single Word or Portions of a Single Word

LetterPerfect offers several options for deleting single words or portions of single words:

- Press Delete Word (Ctrl-Backspace) to delete a word at the cursor or to delete a word to the left of the cursor if the cursor is on a space immediately after the word.

- Press Home-Backspace to delete the word or characters left of the cursor to the space following the preceding word.

- Press Home-Del to delete everything from the cursor to the end of the word and all intervening spaces to the beginning of the next word or character following the word.

- Press the space bar several times in Typeover mode (press Ins) to delete the characters to the right of the cursor.

Deleting to the End of the Line

To delete from the cursor position to the end of the line, press Ctrl-End. Any hard return (**[HRt]**) at the end of the line remains and is not deleted.

Deleting to the End of the Page

To delete from the cursor position to the end of the page, do the following:

1. Press Delete to End of Page (Ctrl-PgDn) or the fast-key option: Ctrl-l.

2. The prompt at the bottom of the screen reads as follows: `Delete Remainder of page? No (Yes)`

    Select **Yes** to delete or **No** to cancel the delete operation.

When you use this feature, LetterPerfect deletes all text and formatting codes from the cursor's position to the end of the page unless the page ends with a **[HPg]**, the hard-page formatting code, which is not deleted.

Deleting a Sentence, Paragraph, or Page

To delete separate blocks of text, complete the following steps:

1. Position the cursor at the text you want to delete.

2. Access the Edit pull-down menu and then choose either Select Sentence or Select Paragraph. There is no option for deleting a page. See the section "Deleting Text with the Mouse" for an easier method of using the mouse to delete text.

   Alternatively, press Move (Ctrl-F4) and choose one of these options:

   Sentence (**1**), Paragraph (**2**), or Page (**3**).

   The sentence, paragraph, or page to be deleted is highlighted (fig. 4.4 shows an example).

3. Choose **Delete** (**3**). The highlighted sentence, paragraph, or page is deleted.

```
 File Edit Search Layout Tools Font [Graphics] Help     (Press ALT= for menu bar)
═══════════════════════════════════════════════════════════════════════════════
 Think of a place that you either have visited or can clearly
 visualize, a place for which you have strong feelings. It can be
 a room, a natural setting, an interesting building, the house in
 which you grew up, King Tut's tomb--any place that interests you
 and that you think you can make engrossing to read about. Write
 a personal description of it, attempting to re-create for your
 reader the experience of seeing or entering the place about which
 you've chosen to write.

 Details are essential in picturing whatever is described.  Try to
 think of rich and suggestive words and phrases that will evoke
 emotional responses in your readers.  Appeal to the senses.  Use
 concrete nouns and active verbs.




 Block on                                      Pg 1 Ln 1.67" Pos 5.9"
```

Fig. 4.4. A text block to be deleted.

Using the Undelete Command

Few things are more frustrating than accidentally deleting text. WordPerfect Corporation understands the errors users make and so provides a way to access recent deletions. LetterPerfect maintains a *buffer* (a special file in RAM) that holds the last three deletions. To undelete text, do the following:

1. Position the cursor where you want the previously deleted text placed.

2. Access the **Edit** pull-down menu and choose **Undelete**. Alternatively, press Undelete (F1) or Esc. The following menu appears in the lower left corner of the screen:

   Undelete: 1 Restore; **2** Previous Deletion: **0**

   A block of highlighted text appears on the editing screen—the most recently deleted text (see fig. 4.5).

```
File Edit Search Layout Tools Font Graphics Help      (Press ALT= for menu bar)

Think of a place that you either have visited or can clearly
visualize, a place for which you have strong feelings.  It can be
a room, a natural setting, an interesting building, the house in
which you grew up, King Tut's tomb--any place that interests you
and that you think you can make engrossing to read about.  Write
a personal description of it, attempting to re-create for your
reader the experience of seeing or entering the place about which
you've chosen to write.

Details are essential in picturing whatever is described.  Try to
think of rich and suggestive words and phrases that will evoke
emotional responses in your readers.  Appeal to the senses.  Use
concrete nouns and active verbs.




Undelete: 1 Restore; 2 Previous Deletion: 0
```

Fig. 4.5. *A text block displayed by the Undelete feature.*

3. Choose **Restore (1)** if the highlighted text is what you want to undelete; choose **P**revious Deletion **(2)** or use the up arrow and down arrow and if you want the Undelete feature to display other previously deleted text. When the proper text appears on-screen, choose **Restore (1)**.

Because deleted text is saved to a RAM buffer file, LetterPerfect may run out of memory or disk storage space if too much text is deleted at once. If you try to delete too much text, LetterPerfect displays this warning prompt: `Delete without saving for Undelete? No (Yes)`

If you select **Yes**, LetterPerfect deletes the highlighted text without saving it to the RAM buffer. The deleted text cannot be restored by the Undelete feature. Select **No** to cancel the deletion operation.

Inserting Text

The capability to insert text is a major difference between LetterPerfect and a typewriter. With a typewriter, you cannot insert a word into a previously typed sentence without retyping the sentence. With LetterPerfect, move the cursor to where you want to add the word and type away. The new word is inserted at the cursor, and the existing text is pushed to the right.

If the text pushes off the screen to the right, press the down arrow, and the text wraps correctly to the next line. Beginning with the 11/01/90 interim release, LetterPerfect offers a Screen Rewrite feature that updates the text on the screen without moving the cursor. To use this feature, hold down the Ctrl key and press the F3 key twice. LetterPerfect wraps the text without moving the cursor.

Overwriting Text

Reminder: Use the Typeover feature to replace letters in a misspelled word by placing the cursor at the appropriate position, pressing Ins, and typing the correct characters.

Whereas the Insert feature pushes existing text ahead as new characters are inserted, the Typeover feature overwrites text. Pressing the Ins key switches LetterPerfect to Typeover mode. The Typeover feature replaces existing, on-screen characters with the characters you type.

When you press the Ins key, the word Typeover appears at the lower left corner of the screen to remind you that—with one exception—each character you type replaces a character of text. However, if the cursor encounters any of LetterPerfect's hidden formatting codes, the code and all text following it advance to the right, ahead of the cursor, just as in Insert mode.

To return to the default Insert mode, press Ins again.

Understanding Hidden Codes

"Behind the scenes" of the document, LetterPerfect is receiving instructions about what you want the document to look like. For instance, pressing Underline (F8) turns on underlining; pressing Underline (F8) a second time, or pressing the right arrow, turns off underlining.

When you select a formatting feature, LetterPerfect inserts a *hidden code* into the document. The hidden code tells LetterPerfect to activate the formatting feature the code represents. By hiding the codes, LetterPerfect keeps the document-editing screen uncluttered.

To see the hidden codes in the text, perform the following steps:

1. Access the **E**dit pull-down menu and select **R**eveal Codes. Alternatively, press Reveal Codes (Alt-F3 or F11) or Ctrl-r. The screen splits in half and displays the same text in both windows. The lower part of the screen shows the hidden codes (see fig. 4.6).

2. Access the **E**dit pull-down menu and select **R**eveal Codes to restore the normal screen. Alternatively, press Reveal Codes (Alt-F3 or F11) or Ctrl-r again.

```
 File Edit Search Layout Tools Font Graphics Help        (Press ALT= for menu bar)

 Think of a place that you either have visited or can clearly
 visualize, a place for which you have strong feelings.  It can be
 a room, a natural setting, an interesting building, the house in
 which you grew up, King Tut's tomb--any place that interests you
 and that you think you can make engrossing to read about.  Write
 a personal description of it, attempting to re-create for your
 reader the experience of seeing or entering the place about which
 you've chosen to write.

                                              Pg 1 Ln 1.83" Pos 1"
{  ▲   ▲   ▲   ▲   ▲   ▲   ▲   ▲   ▲   ▲   ▲   }   ▲   ▲   ▲
 a room, a natural setting, an interesting building, the house in[SRt]
 which you grew up, King Tut's tomb[-][-]any place that interests you[SRt]
 and that you think you can make engrossing to read about.  Write[SRt]
 ▌ personal description of it, attempting to re[-]create for your[SRt]
 reader the experience of seeing or entering the place about which[SRt]
 you've chosen to write.[HRt]
 [HRt]
 Details are essential in picturing whatever is described.  Try to[SRt]
 think of rich and suggestive words and phrases that will evoke[SRt]
 emotional responses in your readers.  Appeal to the senses.  Use[SRt]

 Press Reveal Codes to restore screen
```

Fig. 4.6. *The Reveal Codes screen.*

From figure 4.6 you can see that the hidden codes appear as bolded text enclosed in brackets, which make the codes easier to spot among the document's normal text.

LetterPerfect has many codes (see table 4.1). The codes "tell" LetterPerfect about everything from tab stops to point size to where to place carriage returns and page breaks. Don't memorize all the hidden codes; some of them you may never use. If you encounter a hidden code you need to know more about, refer to the list in table 4.1. The important and common hidden codes will become familiar to you as you use them.

Documents formatted by other WordPerfect word processing programs may include hidden formatting codes for features not supported by LetterPerfect 1.0. The hidden formatting codes for the unsupported features are bolded and enclosed in braces (sometimes called *french brackets*). Unsupported codes that remain in a document after it is saved in LetterPerfect's WordPerfect 5.1 format resume normal functioning if the document is retrieved with WordPerfect 5.1. Table 4.2 lists the unsupported formatting codes.

Listing Hidden Codes

Table 4.1 shows a complete listing of the hidden LetterPerfect 1.0 formatting codes and what they represent. Some of the codes provide additional information about the status of the feature indicated within the brackets. For example, **[L/R Mar:1",1"]** means that the left and right margins are each set at 1 inch.

Table 4.1
LetterPerfect's Hidden Formatting Codes

Hidden Code	Function
[ ]	Hard Space
[-]	Hyphen
-	Soft Hyphen (bolded)
-	Hard Hyphen (not bolded)
[Block]	Beginning of Block
[BOLD] [bold]	Bold ON/off

Hidden Code	Function
[Center]	Center Text
[Center Pg]	Center Page Top to Bottom
[Cntr Tab]	Center Tab
[CNTR TAB]	Hard Center Tab
[Date]	Date/Time Function
[Dec Tab]	Decimal Tab
[DEC TAB]	Tab Alignment (Ctrl-F6)
[Dorm HRt]	Dormant Hard Return
[DSRt]	Deletable Soft Return
[Endnote]	Endnote
[Endnote/WP Footnote]	WordPerfect Footnote Treated as an Endnote by LetterPerfect 1.0
[Fig Box]	Paragraph Figure Box
[Fig Opt]	Figure Box Options
[Flsh Rt]	Flush Right Text
[Font]	Base Font
[Footer]	Footer
[Header]	Header
[HPg]	Hard Page
[HRt]	Hard Return
[HRt-SPg]	Hard Return, Soft New Page Combination
[→Indent]	Indent
[→Indent←]	Left/Right Indent
[Index]	Index Entry
[ISRt]	Invisible Soft Return
[ITALC] [italc]	Italic Font ON/off

Table 4.1 (continued)

Hidden Code	Function
[Just]	Justification
[L/R Mar]	Left and Right Margins
[Lang]	Language
[Ln Spacing]	Line Spacing
[←Mar Rel]	Left Margin Release
[Mrg:<code name>]	Merge Code
[Note Num]	Endnote Number
[Outline Off]	Outline Off
[Outline On]	Outline On
[Paper Sz/Typ]	Paper Size and Type
[Par Num]	Paragraph Number
[Pg Numbering]	Page Number Position
[Rgt Tab]	Right Tab
[RGT TAB]	Hard Right Tab
[SPg]	Soft New Page
[SRt]	Soft Return
[SUBSCPT] [subscpt]	Subscript Font ON/off
[Suppress]	Suppress Page Formatting
[SUPRSCPT] [suprscpt]	Superscript Font ON/off
[T/B Mar]	Top and Bottom Page Margins
[Tab]	Left Tab
[TAB]	Hard Left Tab
[Tab Set]	Tab Set
[UND] [und]	Underlining ON/off
[Unknown Code]	Code Not Recognized by LetterPerfect 1.0

Table 4.2
Hidden Formatting Codes Not Supported by LetterPerfect 1.0

Hidden Code	Unsupported Feature
{Adv}	Advance
{BLine}	Baseline Placement
{BlockPro}	Block Protection
{Box Num}	Caption in Graphics Box
{Brdr Opt}	Border Options
{Cell}	Table Cell
{Cndl EOP}	Conditional End of Page
{Col Def}	Column Definition
{Col Off}	End of Text Columns
{Col On}	Beginning of Text Columns
{Color}	Print Color
{Comment}	Document Comment
{Dbl und}	Double Underlining
{Decml/Algn Char}	Decimal Character/Thousands Separator
{Def Mark:Index}	Index Definition
{Def Mark:List}	List Definition
{Def Mark:ToA}	Table of Authorities Definition
{Def Mark:ToC}	Table of Contents Definition
{End Def}	End of Index, List, or Table of Contents
{End Mark}	End of Marked Text
{End Opt}	Endnote Options
{Endnote Placement}	Endnote Placement
{Equ Box}	Equation Box
{Equ Opt}	Equation Box Options
{Ext large}	Extra Large Print Font ON/off
{Fig Box}	Figure Box

Table 4.2 (continued)

Hidden Code	Function
[Fig Opt:WP]	Figure Box Options
{Fine}	Fine Font ON/off
{Footer B}	Footer
{Force}	Force Odd/Even Page
{Ftn Opt}	Footnote/Endnote Options
{Full Form}	Table of Authorities, Full Form
{HLine}	Horizontal Line
{Hrd Row}	Hard Row
{Hyph On}	Hyphenation On
{Hyph Off}	Hyphenation Off
{HZone}	Hyphenation Zone
{Index}	Index Entry
{Insert Pg Num}	Insert Page Number
{Just Lim}	Word/Letter Spacing/Justification Limits
{Kern}	Kerning
{Large}	Large Font
{Leading Adj}	Leading Adjustment
{Link}	Spreadsheet Link
{Link End}	End of Spreadsheet Link
{Ln Height}	Line Height
{Ln Num}	Line Numbering
{Mark}	List Entry or Table of Contents Entry
{Math Def}	Definition of Math Columns
{Math On}	Math On
{Math Off}	Math Off
!	Formula Calculation
=	Calculate Total

Hidden Code	Function
+	Calculate Subtotal
*	Calculate Grand Total
N	Negate Total
t	Subtotal Entry
T	Total Entry
{Mrg}	Unsupported Merge Code
{New End Num}	New Endnote Number
{New Equ Num}	New Equation Number
{New Fig Num}	New Figure Box Number
{New Ftn Num}	New Footnote Number
{New Tbl Num}	New Table Box Number
{New Txt Num}	New Text Box Number
{New Usr Number}	New User Box Number
{Open Style}	Open Style
{Outline}	Outline Attribute
{Outline Lvl}	Outline Style
{Ovrstk}	Overstrike
{Pg Num}	New Page Number
{Pg Num Style}	Page Number Style
{Pg Numbering}	Unsupported Page Numbering
{Par Num Def}	Paragraph Numbering Definition
{Ptr Cmnd}	Printer Command
{Redln}	Redline
{Ref}	Reference, Cross
{Row}	Table Row
{Shadw}	Shadow
{Sm Cap}	Small Capital Letters Font

Table 4.2 (continued)

Hidden Code	Function
{Small}	Small Font
{Stkout}	Strikeout Font
{Style Off}	Style Definition Off
{Style On}	Style Definition On
{Subdoc}	Subdocument for Master Document
{Subdoc Start}	Beginning of Subdocument
{Subdoc End}	End of Subdocument
{Suppress}	Unsupported Suppress Page Format Options
{Target}	Target for Auto Reference
{Tbl Def}	Table Definition
{Tbl Opt}	Table Box Options
{Tbl Off}	Table End
{Tbl Box}	Table Box
{Text Box}	Text Box
{Txt Opt}	Text Box Options
{Undrln}	Underline Spaces/Tabs
{Usr Box}	User-Defined Box
{Usr Opt}	User-Defined Box Options
{VLine}	Vertical Line
{Vry large}	Very Large Font
{W/O Off}	Widow/Orphan Off
{W/O On}	Widow/Orphan On
{Wrd/Ltr Spacing}	Word and Letter Spacing

Editing in Reveal Codes

Editing a document with the Reveal Codes feature active is different from editing on the main editing screen. The Reveal Codes feature splits the screen, the top window showing the document on the main editing screen and the bottom window showing text and hidden codes. The top window shows 8 lines; the lower window shows 10 lines (that leaves 5 lines in each window for the pull-down menu bar, status lines, and the ruler line).

The cursor in the upper window remains in its normal state, but the cursor in the lower window is a rectangular box. When the cursor in the lower window meets a hidden code, the cursor expands to cover the code, whereas in the upper window the cursor remains unaltered (see fig. 4.7).

```
File Edit Search Layout Tools Font Graphics Help      (Press ALT= for menu bar)

Think of a place that you either have visited or can clearly
visualize, a place for which you have strong feelings.  It can be
a room, a natural setting, an interesting building, the house in
which you grew up, King Tut's tomb--any place that interests you
and that you think you can make engrossing to read about.  Write
a personal description of it, attempting to re-create for your
reader the experience of seeing or entering the place about which
you've chosen to write.

                                             Pg 1 Ln 1.5" Pos 2.9"
{    ▲    ▲    ▲    ▲    ▲    ▲    ▲    ▲    ▲    ▲    ▲    }    ▲    ▲
Think of a place that you either have visited or can clearly[SRt]
visualize, a place for which you have strong feelings.  It can be[SRt]
a room, a natural setting, an interesting building, the house in[SRt]
which you grew up, [BOLD]King Tut's[bold] tomb[-][-]any place that interests you
[SRt]
and that you think you can make engrossing to read about.  Write[SRt]
a personal description of it, attempting to re[-]create for your[SRt]
reader the experience of seeing or entering the place about which[SRt]
you've chosen to write.[HRt]
[HRt]

Press Reveal Codes to restore screen
```

Fig. 4.7. The cursor positioned on a hidden formatting code in Reveal Codes.

The Reveal Codes window can be distracting during the initial stages of creating a document. You use Reveal Codes most often when you edit and format a document. When the hidden codes are visible, you can see them and the effect they may have on the document. Some people like to leave the Reveal Codes window visible during editing; others use it only when necessary. The mouse does not work in the Reveal Codes window. With that one exception, LetterPerfect 1.0 allows complete editing capability while the Reveal Codes feature is active.

Reminder: The mouse does not work in the Reveal Codes window.

You also can delete and undelete codes while using the Reveal Codes feature. The Undelete feature recalls codes you accidentally delete. If a line, paragraph, or page of text is deleted and later undeleted, all the hidden codes are restored as well as the text.

If you want to add additional text within *paired codes* (codes that act as on and off switches, like **[BOLD] [bold]**), move the cursor between the paired codes and type the new text instead of pressing the keys for the feature a second time.

Adding Simple Text Enhancements

The second part of the editing process is *formatting*, or preparing the document for printing. Some formatting is done as you enter the text; some is done later. The following sections focus on simple enhancements that can be done as you enter text.

Boldfacing

To create emphasis, you can **boldface** (make darker than ordinary) your text. For best effect, boldfacing should be used sparingly. To boldface text, complete the following steps:

1. Access the Font pull-down menu and select **B**old. Alternatively, press Bold (F6) or Ctrl-b; or press Font (Ctrl-F8) and select the Bold (**1**) option.

2. Type the text you want to boldface. As you type, depending on your monitor, you see on-screen and in boldface the text you enter.

3. To turn off the Boldface feature, access the Font pull-down menu and select **B**old. Alternatively, press Bold (F6) or Ctrl-b; or press Font (Ctrl-F8) and select **B**old (**1**); or press the right arrow. Any of these options moves the cursor past the **[bold]** code, which discontinues the bolding format.

Bold (F6) and the Ctrl-b fast-key combination each serve as an on/off switch. Press either option once to turn on the boldface format. Pressing either option a second time turns off boldface (see fig. 4.7). If you press Bold (F6) or Ctrl-b twice in a row without typing any text, LetterPerfect does not insert the hidden **[BOLD][bold]** formatting code combination, and the text you enter is not boldfaced.

Underlining

LetterPerfect's Underline feature places a single line under text and spaces but not under tabs. Follow these steps to use the Underline feature:

1. Access the Font pull-down menu and select Underline. Alternatively, press Underline (F8) or Ctrl-u; or press Font (Ctrl-F8) and select Underline (**2**).

2. Enter the text you want underlined. Depending on your monitor, the text you type may appear underlined on-screen.

3. To turn off the Underline feature, access the Font pull-down menu and select Underline. Alternatively, press Underline (F8) or Ctrl-u; or press Font (Ctrl-F8) and select Underline (**2**); or press the right arrow. Any of these options moves the cursor past the **[und]** code, which discontinues the underline format.

Underline (F8) and the Ctrl-u fast-key combination each serve as an on/off switch. Press either option once to turn on the underline format. Pressing either option a second time turns off the underline (see fig. 4.8). If you press Undelete (F8) or Ctrl-u twice in a row without typing any text, LetterPerfect does not insert the hidden formatting code combination **[UND][und]**, and the text you enter is not underlined.

Searching and Replacing

Two of the most powerful tools offered by LetterPerfect are the Search and Replace features. If you have faced the frustration of writing a long report and then hunting for a particular phrase or name, you will appreciate LetterPerfect's search-and-replace capabilities.

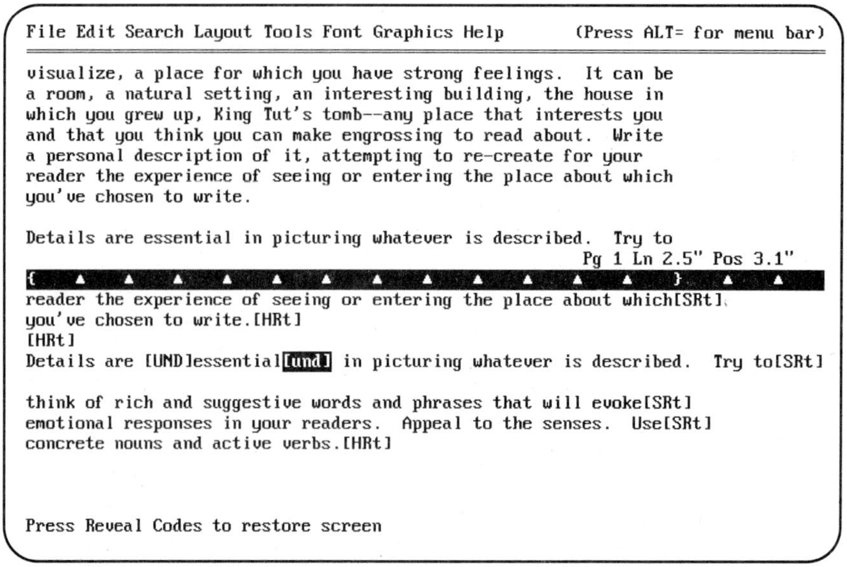

```
File Edit Search Layout Tools Font Graphics Help        (Press ALT= for menu bar)

visualize, a place for which you have strong feelings.  It can be
a room, a natural setting, an interesting building, the house in
which you grew up, King Tut's tomb--any place that interests you
and that you think you can make engrossing to read about.  Write
a personal description of it, attempting to re-create for your
reader the experience of seeing or entering the place about which
you've chosen to write.

Details are essential in picturing whatever is described.  Try to
                                        Pg 1 Ln 2.5" Pos 3.1"
{   ▲   ▲   ▲   ▲   ▲   ▲   ▲   ▲   ▲   ▲   ▲   ▲   }   ▲   ▲
reader the seeing or entering the place about which[SRt]
you've chosen to write.[HRt]
[HRt]
Details are [UND]essential[und] in picturing whatever is described.  Try to[SRt]

think of rich and suggestive words and phrases that will evoke[SRt]
emotional responses in your readers.  Appeal to the senses.  Use[SRt]
concrete nouns and active verbs.[HRt]


Press Reveal Codes to restore screen
```

Fig. 4.8. Underlined text shown by the Reveal Codes screen.

Searching for Text

LetterPerfect's Search feature examines the on-screen document (including headers, footers, and endnotes) for the text and formatting codes you designate. The feature can search from any point in a document, and you can search in either direction—beginning to end or end to beginning. To use the Search feature, perform the following steps:

1. Access the **S**earch pull-down menu and choose either **F**orward or **B**ackward. Alternatively, press either Search (F2) or Backward Search (Shift-F2), depending on whether you want to search from the cursor to the end or to the beginning of the document.

   A prompt appears in the lower left corner of the screen, either →Srch: (forward search) or ←Srch: (backward search). Regardless of which direction you select for the search, while the feature remains active you can change it as follows: press either the down arrow or the right arrow to search forward, or the up arrow or the left arrow to search backward.

2. Enter any text (up to 60 characters) and formatting codes for which you want to search.

3. Press the right mouse button or double-click the left button to begin the search. Alternatively, press Search (F2) to begin the search, regardless of the direction you are searching.

If one occurrence of the text matches, but you want to look for others, repeat the preceding steps. You need not retype the text for which you are searching, because LetterPerfect remembers the previous search request. The following examples show different methods of using the Search feature.

- You can search for parts of a word or even for words you're not sure how to spell. If you type *and* as the word you are searching for, LetterPerfect locates all words that have *and* as a part of them. For example, LetterPerfect matches *and* with *band*, *Randy*, or *And*rew.

  Reminder: If you don't know how to spell a word, search for parts of a word.

- If you want only the specific word and not a part of a word, enter spaces before and after the search text. For example, *[space]***and***[space]* finds only occurrences of *And* or *and* with spaces before and after.

- If you want to find text that has a changing component or if you are unsure of the exact spelling, use the matching character ^X (press Ctrl-V, Ctrl-X). This character matches any single character. If you type *(^X)*, the following characters match: *(1)*, *(2)*, *(3)*, and *(4)*.

- If you type in lowercase only, LetterPerfect finds all occurrences of the word, uppercase and lowercase alike. For example, searching for *and* finds *And*, *AND*, and *and*. But if you type in uppercase only, LetterPerfect finds only uppercase matches (for example, *AND* but not *and*, *And*, or *ANd*).

- LetterPerfect can search for text, hidden formatting codes, or a combination of text and hidden formatting codes. This capability can speed up the search process. For example, searching for **[BOLD]**Past-Due finds the text *past due*, *Past Due*, and *PAST DUE* only if the letter *p* has the **[BOLD]** code immediately to its left.

- You can insert formatting codes into the search string by selecting an option from the pull-down menu bar (or by pressing the key or key combination that creates the hidden formatting code in the main document).

- Pressing Cancel (F1) or Esc during the search operation stops the search and leaves the cursor at its original location.

- If the search fails to find any text or formatting codes matching the search criteria, LetterPerfect displays the message *Not Found* at the lower left corner of the screen.

Searching and Replacing Text

Sometimes you may want to replace the text with different text. To search for
and replace text, perform the following steps:

1. Access the **S**earch pull-down menu and select **R**eplace. Alternatively, press Replace (Alt-F2). LetterPerfect displays this prompt at
   the lower left corner of the screen: w/Confirm? No (Yes)

2. Select **N**o to have all changes made automatically, Select **Y**es to be
   prompted for confirmation of each change.

   LetterPerfect displays the →Srch: prompt at the lower left corner
   of the screen. By default, the Replace feature searches from the
   cursor's location to the bottom of the document. Press the up
   arrow or left arrow to change the replace operation from the
   cursor's location to the top of the document.

3. Enter any text (60 characters maximum), formatting code, or
   combination of text and formatting codes for which you want to
   search.

4. Access the **S**earch pull-down menu and select **F**orward Search.
   Alternatively, press Search (F2).

5. At the Replace with: prompt, type the replacement text (60
   characters maximum), formatting code, or combination of text
   and formatting codes with which you want to replace the existing
   text and formatting codes. If you want the text deleted, do not
   enter anything; go to step 6.

6. Press the right mouse button or double-click the left button.
   Alternatively, press Search (F2).

7. If you requested confirmation in step 2, you see the Confirm? No
   (Yes) prompt each time the search finds a match. Select **Y**es to
   confirm a replacement; to reject the replacement, select **N**o. If
   you want to cancel the search-and-replace operation, press Cancel
   (F1), Esc, or Exit (F7).

8. Press the mouse's cancel button to stop the replace operation
   immediately. Alternatively, press Cancel (F1) or Esc.

If the Replace feature fails to find a match, or when it does not find any additional matches, the message * Not found * appears at the bottom left corner of the screen.

If you want to repeat the replace operation, repeat the preceding steps. You do not have to retype the search string; LetterPerfect keeps it in a RAM buffer until you edit or replace it. However, the program does *not* remember the replacement string. You can edit the previous search request by using the normal editing and function keys. If you press an alphanumeric key before pressing one of the arrow or editing keys, however, the new text is substituted for the old.

Replace works with the Block feature. When you define a block, the replace operation is confined to the block. Editing with the Block feature is explained in Chapter 5.

Reminder: *Edit previous search requests with the normal editing keys. If you press an alphanumeric key before one of the arrow or editing keys, the new text is substituted for the old.*

Using Search or Replace

You can find many uses for a search or replace operation. Consider these ideas:

- *Check for jargon.* For example, if you write to a person unfamiliar with computers, you want to avoid using words that only experienced users know. You also may list your own business jargon and replace it with more common terms.

- *Check for poor writing.* For example, you may want to search your document for the pronouns *this* and *it*, words that are often vague in reference or confusing to readers.

- *Check for clichés.* If you tend to use canned or trite phrases, you can search for them and replace them with fresh images.

- *Check for matching punctuation.* You easily can forget to close a parenthesis or bracket. Double-check the document for the proper pairing of special punctuation.

- *Check for too many spaces.* Normally, you insert two spaces after a period. If you are printing the document on a laser printer or a printer that justifies text, you probably should use only a single space after a period. You can replace all occurrences of two spaces with a single space. You can use the same technique to replace two hard returns with one hard return.

- *Expand abbreviations.* Suppose that you are writing a report about a client named Mrs. William Danielson III. You can type an abbreviation, such as *wd*, and later replace the abbreviation with the full name of the client. Each abbreviation saves you many keystrokes.

Searching for or Replacing Hidden Codes

LetterPerfect can search for or replace hidden codes. When prompted for the search text, press the function key that normally generates the code. If the code is usually generated from a second-level or third-level menu, those choices appear in a menu line at the bottom of the screen. When you select the options you want, the corresponding codes appear in the search-or-replace text area. Note that if you delete one of a set of paired codes (for example, **[BOLD]** or **[bold]**), both are deleted.

To search for the hidden code **[BOLD]**, do the following:

1. Access the **Edit** pull-down menu and select **Reveal Codes.** Alternatively, press Reveal Codes (Alt-F3 or F11) or Ctrl-r.

2. Access the **Search** pull-down menu and select **Forward.** Alternatively, press Search (F2).

3. At the →Srch: prompt, press Bold (F6) or Ctrl-b.

    You can use the pull-down menus to choose the codes for which you want to search.

4. Press the right mouse button or double-click the left button to begin the search. Alternatively, press Search (F2) or Esc.

Some codes are tricky to find. In general, you can insert codes into a Search or Replace command by pressing the correct function key and following the prompts until you find the command you're looking for. For example, all the Merge commands are available from the merge-code command access box—Merge Codes (Shift-F9)—or from the **M**erge Codes option in the **Tools** pull-down menu.

To search for the second code in a paired code, press the feature key twice, use the left-arrow key to move the cursor to the first part of the pair, and then delete the first code. For example, press F2, F6, left arrow, Backspace, and F2 to search for the **[bold]** end code.

Summary

In this chapter you have learned how easily you can make changes to a document with LetterPerfect. You can now do the following operations:

- Retrieve a previously written document
- Delete text by the character, word, line, sentence, paragraph, or page
- Recover accidental deletions by using the Undelete feature
- Toggle between inserting and overwriting text
- Enhance text by making a word or phrase **boldfaced** or <u>underlined</u>
- Find words, names, or phrases anywhere in a document
- Replace any word, name, or phrase
- Find basic errors in punctuation and grammar
- Find, use, and edit hidden codes

Chapter 5 explains how to work with blocks.

Working with Blocks

You can use LetterPerfect's Block feature to highlight an area of text, the first step in using many of LetterPerfect's timesaving functions, such as moving and copying text. In combination with other features, Block gives LetterPerfect versatile and powerful editing capabilities.

The Block feature is extraordinarily flexible. You define the size and shape of the block, and then you specify what to do with that selected text. Block makes possible global editing and formatting changes, such as deleting and underlining, for chunks of text as small as a single character and as large as the entire document. You also can use Block to single out areas of text for saving or printing, and you can use the feature to transfer text from one document to another.

In this chapter, you learn to do these tasks:

- Highlight a block of text or numbers
- Move or copy a block—both within and between documents
- Delete a block
- Save a block
- Print a block
- Enhance a block with features such as italics
- Change the base font to affect the size of characters in a block
- Center a block
- Spell-check a block

181

Reminder: WordPerfect Corporation updated LetterPerfect 1.0 just before this book went to press. Dated 11/01/90, the interim release includes new options for existing features, and a few new features. The menus on your screen may, therefore, differ slightly from those shown in this book. Also, depending on the printer-form definition, margins, tab stops, and font you specify, the text placement and status-line information in documents you create may differ from that shown in this book's figures.

For information about using the mouse and accessing the pull-down menus, refer to the Introduction.

Understanding Block Operations and Revision Strategies

Most LetterPerfect features work without the Block feature. You can boldface or underline text, for example, as you type. But it is frequently easier and quicker to type a document's raw text first and use Block to reorganize paragraphs or add formatting enhancements. This approach lets your thoughts flow freely, without interruption, as you write.

Even when you retype a document, you may find that typing first and adding enhancements later is faster. When you edit a document, you can use Block to rearrange or enhance text as necessary.

Understanding How the Block Feature Works

On your computer screen, blocked text appears highlighted, as shown in figure 5.1. Blocking text is the first step in many editing and formatting operations, such as moving, copying, deleting, saving, or printing.

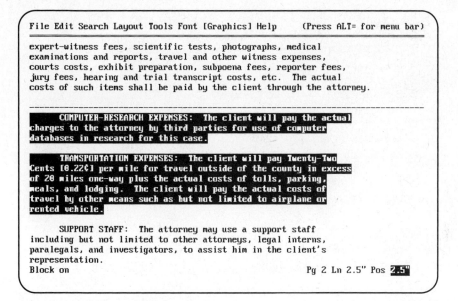

File Edit Search Layout Tools Font [Graphics] Help   (Press ALT= for menu bar)

expert-witness fees, scientific tests, photographs, medical
examinations and reports, travel and other witness expenses,
courts costs, exhibit preparation, subpoena fees, reporter fees,
jury fees, hearing and trial transcript costs, etc. The actual
costs of such items shall be paid by the client through the attorney.

        COMPUTER-RESEARCH EXPENSES: The client will pay the actual
charges to the attorney by third parties for use of computer
databases in research for this case.

        TRANSPORTATION EXPENSES: The client will pay Twenty-Two
Cents [0.22¢] per mile for travel outside of the county in excess
of 20 miles one-way plus the actual costs of tolls, parking,
meals, and lodging. The client will pay the actual costs of
travel by other means such as but not limited to airplane or
rented vehicle.

        SUPPORT STAFF: The attorney may use a support staff
including but not limited to other attorneys, legal interns,
paralegals, and investigators, to assist him in the client's
representation.
Block on   Pg 2 Ln 2.5" Pos 2.5"

Fig. 5.1. *A highlighted block of text.*

Highlighting Text with Block

You can highlight text by using either a mouse or the keyboard. To highlight
a block of text, move the cursor to the first character or formatting code you
want included in the text block, start Block, and move the cursor to the last
character or formatting code to be included in the block. The highlighted text
is ready for the next step in the operation.

Using the Mouse To Highlight a Block of Text

Quick and easy cursor movement and block highlighting are the two most
valuable uses of the LetterPerfect's mouse interface. You can use the mouse to
highlight a block of text by positioning its pointer at the beginning of the block,
pressing and holding down the left mouse button, and moving the mouse
pointer to the end of the block.

Reminder:
To highlight a block with the mouse, position the mouse pointer at the beginning of the block, press and hold down the left mouse button, and move the mouse pointer to the end of the block.

Use these steps to highlight a block of text with a mouse:

1. Move the mouse pointer under the first text character or to the left of the first formatting code to be included in the block.

2. Press and hold down the left mouse button (or the right button on a mouse set up for left-handed users).

   LetterPerfect displays the blinking `Block on` message in the bottom left corner of the screen.

3. Holding down the mouse button, move the mouse pointer to the last character or formatting code to be included in the block.

4. Release the mouse button.

After you release the mouse button, you can enlarge or reduce the size of the block by using any keyboard method described in the following sections.

Using the Keyboard To Highlight a Block of Text

Reminder:
To highlight a block with the keyboard, position the cursor at the first character or code you want in the block, activate Block, and move the cursor to the last character or formatting code in the block.

Follow these steps to highlight a block with the keyboard:

1. Use the cursor keys to move the cursor under the first text character, to the left of the first formatting code to be included in the block.

2. Access the **Edit** pull-down menu and select **Block**. Alternatively, press Block (Alt-F4 or F12).

   LetterPerfect displays the blinking `Block on` message in the bottom left corner of the screen.

3. Perform one of these actions to move the cursor to the end of a block:

   • *Use cursor-movement keys*—up arrow, down arrow, left arrow, right arrow, PgUp, PgDn, Screen Up (keyboard plus key), Screen Down (keyboard minus key), End, and GoTo-GoTo (Ctrl-Home, Ctrl-Home). See Chapter 2 for details about using these keys individually and in combination with the Home key.

- *Type the character(s) or formatting code that appears at the end of the block.* For example, type a period. The block extends to the period at the end of the sentence. To select an entire paragraph, press Enter.

- *Use Search (F2), Backward Search (Shift-F2), or GoTo (Ctrl-Home) plus the character(s) or formatting code that appears at the end of the block.* For example, press Search (F2) and Bold (F6) to extend the block to the next **[BOLD]** code in your document. If there is not a **[BOLD]** code between the cursor's location and the end of the document, LetterPerfect displays the *Not Found* prompt but does not change the block's size.

Completing the Block Operation

The Block on message continues to flash until you complete the block operation by activating any function that works with Block. Table 5.1 lists the LetterPerfect features that work with the Block feature.

Table 5.1
LetterPerfect Features That Work with Block

Feature	Ways To Activate the Feature
Base Font	Access the Font pull-down menu and select Base Font. Alternatively, press Font (Ctrl-F8) and select Base Font (**3**); or press Ctrl-f.
Bold	Access the Font pull-down menu and select **B**old. Alternatively, press Bold (F6), press Font (Ctrl-F8), and then select **B**old (**1**); or press Ctrl-b.
Center	Access the Layout pull-down menu and select **C**enter. Alternatively, press Center (Shift-F6) or Ctrl-c.
Copy	Access the Edit pull-down menu and select **C**opy. Alternatively, press Move (Ctrl-F4) and select Copy (**2**); or press Ctrl-k. If your computer has an enhanced ROM BIOS, you can press Ctrl-Ins.

Table 5.1 (continued)

Feature	Ways To Activate the Feature
Delete	Access the **E**dit pull-down menu and select **D**elete. Alternatively, press Del or Backspace; or press Move (Ctrl-F4) and then select **D**elete (**3**).
Flush Right	Access the **L**ayout pull-down menu and select **F**lush Right. Alternatively, press Flush Right (Alt-F6).
Format	Press Format (Shift-F8).
Italic	Access the **F**ont pull-down menu and select **I**talic. Alternatively, press Font (Ctrl-F8) and select **I**talic (**4**); or press Ctrl-i.
Move (Cut)	Access the **E**dit pull-down menu and select **M**ove. Alternatively, press Move (Ctrl-F4) and select **M**ove (**1**), **C**opy (**2**), and **D**elete (**3**); or press Ctrl-m. If your computer has an enhanced ROM BIOS, you can press Ctrl-Del.
Print	Access the **F**ile pull-down menu and select **P**rint. Alternatively, press Print (Shift-F7).
Replace	Access the **S**earch pull-down menu and select **R**eplace. Alternatively, press Replace (Alt-F2).
Save	Access the **F**ile pull-down menu and select **S**ave. Alternatively, press Save (F10).
Search (Backward)	Access the **S**earch pull-down menu and select **B**ackward. Alternatively, press Backward Search (Shift-F2).
Search (Forward)	Access the **S**earch pull-down menu and select **F**orward. Alternatively, press Search (F2).

Feature	Ways To Activate the Feature
Shell Clipboard	Access the **F**ile pull-down menu and select **G**o to Shell. Alternatively, press Shell (Ctrl-F1) and select **S**ave (**2**) and **A**ppend (**3**).
Spell	Access the **T**ools pull-down menu and select **S**pell. Alternatively, press Spell (Ctrl-F2) or Ctrl-s.
Subscript	Access the **F**ont pull-down menu and select **S**ubscript. Alternatively, press Font (Ctrl-F8) and select **S**ubscript (**6**).
Superscript	Access the **F**ont pull-down menu and select Su**p**erscript. Alternatively, press Font (Ctrl-F8) and select Su**p**erscript (**5**).
Underline	Access the **F**ont pull-down menu and select **U**nderline. Alternatively, press Underline (F8); press Font (Ctrl-F8) and then select **U**nderline (**2**); or press Ctrl-u.

Canceling a Block

To cancel a block with a two-button mouse, click both the mouse buttons at the same time; on a three-button mouse, click the center mouse button. Using the menu system, access the **E**dit pull-down menu and select **B**lock. Using the keyboard, press either Cancel (F1 or Esc) or Block (Alt-F4 or F12).

Rehighlighting a Block

With Block you can perform a single editing or formatting operation. Suppose, however, that you want to make two or more changes to the same block of text. You may, for example, want to emphasize a paragraph by making it both bold and italic. After you make one change to a block, you can use a shortcut to rehighlight the block and make the second change.

Reminder:
Rehighlight a
block of text by
starting Block
and pressing
GoTo twice.

Start by highlighting the block of text and completing the first operation. Leave the cursor at the end of the block. Then complete these steps to rehighlight the same block of text:

1. Use one of the methods described earlier to activate Block.

2. Activate GoTo by holding down Ctrl and pressing Home twice.

GoTo returns the cursor to the position it occupied before the last block operation. If you change your mind about the amount of text you want to highlight, return to the beginning of the block and begin again. Repeat step 2 to return to the beginning of a block already highlighted. The block is no longer highlighted, but the Block feature remains active. Now you can highlight the appropriate text.

Moving a Block

LetterPerfect's capacity to move blocks is a powerful editing tool. With this function, you don't have to worry about preparing your report or letter perfectly the first time. Instead, you can get the ideas down and then use the Block Move feature to organize them later.

Reminder:
When you move
a block of text,
you delete it
from its original
position and
place it in a new
location.

When you move a block of text, you delete it from one place and insert it somewhere else. You can move a block of any size to another place in the current document or to another document.

To move a block of text, follow these steps:

1. Activate Block and highlight the text you want to move.

2. Access the **Edit** pull-down menu and choose **Move** (**1**). Alternatively, press Move (Ctrl-F4) and select **Move** (**1**); or press Ctrl-Del. (The Ctrl-Del method works only on computer systems with a 101-key keyboard and an enhanced ROM BIOS). The highlighted text disappears. At the lower left corner of the screen LetterPerfect displays this prompt: `Move cursor; press Enter to retrieve.`

3. Move the cursor to where you want to insert the block of text.

4. Press Enter. LetterPerfect inserts the text into the document at the cursor's location.

LetterPerfect's fast-key combination performs a block-move operation with fewer keystrokes. To use the fast-key method, follow these steps:

1. Press Ctrl-m. LetterPerfect displays this prompt at the lower left corner of the screen: `Position to top corner of text; press Enter.`

2. Move the cursor to the first character or formatting code you want included in the block.

3. Press Enter. LetterPerfect displays this prompt at the lower left corner of the screen: `Position to bottom corner of text; press Enter.`

4. Move the cursor to the right of the last character or formatting code you want included in the block.

5. Press Enter. The blocked text disappears. LetterPerfect displays this prompt at the lower left corner of the screen: `Move cursor; press Enter to retrieve.`

6. Move the cursor to the place in the document where you want LetterPerfect to insert the text.

7. Press Enter. LetterPerfect inserts the text at the cursor's location.

Copying a Block

The Move feature removes a block of text from one position in a document and places that block in another position. The Copy feature duplicates the block of text in another position: the original stays put, and the copy appears in the new position.

To copy a block of text, follow these steps:

1. Activate Block and highlight the text you want to copy.

2. Access the **E**dit pull-down menu and choose Copy (**2**). Alternatively, press Move (Ctrl-F4) and select **C**opy (**2**); or press Ctrl-Ins. (The Ctrl-Ins method works only on computer systems with a

101-key keyboard and an enhanced ROM BIOS.) The highlight disappears, but the text remains on the screen. LetterPerfect displays this prompt at the lower left corner of the screen: `Move cursor; press Enter to retrieve.`

3. Move the cursor to where you want to add the block of text.

4. Press Enter. At the cursor's location, LetterPerfect inserts a copy of the text into the document.

LetterPerfect's fast-key combination performs a block-copy operation with fewer keystrokes. To use the fast-key method, follow these steps:

1. Press Ctrl-k. LetterPerfect displays this prompt at the lower left corner of the screen: `Position to top corner of text; press Enter.`

2. Move the cursor to the first character or formatting code you want included in the block.

3. Press Enter. LetterPerfect displays this prompt at the lower left corner of the screen: `Position to bottom corner of text; press Enter.`

4. Move the cursor to the right of the last character or formatting code you want included in the block.

5. Press Enter. The block disappears, but the text remains displayed. LetterPerfect displays this prompt at the lower left corner of the screen: `Move cursor; press Enter to retrieve.`

6. Move the cursor to the place in the document where you want LetterPerfect to insert the text.

7. Press Enter. At the cursor's location, LetterPerfect inserts the text.

Deleting a Block

Deleting a block of text is as simple as highlighting the text, pressing Del or Backspace, and confirming the deletion.

To delete a block of text, follow these steps:

1. Activate Block and highlight the block of text.

2. Access the **E**dit pull-down menu and select **D**elete. Alternatively, press either Del or Backspace. LetterPerfect displays this message at the bottom left corner of the screen: Delete Block? No (Yes).

3. If you decide not to delete the block, select **N**o. The prompt disappears, but the block remains highlighted.

If you decide to delete the block, select **Y**es. The text and hidden formatting codes within the highlighted area disappear from the screen.

LetterPerfect's fast-key combination performs a delete operation with fewer keystrokes. To use the fast-key method, follow these steps:

1. Press Ctrl-m. LetterPerfect displays this prompt at the lower left corner of the screen: Position to top corner of text; press Enter.

2. Move the cursor to the first character or formatting code you want included in the block.

3. Press Enter. LetterPerfect displays this prompt at the lower left corner of the screen: Position to bottom corner of text; press Enter.

4. Press Enter. The text and hidden formatting codes within the highlighted area disappear from the screen.

5. Press Cancel (F1 or Esc) to stop the move operation.

The section "Undeleting a Text Block" shows you how to retrieve a block of deleted text.

Blocking Text Automatically

LetterPerfect can automatically block either a sentence or a paragraph for a move, copy, or delete operation. To use the automatic block option, do the following:

1. Place the cursor on a character or hidden formatting code within the sentence or paragraph you want automatically blocked.

2. Access the Edit pull-down menu and choose either Select Sentence or Select Paragraph. Depending on your selection, LetterPerfect highlights either the sentence or entire paragraph and displays this menu at the lower left corner of the screen:

   1 Move; **2** Copy; **3** Delete: **0**

   Alternatively, press Move (Ctrl-F4). LetterPerfect displays this menu at the lower left corner of the screen:

   Move: 1 Sentence; **2** Paragraph; **3** Block; **Retrieve: 4** Block: 0

   Select either Sentence (**1**) or Paragraph (**2**). Depending on your selection, LetterPerfect highlights either the sentence or entire paragraph and displays this menu:

   1 Move; **2** Copy; **3** Delete: **0**

3. If you select Copy (**2**), the highlight disappears, but the text remains in the document. If you select either Move (**1**) or Delete (**3**), the highlight and text disappear.

   LetterPerfect places the text block into the move-delete RAM buffer explained in the next section. The procedure for retrieving the text block is the same as described in the earlier sections of this chapter on moving, copying, and deleting text blocks.

Undeleting a Text Block

LetterPerfect stores deleted text in different temporary RAM buffers, depending on the method you use to delete the text. When you use the Del or Backspace key or the Delete menu option, LetterPerfect stores the text in the delete-option buffer. The delete-option buffer stores the last three blocks of text deleted during the current editing session. When you use the Ctrl-m fast-key method, the move-deletion buffer stores the text. The move-deletion buffer stores only the last block of text deleted during the current editing session.

The method you use to undelete (retrieve) the deleted text block depends on the type of buffer that stores the text.

To undelete a text block stored in the delete-option buffer, do the following:

1. Move the cursor to the place where you want to restore the deleted text block.

2. Access the **E**dit pull-down menu and choose **U**ndelete. Alternatively, do one of the following: press Cancel (F1 or Esc); on a three-button mouse, click the center button; or on a two-button mouse, hold down either button and click the other button.

The most recently deleted text reappears at the cursor position as a highlighted block in the document, and the following menu appears at the bottom left corner of the screen:

Undelete: 1 Restore; **2** Previous Deletion: **0**

3. Select **R**estore (**1**) if you want to restore the most recent deletion at the cursor position. Select **P**revious Deletion (**2**) and then **R**estore (**1**) if you want to restore the second-most-recent deletion as a highlighted text block. To restore the third-most-recent deletion, select **P**revious Deletion (**2**) twice and then choose **R**estore (**1**).

While LetterPerfect displays the Undelete menu, pressing either the right- or down-arrow key highlights the Restore option in a reverse video box. Press Enter, and LetterPerfect restores the text to the document.

Pressing either the left- or up-arrow key highlights the Previous Deletion option in a reverse video box. Pressing any other key terminates the Undelete feature.

As mentioned earlier, the move-deletion method of deleting text stores only the last deleted text block of the current editing session. To undelete from the move-deletion buffer, you may use the menu option or the fast-key option, which is quicker.

To use the **E**dit menu to undelete the text block stored in the move-deletion buffer, do the following:

1. Move the cursor to the place where you want to restore the deleted text block.

2. Access the **E**dit pull-down menu and choose **P**aste Block. LetterPerfect places the block at the cursor's location.

Alternatively, press Move (Ctrl-F4). LetterPerfect displays the following menu across the bottom of the screen:

Move: 1 Sentence; **2** Paragraph; **3** Block; **Retrieve: 4** Block: **0**.

Select **B**lock (**4**). LetterPerfect restores the text block to the document at the cursor's location.

To use the fast-key option to undelete the text block stored in the move-deletion buffer, do the following:

1. Move the cursor to the place where you want to restore the deleted text block.

2. Press Ctrl-a. LetterPerfect restores the block to the document at the cursor's location.

Saving a Block

When you type a document—a legal contract is a good example—you may type a paragraph or some other block of text that you want to use again in another document. If so, save the block to a separate file, independent of the document where you are working.

To save a block of text to a separate file, follow these steps:

1. Activate Block and highlight the block of text you want to save.

2. Access the **File** pull-down menu and choose **Save**. Alternatively, press Save (F10). LetterPerfect displays the prompt `Block name:` at the lower left corner of the screen.

3. Type the name of the file to which you want to save the block; press Enter. LetterPerfect saves the block as a text file in the program's default subdirectory.

   Note: If you include a path name with the file name, LetterPerfect saves the block as a text file in the designated subdirectory instead of in the default subdirectory.

Reminder:
If you save a block to an existing file, you can replace the existing file.

If the name you type is the name of an existing file, the screen displays the message `Replace <`*filename*`>? No (Yes)`. To replace the file, select **Yes**. If you don't want to replace the file, select **No**. If you select **No**, LetterPerfect redisplays the `Block name:` prompt so that you can enter a different file name.

Cue:
Use Retrieve to build a document from blocks of text saved with the Block Save feature.

The Block Save feature works well in combination with LetterPerfect's Retrieve feature. You can use the two features to build a document from previously created blocks of text. A legal office, for example, may use the same paragraphs repeatedly in many different contracts. Use Block to save each reusable paragraph as an individual file. Then use Retrieve to build a contract out of the paragraphs you blocked and saved as individual files. For more information about Retrieve, refer to Chapter 4.

Printing a Block

Sometimes you want to print only one paragraph from a letter or one page from a report instead of a whole document. Use Block Print to print part of a document.

To print a block, follow these steps:

1. Activate Block and highlight the block of text you want to copy.

2. Access the **File** pull-down menu and choose **Print**. Alternatively, press Print (Shift-F7). LetterPerfect displays this prompt at the lower left corner of the screen: `Print block? No (Yes)`.

3. To print the file, select **Yes**. LetterPerfect displays its main Print menu (see fig. 5.2) and sends the document to your printer.

If you don't want to print the file, select **No**. The block remains highlighted so that you can select another editing or formatting option.

The block prints on the currently selected printer. See Chapter 1 for instructions on how to install a printer. For instructions on selecting printer options, see Chapter 8.

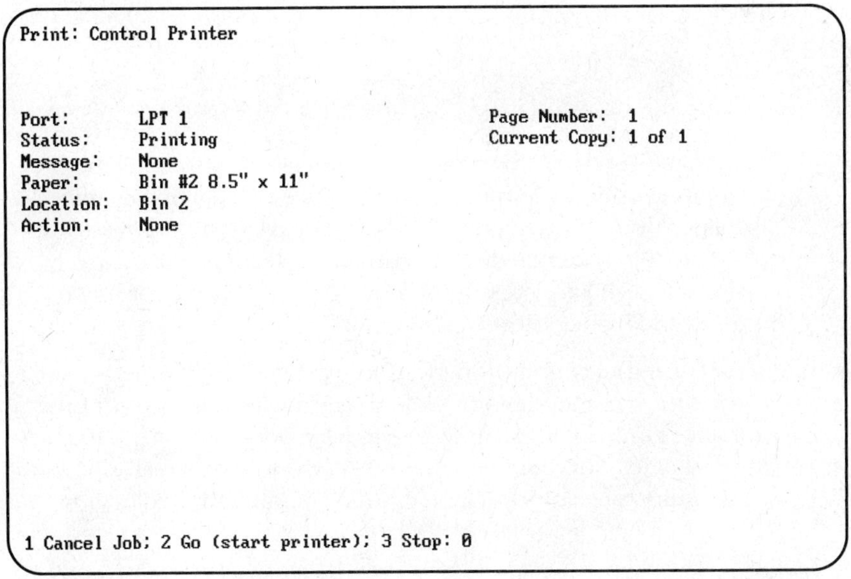

```
Print: Control Printer


Port:       LPT 1                    Page Number:  1
Status:     Printing                 Current Copy: 1 of 1
Message:    None
Paper:      Bin #2 8.5" x 11"
Location:   Bin 2
Action:     None











1 Cancel Job; 2 Go (start printer); 3 Stop: 0
```

Fig. 5.2. LetterPerfect's Print menu.

Enhancing Text with the Block Feature

Using Block, you can change the appearance of selected areas of text. You can emphasize an important paragraph by making it bold, for example, or you can call attention to a single word by underlining it. You can change the type font in a headline. You can center a title. Block gives you the power to make any of these changes to a block of text as small as a single letter or as large as the entire document.

Boldfacing and Underlining Blocked Text

With LetterPerfect you can format your document when you create it. For example, a single keystroke lets you boldface or underline text when you type. Often, however, you may find it faster to type the text raw—without formatting—and then format later with LetterPerfect's Block feature.

To boldface or underline a block of text (or a single character), follow these steps:

1. Activate Block and highlight the text you want to copy.

2. Access the Font pull-down menu and select either the **B**old or the Underline option. Alternatively, to boldface the highlighted text by using the keyboard, press Bold (F6); press Ctrl-b; or press Font (Ctrl-F8) and select **B**old (**1**). To underline the highlighted text by using the keyboard, press Underline (F8); press Ctrl-u; or press Font (Ctrl-F8) and select **U**nderline (**2**).

Reminder:
Enhanced text may not appear on-screen as it is printed.

Although enhanced text prints properly (if your printer supports text-enhancement features such as underlining), the text may not appear correctly on your computer screen unless your computer system includes a monitor with special graphics capabilities. For example, superscript and subscript text appears the same size as ordinary text on most monochrome monitors and color monitors.

Figure 5.3 shows a document that includes bolded and underlined text displayed on a VGA monitor through LetterPerfect's Preview feature. The position number (to the right of the POS at the bottom right of the screen) reflects the enhancement of the text at the cursor's location.

Figure 5.4 shows the same text when it is printed.

Using Block To Change the Font Size and Appearance

LetterPerfect works well with the varieties of fonts available on many printers—particularly on laser printers, which produce high-quality print in many type appearances (sometimes called styles) and sizes. A font's *appearance* is its visual structure, which includes such characteristics as bold and italic. A font's *size* is its height and width.

When you begin creating a document, LetterPerfect uses the font setting (which specifies appearance and size) for the default printer. See Chapter 8 for information on selecting a default printer and font. LetterPerfect makes it easy to select and change any font appearance and size supported by your printer.

A *base font* is the font (of a particular appearance and size) that LetterPerfect uses for printing a character at the cursor's location. See Chapter 6 for information on selecting a base font.

Reminder: LetterPerfect lets you change the base font with the Block feature.

LetterPerfect's Font feature offers two named options for temporarily changing the base font's appearance (bold and italic). The Font feature also offers only two named options for temporarily changing the base font's size (superscript and subscript). Each option places particular hidden paired codes around the text it controls. For example, the hidden paired codes for bolded text are **[BOLD]**<*text*>**[bold]**. Text between the paired bold codes assumes the bolded appearance. Text that appears before and after the paired codes has the appearance of the base font.

> *Note:* Your printer may not support all the font sizes and appearances discussed in this section. Most impact printers (such as dot-matrix and daisywheel printers) support only a few type styles. Although laser printers can print an array of type sizes and appearances, you generally need a font cartridge or downloadable software fonts to take advantage of that capability. Check your printer manual for details.

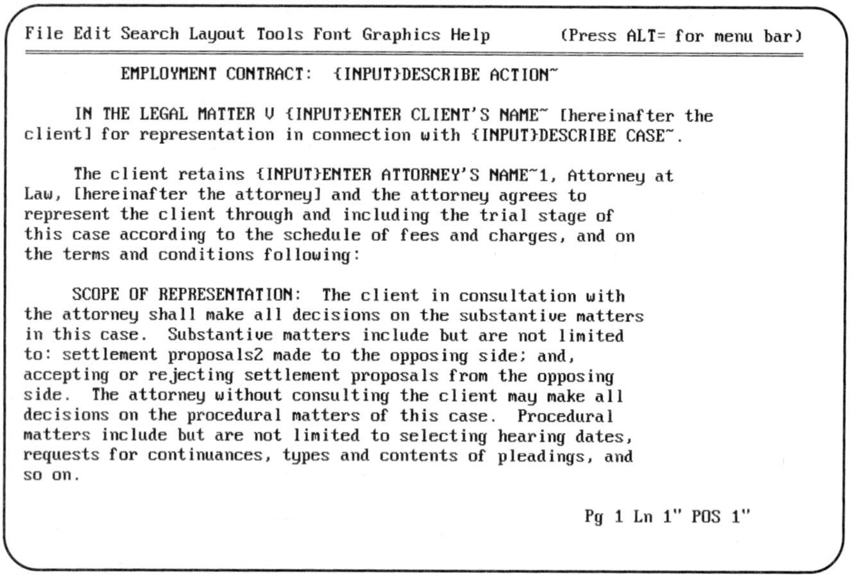

```
File Edit Search Layout Tools Font Graphics Help        (Press ALT= for menu bar)

        EMPLOYMENT CONTRACT:   {INPUT}DESCRIBE ACTION~

    IN THE LEGAL MATTER V {INPUT}ENTER CLIENT'S NAME~ [hereinafter the
client] for representation in connection with {INPUT}DESCRIBE CASE~.

    The client retains {INPUT}ENTER ATTORNEY'S NAME~1, Attorney at
Law, [hereinafter the attorney] and the attorney agrees to
represent the client through and including the trial stage of
this case according to the schedule of fees and charges, and on
the terms and conditions following:

    SCOPE OF REPRESENTATION:  The client in consultation with
the attorney shall make all decisions on the substantive matters
in this case.  Substantive matters include but are not limited
to: settlement proposals2 made to the opposing side; and,
accepting or rejecting settlement proposals from the opposing
side.  The attorney without consulting the client may make all
decisions on the procedural matters of this case.  Procedural
matters include but are not limited to selecting hearing dates,
requests for continuances, types and contents of pleadings, and
so on.

                                        Pg 1 Ln 1" POS 1"
```

Fig. 5.3. *Enhanced text as it appears on-screen.*

LetterPerfect offers only a limited number of named appearance and size font options; however, its Block feature works with the Font feature's base-font option to automatically create paired codes that have the actual name of the temporary and base fonts. The headline shown in figure 5.5 was created through this capability.

The following steps insert font codes that temporarily change the appearance or size (or both) of the base font:

1. Activate the Block feature and highlight the text that is to be printed in an appearance or size (or both) different from that of the base font.

2. Access the Font pull-down menu and select Base Font. Alternatively, press Font (Ctrl-F8) and select Base Font (4); or press Ctrl-f.

   LetterPerfect displays the Base Font menu, which contains a list of the available font types and sizes similar to those shown in figure 5.6. The exact font sizes and styles listed depend on your printer and its supporting resources.

EMPLOYMENT CONTRACT: DESCRIBE ACTION~

 IN THE LEGAL MATTER OF ENTER CLIENT'S NAME~ [hereinafter the client] for representation in connection with DESCRIBE CASE~.

 The client retains **ENTER ATTORNEY'S NAME-**[1], Attorney at Law, [hereinafter the attorney] and the attorney agrees to represent the client through and including the trial stage of this case according to the schedule of fees and charges, and on the terms and conditions following:

 SCOPE OF REPRESENTATION: The client in consultation with the attorney shall make all decisions on the substantive matters in this case. Substantive matters include but are not limited to: settlement proposals[2] made to the opposing side; and, accepting or rejecting settlement proposals from the opposing side. The attorney without consulting the client may make all decisions on the procedural matters of this case. Procedural matters include but are not limited to selecting hearing dates, requests for continuances, types and contents of pleadings, etc.

 RETAINER: ENTER RETAINER AMOUNT IN WORDS~Dollars [$ENTER RETAINER AMOUNT IN NUMBERS~.00] is to be paid to the attorney as a retainer as follows: ENTER CONDITIONS~. **The retainer is non-refundable and deemed earned in full when paid.** If this case is ENTER CONDITIONS~, the retainer will be the full fee for legal services - exclusive of costs and expenses - rendered by the attorney. ENTER CONDITIONS~ will be charged at the hourly rate specified under "Legal Services". The attorney will not file this case until ENTER LIMITATIONS~. All other terms and conditions regarding expenses and After-5:00 p.m. telephone calls remain unaltered and in full force and effect.

———————   - 1 -   ———————
   RMB   CLIENT

Fig. 5.4. Enhanced text as it appears when printed.

Fig. 5.5. *A headline created by a hidden pair of font codes.*

```
Base Font

    Swiss Bold Italic 14pt (HP Roman 8) (FW, Port)
    Swiss Bold Italic 18pt (HP Roman 8) (FW, Port)
    Swiss Bold Italic 24pt (HP Roman 8) (FW, Port)
    Swiss Bold Italic 30pt (HP Roman 8) (FW, Port)
    Swiss Bold Italic 36pt (HP Roman 8) (FW, Port)
    Swiss Italic 06pt (HP Roman 8) (FW, Port)
    Swiss Italic 07pt (HP Roman 8) (FW, Port)
    Swiss Italic 08.50pt (HP Roman 8) (FW, Port)
    Swiss Italic 08pt (HP Roman 8) (FW, Port)
    Swiss Italic 09pt (HP Roman 8) (FW, Port)
    Swiss Italic 10pt (HP Roman 8) (FW, Port)
    Swiss Italic 11pt (HP Roman 8) (FW, Port)
    Swiss Italic 12pt (HP Roman 8) (FW, Port)
    Swiss Italic 14pt (HP Roman 8) (FW, Port)
    Swiss Italic 18pt (HP Roman 8) (FW, Port)
    Swiss Italic 24pt (HP Roman 8) (FW, Port)
    Swiss Italic 30pt (HP Roman 8) (FW, Port)
    Swiss Italic 36pt (HP Roman 8) (FW, Port)
    Swiss Roman 06pt (HP Roman 8) (FW, Port)
    Swiss Roman 07pt (HP Roman 8) (FW, Port)
    Swiss Roman 08.50pt (HP Roman 8) (FW, Port)

 1 Select; N Name search: 1
```

Fig. 5.6. *LetterPerfect's Base Font menu.*

3. Move the cursor bar to highlight the font size and style you want to define for the text in the block.

4. Choose the new font by clicking with the mouse. Alternatively, press Enter or choose **Select** (**1**).

LetterPerfect returns to the main editing screen. When you view the document by using Reveal Codes, you see that LetterPerfect inserts the code for the new base font at the beginning of the block and the code for the original base font at the end of the block, as shown in figure 5.7.

```
 File Edit Search Layout Tools Font Graphics Help        (Press ALT= for menu bar)


                        LetterPerfect 1.0 Hits the Target!

        The newest addition to WordPerfect's impressive lineup of software
   products is LetterPerfect 1.0 - a compact program combining easy-to-use
   basic and advanced word-processing features while offering the printer
   support of its big brother, top-selling WordPerfect 5.1.



                                          Pg 1 Ln 1.18" Pos 7.33"
 {    ▲     ▲     ▲     ▲     ▲     ▲     ▲     ▲     ▲     ▲     ▲     }
 [Just:Full][HRt]
 [Font:Swiss Bold Italic 30pt (HP Roman 8) (FW, Port)][Center]LetterPerfect 1.0 H
 its the Target█[Font:Swiss Roman 14pt (HP Roman 8) (FW, Port)][HRt]
 [HRt]
 [Tab]The newest addition to WordPerfect's impressive lineup of software[SRt]
 products is [ITALC][BOLD]LetterPerfect 1.0[bold][italc] [-] a compact program co
 mbining easy[-]to[-]use[SRt]
 basic and advanced word[-]processing features while offering the printer[SRt]
 support of its big brother, top[-]selling [ITALC][BOLD]WordPerfect 5.1[bold][ita
 lc].[HRt]

 Press Reveal Codes to restore screen
```

Fig. 5.7. *Base font codes displayed with the Reveal Codes feature.*

Centering a Block

You can center a block of text either as you type or after you type the text. To center a block of text as you type, center each line and end the block with a hard return. To center text after you type it, highlight and then center the block. LetterPerfect inserts a hard return at the end of each line of centered text, even if the block you center is a word-wrapped paragraph. The block appears centered both on-screen and in print.

Reminder:
Each line of a centered block of text ends with a hard return.

To center a block of text, follow these steps:

1. Activate Block and highlight one or more lines of text to be centered.

2. Access the **Layout** pull-down menu and select **Center**. Alternatively, press Center (Shift-F6) or Ctrl-c. LetterPerfect displays this prompt at the bottom left corner of the screen: [Just:Center]? No (Yes).

3. Select **Yes**. LetterPerfect centers the line or lines of text in the block.

Restoring Text to Its Original Format

Although blocking text is a quick and easy way to edit and enhance the appearance of your documents, LetterPerfect's Block feature serves no useful purpose in returning text to its original appearance. You must remove the enhancement codes to restore the text's original form.

Reminder:
To restore text to its original format, you can delete just one code in a pair of text-enhance-ment codes.

To delete text-enhancement codes, follow these steps:

1. Move the cursor to the beginning or end of the enhanced text.

2. Access the **Edit** pull-down menu and choose **R**eveal Codes. Alternatively, press Reveal Codes (Alt-F3 or F11) or Ctrl-r.

3. Delete either the beginning or ending text-enhancement code.

As an alternative, you can use LetterPerfect's Replace feature to locate and remove most of a document's hidden formatting codes. To use this method, follow these steps:

1. Access the **Search** pull-down menu and select **R**eplace. Alternatively, press Replace (Alt-F2).

   LetterPerfect displays a prompt at the lower left corner of the screen: w/Confirm? No (Yes)

2. Select **N**o if you want all changes made automatically. Select **Yes** if you want to request confirmation.

LetterPerfect displays the →Srch: prompt at the lower left corner of the screen. By default, the Replace feature searches from the cursor's location to the bottom of the document. Press the up arrow or left arrow to make the Replace operation start from the beginning of the document.

3. Press the key combination you use to create the formatting code in the document.

4. Access the **Search** pull-down menu and select **R**eplace. Alternatively, press Search (F2).

5. At the Replace with: prompt, press the right mouse button or double-click the left button. Alternatively, press Search (F2).

6. If you requested confirmation in step 2, you see the Confirm? No (Yes) prompt each time the search finds a match. Select **Yes** to confirm a replacement or **No** to deny a replacement. To cancel the search-and-replace operation, press Cancel (F1 or Esc) or Exit (F7).

Table 5.2 lists the text-enhancement codes that Replace can find and remove.

Table 5.2
Formatting Codes That Can Be Removed with Replace

Formatting Code	Enhancement Feature
[BOLD] or **[bold]**	Bold ON/off
[Center]	Center Text
[Center Pg]	Center Page Top to Bottom
[Cntr Tab]	Center Tab
[CNTR TAB]	Hard Center Tab
[Date]	Date/Time Function
[Dec Tab]	Decimal Tab
[DEC TAB]	Tab Alignment (Ctrl-F6)
[Endnote]	Endnote
[Endnote/WP Footnote]	WordPerfect Footnote Treated as Endnote by LetterPerfect
[Fig Box]	Paragraph Figure Box

Table 5.2 (continued)

Formatting Code	Enhancement Feature
[Flsh Rt]	Flush Right Text
[Font]	Base Font
[Footer]	Footer
[Header]	Header
[HPg]	Hard Page
[HRt]	Hard Return
[→Indent]	Indent
[→Indent←]	Left/Right Indent
[ITALC] or **[italc]**	Italic Font ON/off
[Just]	Justification
[L/R Mar]	Left and Right Margins
[Lang]	Language
[Ln Spacing]	Line Spacing
[←Mar Rel]	Left Margin Release
[Mrg:<code name>]	Merge Code
[Outline Off]	Outline Off
[Outline On]	Outline On
[Paper Sz/Typ]	Paper Size and Type
[Rgt Tab]	Right Tab
[RGT TAB]	Hard Right Tab
[SUBSCPT] or **[subscpt]**	Subscript Font ON/off
[Suppress]	Suppress Page Formatting
[SUPRSCPT] or **[suprscpt]**	Superscript Font ON/off
[T/B Mar]	Top and Bottom Page Margins
[Tab]	Left Tab
[TAB]	Hard Left Tab
[Tab Set]	Tab Set
[UND] or **[und]**	Underlining ON/off

Displaying Enhanced Text On-Screen

Many LetterPerfect text-enhancement features do not display correctly on a monochrome monitor. In fact, enhanced text may not be legible at all on-screen. Enlarged or reduced text appears in the monitor's normal text size, and italicized, underlined, and bolded text may appear blurred. On color monitors, text enhancements appear in different colors and should be easy to read.

If your screen text is illegible, use the Reveal Codes feature—access the **Edit** pull-down menu and select **R**eveal Codes or, alternatively, press Reveal Codes (Alt-F3 or F11) or Ctrl-r—to see hidden formatting codes.

To supplement the screen display, LetterPerfect offers a feature that shows how your document looks when it is printed: View Document. You can use this feature with either the mouse or the keyboard.

Using the mouse, access the **File** pull-down menu, select **P**rint, and then select **V**iew Document (**3**). Using the keyboard, press Print (Shift-F7) and select View Document (**3**); or press Ctrl-p.

With View Document you can view your document in 100 percent, 200 percent, and fit-in-the-window sizes, but you must return to the main editing screen to edit the text. See Chapter 7 to learn more about the View Document feature.

Although LetterPerfect by itself cannot give you a true "what you see is what you get" (WYSIWYG) on-screen display in the edit screen, commercial add-on hardware and software programs can give you this capability with LetterPerfect. These devices and programs can display text in different sizes and with different font attributes. Most of these devices do, however, slow the operation of your computer system. Remember: No matter how it looks on-screen, your document prints correctly if your printer supports the selected enhancements.

Cue:
If your screen does not show text enhancements, reveal the codes or use the View Document feature.

Using the Block Feature with Spell-Checking

LetterPerfect's Block lets you highlight a section of text for examination with the Spell feature. Use the following steps to spell-check a text block:

1. Activate Block and highlight a section of text.

2. Access the **T**ools pull-down menu and select the **S**pell option.

   Alternatively, press Spell (Ctrl-F2) or Ctrl-s.

LetterPerfect automatically begins the spell-checking operation. Press the mouse's cancel button or press Cancel (F1 or Esc) at any time to stop the spell-checking process. See Chapter 11 for detailed information on using LetterPerfect's Spell feature.

Summary

The Block feature is an adjunct to other features, always part of another text operation. In this chapter, you used Block to highlight text, which you then processed.

This chapter has shown you how to use LetterPerfect's Block feature to edit a document's text and enhance its appearance. With Block you can accomplish these tasks:

- Move a block of text
- Copy a block of text
- Delete a block of text
- Save a block of text
- Print a block of text
- Change the appearance of a block of text by making text bold, underlined, italicized, or centered
- Change the size of the base font
- Spell-check part of a document

Working in tandem with many LetterPerfect features, the Block feature helps you make important changes to your document quickly and easily. In the next chapter, you learn techniques for formatting and enhancing text.

6

Formatting and Enhancing Text

LetterPerfect 1.0 provides many useful tools for both new and experienced users of word processors. If you use a typewriter, you will enjoy the way LetterPerfect handles the mundane chores of setting margins and tabs; centering, justifying, underlining, and boldfacing text; indenting text; and hyphenating words. If you are an old hand with word processors but are new to LetterPerfect, the simple and logical way that the program formats and enhances text will impress you. If you are an experienced user of either WordPerfect 5.0 or WordPerfect 5.1, you will appreciate the similarity of features between those programs and LetterPerfect 1.0.

This chapter shows you how to format existing text and enhance its appearance in the printed document. Procedures described in this chapter include the following:

- Using left and right margins (including the Margin Release feature) and indenting text from the left and from both margins

- Using various types of tabs: left, right, center, decimal, and tabs with dot leaders

- Formatting text to make it centered, flush right, or right-justified

- Changing line spacing

- Inserting hyphens manually or automatically

- Changing the typeface, size, and appearance of a font
- Previewing the document with the View Document feature

Reminder: WordPerfect Corporation updated LetterPerfect 1.0 just before this book went to press. Dated 11/01/90, the interim release includes new options for existing features, and a few new features. The menus on your screen may, therefore, differ slightly from those shown in this book. Also, depending on the printer-form definition, margins, tab stops, and font you specify, the text placement and status-line information in documents you create may differ from that shown in this book's figures.

For information about using the mouse and accessing the pull-down menus, refer to the Introduction.

Formatting Lines and Paragraphs

Cue:
Use the Format menu to format lines and paragraphs on the page.

This chapter focuses on formatting the elements of the page: lines and paragraphs. Chapter 7 guides you through designing documents and formatting the overall page. The Format menu (see fig. 6.1) contains most of the functions used to format a page.

To display the Format menu, access the Layout pull-down menu (see fig. 6.2) and select Format. Alternatively, press Format (Shift-F8).

Changing Default Settings

Cue:
Global settings affect the entire document.

LetterPerfect 1.0 presets all global initial or default settings. *Global* settings are basic formatting options that affect the entire document. Margin, tab, and justification features are examples of global settings. If these settings do not fit your needs, you can either change the settings for the current document or use Setup (Shift-F1) to change many settings permanently.

With LetterPerfect you can control document formatting by setting the program defaults and by inserting hidden codes. The following sections discuss each method.

```
Format

        1 - Justification              Left

        2 - Line Spacing               1

        3 - Top/Bottom Margins         1"          1"

        4 - Left/Right Margins         1"          1"

        5 - Tabs                       Rel; -1", every 0.5"

        6 - Header/Footer

        7 - Page Numbering             No page numbering

        8 - Paper Size                 8.5" x 11"
                Type                   Standard

        9 - Center Page (top to bottom)    No

        I - Document Initial Codes/Base Font    Courier 10cpi


Selection: 0
```

Fig. 6.1. The Format menu.

```
File Edit Search Layout Tools Font Graphics Help        (Press F3 for help)
                 ┌─────────────────────────┐
                 │ Format          Shft-F8  │
                 │ Language        Alt-F8   │
                 │                          │
                 │ Endnote Create  Ctrl-E   │
                 │ Endnote Edit             │
                 │                          │
                 │ ->Indent        F4       │
                 │ ->Indent<-      Shft-F4  │
                 │ <-Margin Rel    Shft-Tab │
                 │                          │
                 │ Center          Ctrl-C   │
                 │ Flush Right     Alt-F6   │
                 │ Tab Align       Ctrl-F6  │
                 │                          │
                 │ Hard Page       Ctrl-Enter│
                 └─────────────────────────┘




                                         Pg 1 Ln 1" Pos 1"
```

Fig. 6.2. The Layout pull-down menu.

Changing Setup Initial Codes

Setup Initial Codes let you change LetterPerfect's default formatting settings. Changes made with Setup Initial Codes are permanent and affect all new documents. Setup changes do not automatically alter the format of current or previously created documents. (You can read more about Setup in Chapter 1.)

After you change the default format settings, LetterPerfect offers two ways to make an existing document use these settings.

To have the changes affect the document on the main editing screen, follow these steps:

1. Use the mouse and highlight the entire document. Alternatively, activate Block (Alt-F4 or F12).

2. Press Del and select **Yes** at the confirmation prompt.

3. Press Exit (F7) and select **No** at each of the two prompts that follow.

4. Press Undelete (F1 or Esc) and choose **Restore (1)**.

The program's new default settings now control the structure of the document.

If you want the new default settings to control the format of a document previously created and saved as a file on disk, press the space bar once and retrieve the document to the main editing screen.

LetterPerfect comes preset with a number of factory defaults, including these:

- **Justification** is set to **Left**.

- Left/ **Right Margins** and Top/ Bottom **Margins** are set to **1** inch.

- **Line Spacing** is set to **1**.

- **Page** Numbering is set to **No** Page Numbering.

If you want all documents you create to have defaults different from those set by LetterPerfect, you can modify Setup Initial Codes by performing these steps:

1. Access the **File** pull-down menu and select Setup. Alternatively, press Setup (Shift-F1).

2. Choose **Initial Codes (5)**.

    LetterPerfect displays the Initial Codes split screen.

3. Access the **L**ayout pull-down menu and select **F**ormat. Alternatively, press Format (Shift-F8).

   LetterPerfect displays the Format menu shown in figure 6.1.

4. To modify the settings, choose one or more options from the menu and enter new values. LetterPerfect inserts a hidden formatting code for each formatting change you make.

5. Press Exit (F7) twice.

   LetterPerfect returns to its main editing screen. The new default settings automatically control the structure of new documents you create (the settings do not affect existing documents).

Using Hidden Formatting Codes

Hidden formatting codes in a document override the default Initial Codes. This chapter concentrates on inserting hidden codes.

Hidden codes affect text from the point where they are inserted until another hidden code is inserted. If, for example, you want a 2-inch margin instead of a 1-inch margin, insert the code **[L/R Mar:2", 2"]**. (Methods of inserting hidden codes are described in this chapter.) The hidden code governs the margins for all text following it. To change the margins back or to modify the margins again, insert another **[L/R Mar]** code.

Changing the Unit of Measure

The on-screen dimensions of a page are often defined in terms of columns (width) and rows (height). Most monitors, for example, display 80 columns and 25 rows of text. Some word processors—including WordPerfect 4.2 and earlier versions—require that you experiment to determine how many columns to include in the margins, how many columns to set in a line, and how many rows to leave for the top and bottom page margins. Font changes require new margin calculations, and the printed document does not always turn out as you expect. This process results in much wasted time.

Cue:
The Absolute Margins feature creates uniform margins, regardless of changes in font size.

LetterPerfect 1.0's Absolute Margins feature eliminates all guesswork. Regardless of the font you select, the program automatically calculates how many columns and rows fit on a page. In addition, you do not need to factor in the size of the font to produce a printed page with perfect margins.

Examine the status line in the lower right corner of LetterPerfect's main editing screen. The screen displays the following information (the numbers vary, depending on the position of the cursor): Pg 1 Ln 1" Pos 1".

LetterPerfect 1.0 offers several unit-of-measure options:

i = inches	Inches, the default setting in LetterPerfect 1.0, are the best units for measuring margins and tabs.
c = centimeters	One centimeter equals 0.39 inch; 1 inch equals 2.54 centimeters.
p = points	One point equals 0.01384 inch or 1/72 inch; 72 points equal 1 inch. Because fonts are often measured in point sizes, you may want to use these units for measuring font width (especially with laser printers).
w=1/1200 inch	One **w** unit equals 1/1200 inch. You may want to use **w** units for precise page or line positioning, such as filling in forms.
u= WordPerfect 4.2 unit (lines and columns)	Most word processors and versions of WordPerfect 5.0 use this unit of measurement. Use this setting if your main printer is either dot-matrix or daisywheel; these printers measure by lines and columns. If you have a laser printer, however, use either inches or points; these units provide control over character placement.

You can easily change the default unit-of-measure setting from inches to another option. To change the unit of measure to centimeters, for example, follow these steps:

1. Access the **File** pull-down menu and select **Setup**. Alternatively, press Setup (Shift-F1).

2. Select **Units of Measure (3)**. LetterPerfect displays this menu:

   1 Inches; **2** Centimeters; **3** Points; **4** 1200ths of an inch; **5** WP 4.2 **units: 0**

3. Choose **Centimeters (3)**.

4. Press Exit (F7) to return to the document.

The status line, which now displays the cursor position in terms of centimeters, should read as follows: Doc 1 Pg 1 Ln 2.54c Pos 2.54c.

Beginning with the 11/01/90 interim release, LetterPerfect recognizes international mnemonic symbols for designating these measurements. However, you *cannot* use the alternative symbols to designate the measurement units from the Setup menu.

The value you designate for the unit of measure determines the units used in menu choices for margins (top, bottom, left, and right), tab settings, and paper size, as well as the units that appear in information displayed in the status line at the lower right corner of the screen. If you change the unit of measurement, all displays of units, including displays contained in hidden codes, immediately and automatically change to reflect the new choice.

Reminder:
If you change the unit of measurement, all displays of units, including displays contained in hidden codes, automatically change to reflect the new choice.

On most menus that require a measurement, such as the menu for changing left and right margins (see the next section, "Changing Margins"), you can enter a value in another format, and LetterPerfect automatically converts the value to its equivalent value in the default-measurement format. For example, if you set the unit of measure to centimeters but want to set the left and right margins at 1 inch, add " or *i* after the number *1*. LetterPerfect automatically converts your entry to *2.54c*.

Beginning with the 11/01/90 interim release, LetterPerfect recognizes the following international mnemonic symbols for designating measurements:

Unit of Measure	LetterPerfect Mnemonic Symbol	International Mnemonic Symbol
Inch	" or i	\
Centimeter	c	:
Point	p	*
1/1200 inch	w	?
WordPerfect unit	u	+

LetterPerfect also automatically converts fractions to decimals. For example, the program converts *6/7"* to *0.857"*.

> *Tip:* Always include the unit type in any measurements used in macro commands. The macro correctly sets the measurement even if you change the default units of measure.

Changing Margins

LetterPerfect 1.0 calculates margins as specific distances from the edges of the paper. You can set 1-inch left and right margins, for example, without being concerned about the number of characters in the line of text. LetterPerfect tracks the size of both the page and the font and automatically determines how many characters can fit on a line or page.

> *Tip*: LetterPerfect measures margins from the edges of the paper. Simply measure the stationery or paper and decide how many inches of white space you want as margins. Because measuring in rows and columns is confusing and is a matter of trial and error, set margins in inches—the program's default measurement—regardless of the type of measurement setting.

Reminder:
To move the cursor to the beginning of the document, press Home, Home, up arrow.

You can change the margin settings at any time. When you enter a margin change, that change affects only text from that point forward. Text entered before the change retains the previous margins. To change margins for an entire document, either go to the beginning of the document and set the margins or change the Initial Codes. (To move the cursor to the beginning of the document before any text but after the initial formatting codes, press Home, Home, up arrow.)

Changing Left and Right Margins

To change left and right margins, follow these steps:

1. Access the Layout pull-down menu and select Format. Alternatively, press Format (Shift-F8).

   LetterPerfect displays its Format menu (see fig. 6.3).

```
 Format

    1 - Justification              Left

    2 - Line Spacing               1

    3 - Top/Bottom Margins         1"        1"

    4 - Left/Right Margins         1"        1"

    5 - Tabs                       Rel; -1", every 0.5"

    6 - Header/Footer

    7 - Page Numbering             No page numbering

    8 - Paper Size                 8.5" x 11"
            Type                   Standard

    9 - Center Page (top to bottom)    No

    I - Document Initial Codes/Base Font    Courier 10cpi


 Selection: 0
```

Fig. 6.3. The Format menu.

2. Select Left/**R**ight Margins (**4**).

   The cursor moves to the first entry immediately right of the Left/
   Right Margins menu option. (Notice that in this case the left and
   right margins are calculated in inches.)

3. Type a new value for the left margin and press Enter.

4. Type a new value for the right margin and press Enter.

5. Press Exit (F7) to return to the document.

> *Caution:* If a Left/Right Margins code is placed after text on a line,
> LetterPerfect 1.0 automatically inserts a hard-return code (**[HRt]**), and the
> Left/Right Margins code is placed at the beginning of the next line.

In LetterPerfect, you can set left and right margins only for the main document.
You cannot define different margin values for headers or footers. You can,
however, use LetterPerfect's Margin Release feature (explained in the next
section) to place text left of a left margin setting.

Using Margin Release

The Margin Release feature releases the left margin and causes text to shift temporarily one tab stop left on the current line. This feature is particularly useful for creating lists. The number appears left of the margin, but the notation stays within normal margins (see fig. 6.4).

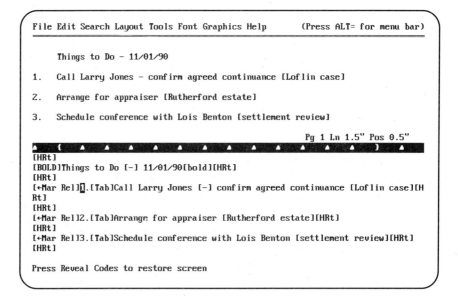

Fig. 6.4. A list created with Margin Release.

To enter text left of the left margin, follow these steps:

1. Move the cursor to the left margin by pressing Enter or Home, Home, left arrow.

2. To move the cursor one tab stop left, access the **L**ayout pull-down menu and select ← **M**argin Rel. Alternatively, press Margin Release (Shift-Tab).

   Repeat this step to move an additional tab stop left.

3. Type the text.

4. Press Tab to return to the normal left margin.

> *Caution:* Do not use Margin Release when the cursor is in the middle of a line of text. If you do so, text right of the Margin Release code usually overwrites text left of the Margin Release code. If no tab stop is left of the cursor, the line begins at the left edge of the page.

Indenting Text

You can emphasize paragraphs by offsetting them. LetterPerfect's two indent options offset text in individual paragraphs from the left margin or both left and right margins.

To indent only the left margin, access the **L**ayout pull-down menu and select → Indent. Alternatively, press Indent (F4).

To indent both the left and right margins, access the **L**ayout pull-down menu and select → Indent ←. Alternatively, press Left-Right Indent (Shift-F4).

Note: Although the Indent options are available from the **L**ayout pull-down menu, the function-key approach requires fewer steps than the pull-down menu approach.

> *Caution*: Never use the space bar for indenting or tabbing. If your printer uses proportional typefaces, the text does not align properly at the left indent or tab stop. Instead, use Tab or the appropriate Indent keys.

Indenting from the Left Margin

To indent only the left margin, select Indent. Indent moves all text following its hidden code one tab stop from the left margin. When you select Indent, the cursor moves to the right one tab stop and then temporarily resets the left margin. Everything you type until you press Enter is offset from the left margin to the tab stop. To indent more than one tab stop, select Indent more than once.

Indent is useful for creating a list. You can, for example, indent and align a series of numbered blocks of text. If you use only Tab to indent the text next to a number, the second and consecutive lines of text are not indented. Instead, they wrap to the next line and align with the number.

Cue:
Use Indent when you create a list.

Figure 6.5 shows the various types of indents.

```
 File Edit Search Layout Tools Font Graphics Help      (Press ALT= for menu bar)

 Basic Law Office Automation I                              Spring 1991

 COURSE OBJECTIVES

 1.   Provide overview of the basic types of computer systems including
      connecting systems with a network

 2.   Introduce students to the computer's software operating system

 3.   Provide overview of software programs [commercial, shareware, and
      freeware] that simplify law-office tasks, increase efficiency,
      and reduce expenses

 COURSE PRESENTATION

      This course provides basic information about computer systems for
      lawyers, paralegals, and support staff.

          The material presented in this class assumes that
          each student has a basic knowledge of law-office
          procedures.  It also assumes that each student
          does not have previous experience with computer
                                               Pg 1 Ln 1" Pos 1"
```

Fig. 6.5. *A variety of indents created with Indent (F4) and Left-Right Indent (Shift-F4).*

To create a list with Indent, follow these steps:

1. Move the cursor to the left margin.

2. Press the item number (for example, 1) and then press Tab.

3. Access the **L**ayout pull-down menu and select → Indent. Alternatively, press Indent (F4). Then type the text of the item.

4. Press Enter to stop indenting and return to the normal margins.

Indenting from Both Margins

Use Left-Right Indent to offset a paragraph from both the right and left margins. When you press Left-Right Indent, the cursor moves right one tab stop and resets the left margin at that location. The right margin is moved to the left an equal distance. Everything you type until you press Enter is indented from the original left and right margins.

To indent from both margins more than tab stop, use Left-Right Indent more than once (see fig. 6.5).

To indent an existing paragraph, follow these steps:

1. Move the cursor to the left margin.

2. Access the **L**ayout pull-down menu and select → **I**ndent ←. Alternatively, press Left-Right Indent (Shift-F4).

Creating a Hanging Paragraph

Combining Margin Release (Shift-Tab) and Indent creates a hanging paragraph, in which the first line is flush with the left margin and the rest of the paragraph is indented to the first tab stop (see fig. 6.6). Hanging paragraphs are useful in various reports, such as bibliographies.

Cue:
Use hanging paragraphs to simplify indenting in reports such as bibliographies.

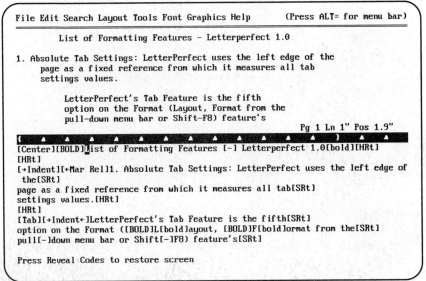

```
 File Edit Search Layout Tools Font Graphics Help      (Press ALT= for menu bar)

        List of Formatting Features - Letterperfect 1.0

 1. Absolute Tab Settings: LetterPerfect uses the left edge of the
       page as a fixed reference from which it measures all tab
       settings values.

          LetterPerfect's Tab Feature is the fifth
          option on the Format (Layout, Format from the
          pull-down menu bar or Shift-F8) feature's
                                            Pg 1 Ln 1" Pos 1.9"
 {    ▲     ▲    ▲    ▲    ▲    ▲    ▲    ▲    ▲    ▲    ▲    }   ▲
 [Center][BOLD]List of Formatting Features [-] Letterperfect 1.0[bold][HRt]
 [HRt]
 [→Indent][←Mar Rel]1. Absolute Tab Settings: LetterPerfect uses the left edge of
  the[SRt]
 page as a fixed reference from which it measures all tab[SRt]
 settings values.[HRt]
 [HRt]
 [Tab][→Indent←]LetterPerfect's Tab Feature is the fifth[SRt]
 option on the Format ([BOLD]L[bold]ayout, [BOLD]F[bold]ormat from the[SRt]
 pull[-]down menu bar or Shift[-]F8) feature's[SRt]

 Press Reveal Codes to restore screen
```

Fig. 6.6. *A hanging paragraph.*

To create a hanging paragraph, follow these steps before you begin to type the text:

1. Move the cursor to the left margin.

2. Access the **L**ayout pull-down menu and select → **I**ndent. Alternatively, press Indent (F4).

3. Access the **L**ayout pull-down menu and select ← **Margin Rel**. Alternatively, press Margin Release (Shift-Tab).

LetterPerfect begins the first line at the left margin and offsets the remainder of the paragraph one tab stop right of the left margin. Pressing Enter restores the margins to their normal settings. Later paragraphs are normal in appearance.

To create a hanging paragraph for existing text, follow these steps:

1. Move the cursor to the first character of the first line in the paragraph.

2. Access the **L**ayout pull-down menu and select → Indent; alternatively, press Indent (F4).

3. Access the **L**ayout pull-down menu and select ← **Margin Rel**; alternatively, press Margin Release (Shift-Tab).

   LetterPerfect automatically reformats the paragraph so that the first line of text begins at the left margin and the remainder of the paragraph offsets one tab stop right of the left margin.

Note: You also can create a hanging paragraph by substituting the Left-Right Indent feature for the Indent feature.

Setting Tab Stops

LetterPerfect comes with tab stops predefined at intervals of 1/2 inch for 14 inches (relative to the margin from –1" to +13"). The four tab formats are left, center, right, and decimal. Each tab format can have a *dot leader*—a series of periods before the tab. Figure 6.7 illustrates the various tab types.

LetterPerfect 1.0 has two tab options for determining tab placement: **A**bsolute (measured from the left edge of the page) and **R**elative to Margin (measured from the left margin—the default).

Absolute tabs, the only type used by WordPerfect 4.2 and 5.0 and many other word processing programs, are set in relation to the left edge of the physical page. The hidden code for Absolute tabs looks similar to this: **[Tab Set:Abs: 0", every 0.5"]**.

Relative to Margin tabs are set in relation to the left margin setting. If the left margin changes, the tabs adjust to the new margin setting. The hidden code for Relative to Margin tabs looks like this: **[Tab Set:Rel: +1", +2", +3", +3.5"]**.

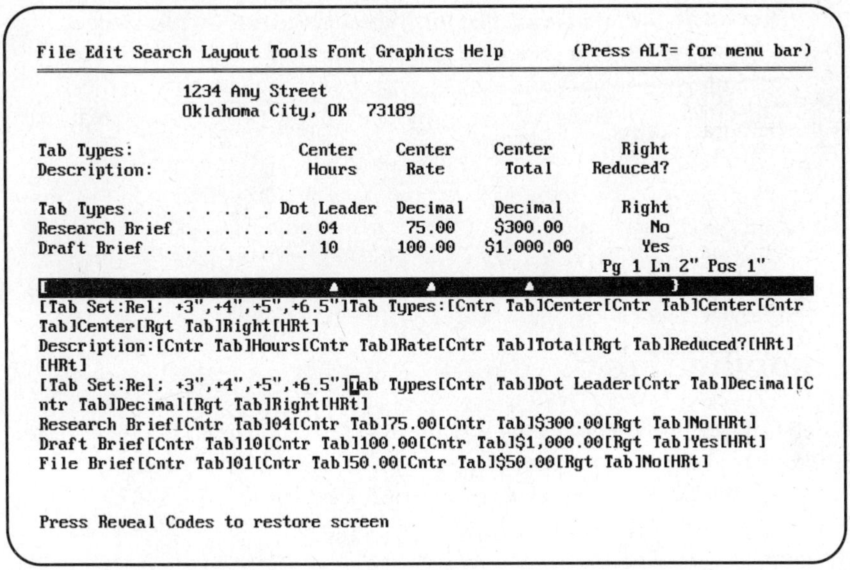

```
File Edit Search Layout Tools Font Graphics Help      (Press ALT= for menu bar)

            1234 Any Street
            Oklahoma City, OK  73189

Tab Types:                  Center    Center    Center      Right
Description:                Hours     Rate      Total      Reduced?

Tab Types. . . . . . . Dot Leader  Decimal   Decimal      Right
Research Brief . . . . . . 04       75.00     $300.00        No
Draft Brief. . . . . . . . 10       100.00    $1,000.00      Yes
                                                     Pg 1 Ln 2" Pos 1"
[                          ▲         ▲         ▲             }
[Tab Set:Rel; +3",+4",+5",+6.5"]Tab Types:[Cntr Tab]Center[Cntr Tab]Center[Cntr
Tab]Center[Rgt Tab]Right[HRt]
Description:[Cntr Tab]Hours[Cntr Tab]Rate[Cntr Tab]Total[Rgt Tab]Reduced?[HRt]
[HRt]
[Tab Set:Rel; +3",+4",+5",+6.5"]Tab Types[Cntr Tab]Dot Leader[Cntr Tab]Decimal[C
ntr Tab]Decimal[Rgt Tab]Right[HRt]
Research Brief[Cntr Tab]04[Cntr Tab]75.00[Cntr Tab]$300.00[Rgt Tab]No[HRt]
Draft Brief[Cntr Tab]10[Cntr Tab]100.00[Cntr Tab]$1,000.00[Rgt Tab]Yes[HRt]
File Brief[Cntr Tab]01[Cntr Tab]50.00[Cntr Tab]$50.00[Rgt Tab]No[HRt]


Press Reveal Codes to restore screen
```

Fig. 6.7. Different kinds of tab settings.

If you designate a Relative to Margin tab stop to be 1 inch from the left margin, the tab is always 1 inch in from that margin even if you later change margin settings.

The following describes LetterPerfect's tab types:

- *Left tabs.* The first line is indented to the tab stop, and text continues to the right. Later lines return to the normal left margin. The left tab is the most common tab type.

- *Center tabs.* Text is centered at the tab stop. A center tab works much like the Center feature. A center tab, however, can force centering anywhere in the line—not just at the center of the margins. Use center tabs to create column headings.

- *Right tabs.* After a right tab stop, text continues to the left. A right tab stop works much like the Flush Right feature. A right tab, however, can be anywhere in the line—not just at the right margin. Use right tabs to create headings over columns of numbers or dates.

- *Decimal tabs.* After a decimal tab stop, text continues to the left until you type the alignment character; then text continues to the right. A decimal tab works much like the Tab Align feature. With decimal tabs, however, you preset the alignment point as a tab stop. The default alignment character is a period, but you can change the default to any character you want (see Chapter 12). Use decimal tabs to line up columns of numbers.

- *Dot leaders.* Any of the four tab types can be preceded by dots (periods) as a leader. Use dot leaders for long lists, such as phone lists, that require visual scanning from left

Changing Tab Settings

When you change the tab settings, the settings affect only the text from the point where you make the change to the point where another tab setting code is placed in the document. To change the entire document, go to the beginning of the document and reset the tab stops or change the Initial Codes. (To move the cursor to the beginning of the document—ahead of any text but following the initial formatting codes—press Home, Home, up arrow.)

If you change the tabs after text is entered, LetterPerfect automatically reformats all tabs following the change. When you use left tabs, a **[Tab]** code reflecting the tab settings is inserted. Center tabs insert a **[Cntr Tab]** code, right tabs insert a **[Rgt Tab]** code, and decimal tabs insert a **[Dec Tab]** code.

LetterPerfect offers several options for setting tab stops. You can set individual tab stops, or you can specify the increment and set multiple tab stops. If the document is set in an 8 1/2-inch-wide portrait form, LetterPerfect lets you set multiple tab stops for the first 7 1/2 inches. If the document is set in a 14-inch-wide landscape form, LetterPerfect lets you set multiple tab stops for the first 10 1/2 inches. Beyond these width limits, LetterPerfect requires that you set individual extended tab stops up to the absolute limit of 54 1/2 inches.

LetterPerfect also imposes a maximum limit of 40 tab stops per tab-setting code. You can delete a single tab stop, all the tab stops, or only the tabs right of the cursor.

To display LetterPerfect's tab-ruler menu, follow these steps:

1. Access the **Layout** pull-down menu and select **Format**. Alternatively, press Format (Shift-F8).

   LetterPerfect displays the Format menu.

2. Select **Tabs** (**5**).

   At the bottom of the screen, LetterPerfect displays its tab-ruler menu, which shows the current tab stops (see fig. 6.8).

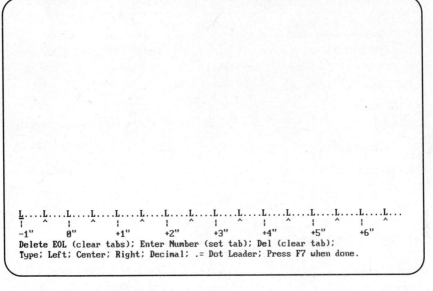

```
L...L...L...L...L...L...L...L...L...L...L...L...L...L...L...
¦    ^    ¦    ^    ¦    ^    ¦    ^    ¦    ^    ¦    ^    ¦    ^
-1"       0"       +1"       +2"       +3"       +4"       +5"       +6"
Delete EOL (clear tabs); Enter Number (set tab); Del (clear tab);
Type; Left; Center; Right; Decimal; .= Dot Leader; Press F7 when done.
```

Fig. 6.8. The LetterPerfect tab-ruler menu.

The cursor is automatically located at the ruler mark 0". You can use the mouse or the keyboard to move the cursor through the tab-ruler menu. Table 6.1 lists the keys (individually and in combination) that move the cursor and tab-stop settings through the tab-ruler menu and that delete tab-stop settings.

Table 6.1
Cursor-Movement Keys in the Tab-Ruler Menu

Key(s)	Action
. (period)	If no tab-stop setting exists at the cursor, creates a right tab-stop setting with dot leaders. If a tab-stop setting is located at the cursor, adds the dot-leader feature to it.
C	Creates a centered tab-stop setting at the cursor.
D	Creates a decimal tab-stop setting at the cursor.
L	Creates a left tab-stop setting at the cursor.
R	Creates a right tab-stop setting at the cursor.

Table 6.1 (continued)

Key(s)	Action
Key specifying the numeric location of the tab-stop setting, and Enter	Moves cursor to the designated tab stop and creates a left tab-stop setting. You can change stop settings by pressing C, D, R, and/or the period (.) key.
Up arrow	Moves cursor to the next tab stop right.
Alt-right arrow*	Moves cursor to the next tab stop right.
Right arrow	Moves cursor one increment right.
Space bar	Moves cursor one increment right.
Down arrow	Moves cursor to the next tab stop left.
Alt-left arrow*	Moves cursor to the next tab stop left.
Left arrow	Moves cursor one increment left.
Home, left arrow	Moves cursor to the left edge of screen.
Home, Home, left arrow	Moves cursor to the beginning of the tab ruler.
Home, right arrow	Moves cursor to the right edge of screen.
Home, Home, right arrow	Moves cursor to the end of the tab ruler.
End	Moves cursor to the end of the tab ruler.
Ctrl-right arrow	Moves tab stop under cursor one increment right.
Ctrl-left arrow	Moves tab stop under cursor one increment left.
Del	Removes tab stop under cursor.
Backspace	Removes tab stop under cursor.
Ctrl-End	Removes all tab stops to the right, beginning at the cursor and continuing to the ruler's end.

* Available only on systems with an enhanced ROM BIOS that recognizes this key combination.

To change tab stops, follow these steps:

1. Access the **Layout** pull-down menu and select **Format**. Alternatively, press Format (Shift-F8).

   LetterPerfect displays the Format menu.

2. Select **Tabs (5)**.

   At the bottom of the screen, LetterPerfect displays the tab-ruler menu.

3. *To delete a single tab stop*, use the mouse or one of the methods described in table 6.1 to move the cursor to the tab stop. Press Del or Backspace to remove the tab setting.

   To delete all the tab stops, move the cursor to the left margin (press Home, Home, left arrow). Press Delete to End of Line (Ctrl-End).

   To delete the tab stops right of the cursor, use the mouse or one of the methods described in table 6.1 to move the cursor to the first tab stop to be deleted. Press Delete to End of Line (Ctrl-End).

4. *To add a single tab stop*, use the mouse or one of the methods described in table 6.1 to move the cursor to the location for the new tab stop. Select **Left** to add a left tab, **Center** to add a center tab, **Right** to add a right tab, or **Decimal** to add a decimal tab. To add a dot leader, press the period (.) before you exit.

   To add multiple left tab stops, type the unit at which you want the tabs to begin, press the comma (,) key, and then type the spacing increment for the additional tab-stop settings. For example, to space tabs 1/2 inch apart beginning at 1 inch, type *1,.5* and press Enter.

   To add multiple center, right, or decimal tab stops and dot leaders, use the method described earlier to create a single tab-stop setting where you want the multiple tab-stop settings to begin. Select **Center**, **Right**, or **Decimal**.

   If you want a dot leader, also press the period (.) key. Type the location of this tab-stop setting, press the comma (,) key, type the spacing increment, and press Enter. For example, to space right-aligned tabs 1/2 inch apart beginning at 1 inch, position the cursor at one inch and press **Right**; then type *1,.5* and press Enter.

5. *To change the tab type*, select **Type** and then select either **Absolute (1)** or **Relative to Margin (2)**.

6. Press Exit (F7) twice to return to the document.

Setting Hard Tabs

Cue:
*Use hard tabs
so that you can
insert any of the
four tab types
regardless of the
tab settings.*

With LetterPerfect 1.0, you can add *hard tabs*. A hard tab enables you to insert any of the four tab formats—left, center, right, or decimal—regardless of the actual tab-stop settings. Suppose, for example, that you want a particular tab to be centered, but you have defined only left tab-stop settings. The hard-centered-tab keystrokes described in table 6.2 let you create a centered tab.

Table 6.2
Types of Hard Tabs

Tab Type	Tab Code	Hard-Tab Code	Keystrokes for Hard Tab
Left tab	**[Tab]**	**[TAB]**	Home, Tab
Center tab	**[Cntr Tab]**	**[CNTR TAB]**	Home, Center (Shift-F6)
Right tab	**[Rgt Tab]**	**[RGT TAB]**	Home, Flush Right (Alt-F6)
Decimal tab	**[Dec Tab]**	**[DEC TAB]**	Home, Tab Align (Ctrl-F6)

When you look at the formatting codes with Reveal Codes (Alt-F3, F12, or Ctrl-r), both regular and hard tabs look the same, except that the letters in the hard tab's code are all uppercase. Once a tab becomes a hard tab, it retains a hard-tab identity regardless of changes to tab settings.

Comparing Tab to Indent

LetterPerfect's Tab and Indent features are similar in some ways, but each has specific uses. Table 6.3 lists the differences between these features.

Table 6.3
Tab and Indent Uses

Feature	Function
Tab	Indents only the first line of a paragraph from the left margin
Indent	Indents the entire paragraph from the left margin
Left-Right Indent	Indents the entire paragraph equally from both margins

Using Tab and Indent with the Outline Feature

If Outline is active, the Tab, Indent, and Left-Right Indent features function slightly differently. See Chapter 10 for a detailed explanation on using these features with Outline. When Outline is on, the word `Outline` appears in the lower left corner of the screen.

Using Tab Align

Tab Align moves the cursor right one tab stop. As you type text, the text moves left of the tab stop until you type the alignment character (the default is a period). After you type the alignment character, the text moves right of the tab stop. Figure 6.9 illustrates how you can use Tab Align to align information at the right with a colon.

To create text aligned at the right on a period, follow these steps:

1. Access the **Layout** pull-down menu and select **Tab Align**. Alternatively, press Tab Align (Ctrl-F6).

   The cursor moves right one tab stop, and the following message appears in the lower left corner of the screen: `Align char = .`

2. Type the text.

3. Type the alignment character (in this case, a period).

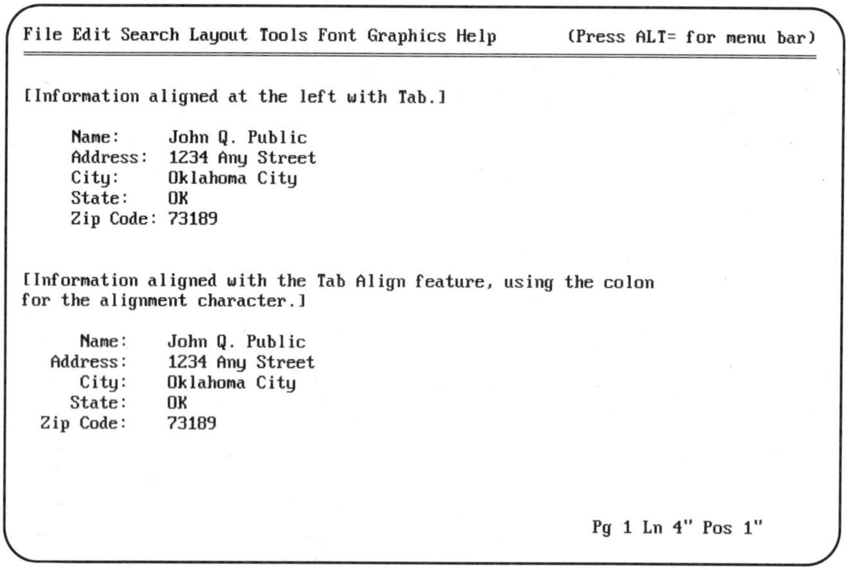

```
┌─────────────────────────────────────────────────────────────────────┐
│ File Edit Search Layout Tools Font Graphics Help    (Press ALT= for menu bar) │
│                                                                       │
│ [Information aligned at the left with Tab.]                           │
│                                                                       │
│      Name:     John Q. Public                                         │
│      Address:  1234 Any Street                                        │
│      City:     Oklahoma City                                          │
│      State:    OK                                                     │
│      Zip Code: 73189                                                  │
│                                                                       │
│                                                                       │
│ [Information aligned with the Tab Align feature, using the colon      │
│ for the alignment character.]                                         │
│                                                                       │
│      Name:     John Q. Public                                         │
│   Address:     1234 Any Street                                        │
│      City:     Oklahoma City                                          │
│     State:     OK                                                     │
│  Zip Code:     73189                                                  │
│                                                                       │
│                                                                       │
│                                                                       │
│                                          Pg 1 Ln 4" Pos 1"            │
└─────────────────────────────────────────────────────────────────────┘
```

Fig. 6.9. *Uses for Tab and Tab Align.*

To align text at the right without displaying the alignment character, repeat step 1, type the text, and then press Enter before you press the alignment character. The typed text is right-justified at the tab stop.

Cue:
To align names and addresses, use a colon with Tab Align. To align numbers, use an equal sign or decimal.

The alignment character can be any character you want, such as the colon shown in figure 6.9. To align names and addresses, use a colon. For aligning numbers, an equal sign (=) is best. To change the alignment character, you must modify the WP.LRS file and insert a language code as described in Chapter 12.

Using Justification

In LetterPerfect 1.0, *justification* refers to the alignment of text with the document's left or right margin. LetterPerfect 1.0 offers four justification formats:

- *Full justification*, which aligns the text on the printed page along both right and left margins.

- *Left justification*, which leaves a ragged right margin. This format is LetterPerfect's default setting.

- *Center justification*, which aligns text evenly right and left of the tab-stop setting at the cursor location. If you use Center to block and center text, LetterPerfect inserts a **[Just:Center]** code at the beginning of the block. And at the end of the block, LetterPerfect inserts a justification code for the previous justification format.

- *Right justification*, which aligns all text on the right margin, leaving the left margin ragged. LetterPerfect inserts a **[Just:Right]** code at the beginning of the block and inserts at the end of the block a justification code for the previous justification format.

> *Caution:* If you use Block on multiple lines of text either to center or to right-align text, LetterPerfect resets the justification at the end of the block to the previously active justification setting. The reset codes do not change if you change the default Initial Codes, insert a justification code at the beginning of the document, add justification codes elsewhere in the document, or delete one of the center or right-align codes.

By default, LetterPerfect uses left justification, an ideal setting if the printer is not capable of proportional spacing or if you want your document to look informal. Use full justification if your printer is capable of proportional spacing and you want a formal look. Hyphenation improves the appearance of fully justified text.

Use hyphenation to reduce the white space between words. Hyphenating words makes justified text more attractive (see this chapter's section "Using Hyphenation").

Figure 6.10 illustrates text that has a ragged right margin and text that is fully justified.

LetterPerfect does not display fully justified text on-screen unless the system has a graphics card. You can, however, use View Document (see this chapter's section "Using Document Preview") or print the page to see text fully justified. Because text is justified by the addition of spaces between words and letters, the attractiveness of justified text depends on the capabilities of your printer.

Cue:
Use full justification when you have a printer capable of proportional spacing and want a formal look.

Cue:
Use hyphenation to reduce the white space between words in fully justified text.

```
The next two paragraphs are set to Justification Left.

This line has so many characters that the very next
extraordinarily long word wraps to the next line, creating a gap
at the right margin.

Turn on hyphenation to improve the look of the text. The extraor-
dinarily long word is hyphenated, creating a visual appearance
that is much more attractive.


The next paragraph is set to Justification Full.

Text that is full-justified aligns neatly at both margins, avoiding
the "ragged-right" look of left-justified text.  When you want your
text to look more formal, set Justification to Full rather than
Left.
```

Fig. 6.10. Justified versus unjustified text, with and without hyphenation.

You can change the justification setting by using the Format menu. If the cursor is within the body of the document, the new setting affects only the portion of the document that follows the cursor position. To change the justification setting for the entire document, either move the cursor to the top of the document before you change the first setting, or change the Initial Codes. (To move the cursor to the beginning of the document, press Home, Home, up arrow.)

To change the justification setting, follow these steps:

1. Access the Layout pull-down menu and select Format. Alternatively, press Format (Shift-F8).

   LetterPerfect displays the Format menu.

2. Select Justification (**1**).

3. Select either **Left** (**1**), **Center** (**2**), **Right** (**3**), or **Full** (**4**).

4. Press Exit (F7) to return to the document.

If you are not sure which type of justification the program is using, display the Format menu and read the setting of the justification option.

Centering Text

LetterPerfect centers a line of text either as you type it or after the text is entered. Follow these steps to center a line of text as you type:

1. Move the cursor to the left margin of a blank line. Access the Layout pull-down menu and select Center. Alternatively, press Center (Shift-F6) or Ctrl-c.

   The cursor moves to the point midway between the two margins.

2. Type the text.

3. Press Enter.

If you type more characters than the margins can hold, the rest of the text wraps to a second line, but only the first line is centered. To center several lines, use Block (described in Chapter 5) or temporarily change justification to Center.

To center text around a specific point on-screen, press the space bar until the cursor is where you want the text centered. Press Center (Shift-F6) or Ctrl-c (notice that the cursor does not move). Then begin typing. Refer to figure 6.11 for examples of various types of text alignments.

> **Cue:**
> To center several lines, use Block or temporarily change justification to Center.

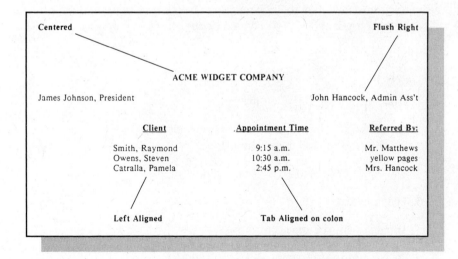

Fig. 6.11. *Examples of LetterPerfect's text-alignment capabilities.*

Follow this procedure to center the text in a previously typed line:

1. Place the cursor at the left margin of the line of text you want to center, or press the space bar until the cursor is at the point where you want the text centered.

2. Access the Layout pull-down menu and select **Center**. Alternatively, press Center (Shift-F6) or Ctrl-c.

   The text moves to the center of the screen.

3. Press the down arrow.

   The text appears centered on-screen.

> *Caution:* If you use the space bar to move the cursor before you activate Center, the text line may start left of the left-margin setting unless the number of spaces you type equals at least half the number of characters in the line of text.

Making Text Flush Right

LetterPerfect makes it easy to align text flush with the right margin. You can make text flush right either as you type it or after the text is entered.

Perform these steps to line up along the right margin the text you are about to type:

1. Move the cursor to the left margin.

2. Access the Layout pull-down menu and select **Flush Right**. Alternatively, press Flush Right (Alt-F6).

   The cursor moves to the right margin.

3. Type the text.

   The text you type travels from right to left.

4. Press Enter to stop typing text flush right.

> *Caution:* If you type more characters than can fit on the line inside the margins, the extra text wraps to the next line below. Only the first line of text is flush right. If you want several lines of text right-aligned, use Block (described in Chapter 5) or temporarily change justification to **Right**.

Follow these steps to change text in a previously typed line to flush right:

1. Position the cursor at the left margin or move the cursor immediately to the left of the word that begins the portion of text you want to be flush right.

2. Select **Align** from the **L**ayout menu and then select **Fl**ush Right. Alternatively, press Flush Right (Alt-F6).

   The text line moves to the right.

3. Press the down arrow.

   The line appears flush right on-screen.

Using Hyphenation

When a line of text becomes too long to fit within the margins, the last word in the line wraps to the next line. With short words, wrapping does not present a problem. With long words, however, these problems can occur:

- If justification is set to left (the LetterPerfect default setting), a large gap can appear at the right margin, making the margin appear too ragged.

- If justification is set to full, large spaces between words become visually distracting.

Hyphenating a long word at the end of a line solves the problem and creates a visually attractive document. When you use the Hyphenation feature, the program fits as much of the word as possible on one line before hyphenating and wraps the rest of the word to the next line (notice the hyphenation of the word *extraordinarily* in fig. 6.10).

Hyphenation is permanently active but not automatic. For hyphenation to function automatically, LetterPerfect requires a speller dictionary with hyphen indicators in its word list, as well as a hyphenation file. The speller module—WP{WP}US.LEX—that comes with LetterPerfect does not include hyphen indicators. The program also does not include any hyphenation file.

If you are a registered owner of WordPerfect 5.1, you can copy its WP{WP} US.LEX file (which includes the hyphen indicators) and WP{WP}US.HYC file into the subdirectory containing the main LetterPerfect program file—LP.EXE. These files activate LetterPerfect's automatic-hyphenation mode.

If you are using the 11/01/90 interim release, you can tell LetterPerfect where to find the subdirectory containing the WordPerfect 5.1 speller and thesaurus files, as explained in Chapter 1.

You also can buy a WordPerfect Language Module that includes WP{WP}US.LEX (and thousands of words to improve the performance of the Speller) and WP{WP}US.HYC, as well as a larger WP{WP}US.THS file that improves the performance of the thesaurus.

> *Caution:* You will find two disadvantages to using the WordPerfect Language Module:
>
> - The files take considerable disk space.
>
> - After you add the files that put hyphenation into automatic mode, the *only* way you can deactivate hyphenation is to delete or rename the files. Hyphenation does *not* have any adjustable settings or parameters.

Without the special files, hyphenation functions at a basic, manual level; you can perform manual hyphenation by positioning the cursor in a word and pressing Ctrl-hyphen. LetterPerfect inserts a hyphen that is invisible unless it is used to break the word at the end of a line, in which case it becomes visible. When you view the word by using Reveal Codes (available on the Edit pull-down menu or through Alt-F3, F11, or Ctrl-r), the hyphen appears as a bold character without brackets. (See this chapter's section "Understanding Hyphens, Spaces, and Soft Returns.")

Cue:
The hyphenation zone is preset and cannot be altered.

LetterPerfect comes with a preset hyphenation zone. You cannot change the parameters of the hyphenation zone. When hyphenation is active, this zone determines whether LetterPerfect divides a word or wraps it to the next line. The hyphenation zone is preset in percentages of line length: the left hyphenation zone is 10 percent; the right hyphenation zone is 4 percent (see fig. 6.12).

On a standard document page, 8 1/2 inches wide with a 1-inch left margin and a 1-inch right margin, a line of text can span 6 1/2 inches. The left hyphenation zone is .65" (10 percent of 6 1/2 inches), and the right zone is .26" (4 percent of 6 1/2 inches). If the line length becomes longer, the zones become larger but retain the same proportions.

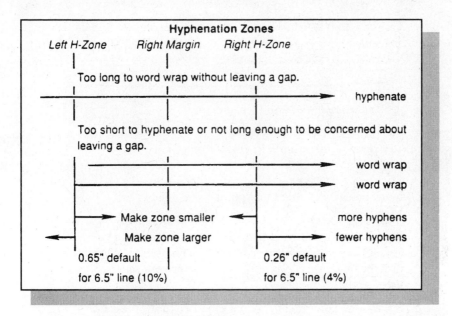

Fig. 6.12. LetterPerfect's hyphenation zone.

The following examples illustrate how LetterPerfect uses the zone in a standard document:

- *If the word begins at or before the left zone* (.65 inch from the right margin) and continues past the right zone (.26 inch from the right margin), the word requires hyphenation. The word is too long to wrap without leaving a large gap.

- *If the word begins at or after the left zone* (.65 inch from the right margin) and continues past the right zone (.26 inch from the right margin), the word wraps to the next line. The word is either too short to hyphenate or short enough that it won't leave a large gap.

In its automatic mode, the Hyphenation feature refers to the added files to locate a word's hyphenation points if the word is located within the hyphenation zone. If LetterPerfect cannot determine the hyphenation points, the program displays this prompt at the bottom left corner of the screen: `Position hyphen; Press ESC.`

The word requiring hyphenation follows the prompt, and the suggested hyphenation point is marked by a hyphen (see fig. 6.13).

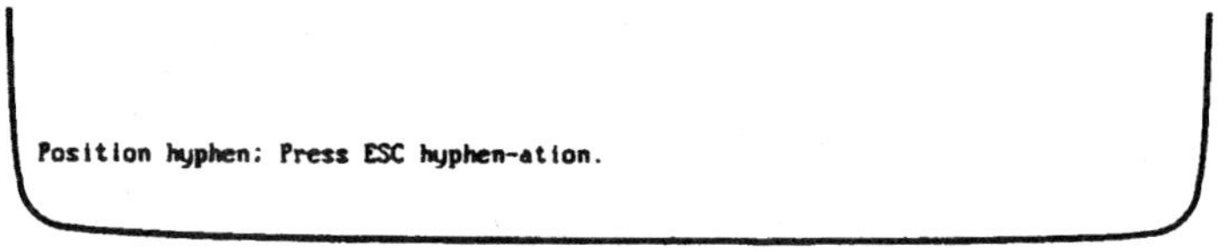

```
Position hyphen: Press ESC hyphen-ation.
```

Fig. 6.13. The manual-hyphenation prompt.

You can respond to the prompt in any of three ways:

- *To accept the suggested hyphenation point*, press Esc. LetterPerfect hyphenates the word at that point.

- If the suggested hyphenation point is not acceptable, *reposition the hyphenation point* by moving the cursor left or right with the arrow keys. (The arrow keys move only a certain number of characters left or right.) When you position the cursor to your satisfaction, press Esc.

- If the word cannot be hyphenated satisfactorily, *press Cancel (F1 or Esc)*. Pressing Cancel permanently rejects hyphenation for that word. LetterPerfect inserts the hidden code [/] before the word. You must manually delete this code before LetterPerfect can hyphenate the word.

> ***Tip***: Because the hyphenation points suggested by LetterPerfect are often incorrect, you can easily make mistakes in hyphenation. Keep a dictionary handy to verify syllable breaks.

Understanding Hyphens, Spaces, and Soft Returns

Cue:
When you edit, keep Reveal Codes active to see which kind of hyphen or dash is entered.

You can create several types of hyphens and dashes. Although these hyphens and dashes appear identical on-screen, LetterPerfect interprets them differently. So that you can determine which kind of hyphen or dash is entered, edit with Reveal Codes active.

Table 6.4 shows the differences between the various types of hyphens and soft returns.

Table 6.4
Types of Hyphens and Soft Returns

Type	Keystroke	Purpose	Hidden Code
Hard hyphen	Hyphen key	Inserts a regular hyphen	**[–]**
Hyphen	Home, hyphen	Causes LetterPerfect to treat a hyphenated word as a single word	–
Soft hyphen	Ctrl-hyphen	Inserts a hyphen that appears when a word breaks at the end of a line	Highlighted –
Dash	Home, hyphen, hyphen	Keeps two hyphens together	–**[–]**
Hard space	Home, space	Keeps two words together	**[ ]**
Invisible soft return	Home, Enter without hyphenating	Inserts a line break	**[ISRt]**
Deletable soft return	(no keystroke)	Forces a line break without hyphenating	**[DSRt]**
Dormant hard return	(no keystroke)	Hard return at the top of a new page becomes dormant to eliminate unnecessary white space; changes back to hard return when not at page top	**[Dorm HRt]**

Using Different Types of Hyphens

When you press the hyphen key, LetterPerfect inserts a hard hyphen into the document. Reveal Codes displays the hyphen as **[–]**. Hard hyphens, always visible on-screen, appear when the document is printed. If a hard hyphen appears in a word that needs to be hyphenated at the end of a line, the program uses the hard hyphen as the breaking point instead of prompting you.

Reminder:
If a hyphen
character
appears in a
word that
requires
hyphenation,
the program
may prompt you
for a hyphen
breaking point.

When you press and release Home followed by a hyphen, LetterPerfect inserts a hyphen character into the document. Reveal Codes displays the hyphen character as an unhighlighted –. Hyphen characters are always visible on-screen and appear when the document is printed. The program does not consider the hyphen character as a hyphen but treats it like a letter of the alphabet. If a hyphen character appears in a word that requires hyphenation, the program may prompt you to designate a hyphen breaking point.

Pressing Ctrl-hyphen inserts a soft hyphen into the document. Reveal Codes displays the soft hyphen as a bold – without brackets. LetterPerfect uses the soft hyphen to divide a word between syllables during hyphenation. You can insert your own soft hyphen at points where you want hyphenation to occur. Soft hyphens are visible and print only when they are the last character in a line; otherwise, soft hyphens are hidden.

> *Tip:* You cannot produce a soft hyphen by using the numeric keypad's minus sign in combination with the Ctrl key. You must instead use the hyphen key at the top of the keyboard. Pressing the numeric keypad's minus sign moves the cursor to the top of the screen. If Num Lock is active (so that pressing a key on the numeric keypad inserts a number into the document), pressing the numeric keypad's minus sign inserts a hard hyphen into the document.

To type a dash, use a combination of two types of hyphens. For the first hyphen, use the hyphen character (Home, hyphen). For the second hyphen, use a hard hyphen (press the hyphen key alone). This technique ensures that regardless of where the line breaks, the two hyphens stay together.

Removing Soft Hyphens

Reminder:
Simply deacti-
vating
hyphenation's
automatic mode
does not remove
or deactivate
soft hyphens.

When a word is hyphenated, LetterPerfect divides it with a soft hyphen. Soft hyphens are displayed on-screen or printed by the printer only if they appear at the end of a line of text. If you reformat the document so that the word is not the last word on a line, the code remains in the word but does not display on-screen and is not printed in the document. If you decide to have an unhyphenated document, you must remove these soft hyphens. Renaming or deleting the files used by hyphenation's automatic mode does not remove the soft hyphens or stop the soft hyphens from splitting a word at the end of a line.

After you turn off automatic hyphenation, use these steps to remove the soft hyphens from a document:

1. Press Home, Home, up arrow to move the cursor to the beginning of the document.

2. Access the **S**earch pull-down menu and select **R**eplace; alternatively, press Replace (Alt-F2).

   LetterPerfect displays the prompt w/Confirm? No (Yes) at the bottom right corner of the screen.

3. Select **N**o.

   LetterPerfect displays the prompt → Srch: at the bottom right corner of the screen.

4. Press Ctrl-hyphen to create a soft hyphen.

5. Press Search (F2) or Exit (F7).

   LetterPerfect displays this prompt at the bottom right corner of the screen: Replace with:.

6. Press Search (F2) or Exit (F7).

   LetterPerfect removes all the soft hyphens in the document.

To remove only unused soft hyphens without deactivating hyphenation's automatic mode, follow this procedure but select **Y**es in step 3. LetterPerfect stops at each soft hyphen and prompts you to confirm the replacement of the hyphen.

Creating and Using the Hard Space

To keep two or more words together, insert a hard space between the words. Create a hard space by pressing and releasing Home and pressing the space bar. Reveal Codes displays the hard space as **[ ]**.

LetterPerfect considers two or more words separated by hard spaces as a single word, which wraps to the next line as a single unit. Suppose, for example, that you always want the name of your business, Jones' Retail Hardware Supply, to appear on one line. Type *Jones'*; press Home, space; type *Retail*; press Home, space; type *Hardware*; press Home, space; and type *Supply*.

Creating and Using Invisible Soft Returns

You can manually insert an invisible soft return to control a line break. For example, you may not want certain words to be broken by a hyphen or space, such as words that have a slash (and/or, either/or) or words connected with an ellipsis ("a fantastic...ground-breaking film"). An invisible soft return breaks the line where you specify. Create the invisible soft return by pressing and releasing Home and pressing Enter. LetterPerfect inserts an invisible soft return, which Reveal Codes displays as **[ISRt]**. If editing changes the line ending, the paragraph reformats; you do not have to remove the return.

Understanding the Deletable Soft Return

If automatic-hyphenation mode is not active and a word is wider than the length of the line, the program inserts a deletable soft return to break the word at the character on the right margin. Reveal Codes displays a deletable soft return as **[DSRt]**.

Understanding the Dormant Hard Return

When a **[HRt]** code follows a **[SPg]** code, LetterPerfect automatically converts the hard-return code into a dormant hard-return code at the top of a new page to avoid unnecessary white space. Reveal Codes displays a deletable soft return as **[Dorm HRt]**. If you reformat the document so that **[Dorm HRt]** is not the first code at the top of the page, LetterPerfect automatically changes the code back to **[HRt]**.

Changing Line Spacing

Cue:
LetterPerfect's default line spacing is single spacing.

Single spacing is LetterPerfect's default line spacing. To double- or triple-space a document, you do not have to place two hard returns after each line manually. You can instead use the Format menu's Line Spacing (**2**) option to increase the number of spaces LetterPerfect inserts between each line. To change the program's default single-spacing for the entire document, you must perform one of these actions:

- Move the cursor to the top of the document (press Home, Home, up arrow) and insert a line-spacing code.

- Insert a line-spacing code into the Initial Codes before you create the document.

You do not see changes in line spacing on-screen except when the setting is a whole number (such as 1, 2, or 3) or a decimal number equal to or greater than 0.5 (such as 1.6, which LetterPerfect displays as a line spacing of 2 on-screen). To see the actual line spacing, you must either display the page with View Document (see this chapter's "Using Document Preview" section) or print the page.

To change the line spacing, complete these steps:

1. Access the **L**ayout pull-down menu and select **F**ormat. Alternatively, press Format (Shift-F8).

2. Select **L**ine Spacing (**2**).

   The cursor moves right of the Line Spacing menu item.

3. Type any number with up to two decimal places and then press Enter.

   To double-space, type *2*. For one and a half spaces between lines, type *1.5*. You can increase line spacing a small amount by typing a number such as *1.02*. Likewise, you can decrease line spacing a small amount by entering a number that is less than 1, such as *.95*.

   Note: If the number you type reduces the line spacing too much, the lines of text may print partially one on top of another.

4. Press Exit (F7) to return to the document.

Tip: LetterPerfect 1.0 automatically converts fractional numbers into their decimal equivalents. If, for example, you type *1 5/8* and press Enter, LetterPerfect converts the number to *1.62*.

Enhancing Text

Because LetterPerfect can get the most out of your printer, you can use the printer's features to enhance your documents. Although LetterPerfect displays some text enhancements on-screen (depending on your monitor), the full impact of the document is of course realized on the printed page. The Font feature controls the size and appearance of characters when they print.

Changing the Base Font

Cue:
The base font
*is the font
used to print
a document.*

When you installed your printer, you selected an initial base font from a list of fonts available on your printer. The *base font* is the font the program uses to print the document. Depending on the capabilities of your printer and its selection of fonts, you can change the size and appearance of a font or include more than one font type in your document.

LetterPerfect offers two methods for changing the default base font. In general, the choices under the Format feature's Initial Codes/Base Font option let you select a new font that controls the size and appearance of all text in the document, except text following a font code inserted through LetterPerfect's Font feature.

Follow these steps to select a new initial base font:

1. Access the Layout pull-down menu and select Format. Alternatively, press Format (Shift-F8). LetterPerfect displays its Format menu.

2. Select Document Initial Codes/Base Font. At the bottom of the screen, LetterPerfect displays a menu:

   1 Initial Codes; **2** Initial Base Font: **0**

3. Choose either option, and LetterPerfect displays the Base Font menu, which list all fonts available to the selected printer (see fig. 6.14). The cursor bar highlights, and an * marks, the font currently active at the cursor.

```
Base Font

   Bits Charter Roman 06pt (HP Roman 8) (FW, Port)
   Bits Charter Roman 07pt (HP Roman 8) (FW, Port)
   Bits Charter Roman 08.50pt (HP Roman 8) (FW, Port)
   Bits Charter Roman 08pt (HP Roman 8) (FW, Port)
   Bits Charter Roman 09pt (HP Roman 8) (FW, Port)
   Bits Charter Roman 10pt (HP Roman 8) (FW, Port)
   Bits Charter Roman 11pt (HP Roman 8) (FW, Port)
   Bits Charter Roman 12pt (HP Roman 8) (FW, Port)
   Bits Charter Roman 14pt (HP Roman 8) (FW, Port)
   Bits Charter Roman 18pt (HP Roman 8) (FW, Port)
   Bits Charter Roman 24pt (HP Roman 8) (FW, Port)
   Bits Charter Roman 30pt (HP Roman 8) (FW, Port)
   Bits Charter Roman 36pt (HP Roman 8) (FW, Port)
 * Courier 10cpi
   Courier 10cpi Bold
   Dutch Bold 06pt (HP Roman 8) (FW, Port)
   Dutch Bold 07pt (HP Roman 8) (FW, Port)
   Dutch Bold 08.50pt (HP Roman 8) (FW, Port)
   Dutch Bold 08pt (HP Roman 8) (FW, Port)
   Dutch Bold 09pt (HP Roman 8) (FW, Port)
   Dutch Bold 10pt (HP Roman 8) (FW, Port)

 1 Select; N Name search: 1
```

Fig. 6.14. *LetterPerfect's Base Font menu.*

Note: If you have a printer that uses both portrait and landscape fonts, LetterPerfect displays a list of fonts for the form's orientation—either all portrait or all landscape fonts. Certain printers, including PostScript, print in either portrait or landscape mode with all of their fonts. (For more information on printing, see Chapter 8.)

Tip: The Base Font menu frequently contains more font names than LetterPerfect can display on one screen. Use the mouse, the arrow keys, the PgDn or PgUp key, or the Screen Down or Screen Up key to move the cursor bar up or down the font list. Press the Home key twice followed by the up arrow to move the cursor bar to the top of the list. Press the Home key twice followed by the down arrow to move the cursor bar to the bottom of the list. You also can press Name Search and type the first letters of the font's name to move the cursor bar to a font.

4. Move the cursor bar to highlight the name of a different font. To choose the font, double-click the mouse, choose **S**elect (**1**), or press Enter.

The base font selected by this method always controls the size and appearance of the text in the current document's substructures, such as headers, footers, and endnotes. That font also controls the size and appearance of all text in the main document unless you insert a different base font code, as described in the following steps. If you want to change the active base font for all documents you create, see the section on changing LetterPerfect's default settings in Chapter 1.

To change the base font for part or all of the text in the main body of the document, follow these steps:

1. Move the cursor to the point in the document where you want LetterPerfect to begin using a different base font.

2. Access the Font pull-down menu and select Base Font. Alternatively, press Font (Ctrl-F8) and select Base Font (4); or press Ctrl-f.

   LetterPerfect displays its Font menu (see fig. 6.14).

3. Move the cursor bar to highlight the new font; select it. LetterPerfect inserts a code for this font into the document at the cursor's location.

Using Proportional Spacing

Cue:
Use proportional spacing to give a printed page a pleasing, professional-looking appearance.

Some printers allow *proportional spacing*—a feature that uses characters of different widths to give a printed page a more pleasing appearance. In proportional spacing, the letter *w*, for example, occupies more space than the letter *i*. The result is a more aesthetic and professional-looking line of text. Nonproportional fonts use characters that occupy the same amount of space and leave gaps that are visually distracting.

When you examine the list of fonts available for the printer, you may see proportionally spaced fonts designated by the initials *PS* or the word *Proportional*. Downloadable software fonts created by third-party programs may not have a proportional-space designation.

> *Tip*: With dot-matrix printers, proportional spacing often slows down the job of printing. Use a nonproportional font for drafts of the document and reserve the proportionally spaced font for the final printing. Examine figure 6.15 and compare the examples of draft and proportional printing.

```
This line is printed in Courier 10 cpi (characters per inch) on a
Toshiba P351 dot-matrix printer in high text quality mode.

This line is printed in Courier PS (proportional spacing) on a Toshiba P351
dot-matrix printer in high text quality mode.
```

Fig. 6.15. Examples of draft and proportional printing.

Choosing Font Attributes

LetterPerfect notes two categories of font attributes: *size* and *appearance*. When you alter a font's size or appearance, the Pos indicator at the lower right portion of the screen takes on the attributes of the font at the cursor. The on-screen appearance of the text and Pos indicator depends on the kind of monitor and video-display card your system uses and on the color option you select in Setup.

Cue: LetterPerfect's two categories of font attributes are size and appearance.

Changing the Font Size

LetterPerfect can make a font *smaller* for a footnote number or a mathematical formula or *larger* to emphasize a heading, column head, title, or letterhead. The Font feature offers two methods for making a font size smaller or larger: paired font-size codes and paired base-font codes.

To use paired font-size codes, follow these steps:

1. Access the Font pull-down menu. LetterPerfect displays a list of options. The Superscript and Subscript options change the font's size and the vertical position of its characters. The Base Font option displays the list of available fonts. The Normal option restores the base font that was active before you selected one of the size and appearance options from this menu.

   Alternatively, press Font (Ctrl-F8). LetterPerfect displays a menu across the bottom of the screen:

   1 Bold; **2** Underline; **3** Normal; **4** Base Font; **5** Italc; **6** Suprscpt;**7** Subscpt: **0**

2. Alternatively, select one of the letter-menu choices.

Depending on your printer's capabilities, changing *size* has the following effects on a font:

- *Superscript* reduces the size of the base font and places text slightly above the line of printed text. Use this option for footnote numbers and mathematical formulas.

- *Subscript* reduces the size of the base font and places text slightly below the line of printed text. Use this option for mathematical formulas.

The Suprscpt (**6**) and Subscpt (**7**) options insert hidden paired codes and control the size of all text appearing between those codes. Reveal Codes displays the paired superscript codes as **[SUPRSCPT]**<*text*>**[suprscpt]** and the paired subscript codes as **[SUBSCPT]**<*text*>**[subscpt]**.

LetterPerfect automatically tracks the vertical height of the larger or smaller letters and adjusts the margins and the number of lines per page. Larger fonts use more vertical space and allow fewer letters per line; smaller fonts use less vertical space and allow more letters per line.

The Normal (**4**) option or Ctrl-n fast-key combination adjusts the amount of text the superscript and subscript options control by moving the size-ending code to the cursor. For example, suppose that this sentence includes hidden superscript and subscript codes: *LetterPerfect supports printers that permit the printing of* **[SUPRSCPT]***Superscript and* **[suprscpt]** **[SUBSCPT]***subscript options.* **[subscpt]**

Both pairs of font-size codes include a second word by mistake. You can use several methods to correct the errors:

- Delete one code of each pair, block the correct word, display the Font menu, and select the size-formatting code.

- Delete the second word and use Undelete to restore it to the document to the right of the ending font-size code.

- Use the Font menu's Normal (**3**) option or the Ctrl-n fast-key combination as described in the following series of steps.

The Normal option and its fast-key equivalent Ctrl-n are the quickest and easiest ways to correct the mistake. To use either method, follow these steps:

1. Move the cursor to the immediate right of the last character in the last word you want controlled by the paired font-size code.

2. Access the Font pull-down menu and select Normal. Alternatively, press Font (Ctrl-F8) and select Normal (3) from the Font menu; or press Ctrl-n.

LetterPerfect moves the ending font-size code to the cursor.

You can read more about the Base Font (4) option in the section "Changing the Base Font," which precedes this section.

To use the paired base-font codes, follow these steps:

1. Use Block to highlight the text you want controlled by the base font code. Figure 6.16 shows a block of text displayed by Reveal Codes.

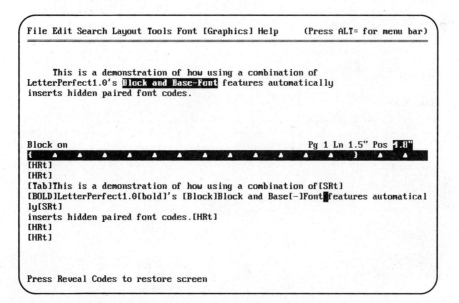

Fig. 6.16. Blocked text as shown by Reveal Codes.

2. Access the Font pull-down menu and select Base Font. Alternatively, press Font (Ctrl-F8) and select Base Font (4); or press Ctrl-f.

3. LetterPerfect displays the Base Font menu, which lists all the available fonts for your printer (see fig. 6.14). The cursor bar highlights, and an * marks, the font currently active at the cursor.

4. Use the mouse, the arrow keys, the PgDn or PgUp key, or the Screen Up or Screen Down key to move the cursor bar up or down the font list. Press Home, up arrow or Home, or down arrow to move the cursor bar to the top or bottom of the font list.

Alternatively, you can select **Name Search** and type the first letters of the font you want to use. When the cursor bar highlights the name of the font that you typed, press Enter.

5. Double-click the mouse. Alternatively, choose **Select** (**1**) or press Enter.

At the beginning of the block, LetterPerfect inserts the name of the font code highlighted by the cursor bar. At the end of the block, LetterPerfect inserts the code for the base font active in the document when you began highlighting the text block.

Figure 6.17 shows the paired base-font codes, as displayed by Reveal Codes, inserted by the program.

```
File Edit Search Layout Tools Font Graphics Help        (Press ALT= for menu bar)


    This is a demonstration of how using a combination of
LetterPerfect1.0's Block and Base-Font features automatically
inserts hidden paired font codes.




                                                  Pg 1 Ln 1.5" Pos 4.35"
{   ▲    ▲    ▲    ▲    ▲    ▲    ▲    ▲    ▲    ▲    ▲   }    ▲    ▲
[HRt]
[HRt]
[Tab]This is a demonstration of how using a combination of[SRt]
[BOLD]LetterPerfect1.0[bold]'s [Font:Swiss Roman 11pt (HP Roman 8) (FW, Port)]Bl
ock and Base[-]Font[Font:Courier 10cpi]█features automatically[SRt]
inserts hidden paired font codes.[HRt]
[HRt]
[HRt]



Press Reveal Codes to restore screen
```

Fig. 6.17. Paired base-font codes inserted by LetterPerfect.

Changing the Font Appearance

To emphasize certain text, you can change the appearance of a font. Enhancements such as bold, italic, and underline are appropriate for book and magazine titles, foreign words, and captions.

To change the appearance of any font, follow these steps:

Cue:
You can emphasize a portion of text by changing the appearance of a font.

1. Access the Font pull-down menu. LetterPerfect displays a list of options. The **Bold** and **Italics** options change the font's appearance. The Base Font option displays the list of available fonts. The Normal option restores the base font that was active before you selected one of the size and appearance options from this menu.

   Alternatively, press Font (Ctrl-F8). LetterPerfect displays a menu across the bottom of the screen:

   1 Bold; **2** Underline; **3** Normal; **4** Base Font; **5** Ital; **6** Suprscpt; **7** Subscpt: **0**

2. Select the **Bold** (**1**), Underline (**2**), Normal (**3**), Base Font (**4**), or Italc (**5**) option to change the appearance of the base font.

In general, the *appearance* options on the Font menu insert paired codes that have these effects on a font:

- *Bold* darkens the font. The Bold feature (F6) or the Ctrl-b fast-key combination activates the bold appearance attribute with fewer keystrokes than either the pull-down menu options or Font (Ctrl-F8).

- *Underline* activates the underlining of characters in a word. The Underline feature (F8) or Ctrl-u fast-key combination activates the underline appearance attribute with fewer keystrokes than either the pull-down menu options or Font (Ctrl-F8).

- *Italic* selects a font whose characters are slanted to the right. The Ctrl-i fast-key combination activates the italic appearance attribute with fewer keystrokes than either the pull-down menu options or Font (Ctrl-F8).

   The Normal (**3**) and Base Font (**4**) options perform as described in the section "Choosing Font Attributes," which immediately precedes this section.

Tip: Use the paired-base-font method to select fonts for font-appearance attributes available in other word processing programs—for example, WordPerfect 5.1—but not in LetterPerfect 1.0 (such as outline; shadow; small capital letters; and fine, large, very large, and extra large text). See "Changing the Base Font" in this chapter.

Placing Different Attributes or Font Sizes on the Same Line

With LetterPerfect, you can mix as many appearance or font-size attributes as are supported by your printer or that fit on a single line. The LetterPerfect program includes the file PRINTER.TST, which tests the capability of your printer to support appearance attributes and font sizes. See Chapter 8 for instructions on how to print this file.

Restoring Font Size and Appearance to Normal

Each font-appearance or font-size attribute is controlled by a set of paired codes. The capitalized code turns the attribute on; the lowercase code turns the attribute off. LetterPerfect offers two ways to resume entering text in the base font and size of the text that appears before the paired codes.

Choosing which restoration method to use depends on whether one attribute or more than one attribute is specified. When you turn off the attributes, LetterPerfect uses the base-font size and appearance settings that were in effect before the size or attributes were changed.

If only one attribute is on, follow these steps to restore the font size and appearance to normal:

1. Press Reveal Codes (Alt-F3 or F11) to display the attribute that is turned on.

2. Press the right arrow to move the cursor past the code that turns the attribute off. Any text you enter to the right of the Attribute Off code has the normal font size and appearance.

If, however, the text you have entered has a combination of attribute-appearance and size changes, use this method to resume entering text in the original base font's attributes and size:

Access the Font pull-down menu and select Normal. Alternatively, press Font (Ctrl-F8) and select Normal (**3**), or press Ctrl-n.

This method moves the cursor to the right, beyond all font appearance and size attribute codes.

If several attributes are on at the same time, press the right arrow enough times to move the cursor past all the codes. In other words, if you have attributes in effect, choose the Normal font or press the right arrow. Both methods move the cursor past the attribute codes.

Using Document Preview

On most computer systems, LetterPerfect uses standard-size ASCII characters to display text on the screen. The display appearance of the text attributes such as bold, underline, and italic depends on the exact type of monitor, video-graphics card, and video software used in the system. Only the most advanced systems show more than bold or underlined text. Color monitors use different color combinations to designate the various font appearance and size attributes.

On systems with a graphics monitor, you can use the View Document feature to display an on-screen picture of each page in the document. Although you cannot edit the page while using View Document, you can view it, edit it, and then view it again.

Cue:
If you have a graphics monitor, you can use View Document to display on-screen a picture of each page in the document.

To use the View Document feature, follow these steps:

1. Access the **F**ile pull-down menu and select **P**rint. Alternatively, press Print (Shift-F7) or Ctrl-p.

2. Select View Document (**6**). If you use Ctrl-p, you do not have to do this step.

   The screen displays a graphic representation of the page. Figure 6.18 is an example of a document displayed at 100 percent with View Document.

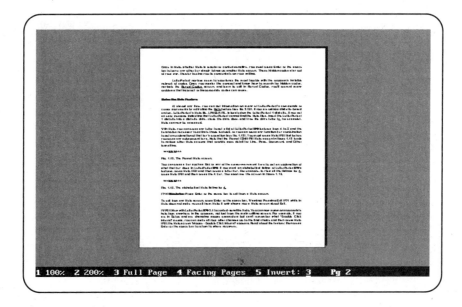

Fig. 6.18. Document displayed by LetterPerfect's View Document feature.

Summary

In this chapter, you learned about the powerful and easily accessible features that LetterPerfect 1.0 offers for formatting and enhancing documents. You now should be able to perform these tasks to control how text appears on the page:

- Alter the units of measurement from inches to LetterPerfect units, points, 1200ths of an inch, or centimeters

- Change left and right margins, use the Margin Release feature, and indent text

- Change tab settings and tab types (left, right, center, decimal, and dot leader)

- Center text, make text flush right, change justification settings, and change line spacing and leaders

- Use the Hyphenation feature and change the hyphenation zone

You should also be able to take advantage of your printer's capabilities with these tasks:

- Enhance text by specifying font attributes such as size and appearance

- Verify formatting with Document Preview

In Chapter 7, you learn about designing document pages.

Designing Document Pages

You have only one chance to make a first impression. Regardless of whether you are writing a memo for your boss, a class assignment for a teacher, a report for a client, an article for an editor, or a resume for an employer, you know that the appearance of a document forms the reader's first impression of its contents. Sometimes the appearance of a document—that is, whether it appears friendly, inviting, and easy-to-read—determines whether it is read or put aside.

Ease of reading depends on clarity. When the reader looks at a page, is it clear what type of information the page contains or where the reader must turn for more information? Is it clear where sections begin and end? This chapter shows you how to use LetterPerfect's formatting features to design documents that are clear, interesting, and, above all, readable.

Reminder: WordPerfect Corporation updated LetterPerfect 1.0 just before this book went to press. Dated 11/01/90, the interim release includes new options for existing features, and a few new features. The menus on your screen may, therefore, differ slightly from those shown in this book. Also, depending on the printer-form definition, margins, tab stops, and font you specify, the text placement and status-line information in documents you create may differ from that shown in this book's figures.

For information about using the mouse and accessing the pull-down menus, refer to the Introduction.

Changing Initial Document Settings

LetterPerfect comes equipped with a set of default format settings—margins, tab settings, paper size, and others. If you make no format changes, these settings govern the appearance of the document. You can, however, override these default settings individually by using the Format feature to insert specific hidden formatting codes into the document.

As an alternative to inserting individual formatting codes, you can use Setup's Initial Codes option to change the default format of a document before you begin working. The changes you make apply to the current document and are saved with it. They override LetterPerfect's default settings, and they override the initial-setting choices made with the Setup menu, which you can display by accessing the File pull-down menu and selecting Setup or, alternatively, by pressing Setup (Shift-F1).

See Chapter 6 for instructions on the Setup feature and on changing the default format settings.

Formatting Pages

LetterPerfect offers format options on several levels: the entire document, a page, a paragraph, a sentence, and a single word. Formatting a page requires making decisions about how the pages in your document should look. What size are top and bottom margins? Is text centered, top to bottom, on the page? Are there headers and footers and, if so, on which pages? Are there automatic page numbers? Is there text or a chart that must be kept together on a page? Must pages start at a certain point in the text? LetterPerfect conveniently includes all page-formatting choices in the Format menu, shown in figure 7.1.

To display the Format menu, access the Layout pull-down menu and select Format (see fig. 7.2). Alternatively, press Format (Shift-F8).

The Format menu offers 10 options that control the appearance of a document page. The Document Initial Codes/Base Font option is discussed in Chapter 2. The Justification (**1**), Line Spacing (**2**), Left/Right Margins (**4**), and Tabs (**5**) options are discussed in Chapter 6. The following sections discuss the Top/Bottom Margins (**3**), Header/Footer (**6**), Page Numbering (**7**), Paper Size/Type (**8**), and Center Page (top to bottom) (**9**) options.

```
Format

      1 - Justification              Left

      2 - Line Spacing               1

      3 - Top/Bottom Margins         1"         1"

      4 - Left/Right Margins         1"         1"

      5 - Tabs                       Rel; -1", every 0.5"

      6 - Header/Footer

      7 - Page Numbering             No page numbering

      8 - Paper Size                 8.5" x 11"
              Type                   Standard

      9 - Center Page (top to bottom)   No

      I - Document Initial Codes/Base Font   Courier 10cpi

  Selection: 0
```

Fig. 7.1. *The Format menu.*

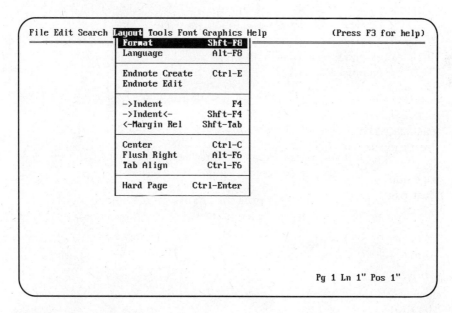

Fig. 7.2. *The Layout pull-down menu.*

Setting Top and Bottom Margins

The top margin is the distance between the top edge of the paper and the first line of text. Similarly, the bottom margin is the distance between the bottom edge of the paper and the bottom line of text.

LetterPerfect measures margins in decimal numbers; if you enter *1.5* or *1 1/2* for a margin setting, you set margins to 1 1/2 inches. By default, LetterPerfect sets the top and bottom margins at 1 inch. The program uses these margin settings for all pages in the document unless you designate new settings on the Format menu.

When you define a new top or bottom margin, LetterPerfect inserts a hidden formatting code such as **[T/B Mar:1.5",1"]**. This code controls the top and bottom margins for all pages following it in a document. The hidden top-bottom margin code controls the margins for the page on which it is located *only* if the code precedes any text characters on the page. If the code follows even one text character, its settings do not control the margins on the current page but govern the top and bottom margins of all pages after the current page.

To set top and bottom margins in a document, move the cursor to where you want margin settings to begin—ordinarily, at the beginning of the document or the top of the current page—and follow these steps:

1. Access the Layout pull-down menu and select Format. Alternatively, press Format (Shift-F8).

   LetterPerfect displays the Format menu, shown in figure 7.1.

2. Select Top/Bottom **Margins (3)**.

3. Type the value for the top margin in decimal numbers and press Enter. To keep the current measurement, press Enter.

4. Type the value for the bottom margin in decimal numbers and press Enter. To keep the current measurement, press Enter.

5. Press Exit (F7) to return to the document.

Allowing for Headers, Footers, and Page Numbers

LetterPerfect places headers, footers, and page numbers on the first line relative to a margin, not between a margin's inner edge and the edge of a page. A header begins on the first line below the page's top margin. Footers and page numbers are placed on the last line above the bottom margin. If you have a multiple-line footer, LetterPerfect places it on the page so that the bottom line of the footer is on the last line above the bottom margin. In addition, the program automatically inserts a blank line between the text of the document and a header, footer, or page number.

Consider, for example, a document that uses a fixed-pitch Courier 10-point base font and 1-inch margins. To place a single-line header that ends with a hard-return code a half-inch from the top edge of the page, you must change the top margin setting to 0.5". After LetterPerfect places the header on the page at the top margin, it adds a blank line, and text begins 1 inch from the top edge of the page.

For more information on headers and footers, see the section "Designing Headers and Footers" later in this chapter.

Hand-Feeding Pages into a Platen Printer

A platen printer rolls paper through a printer as a typewriter does. Most daisywheel and dot-matrix printers are platen printers. Often you must hand-feed sheets individually into a platen printer.

When a page is hand-fed into a printer that has a platen, LetterPerfect operates on the assumption that you insert the paper so that the print head is located at the page's top margin, usually 1 inch below the paper's top edge. When the top margin is set for 1 inch or less, LetterPerfect begins printing at the location of the print head. If, however, the top margin of the document is more than 1 inch, LetterPerfect advances the paper by the margin amount minus 1 inch before it begins printing.

For example, if the top margin is set for a half-inch, LetterPerfect does not advance the sheet before printing begins. However, when the margin is 1 1/2 inches, the page advances a half-inch before it begins printing the document.

Centering Pages Top to Bottom

With LetterPerfect you can override the top and bottom margin settings on a page and center the text between the top and bottom margins. Usually, a page centered from top to bottom is a separate page, shorter than the other pages in a document. The Center Page feature is useful for centering the title page of a report, such as that shown in figure 7.3.

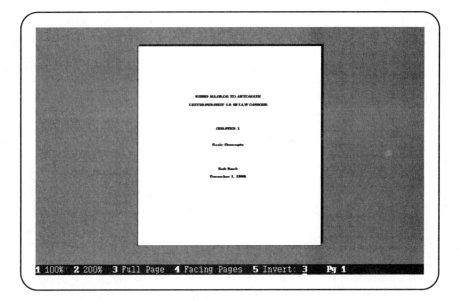

Fig. 7.3. A centered title page.

When you set margins, the settings apply to all following pages until LetterPerfect encounters a new margin setting. But when you use Center Page, the setting applies to just one page—the page on which you activate the feature. When you activate Center Page, a hidden formatting code is placed into the document at the cursor. If you view the page with Reveal Codes, the code appears as **[Center Pg]**.

This code controls the placement of text only for the current page and must precede any text characters on the page. If the code follows even one text character, LetterPerfect ignores it and does not center the text on the page.

LetterPerfect uses the margin settings of the document to calculate the end of a centered page and marks the end with the code **[SPg]**. You also can mark the end of a centered page with a hard page break (**[HPg]**) by accessing the Layout pull-down menu and selecting **H**ard Page or, alternatively, by pressing Ctrl-Enter. Ending the centered page with a hard page break guarantees that the page never merges accidentally with the text on the following page.

Follow these steps to use Center Page:

1. Move the cursor to the top of the page before any text.

2. Access the **L**ayout pull-down menu and select **F**ormat. Alternatively, press Format (Shift-F8).

   LetterPerfect displays the Format menu (see fig. 7.1).

3. Select **C**enter Page (top to bottom) (9).

4. Press **Y** to insert the hidden **[Center Pg]** code into the document at the cursor.

5. Press Exit (F7).

To deactivate Center Page, you must delete the **[Center Pg]** code. Although there are several methods for deleting this code, these steps describe the easiest method:

1. Press Home, Home, Home, up arrow to move the cursor to the top of the document before all formatting codes.

   Although the mouse also can move the cursor to the top line of the document, it *cannot* place the cursor before hidden formatting codes located in front of the text on the top line of the document. Because of this limitation, using the cursor-movement keys is quicker and easier.

2. Access the **S**earch pull-down menu and select **R**eplace. Alternatively, press Replace (Alt-F2).

   LetterPerfect displays this prompt at the lower left corner of the screen: `w/Confirm? No (Yes)`.

3. If the document contains only one hidden Center Page code, select **N**o. If there is more than one hidden Center Page code, select **Y**es.

   LetterPerfect displays the $(\rightarrow)$ `Srch:` prompt at the lower left corner of the screen.

4. Access the **Layout** pull-down menu and select **Format**. Alternatively, press Format (Shift-F8).

LetterPerfect displays the Format menu (see fig. 7.4).

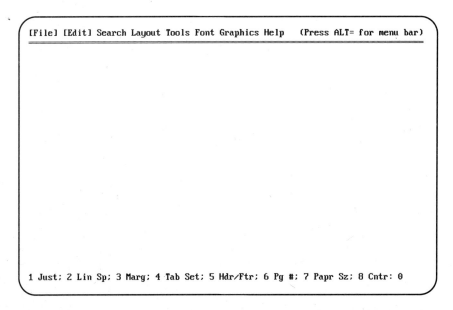
```
[File] [Edit] Search Layout Tools Font Graphics Help    (Press ALT= for menu bar)
═══════════════════════════════════════════════════════════════════════════════



1 Just; 2 Lin Sp; 3 Marg; 4 Tab Set; 5 Hdr/Ftr; 6 Pg #; 7 Papr Sz; 8 Cntr: 0
```

Fig. 7.4. *Format options available to the Search feature.*

5. Select Center Page (top to bottom) (**8**).

LetterPerfect inserts the **[Center Pg]** code after the search prompt.

6. Press Search (F2). LetterPerfect displays the `Replace with:` prompt at the lower left corner of the screen.

7. Press Search (F2). If you selected **No** in step 3, LetterPerfect automatically removes all hidden **[Center Pg]** codes in the document. If you selected **Yes** in step 3, LetterPerfect prompts you to confirm the deletion each time it finds a hidden **[Center Pg]** code.

Designing Headers and Footers

A header is a hidden code containing a block of text (or numbers or graphics) that LetterPerfect inserts at the top of a page. A footer is a hidden code containing a block of text (or numbers or graphics) that LetterPerfect inserts at the bottom of a page. LetterPerfect automatically inserts headers and footers on every page unless you insert a hidden suppress or discontinue code in the document after the header or footer code.

Each page in a document can include a header and a footer. Most of LetterPerfect's formatting features are available for formatting text in a header and footer. You can include automatic page numbering by inserting the numbering code in either a header or a footer. You can edit text in a header or footer just as you edit text on the main editing screen.

Reminder: One page can have both a header and a footer.

Headers and footers print at the top and bottom margins of pages, and LetterPerfect leaves a space of about one line between the header or footer and the text of the document. Headers and footers do not print in the space between the margins and edges of the page.

For example, if the document has a 1-inch top margin and a one-line header, LetterPerfect prints the header 1 inch from the top edge of the page, skips a line, and begins printing the text on the next line. To leave more space between the text and the header or footer, press Enter to add one or more blank lines as part of the header or footer.

LetterPerfect does not display headers or footers on the main editing screen. Follow these steps to see headers or footers on-screen as they appear on the printed page:

1. Move the cursor to the page containing the text you want to view.

2. Access the **F**ile pull-down menu, select **P**rint, and then choose **V**iew Document (**3**). Alternatively, press Print (Shift-F7) and select **V**iew Document (**3**), or press Ctrl-p.

LetterPerfect displays a graphic image of part or all of the page. Follow these steps to see the first 50 characters in a header or footer code:

1. Move the cursor to the line containing the header or footer code.

2. Access the **E**dit pull-down menu and select **R**eveal Codes. Alternatively, press Reveal Codes (Alt-F3 or F11) or Ctrl-r.

You also can edit, discontinue, delete, or suppress headers or footers so that they do not appear on certain pages.

Creating New Headers and Footers

Generally, you should create headers and footers at the beginning of a document, before any text. The hidden header or footer code must precede any text characters on the page. If the code follows even one text character, the header or footer does not appear on the current page but appears on all following pages unless you suppress or discontinue it.

Follow these steps to create a new header or footer:

1. Press Home, Home, Home, up arrow to move the cursor to the first line of the document, before all formatting codes.

   Although the mouse also can move the cursor to the top of the document, it *cannot* place the cursor before hidden formatting codes that precede the text. Using the cursor-movement keys is quicker and easier.

2. Access the Layout pull-down menu and select Format. Alternatively, press Format (Shift-F8).

3. Select Header/Footer (**6**).

   LetterPerfect displays this menu prompt at the lower left corner of the screen:

   1 Header; **2** Footer; **3** Suppress: **0**.

4. To create a header, select Header (**1**); to create a footer, select Footer (**2**).

   LetterPerfect displays a new menu prompt at the lower left corner of the screen:

   1 Discontinue; **2** Create; **3** Edit: **0**.

5. Select Create (**2**).

   LetterPerfect displays an editing screen that is blank except for the following informational bar across the bottom:

   ```
   Header:  Press F7 when done        Pg2 1 Ln 1" Pos 1"
   ```

6. Type the text of the header or footer.

You can use all of LetterPerfect's font-formatting features to enhance the text. For example, you can create a bold header or an underlined footer.

7. Press Exit (F7) to save the header or footer and redisplay the Page Format menu. Press Exit (F7) again to redisplay the document.

When viewed with the Reveal Codes feature, the hidden header and footer codes appear as shown in figure 7.5. Depending on whether the text contains formatting codes, you also can see approximately the first 50 characters of text in the header or footer. When viewed with the View Document feature, the header and footer appear on the page as shown in figure 7.6.

```
 File Edit Search Layout Tools Font Graphics Help        (Press ALT= for menu bar)

 Generally, you should create headers and footers at the beginning
 of a document, before any text. The hidden header or footer code
 must precede any text characters on the page. If the code follows
 even one text character, the header or footer does not appear o n
 the current page but appears on all following pages unless you
 suppress or discontue it.

 Follow these steps to create a new header or footer:

                                                    Pg 1 Ln 1.33" Pos 1"
 [   ▲   ▲                                                            ]
 [Tab Set:Rel; +0.3",+0.6"][Header A:Every page;[Center][ITALC]USING LETTERPERFEC
 T 1.0[italc]][Footer A:Every page;CHAPTER 7[Flsh Rgt]PAGE ^B]Generally, you shou
 ld create headers and footers at the beginning[SRt]
 of a document, before any text. The hidden header or footer code[SRt]
 must precede any text characters on the page. If the code follows[SRt]
 even one text character, the header or footer does not appear o n[SRt]
 the current page but appears on all following pages unless you[SRt]
 suppress or discontue it.[HRt]
 [HRt]
 Follow these steps to create a new header or footer:[HRt]

 Press Reveal Codes to restore screen
```

Fig. 7.5. *Header and footer codes displayed with the Reveal Codes feature.*

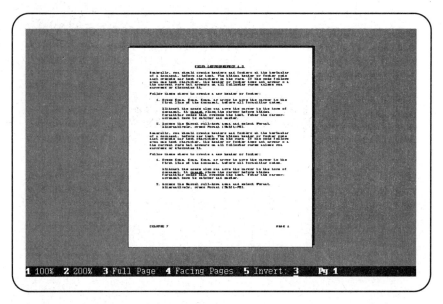

Fig. 7.6. A page with a header and footer displayed with the View Document feature.

> ***Caution:*** If a page contains two or more consecutive header codes or footer codes, LetterPerfect ignores the first code and uses the second or last code for the header or footer. If, however, one or more characters separate the two codes, LetterPerfect places the header or footer created by the first code on the current page and places the header or footer created by the second code on the pages following the current page.

Including Automatic Page Numbering in a Header or Footer

You can include automatic page numbering in a header or footer in addition to formatting the text. These steps show you how to create a header or footer that automatically numbers each page:

1. Perform steps 1 through 5 listed in "Creating New Headers and Footers," which precedes this section. For the purposes of this exercise, select the Footer (2) option.

2. Access the Font pull-down menu bar and select **Bold**. Alternatively, press Bold (F6) or Ctrl-b.

3. Type *REPORT ON EXPANSION OPTIONS*.

4. Access the **Layout** pull-down menu bar and select Flush Right. Alternatively, press Flush Right (Alt-F6).

5. Type *PAGE:* and press the space bar.

6. Access the **Font** pull-down menu bar and select **Characters**. Alternatively, press Ctrl-v.

   LetterPerfect displays the message Key= prompt in the lower left corner of the screen.

7. Press Ctrl-b.

   LetterPerfect inserts the ⌃B numbering code, as shown in figure 7.7.

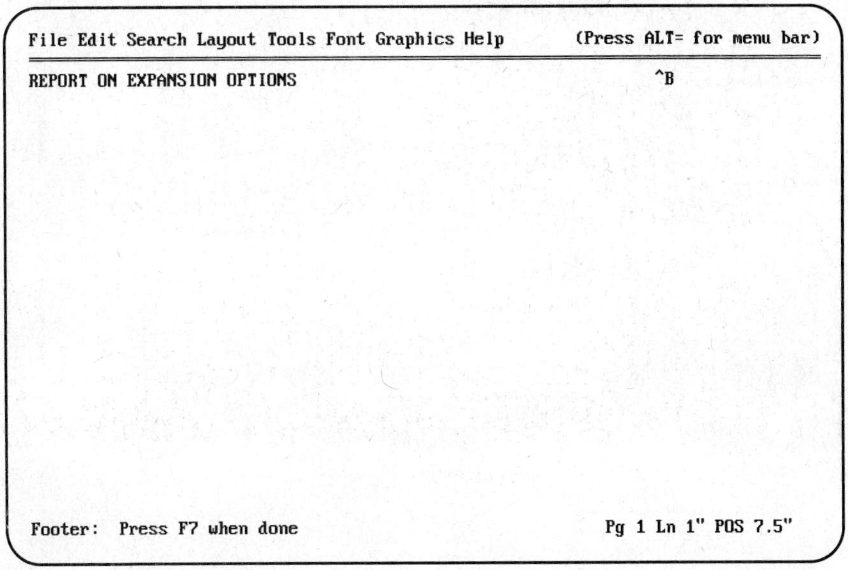

```
 File Edit Search Layout Tools Font Graphics Help      (Press ALT= for menu bar)

 REPORT ON EXPANSION OPTIONS                                      ^B
```

```
 Footer:  Press F7 when done                     Pg 1 Ln 1" POS 7.5"
```

Fig. 7.7. A footer with an automatic-page-numbering code.

> **Caution:** If you press Ctrl-b without first pressing Ctrl-v, LetterPerfect considers Ctrl-b the fast-key combination that activates Bold. If Ctrl-v does not precede Ctrl-b, LetterPerfect inserts the paired **[BOLD][bold]** codes instead of the ^B numbering code.

8. Press Exit (F7) twice to return to the main editing screen.

9. Display the document by accessing the **F**ile pull-down menu bar and selecting **P**rint. Alternatively, press Print (Shift-F7) or Ctrl-p.

10. Select **V**iew Document (**3**).

    LetterPerfect displays the footer, as shown in figure 7.8.

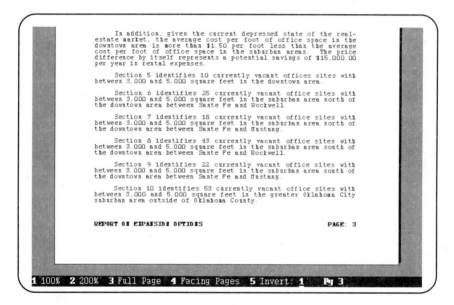

Fig. 7.8. *A footer with automatic page numbering.*

> **Tip:** LetterPerfect's automatic-page-numbering feature does not let you define a style—such as *-2-*—for the page number it places at the bottom of a sheet. You can, however, define a style by using a footer. For example, you can create the code shown at the beginning of this tip by entering these codes when a footer is defined: **[Center]-^B-.**
>
> See "Activating and Positioning Page Numbers" later in this chapter for more information on LetterPerfect's page-numbering capabilities.

Caution: Ending a header or footer with a **[HRt]** causes LetterPerfect to insert an extra line after the header or footer. This means that a header is separated from the main text by two lines instead of one and that the last line of a footer is placed one line above the bottom margin instead of on the bottom line.

Editing Headers and Footers

After you create a header or footer, you can edit its text and formatting.

To edit a header or footer, follow these steps:

1. Access the Layout pull-down menu and select Format. Alternatively, press Format (Shift-F8).

2. Select Header/Footer (**6**).

   LetterPerfect displays this menu prompt at the lower left corner of the screen:

   1 Header; **2** Footer; **3** Suppress: **0**.

3. To edit a header, select **Header** (**1**); to edit a footer, select Footer (**2**). For the purposes of this exercise, select Footer (**2**).

   LetterPerfect displays a new menu prompt at the lower left corner of the screen:

   1 Discontinue; **2** Create; **3** Edit: **0**.

4. Select Edit (**3**).

   LetterPerfect displays the footer with the cursor positioned under the first formatting code or character. Edit the text or formatting as necessary.

5. Press Exit (F7) twice to return to the main editing screen.

Discontinuing Headers and Footers

LetterPerfect uses a hidden formatting code to deactivate the header and footer feature. The hidden formatting code must precede any text characters on the page. If the code follows even one text character, the header or footer prints on the current page but does not appear on any page following the current page.

Follow these steps to discontinue a header or footer:

1. Access the Layout pull-down menu and select Format. Alternatively, press Format (Shift-F8).

2. Select **Header/Footer (6)**.

   LetterPerfect displays this menu prompt at the lower left corner of the screen:

   1 Header; **2** Footer; **3** Suppress: **0**.

3. To discontinue a header, select **Header (1)**; to discontinue a footer, select **Footer (2)**. For the purposes of this exercise, select **Footer (2)**.

   LetterPerfect displays a new menu prompt at the lower left corner of the screen:

   1 Discontinue; **2** Create; **3** Edit: **0**.

4. Select **Discontinue (1)**.

   LetterPerfect inserts a **[Footer A:Discontinue]** code at the cursor in the main document.

5. Press Exit (F7).

Suppressing Headers and Footers

LetterPerfect uses a hidden formatting code to suppress a header and footer on the current page. This code is active only for the current page and must precede any text characters on the page. If the code follows even one text character, LetterPerfect ignores the code and does not suppress the header or footer on any page.

Follow these steps to suppress a header or footer:

1. Access the **Search** pull-down menu bar and select **GoTo**. Alternatively, press GoTo (Ctrl-Home).

2. Type the number of the page on which you want to suppress the header or footer and press Enter.

   Although the mouse also can move the cursor to the top of a page, it *cannot* place the cursor before hidden formatting codes that precede the text. Because of this limitation, using GoTo is quicker and easier.

3. Access the **Layout** pull-down menu and select **Format**. Alternatively, press **Format** (Shift-F8).

4. Select **Header/Footer (6)**.

   LetterPerfect displays a menu prompt at the lower left corner of the screen:

   1 Header; **2** Footer; **3** Suppress: **0**.

5. Select **Suppress (3)**.

   LetterPerfect displays this menu prompt at the lower left corner of the screen: **Suppress:**

   1 Header; **2** Footer; **3 Both: 0**.

6. Select the suppression option to be used on the current page.

   LetterPerfect inserts a hidden suppression code at the cursor in the document. When the program displays the suppression codes with Reveal Codes, they look like this:

   [Suppress:Header]

   [Suppress:Footer]

   [Suppress:Header,Footer]

7. Press **Exit** (F7).

Searching for Text in Headers and Footers

LetterPerfect's Search feature automatically includes text in headers and footers during its operation. Search offers a quick way to find specific headers and footers. Follow these steps to search for text in a header or footer:

1. Access the **Search** pull-down menu and select **Forward** or **Backward**. Alternatively, press **Search** (F2) or **Backward Search** (Shift-F2).

   Depending on which search option you select, LetterPerfect displays the forward-search ($\rightarrow$) `Srch:` or backward-search ($\leftarrow$) `Srch:` prompt at the lower left corner of the screen. If you previously used Search or Replace, the prompt includes the previous search string as a default. If you type a character without first using a cursor-movement key, the previous search string disappears. If, however, you move the cursor even one character before you type a character, LetterPerfect operates on the assumption that you want to edit the previous search string and does not delete it.

> ***Tip:*** After you select a search option, you can reverse its direction by pressing an arrow key. The up arrow changes a forward search to a backward search. The down arrow changes a backward search to a forward search. If you use this method to change the search direction before you enter a search string, you must delete the previous search string manually.

2. Type the text for the search string and press Search (F2).

   A search string entered in lowercase letters matches text that has either upper- or lowercase characters. A search string entered in uppercase letters matches text that has only uppercase characters. LetterPerfect searches through headers, footers, and endnotes to find text matching the string. When it finds matching text, LetterPerfect places the cursor immediately right of the last character or hidden formatting code in the matching string.

3. If the search stops with the cursor in a header or footer, press Exit (F7) once to return to the main editing screen. You also can press Search (F2) or Backward Search (Shift-F2) to begin a new search.

4. When the program cannot find a matching text string, it displays a * Not found * message prompt at the lower left corner of the screen.

Replacing Text in Headers and Footers

LetterPerfect's Replace feature automatically includes text in headers and footers. Follow these steps to replace text in a header or footer:

1. Access the **Search** pull-down menu and select **R**eplace. Alternatively, press Replace (Alt-F2).

   LetterPerfect displays this menu prompt at the lower left corner of the screen: w/Confirm? No (Yes).

2. If you want Replace to operate without confirming each text replacement, select **N**o. If you want to approve of each replacement, select **Y**es.

LetterPerfect displays the (→) Srch: prompt. If you previously used either Search or Replace, the prompt includes the previous search string as a default. If you type a character without first using a cursor-movement key, the previous search string disappears. If, however, you move the cursor even one character before you type a character, LetterPerfect acts as if you want to edit the previous search string and does not delete it.

Tip: On its menus, LetterPerfect offers a replacement operation only between the current location of the cursor and the end of the document. To operate Replace from the cursor to the beginning of the document, press the up arrow while the →Srch: prompt is displayed on the screen. If you use this method to change the search direction before you enter a search string, you must delete the previous search string manually.

3. Type the text for the search string and press Search (F2).

   A search string entered in lowercase letters matches text that has either upper- or lowercase characters. A search string entered in uppercase letters matches text that has only uppercase characters. LetterPerfect searches through headers, footers, and endnotes to find text matching the string.

   LetterPerfect displays a menu prompt in the lower left corner of the screen: Replace with:.

4. Type the text for the replacement string and press Search (F2).

   LetterPerfect begins the replacement operation. When it finds a matching text string, LetterPerfect places the cursor immediately right of the last character in the matching string. If you selected **Yes** in step 2, the program pauses and displays this menu prompt in the lower left corner of the screen when it finds matching text: Confirm? No (Yes).

5. Select **Yes** to replace the original text. Select **No** to leave the original text intact and resume the search for matching text strings.

6. When the program cannot find a matching text string, it displays a * Not found * message in the lower left corner of the screen. The replacement operation stops, and the cursor remains at the location of the last replacement.

7. If the replacement operation stops with the cursor in a header or footer, press Exit (F7) once to return to the main editing screen.

Including Graphics in Headers and Footers

You can include a graphic image or box as part of a header or footer. Use a box around a footer, for example, to call attention to a page number. Or include a previously drawn logo in a header to create stationery for your business. Follow these general steps to add a graphic element to your document:

1. Access the Layout pull-down menu and select Format. Alternatively, press Format (Shift-F8).

2. Select Header/Footer (**6**).

   LetterPerfect displays a menu prompt in the lower left corner of the screen:

   1 Header; **2** Footer; **3** Suppress: **0**.

3. To create a header, select Header (**1**); to create a footer, select Footer (**2**). For this purposes of this exercise, select Footer (**2**).

   LetterPerfect displays this new menu prompt in the lower left corner of the screen:

   1 Discontinue; **2** Create; **3** Edit: **0**.

4. Select Create (**2**).

   LetterPerfect displays a blank editing screen.

5. Access the Graphics pull-down menu bar and select Create (**1**). Alternatively, press Graphic (Alt-F9) or Ctrl-g.

   LetterPerfect displays the Graphics Definition menu shown in figure 7.9.

6. Use the methods described in Chapter 15 to retrieve and edit a graphics image.

7. Press Exit (F7) twice to return to the main editing screen.

```
Graphics Definition

    1 - Filename

    2 - Horizontal Position   Right

    3 - Size                  3.25" wide x 3.25" (high)

    4 - Wrap Text Around Box  Yes

    5 - Border                Yes

        Note: Each time you specify a border option,
              a figure option code ([Fig Opt]) is inserted
              in your document.  This code affects all
              subsequent figures until LetterPerfect
              encounters another figure option code.




Selection: 0
```

Fig. 7.9. *The Graphics Definition menu.*

Activating and Positioning Page Numbers

By default, LetterPerfect's Page Numbering feature is inactive when you begin creating a document. When the feature is active, it numbers pages consecutively with Arabic numerals. You can do these activities with Page Numbering:

- Designate whether the feature is active or inactive.

- Designate one of six locations for placing the page number on the sheet.

- Define the appearance of the page number (in a header or footer only).

You cannot do these activities with Page Numbering:

- Define a Roman-numeral numbering style

- Change the number of a page (page 1 must always be page 1, page 2 must always be page 2, and so on)

- Define the appearance of the page number outside of a header or footer

- Define automatic-page-number placement for odd and even pages

When you activate Page Numbering, the program inserts a hidden formatting code at the cursor. The code must precede any text characters on the page. If the code follows even one text character, the page number does not appear on the current page but appears on all following pages unless you discontinue the code.

Follow these steps to activate Page Numbering for a single document, beginning on the first page:

1. Press Home, Home, Home, up arrow to move the cursor to the top of the document, before all formatting codes.

   Although the mouse also can move the cursor to the top of the document, it *cannot* place the cursor before hidden formatting codes that precede the text. Because of this limitation, using the cursor-movement keys is quicker and easier.

2. Access the **Layout** pull-down menu and select **Format**. Alternatively, press Format (Shift-F8).

   LetterPerfect displays the main Format menu.

3. Select **Page Numbering (7)**.

   LetterPerfect displays the Format: Page Number Position menu, shown in figure 7.10.

4. Choose one of the six page positions by selecting its number. For the purposes of this exercise, choose **5**.

   LetterPerfect inserts this hidden formatting code at the cursor in the main document: **[Pg Numbering:Bottom Center]**.

   The program redisplays the main Format menu. The **Page** Numbering **(7)** option specifies Bottom Center.

5. Press Exit (F7) to return to the main editing screen.

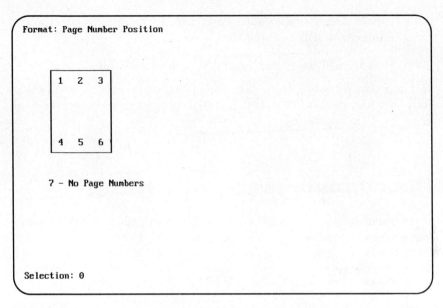

Fig. 7.10. *The Format: Page Number Position menu.*

Use the following procedure to change the program default so that automatic page numbering is active when you begin creating a document:

1. Access the **F**ile pull-down menu bar and select Se**t**up. Alternatively, press Setup (Shift-F1).

   LetterPerfect displays the Setup menu.

2. Select **I**nitial Code (**5**).

   LetterPerfect displays an editing screen that resembles the main editing screen with Reveal Codes active.

3. Access the **L**ayout pull-down menu and select **F**ormat. Alternatively, press Format (Shift-F8).

4. Select **P**age Numbering (**7**).

   LetterPerfect displays the Format: Page Number Position menu, shown in figure 7.10.

5. Choose one of the six page positions by selecting its number. For the purposes of this exercise, choose **5**.

LetterPerfect inserts the formatting code **[Pg Numbering:Bottom Center]** and returns to the Format menu.

6. Press Exit (F7) three times to return to the main editing screen.

The next time you run LetterPerfect or clear the screen, all documents you create will have page numbers at the bottom center of each sheet unless you deactivate Page Numbering.

Discontinuing Page Numbering

When you deactivate Page Numbering, the program inserts a hidden formatting code at the cursor. You must place the hidden code before any text characters on the page. If the code follows even one text character, page numbering does not stop on the current page but stops on the page after the current page.

Follow these steps to deactivate automatic Page Numbering for one or more pages:

1. Access the **S**earch pull-down menu and select **G**oTo. Alternatively, press GoTo (Ctrl-Home).

2. Type the number of the page where you want to deactivate automatic page numbering. Press Enter.

   Although the mouse also can move the cursor to the top of a page, it *cannot* place the cursor before hidden formatting codes that precede the text. Because of this limitation, using GoTo is quicker and easier.

3. Access the **L**ayout pull-down menu and select **F**ormat. Alternatively, press Format (Shift-F8).

   LetterPerfect displays the main Format menu.

4. Select **P**age Numbering (7).

   LetterPerfect displays the Format: Page Number Position menu, shown in figure 7.10.

5. Select **N**o Page Numbers (7).

LetterPerfect inserts this hidden formatting code at the cursor in the main document: **[Pg Numbering:No page numbering]**.

The program redisplays the main Format menu. The **P**age Numbering (**7**) option lists `No Page Numbering`.

6. Press Exit (F7) to return to the main editing screen.

Preventing Widows and Orphans

LetterPerfect uses the margin settings to calculate the amount of text that fits on a single page. When one page is full, a new page begins. LetterPerfect's Widow/Orphan Protection feature prevents widows (a single line from a paragraph placed at the top of a page) and orphans (a single line from a paragraph remaining at the bottom of a page).

The Widow/Orphan Protection feature prevents widows and orphans by keeping at least two lines of a paragraph at the top and bottom of a page. If only the first line of a paragraph can fit at the bottom of a page, LetterPerfect moves the line to the top of the next page. If all but the last line of a paragraph fits at the bottom of a page, the program moves the last two lines to the top of the following page. If the split paragraph consists of only three lines, LetterPerfect places all three lines at the top of the next page.

Widow/Orphan Protection is permanently active and cannot be deactivated. The hidden {**W/O On**} code in the program's Initial Codes setting makes LetterPerfect documents compatible with the defaults in WordPerfect 5.1. Deleting the code does *not* deactivate this protection feature.

Understanding Soft and Hard Page Breaks

You can use two methods for dividing text between pages:

- Automatic page breaks—marked by the hidden formatting code **[SPg]** or **[HRt-SPg]**—calculated automatically by the program from the document's margin and font settings

- Manual page breaks—marked by the hidden formatting code **[HPg]**—that you insert by pressing Ctrl-Enter

Using Soft Page Breaks

Reminder:
LetterPerfect
automatically
recalculates a
soft page when
you add to or
delete from the
text in the
document.

LetterPerfect inserts a hidden soft page break at the end of a page of text (or when the program encounters a protected widow or orphan paragraph line). Text then continues on the following page. When you add or delete text, soft page breaks are automatically recalculated so that pages always break correctly.

LetterPerfect displays a soft page break as a single-dashed line on the main editing screen. When you view the document by using Reveal Codes—access the Edit pull-down menu and select Reveal Codes or, alternatively, press Revcal Codes (Alt-F3 or F11) or Ctrl-r—LetterPerfect displays a soft page break as either **[SPg]** or **[HRt-SPg]**.

Note: A soft page break is represented by the code **[SPg]** unless the page break was originally a hard-return code—**[HRt]**. In that case, the code is **[HRt-SPg]**.

> *Tip:* An undocumented LetterPerfect feature lets you search for the **[SPg]** codes. This capability has a practical application for macros such as the PAGENUM macro described in Chapter 13.
>
> Follow these steps to create the **[SPg]** code in a search operation:
>
> 1. At the (→) Srch: or (←) Srch: prompt, access the Font pull-down menu and select **Characters**. Alternatively, hold down the Ctrl key and press V. At the bottom left corner of the screen, LetterPerfect displays the prompt Key=.
>
> 2. Hold down the Ctrl key and press K. LetterPerfect inserts the **[SPg]** code into the search string.

Using Hard Page Breaks

Reminder:
A hard page
break forces the
page to break at
a particular
point.

To force a page to break at a certain spot—for example, at the beginning of a new section in a report—enter a hard page break. The page always breaks there, no matter what.

LetterPerfect displays a hard page break as a double-dashed line on the main editing screen. When you view the document with Reveal Codes—access the Edit pull-down menu and select Reveal Codes or, alternatively, press Reveal Codes (Alt-F3 or F11) or Ctrl-r—LetterPerfect displays a hard page break as **[HPg]**.

To insert a hard page break, move the cursor immediately right of the last character or hidden formatting code you want on the current page. Access the **Layout** pull-down menu bar and select **Hard Page** or, alternatively, press Ctrl-Enter. Text and formatting codes immediately right of the cursor move from the current page to the top of the next page.

Delete the **[HPg]** code to restore the program to automatic-page-break operation. Although you can use several methods to delete this code, this is the easiest one:

1. Use the mouse or the cursor-movement keys to move the cursor above the **[HPg]** code.

2. Access the **S**earch pull-down menu and select **R**eplace. Alternatively, press Replace (Alt-F2).

   LetterPerfect displays this prompt in the lower left corner of the screen: w/Confirm? No (Yes).

3. If the document contains only one hidden **[HPg]** code, select **N**o. If there is more than one hidden hard page code, select **Y**es.

   LetterPerfect displays the (→) Srch: prompt in the lower left corner of the screen.

4. Press Ctrl-Enter.

   LetterPerfect inserts the **[HPg]** code after the search prompt.

5. Press Search (F2).

   LetterPerfect displays the Replace with: prompt in the lower left corner of the screen.

6. Press Enter.

   LetterPerfect inserts the **[HRt]** code after the search prompt.

7. Press Search (F2).

   If you selected **N**o in step 3, LetterPerfect automatically removes all **[HPg]** codes in the document. If you selected **Y**es in step 3, LetterPerfect prompts you to confirm the deletion each time it finds a hidden **[HPg]** code.

You also can manually delete a hard page code by doing the following:

- Moving the cursor to the beginning of the line just below the double-dashed line and pressing Backspace

- Moving the cursor to the last space before the double-dashed line and pressing Del

Press Enter to insert a **[HRt]** code to separate the text on either side of the cursor.

Understanding Paper Size/Type

In LetterPerfect, you must specify the size, type, orientation, and location (in the printer) of the paper for printing. The paper may be letterhead or legal-sized sheets of standard-size paper on which the text prints in typical portrait (vertical) orientation. Or the paper may be a business envelope, measuring only 4 by 9 1/2 inches, that LetterPerfect prints in landscape (horizontal) orientation.

Modifying and Using Printer Forms

To turn your on-screen or on-disk document into a printed document, LetterPerfect must know the make and model of your printer and the characteristics of the paper on which you want the document printed. The make and model of your printer are defined in a PRS file selected through the LetterPerfect installation program or copied from WordPerfect 5.1. If the correct PRS file is not installed or copied onto your system, refer to Chapter 1 and follow its instructions for selecting and installing a printer definition before you continue with this section.

When you install the printer definition from the program disks, LetterPerfect automatically installs the {LP}SPC.FRM file. This file contains variable information defining the format of different forms available for the printer. When you copy a WordPerfect 5.1 PRS file, the variable information defining the format of different forms available for the printer is included as part of the PRS file. These predefined forms (sometimes called *templates*) include definitions for each type of sheet (page, envelope, or label) available for the printer.

You cannot define additional permanent forms for your printer. You can, however, change some of the parameters for the permanent form definitions by specifying an option on the Format menu. You can define a customized, temporary form as explained in the section, "Defining and Using Temporary Printer Forms," following this section.

> *Tip:* At the same time it released the 11/01/90 interim software, WordPerfect Corporation began selling a separate set of LetterPerfect Supplementary diskettes that include an expanded {LP}SPC.FRM file with additional forms.
>
> In addition, although the LetterPerfect program does not let you create additional permanent forms, if you also own WordPerfect 5.1 you can use its PTR program to modify LetterPerfect PRS files to add additional permanent forms. The LetterPerfect Supplementary diskettes also include the PTR program. Also, if the PRS file was copied from WordPerfect 5.1, you can use that program to create new forms in the LetterPerfect 1.0 PRS file.
>
> For information on creating and editing form definitions with WordPerfect 5.1, see Que's *Using WordPerfect 5.1*, Special Edition. For information on using the PTR program, see the WordPerfect 5.1 manual and *WordPerfect Printer Definition Program: A Technical Reference*, each available from WordPerfect Corporation.

Note: The menus shown as figures in the following section may differ from the menus displayed on your screen. The differences, if any, are limited to optional variables, which you can change. All fixed menu options should match those shown in the figures.

When you select a printer form, LetterPerfect inserts a hidden formatting code at the cursor in the document. This code must precede any text characters on the page. If the code follows even one text character, LetterPerfect does not use the code to format the current page but formats all following pages with the parameters of the code.

To use the printer definitions, follow these steps:

1. Press Home, Home, Home, up arrow to move the cursor to the top of the document, before all formatting codes.

   Although the mouse also can move the cursor to the top of the document, it *cannot* place the cursor before hidden formatting codes that precede the text. Because of this limitation, using cursor-movement keys is quicker and easier.

2. Access the **L**ayout pull-down menu and select **F**ormat. Alternatively, press Format (Shift-F8).

LetterPerfect displays the Format menu.

3. Select Paper Size (**8**).

LetterPerfect displays the Paper Size/Type menu, shown in figure 7.11. Table 7.1 describes each category listed in the menu.

```
Format: Paper Size/Type

Paper type and Orientation    Paper Size      Location    Font Type   Labels

1 X 1 Labels - Wide           4" x 1"         Bin 1       Portrait    1 x 1
3 X 10 Labels                 8.5" x 11"      Bin 1       Portrait    3 x 10
A3 Standard                   11.69" x 16.54  Bin 1       Portrait
A4 Envelope - Wide            8.58" x 4.33"   Manual      Portrait
A4 Labels                     8.27" x 11.69"  Continuous  Portrait    2 x 7
A4 Standard                   8.27" x 11.69"  Continuous  Portrait
A4 Standard - Wide            11.69" x 8.27"  Continuous  Portrait
Envelope - Wide               9.5" x 4"       Manual      Portrait
Half Sheet                    5.5" x 8.5"     Continuous  Portrait
Standard                      8.22" x 12"     Continuous  Portrait
Standard                      8.5" x 11"      Bin 1       Portrait
Standard                      8.5" x 14"      Continuous  Portrait
Standard - Wide               11" x 8.5"      Continuous  Portrait
Standard - Wide               14" x 8.5"      Continuous  Portrait
[ALL OTHERS]                  Width ≤ 14"     Manual



1 Select; 2 Edit; N Name Search: 1
```

Fig. 7.11. *The Paper Size/Type menu.*

Table 7.1
Headings in the Paper Size/Type Menu

Heading	*Explanation*
Paper type and Orientation	The name of the form. If the width of the sheet exceeds its height, the name includes the descriptive term *Wide*. You cannot modify this parameter.
Paper Size	The actual dimensions of the sheet on which LetterPerfect prints the document. You cannot modify this parameter.
Location	A description of how the paper comes into the printer. *Manual* means that the user inserts each sheet. *Continuous* means that the paper is on a

Heading	Explanation
	roll and fed by a tractor feeder. *Continuous* also is used for laser printers with a single paper tray. *Bin* refers to one or more cassettes that contain paper and are inserted in a feeder attached to the printer. With multiple-bin sheet feeders, LetterPerfect automatically selects the paper from the bin designated for the form. You can modify this parameter by selecting the Edit (**2**) option.
Font Type	A description of whether LetterPerfect prints with characters in portrait (parallel) or landscape (perpendicular) orientation, relative to the insertion edge of the paper. This setting has meaning only for certain types of printers, primarily laser printers.

Most laser printers accept paper sizes of only 8 1/2 or fewer inches as the insertion edge. Font Type tells LetterPerfect whether to print the text lines parallel or perpendicular to the insertion edge of the paper. After you define the form and select it for a document, LetterPerfect automatically limits the Base Font choices to those fonts in the orientation designated under Font Type. |
| Labels | A description of whether the form is in a label format. LetterPerfect uses this information to simplify the creation and printing of labels. |

4. Use the arrow keys to move the cursor bar to the form you want to use.

Tip: You may use **N**ame Search and begin typing the name of the form until the cursor bar highlights the form. You also may use the PgDn, PgUp, Screen Up (keyboard –), and Screen Down (keyboard +) keys to scroll through the list. These keys are especially useful when the available-forms list has more entries than can be displayed on-screen.

5. Choose **S**elect (**1**).

You return to the main Format menu.

6. Press Exit (F7).

You return to the main editing screen.

When you use Reveal Codes—access the Edit pull-down menu and select **R**eveal Codes or, alternatively, press Reveal Codes (Alt-F3 or F11) or Ctrl-r—LetterPerfect displays a typical printer-definition code such as this one: **[Paper Sz/Typ:8.5" x 11", Standard]**.

Tip: Press Exit (F7), Cancel (F1), or Esc twice to exit from the Paper Size/Type menu and return to the main editing screen without selecting a form definition.

Tip: Chapter 13 describes how to define a macro that automates the process of selecting a printer-definition form.

Follow these steps to modify a form definition:

1. Access the Layout pull-down menu and select Format. Alternatively, press Format (Shift-F8).

   LetterPerfect displays the Format menu.

2. Select Paper **S**ize (**8**).

   LetterPerfect displays the Paper Size/Type menu, shown in figure 7.11.

3. Select **E**dit (**2**).

   LetterPerfect displays the Format: Edit Paper Definition menu, shown in figure 7.12.

4. Press **L**ocation (**1**).

   LetterPerfect displays this menu prompt at the bottom of the screen:

   Location: 1 Continuous; **2 B**in Number; **3 M**anual: **0**

   The default setting is Continuous (**1**), the selection for a printer that uses continuous paper inserted by a tractor feed or a laser printer with a single bin, such as the HP LaserJet Series II. Choose **B**in Number (**2**) if sheets are inserted individually by a feeder from one or more cassettes. Choose **Manual (3)** if sheets are inserted by hand. For this exercise, assume that your printer has a sheet feeder and that the paper is drawn from bin (cassette) number 1.

5. Select **Bin Number (2)**.

   LetterPerfect displays the prompt `Bin number:` at the bottom of the screen.

6. Press 1 and then press Enter.

   The default for **Location (1)** changes to Bin 1.

7. To be prompted to hand-feed paper into the printer, choose **Prompt to Load (2)**. LetterPerfect displays the prompt `No (Yes)`. Select **Yes**.

When the prompt option is set to **Yes**, LetterPerfect prompts you to insert a sheet for each page in the document, and the program does not print until you give it a **Go** command. For this section, assume that you do not want the program to prompt you to hand-feed sheets into the printer.

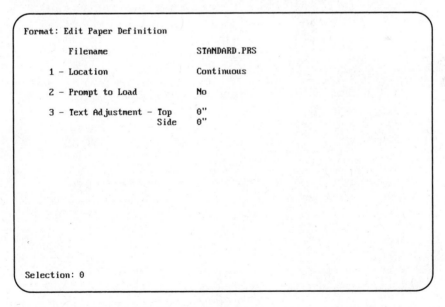

```
Format: Edit Paper Definition

        Filename                STANDARD.PRS

   1 - Location                 Continuous

   2 - Prompt to Load           No

   3 - Text Adjustment - Top    0"
                        Side    0"

















Selection: 0
```

Fig. 7.12. The Format: Edit Paper Definition menu.

When you use a form, you may need to move the printed image horizontally or vertically on the sheet. Make major changes (changes of a quarter-inch or more) by adjusting the printer's hardware settings. If minor changes (changes of less than a quarter-inch) are required or if the printer's hardware cannot make the major changes, LetterPerfect offers a way to fine-tune the placement of the printed image on the sheet.

With the option for Text Adjustment-Top (3), you can move text on the sheet. Up and down options move text vertically on the sheet. Left and right options move text horizontally on the sheet.

Consider this example: LetterPerfect prints a full page of text with a standard 8.5-by-11-inch portrait form with 1-inch margins. When the document prints, however, the top margin is 1.35", and its left margin is 0.9". Instead of resetting margin settings to reposition the printing area, use the text-adjustment option. Table 7.2 explains how to calculate adjustment values.

Table 7.2
Calculating Text Adjustments

If the text prints with this:	*Adjust this way:*
Top line below designated top margin	Subtract the actual location of the top line relative to the top edge of the sheet from the top margin value; enter the result as the value for the Up (1) option.
Top line above designated top margin	Subtract the actual location of the top line relative to the top edge of the sheet from the top margin value; enter the result as the value for the Down (2) option.
Left edge to right of designated left margin	Subtract the measurement for actual location of text relative to the left edge of the sheet from the top margin value; enter the result as the value for the Left (3) option.
Left edge to left of designated left margin	Subtract the measurement for the actual location of text relative to the left edge of the sheet from the top margin value; enter the result as the value for the Right (4) option.

After you calculate the amount of adjustment required for the document in the preceding example, follow these steps to adjust the location of the text:

1. Select **Text** Adjustment-Top (**3**).

   LetterPerfect displays this menu prompt across the bottom of the screen:

   Adjust Text: 1 Up; **2** Down; **3** Left; **4** Right: **0**.

2. Select **Up** (**1**).

   LetterPerfect displays this menu prompt at the lower left corner of the screen: Text Adjustment Distance: 0".

3. Enter *0.35* and press Enter.

4. Repeat step 1.

5. Select **Right** (**4**).

   LetterPerfect displays this menu prompt in the lower left corner of the screen: Text Adjustment Distance: 0".

6. Enter *0.1* and press Enter.

   After you make the adjustments, the Format: Edit Paper Definition menu appears as shown in figure 7.13.

```
Format: Edit Paper Definition

        Filename              STANDARD.PRS

    1 - Location              Continuous

    2 - Prompt to Load        No

    3 - Text Adjustment - Top    0.35"  Up
                          Side   0.1"   Right












Selection: 0
```

Fig. 7.13. The Format: Edit Paper Definition menu showing adjustments to the text locations.

Tip: LetterPerfect automatically converts fractional numbers such as 1/10" into decimal equivalents—0.1" in this example.

Defining and Using Temporary Printer Forms

Reminder: You can define temporary as well as permanent print forms.

You can define a temporary form that is available only during the current editing session. To define a temporary form, follow these steps:

1. Access the Layout pull-down menu and select Format. Alternatively, press Format (Shift-F8).

   LetterPerfect displays the Format menu.

2. Select **Paper Size (8)**

   LetterPerfect displays the Paper Size/Type menu.

3. Move the cursor to the [ALL OTHERS] form.

4. To edit the settings for location or prompt (the default for this form is **Yes**), select Edit and use the methods described in the section "Modifying and Using Printer Forms." Otherwise, skip to step 5.

5. Choose **Select (1)**.

   LetterPerfect displays this menu prompt at the lower left corner of the screen: `Width: 8.5"`.

6. Press Enter to accept the default 8.5" value, or type a different value and press Enter. For this exercise, press 5 and then press Enter.

   LetterPerfect displays this menu prompt in the lower left corner of the screen: `Height: 11"`.

7. Press Enter to accept the default 8.5" value, or type a different value and press Enter. For this exercise, press 8 and then press Enter.

   LetterPerfect displays this menu prompt in the lower left corner of the screen: `Other form type:`.

8. Type a name and press Enter. For this section, type *Booklet* and press Enter.

LetterPerfect returns to the Format menu.

9. Press Exit (F7) to return to the main editing screen.

When you use Reveal Codes—access the Edit pull-down menu and select Reveal Codes or, alternatively, press Reveal Codes (Alt-F3 or F11) or Ctrl-r—LetterPerfect displays the code this way: **[Paper Sz/Typ:5" x 8", Booklet]**.

Because the definition is temporary, it does not appear on the list of permanent forms. Although this definition is not saved as a permanent form type available from the Format menu, the code remains in the document and active if you save the document to disk.

After you print the document with the temporary form definition, use this method if you need to adjust the location of the text on the page:

1. Move the cursor immediately right of the form's code in the document.

2. Repeat steps 1 through 4 from the preceding set of directions.

3. Edit the settings of the form.

4. Repeat steps 5 through 9 from the preceding set of directions. You can press Enter at the width and height prompts because the default width and height values are the new values you entered when you created the form definition.

> *Tip:* Chapter 13 also describes a macro that automatically creates temporary printer-definition forms.

Using a Temporary Printer-Definition Form as a Template

Although LetterPerfect does not let you save the temporary printer-definition form definitions with permanent form definitions, you can save the code in a file that serves as a template for multiple documents. You also can include additional hidden formatting codes and text with the template.

The following example is based on the assumption that you have created the temporary Booklet printer-definition form, described in the previous section.

Use the following steps to create the Booklet template:

1. Access the **File** pull-down menu and select **S**ave. Alternatively, press Save (F10). At the bottom of the screen, LetterPerfect displays the prompt `Document to be saved:`.

2. Type *booklet.tmp* and press Enter.

When you need to use the template for a document, retrieve it on a blank editing screen.

Caution: If you begin creating your new document and accidentally save it without changing the template's name, LetterPerfect replaces the template with the contents of the new document. To avoid the accidental loss of the template, save the blank template with the name of your new document before you begin adding text or new formatting codes.

Tip: You can create an unlimited number of templates. Give each a distinctive, descriptive name and use the TMP extension as an abbreviation for *template*. Using a uniform extension as part of the template name makes it possible to create a macro (see Chapter 13) that automates the retrieval and use of templates. If you run LetterPerfect on a system with dual floppy disk drives or a hard disk drive, you also should consider creating a subdirectory (see Chapter 9) for storing your templates.

Changing the Language Code

LetterPerfect supports text written in 27 languages. If you write in a language other than U.S. English or if your documents include sections written in another language, you can check your work with spelling files and thesaurus files specific to the language.

LetterPerfect's default language is U.S. English. When you check spelling in a document, LetterPerfect refers to its U.S. English dictionary. But if a document includes a section in Spanish and you have a Spanish WordPerfect Language Module program installed, you can instruct LetterPerfect to refer to Spanish speller, thesaurus, and hyphenation dictionaries instead.

Inserting a language code at the beginning of the section written in another language tells LetterPerfect to automatically use the dictionaries of another language and to format text by using that language's functions—for example, date format, thousands' separator, text and decimal align character—as defined in the WP.LRS file. See Chapter 12 for more information on the WP.LRS file.

Follow these steps to change the language code:

1. Move the cursor to the location in the document where you want LetterPerfect to begin using the different language.

2. Access the **L**ayout pull-down menu and select **L**anguage. Alternatively, press Language (Alt-F8).

   LetterPerfect displays this menu prompt: `Language: US.`

3. Type the two-letter code of the new language and press Enter.

The language code remains in effect until LetterPerfect encounters a different language code. So if only a section of a document is in another language, be sure to insert *US*, the code for U.S. English, where U.S. English resumes.

Note: As described in other chapters, a language code controls the operation of many LetterPerfect features. Some of these features require that you insert a specific language code even for the default language. When you activate the Language feature, LetterPerfect displays the code abbreviation for the language active at the cursor's location. Unlike most other LetterPerfect features, however, pressing Enter does *not* insert the language code displayed with the prompt into the document. You always must type the two-letter abbreviation and press Enter to insert any language code into your document.

> *Tip:* If you cannot remember the exact language code, press Help (F3) when the prompt is active. LetterPerfect displays a list of all valid language code abbreviations.

> *Caution:* LetterPerfect does not warn you if you enter an invalid code.

Checking the Document's Format with View Document

View Document graphically displays the pages of your document as closely as possible to how they appear when you print them.

Use View Document to preview page breaks, headers and footers, page numbers, lines, and graphic images. Use it frequently to check your progress when you create a complex document; you can save time by identifying mistakes before you print them, and the feature can alert you early to problems. Figure 7.14 shows a full-page view of a document. See Chapter 8 for more information on using View Document.

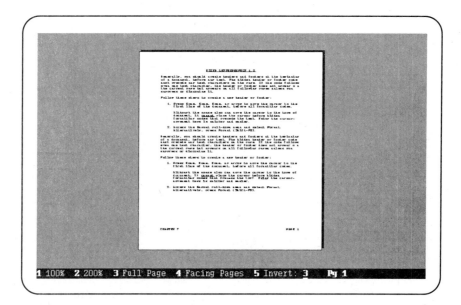

Fig. 7.14. A full-page view of a document.

Summary

In this chapter, you learned these techniques for formatting pages and designing documents:

- Centering a title page between the top and bottom margins
- Adding and editing headers and footers
- Numbering pages
- Preventing widows and orphans
- Choosing and editing paper and form sizes

- Using other aspects of the Format feature
- Changing the default language

Chapter 8 discusses techniques for printing your documents.

Printing and Print Options

8

B ecause of LetterPerfect 1.0's many sophisticated text-formatting features, you can easily lose sight of a basic purpose of the program: printing the words. The programmers at WordPerfect Corporation have gone to great lengths to make printing as easy and flexible as possible. The result is that LetterPerfect's printing capabilities rival those of its big brother, WordPerfect 5.1.

This chapter—which covers all aspects of printing—shows you how to accomplish these tasks:

- Select and define a printer

- Select and define the method (hand-fed, tractor-fed, or sheet-fed) by which the printer inserts paper, labels, and so on

- Designate the size and appearance of fonts available to the printer

- Designate the location of downloadable soft fonts

- Designate the method for printing the document

- Initialize the printer

- Select the size and kinds of material on which to print a document—from continuous forms to letterheads, envelopes, transparencies, and labels

- Designate the entire document or just a portion of it for printing
- Designate the quality of the printed image
- Designate the number of copies printed
- Start, stop, and cancel a printing operation

> ***Reminder:*** WordPerfect Corporation updated LetterPerfect 1.0 just before this book went to press. Dated 11/01/90, the interim release includes new options for existing features, and a few new features. The menus on your screen may, therefore, differ slightly from those shown in this book. Also, depending on the printer-form definition, margins, tab stops, and font you specify, the text placement and status-line information in documents you create may differ from that shown in this book's figures.
>
> For information about using the mouse and accessing the pull-down menus, refer to the Introduction.

Understanding the Printer Function

LetterPerfect's printer operation, which limits printing to a document displayed on-screen, makes it almost impossible for printing problems to cause a document to be lost or scrambled. The program prints only a document displayed on the main editing screen. As it prints the document, LetterPerfect displays a menu that provides information on the status of the print job and options that let you control the printing. This printing method prevents you from editing the document or from using any other LetterPerfect feature until printing finishes.

Activating Print

Reminder:
The main Print menu provides access to LetterPerfect 1.0 print functions.

Activate LetterPerfect's printing features by accessing the **File** pull-down menu and selecting the **P**rint option (see fig. 8.1) or, alternatively, by pressing Print (Shift-F7). When you start Print, LetterPerfect displays the main Print menu (see fig. 8.2), which uses the entire screen to show various printing options.

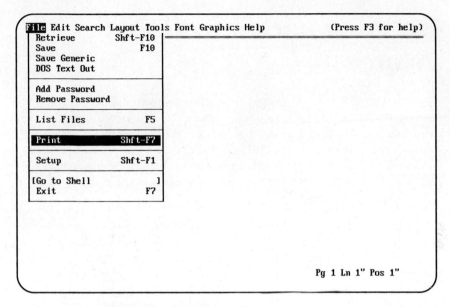

File Edit Search Layout Tools Font Graphics Help   (Press F3 for help)
```
Retrieve        Shft-F10
Save            F10
Save Generic
DOS Text Out

Add Password
Remove Password

List Files      F5

Print           Shft-F7

Setup           Shft-F1

[Go to Shell          ]
Exit            F7
```

Pg 1 Ln 1" Pos 1"

Fig. 8.1. The File pull-down menu.

```
Print

    1 - Full Document
    2 - Multiple Pages
    3 - View Document
    4 - Initialize Printer


Options

    5 - Select Printer
    6 - Binding Offset        0"
    7 - Number of Copies      1
    8 - Graphics Quality      Medium
    9 - Text Quality          High
```

Selection: 0

Fig. 8.2. The main Print menu.

Defining and Selecting a Printer

Printers are like people from around the world: they speak different languages. Most printer manufacturers offer equipment that has unique features, and the manufacturers have also developed proprietary printer command languages. Even different models made by the same manufacturer may use incompatible commands. For example, sending the same command from the same computer to different printers may change the width of margins in one printer and turn on underlining in another.

Each printer requires hundreds of software command codes to generate a document. It would be impossible for you to remember all the codes required to operate even the simplest printer, and writing a software program to operate the printer is a complicated task. Fortunately, LetterPerfect remembers the command codes for you.

In developing LetterPerfect, programmers at WordPerfect Corporation worked with hundreds of printers provided by manufacturers. As a result, LetterPerfect directly supports the unique features of these printers through printer-definition files found on the Printer disks shipped with LetterPerfect. All you have to do is use the Select Printer function to tell LetterPerfect the make and model of the printer attached to your computer.

Using the Select Printer Function

Reminder:
Use the Select
Printer function
to define and
select a printer.

The Select Printer function actually combines two important tasks:

- *Defining* the make and model of the printer available for producing your documents

- *Selecting* the printer definition required to operate the printer for your current document

Select Printer defines printers at any of these stages:

- When you install LetterPerfect

- When you add, edit, or delete a printer definition

- When you use different printers to produce documents

For a quick draft of a long document, you may want to use a dot-matrix printer and then switch to another printer for final, letter-quality copy.

Using Select Printer To Create the Printer's Program File

To take full advantage of a printer's capabilities, you must create a program file that tells LetterPerfect many things, including the following:

- The make and model of the printer

- The available fonts and their locations

- The location and type (parallel or serial) of communications port used by the printer

- The type and number of bins if the printer uses a sheet feeder

The following steps show you how to define an IBM 4019 laser printer connected to the computer's standard parallel-printer port, called LPT1. If you use a different printer, you may not need to make some of the choices indicated here. Follow the steps appropriate for your printer:

1. Access the File pull-down menu and select **P**rint. Alternatively, press Print (Shift-F7).

   LetterPerfect displays its main Print menu (see fig. 8.2).

2. Choose **S**elect Printer (**S**).

   LetterPerfect displays Print: Select Printer menu (see fig. 8.3).

   At the top of the screen, LetterPerfect lists all the printers, if any, that you previously defined. Because LetterPerfect controls only one printer at a time, an asterisk (*) indicates the active printer.

3. Select **A**dditional Printers (**2**).

   LetterPerfect displays the menu shown in figure 8.4.

```
Print: Select Printer










  1 Select; 2 Additional Printers; 3 Edit; 4 Copy; 5 Delete; 6 Help; 7 Update: 1
```

Fig. 8.3. The Print: Select Printer menu.

```
Select Printer: Additional Printers

Printer files not found

    Use the Other Disk option to specify a directory for the printer
    files.  Continue to use this option until you find the disk with the
    printer you want.








  1 Select; 2 Other Disk; 3 Help; 4 List Printer Files; N Name Search: 1
```

Fig. 8.4. The Select Printer: Additional Printers menu.

If the menu includes the error message shown in figure 8.4, one of six things has happened:

- On a system with a hard disk, you did not select a printer, and LetterPerfect did not copy any ALL file to the hard disk during the installation process (see Chapter 1).

- On a system with a hard disk, the ALL file has either been moved or deleted after the installation of the software.

- With the 07/24/90 software running on a system that has a hard disk, the ALL file containing the definition for the printer is in a subdirectory other than that containing the LetterPerfect program files.

- With the 11/01/90 software running on a system that has a hard disk, either the ALL file containing the definition for the printer is in a subdirectory other than that containing the LetterPerfect program files, or the ALL file is in a subdirectory other than the one you designated for printer files with the Setup feature (see Chapter 1).

- With the 07/24/90 software running on a system that has floppy disk drives only, the ALL file containing the definition for the printer is not on a diskette in the drive to which LetterPerfect looks for its program files.

- With the 11/01/90 software running on a system that has floppy disk drives only, the ALL file containing the definition for the printer is not on a diskette in the drive to which LetterPerfect looks for its program files, or the ALL file is not on the drive and/or subdirectory you designated for printer files with the Setup feature (see Chapter 1).

If you did not install the printer's ALL file, or if the ALL file has been deleted, you must run the install program to create an ALL file. When you run the install program, if you cannot find a definition for the printer, call the LetterPerfect customer support line to determine whether a driver for the printer is available.

Tip: If you previously defined printer definitions that are not listed on the printer list, choose the List Printer Files (4) option. LetterPerfect displays the Select Printer: List Printer Files menu, which list all program files named with the PRS (*printer resource*) extension. The PRS files must be located where LetterPerfect looks for its program files (if you have 07/24/90 or 11/01/90 software) or in the location designated for printer files (11/01/90 software only).

Tip: The printer ALL files—which contain many individual printer definitions in compressed form—require more than 450K of disk space. To avoid wasting disk space, install only the ALL file or files required to define the printers you use. You can always add new printers later.

If the printer's ALL file is on the hard disk but in a subdirectory different from that containing the LetterPerfect program files or on a disk not in the drive from which LetterPerfect runs its program files, select the Other (2) option. LetterPerfect displays this menu prompt: `Directory for printer files:`

Tell LetterPerfect where to find the printer's ALL file by typing the drive letter and path and pressing Enter. On a system with a hard disk and the ALL file in the WordPerfect 5.1 print subdirectory, for example, type *c:\wp51\print*.

On a system with dual floppy disk drives, type either *a:* or *b:*.

On a system with a single floppy disk drive, type *a:*.

4. Move the highlight bar to the name and model of your printer (see fig. 8.5).

   Use the mouse or the up-arrow, down-arrow, left-arrow, right-arrow, PgUp, PgDn, Screen Up (keyboard –), and Screen Down (keyboard +) keys to move through the list of printers.

Tip: If you cannot locate the make and model of the printer, try a substitute printer definition. For example, if you cannot find a definition for a dot-matrix printer, use the Epson-FX definition, which is close to being a universal dot-matrix printer definition. If you need a definition for a print-wheel or thimble-type letter-quality printer that is not listed, use the Diablo 630 printer definition.

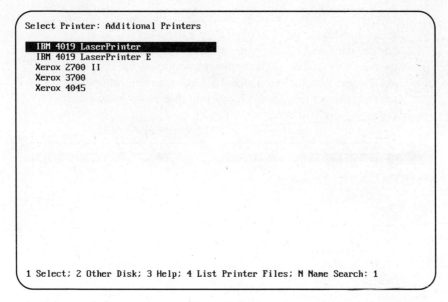

```
Select Printer: Additional Printers

   IBM 4019 LaserPrinter
   IBM 4019 LaserPrinter E
   Xerox 2700 II
   Xerox 3700
   Xerox 4045
```

```
1 Select; 2 Other Disk; 3 Help; 4 List Printer Files; N Name Search: 1
```

Fig. 8.5. *A list of printer definitions in an ALL file.*

5. To select the highlighted printer, choose **Select (1)** or press Enter.

   LetterPerfect displays a name-selection prompt: `Printer filename: IB401LAS.PRS`.

   The file name is LetterPerfect's suggested description for the program file it creates for the printer. This program file ends with the extension PRS—which stands for *printer resource*—a requirement for LetterPerfect to use the program file. In this chapter, the printer's program file is called the PRS file. Although you can edit the file name of the program file, it is better and easier to accept the suggested name.

6. Press Enter to accept the default name for the printer-definition file.

   If a PRS file with the same name exists, LetterPerfect displays a confirmation prompt: `Replace IB401LAS.PRS? No (Yes)`.

   If you choose **No**, LetterPerfect redisplays the name-selection prompt. If you choose **Yes**, LetterPerfect replaces the existing PRS file with the new program file that it is creating.

LetterPerfect begins creating the program file and adds the fonts available with the printer, displaying a progress report at the bottom left corner of the screen. Next, the program displays a message screen that—at a minimum—contains the date of the ALL file and may include helpful information and hints about the selected printer (see fig. 8.6). Reading this information carefully now may save you time later.

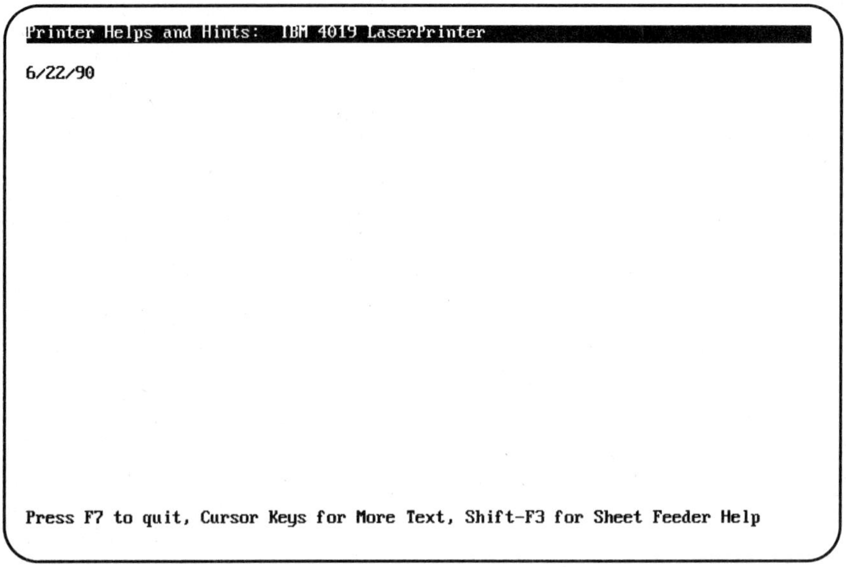

```
┌─────────────────────────────────────────────────────────────────┐
│ Printer Helps and Hints:   IBM 4019 LaserPrinter                  │
│ 6/22/90                                                           │
│                                                                   │
│                                                                   │
│                                                                   │
│                                                                   │
│                                                                   │
│                                                                   │
│                                                                   │
│                                                                   │
│                                                                   │
│                                                                   │
│                                                                   │
│                                                                   │
│                                                                   │
│ Press F7 to quit, Cursor Keys for More Text, Shift-F3 for Sheet Feeder Help │
└─────────────────────────────────────────────────────────────────┘
```

Fig. 8.6. The Select Printer: Help screen.

If the printer can use a sheet feeder, pressing Switch (Shift-F3) displays a similar message screen that contains at least the date of the ALL file and may include helpful information and hints about the sheet feeder.

7. To continue creating the printer's program file, press Exit (F7).

   The Select Printer: Edit menu, shown in figure 8.7, displays the current settings for the selected printer.

8. Press Enter to accept the generic settings for the printer. (The following section, "Editing Printer Settings," shows you how to modify these settings.)

   LetterPerfect returns you to the Select Printer menu, which lists the printer you just defined (see fig. 8.8).

```
Select Printer: Edit

        Filename              IB401LAS.PRS

   1 - Name                   IBM 4019 LaserPrinter

   2 - Port                   LPT1:

   3 - Sheet Feeder           None

   4 - Cartridges and Fonts

   5 - Initial Base Font      Courier 10cpi

   6 - Path for Downloadable
       Fonts

   7 - Print to Hardware Port No




Selection: 0
```

Fig. 8.7. *The Select Printer: Edit menu.*

```
Print: Select Printer

* IBM 4019 LaserPrinter













  1 Select; 2 Additional Printers; 3 Edit; 4 Copy; 5 Delete; 6 Help; 7 Update: 1
```

Fig. 8.8. *The Print: Select Printer menu.*

9. Now that you have defined your printer, *select* it to tell
   LetterPerfect that you intend to print on the printer.

   Move the highlight bar to the name of the printer you defined;
   press Enter or choose Select Printer (**1**) to make this the active
   printer. If your system has a mouse, you also can use it to select
   the printer definition.

   The program displays the main Print menu, which includes the
   newly defined print driver (see fig. 8.9). Until you designate a
   different printer definition, LetterPerfect uses this printer for all
   new documents you create.

```
Print

        1 - Full Document
        2 - Multiple Pages
        3 - View Document
        4 - Initialize Printer


Options

        5 - Select Printer            IBM 4019 LaserPrinter
        6 - Binding Offset            0"
        7 - Number of Copies          1
        8 - Graphics Quality          Medium
        9 - Text Quality              High







Selection: 0
```

Fig. 8.9. The Print menu with new printer definition.

Editing Printer Settings

Reminder:
*You can change
printer settings
easily and as
often as you
like.*

The previous section shows you how to define and select a printer definition
configured with generic settings. You can change these settings at any time:
when you first create a printer definition or later.

Use the following method to change the parameters of the printer:

1. Access the **File** pull-down menu and select **Print**. Alternatively, press Print (Shift-F7).

2. Choose **Select Printer (S)**.

   LetterPerfect displays the Print: Select Printer menu.

3. Using the mouse, cursor-movement keys, or **Name** Search (the last option is not listed on the menu, but it is available), move the cursor bar to highlight the printer definition you want to edit.

4. Select **Edit (3)**.

   LetterPerfect displays the Select Printer: Edit menu, from which you can select the options described in the following sections.

Name (1)

LetterPerfect uses the full name (up to 36 characters) to refer to this printer. You can see the full name displayed when you press Print (Shift-F7).

Port (2)

The *port* is the communications socket on the back of the computer through which LetterPerfect sends its data to the printer. There are two types of communication ports: *parallel* and *serial*.

LetterPerfect works with a maximum of three parallel communication ports, named LPT1, LPT2, and LPT3. Most computer systems have only one or two parallel communication ports.

LetterPerfect works with a maximum of four serial communication ports, named COM1, COM2, COM3, and COM4. Most computer systems have only one or two serial communications ports. If you select a COM port, LetterPerfect automatically prompts you to define additional parameters, including the *baud rate* (the speed at which the computer sends data to the printer) and information about how the data is organized (parity, stop bits, and start bits). Do not guess at these settings. Refer to the printer's technical reference manual (or, in some cases, to the LetterPerfect Printer Help screen) for the appropriate values.

Sheet Feeder (3)

The Sheet Feeder setting tells LetterPerfect that the printer is equipped with a cut-sheet feeder. LetterPerfect displays a list of compatible sheet feeders (see fig. 8.10).

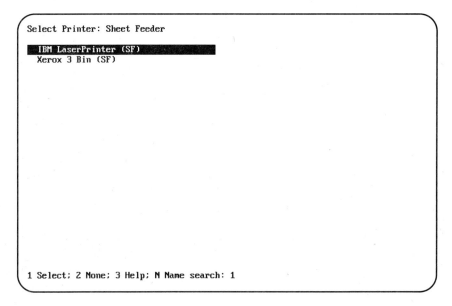

```
Select Printer: Sheet Feeder

  IBM LaserPrinter (SF)
  Xerox 3 Bin (SF)
```
```
1 Select; 2 None; 3 Help; N Name search: 1
```

Fig. 8.10. *The Select Printer: Sheet Feeder menu.*

The procedure for selecting a sheet feeder is the same as that for selecting a printer:

1. Use the mouse, cursor-movement keys, or **N**ame Search function to move the highlight bar to the appropriate choice.

2. Click the mouse, choose **S**elect (**1**), or press Enter.

   The **H**elp (**3**) option displays a "helps and hints" message screen that may contain information about using the sheet feeder.

Cartridges and Fonts (4)

Through the option **C**artridges and Fonts (**4**), you can designate the typefaces (fonts) available to the printer. Depending on the printer's capabilities, these fonts may be located in the printer, on plug-in cartridges or cards, or as software files that LetterPerfect downloads as needed from the system's hard disk. If your printer cannot use cartridge, card, or software fonts, LetterPerfect displays an informational prompt at the bottom of the screen: This printer has no other cartridges or fonts.

Select **C**artridges and Fonts (**4**), and LetterPerfect displays the Select Printer: Cartridges and Fonts menu (see fig. 8.11). Depending on the printer's capabilities, this menu includes categories for these items:

- Built-in fonts (which the program treats in the same manner as cartridges or soft fonts)

- Cartridge fonts (including the number of plug-in font cartridges or cards available)

- Software fonts (including the amount of RAM in the printer available for storing downloaded font files)

```
Select Printer: Cartridges and Fonts

Font Category                        Quantity         Available

Built-In
Cartridges                               2                2
Soft Fonts                             512 K            512 K




NOTE: Most fonts listed under the Font Category (with the exception of Built-In)
are optional and must be purchased separately from your dealer or manufacturer.
If you have fonts not listed, they may be supported on an additional printer
diskette.  For more information call WP at (801) 225-5000.

If soft fonts are marked '*', you must run the Initialize Printer option in LP
each time you turn your printer on.  Doing so deletes all soft fonts in printer
memory and downloads those marked with '*'.

If soft fonts are not located in the same directory as your printer files, you
must specify a Path for Downloadable Fonts in the Select Printer: Edit menu.

1 Select; 2 Change Quantity; N Name search: 1
```

Fig. 8.11. *The Select Printer: Cartridges and Fonts menu.*

To select an option from this menu, follow these steps:

1. Use the mouse, cursor-movement keys, or **N**ame Search to move the cursor bar to highlight the category that you want to examine or edit.

2. Click the mouse or press Enter.

3. Press Exit (F7) to leave the menu.

The Built-In fonts option displays the Select Printer: Built-In menu, which includes a list of fonts permanently coded into the printer's hardware (see fig. 8.12). Each font is marked with an asterisk that tells LetterPerfect that the font is available every time the program sends a document to the printer. Although you can edit the list to remove the asterisk, you have no reason to do so.

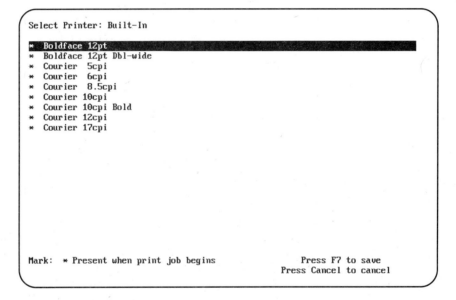

```
Select Printer: Built-In

*  Boldface 12pt
*  Boldface 12pt Dbl-wide
*  Courier  5cpi
*  Courier  6cpi
*  Courier  8.5cpi
*  Courier 10cpi
*  Courier 10cpi Bold
*  Courier 12cpi
*  Courier 17cpi




Mark:  * Present when print job begins          Press F7 to save
                                                Press Cancel to cancel
```

Fig. 8.12. The Select Printer: Built-In menu.

Under the Cartridges font category, the default quantity is the number of physical slots in the printer. This number initially limits the number of removable font cartridges or cards that you can mark with an asterisk. Frequently, you may have more cartridges or cards available than the number of slots in the printer. Use the Change **Q**uantity (**2**) option to change the slot number to match the number of font cartridges or cards actually available.

> *Caution:* A disadvantage to using removable font cartridges or cards is that if there are more cards than slots, you must make sure that the cartridge or card containing the fonts required by your document is actually in the printer slot. If the printer slot contains the wrong cartridge or card, the document prints improperly.

Select the Cartridges category, and LetterPerfect displays the Select Printer: Cartridges menu, which includes a list of the removable cartridges or cards with fonts that usually are permanently coded (see fig. 8.13). Certain printers, however, can download soft fonts to the removable cartridge or card. By default, none of the font cartridges or cards is marked as present when the print job begins. Marking a font cartridge or card with an asterisk tells LetterPerfect that the fonts it contains are present when it begins sending a document to the printer.

```
Select Printer: Cartridges                    Quantity
                                      Total:      2
                                  Available:      2

                                                   Quantity Used

        800 Universal                                   1
        801 Italic                                      1
        802 Prestige                                    1
        803 Letter Gothic                               1
        804 Delegate                                    1
        805 Script/OCR                                  1
        806 Orator                                      1












   Mark:  * Present when print job begins        Press F7 to save
                                              Press Cancel to cancel
```

Fig. 8.13. *The Select Printer: Cartridges menu.*

Follow these steps to mark a font cartridge or card:

1. Move the cursor bar by using either the mouse or cursor-movement keys to highlight the font cartridge or card.

2. Double-click the left mouse button or press the asterisk, 0 (zero), or Enter to mark the highlighted item.

3. Press Exit (F7) to leave the menu.

Repeat steps 1 and 2 to unmark a font cartridge or card marked as initially present when the print job begins.

Under the Soft Fonts category, the default quantity is the minimum amount of RAM in the printer. If your printer has more RAM available than the listed quantity, use the Change **Q**uantity (**2**) option to enter the amount of RAM actually available to the printer.

Select the Cartridges category, and LetterPerfect displays the Select Printer: Soft Fonts menu shown in figure 8.14. The printer drivers that come with LetterPerfect do not contain soft font definitions. To use downloadable soft fonts, you must order special printer drivers from WordPerfect Corporation or use a WordPerfect 5.1 printer definition that includes the soft fonts information. Call the WordPerfect order department at 1-800-321-4566 to order the special printer driver (the nominal charge covers disk handling and shipping)

```
Select Printer: Soft Fonts                       Quantity
                                        Total:    512 K
                                    Available:    512 K

                                               Quantity Used

LetterPerfect printer drivers are not shipped with soft font information. If
you have soft fonts and want to print with them using LetterPerfect, contact
WordPerfect orders at 1-800-321-4566 for ordering information on the printer
driver you desire. There is a nominal charge for handling and shipping of the
diskette(s).

Note: WordPerfect 5.1 drivers work with LetterPerfect. If you have a
WordPerfect printer driver, please feel free to use that driver with
LetterPerfect.




Mark:  * Present when print job begins              Press F7 to save
       + Can be loaded/unloaded during job        Press Cancel to cancel
```

Fig. 8.14. *The Select Printer: Soft Fonts menu.*

If you have a printer definition with soft fonts, LetterPerfect segregates them into *font groups*, sometimes called *font libraries*. When you choose the soft font category, LetterPerfect displays a menu that lists each font family. From this list, you select soft fonts in the same manner described for font cartridges and cards. The method for marking and unmarking soft fonts also is the same.

Marking a soft font with an asterisk tells LetterPerfect that the font is present in the printer when the program begins sending the document to the printer. For each font marked with an asterisk, LetterPerfect subtracts a font's RAM size from the total memory available. Both figures are displayed at the top right of the screen.

Marking a font with a + tells LetterPerfect that it can download and unload the font when it sends the document to the printer.

Initial Base Font (5)

Using the option Initial Base Font (5), you can select the default typeface (for example, Times), style (such as Roman), and size (10 points in height, where 1 point is 1/72 inch) used by LetterPerfect to print standard text. All designated options for Cartridges and Fonts (4)—built-in, cartridge, card, and soft—are listed on the Select Printer: Initial Font menu (see fig. 8.15). If you choose additional fonts with Cartridges and Fonts (4), you will use one of those for the initial font.

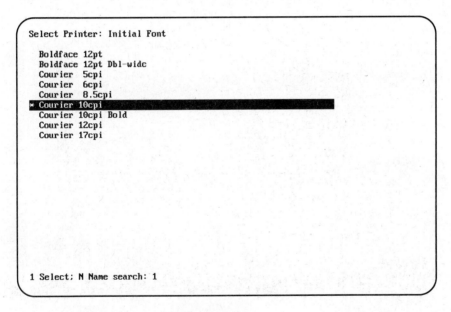

```
Select Printer: Initial Font

  Boldface 12pt
  Boldface 12pt Dbl-wide
  Courier  5cpi
  Courier  6cpi
  Courier  8.5cpi
* Courier 10cpi
  Courier 10cpi Bold
  Courier 12cpi
  Courier 17cpi




 1 Select; N Name search: 1
```

Fig. 8.15. The Select Printer: Initial Font menu.

Path for Downloadable Fonts (6)

If you store soft font files on the system's hard disk, use the option Path for Downloadable Fonts (6) to tell LetterPerfect where to find the soft font files. You must enter the full path name to the subdirectory where the fonts are stored. LetterPerfect accepts only one path name.

Cue:
Keep soft font files in a separate subdirectory.

Print to Hardware Port (7)

The default setting for the last option, Print to Hardware Port (7), is **No**. If you change the setting to **Yes**, LetterPerfect may print documents faster. If a document prints incorrectly with this feature active, change the setting to **No** and reprint the document. If the document now prints correctly with the option set to **No**, the computer system will not let LetterPerfect use direct hardware printing.

If the Print to Hardware Port option is active, you can temporarily deactivate it without changing the printer settings. To do this, start LetterPerfect with the /nh switch. See Chapter 1 for information on starting LetterPerfect with switches. When you start the program with this switch, you cannot make LetterPerfect print to the hardware port during the current editing session; you must completely exit and restart the program without the /nh switch.

> *Caution:* Some TSR programs, such as Backloader 2.1 from Roxxolid Corporation, which controls the loading and unloading of soft fonts to the printer and certain software print spoolers, do not work if LetterPerfect prints to the hardware port. If LetterPerfect sends a document directly to the hardware port with these types of TSR programs active, the document prints incorrectly.

Printing the Test Document

Reminder:
Use
LetterPerfect's
PRINTER.TST
file to test your
printer definition
before you print
documents.

Before you begin to print documents, you can have LetterPerfect print its PRINTER.TST document to test the printer definition. Follow these steps to print the test document:

1. Retrieve the file PRINTER.TST to the screen by one of these methods:

   - Access the **File** pull-down menu, select **Retrieve**, type the file name, and press Enter.

   - Press Retrieve (Shift-F10), type the file name, and press Enter.

   - Press List Files (F5), move the cursor bar to highlight the file name, and select **Retrieve** (**1**).

2. Press Print (Shift-F7) to display the Print menu; select **Full Document** (**1**).

Features that do not print properly are usually not supported by the printer.

> ***Caution:*** Some printers require that you change factory-default hardware settings to use certain features. Make sure that any mechanical settings—for example, DIP (dual in-line package) switches—are set according to the manufacturer's instructions provided in your printer's manual.

Printing a Document with LetterPerfect

LetterPerfect prints only a document displayed on its main editing screen. The program prints a block of text, selected pages, or the entire document.

Printing the entire document requires only three keystrokes; printing one or more pages, five or more keystrokes. If you want to print just part of a page (one or more words, sentences, or paragraphs), LetterPerfect can do that almost as easily through Block.

When the document is printing, you cannot use any other features of LetterPerfect.

Reminder: LetterPerfect prints only documents displayed on its main editing screen.

Printing the Entire Document from the Screen

To print the entire document from the screen, complete the following steps:

1. Access the **File** pull-down menu and choose **P**rint. Alternatively, press Print (Shift-F7).

   LetterPerfect displays the main Print menu (see fig. 8.16).

2. Select **F**ull Document (**1**) to print the entire document.

   LetterPerfect displays the Print: Control Printer menu, shown in figure 8.17, and automatically creates and formats a print job for the active printer. LetterPerfect displays this menu until the entire document is sent to the printer. During this time, you cannot use any other LetterPerfect features.

```
Print

        1 - Full Document
        2 - Multiple Pages
        3 - View Document
        4 - Initialize Printer


Options

        5 - Select Printer          IBM 4019 LaserPrinter
        6 - Binding Offset          0"
        7 - Number of Copies        1
        8 - Graphics Quality        Medium
        9 - Text Quality            High




Selection: 0
```

Fig. 8.16. LetterPerfect's main Print menu.

```
Print: Control Printer


Port:       LPT 1                   Page Number:  1
Status:     Printing                Current Copy: 1 of 1
Message:    None
Paper:      Standard 8.5" x 11"
Location:   Bin 2
Action:     None







1 Cancel Job; 2 Go (start printer); 3 Stop: 0
```

Fig. 8.17. The Print: Control Printer menu.

3. When the document finishes printing, press Enter, Exit (F7), Cancel (F1), Esc, or the space bar to return to the main editing screen.

Printing One or More Pages

To print one or more pages from the document on the main editing screen, complete these steps:

1. Access the **File** pull-down menu and choose **Print**. Alternatively, press Print (Shift-F7).

   LetterPerfect displays the main Print menu (see fig. 8.16).

2. Select **Multiple Pages (2)**.

   At the bottom of the screen, LetterPerfect displays the `Page(s):` prompt.

3. Type the page number of the page or pages you want printed.

   To print page 3, for example, type the number *3* and press Enter.

   After you press Enter, LetterPerfect displays the Print: Control Printer menu and automatically creates and formats a print job for the active printer. LetterPerfect displays this menu until the entire document is sent to the printer. During this time, you cannot use any other LetterPerfect features.

4. When the document finishes printing, press Enter, Exit (F7), Cancel (F1), Esc, or the space bar to return to the main editing screen.

   LetterPerfect also lets you designate several pages for printing during a single print operation. The procedure is identical to that described earlier for printing a single page, except that you enter more than one page number in step 3. Table 8.1 lists the types of page combinations you can enter to print multiple pages during a single print operation.

Table 8.1
Designations for Printing Multiple Pages

Pages to Print	*Method for Designating Pages*
First page to a specific page	Type a hyphen and the number of the last page to be printed. Example: *-8.*
Consecutive pages	Type the beginning page number, a hyphen, and the last page number. Example: *3-9.*
Nonconsecutive pages	Type each page number followed by a comma. Example: *3,8,10,14.*
Specific page to the document's page	Type the beginning page number followed by a hyphen. Example: *5-.*
All even pages	Type the letter *e* without any page number. Example: *e.*
Consecutive even pages	Type the letter *e*, a comma, the beginning page number, a hyphen, and the ending page number. Example: *e,4-10.* **Note:** If you omit an ending page number, LetterPerfect prints all even-numbered pages beginning with the designated first page and continuing to the last even-numbered page in the document.
All odd pages	Type the letter *o* without any page number. Example: *o.*
Consecutive odd pages	Type the letter *o*, a comma, the beginning page number, a hyphen, and the ending page number. Example: *o,7-15.* **Note:** If you omit an ending page number, LetterPerfect prints all odd-numbered pages beginning with the designated first page and continuing to the last odd-numbered page in the document.

Pages to Print	Method for Designating Pages
Labels	LetterPerfect considers each individual label on a sheet as a separate page. The same commands and page combinations are available for printing labels, with two exceptions: the program recognizes a maximum of only two multiple-page commands, and you must precede the *e* and *o* commands with an *l* (as in *le, 4-12*). If you enter more than two multiple-page print commands separated by commas, LetterPerfect prints the labels required by the first two commands and ignores the remaining commands.

Tip: By separating each of the categories with a comma, you can select one or more of the page combinations listed in table 8.1 to print during a single print operation. However, LetterPerfect limits you to a maximum of 30 characters, including separators for designating the pages. For example, to print pages 3 through 5, page 7, even-numbered pages from 10 through 20, odd-numbered pages from 23 through 27, and all pages from 30 to the end of the document, type the following in step 3:

   3-5,7,e,10-20,o,23-27,30-

Printing a Block from the Screen

Printing individual pages or the entire document from the screen is easy because LetterPerfect knows where the document begins and ends and where page breaks occur. If you need one or more words, sentences, or paragraphs printed from the document, however, you must use Block to define the beginning and end of the text segment.

Reminder: The Block feature tells LetterPerfect where a block begins and ends.

Use these steps to print a portion of the document:

1. Move the cursor to the first character you want included in the block.

2. Access the **E**dit pull-down menu and select **B**lock. Alternatively, press and hold down the left mouse button or press Block (Alt-F4 or F12).

   The message Block on flashes at the lower left corner of the screen.

3. Using the cursor-movement keys or dragging the mouse, move the cursor to the last character you want included in the block.

   If you are not using a mouse, you can use some quick methods for defining the block from the keyboard. The block automatically advances to the next occurrence of any character you type if the character is found within the next 2,000 characters. You can advance the block to the end of the current paragraph simply by inserting a hard return (pressing Enter). Press the period (.) key to advance to the end of the current sentence. Here are some other shortcuts for defining a block:

   • Press Screen Up (keyboard +) to highlight a block from the cursor to the bottom of the screen minus one line.

   • Press Screen Down (keyboard –) to highlight a block from the cursor to the top of the screen.

   • Press PgDn to highlight a block of text between the cursor and the top of the next page.

   • Press PgUp to highlight a block of text between the cursor and the top of the previous page.

4. Access the **F**ile pull-down menu and select **P**rint. Alternatively, press Print (Shift-F7).

   Instead of displaying the full-screen Print menu, LetterPerfect displays a prompt on the status line at the bottom of the screen: Print Block? No (Yes).

5. Select **Y**es to print the block. If you choose any other key, the prompt disappears and the block remains highlighted, but LetterPerfect does not print the block.

   If you choose the **Y**es option, LetterPerfect displays the Print: Control Printer menu shown in figure 8.17 and automatically creates and formats a print job for the active printer. LetterPerfect displays this menu until the entire document is sent to the printer. During this time, you cannot use any other LetterPerfect features.

6. When the document finishes printing, press Enter, Exit (F7), Cancel (F1), Esc, or the space bar to return to the main editing screen.

Controlling Printing Activities

LetterPerfect's Control Printer menu lets you cancel the print job. The menu (see fig. 8.17) has two sections: the informational section on the upper part of the screen and the single-line options menu at the bottom of the screen.

Reminder:
The Control Printer menu lets you manage printing activities.

Port

The Port item tells you which communications port LetterPerfect uses to send the document to the printer. This information is relevant only if more than one printer is attached to the system.

Status

The Status item tells you what LetterPerfect is doing. If the job is printing normally, the message displayed is `Printing`. If you use the Cancel Job (**1**) option, LetterPerfect displays the message `Trying to cancel job`.

> *Caution:* If you activate Print when the printer is not operational for any reason—no power, a jammed mechanism, a defective cable, and so on—LetterPerfect signals the `Printing` status even though the document is *not* printing. The Message item (see next section), however, tells you that there is a problem. When the program is trying to print, it remains locked in printing mode and is otherwise unavailable until you either make the printer operational or cancel the print job.

Message

If the document is printing normally, LetterPerfect displays `None`. If LetterPerfect cannot communicate with the printer, the program displays the message `Printer not accepting characters`. This message is LetterPerfect's cryptic method of telling you that it needs your help to solve the problem. In the Action item (see the section "Action"), LetterPerfect suggests the action it thinks that you should take.

Paper

The Paper item lists the form and size of the paper defined for the document currently printing. If you use standard continuous-sheet 8 1/2-by-11-inch paper, LetterPerfect displays the message `Standard 8.5" by 11"`.

Location

The Location item lists how the paper enters the printer. For standard, continuous-sheet paper, this item shows `Continuous feed`. If you feed each sheet by hand, the listing is `Manual`. For printers with sheet feeders, the setting designates the sheet-feeder bin number: `Bin 1`, `Bin 2`, and so on.

Action

The Action item specifies what LetterPerfect wants you to do in connection with the current print job. If the document is printing normally, the activity is `None`. If the printer is not accepting characters, the activity is `Check cable, make sure printer is turned ON`. After the document has printed, the activity is `Press any key to exit`.

Page Number

LetterPerfect shows the number of the document page it is currently sending to the printer. The displayed number may not be the page actually being printed. The printer's RAM may accept and store pages faster than the printer can print an individual page, as can a software-created print spooler. LetterPerfect sends the pages as fast as the printer or spooler can accept them. Thus if the printer or spooler stores five pages, LetterPerfect sends that much and indicates that the current page number is 5 even though the printer may still be printing page 1.

Current Copy

The Current Copy item lists two pieces of information: the number of copies of the document that LetterPerfect is printing and the number of the copy currently printing.

The Control Printer Menu

The bottom line of the screen presents three printer-control options: Cancel Job (**1**), Go (start printer) (**2**), and Stop (**3**).

Cancel Job (1)

Select Cancel Job (**1**) to cancel the print job. LetterPerfect may prompt you to confirm the cancellation. To cancel the print job, select Cancel again. If the printer does not respond immediately, you may see the message `Press Enter if printer doesn't respond`.

Go (Start Printer) (2)

Select Go (start printer) (**2**) to resume printing after you suspend printing with Stop (**3**). You also may need to send a Go command after you cancel a print job. LetterPerfect begins printing the page where the printing stopped or prompts you for a manual feed.

Stop (3)

Select Stop (**3**) to stop or suspend printing without canceling the print job. Use this option if the printer runs out of paper or jams or if you need to replace the ribbon or otherwise intervene in the printing operation. If you do not want to resume the print job, press Cancel (F1) or Esc instead of stopping.

Using the Print Menu

In previous sections, you used the main Print menu's **Full Document (1)** option to print the entire document, the **Multiple Pages (2)** option to print one or more pages within the document, and the **Select Printer (5)** option to choose the active printer definition. Additional options located on the Print menu also are important tools in the overall management of printing activities. These are the additional Print options:

- **View Document (3)**
- **Initialize Printer (4)**
- **Binding Offset (6)**
- **Number of Copies (7)**
- **Graphics Quality (8)**
- **Text Quality (9)**

With these additional options, you can manage printing operations efficiently.

View Document (3)

Reminder:
The View
Document (3)
function shows
how the
document will
appear on the
sheet, without
printing it.

View Document (3) shows you the appearance of the document sheet before it is printed. LetterPerfect displays everything that appears on a page, including text, headers, footers, graphics, page numbers, and endnotes, exactly as it prints on the page—subject to the limitations imposed by the display hardware. If, for example, the computer cannot display graphics, View displays only the text of the document without graphics.

> *Tip:* After you view a document, press Cancel (F1), Esc, or the space bar to redisplay the Print menu, or Exit (F7) to return to the document on the main editing screen.

Use these steps to display a document with View Document:

1. Position the cursor anywhere on the page you want to view.

2. Access the **File** pull-down menu and select **Print**. Alternatively, press Print (Shift-F7).

LetterPerfect displays the main Print menu.

3. Select **View Document (3)**.

> *Tip:* The Ctrl-p fast-key combination requires fewer keystrokes and displays
> the document in View mode directly from the main editing screen.

LetterPerfect shifts the computer into graphics mode and displays the document. On the right end of the status line, LetterPerfect displays the page number of the page displayed. Beginning at the lower left corner of the screen, LetterPerfect displays a menu that offers several options for expanding or reducing the image.

100% Page (1)

Choose the 100% (**1**) option to view the page at full size (see fig. 8.18). Because most monitors cannot show an entire page at full size, you ordinarily see only part of the page. Use the cursor-movement keys to shift the image up, down, right, or left until the desired part of the page comes into view. You should be able to read text at this size.

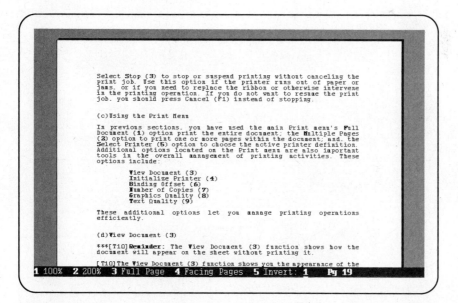

Fig. 8.18. *View Document at 100%.*

> *Tip:* Press PgUp to view the page above the current page displayed by LetterPerfect. Press PgDn to view the page following the current page.

200% Page (2)

The 200% (**2**) option displays the page at twice the normal height and width (see fig. 8.19). At this magnification, you can see only a small portion of the page, but text is clearly legible. If you use a proportional font, LetterPerfect reproduces it as faithfully as possible within the limitations of your particular hardware configuration. Use the cursor-movement keys to shift the image up, down, right, or left until the desired part of the page comes into view.

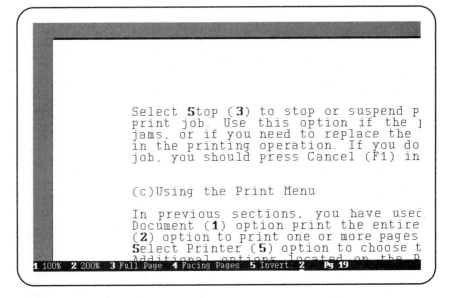

Fig. 8.19. View Document at 200%

> *Tip:* If you press End, the image shifts to the right edge of the document, on the current line. Pressing Ctrl-Home and the up arrow moves the displayed image to the top of the document page. Pressing Ctrl-Home and the down arrow, right arrow, or left arrow moves the image to the bottom, right, or left edge, respectively, of the document page.
>
> Pressing Screen Up (keyboard–) displays the top of the current page. Pressing Screen Down (keyboard+) displays the bottom of the current page.

Full Page (3)

Choose Full Page (3) to view the entire current page (see fig. 8.20). You may not be able to read the text at this size, but you can clearly see the page layout. Use PgUp and PgDn to view the preceding or succeeding page, or use GoTo (Ctrl-Home) with a specific page number to view that page.

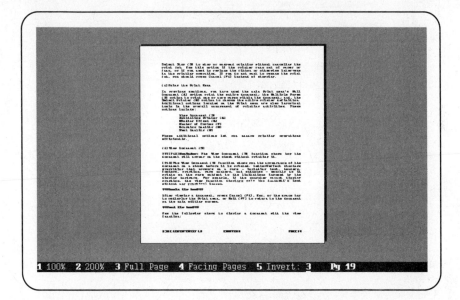

Fig. 8.20. *View Document, with Full Page (3) chosen.*

Facing Pages (4)

Select Facing Pages (4) to display the full-page images of two consecutive pages as they would appear in a book (see fig. 8.21). Before you choose this option, though, remember that in a book page 1 is always a right page and therefore has no facing page. If, then, you choose this option with the cursor on page 1, LetterPerfect does not display a facing page. Remember too that an even-numbered page is always displayed on the left; its facing page is the next page number. For example, facing pages are 20 and 21, not 19 and 20.

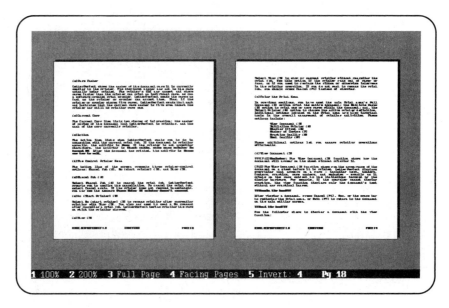

Fig. 8.21. *View Document, with Facing Pages (4) chosen.*

Invert (5)

Select Invert (5) to reverse the colors of the image displayed by View. If, for example, LetterPerfect ordinarily displays the image with black characters on white background, the inverted image displays white characters on a black background (see fig. 8.22).

Initialize Printer (4)

The Initialize Printer (4) option downloads to the printer all soft font files designated as present at the beginning of the print job by the **Cartridges and Fonts (4)** option on the Select Printer: Edit menu. LetterPerfect looks for these files in the disk directory designated in the Path for **D**ownloadable Fonts and Printer Command Files (6) option.

As LetterPerfect downloads the fonts (a process that can take a few minutes or as long as 30 minutes), it displays the Print: Control Printer menu. This menu prevents you from using the other program features, including other printer functions. For this reason, LetterPerfect displays a confirmation prompt at the bottom of the screen: Proceed with Printer Initialization? No (Yes).

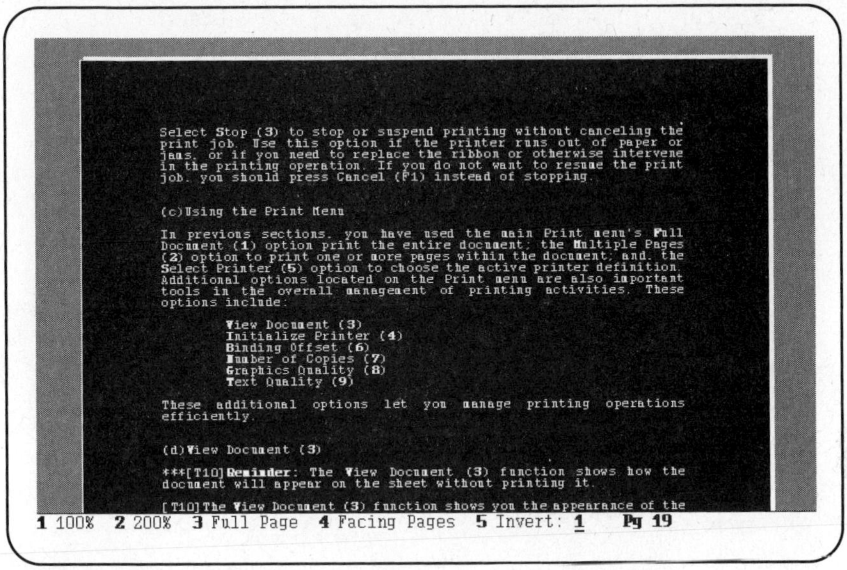

Fig. 8.22. *View Document with inverted colors.*

Select **Yes** to go ahead with the initialization. Select **No** to cancel it.

> **Caution:** When you select the Initialize Printer (4) option, any fonts previously downloaded to the printer are removed from the printer's memory.

Binding Offset (6)

Select **Binding Offset (6)** from the Print menu to make two-sided xerographic copies of a printed document. Setting a binding width shifts odd-numbered pages right and even-numbered pages left by the indicated amount. **Binding Offset (6)** provides an extra margin along the inside edge of the paper for binding the final copy.

Reminder:
Binding Offset (6) provides an extra margin for binding the final copy of a document.

To set a binding width, complete these steps:

1. Access the **File** pull-down menu and select **Print**. Alternatively, press Print (Shift-F7).

2. Select **Binding Offset (6)**.

The cursor moves right of the binding item, and LetterPerfect pauses until you perform one of these actions:

- Press Cancel (F1), Exit (F7), Esc, or Enter to exit the option, leaving its original value unchanged.

  - Type a number for the new value and press Enter.

  3. Type a number and press Enter.

LetterPerfect does not insert a binding-width code into a document. The new binding-width setting remains effective until you change it again or until you exit LetterPerfect. After you set a binding width, every print job you create is shifted.

Beginning with the 11/01/90 software, LetterPerfect applies the binding-offset setting to logical pages, not physical pages. The new method primarily affects the printing of labels, because a single physical page contains many labels, each of which LetterPerfect considers a separate logical page.

As a result of the change, labels on odd-numbered logical pages shift to the right by the amount of the binding width. Labels on even-numbered logical pages shift to the left by the same amount. Unless you need to print labels with a binding offset, you should set the binding-offset option to 0 when printing labels.

Number of Copies (7)

The Number of Copies (7) parameter lets LetterPerfect print more than one copy of the same document in a single operation. LetterPerfect defaults to printing one copy of the document. Follow these steps to change this setting:

1. Access the **File** pull-down menu and select **Print**. Alternatively, press Print (Shift-F7).

   LetterPerfect displays the main Print menu.

2. Select **Number of Copies (2)**.

3. Type the number of copies to be printed and press Enter.

4. Select Full Document (**1**) or **Multiple Pages (2)**.

LetterPerfect displays the Print: Control Printer menu and begins printing the first copy of the document. After you change the parameter, the setting for the number-of-copies parameter remains effective until you change it again or exit LetterPerfect. Every print job—block, pages, and full document—uses the new value until you change it.

Graphics Quality (8)

Use the Graphics Quality (8) option on the Print menu to control the resolution (sharpness) of graphic images. When you select this option, LetterPerfect displays a menu across the bottom of the screen:

Graphics Quality: **1** Do Not Print; **2** Draft; **3** Medium; **4** High: **3**

In general, high-resolution images require more printer RAM, take longer to print, and use more ribbon or toner to print than do medium- or low-resolution images. For most print jobs, the default medium value produces an acceptable image, especially if you are using a laser printer

Tip: A common problem with printing pages that contain both text and graphics—especially with dot-matrix printers—is that the printer does not have enough RAM to print the entire page. If your printer has trouble printing text and graphics at one time, select the Do Not Print (**1**) option for the Graphics Quality (**8**) and choose the Text Quality (**9**) you need. Print the page and reinsert it into the printer. Change the text quality to Do Not Print (**1**), choose the degree of graphics quality you need for printing the graphics images, and print the page again. The drawback to using this method is that it prevents LetterPerfect from printing graphical characters created by the WP.DRS file.

Text Quality (9)

The Text Quality (9) option is identical to the Graphics Quality (9) option except that the former option controls only the printing of text. If you print text and graphics as two separate print jobs, set Text Quality (9) to Do Not Print (**1**) to print graphics.

> *Tip:* On dot-matrix printers, setting Graphics Quality (**G**) and Text Quality (**T**) to Medium produces satisfactory images and characters. This setting also extends the useful life of the ribbon and speeds up the print process.

Troubleshooting Common Printer Problems

When you consider the number of links in the chain from creating to printing a document, it is amazing that things don't go wrong more often. WordPerfect Corporation anticipates most probable difficulties, and LetterPerfect provides you with immediate feedback through the Print: Control Printer screen. Unfortunately, sometimes things just seem to go wrong for no apparent reason. This section presents some common printing problems and suggests possible solutions.

Printer Does Not Print

If your printer does not print, explore these possibilities:

- Make sure that the printer is plugged in and turned on.

- Make sure that the printer is on-line.

- Make sure that LetterPerfect is not waiting for a **G**o (start printer) (**3**) command on the Control Printer screen.

- Make sure that the current print job (if any) is not stopped with the **S**top (**5**) option. Check the Control Printer screen.

- Check the printer. Is it out of paper? Has the paper jammed? Does it need a new ribbon or toner cartridge?

- Check all plugs and connections, including the keyboard and both ends of the printer cable.

- Make sure that you selected the correct printer definition.

- Make sure that the printer is correctly defined. If the printer is of the serial variety, be sure that the baud rate, parity, and start/stop bits are entered accurately.

- Shut off the printer, wait several seconds, and then turn it back on. This action clears any commands (and downloaded fonts) previously sent to the printer.

- If the system uses a hardware print buffer or software print spooler, deactivate it and try printing the document again.

- If you set the Print to Hardware Port (7) option on the Select Printer: Edit menu to **Yes**, change it to **No** and try printing the document again.

- As a last resort, save your documents, exit LetterPerfect, and shut off the printer and computer. Start everything again and try printing.

Printer Is Printing Nonsense

If your printer prints nonsense, try these troubleshooting suggestions:

- Check all plugs and connections, including the keyboard and both ends of the printer cable.

- If the printer is attached to a serial communications port, make sure that its hardware settings are for serial input and not parallel input.

- Make sure that the printer definition is correct. If the printer is attached to a serial communications port, check the settings for the baud rate, parity, and start/stop bits.

- If the nonsense occurs at every other character, you may have a serial printer, and incorrect values may be entered for baud rate, parity, or start/stop bits. Check the printer's technical reference manual.

- Big chunks of good text followed by big chunks of nonsense characters usually indicate problems in defining a serial printer.

- If the printer is attached to a parallel communications port, check the length of the cable connecting the computer to the printer. Distances greater than 15 to 20 feet require either a hardware booster or a special type of parallel cable to work properly.

- If the system uses a hardware print buffer or software print spooler, deactivate it and try printing the document again.

- If you set the Print to Hardware Port (7) option on the Select Printer: Edit menu to **Yes**, change it to **No** and try printing the document again.

Summary

This chapter discusses LetterPerfect's broad range of powerful tools that help you get the most performance from your printer. To use these tools, you must properly define the print driver and then select it. You saw that, although defining and selecting the print driver is not a difficult task, many steps along the way deserve careful consideration. You also learned the following:

- How to print an entire document, one or more pages, or a block of text from the screen

- How to use the Control Printer screen—LetterPerfect's nerve center for managing all your printing activities

- How to use the main Print screen, from which you access other printing options

As you work with LetterPerfect, you may find that you seldom or never use some features; that is perfectly natural. But every LetterPerfect user prints, and prints often. Mastering LetterPerfect's printing options and print-management tools makes you more efficient; increases your productivity; and, most important, enables you to concentrate on your writing—the main purpose of any word processing program. The next chapter, which begins Part II, "Using LetterPerfect's Supplemental Features," explains how to manage and protect files and directories.

Part II

Using LetterPerfect's Supplemental Features

Includes

Managing and Protecting Files and Directories

Working with the Outline and Endnote Feature

Using the Speller and Thesaurus

Working with the Character Feature and LRS File

9

Managing and Protecting Files and Directories

This chapter shows you how LetterPerfect's List Files feature helps you work with DOS to manage your files and directories and how the password feature protects your files from unauthorized viewing, printing, and editing. Among other things, this chapter helps you do these tasks:

- Review the parts of the List Files screen: the header, the file listings, and the menu

- Redisplay the list of files exactly as it appeared before you returned to the main editing screen

- Use List Files instead of DOS for such tasks as displaying a list of files; deleting, moving, copying, and renaming files; making, changing, and deleting directories; and viewing and retrieving documents

- Use file marking to perform List Files operations on multiple files

- Use Block when you run LetterPerfect under the WordPerfect Office or Library Shell program to copy text from a file without first retrieving that file

- Assign and remove a password from a file

339

To benefit most from this chapter, be sure that you understand basic DOS features such as files, directories, and wild-card parameters, as well as basic DOS commands. If you are not familiar with these concepts, you may want to read one of Que's best-selling books on DOS: *Using DOS* or *MS-DOS User's Guide*, Special Edition. For an easy-to-use quick reference, see also *DOS QueCards*.

Reminder: WordPerfect Corporation updated LetterPerfect 1.0 just before this book went to press. Dated 11/01/90, the interim release includes new options for existing features, and a few new features. The menus on your screen may, therefore, differ slightly from those shown in this book. Also, depending on the printer-form definition, margins, tab stops, and font you specify, the text placement and status-line information in documents you create may differ from that shown in this book's figures.

For information about using the mouse and accessing the pull-down menus, refer to the Introduction.

With one exception, you cannot access the pull-down menus from within the List Files screen. Ordinarily, you can use the mouse to select menu choices from the regular List Files menus. Certain features not on these menus—such as Search, Mark Text, Block, and Text Out—are accessible only from the keyboard when List Files is active.

Caution: The LetterPerfect program includes an undocumented feature that recognizes keys other than Y and N for responding when the program displays a Yes/No menu prompt. With the 07/24/90 software, pressing the number 1 performs the same function as pressing Y, and pressing the number 2 performs the same function as pressing N. The alternative keys sometimes cause problems for people using systems with the Esc key located adjacent to the 1 key, because it is easy to accidentally press 1 when you intended to cancel the menu by pressing the Esc key.

With the 11/01/90 software, the alternative response keys have been changed so that pressing the plus key (at the top of the keyboard) performs the same function as pressing Y, and pressing the hyphen (at the top of the keyboard) performs the same function as pressing N.

Understanding List Files

With List Files you can accomplish within LetterPerfect much of the file and directory management you ordinarily perform in DOS. Regardless of which List Files option you select, LetterPerfect's context-sensitive Help (F3) feature is always available.

To activate List Files and display a list of all files in the current default directory, follow this step:

> Access the File pull-down menu bar and select List Files (see fig. 9.1). Alternatively, press List Files (F5).

Reminder:
Pressing List Files (F5) once or choosing List Files from the File pull-down menu on the main editing screen shows you the current default directory.

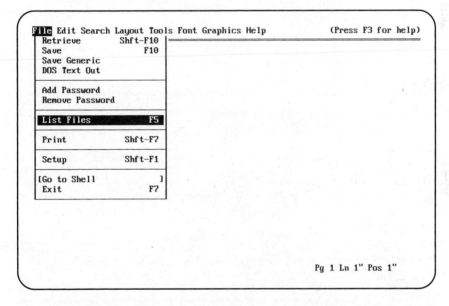

```
File Edit Search Layout Tools Font Graphics Help        (Press F3 for help)
    Retrieve        Shft-F10
    Save              F10
    Save Generic
    DOS Text Out

    Add Password
    Remove Password

    List Files         F5

    Print           Shft-F7

    Setup           Shft-F1

    [Go to Shell          ]
    Exit              F7




                                                Pg 1 Ln 1" Pos 1"
```

Fig. 9.1. *The File pull-down menu, which contains the List Files option.*

At the lower left corner of the screen, LetterPerfect displays `Dir` followed by a file specification for all files in the current default directory, as in `C:\LP10\DOCUMENT\*.*`

The *.* parameter at the end of the file-specification message causes List Files to display a list of all files in the current default directory. If this file list is the one you want, simply click with the right mouse button on the prompt or press Enter. To view a list of fewer than all the files in the current default directory or a list of files in a different directory, you can make List Files use a different file parameter.

To display a list of one file in the current default directory, type the name of the specific file and press Enter. To display a list of more than one file in the current default directory, type a file-specification parameter—such as *.txt or *d:\pl51\wksheets*—and press Enter. The first example causes List Files to display only those files in the current default directory whose names end with the TXT extension. The second example causes List Files to show all files that are in the \PL51\WKSHEETS subdirectory on drive D—or, if no WKSHEETS directory exists, all files named WKSHEETS.*.

If you begin typing a file specification without first pressing any cursor-movement key, what you type replaces the original specification. If, however, you move the cursor even one character or press an editing key before you begin to type, what you type is inserted into the specification. You can edit the file specification, just as you edit regular text, with the LetterPerfect key combinations listed in table 9.1.

Table 9.1
Key Combinations for Editing File Specifications

Key(s)	Effect
Right arrow	Moves cursor one character right
Left arrow	Moves cursor one character left
End	Moves cursor left of the last character in the file specification
Home, left arrow	Moves cursor to first character in the file specification
Del	Deletes character at cursor
Backspace	Deletes character left of cursor
Ctrl-End	Deletes from cursor to end of file specification

Press Enter to accept the default file specification (that is, to list all files in the current directory). The default List Files screen appears (see fig. 9.2). The three sections of this screen are the header, the file list, and the menu.

To return to the main editing screen, press Cancel (F1), Esc, Exit (F7), or the space bar.

```
12/01/90  09:11              Directory C:\LP10\*.*
Document size:        0   Free:  4,636,672  Used:  2,164,287    Files:    120

.   Current    <Dir>                    ..   Parent    <Dir>
DOCUMENT.        <Dir>  11/02/90 09:00 | {LP}SPC .FRM    10,142  11/01/90 12:00
001      .       1,992  11/13/90 12:25 | 05-02   .PIX     1,623  11/04/90 15:07
ADDRESS .TUT       978  11/01/90 12:00 | ARROW-22.WPG       195  11/01/90 12:00
BALLOONS.WPG     3,195  11/01/90 12:00 | BANNER-3.WPG       727  11/01/90 12:00
BEGIN   .TUT        11  11/01/90 12:00 | BICYCLE .WPG     1,355  11/01/90 12:00
BKGRND-1.WPG    11,489  11/01/90 12:00 | BORDER-8.WPG       223  11/01/90 12:00
BULB    .WPG     2,109  11/01/90 12:00 | BURST-1 .WPG       827  11/01/90 12:00
BUTTRFLY.WPG     5,291  11/01/90 12:00 | CALENDAR.WPG       379  11/01/90 12:00
CERTIF  .WPG       661  11/01/90 12:00 | CHKBOX-1.WPG       661  11/01/90 12:00
CLOCK   .WPG     1,825  11/01/90 12:00 | CNTRCT-2.WPG     2,761  11/01/90 12:00
CONVERT .EXE   109,229  11/01/90 12:00 | CURSOR  .COM     1,452  11/01/90 12:00
DEVICE-2.WPG       665  11/01/90 12:00 | DIPLOMA .WPG     2,421  11/01/90 12:00
FILENAME.TUT       335  11/01/90 12:00 | FIXBIOS .COM        50  11/01/90 12:00
FLATTIRE.LRN     2,942  11/01/90 12:00 | FLOPPY-2.WPG       483  11/01/90 12:00
GAVEL   .WPG       895  11/01/90 12:00 | GLOBE2-M.WPG     7,793  11/01/90 12:00
GRAPHCNV.EXE   120,320  11/01/90 12:00 | HANDS-3 .WPG     1,125  11/01/90 12:00
IB40LAPR.PRS   155,087  11/02/90 09:00 | INSTALL .EXE    57,856  11/01/90 12:00
LETTER  .TUT       653  11/01/90 12:00 ▼ LETTER_F.TUT       679  11/01/90 12:00

1 Retrieve; 2 Delete; 3 Move/Rename; 4 Other Directory; 5 Copy; 6 Look;
N Name Search: 6
```

Fig. 9.2. *A file list displayed on the List Files screen.*

Tip: LetterPerfect keeps in RAM a "picture" of the last list of files displayed by List Files. Pressing List Files (F5) twice recalls the last file list displayed during the current editing session, exactly as the list appeared (including marked files) on-screen. Any file or files added to the directory after you return to the main editing screen are not displayed unless you update the list of files by moving the cursor bar to the `. Current <Dir>` entry and pressing Enter twice. You also can select List Files with the mouse and then press the List Files function key (F5) for the previous list. This capability is not available from the pull-down menu bar.

Understanding the Header

The header at the top of the List Files screen displays two lines of information. From left to right on the top line are the date, the time (updated by the minute), and the file specification for the listed directory.

From left to right on the second line are the size (in bytes) of the document on the main editing screen, the free space (in bytes) available on the disk, the disk space (in bytes) taken by files listed on-screen, and the number of files shown in the list.

Understanding the File List

The file list section contains two columns listing files arranged in alphabetical order across the screen. File names beginning with numbers are listed first. This list shows the complete file name, the file size, and the date and time the file was created or last modified. Unlike other WordPerfect Corporation software products, LetterPerfect cannot print its List Files screen.

If, however, your system supports the DOS print-screen feature, you can press that feature's key—usually the PrtSc key, sometimes in combination with the Ctrl or Shift key—to print the contents of the screen. If the list contains more files than will fit on one screen, you must print each screen list individually. Figure 9.3 shows a printout of the main LetterPerfect directory, created through the DOS print-screen feature.

```
12/01/90  09:11              Directory C:\LP10\*.*
Document size:       0   Free: 4,636,672 Used: 2,164,287    Files:      120

     .  Current    <Dir>           |   ..  Parent      <Dir>
  DOCUMENT.        <Dir>  11/02/90 09:00 | {LP}SPC .FRM    10,142  11/01/90 12:00
  001     .         1,992  11/13/90 12:25 | 05-02   .PIX     1,623  11/04/90 15:07
  ADDRESS .TUT        978  11/01/90 12:00 | ARROW-22.WPG       195  11/01/90 12:00
  BALLOONS.WPG      3,195  11/01/90 12:00 | BANNER-3.WPG       727  11/01/90 12:00
  BEGIN   .TUT         11  11/01/90 12:00 | BICYCLE .WPG     1,355  11/01/90 12:00
  BKGRND-1.WPG     11,489  11/01/90 12:00 | BORDER-8.WPG       223  11/01/90 12:00
  BULB    .WPG      2,109  11/01/90 12:00 | BURST-1 .WPG       827  11/01/90 12:00
  BUTTRFLY.WPG      5,291  11/01/90 12:00 | CALENDAR.WPG       379  11/01/90 12:00
  CERTIF  .WPG        661  11/01/90 12:00 | CHKBOX-1.WPG       661  11/01/90 12:00
  CLOCK   .WPG      1,825  11/01/90 12:00 | CNTRCT-2.WPG     2,761  11/01/90 12:00
  CONVERT .EXE    109,229  11/01/90 12:00 | CURSOR  .COM     1,452  11/01/90 12:00
  DEVICE-2.WPG        665  11/01/90 12:00 | DIPLOMA .WPG     2,421  11/01/90 12:00
  FILENAME.TUT        335  11/01/90 12:00 | FIXBIOS .COM        50  11/01/90 12:00
  FLATTIRE.LRN      2,942  11/01/90 12:00 | FLOPPY-2.WPG       483  11/01/90 12:00
  GAVEL   .WPG        895  11/01/90 12:00 | GLOBE2-M.WPG     7,793  11/01/90 12:00
  GRAPHCNV.EXE    120,320  11/01/90 12:00 | HANDS-3 .WPG     1,125  11/01/90 12:00
  IB40LAPR.PRS    155,087  11/02/90 09:00 | INSTALL .EXE    57,856  11/01/90 12:00
  LETTER  .TUT        653  11/01/90 12:00 | LETTER_F.TUT       679  11/01/90 12:00

 1 Retrieve; 2 Delete; 3 Move/Rename; 4 Other Directory; 5 Copy; 6 Look;
 N Name Search: 6
```

Fig. 9.3. *A List Files screen printed with the DOS print-screen feature.*

The file list date and time formats are controlled by a Language Resource file called WP.LRS, located in the same directory as LP.EXE. You can edit this file with LetterPerfect 1.0 to change the display format. See Chapter 12 for information on using and editing the WP.LRS file.

The first two entries at the top of the file listing are always these:

```
. Current <Dir>          .. Parent <Dir>
```

`<Dir>` designates directories and subdirectories. The entry `. Current <Dir>` refers to the currently listed directory. The other entry `.. Parent <Dir>` refers to the directory *above* the current directory in the directory-tree structure. The `<Dir>` for all other entries marks subdirectories below the displayed directory in the directory-tree structure of the disk.

On-screen, the cursor bar highlights the `. Current <Dir>` entry. You can move this bar by moving the mouse pointer and clicking the left mouse button to highlight any name in the list or by using the cursor-movement keys (listed in table 9.2).

Table 9.2
Cursor-Movement Key Combinations

Key Combination	Item Highlighted by the Cursor Bar
Right arrow	The next file in forward sequence
Left arrow	The next file in reverse sequence
Up arrow	The next file above the cursor
Down arrow	The next file below the cursor
Home, up arrow	The first file displayed at the top of the screen in the left column, and then files in the same position on each full screen of files until the cursor bar highlights the `. Current <Dir>` entry
Home, Home, up arrow	The `. Current <Dir>` directory entry
Home, down arrow	The last file displayed at the bottom of the screen in the right column or the last file displayed on-screen if the list does not fill the entire screen
Home, Home, down arrow	The last file in the directory list
PgUp	The first file on the next full screen of files above the cursor in the same column where the cursor is located

Table 9.2 (continued)

Key Combination	Item Highlighted by the Cursor Bar
PgDn	The last file on the next full screen of files below the cursor in the same column where the cursor is located
Screen Down (keyboard +)	The last file in the right column on the current screen and then to the last file listed on each full screen of files below the cursor bar
Screen Up(keyboard –)	The first file listed at the top of the left column on the current screen and then to the first file listed on each full screen of files above the cursor bar
N, n, F2, or keypad = plus the characters in the name of the file	The names in the file list in alphabetical sequence, as each key is pressed. If the first character you type is the backslash (\), the cursor bar moves through subdirectory listings

Using the List Files Menu

The List Files menu at the bottom of the screen in figure 9.2 presents seven command choices. You can select any command by moving the mouse pointer to the option and clicking or by pressing either the appropriate number or the highlighted letter. Each choice acts on the highlighted file or directory.

When you pick a menu command, LetterPerfect often asks for confirmation— and first presents a **No** choice. For example, if you select **Delete (2)** to delete the file named ADDRESS.TUT, LetterPerfect displays this confirmation prompt: `Delete C:\LP10\ADDRESS.TUT? No (Yes).`

Selecting **Yes** deletes the file. Selecting **No** cancels the deletion option.

Using Retrieve

Retrieve (**1**) works like Retrieve from the File pull-down menu and like Retrieve (Shift-F10) from the editing screen: the option inserts the designated file on the main editing screen at the cursor. If a document is on the main editing screen, however, LetterPerfect displays the confirmation prompt Retrieve into current document? No (Yes).

Selecting **Yes** adds the designated file to the document on the main editing screen at the cursor. Selecting **No** cancels the retrieval option.

See "Locking Files" later in this chapter for information on retrieving files that are password-protected.

LetterPerfect protects you from retrieving improper files. It does not retrieve program files, nor does it retrieve any temporary or permanent LetterPerfect system files or macro files.

Retrieve (**1**) retrieves any DOS text file or any file created with WordPerfect 4.2, 5.0, or 5.1 and automatically converts it to LetterPerfect format. During the conversion process, LetterPerfect displays the message DOS Text Conversion in Progress or Document Conversion in Progress. With some kinds of WordPerfect files, no message may appear.

Reminder: Retrieve (1) automatically retrieves certain files in non-LetterPerfect format and automatically converts the files into LetterPerfect format.

Although you cannot activate the pull-down menu bar in List Files, you can use the mouse pointer to move the cursor and to select any choice on the menu display.

Using Delete

The **Delete** (**2**) function or the Del key performs like DOS's DELETE (DEL), ERASE, and REMOVE DIRECTORY (RD) commands. This option works with individual files, groups of files, and subdirectories. If the cursor bar highlights a single file, LetterPerfect displays a confirmation prompt at the bottom of the screen: Delete *<path\filename>*? No (Yes).

Selecting **Yes** deletes the file. Selecting **No** cancels the deletion option.

If you mark a group of files before you activate Delete, LetterPerfect displays this prompt at the bottom of the screen: Delete marked files? No (Yes).

Selecting Yes displays a second confirmation prompt: `Marked files will be deleted. Continue? No (Yes)`. Selecting **Yes** a second time deletes the marked files. Selecting **No** at either of these prompts displays the prompt `Delete <path\filename>? No (Yes)`.

This prompt gives you the option of deleting the file highlighted by the cursor bar. Selecting **Yes** deletes the file. Selecting **No** cancels the delete option.

If the cursor bar highlights an empty subdirectory, LetterPerfect deletes the directory. If, however, the subdirectory contains any files, LetterPerfect displays this error message at the bottom of the screen: `ERROR: Directory not empty`.

You must delete all files in the subdirectory before LetterPerfect can delete the subdirectory itself.

See "Marking Files" for information on marking a group of files for deletion.

Using Move/Rename

Move/Rename (3) works like a combination of DOS's COPY, DEL, ERASE, and RENAME (REN) commands. This option performs two operations on individual files and groups of files: it changes the name of an existing file, and it places a file or group of files into a different subdirectory—with the original file or group of files deleted from the original subdirectory. Note that you cannot move or rename subdirectories; only files may be moved or renamed in LetterPerfect.

See the section "Locking Files" later in this chapter for information on using the Move/Rename option with files that are password-protected.

Follow these steps to rename a file:

1. Move the cursor bar to highlight the name of the file.

2. Select **M**ove/Rename (**3**).

   LetterPerfect displays this prompt at the bottom of the screen: `New name: <drive:\path\filename.ext>`.

   The term *<drive:\path\filename.ext>* is the default file name.

Tip: All the default-name editing techniques described in "Understanding List Files" apply to editing the default name offered by the Move/Rename function.

3. If you enter the name of an existing file, LetterPerfect displays this prompt: `Replace` *<drive:\path\filename.ext>*? `No (Yes)`.

   Selecting **Yes** deletes the file with the same name and replaces it with the file whose name is changed. Selecting **No** cancels the rename option.

A single move operation lets you both move a file and change its name. Use this method to move and rename a single file:

1. Move the cursor bar to highlight the name of the file.

2. Select **M**ove/Rename (**3**).

   LetterPerfect displays this prompt at the bottom of the screen: `New name:` *<drive:\path\filename.ext>*.

   The term *<drive:\path\filename.ext>* represents the default file name.

Tip: All the default-name editing techniques described in "Understanding List Files" apply to editing the default name offered by Move/Rename.

3. If you enter the name of an existing file, LetterPerfect displays this prompt: `Replace` *<drive:\path\filename.ext>*? `No (Yes)`.

   Selecting **Yes** deletes the file that has the same name and replaces it with the file whose name is being changed. LetterPerfect then deletes the original file. Selecting **No** cancels the move option.

Tip: To change only the drive letter, press Del and type the letter of the other drive. Doing so prevents the entire path from being deleted when you type the first letter of the new path name.

Note: You cannot rename a group of marked files; you may only move them to a different drive or subdirectory. Only individual files may be renamed with the current default directory.

If you mark a group of files before you select **Rename/Move (3)**, LetterPerfect displays the prompt Move marked files? No (Yes) at the bottom of the screen when you select this option.

Selecting **Yes** displays a second confirmation prompt: Move marked files to:. Type the drive and path of the subdirectory where you want to move the files; press Enter. LetterPerfect copies the files to the designated subdirectory and deletes the files from the original subdirectory. During the move, if in the target subdirectory LetterPerfect finds a file that has the same name as a marked file, LetterPerfect prompts you to confirm the replacement.

If you select **Yes**, LetterPerfect replaces the file on the target subdirectory and continues with the move operation on the remaining files. If you select **No**, LetterPerfect continues with the move operation but does not move or delete the original file.

See "Marking Files" for information on marking a group of files for use with the Rename/Move feature.

Using Other Directory

The **Other Directory (4)** function performs like DOS's CHANGE DIRECTORY (CD) and MAKE DIRECTORY (MD) commands. This option offers two operations: changing the default subdirectory used by the program and creating new subdirectories.

Changing the Program's Default Subdirectory

The **Other Directory (4)** function offers two methods for changing the current default directory. Follow these steps to use the first method:

1. Move the cursor bar to highlight the name of a subdirectory.

2. Select **Other Directory (4)**.

   LetterPerfect displays this prompt at the bottom of the screen: New directory = *<drive:\path>*.

   The term *<drive:\path>* is the name of the subdirectory highlighted by the cursor bar (see fig. 9.4.)

```
12/01/90  09:00              Directory C:\LP10\*.*
Document size:        0   Free:  4,521,984 Used:  2,162,664      Files:      119

   . Current    <Dir>                    .. Parent      <Dir>
 DOCUMENT.        <Dir> 11/02/90 09:00  {LP}SPC .FRM    10,142 11/01/90 12:00
 ADDRESS .TUT       978 11/01/90 12:00  ARROW-22.WPG       195 11/01/90 12:00
 BALLOONS.WPG     3,195 11/01/90 12:00  BANNER-3.WPG       727 11/01/90 12:00
 BEGIN   .TUT        11 11/01/90 12:00  BICYCLE .WPG     1,355 11/01/90 12:00
 BKGRND-1.WPG    11,489 11/01/90 12:00  BORDER-8.WPG       223 11/01/90 12:00
 BULB    .WPG     2,109 11/01/90 12:00  BURST-1 .WPG       827 11/01/90 12:00
 BUTTRFLY.WPG     5,291 11/01/90 12:00  CALENDAR.WPG       379 11/01/90 12:00
 CERTIF  .WPG       661 11/01/90 12:00  CHKBOX-1.WPG       661 11/01/90 12:00
 CLOCK   .WPG     1,825 11/01/90 12:00  CNTRCT-2.WPG     2,761 11/01/90 12:00
 CONVERT .EXE   109,229 11/01/90 12:00  CURSOR  .COM     1,452 11/01/90 12:00
 DEVICE-2.WPG       665 11/01/90 12:00  DIPLOMA .WPG     2,421 11/01/90 12:00
 FILENAME.TUT       335 11/01/90 12:00  FIXBIOS .COM        50 11/01/90 12:00
 FLATTIRE.LRN     2,942 11/01/90 12:00  FLOPPY-2.WPG       483 11/01/90 12:00
 GAVEL   .WPG       895 11/01/90 12:00  GLOBE2-M.WPG     7,793 11/01/90 12:00
 GRAPHCNV.EXE   120,320 11/01/90 12:00  HANDS-3 .WPG     1,125 11/01/90 12:00
 IB40LAPR.PRS   155,087 11/02/90 09:00  INSTALL .EXE    57,856 11/01/90 12:00
 LETTER  .TUT       653 11/01/90 12:00  LETTER_F.TUT       679 11/01/90 12:00
 LETTER_P.TUT       652 11/01/90 12:00 ▼ LETTER1 .TUT       778 11/01/90 12:00


New directory = C:\LP10\DOCUMENT
```

Fig. 9.4. Preparing to change directories in List Files.

> **Tip:** All the default-name editing techniques described in "Understanding List Files" apply to editing the default name offered by the Other Directory function.

3. Press Enter.

   LetterPerfect displays this prompt at the bottom of the screen: Dir *<drive:\path\filename.ext*.*>*.

4. Press Enter again.

   LetterPerfect displays a list of files in the designated subdirectory, which now becomes the program's default subdirectory.

> **Tip:** To stop the Other Directory feature from changing the default subdirectory, press Cancel (F1) or Esc instead of Enter in step 4.

Follow these steps to use the second method:

1. Move the cursor bar to highlight the . Current <Dir> directory name or a file name.

2. Select **Other Directory (4)**.

   LetterPerfect displays this menu prompt at the bottom of the screen: `New directory =` *<drive:\path>*.

   The term *<drive:\path>* is the name of the current default subdirectory.

3. Using the default-name editing techniques described in "Understanding List Files," type the path name for the new subdirectory and press Enter.

   LetterPerfect displays a list of files in the designated subdirectory, which becomes the program's default subdirectory.

> ***Tip:*** To stop the Other Directory feature from changing the default subdirectory, press Cancel (F1) or Esc instead of Enter in step 3.

Creating a New Subdirectory

Use this procedure to create a new subdirectory:

1. Move the cursor bar to highlight the `. Current <Dir>` directory name or a file name.

2. Select **Other Directory (4)**.

   LetterPerfect displays this prompt at the bottom of the screen: `New directory =` *<drive:\path>*.

   The term *<drive:\path>* is the name of the current default subdirectory.

3. Using the default-name editing techniques described in "Understanding List Files," type the path name for the new subdirectory and press Enter.

   LetterPerfect displays this prompt at the bottom of the screen: `Create` *<drive:\path>*`? No (Yes)`.

4. If you select **Yes**, LetterPerfect creates the new subdirectory but does not display it on-screen nor make it the program's new default subdirectory. If you select **No**, the Other Directory function stops.

> *Tip:* With LetterPerfect you also can change or create directories from the LetterPerfect editing screen. Access the File pull-down menu and select List Files. Alternatively, press List Files (F5). Then press the keypad equal (=) key. LetterPerfect responds as described in the preceding steps 2 through 4.

Using Copy

The Copy **(5)** function works like an enhanced version of DOS's COPY command. This option copies a single file highlighted by the cursor bar, or a group of marked files, to a designated subdirectory. This option also copies a single file to the current directory when you enter a new file name instead of a drive or directory.

See "Locking Files" later in this chapter for information on using the copy option with files that are password-protected.

Use this procedure to copy a single file:

1. Move the cursor bar to highlight the name of the file.

2. Select Copy **(5)**.

   LetterPerfect displays this prompt at the bottom of the screen: `Copy this file to:.`

3. Type the new name (including the path name) and press Enter.

   If you enter a name without a path name, the program creates a new file in the same subdirectory and stops operating. The original file remains unaltered in its subdirectory.

> *Tip:* All the default-name editing techniques described in "Understanding List Files" apply to editing the default name offered by the Move/Rename function.

4. If you enter the name of an existing file, LetterPerfect displays this prompt: `Replace` *<drive:\path\filename.ext>*`? No (Yes).`

Selecting **Yes** deletes the file that has the same name and replaces it with the file whose name is being changed. Selecting **No** cancels the copy option.

5. If you enter the file name without a different path name, the program displays an error message at the lower left corner of the screen: `ERROR: File can't be copied onto itself.` Then the copy operation stops.

   If you mark a group of files before you select Copy (**5**), LetterPerfect displays this prompt at the bottom of the screen: `Copy marked files? No (Yes).`

   Selecting **No** displays the prompt `Copy this file to:.` Then you have the option of copying the file highlighted by the cursor bar. Selecting **Yes** causes LetterPerfect to display a second prompt: `Copy all marked files to:.`

   Type the drive and path of the subdirectory where you want to move the files; press Enter. LetterPerfect copies the files to the designated subdirectory. During the copy operation, if in the target subdirectory LetterPerfect finds a file that has the same name as a marked file, it prompts you to confirm the replacement. If you select **Yes**, LetterPerfect replaces the file on the target subdirectory and continues with the copy operation on the remaining files. If you select **No**, LetterPerfect continues the copy operation on the remaining files but does not copy the file that has the duplicate name.

See "Marking Files" for information on how to mark a group of files to use with the Copy feature.

Using Look

The Look (**6**) function—the List Files default menu option—lets you examine files, directories, and subdirectories quickly. When you display the contents of a file with Look, the program options are limited. When LetterPerfect runs under the Shell program, however, the program combination adds the powerful capability of copying text (including the hidden formatting codes) to a separate file or adding the copied text and codes into the main document. When you display the contents of a directory or subdirectory, all List File menu options are available.

Using Look To Display a File

When the `Dir <Dir name> *.*` prompt appears at the bottom of the screen, highlight a file with the cursor bar, and double-click the left mouse button and then single-click the right button—or press Enter. Look (6) displays the highlighted file without retrieving it to the main editing screen (see fig. 9.5). Except as explained in the next section, LetterPerfect cannot edit or retrieve the file from the Look (6) display.

```
File: C:\LP10\CHAP09P.PRN                        Revised: 12/01/90 09:00

(a)10

(b)Managing and Protecting Files and Directories

This chapter shows you how LetterPerfect's List Files feature helps
you work with DOS to manage your files and directories and how the
password feature protects your files from unauthorized viewing,
printing, and editing. Among other things, this chapter shows you
how to:

     •   Review the parts of the List-Files screen: the header, the
         file listings, and the menu

     •   Redisplay the list of files exactly as it appeared before you
         returned to the main editing screen

     •   Use List Files instead of DOS such tasks as displaying a list
         of files; deleting, moving, copying, and renaming files;
         making, changing, and deleting directories; and viewing and
         retrieving documents


Look: 1 Next Doc; 2 Prev Doc: 0
```

Fig. 9.5. *A file displayed by Look (6).*

See "Locking Files" later in this chapter for information on using Look with files that are password-protected. See "Copying Text from the Look Display with the Shell Clipboard" in the next section for information on retrieving part or all of the document displayed with the Look option.

> **Tip:** Because Look (6) is the List Files feature's default menu choice, you do not have to press 6 to display the file with Look but can press Enter to accept the option.

When List Files displays the file's contents, it adds this information header at the top of the screen:

- The file's full name (including the path)

- The most recent revision date and time

If the highlighted file's name ends with the LPM extension, the file is a LetterPerfect macro. The Look option cannot display the contents of a macro file. However, if the LetterPerfect macro contains a description line, the Look option will show it. As in all WordPerfect Corporation software programs, the Look (6) function cannot display either the contents or the description line in a Shell macro.

Beginning with the 11/01/90 interim software, the Look option will not display the contents of temporary files—such as LP}LP{.BV1 or LP}LP{.TV1—created each time you run LetterPerfect. These temporary files are used by the program, do not contain any information useful to you, and cannot be retrieved to the main editing screen.

The cursor-movement keys function slightly differently when Look displays a document. Table 9.3 describes the keys and how they function.

Table 9.3
Cursor-Movement Key Combinations for Look

Key	Effect
Right arrow	Moves cursor five characters right
Left arrow	Moves cursor five characters left
Up arrow	Moves cursor up one line
Down arrow	Moves cursor down one line
Home, up arrow	Moves cursor up 20 lines
Home, Home, up arrow	Moves cursor to the top line
Home, down arrow	Moves cursor down 20 lines
Home, Home, down arrow	Moves cursor to the bottom line
PgUp	Moves cursor to the top line of the screen and then up 20 lines
PgDn	Moves cursor to the bottom line of the screen and then down 20 lines

Key	Effect
Screen Up (keyboard +)	Moves cursor to the top line of the screen and then up 20 lines
Screen Down (keyboard –)	Moves cursor to the bottom line of the screen and then up 20 lines.
End	Moves cursor to the left edge of the document
F2 or Shift-F2	Moves cursor forward or backward through the document, searching for the designated text string (cannot search for hidden formatting codes); pressing up arrow or down arrow changes search direction
S or s	Moves cursor down through the document until any key is pressed or the end of the document is reached
N or n	Displays the document that follows the current document
P or p	Displays the document that precedes the current document

At the bottom of the screen you see this menu:

Look: 1 **Next** Doc; **2 Prev** Doc: **0**

Selecting Next Doc (**1**) moves the cursor to the first page of the next document in the file list. Selecting **Prev** Doc (**2**) moves the cursor to the first page of the preceding document in the list. If you are on the first or last file in the list, selecting Next Doc (**1**) or **Prev** Doc (**2**) returns you to the file list.

Beginning with the 11/01/90 interim software, the **Next** Doc (**1**) and **Prev** Doc (**2**) options skip LetterPerfect's temporary program files, such as LP}LP{.BV1 and LP}LP{.TV1. The Look option automatically skips these temporary files and displays the next permanent file in sequence. If there are not any permanent files in sequence, LetterPerfect returns to its main List Files screen.

With this menu you can display the first pages of a list of files quickly. To limit the number of files to be scanned, use a file specification (such as *.LTR) to display a shorter list of files before using the Look option.

The mouse cannot scroll the document. The mouse can, however, select the **N**ext Doc and **P**rev Doc menu options as well as access the pull-down menu bar for the limited purpose of using the Help, Search, Exit, and Block (with the Shell only) features.

> *Caution:* When you use Look (6) to display a document in a format other than LetterPerfect 1.0, WordPerfect 5.1, or DOS, the document may not display so that you can read all of its contents. In addition, some cursor-movement keys do not work as described in table 9.3.

You can search for text by using Search and Backward Search. Additionally, if you run LetterPerfect under either the WordPerfect Office (versions 2.0 or later) or WordPerfect Library (version 2.0) Shell programs, the following method lets you use the source feature to define a text block:

1. Access the **E**dit pull-down menu and select Block. Alternatively, press Block (Alt-F4 or F12).

2. Access the **S**earch pull-down menu and select either Forward or Backward. Alternatively, press either Search (F2) or Backward Search (Shift-F2).

3. Type the search characters and press Enter.

If LetterPerfect finds a match for the search characters, the program automatically highlights the text to the line just above the line containing the search characters.

After you activate a search direction, you can switch to the opposite direction by pressing the up arrow to perform a backward search or the down arrow to perform a forward search from the cursor. When you use Look (6), LetterPerfect stores the text string entered during a search operation in a different RAM buffer than that used to store the search text string in the main editing screen.

> *Caution:* When Look (6) displays a document, the feature places the cursor at the bottom of the screen on approximately line 20 unless the document has fewer than 20 lines—and then the cursor is placed on the document's last line. A forward search does not check for the character string above the cursor. To search the entire document, move the cursor to the top line of the document before you begin the search.

When you use Look (6), LetterPerfect does not search for text in headers, footers, or footnotes. When a match is found in regular text, the matching characters are highlighted. If the text string is past the right edge of the regular display screen, the cursor stops at the left edge of the line where the text string is located, but the text string is not highlighted.

With one exception, after you return to the main editing screen, you can press List Files (F5) twice to redisplay the last list of files with the cursor bar highlighting the last file displayed by Look (6). However, if the last file list was a directory on a floppy disk, pressing List Files (F5) twice displays the default directory regardless of the type of drive on which the directory is located. The redisplay capability is *not* available from the pull-down menu bar.

Copying Text from the Look Display with the Clipboard

Running LetterPerfect under either the WordPerfect Office (versions 2.0 or 3.0) or WordPerfect Library (version 2.0) Shell programs gives Look (6) a powerful copying capability. When you display a document by using Look (6), the Shell program lets you highlight and copy part or all of the document to the Shell Clipboard. Here's what you can do with text placed in the Clipboard:

Reminder:
If you run LetterPerfect under either the WordPerfect Office (versions 2.0 or later) or WordPerfect Library (version 2.0) Shell programs, you can copy a block of text and formatting codes to the Clipboard.

- Retrieve it into a document on the main editing screen

- Retrieve it into another program running under the Shell program, one that accepts input from the Clipboard

- Save it as a new file on disk

All text in the highlighted block is saved to the Clipboard, including text right of the visible screen border. All hidden and visible formatting codes—for example, merge codes—within the text block in the source file are copied with the block. Hidden and visible formatting codes outside the block in the source file are not copied.

Because you can locate and retrieve formatted text from a file on disk as you edit a document on the main editing screen, the Clipboard Copy feature gives you a limited second editing window.

Follow these steps to copy a block of text into the Shell Clipboard:

1. Start LetterPerfect from the Office Shell menu. See Chapters 1 and 2 for information on running LetterPerfect with the Shell 3.01 program.

2. Use List Files to display the list of files in the directory that contains the file with the text you want copied.

3. Move the cursor bar to highlight the file.

4. Select Look (6).

5. Move the cursor to the beginning of the section you want to copy.

6. Access the **E**dit pull-down menu bar and select **Block**. Alternatively, press Block (Alt-F4 or F12).

7. Move the cursor to highlight the block you want to copy (see fig. 9.6).

When Look (6) displays a document, dragging the mouse does not activate Block nor move the cursor to highlight a block of text.

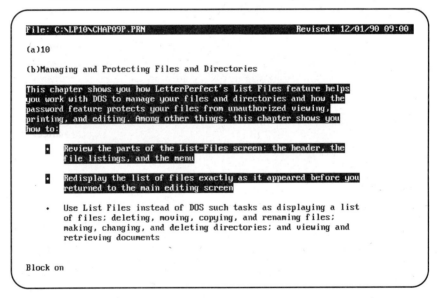

Fig. 9.6. *A highlighted block of text displayed by Look.*

Tip: The Shell program also offers a Screen Copy feature—Alt-Shift-hyphen—which can copy a maximum of one full screen of text, including information in the header and the menu on the bottom line. All text captured through the Screen Copy feature is saved as ASCII text and does not include hidden formatting codes. In contrast, the more powerful

Clipboard Copy feature lets you define a text block that includes hidden formatting codes and more text than is displayed on a single screen. Text and codes captured through Copy are saved to the Clipboard in LetterPerfect 1.0 format.

8. Access the **F**ile pull-down menu bar and select **G**o to Shell. Alternatively, press Shell (Ctrl-F1).

   LetterPerfect displays this menu at the bottom of the screen:

   Clipboard: 1 **S**ave; **2** Append: **0**.

9. Select **S**ave (**1**) to copy the block to the Clipboard, replacing any text previously saved there.

   Select **A**ppend (**2**) to copy the block of text to the Clipboard, adding it to the end of any text previously stored there.

Tip: Choosing Append (**2**) lets you assemble a document quickly by storing different parts of several documents. This capability is especially useful because LetterPerfect has only one main editing screen.

10. Access the **F**ile pull-down menu bar and select **E**xit twice. Alternatively, to return to the main editing screen, press Exit (F7), Cancel (F1), or Esc twice.

11. Access the **F**ile pull-down menu and select **G**o to Shell. Alternatively, press Shell (Ctrl-F1).

    LetterPerfect displays this menu prompt at the bottom of the screen:

    1 Go to Shell; **Clipboard: 2 S**ave; **3** Append; **4** Retrieve: **0**

12. Select **R**etrieve (**4**).

    LetterPerfect inserts the text and its hidden formatting codes at the cursor. Figure 9.7 shows the text marked in figure 9.6 retrieved from the Clipboard.

```
┌─────────────────────────────────────────────────────────────────┐
│ File Edit Search Layout Tools Font Graphics Help    (Press ALT= for menu bar) │
│                                                                   │
│ This chapter shows you how LetterPerfect's List Files feature     │
│ helps you work with DOS to manage your files and directories and  │
│ how the password feature protects your files from unauthorized    │
│ viewing, printing, and editing. Among other things, this chapter  │
│ shows you how to:                                                 │
│                                                                   │
│        •   Review the parts of the List-Files screen: the header, │
│            the file listings, and the menu                        │
│                                                                   │
│                                             Pg 1 Ln 1" Pos 1"     │
│ █████████████████████████████████████████████████████████████████│
│ This chapter shows you how LetterPerfect's List Files feature[SRt]│
│ helps you work with DOS to manage your files and directories and[SRt]│
│ how the password feature protects your files from unauthorized[SRt]│
│ viewing, printing, and editing. Among other things, this chapter[SRt]│
│ shows you how to:[HRt]                                            │
│ [HRt]                                                             │
│ [Tab]•[→Indent]Review the parts of the List[-]Files screen: the header,[SRt]│
│ the file listings, and the menu[HRt]                             │
│ [HRt]                                                             │
│ [Tab]•[→Indent]Redisplay the list of files exactly as it appeared[SRt]│
│                                                                   │
│ Press Reveal Codes to restore screen                              │
└─────────────────────────────────────────────────────────────────┘
```

Fig. 9.7. A Reveal Codes view of a text block retrieved through the Clipboard.

Using Look To Display a File List in a Subdirectory or Directory

Reminder:
Use Look (6) to examine other subdirectories.

With Look (6) you also can examine files and subdirectories in other subdirectories. To examine a subdirectory listed on the current List Files screen, follow these steps:

1. Move the cursor bar to highlight the subdirectory name and press Enter (see fig. 9.8).

2. Press Enter again.

   The program displays a file list for the other subdirectory but does not change its active subdirectory.

To examine the .. Parent <Dir> directory above the directory listed on the current List Files screen, follow these steps:

1. Move the cursor bar to highlight .. Parent <Dir>.

2. Press Enter.

The program displays a file list for the `. .` `Parent` `<Dir>` directory but does not change its active subdirectory.

```
12/01/90  11:50              Directory C:\LP10\*.*
Document size:        0   Free:  4,304,896 Used:  2,241,832      Files:       121

    .   Current   <Dir>             |    ..   Parent    <Dir>
  DOCUMENT.         <Dir>  11/02/90 09:00 | {LP}SPC .FRM   10,142  11/01/90 12:00
  ADDRESS .TUT        978  11/01/90 12:00 | ARROW-22.WPG      195  11/01/90 12:00
  BALLOONS.WPG      3,195  11/01/90 12:00 | BANNER-3.WPG      727  11/01/90 12:00
  BEGIN   .TUT         11  11/01/90 12:00 | BICYCLE .WPG    1,355  11/01/90 12:00
  BKGRND-1.WPG     11,489  11/01/90 12:00 | BORDER-8.WPG      223  11/01/90 12:00
  BULB    .WPG      2,109  11/01/90 12:00 | BURST-1 .WPG      827  11/01/90 12:00
  BUTTRFLY.WPG      5,291  11/01/90 12:00 | CALENDAR.WPG      379  11/01/90 12:00
  CERTIF  .WPG        661  11/01/90 12:00 | CHAP09P .PRN   71,340  12/01/90 09:00
  CHKBOX-1.WPG        661  11/01/90 12:00 | CLOCK   .WPG    1,825  11/01/90 12:00
  CNTRCT-2.WPG      2,761  11/01/90 12:00 | CONVERT .EXE  109,229  11/01/90 12:00
  CURSOR  .COM      1,452  11/01/90 12:00 | DEVICE-2.WPG      665  11/01/90 12:00
  DIPLOMA .WPG      2,421  11/01/90 12:00 | FILENAME.TUT      335  11/01/90 12:00
  FIXBIOS .COM         50  11/01/90 12:00 | FLATTIRE.LRN    2,942  11/01/90 12:00
  FLOPPY-2.WPG        483  11/01/90 12:00 | GAVEL   .WPG      895  11/01/90 12:00
  GLOBE2-M.WPG      7,793  11/01/90 12:00 | GRAPHCNV.EXE  120,320  11/01/90 12:00
  HANDS-3 .WPG      1,125  11/01/90 12:00 | IB40LAPR.PRS  155,087  11/02/90 09:00
  INSTALL .EXE     57,856  11/01/90 12:00 | LETTER  .TUT      653  11/01/90 12:00
  LETTER_F.TUT        679  11/01/90 12:00 ▼ LETTER_P.TUT      652  11/01/90 12:00


Dir C:\LP10\DOCUMENT\*.*
```

Note current directory and highlighted directory

Fig. 9.8. *Preparing to display the contents of a new subdirectory.*

To examine a subdirectory *not* listed on the current List Files screen, follow these steps:

1. Move the cursor bar to highlight the `.` `Current` `<Dir>` directory name or a file name.

2. Press Enter.

3. Using the default-name editing techniques described in "Understanding List Files," type the path name for the new subdirectory.

4. Press Enter.

   The program displays a file list for the other subdirectory but does not change its active subdirectory.

All List Files menu options are available on the list of files displayed by Look (6). After you return to the main editing screen, you can press List Files (F5) twice to redisplay the last list of files.

Using Name Search

When you use the **Name** Search or Search (F2) option, the program quickly moves the cursor bar to highlight a file name or subdirectory in the list as you type the name. During the search, the program examines the entire list of files, regardless of where the cursor is within the list.

To use **Name** Search or Search, follow these steps:

1. Press either N or F2.

2. Type the first letter of the file name—for example, BURST-1.WPG—for which you want to search.

Tip: By default, the List Files feature's Name Search option finds only file names. However, if you type a backslash (\) before a letter, LetterPerfect searches instead for subdirectory names that match the text string. The backslash limits the search to subdirectory names (see fig. 9.9).

If you type *b*, the cursor bar moves to the first file name starting with that letter (see fig. 9.10).

```
12/01/90  11:50              Directory C:\LP10\*.*
Document size:        0   Free:  4,304,896 Used:  2,241,832      Files:     121

    .   Current    <Dir>                ..   Parent     <Dir>
  DOCUMENT.         <Dir> 11/02/90 09:00   {LP}SPC .FRM    10,142  11/01/90 12:00
  ADDRESS .TUT        978  11/01/90 12:00   ARROW-22.WPG       195  11/01/90 12:00
  BALLOONS.WPG      3,195  11/01/90 12:00   BANNER-3.WPG       727  11/01/90 12:00
  BEGIN   .TUT         11  11/01/90 12:00   BICYCLE .WPG     1,355  11/01/90 12:00
  BKGRND-1.WPG     11,489  11/01/90 12:00   BORDER-8.WPG       223  11/01/90 12:00
  BULB    .WPG      2,109  11/01/90 12:00   BURST-1 .WPG       827  11/01/90 12:00
  BUTTRFLY.WPG      5,291  11/01/90 12:00   CALENDAR.WPG       379  11/01/90 12:00
  CERTIF  .WPG        661  11/01/90 12:00   CHAP09P .PRN    71,340  12/01/90 09:00
  CHKBOX-1.WPG        661  11/01/90 12:00   CLOCK   .WPG     1,825  11/01/90 12:00
  CNTRCT-2.WPG      2,761  11/01/90 12:00   CONVERT .EXE   109,229  11/01/90 12:00
  CURSOR  .COM      1,452  11/01/90 12:00   DEVICE-2.WPG       665  11/01/90 12:00
  DIPLOMA .WPG      2,421  11/01/90 12:00   FILENAME.TUT       335  11/01/90 12:00
  FIXBIOS .COM         50  11/01/90 12:00   FLATTIRE.LRN     2,942  11/01/90 12:00
  FLOPPY-2.WPG        483  11/01/90 12:00   GAVEL   .WPG       895  11/01/90 12:00
  GLOBE2-M.WPG      7,793  11/01/90 12:00   GRAPHCNV.EXE   120,320  11/01/90 12:00
  HANDS-3 .WPG      1,125  11/01/90 12:00   IB40LAPR.PRS   155,087  11/02/90 09:00
  INSTALL .EXE     57,856  11/01/90 12:00   LETTER  .TUT       653  11/01/90 12:00
  LETTER_F.TUT        679  11/01/90 12:00 ▼ LETTER_P.TUT       652  11/01/90 12:00


\DOCUMENT                            (Name Search; Enter or arrows to Exit)
```

Fig. 9.9. A name search for a directory.

```
12/01/90  11:50              Directory C:\LP10\*.*
Document size:        0   Free:  4,304,896 Used:  2,241,832      Files:      121


.    Current    <Dir>                  ..    Parent    <Dir>
DOCUMENT.       <Dir>  11/02/90 09:00   {LP}SPC .FRM   10,142  11/01/90 12:00
ADDRESS .TUT      978  11/01/90 12:00   ARROW-22.WPG      195  11/01/90 12:00
BALLOONS.WPG    3,195  11/01/90 12:00   BANNER-3.WPG      727  11/01/90 12:00
BEGIN   .TUT       11  11/01/90 12:00   BICYCLE .WPG    1,355  11/01/90 12:00
BKGRND-1.WPG   11,489  11/01/90 12:00   BORDER-8.WPG      223  11/01/90 12:00
BULB    .WPG    2,109  11/01/90 12:00   BURST-1 .WPG      827  11/01/90 12:00
BUTTRFLY.WPG    5,291  11/01/90 12:00   CALENDAR.WPG      379  11/01/90 12:00
CERTIF  .WPG      661  11/01/90 12:00   CHAP09P .PRN   71,340  12/01/90 09:00
CHKBOX-1.WPG      661  11/01/90 12:00   CLOCK   .WPG    1,825  11/01/90 12:00
CNTRCT-2.WPG    2,761  11/01/90 12:00   CONVERT .EXE  109,229  11/01/90 12:00
CURSOR  .COM    1,452  11/01/90 12:00   DEVICE-2.WPG      665  11/01/90 12:00
DIPLOMA .WPG    2,421  11/01/90 12:00   FILENAME.TUT      335  11/01/90 12:00
FIXBIOS .COM       50  11/01/90 12:00   FLATTIRE.LRN    2,942  11/01/90 12:00
FLOPPY-2.WPG      483  11/01/90 12:00   GAVEL   .WPG      895  11/01/90 12:00
GLOBE2-M.WPG    7,793  11/01/90 12:00   GRAPHCNV.EXE  120,320  11/01/90 12:00
HANDS-3 .WPG    1,125  11/01/90 12:00   IB40LAPR.PRS  155,087  11/02/90 09:00
INSTALL .EXE   57,856  11/01/90 12:00   LETTER  .TUT      653  11/01/90 12:00
LETTER_F.TUT      679  11/01/90 12:00 ▼ LETTER_P.TUT      652  11/01/90 12:00


B                              (Name Search; Enter or arrows to Exit)
```

Fig. 9.10. *The effect on a name search of typing the first letter.*

3. If the cursor bar does not highlight the name of the file you seek, type *u* as the second letter of the name.

   The cursor bar moves to highlight the first file name that starts with the *bu* letter combination (see fig. 9.11). If no file name starts with those letters, the highlight bar moves to the file name that is as close (alphabetically) to that combination as possible.

> **Tip:** If you make a mistake or change your mind, press Backspace. The cursor bar returns to and highlights the first file that matches or most closely approximates this new search name. If the file was highlighted before, sometimes the cursor won't move. For example, the search names BUTA and BUT both highlight the file BUTANE.

4. If the cursor bar still does not highlight the correct file, type the third letter—*r* in this example.

   The cursor bar moves to highlight the first file name starting with these three letters (see fig. 9.12).

5. Press Enter, Cancel (F1), or Esc when the cursor bar highlights the file name you want.

```
┌─────────────────────────────────────────────────────────────────────┐
│ 12/01/90  11:50            Directory C:\LP10\*.*                       │
│ Document size:       0  Free: 4,304,896 Used: 2,241,832     Files:  121│
│                                                                        │
│  .    Current   <Dir>              ..    Parent    <Dir>               │
│ DOCUMENT.       <Dir>  11/02/90 09:00  {LP}SPC .FRM  10,142  11/01/90 12:00│
│ ADDRESS .TUT      978  11/01/90 12:00  ARROW-22.WPG     195  11/01/90 12:00│
│ BALLOONS.WPG    3,195  11/01/90 12:00  BANNER-3.WPG     727  11/01/90 12:00│
│ BEGIN   .TUT       11  11/01/90 12:00  BICYCLE .WPG   1,355  11/01/90 12:00│
│ BKGRND-1.WPG   11,489  11/01/90 12:00  BORDER-8.WPG     223  11/01/90 12:00│
│ BULB    .WPG    2,109  11/01/90 12:00  BURST-1 .WPG     827  11/01/90 12:00│
│ BUTTRFLY.WPG    5,291  11/01/90 12:00  CALENDAR.WPG     379  11/01/90 12:00│
│ CERTIF  .WPG      661  11/01/90 12:00  CHAP09P .PRN  71,340  12/01/90 09:00│
│ CHKBOX-1.WPG      661  11/01/90 12:00  CLOCK   .WPG   1,825  11/01/90 12:00│
│ CNTRCT-2.WPG    2,761  11/01/90 12:00  CONVERT .EXE 109,229  11/01/90 12:00│
│ CURSOR  .COM    1,452  11/01/90 12:00  DEVICE-2.WPG     665  11/01/90 12:00│
│ DIPLOMA .WPG    2,421  11/01/90 12:00  FILENAME.TUT     335  11/01/90 12:00│
│ FIXBIOS .COM       50  11/01/90 12:00  FLATTIRE.LRN   2,942  11/01/90 12:00│
│ FLOPPY-2.WPG      483  11/01/90 12:00  GAVEL   .WPG     895  11/01/90 12:00│
│ GLOBE2-M.WPG    7,793  11/01/90 12:00  GRAPHCNV.EXE 120,320  11/01/90 12:00│
│ HANDS-3 .WPG    1,125  11/01/90 12:00  IB40LAPR.PRS 155,087  11/02/90 09:00│
│ INSTALL .EXE   57,856  11/01/90 12:00  LETTER   .TUT    653  11/01/90 12:00│
│ LETTER_F.TUT      679  11/01/90 12:00 ▼ LETTER_P.TUT    652  11/01/90 12:00│
│                                                                        │
│ BU                       (Name Search; Enter or arrows to Exit)        │
└─────────────────────────────────────────────────────────────────────┘
```

Fig. 9.11. *The effect on a name search of typing a second letter.*

```
┌─────────────────────────────────────────────────────────────────────┐
│ 12/01/90  12:28            Directory C:\LP10\*.*                       │
│ Document size:       0  Free: 4,141,056 Used: 2,241,832     Files:  121│
│                                                                        │
│  .    Current   <Dir>              ..    Parent    <Dir>               │
│ DOCUMENT.       <Dir>  11/02/90 09:00  {LP}SPC .FRM  10,142  11/01/90 12:00│
│ ADDRESS .TUT      978  11/01/90 12:00  ARROW-22.WPG     195  11/01/90 12:00│
│ BALLOONS.WPG    3,195  11/01/90 12:00  BANNER-3.WPG     727  11/01/90 12:00│
│ BEGIN   .TUT       11  11/01/90 12:00  BICYCLE .WPG   1,355  11/01/90 12:00│
│ BKGRND-1.WPG   11,489  11/01/90 12:00  BORDER-8.WPG     223  11/01/90 12:00│
│ BULB    .WPG    2,109  11/01/90 12:00  BURST-1 .WPG     827  11/01/90 12:00│
│ BUTTRFLY.WPG    5,291  11/01/90 12:00  CALENDAR.WPG     379  11/01/90 12:00│
│ CERTIF  .WPG      661  11/01/90 12:00  CHAP09P .PRN  71,340  12/01/90 09:00│
│ CHKBOX-1.WPG      661  11/01/90 12:00  CLOCK   .WPG   1,825  11/01/90 12:00│
│ CNTRCT-2.WPG    2,761  11/01/90 12:00  CONVERT .EXE 109,229  11/01/90 12:00│
│ CURSOR  .COM    1,452  11/01/90 12:00  DEVICE-2.WPG     665  11/01/90 12:00│
│ DIPLOMA .WPG    2,421  11/01/90 12:00  FILENAME.TUT     335  11/01/90 12:00│
│ FIXBIOS .COM       50  11/01/90 12:00  FLATTIRE.LRN   2,942  11/01/90 12:00│
│ FLOPPY-2.WPG      483  11/01/90 12:00  GAVEL   .WPG     895  11/01/90 12:00│
│ GLOBE2-M.WPG    7,793  11/01/90 12:00  GRAPHCNV.EXE 120,320  11/01/90 12:00│
│ HANDS-3 .WPG    1,125  11/01/90 12:00  IB40LAPR.PRS 155,087  11/02/90 09:00│
│ INSTALL .EXE   57,856  11/01/90 12:00  LETTER   .TUT    653  11/01/90 12:00│
│ LETTER_F.TUT      679  11/01/90 12:00 ▼ LETTER_P.TUT    652  11/01/90 12:00│
│                                                                        │
│ BUR                      (Name Search; Enter or arrows to Exit)        │
└─────────────────────────────────────────────────────────────────────┘
```

Fig. 9.12. *The effect on a name search of typing a third letter.*

The name search ends, but the program is ready to perform any List Files menu operations on the highlighted file—Retrieve, Delete, Move/Rename, Copy, or Look.

Marking Files

LetterPerfect performs many List Files operations on a number of files simultaneously if you mark the files before you perform the operation. Follow these steps to mark files:

Reminder:
Use file marking to perform certain List Files functions simultaneously on more than one file.

1. Access the File pull-down menu, select List Files, move the mouse pointer to the directory name, and double-click. Alternatively, press List Files (F5) and then Enter to get to the List Files screen.

Tip: With one exception, pressing List Files (F5) twice redisplays the last list of files displayed by List Files. However, if the last file list was a directory on a floppy disk, pressing List Files (F5) twice displays the default directory regardless of the type of drive on which the directory is located. The redisplay capability is *not* available from the pull-down menu bar.

2. Move the cursor bar to the first file you want to mark.

3. Press the asterisk (*) key.

   LetterPerfect puts a bold asterisk left of the highlighted file name and automatically moves the cursor bar to the next file name in the list.

4. Move the cursor bar to each file you want to include in the List Files operation and mark those files (see fig. 9.13).

Tip: LetterPerfect lets you mark with two keystrokes all files in the list. When one or more files are marked, pressing either Home, asterisk or Mark Files (Alt-F5) unmarks all marked files.

With marked files, the last two fields of the screen heading change. The *Used:* field shows the combined size of the marked files. The *Files:* field changes to *Marked:* and shows the number of marked files.

Not all menu options work with marked files. For example, the program cannot retrieve all marked files at once. These options work with marked files:

> Delete (**2**)
> Move/Rename (**3**) (but not Rename)
> Copy (**5**) (to a different drive or directory)
> Look (**6**) (functions as if the files were not marked)

```
12/01/90  12:56              Directory C:\LP10\*.*
Document size:      0   Free:  4,141,056 Used:     32,731    Marked:      11

  .    Current   <Dir>              | ..    Parent    <Dir>
 DOCUMENT.       <Dir>  11/02/90 09:00 | {LP}SPC .FRM   10,142  11/01/90 12:00
  ADDRESS .TUT      978  11/01/90 12:00 | ARROW-22.WPG     195  11/01/90 12:00
 *BALLOONS.WPG    3,195  11/01/90 12:00 |*BANNER-3.WPG     727  11/01/90 12:00
 *BEGIN   .TUT       11  11/01/90 12:00 |*BICYCLE .WPG   1,355  11/01/90 12:00
 *BKGRND-1.WPG   11,489  11/01/90 12:00 | BORDER-8.WPG     223  11/01/90 12:00
  BULB    .WPG    2,109  11/01/90 12:00 |*BURST-1 .WPG     827  11/01/90 12:00
 *BUTTRFLY.WPG    5,291  11/01/90 12:00 | CALENDAR.WPG     379  11/01/90 12:00
  CERTIF  .WPG      661  11/01/90 12:00 | CHAP09P .PRN  71,340  12/01/90 09:00
  CHKBOX-1.WPG      661  11/01/90 12:00 | CLOCK   .WPG   1,825  11/01/90 12:00
  CNTRCT-2.WPG    2,761  11/01/90 12:00 | CONVERT .EXE 109,229  11/01/90 12:00
  CURSOR  .COM    1,452  11/01/90 12:00 |*DEVICE-2.WPG     665  11/01/90 12:00
  DIPLOMA .WPG    2,421  11/01/90 12:00 | FILENAME.TUT     335  11/01/90 12:00
  FIXBIOS .COM       50  11/01/90 12:00 | FLATTIRE.LRN   2,942  11/01/90 12:00
 *FLOPPY-2.WPG      483  11/01/90 12:00 |*GAVEL   .WPG     895  11/01/90 12:00
 *GLOBE2-M.WPG    7,793  11/01/90 12:00 | GRAPHCNV.EXE 120,320  11/01/90 12:00
  HANDS-3 .WPG    1,125  11/01/90 12:00 | IB40LAPR.PRS 155,087  11/02/90 09:00
  INSTALL .EXE   57,856  11/01/90 12:00 | LETTER   .TUT    653  11/01/90 12:00
  LETTER_F.TUT      679  11/01/90 12:00 | LETTER_P.TUT     652  11/01/90 12:00

 1 Retrieve; 2 Delete; 3 Move/Rename; 4 Other Directory; 5 Copy; 6 Look;
 N Name Search: 6
```

Fig. 9.13. The List Files display, showing multiple marked files.

See the sections on these features for information on using these functions with marked files.

If you mark files and then return to the main editing screen, LetterPerfect can redisplay the same file list, complete with the same marked files; just press List Files (F5) twice. However, if the last file list was a directory on a floppy disk, pressing List Files (F5) twice displays the default directory regardless of the type of drive on which the directory is located. This technique—which works as long as the list of files with marked files was the last file list displayed—is *not* available from the pull-down menu bar.

When you use any command except Look (6) that works with marked files, LetterPerfect asks you to confirm the requested operation on the marked files. If you select Yes, LetterPerfect continues with the operation. If you select No, LetterPerfect asks whether you want to perform the operation on the file highlighted by the cursor bar. Selecting No again terminates the operation. The files marked with asterisks remain marked.

For example, if you select No after marking files and requesting a move operation, LetterPerfect asks whether you want to rename the individual file. Select Yes, and LetterPerfect prompts you to enter a new name for the file. Select No, and LetterPerfect redisplays the entire menu field. The files marked with asterisks remain marked.

Locking Files

You can assign a password to files so that LetterPerfect does not retrieve them or display them with Look (6) unless the specific password is entered. If you decide to guard your files with password protection, remember that if you forget the password, the file is inaccessible to you. Don't forget your password!

Reminder:
If you forget a file's password, LetterPerfect cannot retrieve or display the file.

When a password is assigned, the document must be on the main editing screen. Use this procedure to assign a password:

1. Access the File pull-down menu bar and select **Add Password**. LetterPerfect displays the prompt `Enter Password:`.

   Alternatively, press Text Out (Ctrl-F5). LetterPerfect displays this menu:

   1 DOS Text Out; **2** Password; **3** Save Generic: **0**.

   Select **Password** (**2**). LetterPerfect displays this menu at the bottom of the screen:

   Password: 1 Add/Change; **2** Remove: **0**

   Select **Add/Change** (**1**). LetterPerfect displays the prompt `Enter Password:`.

2. Type up to 24 characters for the password.

Tip: The program accepts any character in the LetterPerfect character sets as part of the password. Press Compose (Ctrl-2) to enter any character that you cannot directly type from the keyboard.

3. Press Enter.

   LetterPerfect displays the prompt `Re-Enter Password:` **at the** bottom of the screen.

4. Type the password again.

5. Press Enter.

   If you make a typing error or don't enter the correct password, LetterPerfect displays an error message and restarts the password-creation process.

6. Access the **F**ile pull-down menu and select **S**ave or E**x**it. Alternatively, press Save (F10) or Exit (F7) and save the document to disk.

> ***Tip:*** With LetterPerfect you can use Cancel or Exit to end the password-creation process at any point. After you assign a password to the document on-screen, however, there is only one way to save the document without the password. You can use the procedure described later to remove the password before saving the document to disk.

When you use the LetterPerfect options to retrieve, display, or copy a file that is protected by a password, LetterPerfect displays this prompt at the bottom of the screen: Enter Password (<*drive:\path\filename.ext*>):.

Note: You do not need to enter a password to delete, move, or rename a locked file.

Type the password and press Enter. If you do not enter the correct password, LetterPerfect displays this error message at the bottom of the screen: ERROR: File is locked–<*drive:\path\filename.ext*>.

Use this procedure to remove the password from the file:

1. Retrieve the file to the main editing screen.

2. Access the **F**ile pull-down menu bar and select **R**emove Password. Alternatively, press Text Out (Ctrl-F5). LetterPerfect displays the menu:

   1 DOS Text Out; **2 P**assword; **3** Save **G**eneric: **0**.

   Select **P**assword (**2**). LetterPerfect displays the menu:

   Password: 1 Add/Change; **2 R**emove: **0**.

   Select **R**emove (**2**).

3. Access the **F**ile pull-down menu and select **S**ave or E**x**it. Alternatively, press Save (F10) or Exit (F7) and save the document to disk.

To verify that the file is unlocked, retrieve it again. LetterPerfect no longer prompts you to enter a password.

Summary

List Files makes your LetterPerfect sessions more convenient, efficient, and effective—and the feature is easier to learn and use than the corresponding DOS commands. The password-protection feature secures your files from unauthorized viewing or editing.

Remember that with List Files, you can perform many file and directory operations that you ordinarily have to do from DOS. For example, you can do these tasks:

- Retrieve LetterPerfect or DOS files

- Delete files and directories

- Move and rename files

- Change the current directory

- Create new directories

- Copy files

- Look at a file's contents

- Copy text from a file on disk through the Shell Clipboard Copy feature without first retrieving the file

- Protect a file with a password, using Text Out

Chapter 10 introduces you two of LetterPerfect's advanced document formatting features: Endnotes and Outlining.

10

Working with the Outline and Endnote Features

I n this chapter you learn about LetterPerfect's Date/Outline feature, which automatically places dates and paragraph numbers into documents. You also learn about the Endnote feature, which provides a simple, standard way of handling quotations and parenthetical information.

Why bother with automatic numbering when you can type the numbers yourself? With automatic numbering, you can create outlines without having to remember what number you should enter. With Outline, some keystrokes have special meanings, and LetterPerfect can automatically generate a new paragraph number or style every time you press Enter.

You also can edit Outline's hidden codes to number regular paragraphs automatically. Automatic outline and paragraph numbering also helps you make changes easily. For example, when you add, delete, or change the order of paragraphs numbered automatically, LetterPerfect renumbers them.

This chapter shows you how to accomplish these tasks:

- Create an outline
- Edit the outline
- Edit hidden Outline codes to create paragraphs numbered automatically

- Use Date to insert the time or date (or both) into a document automatically

- Use Endnote to annotate a document

- Edit an endnote

> *Reminder:* WordPerfect Corporation updated LetterPerfect 1.0 just before this book went to press. Dated 11/01/90, the interim release includes new options for existing features, and a few new features. The menus on your screen may, therefore, differ slightly from those shown in this book. Also, depending on the printer-form definition, margins, tab stops, and font you specify, the text placement and status-line information in documents you create may differ from that shown in this book's figures.
>
> For information about using the mouse and accessing the pull-down menus, refer to the Introduction.

Outlining a Document

Outlines in LetterPerfect consist of normal text that contains hidden **[Par Num:Auto]** formatting codes where paragraph numbers appear. When you use Outline, a hidden **[Outline On]** formatting code precedes the outline, and all text between that code and the end of the document or a hidden **[Outline Off]** formatting code is treated in a special way. Outline automatically generates and inserts these codes. Figure 10.1 shows a sample outline.

Activating the Outline Feature

Use Outline to create paragraph numbers automatically. When Outline is active, a new paragraph number is automatically inserted when you press Enter.

You may want to type a title before you turn on Outline, because the title is not part of the outline. For this example, begin with an empty main editing screen and follow these steps:

1. Access the **L**ayout pull-down menu and select **C**enter. Alternatively, press Center (Shift-F6) or Ctrl-c.

2. Type *CARE AND USE OF 5.25" FLOPPY DISKS* and press Enter.

```
File Edit Search Layout Tools Font Graphics Help        (Press ALT= for menu bar)
════════════════════════════════════════════════════════════════════════════════
                    CARE AND USE OF 5.25" FLOPPY DISKS

I.   Formatting Disks

     A.   New disks  [You must format new disks before you can
          use them].

     B.   Old disks  [Formatting erases everything on the old
          disk, so make a copy of the disk first].


II.  Storage of Disks

     A.   Temperature Range: 50-125 degrees Fahrenheit

     B.   Not near a possible magnetic field

          1.   Telephone
          2.   File drawer with magnetic closure
          3.   Paper clips

III. Handling
Outline                                          Pg 1 Ln 1" Pos 1"
```

Fig. 10.1. *A sample outline.*

3. Place the cursor where you want the outline to begin. In this example, Outline becomes active on the line below the centered heading.

4. Access the **Tools** pull-down menu and select **Outline On** (see fig. 10.2). Alternatively, press Date/Outline (Shift-F5). The following menu appears at the bottom of the screen:

    1 Date Text; **2** Date Code; **3** Outline On; **4** Outline Off: **0**

    Select **Outline On** (3).

At the bottom of the screen, the prompt *Outline* appears, replacing the name of the file if one was displayed. When you activate Outline, a hidden formatting code is inserted at the cursor. Use Reveal Codes—access the Edit pull-down menu and choose **Reveal Codes** or, alternatively, press Reveal Codes (Alt-F3 or F11) or Ctrl-r—to see the **[Outline On]** code and the succeeding paragraph-numbering codes (see fig. 10.3). Reveal Codes is active in this chapter's figures so that you can see what is happening, but you do not have to turn on Reveal Codes to use Outline.

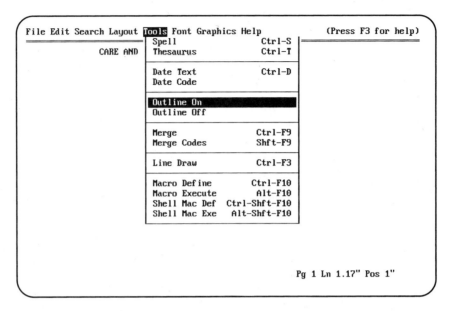

Fig. 10.2. *The Tools pull-down menu.*

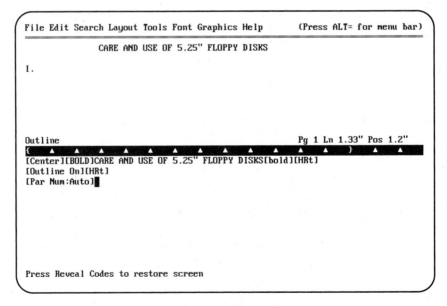

Fig. 10.3. *Hidden formatting codes created by Outline.*

You see the `Outline` prompt when the cursor is in an area following the **[Outline On]** code. The prompt reminds you that Outline is active, which means that the Enter, Tab, and Margin Release keys perform specific additional functions (explained in the next section) unique to Outline.

Creating Level Numbers

The style for the numbers created by Outline has eight levels, which are specified by the number of **[TAB]** codes between the left margin and the **[Par Num:Auto]** code. The following explains these eight levels:

- *First level* (no **[TAB]** code between the left margin and the **[Par Num:Auto]** code): Numbers appear as uppercase Roman numerals followed by a period, as in *I., II., III.*

- *Second level* (one **[TAB]** code between the left margin and the **[Par Num:Auto]** code): Numbers appear as capital letters followed by a period, as in *A., B., C.*

- *Third level* (two **[TAB]** codes between the left margin and the **[Par Num:Auto]** code): Numbers appear as digits or Arabic numerals followed by a period, as in *1., 2., 3.*

- *Fourth level* (three **[TAB]** codes between the left margin and the **[Par Num:Auto]** code): Numbers appear as lowercase letters followed by a period, as in *a., b., c.*

- *Fifth level* (four **[TAB]** codes between the left margin and the **[Par Num:Auto]** code): Numbers appear as digits or Arabic numerals enclosed in parentheses, as in *(1), (2), (3)*.

- *Sixth level* (five **[TAB]** codes between the left margin and the **[Par Num:Auto]** code): Numbers appear as lowercase letters enclosed in parentheses, as in *(a), (b), (c)*.

- *Seventh level* (six **[TAB]** codes between the left margin and the **[Par Num:Auto]** code): Numbers appear as lowercase Roman numerals enclosed in parentheses, as in *(i), (ii), (iii)*.

- *Eighth and all lower levels* (seven or more **[TAB]** codes between the left margin and the **[Par Num:Auto]** code): Numbers appear as lowercase letters, each with a single parenthesis to its right, as in *a), b), c)*.

When Outline is on, the Enter, Tab, Decimal Tab, and Margin Release keys perform these special functions in addition to their regular functions:

- *Enter*: Inserts the **[HRt]** hard-return code at the cursor and on the next line creates a new **[Par Num:Auto]** paragraph number code preceded by the same number of **[TAB]** codes in front of the last **[Par Num:Auto]** code above the cursor.

- *Tab*: Inserts a hard-tab code left of the **[Par Num:Auto]** code. This action changes the level of the number to the next lower level.

- *Decimal Tab (Ctrl-F6)*: When the cursor is placed immediately left of the **[Par Num:Auto]** code and you press Decimal Tab (Ctrl-F6), a **[DEC TAB]** code is inserted at the cursor. The code aligns the numbers on the alignment character but does *not* raise or lower the level of the number. When a new line is created, the **[DEC TAB]** code is omitted.

- *Margin Release (Shift-Tab)*: Deletes one **[TAB]** code; this action changes the level of the number to the next higher level.

    For example, if pressing Enter creates a *II* on the new line, pressing Tab moves the number one tab stop right and changes to the number to *A*. Pressing Margin Release moves the character back to its original position and restores it to *II*.

Adjusting Number Levels

When Outline is active and you press Enter, LetterPerfect responds according to the status of the line when you press the key. If the line contains only the **[Par Num:Auto]** code or one or more **[TAB]** or **[DEC TAB]** codes and the **[Par Num:Auto]** code, a **[HRt]** code is inserted at the beginning of the line. This action moves the cursor and all the codes on the current line down one line.

If, however, the line contains any other formatting code, a single character, or a space, a **[HRt]** code is inserted at the end of the line, the cursor is moved to the next line, and the Outline code structure is duplicated from the original line to maintain the number level. Pressing either Tab or Margin Release before you enter any additional formatting codes or text raises or lowers the number level.

For this example, assume that pressing Enter creates a line with numbering on the third level. To raise the numbering to the second level, access the **Layout** pull-down menu and select **Margin Release**. Alternatively, press Margin Release

(Shift-Tab). To lower the numbering to the fourth level, press Tab. Each time you press Margin Release or Tab, the numbering system changes by one level.

> *Tip:* There are two ways of stopping the **[Par Num:Auto]** code from advancing and incrementing on a line:
>
> - Type a single character.
> - Manually insert a hard tab—the **[TAB]** code created when you press and release the Home key immediately before pressing the Tab key.
>
> When you do either of the above, the **[Par Num:Auto]** code remains at its location, and all of LetterPerfect's formatting keys (including Tab) return to their normal functions until you press Enter. Pressing Enter creates a new Outline number level as described earlier.

Editing WordPerfect Documents with Automatic-Paragraph Numbers

LetterPerfect supports automatically generated paragraph numbers in WordPerfect 5.1 documents. However, LetterPerfect ignores WordPerfect codes defining the style and level of these paragraph numbers. Because of this limitation, these paragraph numbers assume the LetterPerfect style for the paragraph level they occupy when you edit the document in LetterPerfect.

For example, consider a WordPerfect document containing a paragraph-definition code that sets level-three paragraph numbers to capital Roman numerals (I, II, III, and so on). When you import the document into LetterPerfect, the automatic paragraph numbers convert to Arabic numerals (1, 2, 3 and so on). After you edit this type of document in LetterPerfect, the converted paragraph numbers revert to the format designated by the paragraph-definition code if you retrieve the document into WordPerfect 5.1.

Deactivating the Outline Feature

Outline works until you deactivate it. You can activate and deactivate Outline as often as necessary.

If you are unsure whether Outline is active, look at the bottom left corner of the screen: if the `Outline` prompt is displayed, Outline is active at the cursor.

Follow these steps to deactivate Outline:

1. Place the cursor where you want to stop using Outline.

2. Access the **Tools** pull-down menu and select Outline Off. Alternatively, press Date/Outline (Shift-F5); you see this menu at the bottom of the screen:

   1 Date **Text**; **2** Date **Code**; **3** Outline **On**; **4** Outline Off: **0**

   Select Outline Off (**4**).

   A hidden **[Outline Off]** formatting code is inserted at the cursor. From that point forward, Outline is deactivated. Outline remains active between the **[Outline On]** and **[Outline Off]** formatting codes.

> *Tip:* If you deactivate Outline at the wrong location, delete the hidden **[Outline Off]** formatting code. Outline becomes active to the bottom of the document. Paragraphs are *not*, however, reformatted below the **[Outline Off]** code.

> *Caution:* Deleting the **[Outline On]** formatting code deactivates Outline but does *not* reformat the part of the document created when Outline was active. See the following section, "Creating Automatic Paragraph Numbers," to learn to use this method to create automatically numbered paragraphs.

After you deactivate Outline, the Enter and Tab keys revert to their usual functions. You now can enter normal paragraphs after the outline. Moving the cursor back into the text between the **[Outline On]** and **[Outline Off]** codes automatically causes Enter and Tab to perform the special outline functions once again.

> *Tip:* Within endnotes you can create outlines that are completely independent of any outlines in the main body of the document. For information on the Endnote feature, see the sections under "Creating Endnotes" later in this chapter.

Creating Automatic Paragraph Numbers

When Outline is not active, you can automatically number regular paragraphs like those shown in figure 10.4. The following example shows you how to set up numbering by using the third-level Arabic numerals. You can, however, use the same procedure to create automatically numbered paragraphs with any numbering level of Outline.

```
File Edit Search Layout Tools Font Graphics Help      (Press ALT= for menu bar)

     1. This is a sample of document with automatically numbered
paragraphs.  Automatic numbering is created by setting tab stops,
activating LetterPerfect's Outline feature, typing the first word
of the first paragraph, pressing Enter, and then deleting the
[Outline On] formatting code.

     2. Although this method is not as simple as a feature selected
directly from a LetterPerfect menu, it is easy to use once you get
the hang of it.

     3. If you run LetterPerfect under the Shell 3.01 program
(included in the LetterPerfect 1.0 software package), you can write
a Shell macro that creates automatic paragraph numbering in only a
few seconds and as few as five keystrokes.

     4. With the 11/01/90 interim software, you also can write a
LetterPerfect macro that creates automatic paragraph numbering in
only a few seconds and as few as five keystrokes.




                                          Pg 1 Ln 1" Pos 1"
```

Fig. 10.4. *A document with automatic paragraph numbering.*

Follow these steps to create paragraphs with automatic paragraph numbering:

1. Access the **L**ayout pull-down menu. Alternatively, press Format (Shift-F8).

    You see the main Format menu.

2. Select **T**abs (**5**).

    You see the tab-setting menu at the bottom of the screen.

3. Press Home, Home, left arrow.

4. Press Delete to End of Line (Ctrl-End).

5. Press T and R to place tab settings relative to the left margin.

6. Type the following numbers, pressing Enter after each one:

   0.2

   0.5

   0.8

7. Press Exit (F7) twice to return to the main document editing screen.

8. Access the **Tools** pull-down menu and select **Outline On**. Alternatively, press Date/Outline (Shift-F5); next you see this menu at the bottom of the screen:

   1 Date Text; **2** Date Code; **3** Outline **On**; **4** Outline Off: **0**

   Select Outline **On** (**3**).

9. Press Enter.

   A **[Para Num:Auto]** code that creates the first-level number *I.* is inserted.

10. Move the cursor to the **[Outline On]** code and delete it and the **[HRt]** that follows it.

11. With the cursor to the left of the **[Par Num:Auto]** code, press Home-Tab twice to insert two hard-tab codes.

12. Move the cursor to the right of the **[Par Num:Auto]** code and press Home-Tab to insert a hard tab.

    An automatic paragraph number is created (see fig. 10.5).

13. For each subsequent paragraph that requires an automatic paragraph number, block and copy the **[TAB][TAB] [Para Num:Auto][TAB]** codes and insert them at the beginning of each paragraph either before or after you type the paragraph.

Chapter 13 shows you how to create a macro that automatically inserts the **[TAB][TAB][Para Num:Auto][TAB]** code combination.

```
File Edit Search Layout Tools Font Graphics Help        (Press ALT= for menu bar)

    1. This is a sample of document with automatically numbered
paragraphs.  Automatic numbering is created by setting tab stops,
activating LetterPerfect's Outline feature, typing the first word
of the first paragraph, pressing Enter, and then deleting the
[Outline On] formatting code.

    2. Although this method is not as simple as a feature selected
directly from a LetterPerfect menu, it is easy to use once you get
the hang of it.
                                                Pg 1 Ln 1" Pos 1"
{   ▲    ▲    ▲    ▲    ▲    ▲    ▲    ▲    ▲    ▲    }    ▲    ▲
[Tab Set:Rel; +0.2",+0.4",+0.7"][Just:Full][TAB][TAB][Par Num:Auto][TAB]This is
a sample of document with automatically numbered[SRt]
paragraphs.  Automatic numbering is created by setting tab stops,[SRt]
activating LetterPerfect's Outline feature, typing the first word[SRt]
of the first paragraph, pressing Enter, and then deleting the[SRt]
[BOLD][Outline On][bold] formatting code.[HRt]
[HRt]
[TAB][TAB][Par Num:Auto][TAB]Although this method is not as simple as a feature
selected[SRt]
directly from a LetterPerfect menu, it is easy to use once you get[SRt]

Press Reveal Codes to restore screen
```

Fig. 10.5. The automatic-paragraph-numbering code combination.

Tip: By default, numbers created by automatic numbering line up on the first numeral and offset to the right. To align the numbers on the period so that the 0 in 10 is under the 9, move the cursor immediately left of the **[Par Num:Auto]** code and press Tab Align (Ctrl-F6).

Tip: To number paragraphs automatically in different sections of the document and begin each sequence with the number 1, move the cursor to the line above each sequence and insert the **[Outline On][Outline Off]** code combination.

Inserting Dates Automatically

Date/Outline also inserts the current date, the current time, or both into a document at the cursor. The exact date and its format are determined by the information in the WP.LRS file. (See Chapter 12 for information about the WP.LRS file.) Table 10.1 lists the date and time formatting codes recognized by LetterPerfect.

Table 10.1
LetterPerfect's WP.LRS File Date and Time Formatting Codes

Character	Field/Line Number*	Function
1	2/1	Day of the month
2	2/1	Month (as a number)
3	2/1	Month (as a word)
4	2/1	Year (as four numbers)
5	2/1	Year (as the last two numbers)
6	2/1	Day of week (as a word)
7	2/1	Hour (24-hour clock)
8	2/1	Hour (12-hour clock)
9	2/1	Minute
0	2/1	Adds am and pm to time
%	2/1	Adds leading 0 to number values 0 through 9
$	2/1	Adds leading space to number values 0 through 9
am	2/2	Format for trailing am for time format
pm	2/3	Format for trailing pm for time format
<month name>	3/1-12	Complete name of each month
<month abbreviation>	4-1/12	Abbreviated name of each month
<day name>	5/1-12	Complete name of each day
<day abbreviation>	6-1/12	Abbreviated name of each day

* Each field ends with the old-style **[HRT]** end-field code combination (the **[HRt]** code is not visible on the main editing screen). Each line in a multiple-line record ends with a hidden **[HRt]** formatting code.

Follow these steps to insert the date or time:

1. Place the cursor where you want to insert the time or date.

2. Access the **T**ools pull-down menu and select Date **T**ext. Alternatively, press Date/Outline (Shift-F5). Next you see this menu prompt at the bottom of the screen:

   1 Date Text; **2** Date Code; **3** Outline **On**; **4** Outline Off: **0**

   Select Date **T**ext (**1**).

   The date, time, or date and time are inserted into the document at the cursor.

> ***Tip:*** The Ctrl-d fast-key combination is the fastest way to insert the date into the document because it requires the fewest keystrokes. You can use Ctrl-d to insert only text—not the date code.

Date Code (**2**) seems to perform the same as the first option, but it actually operates differently. When you select this option, a hidden code is inserted at the cursor; this code causes the current date to appear on-screen. The code's exact appearance, when it is viewed with Reveal Codes, depends on the formatting information in the WP.LRS file. The default information appears as **[Date:3 1, 4]**.

Unlike the Date **T**ext (**1**) option, which inserts text that does not change unless you edit it, the date code always reflects the system's current date and time. If, for example, you create a document on August 1, 1990, but do not print it until August 3, 1990, the date that appears on-screen and in the printed copy is August 3, 1990.

Using the Endnote Feature

Many documents contain material that requires further explanation. The Endnote feature provides a simple, standard way of handling quotations as well as parenthetical information. Endnotes are grouped at the end of the document immediately following the last character or hidden formatting code. The following section shows you how to create, edit, move, delete, and view endnotes.

Creating Endnotes

An endnote is a reference or other parenthetical text appearing at the end of a document. Creating and editing endnotes in LetterPerfect is easy.

Before you create an endnote, you start, naturally, with text that needs a note. For this example, type the main text as it appears in figure 10.6.

```
In Charles Dickens's story of Nicholas Nickleby, one of the
villains is Mr. Wackford Squeers.

    Mr. Squeers's appearance was not prepossessing. He had
    but one eye, and the popular prejudice runs in favour of
    two.... The blank side of his face was much wrinkled and
    puckered up, which gave him a very sinister appearance,
    especially when he smiled, at which times his expression
    bordered closely on the villanous [sic].... He wore...a
    suit of scholastic black, but his coat sleeves being a
    great deal too long, and his trousers a great deal too
    short, he appeared ill at ease in his clothes, and as if
    he were in a perpetual state of astonishment at finding
    himself so respectable.¹

Compare this description with one of the hero, Nicholas
himself, whose face was "open, handsome, and ingenuous,"²
and whose eyes were "bright with the light of intelligence
and spirit. His figure was somewhat slight, but manly and
well-formed; and apart from all the grace of youth and
comeliness, there was an emanation from the warm young
heart in his look and bearing...."³


    ¹Charles Dickens, The Life and Adventures of Nicholas
Nickleby (Philadelphia: University of Pennsylvania Press,
1982), vol. 1, p. 24.
        ²Dickens, p. 19
        ³Dickens, p. 19
```

Fig. 10.6. *A sample document with endnotes.*

Now that you have the text, create the endnote by completing these steps:

1. Place the cursor in the text where you want a footnote number to appear. For this example, place the cursor after the period following *so respectable* at the end of the indented quotation.

2. Access the Layout pull-down menu and choose Endnote Create (see fig. 10.7). Alternatively, press Ctrl-e. You see the Endnote editing screen shown in figure 10.8.

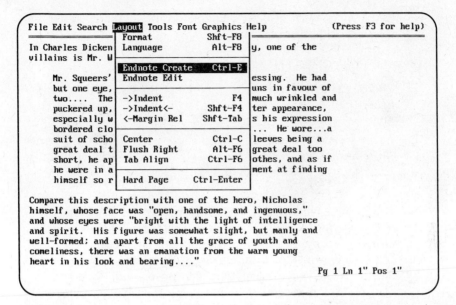

Fig. 10.7. The Layout pull-down menu.

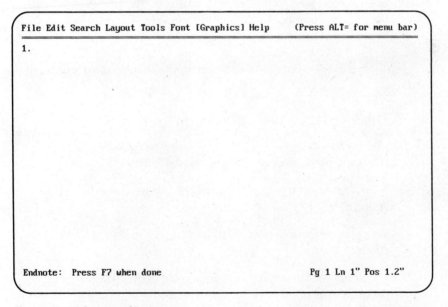

Fig. 10.8. Endnote's editing screen.

Another alternative is to press Endnote (Ctrl-F7); then you see this menu at the bottom of the screen:

Endnote: 1 Create; **2** Edit: 0.

Choose **Create** (**1**). You see the Endnote editing screen shown in figure 10.8.

> ***Tip:*** Pressing the Ctrl-e fast-key combination takes you directly to the Endnote editing screen shown in figure 10.8. This method is quicker than using either the pull-down menus or function keys.

The Endnote editing screen closely resembles the main editing screen. On this screen, you type text in the same manner as in the main document. As you create the endnote, most LetterPerfect editing and formatting features—Spell, Thesaurus, Retrieve, Save, Block, Reveal Codes, Delete, Undelete, Move, Bold, Underline, Font, and so on, except for Graphics—are available from the pull-down menu bar and keyboard.

The correct number is automatically inserted at the beginning of the endnote, which appears as regular text. The program places the endnote number just before the cursor so that you can immediately begin typing the text of the endnote.

> ***Tip:*** You can use List Files from within an endnote to retrieve text into the note.

3. Type the text of the endnote as follows:

   Charles Dickens, *The Life and Adventures of Nicholas Nickleby* (Philadelphia: University of Pennsylvania Press, 1982), vol.1, p. 24.

   When you finish typing, the screen appears as shown in figure 10.9.

4. After you create the endnote, press Exit (F7) to return to the main editing screen.

   The endnote is inserted as a hidden code in the document at the cursor. The text of the endnote is not displayed on the main editing screen, but the location of the endnote is marked with a number that appears in the same manner as superscript text displayed on-screen (see fig. 10.10).

```
File Edit Search Layout Tools Font [Graphics] Help      (Press ALT= for menu bar)

1.Charles Dickens, The Life and Adventures of Nicholas
Nickleby (Philadelphia: University of Pennsylvania Press,
1982), vol. 1, p. 24.




















Endnote:  Press F7 when done                          Pg 1 Ln 1" Pos 1"
```

Fig. 10.9. *The Endnote editing screen with text.*

```
File Edit Search Layout Tools Font Graphics Help       (Press ALT= for menu bar)

In Charles Dicken's story of Nicholas Nickleby, one of the
villains is Mr. Wackford Squeers:

     Mr. Squeers's appearance was not prepossessing.  He had
     but one eye, and the popular prejudice runs in favour of
     two....  The blank side of his face was much wrinkled and
     puckered up, which give him a very sinister appearance,
     especially when he smiled, at which times his expression
     bordered closely on the villanous [sic]....  He wore...a
     suit of scholastic black, but his coat sleeves being a
     great deal too long, and his trousers a great deal too
     short, he appeared ill at ease in his clothes, and as if
     he were in a perpetual state of astonishment at finding
     himself so respectable.1

Compare this description with one of the hero, Nicholas
himself, whose face was "open, handsome, and ingenuous,"2
and whose eyes were "bright with the light of intelligence
and spirit.  His figure was somewhat slight, but manly and
well-formed; and apart from all the grace of youth and
comeliness, there was an emanation from the warm young
heart in his look and bearing...."3

                                                      Pg 1 Ln 1" Pos 1"
```

Fig. 10.10. *An endnote in the text.*

> ***Tip:*** Because the Endnote editing screen and the main editing screen appear so similar, you may forget to return to the main screen after you finish the endnote. If you continue typing text for the main body of the document as part of the endnote, block the text that does not belong in the note, delete the block, exit to the main editing screen, and undelete the block.

5. Repeat steps 1 through 4 to enter other endnotes shown in figure 10.6. For this example, you have two more endnotes to enter. Put footnote 2 after the quotation mark following *ingenuous* and type *Dickens, p. 19.* as the text. Put footnote 3 after the quotation mark following *bearing* and again type *Dickens, p. 19.*

> ***Tip:*** To avoid separating the page number (24, for example) from the page reference (p.), insert a hard space (Home, space bar) instead of a normal space between the *p.* and the number that follows. Words separated by a hard space are treated as a single word and are joined on a single line.

Looking at Endnotes

You can choose from among three methods for viewing the contents of an endnote without printing the document: Reveal Codes, View Document, and Endnote Edit.

Using Reveal Codes

Reveal Codes shows you the hidden endnote code and displays both the text surrounding the endnote and the information in the note itself.

Because only the first few words of the endnote appear when you use Reveal Codes, use this feature when you want to see the beginning of the endnote in the context of the normal text. If the endnote is long, it ends with an ellipsis (...). The entire endnote is there, but Reveal Codes cannot display it. You can see an entire footnote by using other methods.

To view an endnote with Reveal Codes, move the cursor under an endnote number (for this example, the first one) and follow these steps:

1. Access the **Edit** pull-down menu and select **R**eveal Codes. Alternatively, press Reveal Codes (Alt-F3 or F11) or Ctrl-r.

LetterPerfect splits the screen into two windows and displays the first endnote as a highlighted text block: **[Endnote:1;[Note Num]**Charles Dickens, **[UND]**The Life a ...].

2. Press Reveal Codes (Alt-F3 or F11) or Ctrl-r again to exit to the normal document.

The blocked text is the endnote code you created earlier in this section. The part of the endnote displayed in the normal screen is represented by the word *Endnote*, which tells LetterPerfect to superscript the number that follows—in this case, 1.

Following the semicolon is the part of the note that appears at the end of the document, represented by the bracketed **Note Num** notation followed by the beginning of the text of the footnote.

Using Reveal Codes to see the notes is a quick solution; however, because you see only part of the note, you may prefer to check notes by using one of the methods covered in the next two sections.

Using View Document

If your computer system does not have a video graphics card or monitor, it cannot display superscripts or the entire page or zoom in to a particular point on the page. Endnotes can, however, be displayed in context. Skip to step 6 if your computer system does not have a graphics card or monitor.

As you read in Chapter 7, you can use View Document to see the document and its endnotes just as they appear on the printed page without the time and trouble of printing.

Follow these steps to view endnotes with View Document:

1. Move the cursor to the bottom of the document.

2. Access the **File** pull-down menu and select **Print**. Alternatively, press Print (Shift-F7).

You see the main Print menu. Check the printer listing to ensure that the selected printer is the one on which LetterPerfect will print the document so that the document displays accurately.

3. Select **View Document (3)**.

> ***Tip:*** Use the Ctrl-p fast-key combination to activate View Document with the fewest keystrokes.

4. If you do not see the entire page on-screen, select Full Page (**3**) to display the document (see fig. 10.11).

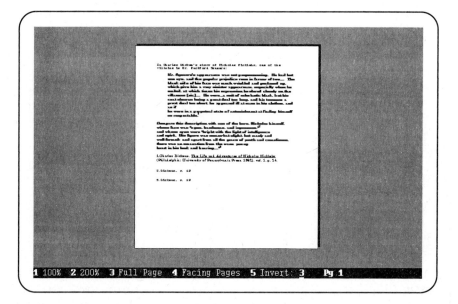

Fig. 10.11. *The View Document full-page display.*

5. Select 100% (**1**) to zoom in more closely on the text (see fig. 10.12).

6. Move the cursor to the bottom of the page with GoTo, down arrow (Ctrl-Home, down arrow) to see the endnotes at the bottom of the page.

7. Press Exit (F7) to return to the document.

Using Endnote Edit

The section "Editing Endnotes" later in this chapter shows you how to use Endnote editing to change an endnote. You also can use the editing function to examine the endnote without making changes. Although this method does not simultaneously display the endnote and the text surrounding the endnote, it is the only method by which you can change the note.

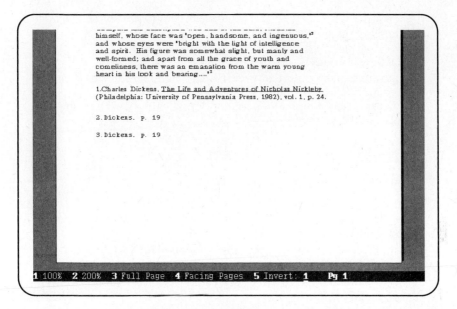

Fig. 10.12. *A View Document 100% page display.*

Adding Endnotes

After you enter several endnotes, you may find that you need one more somewhere in the midst of those previously created. After you create the new endnote, all the notes are renumbered.

Deleting Endnotes

LetterPerfect stores the entire endnote (the number and the text) in one code. You can delete the endnote the same way that you delete any other code.

Follow these steps to delete an endnote:

1. Move the cursor under the endnote to be deleted.

2. Press Del if the cursor is on top of the code or Backspace if the cursor is immediately right of the code.

   You see a confirmation prompt unless you are in Reveal Codes.

3. Select **Yes** to delete the endnote; select **No** to cancel the deletion operation.

   If Reveal Codes is active during the deletion, you are not prompted for confirmation before the endnote is deleted.

   LetterPerfect automatically renumbers all endnotes following the deleted endnote.

Moving Endnotes

When you edit a document, you may want to move or copy an endnote, with or without the normal text surrounding the note. To move just the endnote, delete the code and then undelete the code elsewhere. (Keep in mind that when you use Undelete (F1) or Esc, you can undelete up to the past three deletions, cycling through them by selecting **P**revious Deletion (**2**) from the Undelete menu prompt.)

To copy the note, delete the code as explained in the preceding section and then undelete the note in the original location. Move the cursor to the location where you want another copy of the same endnote to appear and undelete the code again.

Editing Endnotes

You can change an endnote with endnote editing. Suppose that you remember only the title of a book and nothing else when you originally type an endnote. Now you want to enter the complete reference.

Follow these steps to edit an endnote from anywhere in the document:

1. Access the **L**ayout pull-down menu and select Endnote Edit. Alternatively, press Endnote (Ctrl-F7). At the bottom of the screen you see this menu:

   Endnote: **1** Create; **2** Edit: **0**.

   You see the Endnote number? prompt at the bottom of the screen, followed by the number of the first endnote that follows the cursor.

Caution: If the cursor follows the last endnote in the document, you are prompted with a number for an endnote that does not exist! If you then press Enter to accept the number, you see the message `* Not found *`, and you must begin again. To avoid this waste of time, always verify the number with which you are prompted.

2. Press Enter if the default endnote number matches the one you want to edit. To edit a different endnote, type its number and press Enter. For this example, type *3* and press Enter.

3. Because you are now in an Endnote editing screen, use the normal cursor-movement and editing keys to change the endnote. In the example, change the page number from 19 to 24.

4. Press Exit (F7) to return to the main editing screen.

Tip: When you finish editing the endnote, the cursor is positioned just after the code for the endnote. To return the cursor where it was before you edited the endnote, use GoTo, GoTo (Ctrl-Home, Ctrl-Home).

Editing WordPerfect Documents with Footnotes

Unlike its big brother, WordPerfect 5.1, LetterPerfect does not have a footnote feature. However, when you retrieve a WordPerfect document that contains footnotes, LetterPerfect automatically converts the footnotes into endnotes with a special formatting code: **[Endnote/WP Footnote]**. These converted footnotes are numbered in sequence with regular endnotes in the document.

LetterPerfect lets you edit these converted footnotes in the same manner as regular footnotes. After you edit this type of document in LetterPerfect, the converted footnotes revert to the footnote format if you edit the document in WordPerfect 5.1.

Summary

In this chapter, you learned to do these tasks:

- Create an outline
- Edit an outline
- Number paragraphs automatically
- Automatically insert date and time data
- Create an endnote
- Display endnotes by using Reveal Codes and View Document
- Delete and move endnotes
- Edit an endnote

Chapter 11 shows you how LetterPerfect's Spell and Thesaurus features aid in the composing and editing of documents.

11

Using the Speller and Thesaurus

W hether you write for business or pleasure, LetterPerfect's Spell and Thesaurus features help make you a more efficient and accurate writer. The Spell dictionary contains the correct spelling for more than 80,000 words. The Thesaurus dictionary includes synonyms for more than 8,500 words.

The Spell feature searches for spelling and typing errors such as the following:

- Transposed, missing, extra, or wrong letters
- Certain capitalization errors
- Double-word sequences like *the the*

With Spell you can look up words or create and maintain a special dictionary of terms specific to your profession. Spell dictionaries contain only correct spellings—not definitions or indications where you should put hyphens.

You can activate Spell or Thesaurus and select replacement words with the mouse or the keyboard.

If you write in a language other than English and if you installed a WordPerfect Language Module (WLM), you can use the Language feature to insert a language code that tells LetterPerfect to use the Spell, Thesaurus, and Hyphenation files for that language. When this book was published, WordPerfect Corporation offered 27 language modules, including four versions of English and two each of French, German, and Portuguese.

If you frequently repeat one word, Thesaurus lets you find a synonym for it. When you can't think of the right word, use the Thesaurus feature to suggest a substitute word.

Because letters are used to select individual words within Spell or Thesaurus, you select certain menu options only by numbers, not by mnemonic letters or by clicking with the mouse.

This chapter shows you how to use Spell and Thesaurus as part of the cycle of drafting, revising, editing, and proofreading. In this chapter, you learn to do these tasks:

- Access Spell or Thesaurus on a floppy or a hard disk system

- Spell-check a word, page, document, or block of text

- Create and use supplemental Spell dictionaries

- Use the Thesaurus as an aid to composition—for replacing words, viewing words in context, and looking up additional words

Reminder: WordPerfect Corporation updated LetterPerfect 1.0 just before this book went to press. Dated 11/01/90, the interim release includes new options for existing features, and a few new features. The menus on your screen may, therefore, differ slightly from those shown in this book. Also, depending on the printer-form definition, margins, tab stops, and font you specify, the text placement and status-line information in documents you create may differ from that shown in this book's figures.

For information about using the mouse and accessing the pull-down menus, refer to the Introduction.

All instructions and examples in this chapter are drawn from the U.S. English language files WP{WP}US.LEX, WP{WP}US.SUP, and WP{WP}US.THS. If you use a different language module, the two-letter code of that language replaces the *US* in the file name.

Introducing the Spell Feature

When you activate Spell, LetterPerfect first compares each word to be examined with the words in its dictionary. The main dictionary contains a list of common words (words most frequently used) and a list of main words (words generally found in dictionaries). Both lists are combined in the WP{WP}US.LEX main dictionary file. Words that you add manually are in the WP{WP}US.SUP supplemental dictionary.

The Spell feature checks every word against its list of common words. If Spell cannot match the word to one in its common-word list, the feature looks in the list of main words. If Spell cannot match the word to one in its main-word list, and if you create a supplemental word list, the feature tries to match the word to one in this supplemental dictionary. Words in any of the dictionaries are considered correct.

If Spell does not find a word, it gives you several options:

- If Spell offers one or more suggested words, you can select a replacement for the misspelled word.

- You can edit the word by typing the correct spelling.

- If the highlighted word is correct, you can add it to the supplemental dictionary. You can create several supplemental dictionaries of specialized terms—for instance, terms used for law, engineering, medicine, literary criticism, or entomology—and use these special dictionaries during a spell-check.

Spell is not a grammar-checking program and cannot completely replace a human proofreader. The program cannot detect a correctly spelled but incorrectly used word. Spell considers correct any word it finds in any of its dictionaries. For example, suppose that you type *them* instead of *then*, or *their* instead of *there*. Spell does not prompt you to correct these words, because it finds each word in a dictionary. For this reason, proofread your document after using the Spell feature.

Cue:
Spell is not a substitute for a human proofreader; read the document carefully after you perform a spell-check.

The Spell dictionaries contain alternative spellings for some words. For example, the Spell feature includes *doughnut* and *donut*, and *numbskull* and *numskull*.

Using the Spell Feature

On systems with a hard disk drive, LetterPerfect automatically looks for the Spell and Thesaurus dictionary and program files in the subdirectory containing the main program files. Beginning with the 11/01/90 software, LetterPerfect includes a Setup option that lets you set a different subdirectory for the dictionary and program files. (See Chapter 1 for information on using the Setup feature.)

The Spell feature requires two files in order to function: WP{WP}US.LEX and WP{WP}US.SPW. WP{WP}US.LEX contains the main dictionary and common-word list. WP{WP}US.SPW contains the programming code. Spell stores words you select with its add-word option in a third file, WP{WP}US.SUP. The first time you use the add-word option, the program automatically creates WP{WP}US.SUP in the subdirectory containing Spell's other two files.

> *Tip:* If your computer has expanded or extended memory, you can copy the Spell and Thesaurus files into a RAM (virtual) disk. The Spell and Thesaurus features work quicker when their files are on a RAM disk. Chapter 13 explains how to create macros that copy files to, and run the Spell and Thesaurus features from, a RAM disk. Refer to your DOS manual for instructions on creating a RAM disk.

The steps for using Spell depend on the disk-drive configuration of your computer systems, which must have one of these setups:

- A hard disk drive
- A single floppy disk drive that uses either 3 1/2-inch 720K or 1.44M disks or a 5 1/4-inch 1.2M disk
- Two floppy disk drives that use two 5 1/4-inch 360K or larger disks

A floppy disk system limits the size of the dictionaries you can use. On a hard disk system, you do not have to swap disks or worry about dictionary size.

It is good practice to always save a document to disk before you use Spell on it. When you run LetterPerfect on a system with a single 720K floppy disk drive, the steps required for using Spell depend on what files you keep on the LetterPerfect 2 disk that contains the two Spell files. If you keep document files on a separate data disk, you must follow these five steps before you use Spell:

1. Remove the LetterPerfect 2 disk.

2. Insert the data disk.

3. Save the document as a file on the data disk.

4. Remove the data disk.

5. Insert the LetterPerfect 2 disk.

If you run LetterPerfect on a single floppy disk drive system, be sure to perform these five steps before you use Spell; you are not reminded.

> *Caution:* Before you remove a data disk, be sure that LetterPerfect is not performing a timed backup of your document. The message * Please wait * appears at the bottom of the screen during a timed backup. You can lose your document if you remove the data disk when the program is writing a file to the disk.

The following italicized text is an example for practicing with Spell. Type the text, including the spelling errors.

> *A baard disk can be purchased from mail order firms or from computer stores in the area: BOston, Newton, Wellesley, Framingham, Needham, and so forth. The change you experience in going from a floppy disk system to one with a harddisk is both frustrating and exciting. It is something new to to learn and you are busy, and if you do not keep your files organised they become harder to locate in the maze of subdirectories. Or, worse yet, you didn't take the tiem to figure out subdirectories, so all your files are lumped together—rather like throwing papers in a fileing cabinet with n folders.*

Follow these steps to use Spell to check the entire document:

Reminder: Save the document before you use Spell.

1. *Save the document to disk.* Access the **F**ile pull-down menu, select **S**ave, and respond to the menu prompts. Alternatively, press Save (F10) and respond to the menu prompts.

2. Access the **T**ools pull-down menu and select **S**pell. Alternatively, press Spell (Ctrl-F2) or Ctrl-s.

Follow these steps to use Spell to check only a portion of the words in the document:

1. *Save the document to disk.* Access the **F**ile pull-down menu, select **S**ave, and respond to the menu prompts. Alternatively, press Save (F10) and respond to the menu prompts.

2. Highlight one or more words by using Block. Access the **E**dit pull-down menu and select **B**lock. Alternatively, press Block (Alt-F4 or F12) or click the mouse. Use one of the methods described in Chapter 5 to highlight the area of the document you want LetterPerfect to spell-check.

3. Access the **T**ools pull-down menu and select **S**pell. Alternatively, press Spell (Ctrl-F2) or Ctrl-s.

Regardless of the method you use to begin spell-checking, LetterPerfect displays the `* Please Wait *` message and begins checking the words in the document. If every word in the document matches a word in either the common-word list, main-word list, or supplemental dictionary, the spell-check automatically stops. You also can press Cancel (F1) or Esc to cancel the spell-check and resume editing the main document. Regardless of whether Spell stops automatically or you stop it, LetterPerfect displays a message at the bottom of the screen: `Word count:` *<number of words>* `Press any key to continue`

The word count is the number of words Spell examined before the spell-check ended. Press any key to return the program to the main editing screen. See "Understanding the Word Count" later in this chapter for more information about word count.

If LetterPerfect finds a word that does not match another word in the common-word list, main-word list, or supplemental dictionary, the program splits the screen, frequently displays a list of suggested alternatives, and waits for you to select an option from the Not Found menu at the bottom of the screen (see fig. 11.1). See "Selecting a Correct Spelling" later in this chapter.

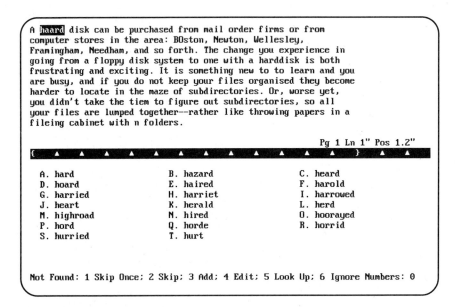

Fig. 11.1. *The alternative word list and Not Found menu.*

Tip: A supplemental dictionary is a regular LetterPerfect document file that you can protect with a password (see Chapter 9 for more information on locking files with a password). If the supplemental dictionary is password-protected, LetterPerfect displays this prompt at the bottom of the screen the first time it encounters a word it cannot locate in either the common-word list or main-word list: `Enter Password (WP{WP}US.SUP):`

If you enter any word other than the password, or if you press Enter, Cancel (F1), or Esc, LetterPerfect displays an error message—`ERROR: File is locked`—for a few seconds. Then this menu appears across the bottom of the screen:

1 Reenter Password; **2** Continue Without Supplemental Dictionary: **1**

Select **Reenter Password (1)** if you know the password and mistyped it. Select **Continue Without Supplemental Dictionary (2)** if you do not know the password.

Select Skip Once **(1)** to keep the highlighted word in the document and have LetterPerfect prompt you for the next occurrence of the word. Select Skip **(2)** to keep the highlighted word in the document and have LetterPerfect ignore all other occurrences of the word. See "Skipping Words Spelled Correctly" later in this chapter.

Select Add **(3)** to add the word to the end of the supplemental dictionary. Thereafter, LetterPerfect ignores all occurrences of the word in the current document and all other documents. See "Adding Words Spelled Correctly" later in this chapter.

Select Edit **(4)** or press the left arrow or the right arrow to edit the word. The highlight disappears, and LetterPerfect enters Spell's edit mode. LetterPerfect displays this prompt at the bottom of the screen: `Spell Edit: Press F7 when done.`

When you edit a word, LetterPerfect limits you to left-arrow and right-arrow keys for cursor movement; in addition, only the Insert/Typeover and Delete options function. In Spell's edit mode, you can edit the highlighted word (or other words in the document). When you finish editing, press Enter, Cancel (F1), Esc, or Exit (F7), and LetterPerfect resumes spell-checking. See "Editing a Word" later in this chapter.

Select Look Up **(5)** to enter a new word to spell-check. (See "Looking Up a Word" later in this chapter.) Select Ignore Numbers **(6)** to tell LetterPerfect to disregard words containing numbers. (See "Handling Words with Numbers" later in this chapter.)

Designating a Dictionary Subdirectory

By default, LetterPerfect looks for the Spell feature's files at the same location where it finds the LP.FIL file. Beginning with the 11/01/90 software, LetterPerfect includes a Setup option that lets you set a different subdirectory for Spell's dictionary and program files. (See Chapter 1 for information on using the Setup feature.) The instructions in this section are based on the assumption that you either are using the 07/24/90 software or are not using the Setup option with the 11/01/90 software.

On a hard disk system, LP.FIL is usually in the C:\LP10 subdirectory. On a dual-floppy-disk system, LP.FIL is usually on the LetterPerfect 2 disk in drive B. When you activate the Spell feature and the LetterPerfect 2 diskette is not in the proper floppy drive, or if the Spell feature's files are not in the main LetterPerfect subdirectory on a hard disk, LetterPerfect displays the following message at the bottom of the screen:

WP{WP}US.LEX not found: **1** Enter **P**ath; **2** Skip Language; **3** Exit Spell: **3**

If you forgot to insert the LetterPerfect 2 disk, insert it into drive B and select Enter Path (**1**). LetterPerfect displays the prompt `Temporary path:`. Type *b:* and press Enter.

If the document contains one or more codes for different languages, and the WordPerfect Language Modules are not on the disk, LetterPerfect also displays the Not Found prompt. If this happens to you, insert into the floppy drive the disk containing the proper language module and repeat the steps described in the preceding paragraph. Or you can select Skip Language (**2**), and LetterPerfect discontinues spell-checking the text until it encounters another language code. Even though LetterPerfect is not checking for correct spelling, the program continues to check for irregular capitalization. Select Exit Spell (**3**) to discontinue spell-checking.

On a hard drive system, select Enter Path (**1**). At the `Temporary path:` prompt, type the path to the location of the Spell files. If, for example, you store several WordPerfect Language Modules in a subdirectory named DICTION so that several WordPerfect programs can use them, type *c:\diction* and press Enter. Chapter 13 explains how to create a macro that starts Spell and automatically uses the larger dictionary of WordPerfect 5.1's Spell feature.

Selecting a Correct Spelling

Using the sample paragraph shown in the section "Using the Spell Feature," start Spell. When LetterPerfect encounters a word not found in either the main or supplemental dictionaries, the program highlights the word, usually displays a list of alternative spellings, and displays the Not Found menu.

If the list includes a word that you want to substitute for the highlighted word in the main document, move the mouse pointer to the word and click the left button, or press the letter left of the word. In some cases, LetterPerfect may not suggest alternative spellings.

If you do not see the correct spelling and if LetterPerfect displays the message `Press Enter for more words`, press Enter or the space bar to display more alternatives. Otherwise, refer to the later sections of this chapter.

> **Tip:** After you press Enter or the space bar and LetterPerfect displays another list of words, you can display a word on a previous screen by pressing Enter or the space bar until the list with the word you want appears.

For this example, you see many alternative spellings for the typographical error *haard* (see fig. 11.2). The correct spelling is *hard*.

Reminder: Spell usually provides a list of suggested alternatives to a word it cannot find in its dictionary.

```
A haard disk can be purchased from mail order firms or from
computer stores in the area: BOston, Newton, Wellesley,
Framingham, Needham, and so forth. The change you experience in
going from a floppy disk system to one with a harddisk is both
frustrating and exciting. It is something new to to learn and you
are busy, and if you do not keep your files organised they become
harder to locate in the maze of subdirectories. Or, worse yet,
you didn't take the tiem to figure out subdirectories, so all
your files are lumped together--rather like throwing papers in a
fileing cabinet with n folders.

                                        Pg 1 Ln 1" Pos 1.2"

  A. hard          B. hazard         C. heard
  D. hoard         E. haired         F. harold
  G. harried       H. harriet        I. harrowed
  J. heart         K. herald         L. herd
  M. highroad      N. hired          O. hoorayed
  P. hord          Q. horde          R. horrid
  S. hurried       T. hurt

Not Found: 1 Skip Once; 2 Skip; 3 Add; 4 Edit; 5 Look Up; 6 Ignore Numbers: 0
```

Fig. 11.2. *A list of alternative words.*

Move the mouse pointer to the word and click the left button, or press the letter left of the replacement word. For instance, click the mouse or press A to replace *haard* with *hard*. The new word automatically replaces the misspelled word in the text. If the misspelled word is capitalized, Spell leaves the word capitalized after replacing it. After you correct the word, spell-checking resumes.

> ***Tip:*** You do not need to wait for all the spelling alternatives to be displayed on-screen. As soon as you see the correct spelling, select it; LetterPerfect immediately substitutes the correct word for the word in the text.

> ***Caution:*** Spell considers an individual letter a word regardless of whether the letter actually is a word. For example, LetterPerfect treats the *n* shown in the last sentence of figure 11.2 as a word. Spell does not highlight the *n* as incorrect even though it is an error.

Correcting Irregular Case

Reminder:
Spell finds irregularities in the capitalization of words.

Spell also checks for case discrepancies—places where uppercase and lower-case letters may be accidentally switched—and offers you the option of changing the capitalization of the word. When Spell finds a word with apparently inappropriate capitalization, a special menu appears (see fig. 11.3).

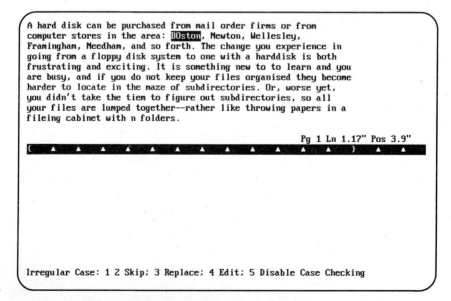

```
A hard disk can be purchased from mail order firms or from
computer stores in the area: BOston, Newton, Wellesley,
Framingham, Needham, and so forth. The change you experience in
going from a floppy disk system to one with a harddisk is both
frustrating and exciting. It is something new to to learn and you
are busy, and if you do not keep your files organised they become
harder to locate in the maze of subdirectories. Or, worse yet,
you didn't take the tiem to figure out subdirectories, so all
your files are lumped together--rather like throwing papers in a
fileing cabinet with n folders.

                                            Pg 1 Ln 1.17" Pos 3.9"
```

```
Irregular Case: 1 2 Skip; 3 Replace; 4 Edit; 5 Disable Case Checking
```

Fig. 11.3. *The Irregular Case menu.*

If the unusual capitalization is actually correct for the word, select Skip (**1** or **2**) from the menu. Spell-checking resumes, and the word is not changed. Both Skip **1** and **2** resume spell-checking without changing the capitalization of the word.

If, however, your text has many words with odd case selections, you may find it simpler to select Disable Case Checking (**5**) so that Spell does not check for words with irregular capitalization.

Select Replace (**3**) to change capitalization. The program does not show you how it will change the capitalization of the word; the correction is determined by the location of capital letters within the word. For example, *cAse* is changed to *Case*, *CAse* to *Case*, *cASE* (a common mistake when you forget that Caps Lock is active) to *CASE*, and *caSE* or *caSe* to *case*. Using the sample text as an example, select Replace (**3**), and LetterPerfect replaces *BOston* with *Boston*.

To change the capitalization of a word manually, select Edit (**4**) or press the left arrow or right arrow. The highlight disappears, and LetterPerfect enters the Spell edit mode. LetterPerfect displays this prompt at the bottom of the screen: `Spell Edit: Press F7 when done.`

When you edit a word, you are limited to the left arrow and right arrow for cursor movement; in addition, only Insert/Typeover and Delete options are functional. Spell's edit mode lets you edit the highlighted word (or other words in the document). When you finish editing, press Enter, Cancel (F1), Esc, or Exit (F7). LetterPerfect resumes spell-checking.

Skipping Words Spelled Correctly

Many correctly spelled words are not included in the LetterPerfect dictionary. The dictionary contains many common American proper names, including personal names like *Catherine*. Less common names, like *Kathryn*, are not included. For example, the next word not found in the sample text is *Wellesley*, a town name. Although *Wellesley* is spelled correctly, it is not found in Spell's main dictionary, unlike the preceding city name, *Newton*, which LetterPerfect automatically accepts because that name is in the dictionary.

When Spell highlights a word as incorrect, the Not Found menu appears at the bottom of the screen. When a highlighted word is spelled correctly, you can skip the word or add it to LetterPerfect's supplemental dictionary.

Selecting Skip Once (**1**) tells LetterPerfect to resume the spell-check without taking any action on the word. If the program finds the word in the document again, Spell stops and prompts you once more. Skip Once (**1**) is the best choice if the word is spelled correctly but may be a misspelling of another word in your document. For example, you may abbreviate *thesaurus* in your text as *thes*. However, you may later mistype *these* as *thes*. You want Spell to catch that error.

Select Skip (**2**) if a word appears several times in the document and you want LetterPerfect to ignore it here but not in other documents. Choosing the second Skip option tells LetterPerfect to resume spell-checking and ignore the word for the rest of the document.

Adding Words Spelled Correctly

Reminder:
You can add a frequently used word to the supplemental dictionary.

Select Add (**3**) from the Not Found menu if you frequently use a word not in Spell's main dictionary. LetterPerfect stores the word in RAM and skips all additional occurrences of the word in the document. At the end of the spell-check, all words selected with the Add option are added to the end of the words list in the supplemental dictionary, WP{WP}US.SUP. If WP{WP}US.SUP does not exist, LetterPerfect automatically creates it in the some directory where Spell's main dictionary is located.

> *Caution:* If you skip and add many words during a spell-check session, the words may fill the computer's RAM. If this happens, LetterPerfect removes skipped words from memory to make room for added words. If no skipped words can be removed, the message `Dictionary Full` appears. Terminating the spell-check lets LetterPerfect add the stored word to the supplemental dictionary. To finish spell-checking the document, refer to "Using the Spell Feature" earlier in this chapter.

Words in the supplemental dictionary are not offered as alternative spellings. If you misspell in the text one of the words you added to the dictionary (for example, you type *Wellesly* instead of *Wellesley*), the correct spelling is not one of the alternative words listed with the Not Found menu. You have to correct the word yourself.

For the example used in this chapter, select Add (**3**) from the Not Found menu to add *Wellesley* to the supplemental dictionary (you should add at least one word to the supplemental dictionary so that you can see what the file looks like later). LetterPerfect stores *Wellesley* in memory and creates a supplemental dictionary at the end of the spell-check session.

You also may want to add *Framingham* and *Needham* (names of towns) to the supplemental dictionary when the program stops at those words.

Editing a Word

When the correct alternative spelling is not offered for an incorrectly spelled word, you must enter the correct spelling yourself. Consider the incorrectly spelled *harddisk*, shown in figure 11.4.

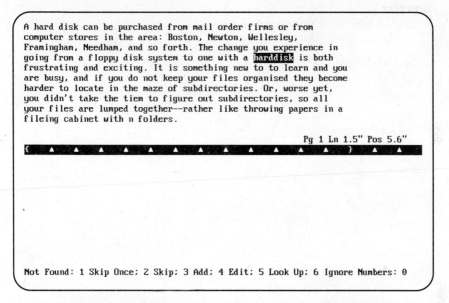

```
A hard disk can be purchased from mail order firms or from
computer stores in the area: Boston, Newton, Wellesley,
Framingham, Needham, and so forth. The change you experience in
going from a floppy disk system to one with a harddisk is both
frustrating and exciting. It is something new to to learn and you
are busy, and if you do not keep your files organised they become
harder to locate in the maze of subdirectories. Or, worse yet,
you didn't take the tiem to figure out subdirectories, so all
your files are lumped together--rather like throwing papers in a
fileing cabinet with n folders.

                                             Pg 1 Ln 1.5" Pos 5.6"

Not Found: 1 Skip Once; 2 Skip; 3 Add; 4 Edit; 5 Look Up; 6 Ignore Numbers: 0
```

Fig. 11.4. Editing a misspelled word.

To enter a correct spelling, complete these steps:

1. Select Edit (4) from the Not Found menu at the bottom of the screen or press the right arrow or left arrow.

   The highlight disappears, and LetterPerfect enters Spell's edit mode. LetterPerfect displays this prompt at the bottom of the screen: Spell Edit: Press F7 when done.

> *Tip:* If LetterPerfect displays a list of word options and you select Edit (4) and then change your mind, press Cancel (F1). LetterPerfect redisplays the list of alternative words.

2. When you edit a word, you are limited to the left arrow and right arrow for moving the cursor; in addition, only the Insert/Type-over and Delete options function. Spell's edit mode lets you edit

the highlighted word (or other words in the document). For instance, move the cursor between *hard* and *disk* and type a space.

3. Press Enter, Exit (F7), Cancel (F1), or Esc to end editing and resume spell-checking.

   Spell rechecks the corrected word and stops at the same place again if the corrected version is not in its dictionary.

In the sample text, the program stops at three more words:

Word in Document	Correct Word
organised	organized
tiem	time
fileing	filing

In the last line of text, LetterPerfect ignores the *n*, which should have been *no*, because the program accepts all single-letter words as valid.

Eliminating Double-Word Sequences

Besides finding misspelled words, Spell stops at double-word sequences—the same word repeated consecutively two or more times. In the sample text, the next problem Spell finds is the double-word sequence *to to* (see fig. 11.5).

When LetterPerfect encounters a double-word sequence, the program does not show alternative spellings but displays the double-word menu at the bottom of the screen:

Double Word: 1 2 Skip; 3 Delete 2nd; 4 Edit; 5 Disable Double Word Checking

If you accidentally type two words instead of one, select Delete 2nd (3). LetterPerfect removes one of the words from the document and resumes spell-checking.

Select Skip (1 or 2) if the double-word sequence is correct. For example, the double-word sequence in this sentence is correct: *She had explained that that job would be difficult for him.* Both Skip options are the equivalent of Skip Once (1) on the Not Found menu. Selecting either Skip option (1 or 2) ignores the double-word sequence and resumes the spell-check. If LetterPerfect encounters *that that* later in the document, the spell-check pauses and highlights the sequence.

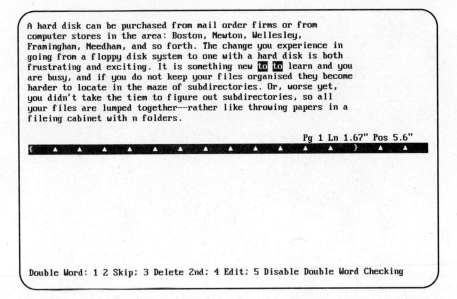

Fig. 11.5. A double-word sequence highlighted by Spell.

If one of the words is a typographical error—if you type *that that* when you mean *than that*, for example—select Edit (**4**) and enter the correct spelling.

Select Disable Double Word Checking (**5**) if the document contains many legitimate double-word sequences. When you use this option, carefully proof-read the document for double-word sequences.

Understanding the Word Count

When Spell finishes, it displays the number of words checked (see fig. 11.6). All words are counted, even articles and conjunctions, but stand-alone numbers are not counted.

For purposes of the word-count function, the program does not consider numbers as words, although numbers that include alphabetic characters are included in the word count. Punctuation characters are word separators and do not cause numbers to be counted as words. For example, LetterPerfect includes *JMD2120* in its word count but not *$55.20* or *(617)*. LetterPerfect also pauses at *JMD2120* unless it finds *JMD2120* in the supplemental dictionary.

```
A hard disk can be purchased from mail order firms or from
computer stores in the area: Boston, Newton, Wellesley,
Framingham, Needham, and so forth. The change you experience in
going from a floppy disk system to one with a hard disk is both
frustrating and exciting. It is something new to learn and you
are busy, and if you do not keep yuur files organized they become
harder to locate in the maze of subdirectories. Or, worse yet,
you didn't take the time to figure out subdirectories, so all
your files are lumped together--rather like throwing papers in a
filing cabinet with n folders.




Word count: 106          Press any key to continue
```

Fig. 11.6. The word count at the end of a spell-check.

LetterPerfect does not treat apostrophes and soft hyphens (Ctrl-hyphen) as separating two or more words. Words separated by hyphens and hard hyphens (Home, hyphen) are, however, counted as individual words in the word count.

LetterPerfect also counts individual letters as words. For example, in the document shown in figure 11.6, the *n* in the last sentence counts as a word.

Terminating a Spell-Check

Reminder:
Press Cancel (F1) to discontinue a spell-check.

Press Cancel (F1) or Esc instead of selecting a menu option to manually stop spell-checking. A count of the words checked up to termination appears with the message `Press any key to continue`.

Press any key to return to the main editing screen.

Looking Up a Word

As you type, you can look up the spelling of a word in Spell's main dictionary. For example, *aggrieve* is one of those pesky *ie*-versus-*ei* words you may use rarely and forget how to spell.

LetterPerfect lets you look up a word by typing either the letters you believe it contains or a word pattern. A *word pattern* is a rough guess at the spelling of a word. In a word pattern, you type an asterisk (*) to replace several unknown letters, or a question mark (?) to replace one unknown letter. During the look-up, LetterPerfect displays all words matching the word pattern.

Reminder:
Speed the process of looking up a word by placing wild card(s) in the middle of the word rather than at the beginning or the end.

Use these steps to look up a word:

1. Intentionally misspell a word (type *teb* for *the*, for example).

2. Highlight the word by using Block; you can click the mouse, access the **E**dit pull-down menu and select **B**lock, or press Block (Alt-F4 or F12). Use one of the methods described in Chapter 5 to highlight the area to be spell-checked.

3. Access the **T**ools pull-down menu and select **S**pell. Alternatively, press Spell (Ctrl-F2) or Ctrl-s.

   LetterPerfect displays the Not Found menu shown in figure 11.7.

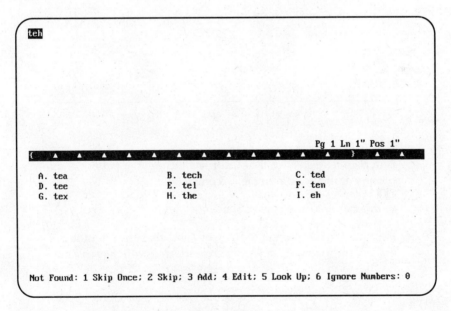

Fig. 11.7. The Not Found menu.

4. Select Look Up (**5**).

   LetterPerfect displays a prompt at the bottom of the screen: `Word or word pattern:`.

5. Type the word or word pattern you want to look up; press Enter.

For example, type *aggr*ve* and press Enter. LetterPerfect displays all words in its dictionary that begin with the letters *aggr*, are followed by some number of letters, and end with *ve* (see fig. 11.8).

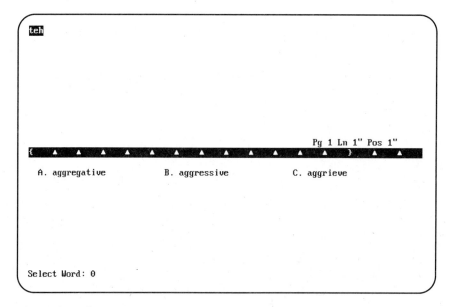

Fig. 11.8. Looking up aggr*ve.

LetterPerfect displays a list of words matching the pattern and a prompt at the bottom of the screen: Select Word: 0.

In this example, the correct spelling—*aggrieve*—is choice C.

6. Move the mouse pointer to the word and click the left mouse button, or press C. LetterPerfect replaces *teh* with *aggrieve* and returns to the main editing screen.

If you do not select a word to replace *teh*, pressing Enter, Exit (F7), Cancel (F1), or Esc redisplays the Word or word pattern: prompt. Pressing any of these keys three times returns the program to the main editing screen.

In some cases, you may see not the correct spelling but a prompt at the bottom of the screen: Press Enter for more words.

Press Enter or the space bar to display more alternatives.

Tip: After you press Enter or space bar and LetterPerfect displays another list of words, you can display a word on a previous screen by pressing Enter or space bar until the list with the word you want appears.

If the dictionary does not contain any words that match the word pattern, LetterPerfect does not offer suggested alternative spellings.

If the word you are searching for does not appear in the word list, you may want to change the word pattern. Fewer words appear when you use question marks, because each question mark represents a single letter; an asterisk, on the other hand, can represent any number of letters. Using *aggr??ve* as the word pattern, for example, displays *aggrieve* as the only word option.

You do not have to enter question marks and asterisks to create a word pattern. LetterPerfect treats any word you enter without the wild-card characters as a *phonetic* spelling (the spelling of a word the way it sounds or the way it is pronounced). For example, you can type *sik* at the Word or word pattern: prompt and press Enter. Figure 11.9 shows the alternatives to this word; press any key to see the rest of the list.

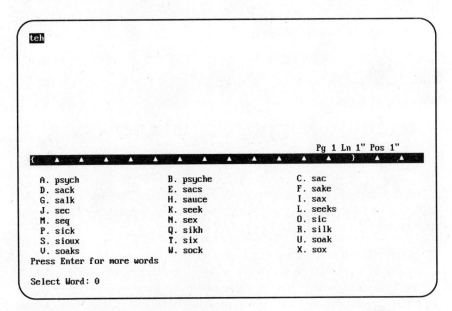

Fig. 11.9. Looking up sik *phonetically.*

In addition to checking for similar spellings, LetterPerfect selects words that are phonetically close (those with similar pronunciations) to the spelling (see fig. 11.9). Using this feature, you can find the spelling of any word you know how to pronounce if the word is in Spell's main dictionary.

> ***Tip:*** If you use an automatic spell-check program or a shorthand word expander such as PRD+ from Productivity Software Inc. as a terminate-and-stay-resident (TSR) program, deactivate the TSR or remove it from memory before you use the Spell or Thesaurus features. If the TSR is active, you may find Spell difficult to use, and you may get inaccurate results.

Chapter 13 shows a macro that automatically activates Spell so that you can use its look-up mode.

Checking Words with Numbers

During a spell-check, LetterPerfect treats words containing numbers—for example, *89th* or *F1-F10*—as regular words (you can skip, add, and edit them). The Ignore Numbers (6) option in the Not Found menu tells Spell to ignore all words that contain numbers. If a document includes many legitimate words containing numbers, you can speed up the spell-check by either of these methods:

- Using the Ignore Numbers option (6)
- Adding to the supplemental dictionary the list of words containing numbers

Creating a Supplemental Dictionary

Spell's supplemental dictionary is a regular LetterPerfect document. You can retrieve and edit it like any other LetterPerfect document. Besides using the Add (3) option from the Not Found menu during a spell-check to add words to the supplemental dictionary, you can retrieve the supplemental dictionary to the main editing screen and add words to it manually.

To add words to the supplemental dictionary, type each word on a separate line in lowercase letters and press Enter. The words in the supplemental dictionary do not have to be in alphabetical order, but the dictionary works faster if they are alphabetized. Figure 11.10 shows the proper structure of the supplemental dictionary.

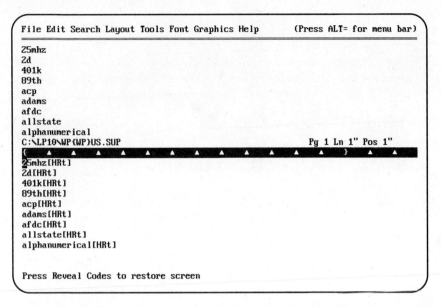

```
File Edit Search Layout Tools Font Graphics Help      (Press ALT= for menu bar)

25mhz
2d
401k
89th
acp
adams
afdc
allstate
alphanumerical
C:\LP10\WP{WP}US.SUP                              Pg 1 Ln 1" Pos 1"
{     ▲      ▲      ▲      ▲      ▲      ▲      ▲      ▲      ▲      }      ▲      ▲
25mhz[HRt]
2d[HRt]
401k[HRt]
89th[HRt]
acp[HRt]
adams[HRt]
afdc[HRt]
allstate[HRt]
alphanumerical[HRt]



Press Reveal Codes to restore screen
```

Fig. 11.10. The organization of the supplemental dictionary.

Tip: To avoid duplication and to save memory and disk space, use Spell on your list of words before you save the list as the supplemental dictionary. Delete any word that LetterPerfect does not highlight for checking.

Using a Supplemental Dictionary

LetterPerfect automatically uses the WP{WP}US.SUP supplemental dictionary during a spell-check. You can, however, create specialized supplemental dictionaries to use with special documents.

To use different supplemental dictionaries, follow these steps:

1. Create the supplemental dictionaries and name them in se-quence—for example, WP{WP}US.001, WP{WP}US.002, WP{WP}US.003.

2. Before you activate Spell, select the supplemental dictionary you want LetterPerfect to use and rename it WP{WP}US.SUP.

Reminder:
The supplemental dictionary WP{WP}US.SUP is automatically used during a spell-check.

3. Activate Spell by accessing the Tools pull-down menu and selecting Spell. Alternatively, press Spell (Ctrl-F2) or Ctrl-s.

Chapter 13 shows a macro that automatically displays a list of supplemental dictionaries and automatically lets you rename the one you select to WP{WP}US.SUP.

Using the Thesaurus

LetterPerfect's Thesaurus adds freshness and variety to your writing by suggesting alternative words. The Thesaurus also helps you to be more precise in your writing; when you can't find quite the word you need, use the Thesaurus.

The Thesaurus file contains *synonyms*, words with meanings similar to but not exactly the same as the original word's meaning. Some words are more or less formal than others or have positive or negative connotations. The Thesaurus only *lists* these words. You decide which one most closely fits your meaning.

To use the Thesaurus, you must know how to spell the word you want to look up. If you are not sure how to spell a word, first look up the spelling by using the wild cards * and ? with Spell. See "Looking Up a Word" earlier in this chapter.

Starting the Thesaurus

The Spell feature requires the WP{WP}US.THS file. On systems with a hard disk drive, LetterPerfect automatically looks for the Thesaurus program file in the subdirectory containing the main program files. Beginning with the 11/01/90 software, LetterPerfect includes a Setup option that lets you set a different subdirectory for the program files. (See Chapter 1 for information on using the Setup feature.)

> *Tip:* If your computer has expanded or extended memory, you can copy the WP{WP}US.THS file into a RAM (virtual) disk. The Thesaurus feature works quicker when this file is on a RAM disk. Chapter 13 explains how to create macros that copy the WP{WP}US.THS file to, and run the Thesaurus feature from, a RAM disk. Refer to your DOS manual for instructions on creating a RAM disk.

The steps for using the Thesaurus depend on the disk-drive configuration of your computer system, which must have one of these configurations:

- A hard disk drive

- A single floppy disk drive that uses either 3 1/2-inch 720K or 1.44M disks or a 5 1/4-inch 1.2M disk

- Two floppy disk drives that use two 5 1/4-inch 360K or larger disks

On a hard disk system, you do not have to swap disks.

On a dual-floppy-disk-system, always save a document to disk before you use the Thesaurus. When you run LetterPerfect on a system with a single 720K floppy disk drive, the steps for using Spell depend on what files you keep on the LetterPerfect 2 disk that must contain the Thesaurus file. If you keep your document files on a separate data disk, these five steps are required before you use the Thesaurus:

1. Remove the LetterPerfect 2 disk.

2. Insert the data disk.

3. Save the document as a file on the data disk.

4. Remove the data disk.

5. Insert the LetterPerfect 2 disk.

Be sure to perform these five steps if you run LetterPerfect on a single floppy drive system. The instructions in this chapter that advise you to save a document before you use the Thesaurus do not remind you to perform the five steps.

Caution: Before you remove a data disk, be sure that LetterPerfect is not performing a timed backup of your document. `* Please wait *` appears at the bottom of the screen during a timed backup. The document can be lost if you remove the data disk when the program is writing a file to the disk.

To practice using the Thesaurus, retrieve or create the corrected sample text that you used when you practiced Spell and follow these steps:

1. Place the cursor anywhere between the first character and the space following the word you want to look up. For example, place the cursor under the period (.) following the word *exciting*.

2. Access the Tools pull-down menu and select Thesaurus. Alternatively, press Thesaurus (Alt-F1) or Ctrl-t.

   The screen splits. The text (if any) appears in the top half of the screen. The Thesaurus menu and word list appear in columns in the bottom half (see fig. 11.11).

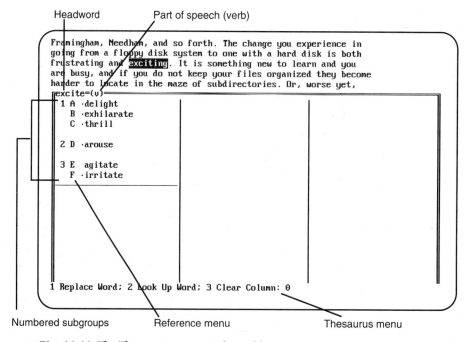

Headword   Part of speech (verb)

```
Framingham, Needham, and so forth. The change you experience in
going from a floppy disk system to one with a hard disk is both
frustrating and exciting. It is something new to learn and you
are busy, and if you do not keep your files organized they become
harder to locate in the maze of subdirectories. Or, worse yet,
excite=(v)
 1 A ·delight
   B ·exhilarate
   C ·thrill

 2 D ·arouse

 3 E  agitate
   F ·irritate




 1 Replace Word; 2 Look Up Word; 3 Clear Column: 0
```

Numbered subgroups   Reference menu   Thesaurus menu

Fig. 11.11. *The Thesaurus menu and word list.*

If the menu is empty and LetterPerfect displays the Word: prompt at the bottom of the screen, the cursor was not within a word boundary when you activated the Thesaurus. Or LetterPerfect cannot find the word you request. In either case, type the word you want to look up at the Word: prompt and press Enter.

Understanding the Parts of the Thesaurus Menu

LetterPerfect displays the word you looked up—called a *headword* because it has a body of similar words attached to it—at the top of the first column. Some synonyms for a headword are headwords themselves and are noted with a small bullet. In figure 11.11, all words but one are headwords.

Reminder:
Words displayed with a bullet in the Thesaurus menu screen also are headwords.

The words are arranged into parts of speech and *subgroups*, or numbered groups of words with the same basic meaning. The column of letters left of the words is called the *Reference menu*. Choose a word by selecting its Reference-menu letter. The following indicates the parts of speech from the Thesaurus menu:

Part of Speech	Abbreviation
Adjective	(a)
Noun	(n)
Verb	(v)

Replacing a Word

If you see a word for replacing the highlighted word, select the replacement. You can, for example, select *delight* from the list to replace *exciting* and then add *ful* to make the word *delightful*.

To replace a word in the text with one from the Thesaurus menu, follow these steps:

1. Move the mouse pointer to the option and click the mouse button, or select Replace Word (**1**) from the Thesaurus menu.

   At the bottom of the screen, LetterPerfect displays the prompt `Press letter for word`.

2. Press the letter that corresponds to the replacement word. For example, press A to select the word *delight*. Unlike what you can do in Spell, you *cannot* select a replacement word by clicking with the mouse.

The Thesaurus menu disappears. LetterPerfect replaces *exciting* with *delight* (see fig. 11.12) and returns the program to the main editing screen. Remember to add *ful* to *delight*!

```
File Edit Search Layout Tools Font Graphics Help      (Press ALT= for menu bar)
─────────────────────────────────────────────────────────────────────────────
Framingham, Needham, and so forth. The change you experience in
going from a floppy disk system to one with a hard disk is both
frustrating and delightful. It is something new to learn and you
are busy, and if you do not keep your files organized they become
harder to locate in the maze of subdirectories. Or, worse yet,
you didn't take the time to figure out subdirectories, so all
your files are lumped together--rather like throwing papers in a
filing cabinet with no folders.




                                              Pg 1 Ln 1.67" Pos 3.6"
```

Fig. 11.12. Exciting *replaced with* delightful.

Expanding the Word List

If you don't see the right word on the Thesaurus menu, or if you want to try other words, you can expand the word list.

Reminder:
Display more words on the Thesaurus menu screen by selecting new headwords from the existing alternatives.

Suppose, for example, that you think the meaning of *delight* is close to the word you are looking for but not exactly right. You can replace *exciting* with *delightful* and then use the Thesaurus for *delightful*, but that process is tedious. Fortunately, LetterPerfect lets you request more words from the Thesaurus menu before you choose the replacement.

For this example, restore *exciting* in the sample text (by either pressing Undelete (F1) or typing *exciting*) and delete *delightful*. Place the cursor in the word *exciting* and start the Thesaurus.

Words marked with a bullet also are headwords; look up the headwords for more ideas (see fig. 11.11). Words without bullets are not headwords. If you try to look up a word that is not marked with a bullet, LetterPerfect redisplays this message prompt at the bottom of the screen:

1 Replace Word; **2** Look Up Word; **3** Clear Column: **0**.

Use these steps to expand the list of words displayed on the Thesaurus menu:

1. From the words listed on the Thesaurus menu, choose one close to the meaning you want.

2. Press the letter beside the word. For example, press A to select *delight* so that you can see some synonyms for that word.

   Words associated with *delight* appear in the next column right of the previous headword (see fig. 11.13). Notice that the Reference menu (the column of letters) moves to the second column.

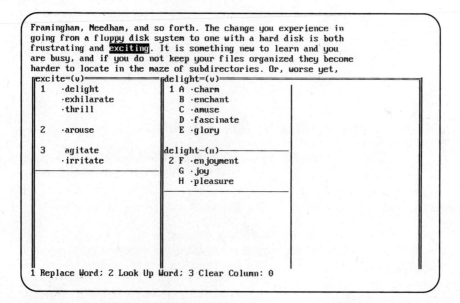

Fig. 11.13. *A second headword selection.*

3. Select a replacement word or select another headword to see additional words. For example, press D to select *fascinate* as the next headword (see fig. 11.14).

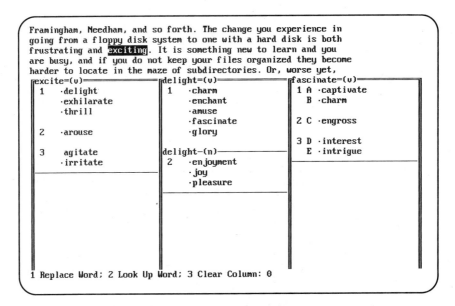

Fig. 11.14. A third headword selection.

Maneuvering inside the Thesaurus

When you select a new headword, LetterPerfect automatically moves the Reference menu (the column of letters) to the new column of words. Each column contains only one headword and its associated words. Use the left arrow and right arrow to move the Reference menu between columns.

You can select up to three headwords to view at one time, as shown in figure 11.14. When you select a fourth headword, the third column is replaced with the new selection. Or you can select Clear Column (**3**) from the Thesaurus menu to clear the current column (the one containing the Reference menu) and select another word. If you clear either the left or middle column, LetterPerfect moves the remaining columns to the right.

The headword choices in a column automatically wrap to the adjacent column to the left unless that column has its own headword. If the columns are full, the remaining words in the headword list continue down the column past the bottom of the screen.

Use the up arrow and down arrow to move from one numbered group to the next within the columns. You can go directly to a particular subgroup by pressing GoTo (Ctrl-Home), typing the subgroup number, and then pressing Enter. Use PgUp, PgDn, Screen Up (the keypad – key), and Screen Down (the keypad + key) to move to the top or bottom of the column.

If, for example, you tell LetterPerfect to display the headword *glory*, its options exceed the length of the column, as shown in figure 11.15.

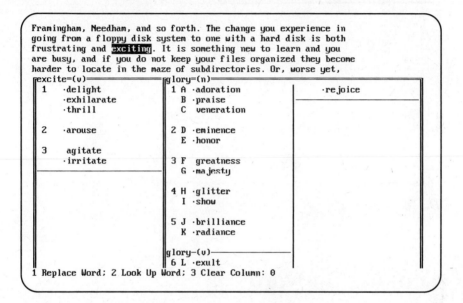

Fig. 11.15. *Headword options exceeding the length of a column.*

The unbroken lines below the groups of words in a column indicate the end of a group of alternative words for a headword.

Follow these steps to move the Reference menu and select a replacement word:

1. Press the left arrow or right arrow until the Reference menu is in the column containing the replacement word.

   For example, press the left arrow to move to the first column containing *exhilarate*.

2. Replace the word in the text with the word you want.

   For example, if you decide that *exhilarate* is the best replacement for *exciting*, select Replace Word (**1**) and press B. Edit *exhilarate* by deleting the *e* and adding the *ing* suffix. The final text should be similar to what you see in figure 11.16.

```
┌─────────────────────────────────────────────────────────────────┐
│  File Edit Search Layout Tools Font Graphics Help    (Press ALT= for menu bar) │
│  Framingham, Needham, and so forth. The change you experience in  │
│  going from a floppy disk system to one with a hard disk is both  │
│  frustrating and exhilarating. It is something new to learn and you │
│  are busy, and if you do not keep your files organized they become │
│  harder to locate in the maze of subdirectories. Or, worse yet,  │
│  you didn't take the time to figure out subdirectories, so all   │
│  your files are lumped together--rather like throwing papers in a │
│  filing cabinet with no folders.                                  │
│                                                                   │
│                                                                   │
│                                                                   │
│                                                                   │
│                                                                   │
│                                                                   │
│                                                                   │
│                                                Pg 1 Ln 1.67" Pos 3.8" │
└─────────────────────────────────────────────────────────────────┘
```

Fig. 11.16. Exciting *replaced with* exhilarating.

Looking Up Words

When you use the Thesaurus, you can look up other words that come to mind by following these steps:

1. Select Look Up Word (**2**).

2. At the Word: prompt, type the new word you want to look up and press Enter.

   If the word is a headword, LetterPerfect displays the word with all its subgroups of synonyms. If the word is not a headword, LetterPerfect redisplays the main Thesaurus prompt.

Summary

Although you may still need a conventional dictionary to look up the meanings of words, LetterPerfect's Spell and Thesaurus features are handy tools that can help you improve your writing. In this chapter, you learned to use Spell to complete these tasks:

- Replace misspelled words with suggested alternatives

- Correct a word yourself

- Omit parts of a document from a spell-check

- Create and use supplemental dictionaries

- Count the words in a document

You also learned to use the Thesaurus to complete these tasks:

- Look up synonyms

- Review additional words for your selection

- Replace one word with another that is more appropriate

Chapter 12 shows you how to create special characters and modify some of LetterPerfect's advanced default settings.

12

Working with the Character Feature and LRS File

T his chapter explains LetterPerfect's Character feature and shows you how to use the Language Resource (LRS) file to change the program defaults for some LetterPerfect features.

The Character feature—sometimes called the Compose feature—is used to graphically create and print special characters not found on the keyboard. This chapter shows you how to do these tasks:

- Create special characters

- Use two key sequences (Ctrl-2 and Ctrl-v) to access the Character feature

- Use mnemonic key combinations with the Character feature

- Use language codes to simplify working with foreign languages

429

> **Reminder:** WordPerfect Corporation updated LetterPerfect 1.0 just before this book went to press. Dated 11/01/90, the interim release includes new options for existing features, and a few new features. The menus on your screen may, therefore, differ slightly from those shown in this book. Also, depending on the printer-form definition, margins, tab stops, and font you specify, the text placement and status-line information in documents you create may differ from that shown in this book's figures.
>
> For information about using the mouse and accessing the pull-down menus, refer to the Introduction.

Using Special Characters

LetterPerfect offers two methods of entering special characters that are not available on a standard PC keyboard. Special characters include nonkeyboard characters in the IBM Extended Character Set and characters in the WordPerfect Character Set. All special characters are represented internally as LetterPerfect character set codes, regardless of which method you use to enter them. You can use the Character feature anywhere in the LetterPerfect program.

Using the IBM Extended Character Set

Every character you see on-screen is represented internally (inside the computer) by a number, called its *ASCII code*. For example, the uppercase letter *A* is ASCII 65 and the lowercase *a* is ASCII 97.

ASCII is an acronym for *American Standard Code for Information Interchange*. The original ASCII code, 128 characters (0 through 127), was extended to 256 (128 through 255) characters when IBM introduced the IBM PC. The IBM PC's 256-character set is therefore referred to as the *IBM Extended Character Set* or the *Extended ASCII Character Set* (see table 12.1). Characters 128 through 255 are sometimes called the upper ASCII characters.

Table 12.1
The IBM Extended Character Set

Dec	Hex	Screen	Key	Ctrl	Dec	Hex	Screen
0	0		^@	NUL	50	32	2
1	1	☺	^A	SOH	51	33	3
2	2	☻	^B	STX	52	34	4
3	3	♥	^C	ETX	53	35	5
4	4	♦	^D	EOT	54	36	6
5	5	♣	^E	ENQ	55	37	7
6	6	♠	^F	ACK	56	38	8
7	7	·	^G	BEL	57	39	9
8	8	◘	^H	BS	58	3A	:
9	9	○	^I	HT	59	3B	;
10	A	◙	^J	LF	60	3C	<
11	B	σ	^K	VT	61	3D	=
12	C	♀	^L	FF	62	3E	>
13	D	♪	^M	CR	63	3F	?
14	E	♫	^N	SO	64	40	@
15	F	☼	^O	SI	65	41	A
16	10	►	^P	DLE	66	42	B
17	11	◄	^Q	DC1	67	43	C
18	12	↕	^R	DC2	68	44	D
19	13	‼	^S	DC3	69	45	E
20	14	¶	^T	DC4	70	46	F
21	15	§	^U	NAK	71	47	G
22	16	▬	^V	SYN	72	48	H
23	17	↨	^W	ETB	73	49	I
24	18	↑	^X	CAN	74	4A	J
25	19	↓	^Y	EM	75	4B	K
26	1A	→	^Z	SUB	76	4C	L
27	1B	←	^[	ESC	77	4D	M
28	1C	∟	^\	FS	78	4E	N
29	1D	↔	^]	GS	79	4F	O
30	1E	▲	^^	RS	80	50	P
31	1F	▼	^_	US	81	51	Q
32	20	Space			82	52	R
33	21	!			83	53	S
34	22	"			84	54	T
35	23	#			85	55	U
36	24	$			86	56	V
37	25	%			87	57	W
38	26	&			88	58	X
39	27	'			89	59	Y
40	28	(			90	5A	Z
41	29	)			91	5B	[
42	2A	*			92	5C	\
43	2B	+			93	5D	]
44	2C	,			94	5E	^
45	2D	-			95	5F	_
46	2E	.			96	60	`
47	2F	/			97	61	a
48	30	0			98	62	b
49	31	1			99	63	c

Table 12.1 (continued)

Dec	Hex	Screen	Dec	Hex	Screen	Dec	Hex	Screen
100	64	d	152	98	ÿ	204	CC	╠
101	65	e	153	99	Ö	205	CD	═
102	66	f	154	9A	Ü	206	CE	╬
103	67	g	155	9B	¢	207	CF	╧
104	68	h	156	9C	£	208	D0	╨
105	69	i	157	9D	¥	209	D1	╤
106	6A	j	158	9E	Pt	210	D2	╥
107	6B	k	159	9F	ƒ	211	D3	╙
108	6C	l	160	A0	á	212	D4	╘
109	6D	m	161	A1	í	213	D5	╒
110	6E	n	162	A2	ó	214	D6	╓
111	6F	o	163	A3	ú	215	D7	╫
112	70	p	164	A4	ñ	216	D8	╪
113	71	q	165	A5	Ñ	217	D9	┘
114	72	r	166	A6	ª	218	DA	┌
115	73	s	167	A7	º	219	DB	█
116	74	t	168	A8	¿	220	DC	▄
117	75	u	169	A9	⌐	221	DD	▌
118	76	v	170	AA	¬	222	DE	▐
119	77	w	171	AB	½	223	DF	▀
120	78	x	172	AC	¼	224	E0	∝
121	79	y	173	AD	¡	225	E1	β
122	7A	z	174	AE	«	226	E2	Γ
123	7B	{	175	AF	»	227	E3	π
124	7C	|	176	B0	▒	228	E4	Σ
125	7D	}	177	B1	▓	229	E5	σ
126	7E	~	178	B2	▓	230	E6	µ
127	7F	Δ	179	B3	│	231	E7	τ
128	80	Ç	180	B4	┤	232	E8	Φ
129	81	ü	181	B5	╡	233	E9	Θ
130	82	é	182	B6	╢	234	EA	Ω
131	83	â	183	B7	╖	235	EB	δ
132	84	ä	184	B8	╕	236	EC	∞
133	85	à	185	B9	╣	237	ED	φ
134	86	å	186	BA	║	238	EE	∈
135	87	ç	187	BB	╗	239	EF	∩
136	88	ê	188	BC	╝	240	F0	≡
137	89	ë	189	BD	╜	241	F1	±
138	8A	è	190	BE	╛	242	F2	≥
139	8B	ï	191	BF	┐	243	F3	≤
140	8C	î	192	C0	└	244	F4	⌠
141	8D	ì	193	C1	┴	245	F5	⌡
142	8E	Ä	194	C2	┬	246	F6	÷
143	8F	Å	195	C3	├	247	F7	≈
144	90	É	196	C4	─	248	F8	°
145	91	æ	197	C5	┼	249	F9	∙
146	92	Æ	198	C6	╞	250	FA	·
147	93	ô	199	C7	╟	251	FB	√
148	94	ö	200	C8	╚	252	FC	ⁿ
149	95	ò	201	C9	╔	253	FD	²
150	96	û	202	CA	╩	254	FE	■
151	97	ù	203	CB	╦	255	FF	

The original ASCII character set includes the characters found on an English-language typewriter: uppercase and lowercase letters, digits, and punctuation. The term *ASCII file* refers to a file consisting exclusively of characters from the original ASCII character set. The IBM Extended Character Set added many foreign language characters, mathematical symbols, and line-drawing characters.

If you are familiar with the IBM Extended Character Set, you may prefer to enter the character with the Alt-key method rather than with Character. When you enter a special character by using its ASCII code, LetterPerfect converts the code to the corresponding character in the LetterPerfect character set.

To use the Alt-key method, look up the number of the character you want in a chart of the IBM Extended Character Set (see table 12.1). To enter the character, hold down the Alt key, and then type the ASCII number on the numeric keypad. The corresponding character appears on-screen when you release the Alt key. You must type the numbers on the numeric keypad. The Alt-key method does not work with the numbers on the top row of the keyboard.

> *Caution:* Some portable computers have keyboards that lack a numeric keypad. The Alt-key method may not work on this type of computer keyboard.

For example, to insert the character ê, press and hold down the Alt key and type *136*. For the mathematical intersection symbol ∩, hold down Alt and type *239*. When the cursor is on an extended ASCII character viewed with Reveal Codes, the character appears with its LetterPerfect character set number, as shown in figure 12.1.

Using LetterPerfect's Character Sets

In 1988, to facilitate foreign language and scientific word processing, WordPerfect Corporation designed its own character sets, consisting of 1,729 characters. The characters are arranged by subject in 13 groups, numbered 0 through 12. The LetterPerfect software package includes two files—LP.DRS and LPSMALL.DRS—each containing subsets of the 1,729 characters. Table 12.2 shows the subset of characters contained in LP.DRS. The LPSMALL.DRS file contains fewer characters.

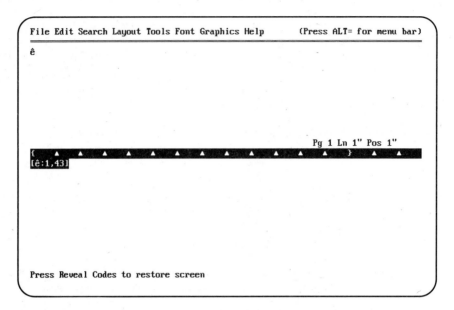

Fig. 12.1. *An extended ASCII character viewed with Reveal Codes.*

Table 12.2
LetterPerfect Character Sets

Character Set 0 (ASCII)

	0 1 2 3 4 5 6 7 8 9	1 0 1 2 3 4 5 6 7 8 9	2 0 1 2 3 4 5 6 7 8 9
0			
30	! " # $ % & ' ( )	* + , - . / 0 1 2 3	4 5 6 7 8 9 : ;
60	< = > ? @ A B C D E	F G H I J K L M N O	P Q R S T U V W X Y
90	Z [\ ] ^ _ ` a b c	d e f g h i j k l m	n o p q r s t u v w
120	x y z { | } ~		

Character Set 1 (Multinational)

	0 1 2 3 4 5 6 7 8 9	1 0 1 2 3 4 5 6 7 8 9	2 0 1 2 3 4 5 6 7 8 9
0	` ´ ~ ^ ¯ / ¨ ˝ ' '	, ` , ° ' " ˛ ¸	´ ¯ ˇ Í ı J Á á Â â
30	Ä ä À à Å å Æ æ Ç ç	É é Ê ê Ë ë È è Í í	Î î Ï ï Ì ì Ñ ñ Ó ó
60	Ô ô Ö ö Ò ò Ú ú Û û	Ü ü Ù ù Ÿ ÿ Ã ã Đ đ	Ø ø Õ õ Ý ý Ð ð Þ þ

Each LetterPerfect character is identified by a two-part numeric code. The first part is the number of the character set in which the character is contained. The second part is the number of the character within that character set. For example, the ê is character 43 in Character Set 1 (multinational), which makes the character's LetterPerfect identification number 1,43.

By default, LetterPerfect uses the LP.DRS file if LP.DRS is located on the same drive and subdirectory as the LP.FIL file. If LP.DRS is not found, the program uses LPSMALL.DRS if it is located on the same drive and subdirectory as the LP.FIL file. If neither file is located, you are limited to the 256 characters in the ASCII and extended ASCII character sets for creating, displaying, and printing characters.

In addition, some characters in the ASCII and extended ASCII character sets are located in WordPerfect character sets not included in either DRS file in the LetterPerfect software package. As an example, the legal section symbol, is located in Character Set 4 (Typographic Symbols) and is the sixth character in the set. The LetterPerfect code for the section symbol is 4,6. Because the legal section symbol is also ASCII 21, LetterPerfect treats the § symbol as if it is in the DRS file, even though it isn't.

> *Tip:* With the 07/24/90 LetterPerfect program, if you also own either WordPerfect 5.1 or DrawPerfect 1.1 and can afford the disk space, you can copy the WP.DRS file from either of these programs to the drive and subdirectory with LP.FIL, rename it LP.DRS, and have between 1,700 (if you use the WordPerfect 5.1 DRS file) and 2,000-plus (if you use the DrawPerfect 1.1 DRS file) characters available for LetterPerfect to use.
>
> Beginning with the release of the 11/01/90 software, LetterPerfect directly supports either WP.DRS file. WordPerfect Corporation now offers a set of supplementary disks for LetterPerfect that includes the font file, WP.DRS, used by DrawPerfect 1.1. This font file requires approximately 743K of disk space and—in addition to all the 2,000-plus WordPerfect characters—includes 30 fonts of graphical characters. If your system has the disk space to support the WP.DRS font file, you should consider buying the supplementary disk set from WordPerfect Corporation.

Displaying Special Characters On-Screen

Most video-card and monitor combinations are limited to displaying the 256 characters in the Extended ASCII Character Set on the main editing screen. If you have a special display adapter, such as the Hercules Graphics Card Plus, you can display up to 512 different characters (the IBM Extended Character Set plus 256 other characters). The additional 256 characters, taken from various LetterPerfect character sets, are hard-coded into LetterPerfect. You cannot choose a different set of display characters without using a software product from a third-party vendor.

When you use a character that the monitor cannot display on the main editing screen, LetterPerfect represents the character as a small solid box (■). If, however, your printer can print graphic images, LetterPerfect displays the actual character—if you use View Document from the Print menu.

Follow these steps to display a document on the main editing screen with the preview function:

1. Access the **File** pull-down menu and select **P**rint. Alternatively, press Print (Shift-F7).

   You see the Print menu as shown in figure 12.2.

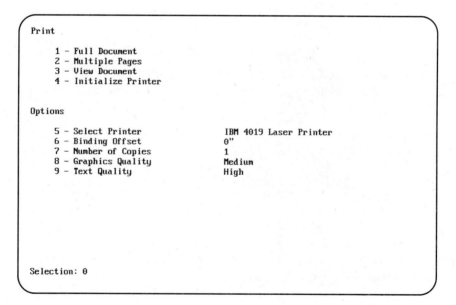

```
Print

        1 - Full Document
        2 - Multiple Pages
        3 - View Document
        4 - Initialize Printer


Options

        5 - Select Printer          IBM 4019 Laser Printer
        6 - Binding Offset          0"
        7 - Number of Copies        1
        8 - Graphics Quality        Medium
        9 - Text Quality            High




Selection: 0
```

Fig. 12.2. LetterPerfect's Print menu.

2. Select **V**iew Document (**3**).

   You see the document, as shown in figure 12.3.

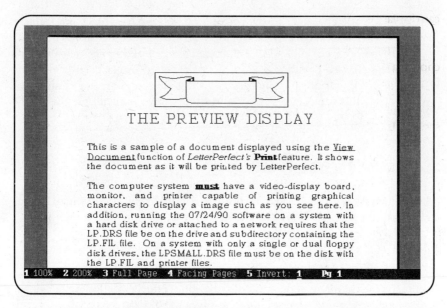

Fig. 12.3. *A document displayed with Preview.*

Caution: With the 07/24/90 software, for the Preview feature to work, either the LP.DRS or LPSMALL.DRS file must be in the drive and subdirectory containing LetterPerfect's LP.FIL file. With the 11/01/90 software, for Preview to work, one of the DRS font files—LP.DRS, LPSMALL.DRS, or WP.DRS—must be in the drive and subdirectory containing LetterPerfect's printer files. If LetterPerfect does not find one of its DRS files, you briefly see the message ERROR: Can't find .DRS file.

If your printer does not have graphics capability or does not have a font that contains that character, you cannot view the character with Preview. A blank space is inserted at the location of the character when the document prints.

Printing Special Characters

If a character is not found in the ASCII or extended ASCII character sets but is in a character set available to the program, the character is printed graphically if your printer has graphics capability. During the printing process, LetterPerfect first looks for the character in the active font. If the character is not found, LetterPerfect looks for it in a substitute font. If LetterPerfect still cannot find the character, the program analyzes the character to see whether it can be printed as a regular character with a diacritical mark; LetterPerfect then prints the diacritical mark graphically if necessary. If the special character cannot be broken down this way, LetterPerfect prints the entire character graphically.

Setting Print Quality

The print quality for special characters created graphically is determined by the print-quality setting for both text and graphics on the main Print menu:

- If Text Quality (9) is set to High, special characters are printed with the printer's high-quality setting.

- If Text Quality is set at Medium or Draft, LetterPerfect uses the print-quality setting established for Graphics Quality (8).

- If either Text Quality or Graphics Quality is set to Do Not Print, special characters are not printed.

Entering Special Characters with the Character Feature

You can use either of two Character methods to enter special characters: a *numeric* method or a *mnemonic* method. Both require that you activate Character with either the mouse or the keyboard. Using the numeric method, you type the first number of the character, then a comma, and then the second number of the character; finally, you press any key. With the mnemonic method, type the two components of the character and press any key.

Comparing Ctrl-2 to Ctrl-V

Use any of three key sequences to access Character: the Font, Character pull-down menu sequence, Ctrl-2, or Ctrl-v (the fast-key combination). Of the three, only Ctrl-2, the primary Character key sequence, works everywhere in the program, including submenus. The fast-key and pull-down menu sequences work in the main editing screen but not in all submenus.

Many users prefer Ctrl-v because it displays the prompt Key= to remind you to enter the character numbers or mnemonic combination. If you prefer to see this prompt, use Ctrl-v rather than Ctrl-2. When the prompt Key= appears at the lower left corner of the screen, type the two characters or enter the numeric code of a character from the LetterPerfect character set.

Using the Numeric Method

Follow these steps to create the Ñ through the numeric method:

1. Access the Font pull-down menu and select Characters. Alternatively, press Ctrl-2 or Ctrl-v.

   If you choose the pull-down menu or Ctrl-v sequence, the Key= prompt is displayed at the lower left corner of the screen. If you use the Ctrl-2 sequence, a prompt is *not* displayed.

2. Enter the LetterPerfect character set number (*1* in this example), a comma (*,*), and the character-set sequence number of the character (*56* in this example).

3. Press Enter.

   If you enter a valid LetterPerfect character code, Ñ is displayed on-screen at the cursor. If the character cannot be displayed on the main editing screen, a small box is inserted in the document at the cursor.

Using the Mnemonic Method

To use special characters more easily, you can follow several internal mnemonic shortcuts for Character. With these shortcuts you can create certain characters by typing characters that resemble components of the character. If the character is a digraph (a combination of two characters) or a diacritical (a character plus a diacritical mark, such as a circumflex [^]), you can probably enter it with a mnemonic character, without knowing its LetterPerfect numeric code.

Follow these steps to create the Ñ with the mnemonic method:

1. Access the Font pull-down menu and select **Characters**. Alternatively, press Ctrl-2 or Ctrl-v.

   If you choose the pull-down menu or Ctrl-v sequences, you see the Key= prompt at the lower left corner of the screen. If you choose the Ctrl-2 sequence, you do *not* see a prompt.

2. Type a capital *N* followed by the tilde (~).

   If you enter a valid LetterPerfect character combination, you see the Ñ on-screen at the cursor. If the character is one that cannot be displayed on the main editing screen, LetterPerfect inserts a small box in the document at the cursor.

   When you use the Compose mnemonic method, you do not need to use a comma between the two characters or to press Enter afterward.

> *Tip:* LetterPerfect's mnemonic combinations are often ingenious. For example, to enter the ½ character, activate Character and then type /2.
>
> Only certain predefined pairs of characters work with Character. The order in which you enter the characters is unimportant, but the case of the letters is sometimes important. For example, to enter the ç (cedilla c) character, you can select Compose and then type either *c,* or *,c.*

Table 12.3 lists the mnemonic characters for entering diacritical marks. Table 12.4 lists the mnemonic characters for entering other special characters. Refer to these lists when you use the Character mnemonic method.

Changing Fonts

With many word processing programs, you must change fonts to access special characters. In LetterPerfect, font changes are intended to alter the typeface or the font size. Changing to another font to access a particular character should not be necessary if the driver for the printer is defined correctly.

Table 12.3
WordPerfect Mnemonic Characters for Diacritical Marks

Mnemonic Character	Description	Examples
´	Acute accent	á Á é É í Í ó Ó ú Ú ŕ Ŕ
`	Grave accent	à À è È ì Ì ò Ò ù Ù Ỳ ỳ ř Ř
v	Caron (hachek)	č Č ď Ď ě Ě ǧ Ǧ Ǐ Ľ ň Ň ř Ř š Š ǐ Ť
,	Cedilla	ç Ç ş Ş ţ Ţ ķ Ķ
;	Ogonek (Polish hook)	ą Ą ę Ę į Į ų Ų
:	Centered dot	ŀ Ŀ
^	Circumflex	â ê î ô û ŷ
-	Crossbar	đ Đ ŧ Ŧ ħ Ħ
.	Dot above	ė Ė ı İ
_	Macron (overbar)	ā Ā ē Ē ī Ī ō Ō ū Ū
/	Slash	ø Ø
\	Stroke	ł Ł
~	Tilde	ñ Ñ ã Ã ĩ Ĩ õ Õ ũ Ũ
"	Umlaut or diaeresis	ä Ä ë Ë ï Ï ö Ö ü Ü ÿ Ÿ
@	Circle above	å Å ů Ů
o	Circle above	å

Table 12.4
Other WordPerfect Mnemonic Characters

Mnemonic Character	Displayed Result	Description	Numeric Codes
		Bullets	
*.	•	Small filled bullet	[4,3]
**	●	Medium filled bullet	[4,0]
*o	○	Small hollow bullet	[4,45]
*O	○	Large hollow bullet	[4,1]
		Fractions	
/2	½	One-half symbol	[4,17]
/4	¼	One-quarter symbol	[4,18]

Table 12.4 (continued)

Digraphs

Mnemonic Character	Displayed Result	Description	Numeric Codes
ss	ß	German double s	[1,23] (lowercase only)
AE	Æ	AE Digraph	[1,36]
ae	æ	ae Digraph	[1,37]
IJ	IJ	IJ Digraph	[1,138]
ij	ij	ij Digraph	[1,139] (Displays on-screen as y diaeresis [1,75] but is in fact a different character)
OE	Œ	OE Digraph	[1,166]
oe	œ	oe Digraph	[1,167]

Typographic Characters

Mnemonic Character	Displayed Result	Description	Numeric Codes
!!	¡	Inverted exclamation mark	[4,7]
??	¿	Inverted question mark	[4,8]
<<	«	Left double guillemet	[4,9]
>>	»	Right double guillemet	[4,10]
a=	ª	Feminine Spanish ordinal	[4,15]
o=	º	Masculine Spanish ordinal	[4,16]
n-	–	En dash	[4,33] (lowercase)
m-	—	Em dash	[4,34] (lowercase)
--	—	Em dash	[4,34]

Currency

Mnemonic Character	Displayed Result	Description	Numeric Codes	
L-	£	Pound/Sterling	[4,11]	(uppercase L)
Y=	¥	Yen	[4,12]	(uppercase Y)
Pt	₧	Pesetas	[4,13]	(uppercase P, lowercase t)
f-	ƒ	Florin/Guilders	[4,14]	(lowercase f)
c/	¢	Cents symbol	[4,19]	(lowercase c)
xo	¤	Currency symbol	[4,24]	(lowercase)

When you use a character not available in your current font, LetterPerfect's printer drivers look for that character in your other fonts. If the character is not available in another font, LetterPerfect prints it graphically if the active printer has graphics capability.

Working with Foreign Languages

LetterPerfect's support for foreign languages and multilingual documents is surprisingly good for a low-end word processor. If you create most of your documents in a language other than English, consider purchasing LetterPerfect in that language version so that the prompts and documentation are in the language you use.

Using Foreign Language Dictionaries and Thesauruses

If you write primarily in English but often work with multilingual documents, you can purchase a WordPerfect Language Module for that language. The Language Module contains the language dictionaries, thesaurus, and hyphenation files that work with the English version of LetterPerfect. Canadian versions, for example, are shipped with a United Kingdom English dictionary and a Canadian French dictionary. The documentation and screen prompts are in English or French, depending on the version.

To use multiple dictionaries and thesauruses with the 07/24/90 software on a system that has a hard disk drive, you must copy the Speller, thesaurus, and hyphenation files to a drive and disk accessible to the system while LetterPerfect is operating. On a system that has a single floppy disk drive, these files should be on the LetterPerfect 2 disk.

To use multiple dictionaries and thesauruses with the 11/01/90 software on a system that has a hard disk drive, the Speller, thesaurus, and hyphenation files should be in the drive and disk designated for these files with LetterPerfect's Setup feature. (See Chapter 1 for information on using the Setup feature.) On a system that has a single floppy disk drive, these files should be on the LetterPerfect 2 disk.

Each dictionary, thesaurus, and hyphenation file name contains a two-letter language code for the corresponding language. For example, the U.S. English dictionary is named WP{WP}*US*.LEX, and the Spanish dictionary is named WP{WP}*ES*.LEX. Similarly, the U.S. English thesaurus is named WP{WP}*US*.THS, and the Spanish thesaurus is named WP{WP}*ES*.THS. Some languages also have a hyphenation file, such as WP{WP}*US*.HYC for U.S. English.

In addition to dictionary, thesaurus, and hyphenation files for specific languages, you should have a file called WP{WP}.SPW or WP{WP}.SPR. The file you have depends on the specific language version of LetterPerfect. *SPW* stands for *Spell By Word* (lookup), whereas *SPR* stands for *Spell By Rule* (algorithm). The U.S English version ships with the WP{WP}.SPW file.

The United States version of LetterPerfect contains stripped-down versions of the spelling and thesaurus dictionaries. However, the U.S. WordPerfect Language Modules include the same dictionaries, thesauruses, and hyphenation files used in WordPerfect 5.1. These files are required to activate LetterPerfect's automatic-hyphenation feature.

> *Tip:* If you own WordPerfect 5.1 and can afford the disk space, you are encouraged to copy the WordPerfect 5.1 WP{WP}US.LEX, WP{WP}US.THS, WP{WP}US.SPW, and WP{WP}US.HYC files to the drive and disk containing the LetterPerfect program files.

Entering LetterPerfect Language Codes

The key to LetterPerfect's excellent foreign language support is the Language feature. The language code automatically determines these items:

- Dictionary, thesaurus, and hyphenation files to be used
- The format of the date
- The tab-alignment character

You can change languages as many times as you want by inserting language codes in the document. A language code stays in effect until LetterPerfect encounters another one.

Language codes make it possible to switch languages in the middle of a document. When you spell-check a document that is part German and part

Swedish, for example, LetterPerfect automatically uses the German dictionary to spell-check the German sections and the Swedish dictionary to spell-check the Swedish sections if you have the corresponding dictionaries. If you do not have the correct dictionary, LetterPerfect displays this message at the bottom of the screen:

WP{WP}SV.LEX not found: **1** Enter **Path**; **2** Skip **Language**; **3** Exit Spell: **3**.

Select Enter **Path** (**1**) to enter the DOS path for the missing dictionary, select **Skip Language** (**2**) to skip that language (the spell-check is resumed at the next language code), or select **Exit Spell** (**3**) to stop the spell-check and exit Spell.

If you add words to the dictionary during the spell-check, they are added to the appropriate supplementary dictionary. If the supplemental dictionary does not exist, it is created.

You also can add language codes anywhere in the document. If you enter a language code with Setup's initial codes function, the language you designate becomes the default language for all new documents. (See Chapter 1 for information on using Setup.)

Follow these steps to enter a language code:

1. Access the **Layout** pull-down menu and select **Language**. Alternatively, press **Language** (Alt-F8).

   At the lower left corner of the screen, you see a prompt with a two-letter abbreviation for the active language: Language: US.

2. Type the two-letter code for the language you want to use; press Enter.

With the 07/24/90 software, the prompt disappears, and LetterPerfect inserts a pair of hidden language codes at the cursor's location. For example, if you type the **ES** Spanish abbreviation, the paired codes appear as **[Lang:ES][Decml/Algn Char:.,,]** when viewed with the Reveal Codes feature.

With the 11/01/90 software, the prompt disappears, and LetterPerfect inserts a pair of hidden language codes at the cursor's location *only* if the selected language has a record in the WP.LRS file. Otherwise, LetterPerfect inserts only the code for the selected language.

For example, if you type the **ES** Spanish abbreviation, the paired codes appear as **[Lang:ES][Decml/Algn Char:.,,]** when viewed with the Reveal Codes feature. However, if the Spanish record in the WP.LRS file has been deleted, LetterPerfect inserts only **[Lang:ES]**.

> ***Caution:*** To use a tab-alignment character different from the default character of the current language, you must insert a language code for the default language. You cannot press Enter to insert the default language code displayed by the language prompt, as you can with most LetterPerfect prompts. To insert the codes for the language into the document at the cursor, you must type the default two-letter code before you press Enter.
>
> The next section shows you how to use the Language Resource file to change the tab-alignment character.

Table 12.5 lists the language codes officially supported by LetterPerfect.

Table 12.5
Language Codes Supported by LetterPerfect

Language	Code File	Speller File	Thesaurus File	Hyphenation Driver	Keyboard
Afrikaans	AF	Yes	No	No	Yes
Catalan	CA	Yes	No	Yes	Yes
Danish	DK	Yes	Yes	Yes	Yes
Dutch	NL	Yes	Yes	Yes	Yes
English-Australia	OZ	Yes	Yes	Yes*	Yes
English-U.K.	UK	Yes	Yes	Yes*	Yes
English-U.S.A.	US	Yes	Yes	Yes*	No
Finnish	SU	Yes	No	Yes	Yes
French-Canada	CF	Yes	Yes	Yes	Yes
French-National	FR	Yes	Yes	Yes	Yes
German-National	DE	Yes	Yes	Yes	Yes
German-Switzerland	SD	Yes	Yes	Yes	Yes

Language	Code File	Speller File	Thesaurus File	Hyphenation Driver	Keyboard
Afrikaans	AF	Yes	No	No	Yes
Greek†	GR	No	No	Yes	Yes
Icelandic	IS	Yes	No	No	Yes
Italian	IT	Yes	Yes	Yes	Yes
Norwegian	NO	Yes	Yes	Yes*	Yes
Portuguese-Brazil	BR	Yes	No	Yes	Yes
Portuguese-National	PO	Yes	No	Yes	Yes
Russian†	RU	No	No	Yes	Yes
Spanish	ES	Yes	Yes	Yes	Yes
Swedish	SV	Yes	Yes	Yes	Yes

*The Speller file contains a list of hyphenated words and is used for both spell-checking and hyphenating a document.

†Greek and Russian Language Modules also include screen fonts, printer drivers, and special utilities.

Using the Language Resource File (WP.LRS)

LetterPerfect has a special file, WP.LRS, that among other things contains information about all languages supported by LetterPerfect, including formatting information for some menu displays and features. The WP.LRS file is in the special secondary-merge file format (see fig. 12.4) used by the Notebook 3.0 program and contained in the WordPerfect Office 3.0 software package.

If you work with a language for which no language code or definition is available, you can edit the WP.LRS file in either Notebook or LetterPerfect to create your own settings. Just add a new record to the WP.LRS file with the appropriate information (names and abbreviations for the months and the days of the week, how you want the date formatted, and the text for the footnote continuation messages).

```
 File Edit Search Layout Tools Font Graphics Help      (Press ALT= for menu bar)
══════════════════════════════════════════════════════════════════════════
           ^N
 US1
 01 F01 1,1,1,3,
 02 F02 1,5,1,37,
 03 F03 2,1,13,26,
 04 F04 2,30,13,35,
 05 F05 15,1,21,26,
 06 F06 15,30,21,35,
 07 F07 1,39,1,57,
 08 F08 1,59,1,77,
 09 F09 2,39,2,77,
 10 F10 3,39,3,77,
 11 F11 4,39,4,77,
 12 F12 5,39,5,77,
 13 F13 6,39,6,77,
 14 F14 7,39,7,77,
 15 F15 8,39,8,77,
 16 F16 9,39,9,77,
 17 F17 10,39,10,77,
 18 F18 11,39,11,77,
 19 F19 12,39,12,77,
 20 F20 13,39,13,77,
 C:\LP10\WP.LRS                                    Pg 1 Ln 1" Pos 1"
```

Fig. 12.4. The WP.LRS file.

The record for each language begins immediately after an end-record (^E) code and contains 31 fields separated by the end-field (^R) code. Depending on the language, some fields are empty, and others contain multiple lines of information.

Table 12.6 lists all the formatting fields for the U.S. language record (the last one in the WP.LRS file). The empty fields are not currently used by either version of the LetterPerfect software.

Table 12.6
Default U.S. Language Formatting Fields in the WP.LRS File

Field Number	Field Contents	Default Setting	Record
1	Language code		US ^R
2	Format for date	3 1, 4	
	Format for am	am	
	Format for pm	pm ^R	
3	Format for month names	January	
		February	
		March	
		April	
		May	

Field Number	Field Contents	Default Setting	Record
		June	
		July	
		August	
		September	
		October	
		November	
		December ⌃R	
4	Format for month abbreviations	Jan	
		Feb	
		Mar	
		Apr	
		May	
		Jun	
		Jul	
		Aug	
		Sep	
		Oct	
		Nov	
		Dec ⌃R	
5	Format for day names	Sunday	
		Monday	
		Tuesday	
		Wednesday	
		Thursday	
		Friday	
		Saturday ⌃R	
6	Format for day abbreviations	Sun	
		Mon	
		Tue	
		Wed	
		Thu	
		Fri	
		Sat ⌃R	
7–20	Empty	⌃R	
21	List Files date sequence	2 ⌃R	
22	List Files date separators	- -⌃R	

Table 12.1 (continued)

Field Number	Field Contents	Default Setting	Record
23	List Files time format	12 ^R	
24	List Files hour/minutes separator	.	
	Format for List Files am	a	
	Format for List Files pm	p ^R	
25	List Files file size thousand separator	, ^R	
26-27	Empty	^R	
28	Decimal alignment character	. ^R	
29-30	Empty	^R	
31	Empty	^R	
	End of Record	^E	

Follow these steps to edit WP.LRS so that the United States language tab-alignment feature uses the colon (:) as the tab-alignment character:

1. Retrieve the WP.LRS file to the main editing screen.

2. Access the Search pull-down menu and select Forward. Alternatively, press Search (F2).

   At the lower left corner of the screen, you see the prompt `->Srch:.`

3. Type *US*.

4. Press Character (Ctrl-2) and press Ctrl-R.

   US^*R* is inserted as the search string.

5. Press Search (F2).

   You see the `*Please Wait*` prompt, and the cursor moves to the beginning of the *US* language record.

6. Move the cursor left of the ^R in field 28.

7. Type the colon (:) and delete the period.

8. Use Save to save the modified WP.LRS to the disk containing LP.FIL.

The WP.LRS file is read into RAM when you start the program. Any changes made to the settings in the WP.LRS file do not take effect until the next time you start the program.

The WP.LRS file also controls the way LetterPerfect displays the file time and date listings with the List Files feature. By default, the file list appears as shown in figure 12.5.

```
11-01-90  09:00a              Directory C:\LP10\*.*
Document size:        0   Free:  3,993,600 Used:  2,188,244     Files:      128

  .    Current    <Dir>                   ..    Parent    <Dir>
DOCUMENT.          <Dir>  11-02-90 09:00a  {LP}SPC .FRM   10,142  11-01-90 12:00p
ADDRESS .TUT         978  11-01-90 12:00p  ARROW-22.WPG      195  11-01-90 12:00p
BALLOONS.WPG       3,195  11-01-90 12:00p  BANNER-3.WPG      727  11-01-90 12:00p
BEGIN   .TUT          11  11-01-90 12:00p  BICYCLE .WPG    1,355  11-01-90 12:00p
BKGRND-1.WPG      11,489  11-01-90 12:00p  BORDER-8.WPG      223  11-01-90 12:00p
BULB    .WPG       2,109  11-01-90 12:00p  BURST-1 .WPG      827  11-01-90 12:00p
BUTTRFLY.WPG       5,291  11-01-90 12:00p  CALENDAR.WPG      379  11-01-90 12:00p
CERTIF  .WPG         661  11-01-90 12:00p  CHKBOX-1.WPG      661  11-01-90 12:00p
CLOCK   .WPG       1,825  11-01-90 12:00p  CNTRCT-2.WPG    2,761  11-01-90 12:00p
CONVERT .EXE     109,229  11-01-90 12:00p  CURSOR  .COM    1,452  11-01-90 12:00p
DEVICE-2.WPG         665  11-01-90 12:00p  DIPLOMA .WPG    2,421  11-01-90 12:00p
FILENAME.TUT         335  11-01-90 12:00p  FIXBIOS .COM       50  11-01-90 12:00p
FLATTIRE.LRN       2,942  11-01-90 12:00p  FLOPPY-2.WPG      483  11-01-90 12:00p
GAVEL   .WPG         895  11-01-90 12:00p  GLOBE2-M.WPG    7,793  11-01-90 12:00p
GRAPHCNV.EXE     120,320  11-01-90 12:00p  HANDS-3 .WPG    1,125  11-01-90 12:00p
IB40LAPR.PRS     155,087  11-02-90 09:00a  INSTALL .EXE   57,856  11-01-90 12:00p
LETTER  .TUT         653  11-01-90 12:00p  LETTER_F.TUT      679  11-01-90 12:00p
LETTER_P.TUT         652  11-01-90 12:00p ▼ LETTER1 .TUT      778  11-01-90 12:00p

1 Retrieve; 2 Delete; 3 Move/Rename; 4 Other Directory; 5 Copy; 6 Look;
N Name Search: 6
```

Fig. 12.5. *The default List Files display format.*

The number in Field 21 determines which of three sequences LetterPerfect uses to show the date's components. The sequences are these:

Number	Date Sequence
1	day month year
2	month day year
3	year month day

The default date format is 2. **Note:** In the original LetterPerfect manual, the sequences listed for 1 and 2 are interchanged by mistake.

The characters on each line in Field 22 determine the two characters that separate the three date components. The default character format is two hyphens.

The number in Field 23 determines whether LetterPerfect uses a standard (12 hour) or military (24 hour) format to display the file time. The default time format is 12—standard time.

The following steps illustrate how to modify the WP.LRS file so that the file's date components are separated by forward slashes, with the time in military format:

1. Retrieve the WP.LRS file to the main editing screen.

2. Access the Search pull-down menu and select Forward. Alternatively, press Search (F2).

   At the lower left corner of the screen, you see the prompt ->Srch:.

3. Type *US*.

4. Press Character (Ctrl-2) and then Ctrl-r.

   The program inserts *US^R* as the search string.

5. Press Search (F2).

   You see the *Please Wait* prompt, and the cursor moves to the beginning of the US language record.

6. Move the cursor to the first line in Field 22 and replace the hyphen with a forward slash.

7. Move the cursor to the second line in Field 22 and replace the hyphen with a forward slash.

8. Move the cursor to Field 23 and change 12 to 24.

9. Use Save to save the modified WP.LRS file to the disk containing LP.FIL.

The next time you start LetterPerfect and use the List Files feature, the list of files displays the date and time formats shown in figure 12.6.

```
11/01/90  09:05              Directory C:\LP10\*.*
Document size:      0   Free:  3,993,600 Used:  2,188,194      Files:    128

.    Current    <Dir>                  ..    Parent    <Dir>
DOCUMENT.        <Dir> 11/02/90 09:00   {LP}SPC .FRM   10,142  11/01/90 12:00
ADDRESS .TUT       978 11/01/90 12:00   ARROW-22.WPG      195  11/01/90 12:00
BALLOONS.WPG     3,195 11/01/90 12:00   BANNER-3.WPG      727  11/01/90 12:00
BEGIN   .TUT        11 11/01/90 12:00   BICYCLE .WPG    1,355  11/01/90 12:00
BKGRND-1.WPG    11,489 11/01/90 12:00   BORDER-8.WPG      223  11/01/90 12:00
BULB    .WPG     2,109 11/01/90 12:00   BURST-1 .WPG      827  11/01/90 12:00
BUTTRFLY.WPG     5,291 11/01/90 12:00   CALENDAR.WPG      379  11/01/90 12:00
CERTIF  .WPG       661 11/01/90 12:00   CHKBOX-1.WPG      661  11/01/90 12:00
CLOCK   .WPG     1,825 11/01/90 12:00   CNTRCT-2.WPG    2,761  11/01/90 12:00
CONVERT .EXE   109,229 11/01/90 12:00   CURSOR  .COM    1,452  11/01/90 12:00
DEVICE-2.WPG       665 11/01/90 12:00   DIPLOMA .WPG    2,421  11/01/90 12:00
FILENAME.TUT       335 11/01/90 12:00   FIXBIOS .COM       50  11/01/90 12:00
FLATTIRE.LRN     2,942 11/01/90 12:00   FLOPPY-2.WPG      483  11/01/90 12:00
GAVEL   .WPG       895 11/01/90 12:00   GLOBE2-M.WPG    7,793  11/01/90 12:00
GRAPHCNV.EXE   120,320 11/01/90 12:00   HANDS-3 .WPG    1,125  11/01/90 12:00
IB40LAPR.PRS   155,087 11/02/90 09:00   INSTALL .EXE   57,856  11/01/90 12:00
LETTER  .TUT       653 11/01/90 12:00   LETTER_F.TUT      679  11/01/90 12:00
LETTER_P.TUT       652 11/01/90 12:00 ▼ LETTER1 .TUT      778  11/01/90 12:00

1 Retrieve; 2 Delete; 3 Move/Rename; 4 Other Directory; 5 Copy; 6 Look;
N Name Search: 6
```

Fig. 12.6. *The modified List Files display format.*

Summary

LetterPerfect's support for special characters and foreign languages is exceptional for a low-end word processor. Because LetterPerfect can print more than 2,000 characters from the WordPerfect Character Set on printers that have graphics capability, documents with special characters print correctly on a wide variety of printers. When you use LetterPerfect instead of a special-purpose program for foreign language word processing, you take advantage of LetterPerfect's strong word processing features (often missing in special foreign language programs) and avoid the problems of file incompatibility (the bane of special-purpose programs). If you work with special characters and foreign languages, the features described in this chapter should make your work easier.

In this chapter, you learned to do these tasks:

- Enter special characters into a document

- Print special characters on printers that have graphics capability

- Use numeric and mnemonic methods to create special characters

- Work with multilingual documents

- Work with the WP.LRS file

Chapter 13 shows you how to use the Shell (07/24/90 and 11/01/90 software) and LetterPerfect (11/01/90 software only) macro features. You also learn how to create macros that simplify using LetterPerfect.

Part III

Using LetterPerfect's Advanced Features

Includes

Creating and Using Macros

Assembling Documents Using Merge

Integrating Text and Graphics

13

Creating and Using Macros

T he Macro feature is a powerful tool that enables you to customize the operation of LetterPerfect to meet your special needs. A macro is a special file that contains a record of keystrokes. When you activate the Macro feature and select a macro file, the keystrokes are played back in the same sequence as you originally typed them—except much faster. With as few as two or three keystrokes, you can start a macro containing thousands of keystrokes that do one or more of the following things:

- Perform tedious or repetitious tasks without making a mistake

- Add text to a document

- Format or enhance part (character, word, sentence, paragraph, page, and so on) or all of a document

- Start other LetterPerfect features

- Simulate WordPerfect 5.1 features not included in LetterPerfect

457

Reminder: WordPerfect Corporation updated LetterPerfect 1.0 just before this book went to press. Dated 11/01/90, the interim release includes new options for existing features and a few new features including a built-in macro feature. Therefore, the menus on your screen may differ slightly from those shown in this book. Also, depending on the printer-form definition, margins, tab stops, and font you specify, the text placement and status-line information in documents you create may differ from those shown in this book's figures.

For more information about using the mouse and accessing the pull-down menus, refer to the introduction.

Caution: The first release of LetterPerfect 1.0, dated 07/24/90, DOES NOT include an internal, or built-in, macro feature; however, the 07/24/90 LetterPerfect software package does provide the WordPerfect Shell 3.01 program that includes a macro feature. If you are using the first release of the program, you must run LetterPerfect through the Shell (see Chapter 1) in order to use macros.

The first interim release of LetterPerfect 1.0, dated 11/01/90, DOES include an internal macro feature. If you are using this release, a macro feature is available to you automatically, without running the program through the Shell. You have the additional capability of adding the Shell macro feature if you choose to run this interim release of LetterPerfect through the WordPerfect Shell 3.01 program.

You can determine the date of your release by pressing Help (F3) and noting the date at the top right corner of the screen. For easy reference, you can use this chart:

	Built-in LetterPerfect Macros	Shell Macros
07/24/90 Original Release	No	Yes
11/01/90 Interim Release	Yes	Yes

Tip: The Shell 3.01 program requires approximately 120K of disk space and 51K of RAM. If your system has a single floppy disk drive with less than 640K of RAM, more disk switching is required to run LetterPerfect through the Shell and you may not have enough RAM to edit large documents.

When the 11/01/90 interim version was released, WordPerfect Corporation offered users of the 07/24/90 software an upgrade to the 11/01/90 program for a nominal charge of less than $20.00. If you are using the 07/24/90 software on a single floppy-disk-drive system, you should consider upgrading to the 11/01/90.

Caution: Unlike LetterPerfect and its macro feature, Shell and its macro feature do *not* recognize the mouse. Although you can use the mouse to select menu options while you create either type of macro, only LetterPerfect macros record options selected with the mouse. You cannot use the mouse to highlight a block of text while defining either type of macro.

If you perform a task repeatedly with LetterPerfect, even one as simple as deleting a line, you can do it more quickly with a macro. Macros can automate simple tasks, such as typing *Sincerely yours* and your name. Macros also can perform complex operations that include both text and LetterPerfect commands. After you create a macro, you can use it to do almost instantly things that require many seconds or minutes of manual keystrokes.

The Macro feature enables you to customize LetterPerfect to your personal needs. Every word processing program has features that you can use in easy one- or two-key procedures. For example, LetterPerfect enables you to delete a word in one step (press Ctrl-Backspace), but you need more keystrokes to delete a sentence or a paragraph. If you often delete whole sentences or paragraphs, you can create macros to make those tasks, or any others, just as easy as deleting a word.

Suppose that you want to change the format in a document from single- to double-spacing. Without a macro, you would need to complete a sequence of many commands: press Format (Shift-F8), press L for Line Spacing (2), type *2* to change to double-spacing, press Enter, and press Exit (F7). A macro enables you to assign all these keystrokes to the Alt-D key combination for double-spacing. Then, whenever you want to change to double-spacing, you simply press Alt-D to run the macro. The Macro feature not only "remembers" that Alt-D includes these keystrokes but also executes them automatically—and a lot faster than you can enter them one at a time.

In addition to the obvious advantages of macros, they are fun to create and use. In this chapter, you learn these basic macro skills:

- Creating macros

- Running macros

- Stopping macros

- Replacing macros

- Controlling how the macros run

To help you become familiar with LetterPerfect macros, this chapter also includes the following features:

- Samples of useful macros

- Techniques to apply when you create your own macros

- Tips on using macros

Don't expect to create perfect macros every time you try. You can improve your odds of success if you work through the steps before you begin creating the macro. If the steps work when you perform them one by one, they are likely to work in a macro. Before you create a complicated macro, you may want to write down each of the steps. Even experienced macro users, however, often create their macros through trial and error. Don't be afraid to experiment.

The best method for learning macro techniques is to practice creating the sample macros in this chapter. Because macros draw on other LetterPerfect procedures, you may learn some new tricks for using LetterPerfect as you work through this chapter. You also can learn to create simple macros that make it quicker and easier to use some of LetterPerfect's features.

Understanding Types of Macros

You can create and run the following three types of macros:

- Alt-*letter* (LetterPerfect) or Alt-Shift-*letter* (Shell) macros

- Named macros

- Temporary macros (only with versions of LetterPerfect dated later than 11/01/90)

A LetterPerfect Alt-*letter* macro has a name that consists of the Alt key plus a letter from A to Z, for example, ALTK .LPM. A Shell Alt-Shift-*letter* macro has a name that consists of the Alt and Shift keys plus a letter from A to Z, for example, ALTSHFTK .SHM.

A *named* macro has a name of one to eight characters, such as TABS or MARGINS. Although invoking a named macro requires more keystrokes than Alt-*letter* and Alt-Shift-*letter* macros, you may find it easier to remember what a named macro does.

A *temporary* macro is simply a macro that you create without a name. If you are using a version of LetterPerfect dated 11/01/90 or later, you can create temporary macros. LetterPerfect automatically assigns the macro a default "name" of LP{LP}.LPN and stores it on disk under that name. This macro is considered temporary because, when you create another macro with no name, LetterPerfect replaces the original unnamed macro with the new one; you can have only one temporary macro at a time.

When you create any type of macro in LetterPerfect, the program automatically gives the file an LPM extension (LPM stands for LetterPerfect macro). Macros created with the Shell receive an SHM extension (SHM stands for Shell macro). You do not need to be concerned about the LPM or SHM extensions except when you manipulate macros as files, either in DOS or through the List Files (F5) feature. You will learn more about handling macros as files later in this chapter.

> *Tip:* The simplest macros to use are the Alt-*letter* (LetterPerfect) or Alt-Shift-*letter* (Shell) macros. You should choose this type of macro for the most frequently used macros. Be sure that you select mnemonic letters that will remind you of what the macros do. For instance, you might use the name Alt-C for a LetterPerfect macro that centers text, or Alt-Shift-H for a Shell macro that inserts a heading.

> *Tip:* When you run the 11/01/90 LetterPerfect program through the Shell, you can create separate macros, with the same letter or name, that perform different functions. For example, you can use Alt-H for a LetterPerfect macro that highlights a word with the Block feature, and Alt-Shift-H for a Shell macro that inserts a heading.

Creating LetterPerfect and Shell Macros

In this section, you learn the five basic steps required to create macros. Then you create your first macro—something short but useful.

Before you create a macro to edit a document, you should have either the actual document on which you will use the macro or a few lines of text formatted in the same manner as the document with which you will use the macro.

> *Caution:* Use LetterPerfect's Save feature to keep the original version of a document as a file on disk; the original will be available in case you make a mistake while you create the macro. After you save the original document, you can safely practice making macros with the document that remains on-screen. (Just be sure that you do not save the document again with the same name!)

Use these steps to create a macro:

1. With the 11/01/90 software, access the **Tools** pull-down menu and select Macro De**fine** or Shell Mac **D**ef (see fig. 13.1). Alternatively, press Macro Define (Ctrl-F10) or Macro Define (Ctrl-Shift-F10).

   With the 07/24/90 software, access the **Tools** pull-down menu and select Macro De**fine** (see fig. 13.2). Alternatively, press Macro Define (Ctrl-F10) or Shell Macro Define (Ctrl-Shift-F10).

   At the bottom of the screen, you see a message prompt, either `Define macro:` for a LetterPerfect macro or `Define shell macro:` for a Shell macro.

2. Type the name of the macro. For an Alt-*letter* macro, hold down the Alt key and press a letter from A to Z. For an Alt-Shift-*letter* macro, hold down the Alt and Shift keys and press a letter from A to Z. For a descriptive macro, type one to eight characters (letters or numbers) and press Enter.

   If the name you give the macro is the same as an existing macro, at the bottom of the screen the program displays the prompt: `Replace C:\LP10\<`*macro name*`>.LPM? No (Yes).` **Press Enter** to select the default **No** option and terminate the macro-creation process. Select **Yes** to replace the existing macro and continue the macro-creation process.

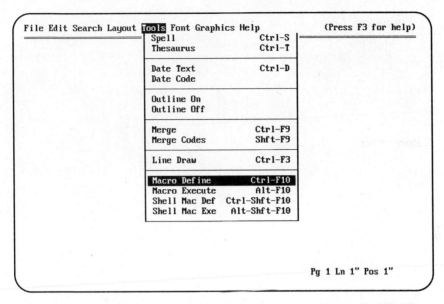

Fig. 13.1. *The 11/01/90 program's pull-down menu for defining a macro.*

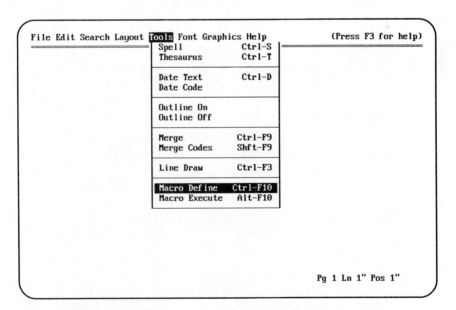

Fig. 13.2. *The 07/24/90 program's pull-down menu for defining a macro.*

Tip: By default, LetterPerfect stores and uses built-in macros on the drive or in the subdirectory where it looks for LP.FIL. If you want LetterPerfect to store and use macros from a different drive or subdirectory, enter a *full* pathname for the macro in step 2. For example, to store a macro named *test* in a subdirectory named *C:\MACROS*, type *C:\MACROS\TEST* and press Enter. The Shell program stores and uses Shell macros on the drive or in the subdirectory where it looks for the Shell program files unless you have designated a different location for macros with the Shell Setup (**4**), Options (**2**) feature. If you want to store and use Shell macros from a different drive or subdirectory, enter a *full* pathname for the macro in step 2. For example, to store a macro named *test* in a subdirectory named *C:\MACROS*, type *C:\MACROS\TEST* and press Enter.

As noted previously, the 11/01/90 program offers a third method of naming a macro—the Enter key. If you press Enter when the program prompts you for a macro name you create a temporary macro named *LP{LP}.LPM*. When you create a temporary macro, LetterPerfect does *not* prompt for a description. If you want to keep a temporary macro permanently, give *LP{LP}.LPM* a different name that ends with the *.LPM* extension.

3. After you name the macro, at the bottom of the screen, the program displays the message prompt: `Description:`. Type a short—up to 39 characters— description of what the macro does and press Enter.

   LetterPerfect can execute a macro without a description. To create a macro without a description, press Enter without typing any characters in step 3. Although the description does not serve any purpose with Shell macros when running LetterPerfect, you can see the description for a LetterPerfect macro using the List Files feature's **Look** (**6**) function (see Chapter 9). The description for either type of macro also is useful if you use the WordPerfect Editor 3.01 program to edit macros. Editor is part of the Office PC or LAN 3.01 software package. WordPerfect Corporation also may offer Editor 3.01 as a separate product before the end of 1991.

4. At the bottom of the screen, a flashing `Macro Def` displays for LetterPerfect macros. If you are creating a Shell macro, the program displays the message prompt `* Starting shell macro *`

for only a few seconds. Type the characters and/or formatting commands in the exact sequence that you want them executed when played back by the macro feature. The program records and stores the keystrokes in a file with the name you designated in step 2 and ending with either the .LPM or .SHM extension.

Note: All the commands that you use to define a macro also affect the current document. For example, when you create a macro to change tab settings, you also change the tab settings at the cursor position in the document. Press the Ctrl-r fast-key combination to activate the reveal-code feature and verify the tab setting changes in the current document. Press Ctrl-r again to return to the normal editing screen.

Tip: When you want to use a formatting code (such as Enter or Flush Right) or certain punctuation together with the text in a macro, include the formatting or punctuation as part of the macro.

5. With the 11/01/90 software, access the **Tools** pull-down menu and select Macro Define or Shell Mac Def. Alternatively, press Macro Define (Ctrl-F10) or Shell Macro Define (Ctrl-Shift-F10).

   With the 07/24/90 software, access the **Tools** pull-down menu and select Shell Macro Define. Alternatively, press Macro Define (Ctrl-F10) or Shell Macro Define (Ctrl-Shift-F10).

   If you are creating a LetterPerfect macro, the flashing `Macro Def` message disappears. If you are creating a Shell macro, at the bottom of the screen, the program displays the message prompt `* Shell macro ended *` for a few seconds.

Now that you have learned the basics, you probably are ready to create a nuts-and-bolts macro that performs a common task such as writing your name and address at the top of a letter. Here are the steps to follow:

1. Clear the main editing screen. Access the **File** pull-down menu, choose Exit, and select N twice. Alternatively, press Exit (F7) and select N twice.

2. With the 11/01/90 software, access the **Tools** pull-down menu and select Macro Define or Shell Mac Def. Alternatively, press Macro Define (Ctrl-F10) or Shell Macro Define (Ctrl-Shift-F10).

With the 07/24/90 software, access the **Tools** pull-down menu and select Shell Macro **D**efine. Alternatively, press Macro Define (Ctrl-F10) or Shell Macro Define (Ctrl-Shift-F10).

3. Type *AD* and press Enter.

4. Type *Creates Return Address at Top of Letter* and press Enter.

Caution: You can change your mind about creating a macro at any point up until you press Enter at the end of step 4. You can press Cancel (F1) or Esc to stop the macro-creation process. After you press Enter, however, the only way to stop creating the macro is as described in step 11.

---

5. Access the **L**ayout pull-down menu and select **C**enter. Alternatively, press Center (Shift-F6) or Ctrl-c.

6. Type your name and press Enter.

7. Repeat step 5.

8. Type your street or post office box address and press Enter.

9. Repeat step 5.

10. Type your city, state, and ZIP code and press Enter. The text on your screen should resemble the text shown in figure 13.3.

11. With the 11/01/90 software, access the **Tools** pull-down menu and select Macro **D**efine or Shell Mac **D**ef. Alternatively, press Macro Define (Ctrl-F10) or Shell Macro Define (Ctrl-Shift-F10).

With the 07/24/90 software, access the **Tools** pull-down menu and select Shell Macro **D**efine. Alternatively, press Macro Define (Ctrl-F10) or Shell Macro Define (Ctrl-Shift-F10).

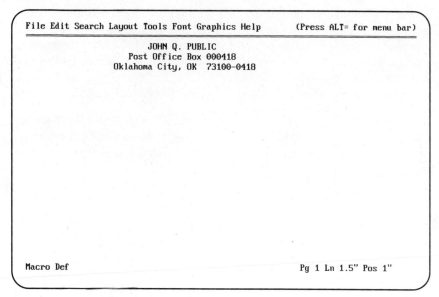

File Edit Search Layout Tools Font Graphics Help   (Press ALT= for menu bar)

                              JOHN Q. PUBLIC
                          Post Office Box 000418
                        Oklahoma City, OK 73100-0418

Macro Def   Pg 1 Ln 1.5" Pos 1"

Fig. 13.3. *The* AD *macro being created.*

Creating Macros That Work With Different Languages

At this writing, LetterPerfect supports 27 different languages. Although each LetterPerfect feature is listed in the same numerical sequence on menus regardless of the language version, the names and mnemonic letters that select an option (including Yes/No options) vary between these versions. Because of these language variations, macros that select menu options mnemonically frequently do not work between different language versions.

Fortunately, the LetterPerfect and Shell macro features provide a method of creating macros that work properly regardless of the language version of LetterPerfect on which you run them. You can select any option on any LetterPerfect menu by typing a number or character that represents its numerical sequence. This method works even if a number is not listed for an option on the menu.

The most obvious example is the pull-down menu bar that lists only mnemonic letters to select options. Although the pull-down menu options are not listed, you can select any of them by pressing the number or character that represents its numerical sequence. For example, the **Help** option is the eighth option in sequence. To select **Help**, press either the **H** or **8**. Under Help, the **Fast Keys** option is the third in sequence; you can press either **F** or **3** to select **Fast Keys**.

The menus you select when you press the function keys are less obvious. For example, when you press Format (Shift-F8), the tenth and final option on the menu is Document Initial Codes/Base Font. The initial-codes option does not list a numerical option. However, you can press either **I** or its character equivalent / (forward slash) to select the initial-codes option.

No LetterPerfect menu has more than 16 options. You can select the first nine menu options by pressing numbers 1 through 9. You can select the tenth through sixteenth options by pressing characters. The method for selecting Yes/No options depends on whether you are using the 07/24/90 version of LetterPerfect or the 11/01/90 version.

Table 13.1 lists all of the number and character alternatives for selecting LetterPerfect menu options. Use the numerical alternatives when you create a macro that selects one or more options from a LetterPerfect menu *and* the macro will be used with different language versions of LetterPerfect.

Running Macros

After you have created a macro you are ready to use it. The way you run a macro depends on its type and name. In general, you can use an Alt-*letter* or Alt-Shift-*letter* macro more quickly, but you can create only 26 of each type. You can create an unlimited number of macros with descriptive names. Running the named macro requires more keystrokes, but the name makes it easier for you to remember the macro's function.

Table 13.1
The Numerical/Character Alternatives for
Selecting LetterPerfect Menu Options

If the Menu Option Is Listed:	Alternative Number/Character Is:
First	1
Second	2
Third	3
Fourth	4
Fifth	5
Sixth	6
Seventh	7
Eighth	8
Ninth	9
Tenth	/
Eleventh	\
Twelfth	:
Thirteenth	*
Fourteenth	?
Fifteenth	+
Sixteenth	=
Yes (07/24/90 program)	1
Yes (11/01/90 program)	+
No (07/24/90 program)	2
No (11/01/90 program)	-

Starting Alt-*letter* and Alt-Shift-*letter* Macros

To run an Alt-*letter* or Alt-Shift-*letter* macro, simply hold down the Alt key (LetterPerfect macro), or Alt and Shift keys (Shell macro), and press the letter. For example, if you named the return-address macro (created in the last section) Alt-A, to invoke the macro you hold down the Alt key and type *A*. The program knows that this key combination means "run a macro."

Starting Named Macros

Named macros, such as the AD macro created earlier in this chapter, require more keystrokes to start than Alt-*letter* or Alt-Shift-*letter* macros. The following procedure shows how to start a named macro:

1. Clear the main editing screen. Access the File pull-down menu, choose Exit, and select N twice. Alternatively, press Exit (F7) and select N twice.

2. With the 11/01/90 software, access the Tools pull-down menu and select Macro Execute or Shell Mac Exe. Alternatively, press Macro Execute (Alt-F10) or Shell Macro Execute (Alt-Shift-F10).

   With the 07/24/90 software, access the Tools pull-down menu and select Shell Macro Execute. Alternatively, press Macro Execute (Alt-F10) or Shell Macro Execute (Alt-Shift-F10).

> ***Tip:*** A common mistake many users make when first using the Macro feature is to press Macro Define (Ctrl-F10 or Ctrl-Shift-F10) instead of Macro Activate (Alt-F10 or Alt-Shift-F10). If you make this mistake, press Cancel (F1) or Esc.

3. At the bottom of the screen, the program displays a message prompt—either `Macro:` for LetterPerfect macros or `Shell Macro:` for Shell macros. Type *AD* and press Enter.

   LetterPerfect inserts the return address as shown in figure 13.3.

Tip: By default, LetterPerfect starts built-in macros stored on the drive or in the subdirectory where it looks for the LP.FIL. The Shell macro feature starts Shell macros stored either on the drive or in the subdirectory where it looks for the Shell program files or the subdirectory selected using the Shell Setup feature. If you want LetterPerfect to store and use macros stored in a different location, enter a *full* pathname for the macro in step 2. For example, to store macro named *test* in a subdirectory named *C:\MACROS*, type *C:\MACROS\TEST* and press Enter.

Note: If you type the name of a non-existent LetterPerfect macro, the program displays a message at the bottom left corner of the screen: `ERROR: File not found — <`*macro name*`>.LPM`. If you type the name of a non-existent Shell macro, Shell displays a message at the bottom left corner of the screen: `ERROR: File not found.`

Automatic Starting of Macros

The `/m-<`*macro name*`>` program switch causes the 11/01/90 version of LetterPerfect to execute automatically any LetterPerfect macro when the program starts. The variable `<`*macro name*`>` can include a path to the macro's location.

The LetterPerfect `/m` switch cannot execute a Shell macro when you start LetterPerfect through Shell. However, you can use the Shell program's `/m-<`*macro name*`>` program switch to start Shell with a macro that automatically starts LetterPerfect and executes a LetterPerfect macro.

Terminating Macro Creation and Operation

You can stop the macro-definition process at any time up to the point you press Enter after typing a description for the macro. You can press Cancel (F1) or Esc to abort the macro creation process. After a macro is created, to remove the macro from the disk you must either create a new macro with the same name or delete its file. You will learn these common procedures as you work with macros in this chapter.

LetterPerfect also enables you to press Cancel (F1) or Esc to stop execution of a LetterPerfect macro before completing the operation. You press Cancel (Alt-Shift-F1) to stop execution of a Shell macro before completing the operation. As a practical matter, however, most macros execute in less than a second so pressing Cancel (F1 or Alt-Shift-F1) or Esc does not stop the macro operation.

> *Caution:* Even an incomplete macro can create unwanted codes in a document.

Replacing Macros

Occasionally, you will make a mistake while creating a macro, or you may want to change the way a macro operates. Although WordPerfect 5.1 has a built-in editor, LetterPerfect does not; therefore, the only way to correct macro errors or to amend LetterPerfect or Shell macros from within LetterPerfect is to recreate and replace the macro.

For example, suppose that after you create the return-address macro you decide that you want to include the current date on a third line. Then you must decide which of these ways you want the macro to run:

- If you want to add the date manually when you need it, keep the macro the way it is.

- If you want the macro to insert only your return address at certain times, and at other times to insert both the return address and the date, create a second macro that includes both the return address and the date.

- If you need only one macro that inserts both the return address and the date, you must recreate the AD macro name, adding the steps to insert the date.

To replace a macro, you create a new macro with the same name. The creation process is the same except that the program prompts you to confirm replacement of the original macro. Use the following steps to replace a macro with another one of the same name:

1. Clear the main editing screen. Access the File pull-down menu, choose Exit, and select N twice. Alternatively, press Exit (F7) and select N twice.

2. With the 11/01/90 software, access the **T**ools pull-down menu and select Macro De**f**ine or Shell Mac **D**ef. Alternatively, press Macro Define (Ctrl-F10) or Shell Macro Define (Ctrl-Shift-F10).

   With the 07/24/90 software, access the **T**ools pull-down menu and select Macro **D**efine. Alternatively, press Macro Define (Ctrl-F10) or Shell Macro Define (Ctrl-Shift-F10).

3. Type *AD* and press Enter. At the bottom of the screen the pro- gram displays the prompt: `Replace C:\LP10\`*`<macro`* *`name>`*`.LPM? No (Yes)`. Press Enter to select the default **No** option and terminate the macro-creation process. Select **Yes** to replace the existing macro and continue the macro-creation process.

4. For the purposes of these instructions, select **Yes**.

5. Type *Creates Return Address at Top of Letter* and press Enter.

6. Access the **L**ayout pull-down menu and select **C**enter. Alterna- tively, press Center (Shift-F6) or Ctrl-c.

7. Type your name and press Enter.

8. Repeat step 6.

9. Type you street or post office box address and press Enter.

10. Repeat step 6.

11. Type your city, state, and ZIP code and press Enter three times.

12. Repeat step 6.

13. Access the **T**ools pull-down menu and select Date **C**ode. Alterna- tively, press Date/Outline (Shift-F5) and select Date Code (**2**).

    The current date appears on-screen below the return address. The date is correct if your computer has a built-in clock that remembers the date or if you answered a prompt for the date when you started the computer.

14. Press Enter twice.

15. With the 11/01/90 software, access the **T**ools pull-down menu and select Macro De**f**ine or Shell Mac **D**ef. Alternatively, press Macro Define (Ctrl-F10) or Shell Macro Define (Ctrl-Shift-F10).

With the 07/24/90 software, access the Tools pull-down menu and select Macro Define. Alternatively, press Macro Define (Ctrl-F10) or Shell Macro Define (Ctrl-Shift-F10).

> *Tip:* When you create a macro, always supply information for items such as date format (or search) even if the required information to be used by the macro is already displayed. This technique guarantees that the macro operates in the same manner every time you run it.

Using the Macro Commands Features

The macro features offer you a great deal of flexibility in creating LetterPerfect and Shell macros. With each macro feature, you decide not only *what* a macro does but *how* the macro performs the task. The Macro Commands feature accesses options that do the following:

- Pause so that you can input text and formatting codes

- Run visibly or invisibly

When you press Macro Commands (Ctrl-PgUp) while recording a LetterPerfect macro, the following menu replaces the blinking `Macro Def` message:

1 Pause; **2** Display: **0**

When you press Macro Commands (Ctrl-Shift-PgUp) while recording a Shell macro, the following menu appears on the status line:

(Shell) **1** Pause; **2** Display; **3** Assign; **4** Comment: **0**

The following sections show you how to use the Pause (**1**) and Display (**2**) options in macros. The Shell Macro's Assign (**3**) and Comment (**4**) options are `not` explained. The Assign option is an advanced feature which, to be useful, requires at least some understanding of software programming that is beyond the scope of this book. The Comment option, that enables you to enter descriptions of how the macro functions, does not serve any purpose in the creation or operation of macros with LetterPerfect 1.0. Comments can be seen only when you edit a Shell macro with the Editor 3.01 program.

> *Tip:* Unlike most features, you *cannot* access the Macro Command feature
> from the pull-down menu bar. The only way to access the Macro Command
> feature is to press Ctrl-PgUp for a LetterPerfect macro and Ctrl-Shift-PgUp for
> a Shell macro.

Pausing a Macro

One of the most useful options to control how a macro runs is the Pause option.
You can make a macro pause while it is running so that you can enter a
command or some text. Then the macro can continue to run. To access the
Macros Command option, follow these steps:

1. With the 11/01/90 software, access the **Tools** pull-down menu and
   select Macro Define or Shell Mac Def. Alternatively, press Macro
   Define (Ctrl-F10) or Shell Macro Define (Ctrl-Shift-F10).

   With the 07/24/90 software, access the **Tools** pull-down menu and
   select Macro **Define**. Alternatively, press Macro Define (Ctrl-F10)
   or Shell Macro Define (Ctrl-Shift-F10).

2. Give the macro a name and description.

3. Enter the keystrokes for the macro up to the point where you
   want the macro to pause.

4. Press Macro Commands (Ctrl-Pgup) (LetterPerfect) or (Ctrl-Shift-
   PgUp) (Shell). The program displays either the LetterPerfect
   Macro Command menu or the Shell Macro Command menu.

5. Select **Pause (1)**. The Macro Command menu disappears. If you
   are creating a LetterPerfect macro the blinking `Macro Def`
   reappears to remind you that you are defining a LetterPerfect
   macro. If you are creating a Shell macro the program does not
   display any reminder message.

   From this point you can enter text and formatting codes and
   make menu selections (with the keyboard or mouse) that appear
   on the main editing screen; none of this information is recorded
   with the macro.

6. Press Enter to end the pause and resume recording keystrokes for
   the macro.

7. With the 11/01/90 software, access the **Tools** pull-down menu and select Macro Define or Shell Mac **Def**. Alternatively, press Macro Define (Ctrl-F10) or Shell Macro Define (Ctrl-Shift-F10).

With the 07/24/90 software, access the **Tools** pull-down menu and select Macro **Define**. Alternatively, press Macro Define (Ctrl-F10) or Shell Macro Define (Ctrl-Shift-F10).

The next two sections show you how to create macros that use the Pause option.

A Macro That Creates Headings

A useful macro that includes a pause is one that sets up the format for a heading. Suppose that you want most of your headings to be centered and underlined in boldface type. Instead of giving each of those formatting commands, you can create a macro to perform them for you.

Place the cursor at the beginning of the line where you want the heading. A blank screen is fine. Then complete the following steps to create a macro that displays a heading:

1. With the 11/01/90 software, access the **Tools** pull-down menu and select Macro Define or Shell Mac **Def**. Alternatively, press Macro Define (Ctrl-F10) or Shell Macro Define (Ctrl-Shift-F10).

   With the 07/24/90 software, access the **Tools** pull-down menu and select Macro **Define**. Alternatively, press Macro Define (Ctrl-F10) or Shell Macro Define (Ctrl-Shift-F10).

2. Press Alt-h or Alt-Shift-h.

3. Type *Centered, underlined, bolded heading* and press Enter.

4. Access the **Layout** pull-down menu and select **Center**. Alternatively, press Center (Shift-F6) or Ctrl-c.

5. Access the **Font** pull-down menu and select **Underline**. Alternatively, press Underline (F8) or Ctrl-u.

6. Press Macro Commands (Ctrl-Pgup) (LetterPerfect) or (Ctrl-Shift-PgUp) (Shell). The program displays either the LetterPerfect Macro Command menu or the Shell Macro Command menu.

7. Select **P**ause (**1**). The macro feature stops recording keystrokes until you press Enter.

> *Tip:* Before you press Enter, you may find that typing a "stand in" heading makes it easier to create the rest of the macro. This heading does not become part of the macro.

8. For the purposes of these instructions, type *temporary heading* in lowercase letters.

9. Press Enter. The macro feature resumes recording keystrokes.

10. Access the **E**dit pull-down menu and select **B**lock. Alternatively, press Block (Alt-F4 or F12).

11. Move the cursor with the left-arrow key to **highlight** temporary heading.

12. Access the **F**ont pull-down menu and select **B**old. Alternatively, press Bold (F6) or Ctrl-b.

13. Press End to move the cursor past all of the hidden formatting codes following the g in heading.

14. Press Enter twice.

15. With the 11/01/90 software, access the **T**ools pull-down menu and select Macro **D**efine or Shell Mac Def. Alternatively, press Macro Define (Ctrl-F10) or Shell Macro Define (Ctrl-Shift-F10).

    With the 07/24/90 software, access the **T**ools pull-down menu and select Macro **D**efine. Alternatively, press Macro Define (Ctrl-F10) or Shell Macro Define (Ctrl-Shift-F10).

After you create the heading macro use the following steps to test it:

1. Clear the main editing screen. Access the **F**ile pull-down menu, choose E**x**it, and select N twice. Alternatively, press Exit (F7) and select N twice.

2. Press Alt-H (LetterPerfect) or Alt-Shift-H (Shell). The cursor moves to the center of the line, the number to the left of Pos on the status line is underlined (which indicates that the text you type will be underlined), and the macro pauses for you to type the heading line.

3. Type *HEADING MACRO TEST* and press Enter. The heading is underlined and the cursor moves to the left margin two lines beneath the heading.

A Macro That Formats Letters

Earlier in this chapter, you created a macro that inserts your return address and the current date at the top of a page. Using the additional features you have learned, you now can create a more powerful macro that combines text with formatting commands. The macro shown in this section formats a letter in the following ways:

- Formats the page for a two-inch top margin

- Inserts and centers your return address

- Inserts and centers the current date two lines below the address

- Pauses three times so that you can enter three lines of a recipient's address

- Enters the salutation

Follow these steps to create the letter-formatting macro:

1. Clear the main editing screen. Access the **File** pull-down menu, choose E**x**it, and select N twice. Alternatively, press Exit (F7) and select N twice.

2. With the 11/01/90 software, access the **Tools** pull-down menu and select Macro **D**efine or Shell Mac **D**ef. Alternatively, press Macro Define (Ctrl-F10) or Shell Macro Define (Ctrl-Shift-F10).

   With the 07/24/90 software, access the **Tools** pull-down menu and select Macro **D**efine. Alternatively, press Macro Define (Ctrl-F10) or Shell Macro Define (Ctrl-Shift-F10).

3. Type *Letter* and press Enter.

4. Type *Formats Letter* and press Enter.

5. Access the **Layout** pull-down menu and select **F**ormat. Alternatively, press Format (Shift-F8). LetterPerfect displays the Format menu.

6. Select Top/Bottom Margins (**3**).

7. Type *2i* and press Enter twice.

8. Press Exit (F7).

9. Access the **L**ayout pull-down menu and select **C**enter. Alternatively, press Center (Shift-F6) or Ctrl-c.

10. Type your name and press Enter.

11. Repeat step 9.

12. Type your street or post office box address and press Enter.

13. Repeat step 9.

14. Type your city, state, and ZIP code and press Enter three times.

15. Repeat step 9.

16. Access the **T**ools pull-down menu and select **D**ate Code. Alternatively, press Date/Outline (Shift-F5) and select Date Code (2).

    The current date appears on-screen below the return address. The date is correct if your computer has a built-in clock that remembers the date or if you answered a prompt for the date when you started the computer.

17. Press Enter four times to move the cursor to the left margin three lines below the date.

18. Press Macro Commands (Ctrl-Pgup) (LetterPerfect) or (Ctrl-Shift-PgUp) (Shell). The program displays either the LetterPerfect Macro Command menu or the Shell Macro Command menu.

19. Select **P**ause (**1**). Remember that everything you type during a pause (until you next press Enter) does not become part of the macro.

20. Type any name, such as *Ms. Joan Smith*, and press Enter twice. (The first Enter ends the pause; the second Enter is recorded in the macro).

21. Press Macro Commands (Ctrl-Pgup) (LetterPerfect) or (Ctrl-Shift-PgUp) (Shell).

22. Select **Pause** (**1**).

23. Type any street address, such as *1234 Any Street*, and press Enter twice.

24. Press Macro Commands (Ctrl-Pgup) (LetterPerfect) or (Ctrl-Shift-PgUp) (Shell).

25. Select **Pause** (**1**).

26. Type any city, state, and zip code, such as *Oklahoma City, OK 73189*, and press Enter twice.

27. Press Enter four times to move the cursor to the left margin three lines below the date.

28. Type *Dear M.*

29. Press Macro Commands (Ctrl-Pgup) (LetterPerfect) or (Ctrl-Shift-PgUp) (Shell).

30. Select **Pause** (**1**).

31. Type *s. Smith* and press Enter.

32. Type a colon and press Enter three times to move the cursor to the left margin two lines below the date. The document on LetterPerfect's main editing screen should appear as shown in figure 13.4.

33. With the 11/01/90 software, access the **Tools** pull-down menu and select Macro Define or Shell Mac Def. Alternatively, press Macro Define (Ctrl-F10) or Shell Macro Define (Ctrl-Shift-F10).

    With the 07/24/90 software, access the **Tools** pull-down menu and select Macro **Define**. Alternatively, press Macro Define (Ctrl-F10) or Shell Macro Define (Ctrl-Shift-F10).

Now clear the screen and try the new macro by completing these steps:

1. Clear the main editing screen. Access the **File** pull-down menu, choose Exit, and select N twice. Alternatively, press Exit (F7) and select N twice.

2. With the 11/01/90 software, access the **Tools** pull-down menu and select Macro Execute or Shell Mac Exe. Alternatively, press Macro Execute (Alt-F10) or Shell Macro Execute (Alt-Shift-F10).

```
File Edit Search Layout Tools Font Graphics Help      (Press ALT= for menu bar)
                         JOHN Q. PUBLIC
                       Post Office Box 000418
                    Oklahoma City, OK  73100-0418


                         November 2, 1990


         Ms. Joan Smith
         1234 Any Street
         Oklahoma City, OK  73189


         Dear Ms. Smith:




                                              Pg 1 Ln 4.5" Pos 1"
```

Fig. 13.4. *The format created by the Letter macro.*

With the 07/24/90 software, access the **Tools** pull-down menu and select Macro Execute. Alternatively, press Macro Execute (Alt-F10) or Shell Macro Execute (Alt-Shift-F10).

> **Tip:** A common mistake many users make when first using the Macro feature is to press Macro Define (Ctrl-F10 or Ctrl-Shift-F10) instead of Macro Activate (Alt-F10 or Alt-Shift-F10). If you make this mistake, press Cancel (F1) or Esc.

3. At the bottom of the screen, the program displays a message prompt—either `Macro:` for LetterPerfect macros or `Shell Macro:` for Shell macros. Type *Letter* and press Enter.

4. Your name, return address, and the current date appear on the main editing screen with the cursor at the left margin two lines below the current date.

5. Type the recipient's name and press Enter. The cursor moves down one line and pauses for you to enter the recipient's street address.

6. Type the street address and press Enter. The cursor moves down one line and pauses for you to enter the city, state, and zip code.

7. Type the city, state, and zip code and press Enter. Three lines below the last address line `Dear M` appears and the macro pauses for you to complete the letter's salutation.

8. Complete the salutation and press Enter. The colon appears at the end of the salutation and the cursor moves to the left margin two lines below the salutation.

Now that the macro has completed operation you can begin to enter the text of your letter.

Making Macro Operations Visible

With the Macro Commands Display feature, you control whether the macro runs invisibly, or displays each command and menu just as if it were being typed quickly. By default, LetterPerfect and Shell macros run invisibly.

Tip: LetterPerfect and Shell macros run much more quickly when they operate invisibly, but even when a macro displays its operation and runs "slowly" it operates faster than you can possibly type. Displaying macro operations is useful when you are learning to create your own macros.

The macro shown in this section creates a macro that serves no purpose except to show you how a macro displays its operations on the screen. For the purposes of this demonstration, use the pull-down menus for each step in this macro. Follow these steps to create the macro:

1. Clear the main editing screen. Access the File pull-down menu, choose Exit, and select N twice.

2. With the 11/01/90 software, access the Tools pull-down menu and select Macro Define or Shell Mac Def.

   With the 07/24/90 software, access the Tools pull-down menu and select Macro Define.

3. Type *display* and press Enter.

4. Type *Shows Macro Operations* and press Enter.

5. Press Macro Commands (Ctrl-Pgup) (LetterPerfect) or (Ctrl-Shift-PgUp) (Shell). The program displays either the LetterPerfect Macro Command menu or the Shell Macro Command menu.

6. Select **Display** (**2**). At the lower left corner of the screen, LetterPerfect displays the menu prompt: `Display execution? No (Yes).`

7. Select **Yes**.

8. Access the **Layout** pull-down menu and select **Format**. LetterPerfect displays the Format menu.

9. Select Left/Right **Margins** (**4**).

10. Type *2* and press Enter twice.

11. Select **Tabs** (**5**). LetterPerfect displays its main editing screen with the tab-selection menu across the bottom of the screen.

12. Press Ctrl-End.

13. Type *3* and press Enter.

14. Press Exit (F7) twice to return to the main editing screen.

15. Access the **Layout** pull-down menu and select **Center**.

16. Type *This is the first line of the test macro.*

17. Press Home, left arrow to move the cursor to the beginning of the line.

18. Access the **Edit** pull-down menu and select **Block**.

19. Press End to highlight the entire line.

20. Access the **Font** pull-down menu and select **Underline**.

21. Press Enter three times.

22. Type *This is the second line of the test macro.*

23. Press Home, left arrow to move the cursor to the beginning of the line.

24. Access the **Edit** pull-down menu and select **Block**.

25. Press End to highlight the entire line.

26. Access the Font pull-down menu and select **Underline**.

27. Press Enter three times.

28. Type *This is the third line of the test macro.*

29. Press Home, left arrow to move the cursor to the beginning of the line.

30. Access the Edit pull-down menu and select **Block**.

31. Press End to highlight the entire line.

32. Access the Font pull-down menu and select **Underline**.

33. Press Enter three times.

34. Access the Edit pull-down menu and select **Block**.

35. Press Home, Home, up arrow to highlight the entire document.

36. Access the Font pull-down menu and select **Bold**.

37. Press Home, Home, down arrow to move the cursor to the bottom of the document.

38. Access the Layout pull-down menu and select **Center**.

39. In all capital letters, type *THIS COMPLETES EXECUTION OF THE TEST MACRO.*

40. Press Home, left arrow to move the cursor to the beginning of the line.

41. Access the Edit pull-down menu and select **Block**.

42. Press End to highlight the line you just typed.

43. Access the Font pull-down menu and select **Bold**.

44. Press Home, Home, Home, up arrow.

45. Access the Edit pull-down menu and select **Reveal Codes**.

46. With the 11/01/90 software, access the Tools pull-down menu and select Macro Define or Shell Mac **Def**.

With the 07/24/90 software, access the **T**ools pull-down menu and select Macro **D**efine.

Now complete these steps to try the DISPLAY macro:

1. Clear the main editing screen. Access the **F**ile pull-down menu, choose E**x**it, and select N twice. Alternatively, press Exit (F7) and select N twice.

2. With the 11/01/90 software, access the **T**ools pull-down menu and select Mac**r**o Execute or Shell Mac Exe. Alternatively, press Macro Execute (Alt-F10) or Shell Macro Execute (Alt-Shift-F10).

   With the 07/24/90 software, access the **T**ools pull-down menu and select Macro Execute. Alternatively, press Macro Execute (Alt-F10) or Shell Macro Define (Alt-Shift-F10).

3. Type *display* and press Enter.

4. Watch while the macro creates the test document on your screen.

Connecting LetterPerfect and Shell Macros

Either a LetterPerfect or Shell macro can be connected to itself or connected to a different macro. When a macro is connected to itself, it contains a *loop*.

You have two options for connecting two or more macros to each other. In addition, if the LetterPerfect program you are using is dated 11/01/90, and you are running it through the Shell program, you can connect LetterPerfect macros to Shell macros and vice versa.

The first method is to *chain* one macro to another macro. For example, if macro B is chained to macro A, when macro A completes its operations it runs macro B.

The second method is to *nest* one macro within another. For example, if macro B is nested within macro A, macro A starts to run, and then pauses and runs macro B. After macro B completes its operations, the remainder of macro A completes its operation.

A macro can include multiple nested macros but only one chained macro. When you chain macros only the `last` macro in the chain can be a looping macro.

Creating A Looping Macro

A *looping* macro is connected to itself and continues to operate until either it fails to find a search string or you manually terminate its operation. A looping macro that requires manual termination continues to operate again and again—theoretically, for eternity—unless you press Cancel (F1) or Esc for a LetterPerfect macro, or Cancel (Alt-Shift-F1) for a Shell macro.

This odd repetition has a practical use. Macros stop automatically when a search operation fails. When you include a search within a macro, and then chain the macro to itself, the macro performs the search, does whatever you created the macro to do, and then searches again. The macro performs the specified action on each item that the macro finds, and then stops when the search fails. You will discover more uses for this looping technique after you have learned to use LetterPerfect's advanced features.

The following example shows you how to create a macro that finds a company's name in a document, enhances the name's appearance by bolding and underlining it, and then repeats until it fails to find the name.

1. Clear the main editing screen. Access the **File** pull-down menu, choose Exit, and select N twice. Alternatively, press Exit (F7) and select N twice.

2. Press Enter and type *Acme Software Company*.

3. Move the cursor to the top of the document.

4. With the 11/01/90 software, access the **Tools** pull-down menu and select Macro Define or Shell Mac **Def**. Alternatively, press Macro Define (Ctrl-F10) or Shell Macro Define (Ctrl-Shift-F10).

   With the 07/24/90 software, access the **Tools** pull-down menu and select Macro **Define**. Alternatively, press Macro Define (Ctrl-F10) or Shell Macro Define (Ctrl-Shift-F10).

5. Type *acme* and press Enter.

6. Type *Enhances Company's Name* and press Enter.

7. Access the **S**earch pull-down menu and select **F**orward. Alternatively, press Search (F2).

8. Type *acme software company* and press Search (F2).

9. Access the **E**dit pull-down menu and select **B**lock. Alternatively, press Block (Alt-F4 or F12).

10. Move the cursor to highlight `Acme Software Company`.

11. Access the **F**ont pull-down menu and select **B**old. Alternatively, press Bold (F6) or Ctrl-b.

12. Repeat steps 9 and 10.

13. Access the **F**ont pull-down menu and select **U**nderline. Alternatively, press Bold (F8) or Ctrl-u.

14. With the 11/01/90 software, access the **T**ools pull-down menu and select Macro Execute or Shell Mac Exe. Alternatively, press Macro Execute (Alt-F10) or Shell Macro Execute (Alt-Shift-F10).

   With the 07/24/90 software, access the **T**ools pull-down menu and select Macro Execute. Alternatively, press Macro Execute (Alt-F10) or Shell Macro Define (Alt-Shift-F10).

15. Type *acme* and press Enter.

16. With the 11/01/90 software, access the **T**ools pull-down menu and select Macro Define or Shell Mac **D**ef. Alternatively, press Macro Define (Ctrl-F10) or Shell Macro Define (Ctrl-Shift-F10).

   With the 07/24/90 software, access the **T**ools pull-down menu and select Macro **D**efine. Alternatively, press Macro Define (Ctrl-F10) or Shell Macro Define (Ctrl-Shift-F10).

Now complete these steps to try the ACME macro:

1. Clear the main editing screen. Access the **F**ile pull-down menu, choose E**x**it, and select N twice. Alternatively, press Exit (F7) and select N twice.

2. Press Enter and type *Acme Software Company*.

3. Repeat step 2 until the screen contains at least 10 entries on lines separated by blank lines.

4. Move the cursor to the top of the document before any text or formatting codes.

5. With the 11/01/90 software, access the Tools pull-down menu and select Macro Execute or Shell Mac Exe. Alternatively, press Macro Execute (Alt-F10) or Shell Macro Execute (Alt-Shift-F10).

   With the 07/24/90 software, access the Tools pull-down menu and select Macro Execute. Alternatively, press Macro Execute (Alt-F10) or Shell Macro Execute (Alt-Shift-F10).

6. Type *acme* and press Enter.

7. The program displays the `*Please Wait*` at the lower left corner of the screen but the document appears unaltered. When the macro completes operation, the program redisplays the document as edited by the macro.

Creating Nested Macros

The macro feature supports a technique called *nesting*—starting and running one macro (the *inside* macro) from within another macro (the *host* macro). For example, when the host macro encounters the instruction to execute the inside macro, the host macro pauses while the inside macro performs its operations. After the inside macro completes its function, the host macro resumes operation.

In general, the nested-macro technique permits the host macro to be either an Alt-*letter* or Alt-Shift-*letter*, or a named macro, but requires that the inside macro be an Alt-*letter* or Alt-Shift-*letter* macro. However, when the 11/01/90 LetterPerfect program runs through the Shell 3.01 program, the inside macro also can be either an Alt-*letter* or Alt-Shift-*letter* macro, or a named macro of a different type. Table 13.2 lists host/inside macro combinations.

> *Tip:* With the WordPerfect Editor 3.01 program you can create and edit LetterPerfect and Shell host macros that work with a named inside macro of the same type as the host. Thus, an edited host LetterPerfect macro works with a named inside macro, and an edited host Shell macro works with a named Shell inside macro. Editor is part of the Office PC or LAN 3.01 software package. WordPerfect Corporation also may offer Editor as a separate product before the end of 1991.

Table 13.2
The 11/01/90 Host/Inside Macro Combinations

If the Host Macro Is:	*The Inside Macro Can Be:*
name.LPM	
or Alt-*letter*.LPM	Alt-*letter*.LPM
	Alt-Shift-*letter*.SHM
	name.SHM
name.SHM	
or Alt-Shift-*letter*.SHM	Alt-Shift-*letter*.SHM
	ALT-*letter*.LPM
	name.LPM

If you want to use a host and named macro of the same type—LetterPerfect and LetterPerfect or Shell and Shell—you are limited to chaining the two macros as described in the next section, "Chaining Macros."

Use the following steps to create a host macro that starts an inside macro:

1. Begin to create the *host* macro using the steps shown in "Creating LetterPerfect and Shell Macros" earlier in this chapter.

2. When you create the host macro with the 11/01/90 software, access the **T**ools pull-down menu and select Macro Execute or Shell Mac Ex. Alternatively, press Macro Execute (Alt-F10) or Shell Macro Execute (Alt-Shift-F10).

   With the 07/24/90 software, access the **T**ools pull-down menu and select Macro Execute. Alternatively, press Macro Execute (Alt-F10) or Shell Macro Execute (Alt-Shift-F10).

3. At the bottom of the screen, the program displays a message prompt—either `Macro:` for LetterPerfect macros or `Shell Macro:` for Shell macros. Hold down Alt for a LetterPerfect macro, or hold down Alt-Shift for a Shell macro, then press the letter for the name of the *inside* macro.

Caution: If the inside macro is looped, when the inside macro completes operation both the inside and host macros terminate. The remaining actions in the host macro are *not* performed.

If the inside macro exists, the program immediately executes its functions. If you have not yet created the inside macro, nothing happens. After you create the inside macro and start the host macro, the host macro automatically runs the inside macro at the proper time.

> ***Tip:*** By default, LetterPerfect uses its macros on the drive or in the subdirectory where it looks for the LP.FIL. The Shell program uses its macros on the drive or in the subdirectory where it looks for the Shell program files unless you have designated a different location for macros with the Shell Setup (4), Options (2) feature. If you want either macro feature to use host or inside macros from a different drive or subdirectory, enter a *full* pathname for the macro in step 2. For example, to store a macro named *test* macro in a subdirectory named *C:\MACROS*, type *C:\MACROS\TEST* and press Enter.

4. Complete defining the host macro.

5. With the 11/01/90 software, access the **Tools** pull-down menu and select Macro Define or Shell Mac **D**ef. Alternatively, press Macro Define (Ctrl-F10) or Shell Macro Define (Ctrl-Shift-F10).

   With the 07/24/90 software, access the **Tools** pull-down menu and select Macro **D**efine. Alternatively, press Macro Define (Ctrl-F10) or Shell Macro Define (Ctrl-Shift-F10).

6. Using what you have learned to this point, create the inside macro if you have not previously done so.

After you have created the host and inside macros, start the host macro as described earlier in this chapter. During its operation, the host macro automatically operates the inside macro.

When you run the host macro without creating the inside macro, the program executes the host macro's functions and displays an error message. If the inside macro is a LetterPerfect macro, the message is: ERROR: File not found — ALT<*letter*>.LPM. If the inside macro is a Shell macro, the message is: ERROR: File not found.

Creating Chained Macros

Chaining macros usually is easier than creating a single macro that performs several editing tasks on a document, especially if the macro you are creating ends with a series of commands that already are stored in a different macro.

For example, suppose that you have a group of documents that contain different versions of a company's name, such as `Acme Software Company` and `Acme Software Co`. You decide that the company name should always be listed as `Acme Software Company`. In addition, the company name's appearance needs to be enhanced with underlining and bold type. Finally, you want to add a bracketed notation of the company's office hours and telephone number following the company name. When the editing is completed, each occurrence of the company's name should appear as follows:

<u>Acme Software Company</u> `[8:00 a.m. through 4:00 p.m. CST -405/555-9234]`

Careful preplanning is the key to creating chained macros that perform complex editing operations. Start by deciding how you want the *final* document to appear. Then, examine the document to determine each editing step required to produce the final appearance. Finally, determine how many separate macros are required to perform all of the editing steps.

At first glance, the changes described in this section may appear to require only two macros that perform separate search-and-replace operations to make the desired changes. However, a careful analysis of the documents reveals two reasons why a minimum of *four* macros is required to make the proper editing changes.

First, the final company name and bracketed information exceed the capacity of a replacement string in a single search-and-replace operation. Second, the period following *Co* may also mark the end of a sentence (as it does for one sentence in the paragraph that outlines the editing problem). If you use a single search-and-replace operation to change *Co.* to *Company*, you may lose periods at the ends of sentences. So, the first macro needs to change only those occurrences where *Co.* is at the end of a sentence.

> *Tip:* The fewer the keystrokes you use in a macro, the easier the macro is to create. When you create a chained macro that does not work properly, you may find it easier to fix if you use a separate macro to perform each editing step. If you use this method and the document is not edited properly, it may take you only a few seconds to identify and correct the macro in the chain that does not work as you expected.

Because you probably do not have a document that contains the variations of the Acme company name, create one as follows:

1. Type *Acme Software Company* and press Enter twice.

2. Type *Acme Software Co.*, press the space bar twice, and press Enter twice.

3. Type *Acme Software Co.* and press Enter twice.

4. Save the document, which should appear as shown in figure 13.5, as ACMETEST.

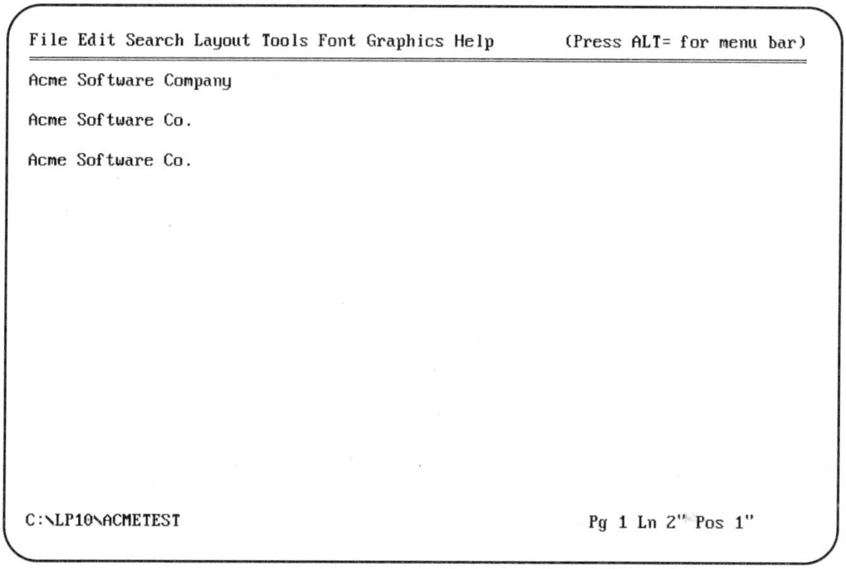

```
File Edit Search Layout Tools Font Graphics Help      (Press ALT= for menu bar)

Acme Software Company

Acme Software Co.

Acme Software Co.




















C:\LP10\ACMETEST                                    Pg 1 Ln 2" Pos 1"
```

Fig. 13.5. The Acmetest document.

Now you are ready to begin creating the four macros that will edit your document.

Creating the Macro that Starts the Chain

The first macro in the chain is the *Starting* macro. All of the other macros in the chain are *secondary* macros. A secondary macro can, and frequently does, start another secondary macro. Except for the last secondary macro in the chain, neither the start nor the secondary macros can be looping macros. The last secondary macro in the chain can be chained to the start macro.

> *Tip:* The sequence in which you create the macros that make up the chain does not matter. You can even create the macros in different editing sessions. The only important thing is that all macros in the chain have been created when you run the chain.

Follow these steps to create the starting macro:

1. Clear the main editing screen. Access the **File** pull-down menu, choose **Exit**, and select N twice. Alternatively, press Exit (F7) and select N twice.

2. Retrieve the *ACMETEST* document to the main editing screen.

3. With the 11/01/90 software, access the **Tools** pull-down menu and select Macro Define or Shell Mac Def. Alternatively, press Macro Define (Ctrl-F10) or Shell Macro Define (Ctrl-Shift-F10).

   With the 07/24/90 software, access the **Tools** pull-down menu and select Macro **Define**. Alternatively, press Macro Define (Ctrl-F10) or Shell Macro Define (Ctrl-Shift-F10).

4. Type *acme-1* and press Enter.

5. Type *Fix Co. at end of sentence* and press Enter.

6. Access the **Search** pull-down menu and select **Replace**. Alternatively, press Replace (Alt-F2).

7. Select **No** to have the replace operation performed automatically without any decision from you.

8. Type *co.* (Be sure to include the period.)

9. Press the space bar twice, and press Search (F2).

10. Type *Company.* (Be sure to include the period.)

11. Press the space bar twice and press Search (F2).

12. With the 11/01/90 software, access the **Tools** pull-down menu and select Macro Execute or Shell Mac Exe. Alternatively, press Macro Execute (Alt-F10) or Shell Macro Execute (Alt-Shift-F10).

   With the 07/24/90 software, access the **Tools** pull-down menu and select Macro Execute. Alternatively, press Macro Execute (Alt-F10) or Shell Macro Execute (Alt-Shift-F10).

13. Type *acme-2* and press Enter.

14. With the 11/01/90 software, access the **Tools** pull-down menu and select Macro Define or Shell Mac **Def**. Alternatively, press Macro Define (Ctrl-F10) or Shell Macro Define (Ctrl-Shift-F10).

With the 07/24/90 software, access the **Tools** pull-down menu and select Macro **D**efine. Alternatively, press Macro Define (Ctrl-F10) or Shell Macro Define (Ctrl-Shift-F10).

Creating Secondary Macros in the Chain

The instructions in this section require that you have created the *ACMETEST* document and have it on the main editing screen. Follow these steps to create the first secondary macro:

1. With the 11/01/90 software, access the **Tools** pull-down menu and select Macro Define or Shell Mac **D**ef. Alternatively, press Macro Define (Ctrl-F10) or Shell Macro Define (Ctrl-Shift-F10).

   With the 07/24/90 software, access the **Tools** pull-down menu and select Macro **D**efine. Alternatively, press Macro Define (Ctrl-F10) or Shell Macro Define (Ctrl-Shift-F10).

2. Type *acme-2* and press Enter.

3. Type *Fix Co. in the middle of sentence* and press Enter.

4. Press Home, Home, Home, up arrow.

5. Access the **Search** pull-down menu and select **R**eplace. Alternatively, press Replace (Alt-F2).

6. Select **N**o to have the replace operation performed automatically without any decision from you.

7. Type *co.* and press Search (F2).

8. Type *Company* and press Search (F2).

9. With the 11/01/90 software, access the **Tools** pull-down menu and select Macro Execute or Shell Mac **E**xe. Alternatively, press Macro Execute (Alt-F10) or Shell Macro Execute (Alt-Shift-F10).

   With the 07/24/90 software, access the **Tools** pull-down menu and select Macro Execute. Alternatively, press Macro Execute (Alt-F10) or Shell Macro Execute (Alt-Shift-F10).

10. Type *acme-3* and press Enter.

11. With the 11/01/90 software, access the **Tools** pull-down menu and select Macro Define or Shell Mac **Def**. Alternatively, press Macro Define (Ctrl-F10) or Shell Macro Define (Ctrl-Shift-F10).

With the 07/24/90 software, access the **Tools** pull-down menu and select Macro **Define**. Alternatively, press Macro Define (Ctrl-F10) or Shell Macro Define (Ctrl-Shift-F10).

Follow these steps to create the third secondary macro:

1. With the 11/01/90 software, access the **Tools** pull-down menu and select Macro Define or Shell Mac **Def**. Alternatively, press Macro Define (Ctrl-F10) or Shell Macro Define (Ctrl-Shift-F10).

With the 07/24/90 software, access the **Tools** pull-down menu and select Macro **Define**. Alternatively, press Macro Define (Ctrl-F10) or Shell Macro Define (Ctrl-Shift-F10).

2. Type *acme-3* and press Enter.

3. Type *Creates enhanced company name* and press Enter.

4. Press Home, Home, Home, up arrow.

5. Access the Search pull-down menu and select **Replace**. Alternatively, press Replace (Alt-F2).

6. Select **No** to have the replace operation performed automatically without any decision from you.

7. Type *Acme Software Company* and press Search (F2).

8. Press Underline (F8) and Bold (F6).

9. Type *Acme Software Company*.

10. Press Bold (F6), Underline (F8), and Search (F2).

11. With the 11/01/90 software, access the **Tools** pull-down menu and select Macro Execute or Shell Mac **Exe**. Alternatively, press Macro Execute (Alt-F10) or Shell Macro Execute (Alt-Shift-F10).

With the 07/24/90 software, access the **Tools** pull-down menu and select Macro Execute. Alternatively, press Macro Execute (Alt-F10) or Shell Macro Execute (Alt-Shift-F10).

12. Type *acme-4* and press Enter.

13. With the 11/01/90 software, access the **T**ools pull-down menu and select Macro De**f**ine or Shell Mac **D**ef. Alternatively, press Macro Define (Ctrl-F10) or Shell Macro Define (Ctrl-Shift-F10).

   With the 07/24/90 software, access the **T**ools pull-down menu and select Macro **D**efine. Alternatively, press Macro Define (Ctrl-F10) or Shell Macro Define (Ctrl-Shift-F10).

Follow these steps to create the last secondary macro:

1. With the 11/01/90 software, access the **T**ools pull-down menu and select Macro De**f**ine or Shell Mac **D**ef. Alternatively, press Macro Define (Ctrl-F10) or Shell Macro Define (Ctrl-Shift-F10).

   With the 07/24/90 software, access the **T**ools pull-down menu and select Macro **D**efine. Alternatively, press Macro Define (Ctrl-F10) or Shell Macro Define (Ctrl-Shift-F10).

2. Type *acme-4* and press Enter.

3. Type *Adds office bours and telephone number* and press Enter.

4. Press Home, Home, Home, up arrow.

5. Access the **S**earch pull-down menu and select **R**eplace. Alternatively, press Replace (Alt-F2).

6. Select **N**o to have the replace operation performed automatically without any decision from you.

7. Type *company* and press Bold (F6) twice.

8. Move the cursor to highlight the **[BOLD]** code and delete it.

9. Press End and Underline (F8) twice.

10. Move the cursor to highlight the **[UND]** code and delete it.

11. Press Search (F2).

12. Type *Company* and press Bold (F6) twice.

13. Move the cursor to highlight the **[BOLD]** code and delete it.

14. Press End and Underline (F8) twice.

15. Move the cursor to highlight the **[UND]** code and delete it.

16. Press End and press the space bar.

17. Type *[8:00 a.m. through 4:00 p.m. CST - 405/555-9234]*

18. Press Search (F2).

19. With the 11/01/90 software, access the **Tools** pull-down menu and select Macro Define or Shell Mac **Def**. Alternatively, press Macro Define (Ctrl-F10) or Shell Macro Define (Ctrl-Shift-F10).

    With the 07/24/90 software, access the **Tools** pull-down menu and select Macro **Define**. Alternatively, press Macro Define (Ctrl-F10) or Shell Macro Define (Ctrl-Shift-F10).

Now complete these steps to try the macro chain:

1. Clear the main editing screen. Access the **File** pull-down menu, choose Exit, and select N twice. Alternatively, press Exit (F7) and select N twice.

2. Retrieve the *ACMETEST* document to the main editing screen.

3. With the 11/01/90 software, access the **Tools** pull-down menu and select Macro Execute or Shell Mac **Exe**. Alternatively, press Macro Execute (Alt-F10) or Shell Macro Execute (Alt-Shift-F10).

    With the 07/24/90 software, access the **Tools** pull-down menu and select Macro Execute. Alternatively, press Macro Execute (Alt-F10) or Shell Macro Execute (Alt-Shift-F10).

4. Type *acme-1* and press Enter.

5. The program displays the `*Please Wait*` at the lower left corner of the screen but the document appears unaltered. When the macro completes operation, the program redisplays the edited document as shown in figure 13.6.

You have now learned how to create basic LetterPerfect and Shell macros. The next sections show you how to create macros that you may find useful when you create and edit documents with LetterPerfect.

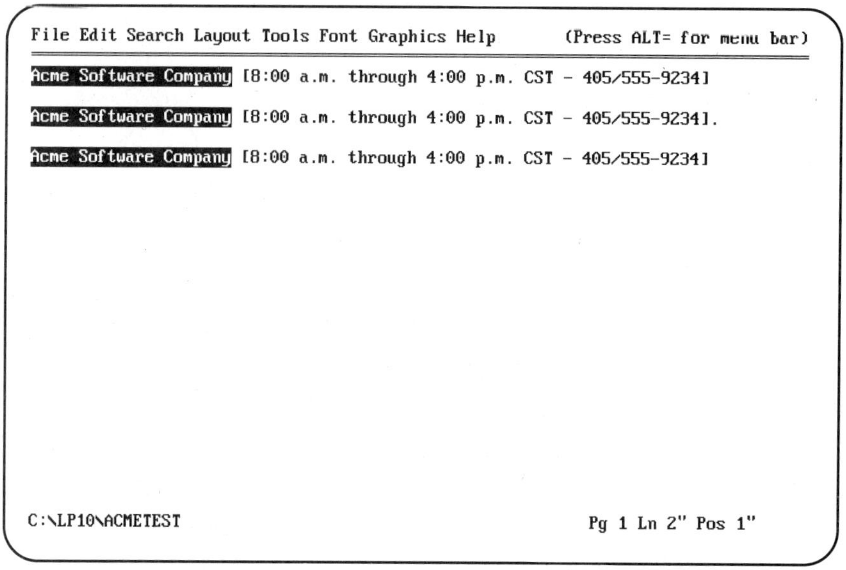

```
 File Edit Search Layout Tools Font Graphics Help        (Press ALT= for menu bar)

 Acme Software Company [8:00 a.m. through 4:00 p.m. CST - 405/555-9234]

 Acme Software Company [8:00 a.m. through 4:00 p.m. CST - 405/555-9234].

 Acme Software Company [8:00 a.m. through 4:00 p.m. CST - 405/555-9234]




 C:\LP10\ACMETEST                                        Pg 1 Ln 2" Pos 1"
```

Fig. 13.6. The edited ACMETEST document.

Creating Some Useful Macros

You do not have to be a macro expert to create macros that help you with your everyday work. In this section, you learn to create some useful macros that automatically:

- Enhance the appearance of a word using a bold type font

- Change the default directory

- Invoke the Spell feature's Lookup option

- Delete a sentence or a paragraph

- Select a printer-definition form

- Create a temporary printer-definition form

- Start and display LetterPerfect under Shell

A Macro That Bolds an Existing Word

Complete the following steps to create a macro that bolds a word after you type it:

1. Type *Corporations can increase profits by focusing on customer needs.*

2. Move the cursor immediately to the right of the last e in the word increase.

3. With the 11/01/90 software, access the Tools pull-down menu and select Macro Define or Shell Mac Def. Alternatively, press Macro Define (Ctrl-F10) or Shell Macro Define (Ctrl-Shift-F10).

   With the 07/24/90 software, access the Tools pull-down menu and select Macro Define. Alternatively, press Macro Define (Ctrl-F10) or Shell Macro Define (Ctrl-Shift-F10).

4. Press either Alt-B (LetterPerfect macro) or Alt-Shift-B (Shell macro).

5. Type *Bold preceding word* and press Enter.

6. Access the Edit pull-down menu and select Block. Alternatively, press Block (Alt-F4 or F12).

7. Press Word Left (Ctrl-left arrow).

8. Access the Font pull-down menu and select Bold. Alternatively, press Bold (F6) or the Ctrl-b fast-key combination.

9. With the 11/01/90 software, access the Tools pull-down menu and select Macro Define or Shell Mac Def. Alternaively, press Macro Define (Ctrl-F10) or Shell Macro Define (Ctrl-Shift-F10).

   With the 07/24/90 software, access the Tools pull-down menu and select Macro Define. Alternatively, press Macro Define (Ctrl-F10) or Shell Macro Define (Ctrl-Shift-F10).

You can use this macro to bold any existing word in a document by positioning the cursor immediately after the word you want to bold and press either Alt-B (LetterPerfect macro) or Alt-Shift-B (Shell macro). Using a macro is simpler than blocking a word and giving the appropriate commands each time you want to change a word's appearance to bold.

In addition to bold, you can use the procedure described in this ction to create macros that change a word's size or appearance to the following: underline, italic, superscript, and subscript.

A Macro That Changes Directories

If you have a hard disk, you often need to change from one directory to another directory. You can create a macro for each directory change, and you can use an abbreviated form of the directory's name for the name of the macro. You can make the macro end so that you remain at the editing screen, or you can have the macro take you to the List Files screen for your new directory.f course, you can use macros that change directories only if you have first created those directories.

Suppose that you have a directory called C:\BUSINESS\ACCOUNTS. The following macro, named ACC, changes the current directory to C:\BUSINESS\ACCOUNTS without making it the default editing subdirectory. For this macro, the current drive is drive C. Complete these steps to create the macro:

1. With the 11/01/90 software, access the Tools pull-down menu and select Macro Define or Shell Mac Def. Alternatively, press Macro Define (Ctrl-F10) or Shell Macro Define (Ctrl-Shift-F10).

   With the 07/24/90 software, access the Tools pull-down menu and select Macro Define. Alternatively, press Macro Define (Ctrl-F10) or Shell Macro Define (Ctrl-Shift-F10).

2. Type *ACC* and press Enter.

3. Type *Displays C:\BUSINESS\ACCOUNTS directory* and press Enter.

4. Access the Files pull-down menu and select List Files. Alternatively, press List Files (F5).

5. Type *C:\BUSINESS\ACCOUNTS* and press Enter.

   If you want the macro to change LetterPerfect's default subdirectory to C:\BUSINESS\ACCOUNTS press = before you type the subdirectory's name in step 5.

6. With the 11/01/90 software, access the **Tools** pull-down menu and select Macro Define or Shell Mac **D**ef. Alternatively, press Macro Define (Ctrl-F10) or Shell Macro Define (Ctrl-Shift-F10).

   With the 07/24/90 software, access the **Tools** pull-down menu and select Macro **D**efine. Alternatively, press Macro Define (Ctrl-F10) or Shell Macro Define (Ctrl-Shift-F10).

A Macro For Looking Up The Spelling of a Word

As explained in Chapter 11, when you start LetterPerfect's Spell feature it automatically begins spell checking the document (or text block if you highlighted it prior to starting the Spell feature). Although the Spell feature includes a Lookup option, you cannot access this option until after the spell checking begins. This limitation, discussed in the "Looking Up a Word" section of Chapter 11, makes it awkward to check the spelling of a word while you are creating a document.

Fortunately, you can create a macro so that you can quickly use the Lookup option to check the spelling of a word. The following steps show you how to create the macro:

1. Clear the main editing screen. Access the **File** pull-down menu, choose **Exit**, and select N twice. Alternatively, press Exit (F7) and select N twice.

2. With the 11/01/90 software, access the **Tools** pull-down menu and select Macro Define or Shell Mac **D**ef. Alternatively, press Macro Define (Ctrl-F10) or Shell Macro Define (Ctrl-Shift-F10).

   With the 07/24/90 software, access the **Tools** pull-down menu and select Macro **D**efine. Alternatively, press Macro Define (Ctrl-F10 or Ctrl-Shift-F10).

   Depending on the type of macro you are creating, at the lower left corner of the screen LetterPerfect displays the prompt `Define macro:` for a LetterPerfect macro or `Define shell macro:` for a Shell macro.

3. Type *Lookup* and press Enter. LetterPerfect displays the prompt `Description:`.

4. Type *Activates the Spell Lookup Option* and press Enter.

   Depending on the type of macro you are creating, at the lower left corner of the screen LetterPerfect displays a prompt `Macro Def` for a LetterPerfect macro that flashes until you complete the macro, or a temporary prompt `* Starting shell macro *` for a Shell macro that disappears after a few seconds.

5. Type *teh*.

6. Access the **Edit** pull-down menu and select **Block**. Alternatively, press Block (Alt-F4 or F12).

7. Use the left arrow to highlight `teh`.

8. Access the **Tools** pull-down menu and select **Spell**. Alternatively, press Spell (Ctrl-F2) or Ctrl-S. LetterPerfect displays the Spell feature's menu line as shown in figure 13.7.

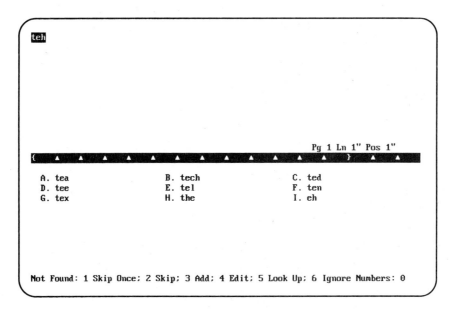

Fig. 13.7. The Spell feature's menu line.

9. Press Cancel (F1) or Esc twice. LetterPerfect displays the main editing screen.

10. With the 11/01/90 software, access the Tools pull-down menu and select Macro Define or Shell Mac Def. Alternatively, press Macro Define (Ctrl-F10) or Shell Macro Define (Ctrl-Shift-F10).

With the 07/24/90 software, access the Tools pull-down menu and select Macro Define. Alternatively, press Macro Define (Ctrl-F10 or Ctrl-Shift-F10).

LetterPerfect saves the macro as either LOOKUP.LPM or LOOKUP.SHM.

Caution: During creation of either LetterPerfect or Shell macros, the program automatically suspends recording the keystrokes until the Spell feature completes operation, and the program returns to its main editing screen; at that point the program resumes recording keystrokes.

While creating a document, use the following steps to use the Lookup macro:

1. With the 11/01/90 software, access the Tools pull-down menu and select Macro Execute or Shell Mac Exe. Alternatively, press Macro Execute (Alt-F10) or Shell Macro Execute (Alt-Shift-F10).

With the 07/24/90 software, access the Tools pull-down menu and select Macro Execute. Alternatively, press Macro Execute (Alt-F10) or Shell Macro Execute (Alt-Shift-F10).

Depending on the type of macro you are creating, at the lower left corner of the screen LetterPerfect displays the prompt Define macro: for a LetterPerfect macro, or Define shell macro: for a Shell macro.

2. Type *lookup* and press Enter. LetterPerfect inserts teh in the main document at the cursor and displays a menu listing the Spell feature's options.

3. Press 5 to select the Lookup option. LetterPerfect displays the menu prompt: Word or word pattern:.

4. Type the phonic spelling for the word pattern you want LetterPerfect to look up (see Chapter 11 for the different methods you can use to create the word pattern) and press Enter.

For example, type *kat* and press Enter. LetterPerfect displays a list of words that match the word pattern and the menu prompt `Select word:`.

5a. If the word you want is among the listed choices, select it by either highlighting it with the mouse pointer and clicking the left button, or typing the letter immediately to the left of the word. LetterPerfect replaces `teh` with the word you designated and displays the prompt: `Word count: 1 Press any key to continue`. Press any key to resume writing or editing the document.

5b. If the word you want is not among the listed choices but the display includes the prompt `Press Enter for more words`, press Enter to display a new list of words. When you find the word you want to use, use the procedure described in step 5a to select it.

5c. If the word you want is not among the listed choices and the display does not include the prompt `Press Enter for more words`, the program cannot find a match for the word pattern. Press Enter to redisplay the menu prompt: `Word or word pattern:` and repeat step 4.

6. With the 11/01/90 software, access the **T**ools pull-down menu and select Macro De**f**ine or Shell Mac **D**ef. Alternatively, press Macro Define (Ctrl-F10) or Shell Macro Define (Ctrl-Shift-F10).

With the 07/24/90 software, access the **T**ools pull-down menu and select Macro **D**efine. Alternatively, press Macro Define (Ctrl-F10 or Ctrl-Shift-F10).

A Macro For Deleting A Sentence or Paragraph

Use the following steps to create a macro that deletes the sentence in which the cursor is located:

1. Move the cursor to a position within the sentence you want to delete.

2. With the 11/01/90 software, access the **T**ools pull-down menu and select Macro Define or Shell Mac **D**efine. Alternatively, press Macro Define (Ctrl-F10) or Shell Macro Define (Ctrl-Shift-F10).

   With the 07/24/90 software, access the **T**ools pull-down menu and select Macro **D**efine. Alternatively, press Macro Define (Ctrl-F10) or Shell Macro Define (Ctrl-Shift-F10).

   Depending on the type of macro you are creating, at the lower left corner of the screen LetterPerfect displays the prompt `Define macro:` for a LetterPerfect macro, or `Define shell macro:` for a Shell macro.

3. Press Alt-s or Alt-Shift-s.

4. Type *Deletes Current Sentence* and press Enter.

5. Access the **E**dit pull-down menu and choose Select Se**n**tence.

   LetterPerfect highlights the sentence and at the bottom of the screen displays a menu prompt:

   1 Move; **2 C**opy; **3 D**elete: **0**

6. Select **D**elete (**3**).

7. With the 11/01/90 software, access the **T**ools pull-down menu and select Macro Define or Shell Mac **D**ef. Alternatively, press Macro Define (Ctrl-F10) or Shell Macro Define (Ctrl-Shift-F10).

   With the 07/24/90 software, access the **T**ools pull-down menu and select Macro **D**efine. Alternatively, press Macro Define (Ctrl-F10 or Ctrl-Shift-F10).

   LetterPerfect saves the macro as either ALT.LPM or ALTSHFT.SHM.

To create a macro that deletes the paragraph at the cursor's location, repeat the previous steps, replacing Alt-s or Alt-Shift-s with Alt-p or Alt-Shift-p in step 2, and Select Paragraph in step 4. Use the same series of steps (making the appropriate replacements in step 2 and selections in step 4) to create macros that move or copy a word, sentence, paragraph, or page.

A Macro That Automates Selecting a Printer-Definition Form

The procedure for selecting a printer form is described in the "Understanding Paper Size/Type" section of Chapter 7. The following steps show you how to create a macro that automates the selection process:

1. With the 11/01/90 software, access the **Tools** pull-down menu and select Macro Define or Shell Mac Def. Alternatively, press Macro Define (Ctrl-F10) or Shell Macro Define (Ctrl-Shift-F10).

   With the 07/24/90 software, access the **Tools** pull-down menu and select Macro **Define**. Alternatively, press Macro Define (Ctrl-F10 or Ctrl-Shift-F10).

   Depending on the type of macro you are creating, at the lower left corner of the screen LetterPerfect displays the prompt `Define macro:` **for a LetterPerfect macro or** `Define shell macro:` **for a** Shell macro.

2. If you are creating a LetterPerfect macro, hold down the Alt key and type *f*. If you are creating a Shell macro with either version, hold down the Alt and Shift keys and type *f*. The program displays the prompt `Description:`.

3. Type *Selects Document's Printer Form* and press Enter.

   If you are creating a LetterPerfect macro, at the lower left corner of the screen the program displays a flashing `Macro Def` until you complete the macro. If you are creating a Shell macro, the program displays `* Starting shell macro *` that disappears after a few seconds.

4. Press Home, Home, Home, up arrow.

5. Access the **Layout** pull-down menu and select Format. Alternatively, press Format (Shift-F8). LetterPerfect displays its Format menu.

6. Choose Paper Size Type (8). LetterPerfect displays the Paper Size/Type menu.

7. If you are creating a LetterPerfect macro, hold down the Ctrl key and press PgUp. If your creating a Shell macro, hold down the Ctrl and Shift keys and press PgUp.

If you are creating a LetterPerfect macro, at the lower left corner of the screen the program displays a menu prompt:

1 Pause; **2 D**isplay: **0**

If you are creating a Shell macro, the program displays a menu prompt:

(Shell) **1 P**ause; **2 D**isplay; **3** Assign; **4** Comment: **0**

8. Select **Pause** (**1**). Although the macro definition remains active, LetterPerfect does not record either the keystrokes or cursor movements in step 9 as part of the macro.

9. Move the cursor bar to highlight the printer-definition form you want added to your document.

10. Press Enter. LetterPerfect ends the pause and resumes adding keystrokes to the macro.

11. Press **Select** (**1**). LetterPerfect redisplays the Format menu.

12. Press Exit (F7), Cancel (F1), or Esc. LetterPerfect displays the main editing screen.

13. With the 11/01/90 software, access the Tools pull-down menu and select Macro Define or Shell Mac Def. Alternatively, press Macro Define (Ctrl-F10) or Shell Macro Define (Ctrl-Shift-F10).

    With the 07/24/90 software, access the Tools pull-down menu and select Macro Define. Alternatively, press Macro Define (Ctrl-F10 or Ctrl-Shift-F10).

    Depending on the name you give the macro in step 2, Letter-Perfect saves the macro as either ALTF.LPM or ALTSHFTF.SHM.

The following steps show you how to use the macro:

1. To start the LetterPerfect macro, hold down the Alt key and type *f*. To start the Shell macro, hold down the Alt and Shift keys and type *f*.

2. Move the cursor bar to highlight the name of the printer-definition form you want to use in the document.

3. Press Enter. LetterPerfect inserts the printer-definition form as the first code in your document.

A Macro That Creates A Temporary Printer-Definition Form

As explained in Chapter 7, LetterPerfect does not let you create page forms that are permanently stored with its printer-definition file. However, you can create a macro that recreates the same temporary form by following these steps:

1. With the 11/01/90 software, access the **Tools** pull-down menu and select Macro De**fine** or Shell Mac **Def**. Alternatively, press Macro Define (Ctrl-F10) or Shell Macro Define (Ctrl-Shift-F10).

   With the 07/24/90 software, access the **Tools** pull-down menu and select Macro **Define**. Alternatively, press Macro Define (Ctrl-F10 or Ctrl-Shift-F10).

   If you are creating a LetterPerfect macro, at the lower left corner of the screen the program displays the `Define macro:` prompt. If you are creating a Shell macro, the program displays the `Define shell macro:` prompt.

2. Type *legal-l* and press Enter. At the lower left corner of the screen, the program displays the `Description:` prompt.

3. Type *Creates temporary legal landscape printer form* and press Enter.

   If you are creating a LetterPerfect macro, at the lower left corner of the screen the program displays a `Macro Def` message that flashes until you complete the macro. If you are creating a Shell macro, the program displays a `* Starting shell macro *` message that disappears after a few seconds.

4. Press Home, Home, Home, up arrow.

5. Access the **Layout** pull-down menu and select **Format**. Alternatively, press Format (Shift-F8). LetterPerfect displays its Format menu.

6. Choose Paper **S**ize Type (**8**). LetterPerfect displays the Paper Size/Type menu.

7. Press Home, Home, Home, down arrow to move the cursor bar to highlight the [ALL OTHERS] printer-definition form.

8. Press Enter. The program displays the Width: 8.5" prompt.

9. Type *14* and press Enter. The program displays the Height: 11" prompt.

10. Type *8.5* and press Enter. The program displays the Other form type: prompt.

11. Type *Legal Landscape* and press Enter. The program redisplays the Format menu.

12. Press Exit (F7), Cancel (F1), or Esc. LetterPerfect displays the main editing screen.

13. With the 11/01/90 software, access the **Tools** pull-down menu and select Macro De**f**ine or Shell Mac **D**ef. Alternatively, press Macro Define (Ctrl-F10) or Shell Macro Define (Ctrl-Shift-F10).

    With the 07/24/90 software, access the **Tools** pull-down menu and select Macro De**f**ine. Alternatively, press Macro Define (Ctrl-F10 or Ctrl-Shift-F10).

    Depending on the type of macro you are creating, the program saves the macro as either LEGAL-L.LPM or LEGAL-L.SHM.

The following steps show you how to use the macro:

1. With the 11/01/90 software, access the **Tools** pull-down menu and select Macro Execute or Shell Mac Exe. Alternatively, press Macro Execute (Alt-F10) or Shell Macro Execute (Alt-Shift-F10).

    With the 07/24/90 software, access the **Tools** pull-down menu and select Macro Execute. Alternatively, press Macro Execute (Alt-F10) or Shell Macro Execute (Alt-Shift-F10).

2. Type *legal-l* and press Enter. At the bottom of the screen, the program displays the * Please Wait * message for a few seconds. When the message disappears, the macro has created the Legal Landscape printer-definition form as the first code in your document.

A Shell Macro That Starts and Displays LetterPerfect

By default, when you start the Shell 3.01 program it displays its main menu screen, so that you can select the program or programs that you want Shell to run. If you have designated one or more programs to start resident (see Chapter 1), Shell loads each resident program into memory, but returns to the main menu screen. However, you may want LetterPerfect's main editing screen displayed when you start the Shell.

The following instructions show you how to create and use a Shell macro that automatically starts LetterPerfect and displays the main editing screen:

1. From the DOS prompt, change to the drive (and subdirectory, if you are running LetterPerfect on a system with a hard-disk drive) containing the Shell program.

2. Type *shell* and press Enter.

3. Press Shell Macro Define (Ctrl-Shift-F10). At the lower left corner of the screen the program displays the prompt `Define shell macro:`.

4. Type *start_lp* and press Enter. The program displays the prompt `Description:`

5. Type *Automatically Starts LetterPerfect* and press Enter. At the lower left corner of the screen the program displays a temporary prompt `* Starting shell macro *` that disappears after a few seconds and is replaced by `*Macro Def*` which remains on screen with the Shell menu.

6. Type *L* (or whatever letter designates the LetterPerfect selection).

7. When LetterPerfect's main editing screen is displayed, press Shell Macro Define (Ctrl-Shift-F10). LetterPerfect saves the macro as START_LP.SHM.

8. Exit both LetterPerfect and Shell and return to the DOS prompt.

Now that you have created the Shell macro, you can use it either selectively or automatically each time you start the Shell program. The following steps show you how to use the macro selectively:

1. From the DOS prompt, change to the drive (and subdirectory, if you are running LetterPerfect on a system with a hard disk drive) containing the Shell program.

2. Type *shell /m-start_lp* and press Enter. The Shell program starts and automatically displays LetterPerfect's main editing screen.

If you start Shell from a DOS batch file, you can use it so that Shell automatically runs the START_LP macro. The following steps show you how to use LetterPerfect to modify the batch file:

1. Access the **File** pull-down menu and select **Retrieve**. Alternatively, press Retrieve (Shift-F10).

2. Type the batch file's name (including the *.BAT* extension) and press Enter.

3. Move the cursor to the end of the line containing the entry SHELL.

4. Press the space bar and type */m-start_lp*.

5. Access the **File** pull-down menu and select **DOS Text Out**. Alternatively, press Text Out (Ctrl-F5) and select **DOS Text Out** (**1**).

6. At the Document to be saved prompt, LetterPerfect displays the prompt: Replace C:\<*path name*>\<file name>.BAT? No (Yes)

7. Select **Yes**.

8. Exit both LetterPerfect and Shell and return to the DOS prompt.

9. Change to the drive (and subdirectory, if you are using a system with a hard disk drive) containing the batch file.

10. Type the batch file's name and press Enter. The Shell program starts and automatically displays LetterPerfect's main editing screen.

Summary

In this chapter you have learned how to create and use macros to edit documents and access LetterPerfect features more quickly and easily. A macro is a mini-program that stores a group of keystrokes in a special file and replays the keystrokes when you run the macro. The macro techniques presented include the following:

- Create Alt-*<letter>*, Alt-Shift-*<letter>*, and named macros
- Replace macros
- Run different types of macros
- Create macros that work with any language version of LetterPerfect
- Create looping, nested, and chained macros
- Create some macros for everyday use

Chapter 14 shows you how to use LetterPerfect's powerful Merge feature.

14

Assembling
Documents with
Merge

All but the most basic word processors have merge capabilities. LetterPerfect includes a functional Merge feature that uses a compact set of 13 merge codes. With these codes you can create documents by combining information from different files and from the keyboard.

This chapter is useful for two kinds of users: those who have never performed a merge, and those who are familiar with Merge in other word processors but need to learn LetterPerfect's Merge features.

Reminder: WordPerfect Corporation updated LetterPerfect 1.0 just before this book went to press. Dated 11/01/90, the interim release includes new options for existing features, and a few new features. The menus on your screen may, therefore, differ slightly from those shown in this book. Also, depending on the printer-form definition, margins, tab stops, and font you specify, the text placement and status-line information in documents you create may differ from that shown in this book's figures.

For information about using the mouse and accessing the pull-down menus, refer to the Introduction.

Understanding a Merge

LetterPerfect's Merge feature produces a document by combining information that changes with information that does not change. Merge works with structured *variable text* and *standard format* documents—also called *universal* or *boilerplate* text. The basic merge process, shown in figure 14.1, increases productivity because you enter only *once* the information that does not change.

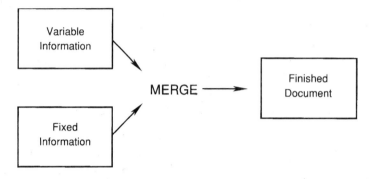

Fig. 14.1. Fixed information combined with variable information to produce a finished document.

Variable information can include a variety of text. Suppose that you decide to turn your address book into a LetterPerfect merge application. The variable information includes names, addresses, and telephone numbers.

The *fixed information*, which is the same for each document, includes formatting codes and fixed text.

Providing the Fixed Information

A *primary file* (also called a merge template) contains the fixed information—formatting codes, text, or both—that goes into each LetterPerfect document. When you activate Merge, the program searches the primary file for merge codes. These codes tell LetterPerfect where to locate each item of variable information and where to place this information into the final document.

Getting Variable Information into a Merge

Merge accepts variable information from two sources. The most common, and generally most useful, source is the structured *secondary file*. The second source is information entered from the keyboard by the user when Merge pauses for the input.

Designing a Secondary File

A secondary file contains *records* of organized information arranged into subgroups called *fields*. LetterPerfect uses special codes to mark the end of each field and record. You can include other codes in the secondary file to handle special situations, but only two codes are required: {END RECORD}, for marking the end of a record, and {END FIELD}, for marking the end of each field within a record.

A *record* is one complete set of variable information. For example, if you use Merge to produce a set of mailing labels, a record contains all the variable information required to create one label. If you use Merge to generate a form letter, a record contains all the variable information to be included in one letter. If you use Merge to assemble a standard legal contract, a record contains all the variable information to be included in one contract.

A *field* is one item of unique information in a record. A field can contain these kinds of information:

- No information (a blank field)

- One or more words, sentences, or paragraphs

- A number or numeric value

The secondary file for mailing labels requires, for example, records with these information fields:

- Recipient's name

- Street address

- City

- State

- ZIP code

Using Merge Files Created by Other WordPerfect Programs

LetterPerfect's Merge works with primary and secondary merge files created by other WordPerfect Corporation programs, although you must retrieve and save some files as LetterPerfect files in order for the merge to work properly. If the file contains some merge codes recognized by the other programs but not by LetterPerfect, you must edit the files to remove the codes not supported. If you use these files without removing the unsupported codes, LetterPerfect ends the merge with an error message.

LetterPerfect works directly, for example, with the secondary files maintained by Notebook, one of several useful programs marketed by WordPerfect Corporation in its Library 2.0, Office 2.0, and Office 3.0 program packages. A Notebook file is a standard merge file that has some additional codes used strictly by Notebook. LetterPerfect ignores these codes and treats the Notebook file exactly like a standard LetterPerfect secondary file.

Using DOS Delimited Secondary Files

Unlike the Merge feature in some other word processing programs, LetterPerfect's Merge cannot use changeable information stored in *delimited* DOS text files (those that contain non-LetterPerfect codes marking the end of each record and each field).

Building a Simple Merge

This section shows you how to plan a merge and how to create the primary and secondary files for performing a simple merge. You learn also how to tell LetterPerfect to combine the files in a merge operation.

Understanding and Accessing LetterPerfect's Merge Codes

Merge works with documents that contain text formatted with special merge codes. LetterPerfect uses 13 of the merge codes introduced in the powerful

WordPerfect Programming Language (WPL) used by WordPerfect 5.1. Some LetterPerfect merge codes are followed by arguments, textual or numerical parameters ending with one or more tildes. The structure of a merge code and its argument is called the code's *command syntax*.

To get the most from LetterPerfect's Merge, you should understand the merge codes and command syntax. Table 14.1 lists each merge code and its command syntax, if any, and other information about the code, including a brief description of the function of the code. If the LetterPerfect code functions similarly to an old-style merge code or code combination used in WordPerfect 4.2 or WordPerfect 5.0, the old-style code is listed at the end of the description.

Table 14.1
LetterPerfect's Merge Codes

Code Name/ Syntax	Reveal Codes Appearance	File Type	Description
{DATE}	[Mrg:DATE]	P	Inserts the computer system's current date and/or time in the format designated for LetterPerfect's Date/ Outline feature. This is the old-style ⌃D merge code used by WordPerfect 4.2 and 5.0.
{END FIELD}	[Mrg:END FIELD][HRt]	S	Marks the end of each field in a record; is followed by a [HRt] formatting code that is not visible on the main editing screen. This is the old-style ⌃R merge code used by WordPerfect 4.2 and 5.0.
{END RECORD}	[Mrg:END RECORD][HPg]	S	Marks the end of each record in a secondary file; is followed by a [HPg] formatting code that is not visible on the main editing screen. This is the old-style ⌃E merge code used by WordPerfect 4.2 and 5.0.

Table 14.1 (continued)

Code Name/ Syntax	Reveal Codes Appearance	File Type	Description
{FIELD}name/ number~	**[Mrg:FIELD]name/ number~[HRt]**	P	Inserts at the code's location in the primary file the text and/or formatting codes contained in the secondary file's named or numbered field.
			This is the old-style ^F<number> merge code used by WordPerfect 4.2 and 5.0.
{FIELD NAMES} name1~...nameN~~ {END RECORD}	**[Mrg:FIELD NAMES] name1~...nameN~~ [Mrg:END RECORD][HPg]**	S	Creates the name structure in a secondary file file and assigns names to the first 100 fields in a record. This LetterPerfect code structure has the same function as the following old-style merge code structure used by WordPerfect 4.2 and 5.0:
			^N <field name> ... ^N^R ^E[HPg]
{INPUT}message~	**[Mrg:INPUT]message~**	P	Pauses the merge operation; displays a message on the bottom line of the screen, beginning at the left corner; and lets you enter an unlimited number of keystrokes until you press the End Field (F9) key. This LetterPerfect code has the same function as the following old-style merge code structure used by WordPerfect 4.2 and 5.0: ^Omessage^O^C

Code Name/ Syntax	Reveal Codes Appearance	File Type	Description
{NEST PRIMARY} filename~	**[Mrg:NEST PRIMARY] filename~**	P	Causes the program to begin using another primary file for the merge operation. After Merge completes the steps required by the other primary file, Merge returns to the original primary file and resumes using it.
{NEXT RECORD}	**[Mrg:NEXT RECORD]**	P	Causes the merge operation to begin processing the next record in the secondary file immediately. You can insert this code from the keyboard during a pause in the merge operation. This is the old-style ^N merge code used by WordPerfect 4.2 and 5.0.
{PAGE OFF}	**[Mrg:PAGE OFF]**	P/S	Discontinues insertion of the **[HPg]** code between copies of the document created during a merge operation on multiple records. This LetterPerfect code has the same function as the following old-style merge code structure used by WordPerfect 4.2 and 5.0: ^N^P^P

Table 14.1 (continued)

Code Name/ Syntax	Reveal Codes Appearance	File Type	Description
{PAGE ON}	[Mrg:PAGE ON]	P/S	Restores insertion of the [HPg] code between copies of the document created during a merge operation on multiple records.
{PRINT}	[Mrg:PRINT]	P/S	Sends all text created by the merge operation up to the location of the {PRINT} code to the printer. This is the old-style ^T merge code used by WordPerfect 4.2 and 5.0.
{QUIT}	:QUIT]	P/S	Ends the merge operation after adding the remainder of the primary file's structure and universal language to the document but does not execute the remaining merge command codes. You can insert this code from the keyboard during a pause in the merge operation. This is the old-style ^Q merge code used by WordPerfect 4.2 and 5.0.
{STOP}	[Mrg:STOP]	P/S	Similar to the {QUIT} code, except that {STOP} immediately terminates the merge without adding the remainder of the text and merge codes in the primary file. You can insert this code from the keyboard during a pause in the merge operation.

To access the merge commands, you can choose either of these methods:

- Access the **T**ools pull-down menu and select **M**erge Codes (see fig. 14.2).

- Press Merge Codes (Shift-F9).

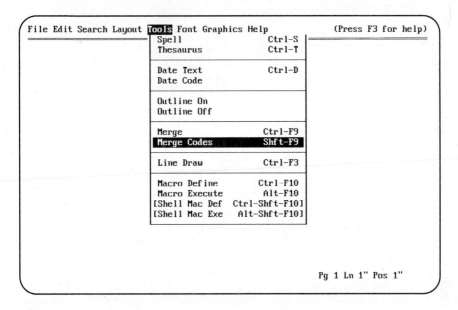

File Edit Search Layout **Tools** Font Graphics Help   (Press F3 for help)

```
              Spell              Ctrl-S
              Thesaurus          Ctrl-T

              Date Text          Ctrl-D
              Date Code

              Outline On
              Outline Off

              Merge              Ctrl-F9
              Merge Codes        Shft-F9

              Line Draw          Ctrl-F3

              Macro Define       Ctrl-F10
              Macro Execute      Alt-F10
              [Shell Mac Def  Ctrl-Shft-F10]
              [Shell Mac Exe  Alt-Shft-F10]
```

Pg 1 Ln 1" Pos 1"

Fig. 14.2. *The Tools pull-down menu listing the Merge Codes option.*

LetterPerfect displays the Merge command access box shown in figure 14.3. This box contains all 13 of LetterPerfect's merge command codes, each code listed alphabetically with its syntax (including the tilde), if any.

Caution: A frequent cause of improper merge operations is the accidental deletion or misplacement of one or more tildes in the command syntax of a merge code in a primary or secondary file. The deletion of even one tilde in either of these files can cause the merge to function improperly or to fail completely. If you encounter either of these problems, check for missing tildes and correct tilde placement.

Typing the name of a code moves the cursor bar automatically to the code, as does moving the mouse pointer to a code and clicking the left mouse button once. Pressing the down or right arrow moves the cursor bar down the list of codes; pressing the up or left arrow moves the cursor up the list of codes.

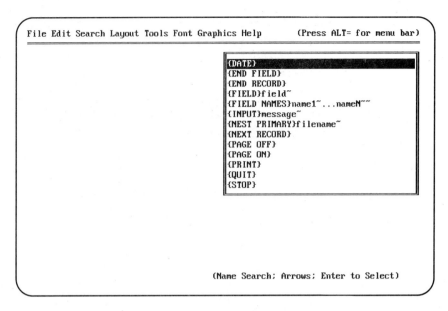

File Edit Search Layout Tools Font Graphics Help   (Press ALT= for menu bar)

```
{DATE}
{END FIELD}
{END RECORD}
{FIELD}field~
{FIELD NAMES}name1~...nameN~~
{INPUT}message~
{NEST PRIMARY}filename~
{NEXT RECORD}
{PAGE OFF}
{PAGE ON}
{PRINT}
{QUIT}
{STOP}
```

(Name Search; Arrows; Enter to Select)

Fig. 14.3. The command access box for Merge.

Select a command code by moving the cursor bar to it and either double-clicking the left mouse button or pressing Enter. If the code requires syntax, the program pauses and displays a prompt that instructs you to enter the syntax. Type the syntax and press Enter. The command code access box disappears, and LetterPerfect inserts the code with its syntax and tilde into the document at the cursor. If the code does not require syntax, LetterPerfect automatically inserts the code at the cursor, and the command code access box disappears.

To exit the command code access box without selecting a command code or to discontinue selecting a command code as you define its syntax, click the right mouse button or press either Cancel (F1), Esc, or Exit (F7).

Tip: Although the merge {**END FIELD**} code is listed in LetterPerfect's command code access box, you will find it quicker and easier to insert this code by pressing End Field (F9).

Deciding How To Use the Merge Feature

Perhaps the greatest single use of any word processing program is memo and letter writing. Unfortunately, many users do not even think about, let alone use, Merge in connection with routine writing tasks. Properly used, though,

Merge makes writing even a single memo or letter quicker and easier. Merge really saves time, though, when you send the same basic letter to different people, with information customized for each recipient.

Suppose, for example, that you are an elementary school teacher who needs to schedule an appointment with the parents of each of your students. You want to write a letter to the parents of each child, suggesting a date and time for the conference. The year before, you mimeographed a form letter and inserted by hand each child's name and the suggested date and time for the conference. This year, you want to make your letters look more professional. You decide to write a standard business letter. Is this a good time to use a merge?

To answer that question, you must analyze the information to be included in the letter. You want to tell each child's parents something about the purpose of the conference, encourage them to attend, and ask them to start thinking about questions they want to ask. You have a fair amount of *fixed information* that is the same in each letter.

To make the communication more personal, however, you want to include in each letter the name and address of the parent(s) and the date and time of the meeting. It also would be nice to include the child's name in the letter and a personal salutation—for example, *Dear Mr. and Mrs. Richards*—instead of *Dear Parent*. From these requirements, you can readily see that you also have some *variable information* to include.

With both fixed and variable information to handle, you decide to use a merge to create the letters.

Planning the Merge

A few minutes spent planning a merge operation often saves much time in entering data later. When you plan, you decide what information is fixed and what information is variable, and then you assign names to each item of variable data.

Determining the Variable Data

The first step in planning a merge is to decide the type and scope of the variable text. You must decide which text goes in the primary file (the universal, or boilerplate, text) and which goes in the secondary file (the variable information).

Begin by looking at the information that changes from letter to letter. Figure 14.4 shows a list of students, the name and address of each child's parents, and the date and time of each proposed conference.

CLASS LISTING FOR THOMAS, JEAN
BUENA PARK GRADE 1 SECTION A

STUDENT	PARENT	ADDRESS		
BOLCOM AMY	MR MRS GEORGE BOLCOM	4319 N RACINE	CHICAGO	60613 - 10/13 3:30 PM
BYERS TERRY	MR MRS DONALD BYERS	1306 W IRVING PARK	CHICAGO	60613 - 10/17 3:00 PM
CAMPBELL MARY ANN	MS PAULA CAMPBELL	4416 N KENMORE	CHICAGO	60644 - 10/20 3:00 PM
DAYHOFF LAWRENCE	MR MRS KENNETH DAYHOFF	1317 W BUENA	CHICAGO	60613 - 10/15 3:00 PM
DENNIS WILLIAM	MR MRS JOHN DENNIS	4220 N RACINE	CHICAGO	60613 - 10/21 3:00 PM
FLEMING CHARLES	MR MRS JAMES FLEMING	4431 N KENMORE	CHICAGO	60644 - 10/15 4:00 PM
GREGORY TODD	MRS JANET GREGORY	4317 N RACINE	CHICAGO	60613 - 10/21 3:30 PM
HARRIS PETER	MR MRS CLAUDE HARRIS	1227 W BELLE PLAINE	CHICAGO	60613 - 10/13 4:00 PM
HENNESSEY JENNIFER	MR MRS CARROLL HENNESSEY	4530 N SOUTHPORT	CHICAGO	60644 - 10/16 3 30 AM
HOPKINS NANCY	MR MRS JOHN HOPKINS	4671 N JANSSEN	CHICAGO	60644 - 10/14 3 30 PM
JAMISON GERALD	MR MRS EUGENE FORD	1115 W PENSACOLA	CHICAGO	60613 - 10/17 4:00 PM
JONES RICHARD	MR MRS DAVID JONES	3961 N KENMORE	CHICAGO	60613 - 10/20 4:00 PM
KEENEY CHRISTINE	MR MRS LAVERNE KEENEY	1223 W HUTCHINSON	CHICAGO	60613 - 10/13 3:00 PM
KING MARVIN	MR MRS CHARLES KING	1139 W BUENA	CHICAGO	60613 - 10/21 4:00 PM
LOVEQUIST HEATHER	MR MRS GARRY LOVEQUIST	1326 W CUYLER	CHICAGO	60613 - 10/15 3:30 PM
MELBERG HAROLD	MR MRS SAUL MELBERG	4221 N MALDEN	CHICAGO	60613 - 10/22 3:00 PM
MOON SUSAN	MR MICHAEL MOON	4503 N SEMINARY	CHICAGO	60644 - 10/14 3:00 PM
NELSON FREDERICK	MR MRS FREDERICK NELSON	1330 W WARNER	CHICAGO	60613 - 10/16 3:00 PM
OLSZEWSKI JOHN	MR MRS FRANK OLSZEWSKI	4227 N MALDEN	CHICAGO	60613 - 10/17 3:30 PM
PLATT DOUGLAS	MR MRS WAYNE PLATT	1223 W BERTEAU	CHICAGO	60613 - 10/14 4:00 PM
SIMMONS MARK	MR MRS GLENN SIMMONS	1508 W AGATITE	CHICAGO	60644 - 10/16 4:00 PM
WILKINSON LUCY	MR MRS SCOTT WILKINSON	1440 W BELLE PLAINE	CHICAGO	60613 - 10/20 3:30 PM

Fig. 14.4. Variable information.

When you examine the list, two patterns stand out. First, all the parents live in the same city and state, but their ZIP codes vary. If you include the city and state in the variable data, you have to type *Chicago, Illinois* in each record in the secondary file. But if you include the city and state as fixed text, you type *Chicago, IL* only once—in the primary file. Because the ZIP code varies with each letter, you must include it as variable information in the secondary file.

Second, all the appointments are in October 1990. You can thus include the name of the month (fixed text) in the primary file, and the day of the month (variable information) in the secondary file. The list of secondary data fields is shown in figure 14.5.

Assigning Field Names

After you determine the type of variable information to use, you are ready to think about field names. Each item of variable information requires a separate field in the record, with a unique *field name*. Each field name should be short but descriptive, indicating the type of information in the field. LetterPerfect accepts one-word or multiple-word field names.

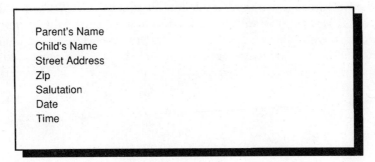

Parent's Name
Child's Name
Street Address
Zip
Salutation
Date
Time

Fig. 14.5. Secondary (variable) information for the sample merge.

You can use the name *Child*, for example, for the field that holds the name of the child, or you can call this field *Child Name*. Figure 14.6 lists the simple, logical choices for the parent letter project.

Parent
Child
StreetAddress
Zip
Salutation
Date
Time

Fig. 14.6. Field names for the sample merge.

Although there is no limit to the number of characters for a field name, Merge recognizes only the first 15 characters, including spaces and numerals, as unique. Even though the following field names are visually unique, LetterPerfect considers them identical in merging operations because the first 15 characters are identical through the letter **b** in the word **number**:

    {FIELD}This field number one~

    {FIELD}This field number two~

If the primary and secondary files contain two or more identical field names, Merge inserts the information from only the first named field in sequence in the secondary merge file.

The merge process recognizes an unlimited number of numbered fields but imposes a limit of 100 named fields in either a primary or secondary file. After Merge processes the first 100 named fields, it does not insert data into any additional named fields in the primary file. After this limit is reached, and if one of the first 100 named fields is repeated later in the primary file, Merge inserts data into the field.

Creating the Primary File

After you choose field names, you are ready to create the primary file, a LetterPerfect file containing the universal text and formatting codes that should appear in the final letter. Begin typing the universal text of the letter. When you reach the first location for the date, follow these steps:

1. Access the **Tools** pull-down menu and select **Merge Codes**. Alternatively, press Merge Codes (Shift-F9).

   LetterPerfect displays the merge command code box with the cursor bar highlighting {**DATE**}.

2. Double-click the left mouse button or press Enter.

   LetterPerfect inserts the {**DATE**} merge code at the cursor in the document, shown in figure 14.7.

3. Press Enter twice.

4. Access the merge command code box by using one of the methods described in step 1.

5. Move the cursor bar to the {**FIELD**} code and press Enter.

   At the lower left corner of the screen, LetterPerfect displays the prompt Enter Field:.

6. Type *Parent* and press Enter.

   LetterPerfect inserts the {**FIELD**} merge code and *Parent*, followed by a tilde, as shown in figure 14.8.

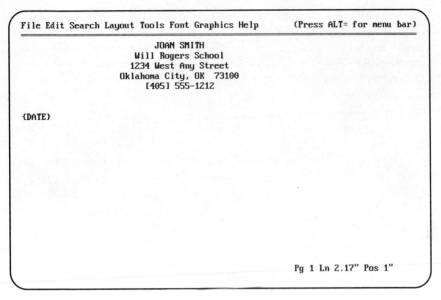

Fig. 14.7. *The primary file, containing the {DATE} code.*

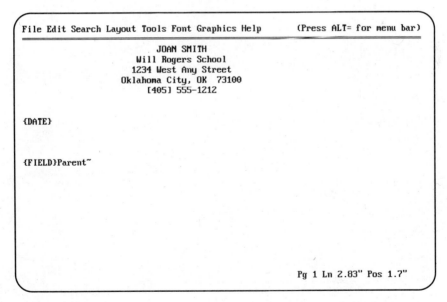

Fig. 14.8. *The primary file, showing the command syntax {FIELD}Parent~.*

7. Continue typing the primary document, inserting {**FIELD**} codes where they are needed.

8. Access the **F**ile pull-down menu and select **S**ave. Alternatively, press Save (F10). Choose a descriptive file name, such as PARENTS.PF.

> ***Tip:*** Although designating primary files with the PF suffix is not required in order for Merge to operate, ending a primary file name with PF makes distinguishing merge primary files from other LetterPerfect files easy. In the same manner and for the same reason, you can end a secondary file with the SF extension. Using this system makes it possible to relate a primary file and secondary file by using identical characters for the name of each file.

Figure 14.9 shows the on-screen appearance of the document after you type it. The *Child* field appears twice in the primary file. LetterPerfect inserts information from a secondary file into the document created by the primary file as often as necessary.

```
File Edit Search Layout Tools Font Graphics Help        (Press ALT= for menu bar)

{FIELD}Parent~
{FIELD}StreetAddress~
Oklahoma City, OK  {FIELD}Zip~

Dear {FIELD}Salutation~:

In case the name above is not familiar to you yet, let me introduce myself.
I'm Joan Smith, a first-grade teacher at Will Rogers Elementary School, and I
have the pleasure of having your child, {FIELD}Child~, in my class this year.

I like to get together with the parents of each of my first-graders early in
the school year to talk about their child's progress.  This also gives us an
opportunity to get to know each other, and it gives you a chance to ask any
questions you may have about how {FIELD}Child~ is doing.

I've tentatively scheduled a meeting on October {FIELD}Date~, 1990, at {FIELD}Ti
schedule is not convenient for you, please feel free to call me or drop me a
note.  I can schedule conferences any day after school.

I'm looking forward to meeting you!

Sincerely,
                                                 Pg 1 Ln 6.33" Pos 1.22"
```

Fig. 14.9. *The primary document, with {**FIELD**} codes displayed.*

When it displays text on the screen, LetterPerfect ignores the space occupied by the merge codes, such as {**FIELD**}, but not the syntax and tilde following a code. As a result, text may scroll past the visual right margin, as shown on the first line of the third paragraph in figure 14.9.

If you print a primary file, the hard copy includes each field name followed by a tilde, as shown in figure 14.10. The {**DATE**} and {**FIELD**} codes do not appear in the printed version of the document.

JOAN SMITH
Will Rogers School
1234 West Any Street
Oklahoma City, OK 73100
[405] 555-1212

Parent~
StreetAddress~
Oklahoma City, OK Zip~

Dear Salutation~:

In case the name above is not familiar to you yet, let me introduce myself. I'm Joan Smith, a first-grade teacher at Will Rogers Elementary School, and I have the pleasure of having your child, Child~, in my class this year.

I like to get together with the parents of each of my first-graders early in the school year to talk about their child's progress. This also gives us an opportunity to get to know each other, and it gives you a chance to ask any questions you may have about how Child~ is doing.

I've tentatively scheduled a meeting on October Date~, 1990, at Time~. If this schedule is not convenient for you, please feel free to call me or drop me a note. I can schedule conferences any day after school.

I'm looking forward to meeting you!

Sincerely,

Joan Smith

Fig. 14.10. A printed copy of the primary document, showing field names.

Tip: Create a reference book of frequently used forms by printing copies of your primary files and inserting them into a notebook. If the primary file uses the {**DATE**} merge code, type the text *Automatically Dated* beside the merge code before you print the file.

If another person supplies the variable information for use with the primary file, replace each {**FIELD**}**name~** with underlined spaces before you print the file. Give the person supplying the variable information a copy of the printed file and let him or her write the variable information in the blanks.

Creating the Secondary File

The secondary file includes variable information that LetterPerfect inserts into the document during the merge. The text is arranged into fields and records. Creating the secondary file requires these actions:

- Creating at the beginning of the secondary file a special record that contains the name of each field

- Entering the text for each field in the record

- Inserting merge codes to mark the end of each field and record

Creating the Field Names Record in a Secondary File

In LetterPerfect 1.0, using named fields in a merge requires creating a special record at the beginning of the secondary file to tell LetterPerfect the field names you assigned. The following steps show you how to insert the special record and the field names into the secondary file:

1. Press Exit (F7) and N twice to clear the main editing screen.

2. Access the **T**ools pull-down menu and select **M**erge Codes. Alternatively, press Merge Codes (Shift-F9).

   LetterPerfect displays the merge command code box with the cursor bar highlighting {**DATE**}—unless you are performing these steps immediately after you created the primary file. If you just created the primary file, the cursor bar highlights {**FIELD**}.

3. Using the cursor-movement keys or mouse, move the cursor bar to highlight {**FIELD NAMES**}**name1~...nameN~~**.

4. Double-click the left mouse button or press Enter.

   At the lower left corner of the screen, LetterPerfect displays the prompt Enter Field 1:$4.

5. Type *Parent* and press Enter.

   Parent disappears, and LetterPerfect changes the prompt to Enter Field 2:.

6. Repeat step 5 to enter each of these field names: *Child*, *StreetAddress*, *Zip*, *Salutation*, *Date*, and *Time*.

Caution: In the secondary file, you must type each field name *exactly*—except for case—as it appears in the primary file. If a field name in the primary file does not have a match in the secondary file, the document created by Merge does not contain any information at the unmatched field name. LetterPerfect does *not* warn you about the unmatched field name. If, for example, you use *Parent* in the primary file and *Parents* in the secondary file, LetterPerfect creates the letter without information at the location of {**FIELD**}**Parent~** in the primary file. LetterPerfect does, however, consider *PARENT* and *Parent* identical field names.

Tip: If you misspell or otherwise type an incorrect field name but do not catch the mistake before you press Enter, continue to enter the remaining field names. After LetterPerfect creates the special field name records, you can edit the field names the same way you edit any word in a LetterPerfect document.

7. After you type the last field name, press Enter at the next prompt for a field name.

   The prompt disappears, and LetterPerfect creates the special record shown in figure 14.11.

Tip: If you mistakenly press Enter before you type all the field names, you can still add field names to the list. See "Adding Fields to a Secondary File" later in this chapter.

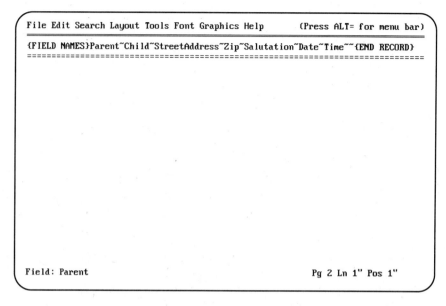

```
File Edit Search Layout Tools Font Graphics Help        (Press ALT= for menu bar)

{FIELD NAMES}Parent~Child~StreetAddress~Zip~Salutation~Date~Time~~{END RECORD}
================================================================================




Field: Parent                                          Pg 2 Ln 1" Pos 1"
```

*Fig. 14.11. The secondary document after you complete the {**FIELD NAMES**}*
record.

The {**FIELD NAMES**} record contains this information:

- The {**FIELD NAMES**} merge code at the beginning of the record.
  LetterPerfect uses the information in this record to locate each
  named field in the records that follow.

- The name of each field, just as you typed it.

- A tilde (~) at the end of each field name. The tilde tells LetterPerfect
  where one name ends and the next one begins.

- An extra tilde and an {**END RECORD**} code after the last field name.
  These items tell LetterPerfect where the record ends.

Entering Fields and Records

After LetterPerfect creates the {**FIELD NAMES**} record in the secondary file,
you are ready to enter variable data.

Notice that in figure 14.11 the name of the first field is displayed in the lower
left corner of the screen. From the special {**FIELD NAMES**} record, LetterPerfect
knows that you are in a secondary file and that the first field in each record is
named *Parent*.

Follow these steps to create a record for the first student:

1. If the cursor is not at the top of page 2, immediately following the page break separating it from page 1, press PgDn.

2. Type the names of the first child's parents exactly as you want the names to appear in the address block. In this example, type *Mr. and Mrs. Thomas H. Benton.* Do *not* press Enter.

3. Press End Field (F9). LetterPerfect inserts an {**END FIELD**} code and a hard return after *Benton*, as shown in figure 14.12. The field name prompt at the lower left corner of the screen changes to Child.

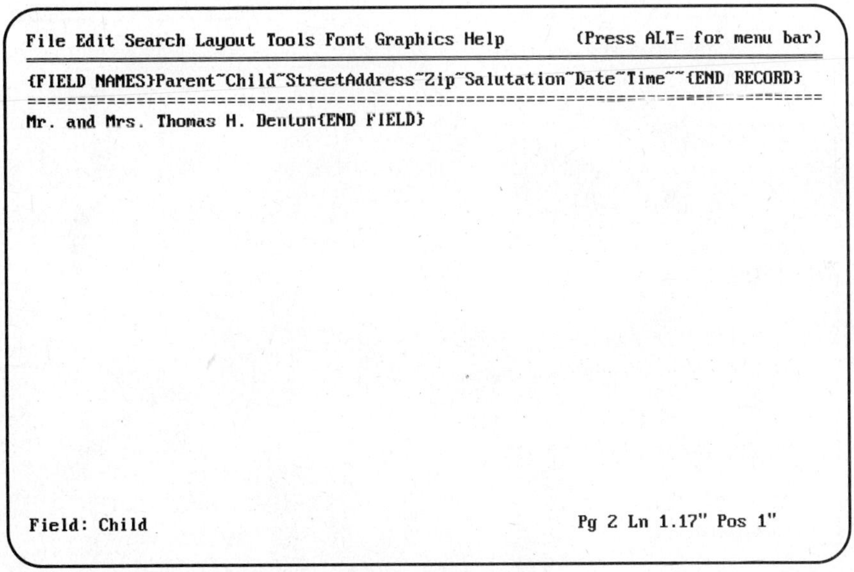

```
 File Edit Search Layout Tools Font Graphics Help        (Press ALT= for menu bar)

{FIELD NAMES}Parent~Child~StreetAddress~Zip~Salutation~Date~Time~~{END RECORD}
===============================================================================
Mr. and Mrs. Thomas H. Benton{END FIELD}









 Field: Child                                        Pg 2 Ln 1.17" Pos 1"
```

Fig. 14.12. The secondary file with one field entered.

4. Type *Sally* and press End Field (F9). LetterPerfect inserts an {**END FIELD**} code and a hard return after *Sally*, and the field name prompt changes to StreetAddress.

5. Repeat step 4 to enter the variable text for the remaining fields: *2322 Red Oak Terrace, 73100, Mr. and Mrs. Benton, 18,* and *4:00.* Be sure to press End Field (F9) and not Enter at the end of each field, including the last one.

6. Access the **T**ools pull-down menu and select **M**erge Codes. Alternatively, press Merge Codes (Shift-F9).

   LetterPerfect displays the merge command code box with the cursor bar highlighting {**FIELD**}.

7. Using the cursor-movement keys or mouse, move the cursor bar to highlight {**END RECORD**}.

8. Double-click the left mouse button or press Enter.

   LetterPerfect inserts the {**END RECORD**} code followed by a hidden hard page code (see fig. 14.13). The prompt at the lower left corner of the screen again reads Parent.

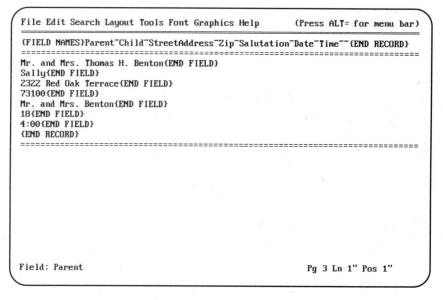

```
 File Edit Search Layout Tools Font Graphics Help      (Press ALT= for menu bar)
 ════════════════════════════════════════════════════════════════════════════
 {FIELD NAMES}Parent~Child~StreetAddress~Zip~Salutation~Date~Time~~{END RECORD}
 ════════════════════════════════════════════════════════════════════════════
 Mr. and Mrs. Thomas H. Benton{END FIELD}
 Sally{END FIELD}
 2322 Red Oak Terrace{END FIELD}
 73100{END FIELD}
 Mr. and Mrs. Benton{END FIELD}
 18{END FIELD}
 4:00{END FIELD}
 {END RECORD}
 ════════════════════════════════════════════════════════════════════════════




 Field: Parent                                     Pg 3 Ln 1" Pos 1"
```

Fig. 14.13. *The secondary file with a complete record entered.*

9. Repeat steps 2 through 8 for each record. Make sure that you start each record on a separate page.

10. Access the File pull-down menu and select **S**ave. Alternatively, press Save (F10). Choose a descriptive file name, such as PARENTS.SF.

Merging the Files

No matter how complex your primary and secondary files are, using Merge is simple. The following steps show you how to use Merge to create letters by using the primary and secondary files created in the previous sections:

1. Press Exit (F7) and N twice to clear the main editing screen.

2. Access the **Tools** pull-down menu and select **Merge**. Alternatively, press Merge (Ctrl-F9).

   At the bottom of the screen, LetterPerfect displays this prompt: `Primary file: (Press F5 to List Files)`.

3. Type *parents.pf* and press Enter.

   At the bottom of the screen, LetterPerfect displays this prompt: `Secondary file: (Press F5 to List Files)`.

> ***Tip:*** If you forget the name of a primary or secondary file, press List Files (F5) to locate the file name. When you locate the correct file, highlight it with the cursor bar and press **Retrieve (1)**. When you select the primary file name this way, LetterPerfect displays the `Secondary File:` prompt. When you select the secondary file name this way, LetterPerfect automatically performs the merge without further action. See Chapter 9 for information on using List Files.

4. Type *parents.sf* and press Enter.

   At the bottom of the screen, LetterPerfect displays the message `* Merging *`.

During the merge, the screen does not change. LetterPerfect combines the variable information in the secondary file with the universal text in the primary file, creating a separate letter ending with a hidden **[HPg]** code for each record in the secondary file and inserting the current date at the location of the **{DATE}** merge code. You can edit each letter just as you edit any other LetterPerfect document.

> ***Caution:*** A document created by a merge exists only in RAM. To preserve the document, you must save it just as you save any other LetterPerfect document.

Handling Special Situations

The simple merge techniques described in the preceding section are adequate for many situations requiring merges. But LetterPerfect has even more powerful merge capabilities. You can pick and choose from these capabilities for your particular merge needs. In this section, you learn to use some additional merge capabilities.

Creating a Secondary File from a DOS Delimited Text File

Virtually all database management programs can produce reports in a delimited format, in which records and fields are separated by defined characters. In structure, a DOS delimited text file equals a LetterPerfect secondary file; both have defined ways of separating records and separating fields.

Different database programs use different characters as delimiters. Although LetterPerfect accepts only the {**END FIELD**} and {**END RECORD**} codes as delimiters for Merge, Replace lets you quickly change the DOS delimiters into LetterPerfect merge codes.

Suppose, for example, that you have a DOS delimited text file that uses a comma and space as its field delimiter, and a line return—which LetterPerfect interprets as its hidden **[HRt]** code—as its record separator. After you retrieve this file to LetterPerfect's main editing screen, follow these steps to change its delimiters:

1. Access the **S**earch pull-down menu and select **R**eplace. Alternatively, press Replace (Alt-F2).

   At the bottom of the screen, LetterPerfect displays this prompt:
   `w/Confirm? No (Yes).`

2. Select **N**o to have LetterPerfect perform the replace operation without prompting for a confirmation of each replacement. Select **Y**es to have LetterPerfect prompt you for confirmation of each replacement.

   At the bottom of the screen, LetterPerfect displays the prompt
   `-> Srch:.`

3. Press Enter.

   LetterPerfect inserts **[HRt]** as the search string.

4. Press Search (F2) or Exit (F7).

   At the bottom of the screen, LetterPerfect displays the prompt `Replace with:`.

5. Access the **T**ools pull-down menu and select **M**erge Codes. Alternatively, press Merge Codes (Shift-F9).

   LetterPerfect displays the merge command code box with the cursor bar highlighting either {**DATE**} or the last merge code highlighted during the current editing session.

6. Using the cursor-movement keys or mouse, move the cursor bar to highlight {**END RECORD**}.

7. Double-click the left mouse button or press Enter.

   LetterPerfect inserts **[Mrg:END RECORD]** as the replacement string.

8. Press Ctrl-Enter.

   LetterPerfect adds the **[HPg]** code after the **[Mrg:END RECORD]** in the replacement string.

9. Press Search (F2) or Exit (F7).

   At the bottom of the screen, LetterPerfect displays this message prompt: `*Please Wait*`.

   During the replacement, LetterPerfect changes all **[HRt]** codes in the DOS delimited text file to **[Mrg:END RECORD][HPg]**.

10. Press the key combination Home, Home, Home, up arrow.

11. Repeat steps 1 and 2.

12. When you see the `-> Srch:` prompt, type a comma and press the space bar once.

    LetterPerfect inserts a comma and space (although the space is not visible) as the search string.

13. Press Search (F2) or Exit (F7).

    At the bottom of the screen, you see this prompt: Replace with:.

14. Press End Field (F9) and Enter.

    LetterPerfect inserts **[Mrg:END FIELD][HRt]** as the replacement string.

15. Press Search (F2) or Exit (F7).

    At the bottom of the screen, you see the message *Please Wait*.

    During the replacement, LetterPerfect changes all comma-and-space codes to **[Mrg:END FIELD][HRt]**.

16. Access the **File** pull-down menu and select **Save**. Alternatively, press Save (F10). Choose a descriptive file name and end it with the SF extension.

Caution: Some database programs produce DOS text files containing paired delimiter codes—such as "<field>"—that mark the beginning and ending of each field. If you have this kind of file, you should perform an additional replace operation—pressing Search (F2) without designating a replacement string—to remove the beginning delimiter code from each field.

Working Empty Fields

Frequently, a secondary file includes records with fields that do not contain information—blank fields. For example, a secondary file with records listing names, addresses, and telephone numbers may include records with fields organized like this:

{FIELD NAMES}Name~StreetAddress~AptNumber~City~State~Zip Code~Home Phone~Work Phone~Salutation~~{END RECORD}

In this type of record, the apartment number field or one of the fields for a telephone number may well be empty. For this example, assume that the primary file is in this format:

{FIELD}Name~
{FIELD}StreetAddress~
{FIELD}AptNumber~
{FIELD}City~, {FIELD}State~ {FIELD}Zip~

A merge operation using these primary and secondary files with no information in the *AptNumber* field creates a document like this:

Mr. John K. Jones
1122 Any Street

Oklahoma City, OK   73100

During the merge, LetterPerfect removes the **{FIELD}AptNumber~** code but not the hidden **[HRt]** formatting code following it. Because the *AptNumber* field does not contain information for LetterPerfect to combine into the final document, the program skips to the next merge code and performs the action required by it, leaving a blank line. To remove the blank line, you could edit the final document by deleting the hidden **[HRt]** between the street address and the line containing the city, state, and ZIP code.

Fortunately, LetterPerfect offers a simple method through which you can avoid this extra work: adding a ? at the end of a field name causes the program to remove automatically the hidden **[HRt]** following the tilde in the field name if the corresponding field in the secondary file does not contain any information.

Change the primary file by adding a ? to the end of *AptNumber* so that the merge code structure looks like this:

{FIELD}Name~
{FIELD}StreetAddress~
{FIELD}AptNumber?~
{FIELD}City~, {FIELD}State~ {FIELD}Zip~

If you use this primary file for a merge with a secondary file that has no information in the *AptNumber* field, you produce this document:

Mr. John K. Jones
1122 Any Street
Oklahoma City, OK   73100

> ***Caution:*** Do not use a ? with any field code placed on the same line with another field code. If you add a ?, and the field in the secondary file is blank, LetterPerfect removes its line in the final document—even if the field for the other field name contains information inserted into the document.

Adding Fields to a Secondary File

No matter how carefully you plan a merge, sometimes you need to add fields after you create the secondary file.

Before you enter any data, you can add a field anywhere within the field list by simply including the field name and a tilde. Assume, for example, that the existing field list looks like this:

{FIELD NAMES}Name~StreetAddress~City~State~ZipCode~~{END RECORD}

To add a Company field after the Name field, move the cursor to the *S* in Street Address and type *Company~* so that the field names record looks like this:

{FIELD NAMES}Name~Company~StreetAddress~City~State~ZipCode~~{END RECORD}

You must press Home, Home, up arrow before LetterPerfect recognizes the added field.

If you already entered information for records into the secondary file, you also should insert the field into *every* existing record. Merge can use field names in any order in the primary file. For this reason, the fields in the records of a secondary file do not need to be in any particular order, as long as every record in the secondary file has the same fields in the same order. In this situation, adding the field name so that it is the last field in the record makes it easy for you to avoid inserting a field at the wrong place in a record.

You do not need to delete an unwanted field from the records in a secondary file. Removing the field's merge code from the primary file prevents LetterPerfect from inserting the information into the final document.

This flexibility lets you create a variety of primary merge files that use the same secondary file for different purposes. For example, a secondary file containing records of business contacts can include biographical information such as birthday, home address, home telephone, and spouse's name, in addition to the usual name, business address, and business telephone number. With this type of secondary file, you can use one primary merge file that creates a client business telephone list and another primary merge file that creates a calendar listing clients' birthdays—both from the same secondary file.

Suppressing Unwanted Text and Codes

By default, LetterPerfect inserts a hard page break in the merged document after the program processes the data for each record in the secondary file. For many applications, such as creating a letter, this insertion is exactly what you want.

In some merge applications, however, you may want multiple records to appear on the same page in the finished document. Inserting the {**PAGE OFF**} merge code into the primary file prevents LetterPerfect from adding a hidden [**HPg**] code to the document after it processes each record in the secondary file.

For example, suppose that you use a merge file to produce a catalog for an office supply distributor (see fig. 14.14). Logically, each catalog item needs its own separate record, but you need more than one item to appear on a page. Place the {**PAGE OFF**} command at the end of each record in the primary file.

To suppress hard page breaks between records, retrieve PARENTS.PF, created earlier in the chapter, and follow these steps:

1. Position the cursor anywhere within the primary file.

2. Access the Tools pull-down menu and select Merge Codes. Alternatively, press Merge Codes (Shift-F9).

   LetterPerfect displays the merge command code box with the cursor bar highlighting either {**DATE**} or the last merge code highlighted during the current editing session.

Magnifique-8 Laser Printer

8 page-per-minute laser printer. Create complete publications, presentation-quality graphics materials, much more on this state-of-the art laser printer. Two paper trays for ease of use. Advanced solid-state electronics. Price includes 1 MB memory, standard letter-size and legal-size paper trays, one toner cartridge.

Price Schedule:

1	2-5	6+
1,800.00	1,760.00	1,715.00

Magnifique-12 Laser Printer

12 page-per-minute laser printer. This printer has features similar to the Magnifique-8, but is for the truly high-volume operation. Can handle 11x17 sheets with optional 11x17 paper tray, *sold below*. This rugged, modern unit will handle the toughest jobs in any office. Price includes 2 MB memory, standard letter-size and legal-size paper trays, one toner cartridge.

Price Schedule:

1	2-5	6+
2,800.00	2,650.00	2,515.00

Letter-Sized Paper Tray

Standard letter-sized paper tray for the Magnifique-8 or Magnifique-12 printers. Capacity 225 sheets. Made of high-impact polystyrene.

Price Schedule:

1	2-6	7-12	12-20	21+
18.00	17.40	17.05	16.90	16.75

Legal-Sized Paper Tray

Legal-sized paper tray for the Magnifique-8 or Magnifique-12 printers. Capacity 225 sheets. Made of high-impact polystyrene.

Price Schedule:

1	2-6	7-12	12-20	21+
21.00	20.40	20.10	19.95	19.90

Fig. 14.14. *A sample catalog page.*

3. Using the cursor-movement keys or mouse, move the cursor bar to highlight {**PAGE OFF**}.

4. Double-click the right mouse button or press Enter.

   LetterPerfect inserts the {**PAGE OFF**} code into the document at the cursor (see fig. 14.15).

5. Access the **File** pull-down menu and select **Save**. Alternatively, press Save (F10). Save the primary file.

```
File Edit Search Layout Tools Font Graphics Help     (Press ALT= for menu bar)

{PAGE OFF}                 JOAN SMITH
                         Will Rogers School
                        1234 West Any Street
                       Oklahoma City, OK  73100
                          [405] 555-1212


{DATE}



{FIELD}Parent~
{FIELD}StreetAddress~
Oklahoma City, OK  {FIELD}Zip~

Dear {FIELD}Salutation~:

In case the name above is not familiar to you yet, let me introduce myself.
I'm Joan Smith, a first-grade teacher at Will Rogers Elementary School, and
I have the pleasure of having your child, {FIELD}Child~, in my class this year.

I like to get together with the parents of each of my first-graders early in the
                                               Pg 1 Ln 1" Pos 1"
```

Fig. 14.15. *The {PAGE OFF} code for suppressing hard page breaks between records.*

> **Tip:** To restore document separation during merges, either delete the **{PAGE OFF}** code and resave the primary file or use the procedure just described to add a **{PAGE ON}** code to a field in a record in the secondary file.
>
> You also can insert the **{PAGE OFF}** code into any field in the secondary file. When the merge processes the record containing the **{PAGE OFF}** code, the information in all records from that point is placed on a single page until the merge is complete, the program processes a record with a field containing a **{PAGE ON}** code, or the text fills the page and inserts a **{SPg}** code.

Merging Directly to the Printer

If you have a complex document or many records in the secondary file, the document created by the merge can be quite large. A file in LetterPerfect is limited only by the available amount of RAM, disk space, or both. However, even if the disk is large enough to store the document, there is usually no point in saving hundreds of form letters as a disk file.

For these reasons, you can insert the {**PRINT**} merge code that sends the document created by the merge directly to the printer as soon as the program processes a record. After LetterPerfect sends the document to the printer, the program clears the document from RAM before processing the next record.

You will find these limitations to this method:

- LetterPerfect does not save the document for later use.
- You cannot edit the document before you print it.
- Merges to the printer usually take longer than regular merges.

Merging to the printer requires inserting {**PAGE OFF**} and {**PRINT**} codes somewhere in the primary document. If you do not include the {**PAGE OFF**} code, the printer inserts a blank sheet between each document.

Follow these steps to send each document to the printer as soon as LetterPerfect creates the document:

1. Move the cursor to the bottom of the primary file.

2. Access the Tools pull-down menu and select Merge Codes. Alternatively, press Merge Codes (Shift-F9).

   LetterPerfect displays the merge command code box with the cursor bar highlighting either {**DATE**} or the last merge code highlighted during the current editing session.

3. Using the cursor-movement keys or mouse, move the cursor bar to highlight {**PAGE OFF**}.

4. Double-click the left mouse button or press Enter.

   LetterPerfect inserts the {**PAGE OFF**} code into the document at the cursor.

5. Repeat steps 2 through 4 to insert the {**PRINT**} code.

6. Access the File pull-down menu and select Save. Alternatively, press Save (F10). Save the primary file.

   The {**PAGE OFF**}{**PRINT**} code combination appears in the primary file, as shown in figure 14.16.

```
File Edit Search Layout Tools Font Graphics Help      (Press ALT= for menu bar)


Dear {FIELD}Salutation~:

In case the name above is not familiar to you yet, let me introduce myself.
I'm Joan Smith, a first-grade teacher at Will Rogers Elementary School, and
I have the pleasure of having your child, {FIELD}Child~, in my class this year.

I like to get together with the parents of each of my first-graders early in the
school year to talk about their child's progress.  This also gives us an
opportunity to get to know each other, and it gives you a chance to ask any
questions you may have about how {FIELD}Child~ is doing.

I've tentatively scheduled a meeting on October {FIELD}Date~, 1990, at {FIELD}Ti
this schedule is not convenient for you, please feel free to call me or drop
me a note.  I can schedule conferences any day after school.

I'm looking forward to meeting you!

Sincerely,


Joan Smith{PAGE OFF}{PRINT}
                                              Pg 1 Ln 8.76" Pos 1.94"
```

Fig. 14.16. *The primary document, showing the* **{PAGE OFF}{PRINT}** *code for merging documents directly to the printer.*

Including Keyboard Input in a Merge

In addition to combining information from a secondary file, Merge combines information entered from the keyboard during the merge. The combination of information from two files is called a *secondary merge*; pausing so that the user can insert information during the merge is part of a *keyboard merge*. A single merge operation can include a secondary merge and a keyboard merge.

Placing the {**INPUT**} merge code into the primary file causes LetterPerfect to pause a merge operation for keyboard input. When LetterPerfect processes the {**INPUT**} code for each copy of the merged document, the program pauses and displays on the main editing screen the document as it looks at that point. In addition, LetterPerfect displays on the status line a prompt message that you previously created. During the pause, you can enter an unlimited amount of information until you press End Pause (F9)—also known as End Field—which ends the pause and resumes the merge.

Creating primary files with keyboard merge codes lets you use Merge to produce frequently used documents quickly and with formatting and structural uniformity. These kinds of documents include memos, checks, invoices, letters, and envelopes.

The letter shown in figure 14.17 illustrates this type of merge primary file. Figure 14.18 shows all the formatting codes for the primary file. For information on inserting the nonmerge codes used in this primary file, refer to Chapters 3 and 4.

{DATE}

{INPUT}ENTER NAME~
{INPUT}ENTER STREET/POST OFFICE ADDRESS~
{INPUT}ENTER CITY AND STATE~ {INPUT}ENTER ZIP CODE~

{INPUT}Enter ATTN: Name, Word Right, Press Enter~
Re: {INPUT}ENTER PARTY NAMES~
       {INPUT}ENTER COUNTY & CASE NUMBER~
       Reference No. {INPUT}ENTER CASE REFERENCE NUMBER~

Dear {INPUT}ENTER SALUTATION~:

{INPUT}TYPE LETTER~

Sincerely,

ROBERT M. BECK
Attorney at Law

RMB:jmd

Enclosure{INPUT}ENTER PLURAL IF NECESSARY~: {INPUT}ENTER ENCLOSURES~

pc: {INPUT}ENTER PERSONS RECEIVING COPIES~

Fig. 14.17. *A primary file for a letter, showing {**INPUT**} codes for a keyboard merge.*

```
[Paper Sz/Typ:8.5" x 11",Bin #1][T/B Mar:1",1"][L/R Mar:1",1"][Ln Spacing:1][Tab Set:Abs: 1.3",1.9"]
[Pg Numbering:No page numbering][Suppress:Header][Font:Dutch Roman 11pt (HP Roman 8) (FW,Port)]
[Center][Mrg:DATE][HRt]
[HRt]
[HRt]
[Mrg:INPUT]ENTER NAME~[HRt]
[Mrg:INPUT]ENTER STREET/POST OFFICE ADDRESS~[HRt]
[Mrg:INPUT]ENTER CITY AND STATE~  [Mrg:INPUT]ENTER ZIP CODE~[Paper Sz/Typ:8.5" x 11",Bin #2][HRt]
[HRt]
[BOLD][Mrg:INPUT]Enter ATTN: Name, Word Right, Press Enter~[bold][HRt]
[HRt]
Re:[Tab][Mrg:INPUT]ENTER PARTY NAMES~[HRt]
[Tab][Mrg:INPUT]ENTER COUNTY & CASE NUMBER~[HRt]
[Tab][UND]Reference No. [Mrg:INPUT]ENTER CASE REFERENCE NUMBER~[und][HRt]
[HRt]
[HRt]
[HRt]
Dear [Mrg:INPUT]ENTER SALUTATION~:[HRt]
[HRt]
[Mrg:INPUT]TYPE LETTER~[HRt]
[HRt]
Sincerely,[HRt]
[HRt]
[HRt]
[HRt]
[BOLD]ROBERT M. BECK[HRt]
Attorney at Law[bold][HRt]
[HRt]
RMB:jmd[HRt]
[HRt]
Enclosure[Mrg:INPUT]ENTER PLURAL IF NECESSARY~:[Tab][Mrg:INPUT]ENTER ENCLOSURES~
[HRt]
pc:[Tab][Mrg:INPUT]ENTER PERSONS RECEIVING COPIES~
```

Fig. 14.18. *The letter template's formatting codes.*

> **Tip:** If the primary file contains only {**INPUT**} merge codes, and if you start Merge and LetterPerfect displays the Secondary file: prompt, do *not* type a file name in response; just press Enter.

Besides uniformity and the faster production of documents, using a keyboard merge primary file offers two other important advantages. First, with minimal instruction a new employee can produce documents in the proper company format by selecting the appropriate primary file for the merge. Second, documents with a uniform format (including margins, tab settings, line spacing, headers on second pages, the date line, address location, salutations, signature lines, enclosures) make it possible to create macros that automatically edit the correspondence and create the envelope for it.

Retrieve the PARENTS.PF primary file created earlier in this chapter and follow these steps to replace a field name code with an {**INPUT**} merge code:

1. Move the cursor to the {**FIELD**}**Date~** code on the first line in the third paragraph.

2. Delete the {**FIELD**}**Date~** code.

3. Access the **Tools** pull-down menu and select **M**erge Codes. Alternatively, press Merge Codes (Shift-F9).

   LetterPerfect displays the merge command code box with the cursor bar highlighting either {**DATE**} or the last merge code highlighted during the current editing session.

4. Using the cursor-movement keys or mouse, move the cursor bar to highlight {**INPUT**}**message~**.

5. Double-click the left mouse button or press Enter.

   At the lower left corner of the screen, LetterPerfect displays the prompt Enter Message:.

6. Type *Type the conference date, press F9* and press Enter.

LetterPerfect inserts the {**INPUT**} merge code and Type the conference date, press F9, followed by a tilde, as shown in figure 14.19.

```
File Edit Search Layout Tools Font Graphics Help      (Press ALT= for menu bar)

Dear {FIELD}Salutation~:

In case the name above is not familiar to you yet, let me introduce myself.
I'm Joan Smith, a first-grade teacher at Will Rogers Elementary School, and
I have the pleasure of having your child, {FIELD}Child~, in my class this year.

I like to get together with the parents of each of my first-graders early in the
school year to talk about their child's progress.  This also gives us an
opportunity to get to know each other, and it gives you a chance to ask any
questions you may have about how {FIELD}Child~ is doing.

I've tentatively scheduled a meeting on October {INPUT}Type the conference date,
Press F9~, 1990, at {FIELD}Time~.  If this schedule is not convenient for you,
please feel free to call me or drop me a note.  I can schedule conferences
any day after school.

I'm looking forward to meeting you!

Sincerely,


Joan Smith{PAGE OFF}{PRINT}
                                              Pg 1 Ln 6.99" Pos 1.88"
```

Fig. 14.19. The letter primary file with the {INPUT} code and message.

7. Access the **File** pull-down menu and select **S**ave. Alternatively, press Save (F10). Save the primary file.

When LetterPerfect uses this primary file and its related secondary file, Merge combines the information in the secondary file until the {**INPUT**} code is processed. At that point, these things happen:

- The document created by the merge operation up to the {**INPUT**} merge code is displayed.

- The prompt `Type the conference date, press F9` is displayed in the lower left corner of the screen.

- The merge operation pauses, and you can enter an unlimited amount of information from the keyboard.

- The merge resumes when you press End Field (F9).

> *Caution:* If a primary file contains merge codes for both types of merges—secondary and keyboard—and you do not designate a secondary file at the beginning of the merge process, Merge leaves empty the fields for secondary file data but pauses at the keyboard input codes so that you can enter data.

Terminating Keyboard Merge Operations

There are many reasons—missing information, telephone calls, appointments, emergencies—why you may be interrupted before completing a keyboard merge session. The Merge feature lets you save data merged to the point of interruption and resume the merge process at your convenience.

Follow these steps to halt the merge process so that you can resume it later:

1. Enter all the data into the current field, but do *not* press the End Pause (F9) key.

2. Access the **T**ools pull-down menu and select **M**erge Codes. Alternatively, press Merge Codes (Shift-F9). LetterPerfect displays this menu:

   1 Quit; **2** Next Record; **3** Stop: **0**

> ***Tip:*** After accessing the Merge feature's termination menu, if you change your mind and want to continue with the current merge operation, press Cancel (F1), Esc, or Exit (F7). The termination menu disappears, and the Merge feature resumes operation at the place where you activated Merge Codes.

3. Select the **Q**uit (**1**) option. LetterPerfect adds the unprocessed portion of the primary file to the document on-screen and terminates the merge process.

4. Save the document with a unique name.

5. When you are ready to resume the merge process, start the Merge feature and enter the unique name selected in step 4 for the primary file name. LetterPerfect resumes the merge process at the merge prompt immediately following the point where you terminated the original merge operation.

If you want to halt the merge process without saving the document, use just step 2 and choose the **S**top (**3**) option. LetterPerfect immediately terminates the merge process, leaving the partial merge document on-screen for whatever action you want to perform on it.

Preparing Special Primary Documents for Merges

The following sections show you how to use LetterPerfect's Merge with two special types of primary files: fill-in forms and mailing labels.

Using Fill-In Forms

Suppose that you have a form like the one shown in figure 14.20, and you want to use the printer to fill in the blanks. You can use Merge to speed up the process. Again, the merge process requires some preparation, but once you set up the procedure, it is easy to use.

Student Grade Report

Name: Grade Level:

Student Number: Class Standing:

Subject: Teacher:

Semester Average:

Final Exam:

Total Grade:

Fig. 14.20. A sample preprinted form.

First, you must determine the spatial location for each merge code to be entered in the primary file so that the correct information is placed at the proper location on the preprinted form. The best approach is to take a copy of the form and, starting from the upper left corner, measure the exact distance to the beginning of each entry to be made on the form. Mark the coordinates of each entry right on the form, as shown in figure 14.21. Also measure and mark the top, bottom, left, and right margins. If you have a constant distance height between lines on the form, measure the line height and note it on the form.

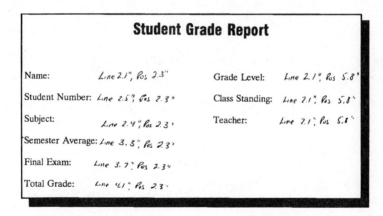

Fig. 14.21. The preprinted form marked with field locations.

> *Tip:* If information for a blank on the preprinted form remains the same for every record, enter the universal text instead of a merge code at the appropriate location on the primary file. For example, on the preprinted *Student Grade Report* form, the blanks for *Grade Level*, *Subject*, and *Teacher* are probably the same for every record.

After you mark all the locations on the form but before you create the primary file, be sure that you have a paper definition with the appropriate size, location, and other characteristics. (See Chapter 7 for more information on defining paper sizes.)

Select the appropriate paper size by following these steps:

1. Access the **L**ayout pull-down menu and select **F**ormat. Alternatively, press Format (Shift-F8) and select **P**aper Size (**8**).

   LetterPerfect displays the Format: Paper Size/Type menu, similar to that shown in figure 14.22 (the actual form definitions listed depend on the printer you are using).

```
Format: Paper Size/Type

Paper type and Orientation    Paper Size      Location    Font Type    Labels

Bin #1                        8.5" x 11"      Bin 1       Portrait
Bin #1 - Wide                 11" x 8.5"      Bin 1       Landscape
Bin #2                        8.5" x 11"      Bin 2       Portrait
Bin #2 - Wide                 11" x 8.5"      Bin 2       Landscape
Envelope - Wide               9.5" x 4"       Bin 3       Landscape
Legal                         8.5" x 14"      Bin 2       Portrait
Legal - Wide                  14" x 8.5"      Bin 2       Landscape
[ALL OTHERS]                  Width ≤ 8.5"    Manual








1 Select; 2 Edit; N Name Search: 1
```

Fig. 14.22. The Format: Paper Size/Type menu.

2. Move the cursor bar to highlight the correct paper size; choose **Select (1)**.

3. Press Exit (F7) until the program returns to the main editing screen.

Now you are ready to create the primary file. Follow these steps:

1. Check the top, bottom, left, and right default margin settings for the form. Make sure that the margins are no larger than those you measured and noted on the form. Refer to Chapter 6 for information on setting margins.

2. If the form has a constant line spacing, you can save a few operations by setting LetterPerfect's line height to that of the form. To set the line spacing, refer to the instructions in Chapter 6.

3. Move the cursor to the first field on the top line of the form. Use the **Line Spacing (2)** option on the Format menu to adjust the vertical placement of the merge code. Use the **Tabs (5)** option on the Format menu to adjust the horizontal placement of the merge code.

4. Enter the appropriate merge code. To merge from a secondary file, enter a **{FIELD}** code. To enter information from the keyboard during the merge, enter an **{INPUT}** code and a message. Refer to "Creating a Primary File" earlier in this chapter for instructions on entering **{FIELD}** codes. Refer to "Including Keyboard Input in a Merge" earlier in this chapter for instructions on **{INPUT}** codes and messages.

Tip: To insert the current date automatically, insert the **{DATE}** merge code. For instructions, refer to "Creating the Primary File" earlier in this chapter.

5. If additional fields are on the first line of the form, use the **Tabs (5)** option on the Format menu to adjust the horizontal placement of the next merge code. Insert the appropriate merge code at each position.

6. When you finish defining fields on the first line of the form, press Enter.

7. Repeat steps 3 through 7 until you finish all fields on the form. The form should look like the one shown in figure 14.23.

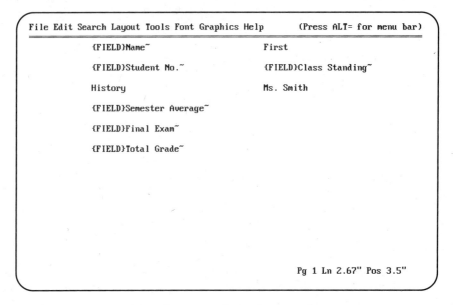

Fig. 14.23. *A primary file with merge codes and universal text.*

You are now ready to perform the merge. Refer to the section "Merging the Files" for information on activating Merge.

Using Mailing Labels

Mailing labels are one of the classic applications of merge capabilities. LetterPerfect makes creating a label with Merge quick and easy.

Selecting and Using a Label Definition

As explained in Chapter 8, LetterPerfect's printer definitions include pre-defined form definitions whose dimensions cannot be changed. Usually the predefined forms include definitions for the most common label formats and sizes. The list of these forms shows the paper size and number of labels, and the orientation of labels on the paper.

Follow these steps to display the list of available forms:

1. Press Exit (F7) and N twice to clear the main editing screen.

2. Access the Layout pull-down menu and select Format. Alternatively, press Format (Shift-F8).

   LetterPerfect displays the Format menu.

3. Select Paper Size (**8**).

   LetterPerfect displays the Format: Paper Size/Type menu (see fig. 14.24).

```
Format: Paper Size/Type

Paper type and Orientation    Paper Size      Location    Font Type    Labels

Bin #1                        8.5" x 11"      Bin 1       Portrait
Bin #1 - Wide                 11" x 8.5"      Bin 1       Landscape
Bin #2                        8.5" x 11"      Bin 2       Portrait
Bin #2 - Wide                 11" x 8.5"      Bin 2       Landscape
Disk Label                    8.5" x 11"      Bin 2       Portrait     2 x 3
Envelope - Wide               9.5" x 4"       Bin 3       Landscape
File Label                    8.5" x 11"      Bin 2       Portrait     2 x 10
Legal                         8.5" x 14"      Bin 2       Portrait
Legal - Wide                  14" x 8.5"      Bin 2       Landscape
[ALL OTHERS]                  Width ≤ 8.5"    Manual




1 Select; 2 Edit; N Name Search: 1
```

Fig. 14.24. The Format: Paper Size/Type menu.

4. Move the cursor bar to highlight the correct form.

Tip: Although you cannot edit the dimensions of the form, you can change the location and orientation of the form. See Chapter 8 for full information about editing these settings.

5. Select the form and press Exit (F7) to return to the main editing screen.

After you select the form of the label by using the method described in the preceding section, you are ready to enter the {**FIELD**} commands (and other merge commands as well) to create the primary and secondary files. For information on creating primary and secondary files and on using Merge, review the earlier sections in this chapter.

Dealing with Idiosyncrasies of Labels

LetterPerfect creates each label as a *logical page*. If, for example, the paper size/ type definition specifies 3 columns of labels and 10 rows, LetterPerfect interprets the definition as 30 logical pages. All these logical pages are printed on the same sheet of paper, or—put another way—on a single *physical page*. This concept can be useful, but it also creates a few limitations. Some label properties you should know about are discussed in this section.

Label Display and Page Size

If the form defines the labels as being 1 inch high and 2.63 inches wide, LetterPerfect sees a page of those exact dimensions. If you try to type more text than can fit on a page of that size, LetterPerfect inserts a soft page break.

Each label is a logical page and appears on the main editing screen as an individual page separated from other pages by a hidden soft page code, [**SPg**]. To see the labels as LetterPerfect prints them, access the File pull-down menu, select **Print**, and select View Document (**3**). Alternatively, press Print (Shift-F7) and select View Document (**3**); or use the Ctrl-p fast-key combination.

Headers, Footers, and Page Numbers

If you define a header for every page, it appears on every *logical* page. If you define such a header for a 3-by-10 sheet of labels, you get 30 headers, one on each label. The same is true for footers or page numbers. If you want to number each *page* of labels, no straightforward method of numbering is available.

Printing Individual Pages

Because LetterPerfect sees each label as a logical page, giving LetterPerfect a command to print a single page causes LetterPerfect to do just that—print a single *logical* page (in other words, one label). This result is *not* evident when you use the Print View feature, which shows a complete page of printed labels. The only reliable method for printing less than the entire sheet of labels is to block the labels you want to print and then print the block. Refer to Chapter 5 for more information about printing blocks.

Using Advanced Merge Commands To Control the Merge Process

You can use several merge command codes to alter the flow of the merge. You can enter some of these codes during a pause in a keyboard merge.

{NEXT RECORD}

This code causes the merge to begin immediately processing the next record in the secondary file. You can insert this code from the keyboard during a pause in the merge. The syntax is: {**NEXT RECORD**}.

{NEST PRIMARY}

This code causes the merge to begin with a different primary file. After Merge completes the steps required by the other primary file, Merge returns to the original primary file and resumes combining with that file. A single merge works with up to 10 nested primary files. The syntax is: {**NEST PRIMARY**}*filename~*.

The argument *filename* is the name of the primary file to which control is to be transferred. If the file is not in the current directory, you must include a path name.

{QUIT}

This code ends the merge after the remainder of the structure and universal language of the primary file is added to the document, but the code does not execute the remaining merge command codes. You can insert this code from the keyboard during a pause in the merge. The syntax is: {QUIT}.

{STOP}

This code is similar to the {QUIT} code except that {STOP} immediately terminates the merge without adding the remainder of the text and merge codes in the primary file. You can insert this code from the keyboard during a pause in the merge. The syntax is: {STOP}.

Summary

In this chapter, you learned to do these tasks with LetterPerfect's Merge feature:

- Create simple merges that produce standard documents
- Create merges that combine information from secondary files and keyboard input
- Create and use merges that produce mailing labels

Chapter 15 shows you how to enhance the appearance of your documents with graphic images.

15

Integrating Text and Graphics

Many things distinguish an outstanding document from an ordinary one. Subject matter, the author's writing abilities, and the visual appearance of the document are three of the most important. Although LetterPerfect 1.0 cannot affect the subject matter or the quality of the writing, its Graphics feature gives you a powerful tool for improving the appearance of any document.

LetterPerfect works directly with graphic images only in WordPerfect's WPG format. The LetterPerfect software package includes a special program, however, that converts into WPG format 13 formats created by more than 60 popular graphics and spreadsheet programs.

One major difference between a dedicated desktop publishing program and a word processing program is the appearance of the document on the computer screen. In a desktop publishing program like PageMaker, what you see on-screen closely resembles what you see on the printed page. When you edit with LetterPerfect, graphics on-screen represent—but don't look like—what you see when you print the document. Figure 15.1 shows text as it appears on LetterPerfect's main editing screen. Figure 15.2 shows the same text and full graphic image displayed with the View Document feature.

File Edit Search Layout Tools Font Graphics Help   (Press ALT= for menu bar)

This is a sample of a document with the ARROW-22.WPG
graphics image in a figure box. This image is one of 30
that is included with the   ┌FIG 1─────────────
LetterPerfect program.
When viewed with the
Reveal Codes feature, each
figure box resembles one of
LetterPerfect's regular
formatting codes, listing the
box's sequence number
and the name of its original
file:

   [Fig Box:1;ARROW-22.WPG]

With one exception, a graphics-image box's vertical
location begins at the line on which the code is located.
However, if the bottom of the box extends past the page's
bottom margin, LetterPerfect automatically places the box
on the first line of the following page. The next section
shows you how LetterPerfect can wrap text around a
graphics-image box.

   Pg 1 Ln 6.66" Pos 3.29"

Fig. 15.1. A graphic figure as it appears on the main editing screen.

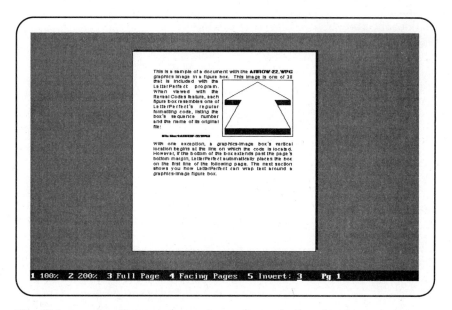

Fig. 15.2. A page with text and a graphic image as displayed with View Document.

In this chapter, you learn to use these techniques to enhance your document:

- Import graphic images as figure boxes

- Select the size and horizontal position for each figure box

- Wrap text around the figure box

- Include and exclude borders around the figure box

Reminder: WordPerfect Corporation updated LetterPerfect 1.0 just before this book went to press. Dated 11/01/90, the interim release includes new options for existing features, and a few new features. The menus on your screen may, therefore, differ slightly from those shown in this book. Also, depending on the printer-form definition, margins, tab stops, and font you specify, the text placement and status-line information in documents you create may differ from that shown in this book's figures.

For information about using the mouse and accessing the pull-down menus, refer to the Introduction.

Instructions in this chapter are based on the assumption that LetterPerfect's graphic image files are installed with the program. If these files are not installed and you want to perform the instructions in this chapter, refer to Chapter 1 for instructions on installing LetterPerfect's graphic images files.

Assessing Hardware Limitations

LetterPerfect offers many advanced formatting and graphics capabilities. With LetterPerfect, you can create different font sizes, lines, and graphic images. Not every computer is equipped, however, to match the power of LetterPerfect. The system's hardware—specifically the video card, monitor, and printer—may limit the use of advanced formatting and graphics.

When the system has a graphics card (such as a CGA, EGA, or VGA card; a Hercules Graphics Card; a Hercules Graphics Card Plus; or a Hercules InColor card), graphic images appear correctly when they are displayed by View Document. A system that does not have a graphics card cannot display graphic images or the lines, boxes, or shades in imported graphics.

If the printer does not support proportional fonts (like Times and Helvetica) or enhanced fonts (bold, italic, and reduced or enlarged text), LetterPerfect cannot print these fonts. If the printer does not have the capability to print graphics, the document does not print correctly.

Importing an Image into a Graphics Box

LetterPerfect Graphics imports graphic images into a figure box that it places into the document at the cursor. After the graphics-image box is in the document, LetterPerfect treats the box like any other character or formatting code. The box is not anchored to a specific location within the document; it "floats" with text and formatting codes—that is, it moves and can be deleted like other characters or codes.

With Graphics you can insert a graphics-image box as you write the document, or you can add the box during a later editing session. Although you cannot use Graphics to alter the appearance of the image, you can adjust the horizontal placement and size of the box and remove lines that define the borders of the box.

Note: The instructions in this chapter show you how to create and edit a graphics-image box by selecting the options on the Graphics Definition menu in numerical sequence. With Graphics, though, you can create and edit a graphics-image box with any sequence of menu options.

Each section is self-contained and can be read independently of the other sections. If, however, you want to perform the instructional steps in each section, you may find it easier to read the sections in forward sequence and save the document as a file until you complete all the instructions.

Tip: LetterPerfect offers another, simpler method than the one described in the following sections for importing a graphic image into a document—direct retrieval of the graphic image. From the main editing screen, use either Retrieve or the List Files retrieve function to retrieve into the document the file containing the graphic image. LetterPerfect automatically creates a graphics-image box around the graphic image and inserts the box at the cursor. You can edit graphics-image boxes created with this method just as you edit boxes created with the method described in the section "Designating a Graphics-Image File."

See Chapter 4 for instructions on using Retrieve. See Chapter 9 for instructions on using the List Files retrieve function.

Designating a Graphics-Image File

Inserting a graphics-image box into the document begins when you activate Graphics and select the graphic image to appear in it. Follow these steps to activate Graphics and designate a graphic image:

1. Move the cursor to the left margin.

2. Access the **G**raphics pull-down menu (see fig. 15.3). Alternatively, press Graphics (Alt-F9).

   At the lower left corner of the screen, LetterPerfect displays the menu:

   Graphics: 1 Create; **2 E**dit: **0.**

3. Select **C**reate (**1**) from either menu. LetterPerfect displays the Graphics Definition menu shown in figure 15.4.

Tip: Pressing the Ctrl-g fast-key combination automatically performs steps 1 and 2, saving you several keystrokes.

4. Choose Filename (**1**).

   At the bottom of the screen, LetterPerfect displays this prompt:

   ```
   Enter filename:  (Press F5 to List Files)
   ```

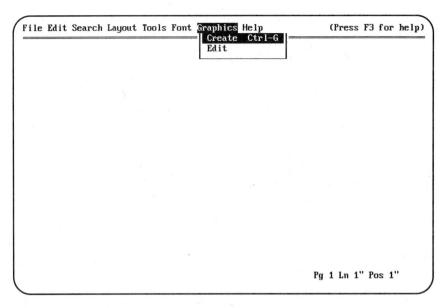

Fig. 15.3. The Graphics pull-down menu.

```
Graphics Definition

     1 - Filename

     2 - Horizontal Position  Right

     3 - Size                 3.25" wide x 3.25" (high)

     4 - Wrap Text Around Box Yes

     5 - Border               Yes

        Note: Each time you specify a border option,
              a figure option code ([Fig Opt]) is inserted
              in your document.  This code affects all
              subsequent figures until LetterPerfect
              encounters another figure option code.




















Selection: 0
```

Fig. 15.4. The Graphics Definition menu.

LetterPerfect waits until you enter a file name for the graphic image. You can enter the file name without a path if you run LetterPerfect on a system that has one of these specifications:

- *A single floppy disk drive.* The file must always be on LetterPerfect 2 disk in either the program subdirectory (the one containing LP.FIL) or the default subdirectory (the one in which the program currently stores document files).

- *Dual floppy disk drives.* The file can be on a disk in either drive in the program subdirectory (the one containing LP.FIL) or the default subdirectory (the one in which document files are stored currently).

- *A hard disk drive.* The file can be in either the program subdirectory (the one containing LP.FIL) or the default subdirectory (the one in which the program currently stores document files).

If the file is in any other subdirectory, you must enter the full path name, as in *C:\lp10\graphics\arrow-22.wpg.*

> *Tip:* When you cannot remember either the name of the graphic file or the subdirectory containing the name, you can use List Files (F5) to search for the file. (See Chapter 9 for information on using List Files.) After you locate the file, move the cursor bar to highlight its name; then select **Retrieve** (**1**). LetterPerfect inserts that file name into the Graphics Definition menu.

5. For the purposes of this chapter, type *arrow-22.wpg* and press Enter.

LetterPerfect inserts ARROW-22.WPG as the file name option. Press Cancel (F1) or Esc to return to the main editing screen without inserting a graphics-image box. If you press any other key, LetterPerfect inserts an empty graphics-image box (see fig. 15.5) into the document and returns to the main editing screen.

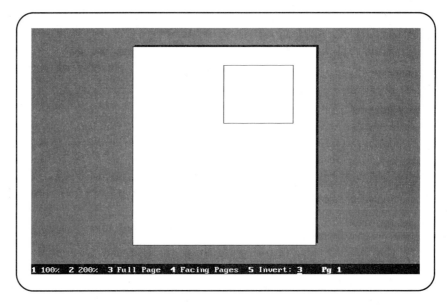

1 100% 2 200% 3 Full Page 4 Facing Pages 5 Invert: 3 Pg 1

Fig. 15.5. *The default box for a figure.*

The vertical location of a graphics-image box on a page begins at the line on which the code is located, with one exception. If the bottom of the box extends past the bottom margin, LetterPerfect automatically places the box so that it begins on the first line of the following page.

The next section shows you how to adjust the horizontal placement of the graphics-image box.

Adjusting the Horizontal Placement of the Graphics-Image Box

The Graphics feature includes four options for placing a graphics-image box horizontally. You can designate the placement of a box when you import the graphic image or at a later time.

If you read this section immediately after following the steps in the last section, skip steps 1 through 4 in the following instructions and start with step 5. To change the horizontal placement of an existing figure, begin with step 1 in these instructions:

1. Move the cursor to the left margin.

2. Access the **G**raphics pull-down menu, shown in figure 15.3. Alternatively, press Graphics (Alt-F9). At the lower left corner of the screen, LetterPerfect displays the menu:

   Graphics: 1 Create; **2** Edit: **0**.

3. Select **E**dit (**2**) from either menu.

   At the bottom of the screen, you see the prompt `Figure number? n`, where *n* is the sequence number of the first figure after the cursor.

   For example, if the document contains three graphics-image boxes, and the cursor is located between the second and third boxes, the number 3 appears in the prompt. When all the graphics-image boxes are above the cursor, the number displayed in the prompt is the number in the sequence, but no box has that number. If you press Enter to accept the default number, LetterPerfect flashes a `*Not Found*` prompt and returns to the main editing screen.

4. Press Enter to edit the default box. To edit a different graphics-image box, type the number of the box and press Enter.

   LetterPerfect displays the Graphics Definition menu shown in figure 15.4.

5. Select **H**orizontal Position (**2**).

   At the bottom of the screen, LetterPerfect displays the menu:

   Horizontal Position: 1 Left; **2** Right; **3** Center; **4** Full: **0**.

   The **L**eft (**1**) and **R**ight (**2**) options, respectively, place the box at the left and right margins of the document (see figs. 15.6 and 15.7). The **C**enter (**3**) option places the graphics-image box an equal distance from the left and right margins (see fig. 15.8). The **F**ull (**4**) option automatically overrides the height and width setting of the graphics-image box (see the next section) and expands the box so that its sides touch the left and right margins (see fig. 15.9). The default horizontal placement setting is the right margin.

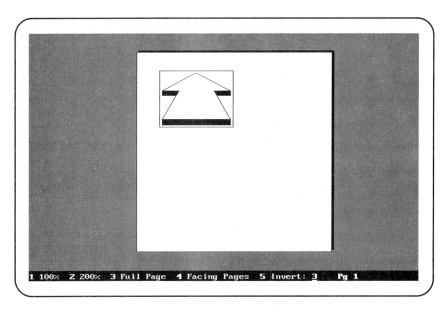

Fig. 15.6. A graphics-image box with left horizontal placement.

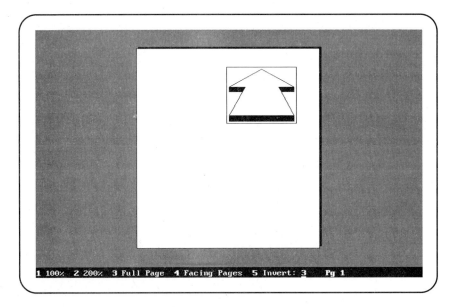

Fig. 15.7. A graphics-image box with right horizontal placement.

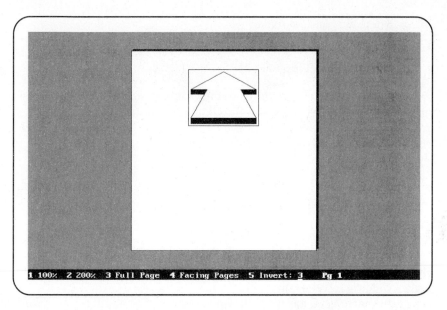

Fig. 15.8. A graphics-image box with center horizontal placement.

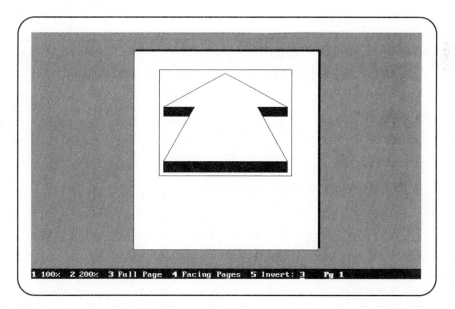

Fig. 15.9. An expanded graphics-image box with full horizontal placement.

6. Select the placement type.

   For the purposes of this chapter, select Left (**1**). LetterPerfect changes the description to Left.

Depending on the size of the graphics-image box, LetterPerfect can wrap text around boxes that have left, right, and center horizontal placement. The next section shows you how to adjust the size of a graphics-image box. See the section "Wrapping Text around a Graphic Image" later in this chapter.

Adjusting the Size of a Graphics-Image Box

By default, Graphics automatically creates a graphics-image box that is 3 1/4 inches wide (one-half the available space between the 1-inch margins on an 8 1/2-by-11-inch sheet) and adjusts the height to display the full graphic image. With Graphics you can adjust the height and width of a graphics-image box. You can adjust the size of the box when you import the image into it or at a later time.

If you read this section immediately after following the steps in the last section, "Designating a Graphics-Image File," skip steps 1 through 4 in the following instructions and start with step 5.

To change the size of an existing figure, begin with step 1 in these instructions:

1. Move the cursor to the left margin.

2. Access the Graphics pull-down menu, shown in figure 15.3. Alternatively, press Graphics (Alt-F9). You see this menu at the lower left corner of the screen:

   Graphics: 1 Create; **2 E**dit:

3. Select Edit (**2**) from either menu.

   At the bottom of the screen, you see the prompt Figure number? n, where *n* is the sequence number of first figure after the cursor.

   For example, if the document contains three graphics-image boxes, and the cursor is located between the second and third ones, the number 3 appears in the prompt. When all the boxes are above the cursor, the number displayed is the number in the sequence, but no box appears with the number. If you press Enter to accept the default number, LetterPerfect flashes a

`*Not Found*` prompt and returns the program to the main editing screen.

4. Press Enter to edit the default box. To edit a different graphics-image box, type the number of the box and press Enter.

LetterPerfect displays the Graphics Definition menu, shown in figure 15.4.

5. Select Size (3).

You see this menu at the bottom of the screen:

1 Set **W**idth/Auto Height; **2** Set **H**eight/Auto Width; **3** Set **B**oth; **4** Auto Both: **0**

From this menu you can set the box width (see step 6); then LetterPerfect calculates the height, according to the size of the graphic or the amount of text the box contains.

Suppose, for example, that you want the box to be 3 inches wide. Because you are not sure how much height the box requires to display the image when it is inserted in a 3-inch box, let LetterPerfect calculate the height. You also can set the box height and let LetterPerfect calculate the width. Or you can set both the width and height.

6. Do one of the following:

- Select **W**idth/Auto Height (**1**) to specify the width of the box. LetterPerfect calculates the height according to the contents of the box.

- Select **H**eight/Auto Width (**2**) to specify the height of the box. LetterPerfect calculates the width according to the contents of the box.

- Select Set **B**oth (**3**) to specify both the width and height.

- Select Auto Both (**4**) to instruct LetterPerfect to calculate both the height and width. Auto Both (**4**) is the default. Selecting this option after you use one other option to change the size of the box does *not* restore the original size of the box.

7. If you chose any of the first three options in step 6, type the width, height, or both (depending on your choice) and press Enter.

Caution: The Horizontal Placement (**2**) option includes a selection—**Full** (**4**)—that automatically expands the graphics-image box to occupy all the space between the left and right margins; the selection also adjusts the height of the box. See the section "Adjusting the Horizontal Placement of the Graphics-Image Box" immediately before this section.

Wrapping Text around a Graphics-Image Box

If there is space between the left and right margins and the borders of a graphics-image box, LetterPerfect by default automatically wraps text around three sides of the box. If the box has center or right horizontal placement, the text wraps around its top, left, and bottom edges, as shown in figures 15.10 and 15.11.

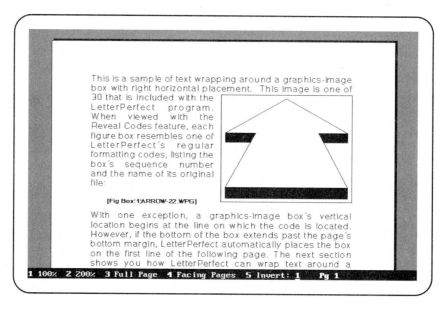

Fig. 15.10. *Text wrapped around a graphics-image box with right horizontal placement.*

If the box has left horizontal placement, the text wraps around its top, right, and bottom edges, as shown in figure 15.12.

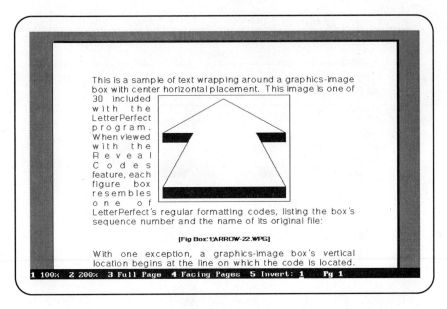

Fig. 15.11. Text wrapped around a graphics-image box with center horizontal placement.

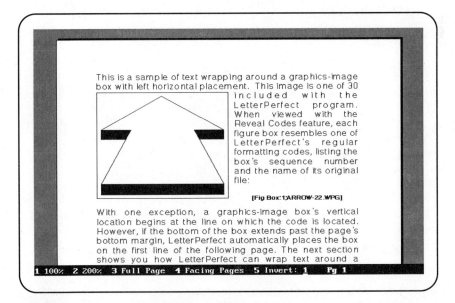

Fig. 15.12. Text wrapped around a graphics-image box with left horizontal placement.

If the box has full horizontal placement, the box splits the text so that the document appears as shown in figure 15.13.

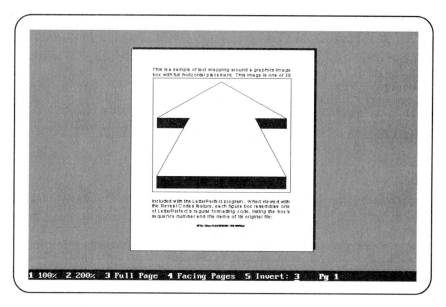

Fig. 15.13. Text above and below a graphics-image box with full horizontal placement.

Caution: To wrap text around a graphics-image box properly, you must put the code for the box at the left margin of the document, as shown in figure 15.14. If the code is improperly placed away from the left margin (see fig. 15.15), the line of text overwrites the graphic image, as shown in figure 15.16.

Use the **W**rap Text Around Box (**4**) option on the Graphics Definition menu to deactivate automatic text-wrapping. If you change the option's setting to **N**o, the text overwrites the graphic image, as shown in figure 15.17.

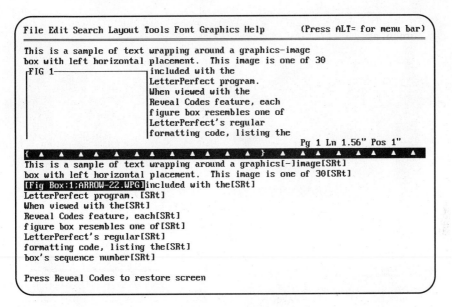

Fig. 15.14. *A graphics-image box code, properly placed at the left margin.*

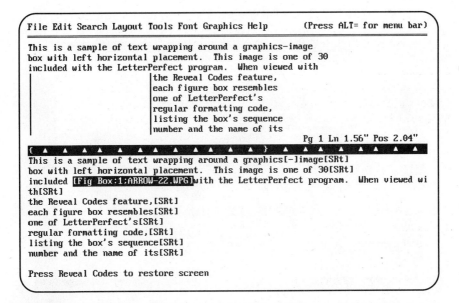

Fig. 15.15. *A graphics-image box code, improperly placed away from the left margin.*

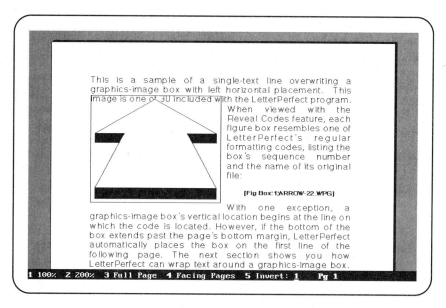

Fig. 15.16. Text overwriting a graphics-image box because of improperly placed codes.

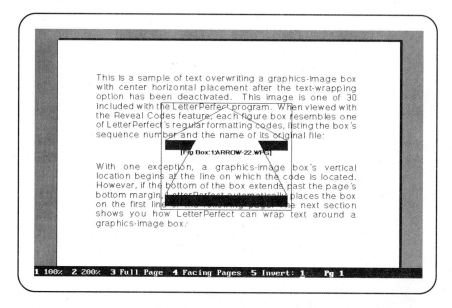

15.17. Text overwriting a graphics-image box after automatic text-wrap has been deactivated.

Tip: When you create two graphics-image boxes adjacent to each other, LetterPerfect prints the images side by side if they have the same or adjacent horizontal placement settings. If, however, you set the wrap-text parameter for the first box to No and give the two adjacent images the same horizontal placement setting, one image is superimposed on top of the other, as shown in figure 15.18. If you set the wrap-text parameter for the first box to No and give the two adjacent images adjacent horizontal placement settings, LetterPerfect overlaps the first image with the second image.

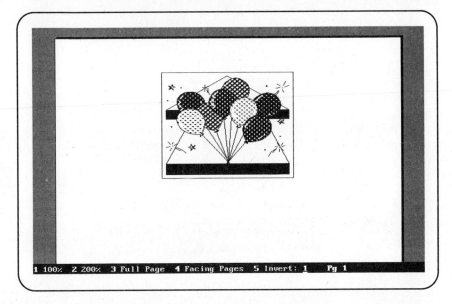

Fig. 15.18. A balloon graphic image superimposed over an arrow graphic image.

Removing Lines at the Borders of a Graphics-Image Box

By default, Graphics automatically creates a graphics-image box with lines defining its edges. You can remove these border lines (and re-create them if you change your mind later).

If you read this section immediately after following the steps in the section, "Designating a Graphics-Image File," skip steps 1 through 3 in the following instructions and begin with step 4.

To change the size of an existing figure, begin with step 1 in these instructions:

1. Access the **Graphics** pull-down menu, shown in figure 15.3. Alternatively, press Graphics (Alt-F9). You see this menu at the lower left corner of the screen:

   Graphics: 1 Create; **2** Edit: **0**

2. Select **Edit (2)** from either menu.

   At the bottom of the screen, you see the prompt Figure number? n, where *n* is the sequence number of the first figure after the cursor.

   For example, if the document contains three graphics-image boxes, and the cursor is located between the second and third boxes, the number 3 appears in the prompt. When all boxes are above the cursor, the number displayed is the number in the sequence, but no box has the number. If you press Enter to accept the default number, LetterPerfect flashes a *Not Found* prompt and returns to the main editing screen.

3. Press Enter to edit the default box. To edit a different box, type the number of the box and press Enter.

   LetterPerfect displays the Graphics Definition menu, shown in figure 15.4.

4. Select **Border (5)**.

   You see a Yes (No) prompt. If the box does not have lines at its border, the prompt appears as No (Yes).

5. Select **No** to remove the lines at the border that mark the edges of the graphic box.

   The hidden code **[Fig Opt:WP,Border Off]** is inserted immediately right of the box. Figure 15.19 shows the box without lines at its borders.

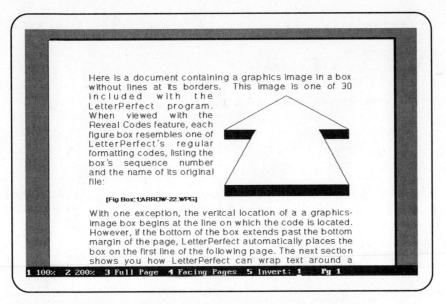

Fig. 15.19. A graphics-image box without lines at its borders.

> *Caution:* Unlike other options on the Graphics Definition menu, the border option controls *all* graphics-image boxes that follow it. To restore border lines to subsequent boxes, use the procedure just described but select **Yes** in step 5.

Returning to the Editing Screen

When you finish creating or editing the graphics-image box, press Exit (F7) to return to the main editing screen. If you are initially creating a graphics-image box and want to return to the main editing screen without inserting the box, press Cancel (F1) or Esc. If you are editing an existing box and decide to abandon your changes and return to the main editing screen, press Cancel (F1) or Esc.

Converting Graphics Files to WPG Format

LetterPerfect imports and prints graphic images only in WPG format. The WordPerfect programs—WordPerfect 5.1, PlanPerfect 5.1, and DrawPerfect 1.1—that create graphic images all do so in WPG format. Graphic images in other formats must be converted to WPG format before they can be imported into a document.

The GRAPHCNV.EXE program included with LetterPerfect automatically converts image files in other graphic formats to WordPerfect graphic format. Follow these steps to convert a graphic image file into WPG format:

1. At the DOS prompt, change to the subdirectory containing the GRAPHCNV.EXE program by typing *cd \<pathname>*.

2. Type *graphcnv* and press Enter.

3. Tell the program where to find the file that requires conversion by typing its name as follows:

   <drive letter>:\<pathname>\<filename.extension>.

   LetterPerfect suggests a default name for the WPG file it will create.

4. Press Enter to accept the default. You also can type a new name (including the path name) for the file and press Enter. This name must end with the WPG extension.

   After LetterPerfect creates the new WPG file, it displays ->ok.

5. Press any key to quit GRAPHCNV and return to DOS.

This section provides only a short overview of the GRAPHCNV program. For a more detailed explanation of the program and its options, read Appendix F in the LetterPerfect reference manual.

Using Line Draw

With Line Draw you can draw a line or box just by moving the cursor. Line Draw is quick and easy.

Lines and boxes drawn with Line Draw are actually composed of ASCII characters and are part of the text. You cannot type over them or around them without disturbing them. Be sure to experiment with line drawing before you use this tool to plan a document.

Caution: If you use proportionally spaced type, lines and boxes drawn with Line Draw don't print correctly. For example, if you use a laser printer with fonts like Times or Helvetica or any of the Bitstream fonts, you must switch to a nonproportional font, such as Courier, to make the Line Draw characters line up correctly. If you do laser-printed desktop publishing, do not use Line Draw.

To draw a line or box, follow these steps:

1. Access the **Tools** pull-down menu and select **Line Draw**. Alternatively, press Line Draw (Ctrl-F3).

   At the bottom of the screen, LetterPerfect displays this menu:

   1 |; **2** ‖; **3** *; **4 Change; 5 Erase; 6 Move: 1**

2. Select **1** for a single line, **2** for a double line, or **3** to define the line.

3. Use the cursor keys to draw the line or box. Although the mouse can move its pointer around the screen, it cannot move the cursor when Line Draw is active.

4. Press Cancel (F1), Esc, or Exit (F7) to deactivate Line Draw and return to the main editing screen.

Changing the Line Style

You can change the style of the line to something other than single, double, or asterisk lines by selecting Change (4) from the Line Draw menu.

To change the line style, follow these steps:

1. Select Change (4) from the Line Draw menu. The following menu appears:

    1 ▮; 2 ▮; 3 ▮; 4 ▮; 5 ▪; 6 ▮; 7 ▮; 8 ▪; 9 Other: 0

2. Select any of the eight line styles shown, or select **9** and type the character you want for the lines. After you make a selection, you automatically return to the main editing screen Line Draw menu. The new line character replaces the asterisk as selection 3.

3. Use the cursor keys to draw the line.

4. Press Cancel (F1), Esc, or Exit (F7) to deactivate Line Draw and return to the main editing screen.

Erasing the Line

You can erase the line drawn with Line Draw in the same way you drew it. Just follow these steps:

1. Choose Erase (5) from the Line Draw menu.

2. Use the cursor keys to trace over the line you want to erase.

    To start drawing again after you erase a line, select one of the line-drawing tools (1, 2, or 3).

3. Press Cancel (F1), Esc, or Exit (F7) to deactivate Line Draw and return to the main editing screen.

Moving the Cursor without Erasing or Drawing

To move the cursor without drawing, select **Move (6)** from the Line Draw menu. Use the cursor keys to move the cursor to a different location. Select **1**, **2**, or **3** to choose a character and resume drawing a line. Select **5** to resume erasing a line.

Summary

LetterPerfect has powerful graphics capabilities. In this chapter, you learned to do these tasks:

- Integrate text with graphic images in boxes

- Edit the size and appearance of the graphics-image box

- Use the GRAPHCNV.EXE program to convert image files in other formats into the WPG format accepted by LetterPerfect

- Use Line Draw

In addition, you learned that although LetterPerfect has powerful graphics capabilities, the visual display of the document depends on the capabilities of the system's monitor and video display card; the appearance of the printed page depends on the system's printer.

Appendix

LetterPerfect for WordPerfect 4.2-5.1 Users

The LetterPerfect File Format

LetterPerfect 1.0 creates files in the same format as WordPerfect 5.1 and also directly imports files formatted by WordPerfect 4.2, WordPerfect 5.0, WordPerfect 5.1, and DOS (ASCII).

With LetterPerfect 1.0, you can retrieve and edit files created in WordPerfect 5.1. When LetterPerfect retrieves a WordPerfect 5.1 document, it automatically encloses in right and left braces ({ }) all WordPerfect 5.1 formatting codes for features not available in LetterPerfect—for example, {**Ftn Opt**} for footnote options. Although these codes are meaningless when you use LetterPerfect, if you do not delete these codes while using LetterPerfect, the functions represented by these codes are restored when the document is retrieved into WordPerfect 5.1.

In LetterPerfect, you also can retrieve and edit WordPerfect 5.0 documents. When you save the document, however, it is automatically converted into LetterPerfect 1.0 format. WordPerfect 5.0 can retrieve a document that is in LetterPerfect format, but the program automatically converts formatting codes for unrecognized LetterPerfect features into an **[Unknown]** code.

Although you cannot change fonts, LetterPerfect does let you directly retrieve and edit WordPerfect 4.2 documents. To convert font-changing codes in a WordPerfect 4.2 document, you must use the Convert program and a CRS file. See Appendix C in the LetterPerfect reference manual. With WordPerfect 4.2, you cannot retrieve or edit documents saved in LetterPerfect 1.0 format.

Differences between WordPerfect 5.1 and LetterPerfect 1.0

LetterPerfect's user interface is similar to that of WordPerfect 5.1. Some WordPerfect 5.1 features are not available in LetterPerfect, arc available in a limited form in LetterPerfect, or function differently in LetterPerfect. The following subsections describe differences in these features.

Cancel

In LetterPerfect 1.0, both F1 and Esc act as the Cancel feature unless you assign the Help feature to the F1 key, using the Setup feature described in Chapter 1.

Cartridges and Fonts

LetterPerfect printer drivers do *not* include soft-font information, as do printer drivers in WordPerfect 5.1. To use a printer driver that has soft-font information, you must copy a WordPerfect 5.1 PRS file to the directory containing the LetterPerfect program files. When you use a WordPerfect 5.1 PRS file with LetterPerfect, you are limited to the forms defined in that file; you can't use those found in the {LP}SPC.FRM file.

Characters

LetterPerfect's Characters feature lets you create codes for more than 2,000 characters. LetterPerfect may not be able to print those characters in a document or display them with View Document, however, because the LetterPerfect driver resource file (either LP.DRS or LPSMALL.DRS) is not as extensive as the WP.DRS files available with WordPerfect 5.1 (1,700-plus characters) and DrawPerfect 1.1 (2,000-plus characters).

If you own either WordPerfect 5.1 or DrawPerfect 1.1, and your system has enough disk space, LetterPerfect can use the WP.DRS font file from those programs to print or display all the characters the program creates. The procedure for using either of these WP.DRS files depends on the date of your LetterPerfect software.

With the 07/24/90 software, copy the WP.DRS font file to the disk and directory containing the LetterPerfect printer files. Beginning with the 11/01/90 software, copy the WP.DRS file to the location set for the program's printer files with the Setup feature. See Chapter 1 for information on using the Setup feature.

When you have LetterPerfect using a WP.DRS font file, you can delete the LetterPerfect-specific font file—either LP.DRS or LPSMALL.DRS—from the disk. If the program finds more than one DRS font file in the proper directory, LetterPerfect uses the first DRS file it finds in the following sequence: WP.DRS, WPSMALL.DRS, LP.DRS, LPSMALL.DRS.

Beginning with the release of the 11/01/90 software, WordPerfect Corporation began offering a separate set of supplementary disks for LetterPerfect. The DrawPerfect 1.1 WP.DRS font file is one of the files included on the supplementary disks.

Date

The format used by LetterPerfect's Date feature is set by the WP.LRS file. If however, the date format stored in a WordPerfect 5.1 date code is different from the LetterPerfect default format, LetterPerfect uses the WordPerfect 5.1 format for that code only.

Footnotes and Endnotes

LetterPerfect automatically converts all footnotes in WordPerfect 5.1 to endnotes that are numbered and edited like any other endnote. Converted footnote codes appear as **[Endnote/WP Footnote]** when you display a document with Reveal Codes. Enter an endnote code in the search string to find a converted WordPerfect 5.1 footnote code. After you save the document, retrieve it with WordPerfect 5.1 to automatically restore footnotes to their original forms.

Function Keys

LetterPerfect features that are similar or identical to those in WordPerfect 5.1 are assigned to the same function keys as the features in WordPerfect 5.1. The function keys assigned to a WordPerfect feature not supported by LetterPerfect are inoperative in LetterPerfect, except for Alt-F8, which activates Letter-Perfect's Language feature instead of the unsupported WordPerfect Style feature. Some LetterPerfect features (for example, Move, Copy, and Paste Block) perform differently when you activate them from the function keys than when you use pull-down menus.

Graphics

LetterPerfect imports graphics images into paragraph-like figure boxes. LetterPerfect ignores the codes in WordPerfect documents for graphics images containing text, equations, graphics on disk, and all other types of graphics boxes (for example, text boxes, table boxes).

The Figure Box Options (**[Fig Opt]**) code may contain both supported and unsupported options. LetterPerfect converts unsupported options to a code that includes *WP*. For example, a graphics-image code containing Caption Number Style (an unsupported feature) and Borders On (a supported feature) appears as **[Fig Opt:WP, Borders On]**.

LetterPerfect prints and displays graphic images only in WPG format. GRAPHCNV.EXE—LetterPerfect's Graphics Conversion Program—does, however, convert images in other graphic formats to WPG format. For more information on GRAPHCNV.EXE, read Appendix F in the LetterPerfect reference manual.

Hyphenation

The WP{WP}US.LEX file included in the LetterPerfect software package does not contain hyphenation indicators. The Hyphenation feature works automatically only if the program finds WP{WP}US.HYC—a special hyphenation file—in the same location as the Spell feature's WP{WP}US.LEX file. For more information on the WP{WP}US.LEX file, see the section "Speller Dictionaries" later in this appendix.

With the 07/24/90 software, WP{WP}US.HYC must be in the subdirectory and drive where WP{WP}US.LEX and LP.FIL are located. If you own WordPerfect 5.1, you can copy its WP{WP}US.LEX and WP{WP}US.HYC files to this location.

Beginning with the 11/01/90 software, an option under the Setup feature lets you set the location for the program's Spell, hyphenation, and thesaurus files. (See Chapter 1 for information on using the Setup feature.) Among other things, this Setup option lets you tell LetterPerfect to use WordPerfect 5.1 language files without copying them to the main LetterPerfect subdirectory or disk. In addition, if disk space is tight and you have this version of LetterPerfect using the WordPerfect language files, you can delete the LetterPerfect Spell and thesaurus files.

If you do not own WordPerfect 5.1, you can purchase special WordPerfect Language Modules that include the WP{WP}US.HYC file in addition to expanded Spell and thesaurus files.

When the WP{WP}US.LEX and WP{WP}US.HYC files are present, the only way to deactivate Hyphenation is to delete or rename these files.

Justification

LetterPerfect's default justification setting is left justification—and WordPerfect 5.1 defaults to full justification. If you retrieve a LetterPerfect document into WordPerfect 5.1, LetterPerfect automatically inserts a **[Just:Left]** code in Initial Codes to retain the justification setting. You can delete the code from Setup Initial Codes in LetterPerfect or from Document Initial Codes in WordPerfect to remove the setting.

Language

LetterPerfect's WP.LRS file contains records for only 19 languages instead of the 27 languages contained in the WP.LRS file shipped with WordPerfect 5.1.

Merge

LetterPerfect's Merge feature can use WordPerfect 4.2, 5.0, and 5.1 primary and secondary files. However, if any of these files contain a WordPerfect merge code not supported by LetterPerfect, the merge aborts and LetterPerfect displays an error message.

Paper Size/Type

LetterPerfect can use WordPerfect 5.1 printer driver files.

LetterPerfect requires the {LP}SPC.FRM file, however, which WordPerfect 5.1 does not use. The {LP}SPC.FRM file contains many form definitions for different paper sizes and label forms. LetterPerfect adds these forms to the PRS files created during the printer selection process.

If you do not use LetterPerfect to select the printer from the ALL file (if, for example, LetterPerfect is using a WordPerfect 5.1 PRS file), form definitions are not added from the FRM (forms) file. In this situation, LetterPerfect's Paper Size /Type menu displays only the standard forms for the printer selection plus forms defined by WordPerfect 5.1.

Beginning with the release of the 11/01/90 software, WordPerfect Corporation is offering a separate set of supplementary disks for LetterPerfect. An expanded {LP}SPC.FRM file—containing a larger number of paper size/type forms—is one of the files included on the supplementary disks.

The supplementary-disk set also includes the Printer Program, which among other things lets you edit LetterPerfect's printer driver files to add and delete paper size/type forms.

Paragraph Numbers

You must use LetterPerfect's Outline feature to create paragraph numbers. LetterPerfect ignores Paragraph Number Definitions in WordPerfect 5.1 documents.

Retrieve

Retrieving a DOS (ASCII) text file with LetterPerfect automatically converts the document into the LetterPerfect format.

Speller Dictionaries

LetterPerfect's Spell feature requires a WP{WP}US.LEX file in order to operate. The LEX file in the LetterPerfect software package is a subset of (contains fewer words than) the LEX file included in the WordPerfect 5.1 software package. If you own WordPerfect 5.1 and your system has enough disk space, you can copy the WordPerfect 5.1 WP{WP}US.LEX file to the drive and/or subdirectory containing the LetterPerfect program files. LetterPerfect also can use any WP{WP}US.SUP file you create with WordPerfect 5.1.

Style

LetterPerfect does not support WordPerfect 5.1's Style feature. If, however, you retrieve a WordPerfect 5.1 document containing a style code that includes formatting codes supported by LetterPerfect (for example, Bold, Underline, Italics, Superscript, or Subscript), LetterPerfect uses these codes to format the document.

LetterPerfect encloses Style codes from WordPerfect 5.1 in left ({) and right (}) braces. When you use LetterPerfect's Reveal Codes, highlight a style code with the cursor and LetterPerfect expands the code to show its formatting codes, enclosing formatting codes supported by LetterPerfect in left ([) and right (]) brackets.

If you delete a style code, LetterPerfect's Undelete feature does not restore the unsupported codes inside the style code.

Suppress Page Format

LetterPerfect suppresses only headers and footers. If a WordPerfect 5.1 document contains a suppression code other than for headers or footers (for example, for page numbers), LetterPerfect displays the code in left ({) and right (}) braces. If the code includes instructions for suppressing a header or footer, LetterPerfect displays it in left ([) and right (]) brackets, replacing any unsupported suppression codes with the letters WP.

Tab Align

By default, LetterPerfect's Tab Align feature uses a period as the alignment character. When LetterPerfect retrieves a WordPerfect 5.1 document, the program ignores alignment codes such as **[Dccml/Algn Char]**. You can change LetterPerfect's alignment character only by editing the WP.LRS file.

Tables

LetterPerfect does not support WordPerfect 5.1's Table feature. When LetterPerfect retrieves a WordPerfect 5.1 document containing a table, LetterPerfect encloses formatting codes for the table in left ({) and right (}) braces. The text of the table is not formatted into rows and cells. Instead, each cell begins a new line. When you are using LetterPerfect's Reveal Codes feature and the cursor highlights a table cell code, the code displays the cell address. In LetterPerfect, you can edit and delete the text and formatting codes of a table.

Thesaurus

LetterPerfect's Thesaurus requires a WP{WP}US.THS file in order to operate. The THS file in the LetterPerfect software package is a subset of the THS file in the WordPerfect 5.1 software package. If you own WordPerfect 5.1 and your system has enough disk space, you can copy the WordPerfect 5.1 WP{WP}US.THS file to the drive and/or subdirectory containing the LetterPerfect program files.

Widow/Orphan

By default, LetterPerfect's Widow/Orphan feature is permanently active. When LetterPerfect retrieves a WordPerfect 5.1 document with a Widow/Orphan off code, the program encloses the formatting codes in left ({) and right (}) braces (**{W/O Off}**), signifying that LetterPerfect ignores the code.

Although LetterPerfect automatically places a **{W/O On}** code in Initial Codes—which retains the Widow/Orphan formatting when LetterPerfect documents are retrieved by WordPerfect 5.1—deleting the code does *not* deactivate the Widow/Orphan feature.

Index

595

D

G

T

Computer Books From Que Mean PC Performance!

Spreadsheets

1-2-3 Database Techniques	$29.95
1-2-3 Graphics Techniques	$24.95
1-2-3 Macro Library, 3rd Edition	$39.95
1-2-3 Release 2.2 Business Applications	$39.95
1-2-3 Release 2.2 PC Tutor	$39.95
1-2-3 Release 2.2 QueCards	$19.95
1-2-3 Release 2.2 Quick Reference	$ 8.95
1-2-3 Release 2.2 QuickStart, 2nd Edition	$19.95
1-2-3 Release 2.2 Workbook and Disk	$29.95
1-2-3 Release 3 Business Applications	$39.95
1-2-3 Release 3 Workbook and Disk	$29.95
1-2-3 Release 3.1 Quick Reference	$ 8.95
1-2-3 Release 3.1 QuickStart, 2nd Edition	$19.95
1-2-3 Tips, Tricks, and Traps, 3rd Edition	$24.95
Excel Business Applications: IBM Version	$39.95
Excel Quick Reference	$ 8.95
Excel QuickStart	$19.95
Excel Tips, Tricks, and Traps	$22.95
Using 1-2-3/G	$29.95
Using 1-2-3, Special Edition	$27.95
Using 1-2-3 Release 2.2, Special Edition	$27.95
Using 1-2-3 Release 3.1, 2nd Edition	$29.95
Using Excel: IBM Version	$29.95
Using Lotus Spreadsheet for DeskMate	$22.95
Using Quattro Pro	$24.95
Using SuperCalc5, 2nd Edition	$29.95

Databases

dBASE III Plus Handbook, 2nd Edition	$24.95
dBASE III Plus Tips, Tricks, and Traps	$24.95
dBASE III Plus Workbook and Disk	$29.95
dBASE IV Applications Library, 2nd Edition	$39.95
dBASE IV Programming Techniques	$24.95
dBASE IV Quick Reference	$ 8.95
dBASE IV QuickStart	$19.95
dBASE IV Tips, Tricks,and Traps, 2nd Edition.	$24.95
dBASE IV Workbook and Disk	$29.95
Using Clipper	$24.95
Using DataEase	$24.95
Using dBASE IV	$27.95
Using Paradox 3	$24.95
Using R:BASE	$29.95
Using Reflex, 2nd Edition	$24.95
Using SQL	$29.95

Business Applications

Allways Quick Reference	$ 8.95
Introduction to Business Software	$14.95
Introduction to Personal Computers	$19.95
Lotus Add-in Toolkit Guide	$29.95
Norton Utilities Quick Reference	$ 8.95
PC Tools Quick Reference, 2nd Edition	$ 8.95
Q&A Quick Reference	$ 8.95
Que's Computer User's Dictionary	$ 9.95
Que's Wizard Book	$ 9.95
Quicken Quick Reference	$ 8.95
SmartWare Tips, Tricks, and Traps 2nd Edition	$24.95
Using Computers in Business	$22.95
Using DacEasy, 2nd Edition	$24.95
Using Enable/OA	$29.95
Using Harvard Project Manager	$24.95
Using Managing Your Money, 2nd Edition	$19.95

Using Microsoft Works: IBM Version	$22.95
Using Norton Utilities	$24.95
Using PC Tools Deluxe	$24.95
Using Peachtree	$27.95
Using PFS: First Choice	$22.95
Using PROCOMM PLUS	$19.95
Using Q&A, 2nd Edition	$23.95
Using Quicken: IBM Version, 2nd Edition	$19.95
Using Smart	$22.95
Using SmartWare II	$29.95
Using Symphony, Special Edition	$29.95
Using Time Line	$24.95
Using TimeSlips	$24.95

CAD

AutoCAD Quick Reference	$ 8.95
AutoCAD Sourcebook 1991	$27.95
Using AutoCAD, 3rd Edition	$29.95
Using Generic CADD	$24.95

Word Processing

Microsoft Word 5 Quick Reference	$ 8.95
Using DisplayWrite 4, 2nd Edition	$24.95
Using LetterPerfect	$22.95
Using Microsoft Word 5.5: IBM Version, 2nd Edition	$24.95
Using MultiMate	$24.95
Using Professional Write	$22.95
Using Word for Windows	$24.95
Using WordPerfect 5	$27.95
Using WordPerfect 5.1, Special Edition	$27.95
Using WordStar, 3rd Edition	$27.95
WordPerfect PC Tutor	$39.95
WordPerfect Power Pack	$39.95
WordPerfect Quick Reference	$ 8.95
WordPerfect QuickStart	$19.95
WordPerfect 5 Workbook and Disk	$29.95
WordPerfect 5.1 Quick Reference	$ 8.95
WordPerfect 5.1 QuickStart	$19.95
WordPerfect 5.1 Tips, Tricks, and Traps	$24.95
WordPerfect 5.1 Workbook and Disk	$29.95

Hardware/Systems

DOS Tips, Tricks, and Traps	$24.95
DOS Workbook and Disk, 2nd Edition	$29.95
Fastback Quick Reference	$ 8.95
Hard Disk Quick Reference	$ 8.95
MS-DOS PC Tutor	$39.95
MS-DOS Power Pack	$39.95
MS-DOS Quick Reference	$ 8.95
MS-DOS QuickStart, 2nd Edition	$19.95
MS-DOS User's Guide, Special Edition	$29.95
Networking Personal Computers, 3rd Edition	$24.95
The Printer Bible	$29.95
Que's PC Buyer's Guide	$12.95
Understanding UNIX: A Conceptual Guide, 2nd Edition	$21.95
Upgrading and Repairing PCs	$29.95
Using DOS	$22.95
Using Microsoft Windows 3, 2nd Edition	$24.95
Using Novell NetWare	$29.95
Using OS/2	$29.95
Using PC DOS, 3rd Edition	$24.95
Using Prodigy	$19.95

Using UNIX	$29.95
Using Your Hard Disk	$29.95
Windows 3 Quick Reference	$ 8.95

Desktop Publishing/Graphics

CorelDRAW Quick Reference	$ 8.95
Harvard Graphics Quick Reference	$ 8.95
Using Animator	$24.95
Using DrawPerfect	$24.95
Using Harvard Graphics, 2nd Edition	$24.95
Using Freelance Plus	$24.95
Using PageMaker: IBM Version, 2nd Edition	$24.95
Using PFS: First Publisher, 2nd Edition	$24.95
Using Ventura Publisher, 2nd Edition	$24.95

Macintosh/Apple II

AppleWorks QuickStart	$19.95
The Big Mac Book, 2nd Edition	$29.95
Excel QuickStart	$19.95
The Little Mac Book	$ 9.95
Que's Macintosh Multimedia Handbook	$24.95
Using AppleWorks, 3rd Edition	$24.95
Using Excel: Macintosh Version	$24.95
Using FileMaker	$24.95
Using MacDraw	$24.95
Using MacroMind Director	$29.95
Using MacWrite	$24.95
Using Microsoft Word 4: Macintosh Version	$24.95
Using Microsoft Works: Macintosh Version, 2nd Edition	$24.95
Using PageMaker: Macinsoth Version, 2nd Edition	$24.95

Programming/Technical

Assembly Language Quick Reference	$ 8.95
C Programmer' sToolkit	$39.95
C Quick Reference	$ 8.95
DOS and BIOS Functions Quick Reference	$ 8.95
DOS Programmer's Reference, 2nd Edition	$29.95
Network Programming in C	$49.95
Oracle Programmer's Guide	$29.95
QuickBASIC Advanced Techniques	$24.95
Quick C Programmer's Guide	$29.95
Turbo Pascal Advanced Techniques	$24.95
Turbo Pascal Quick Reference	$ 8.95
UNIX Programmer's Quick Reference	$ 8.95
UNIX Programmer's Reference	$29.95
UNIX Shell Commands Quick Reference	$ 8.95
Using Assembly Language, 2nd Edition	$29.95
Using BASIC	$24.95
Using C	$29.95
Using QuickBASIC 4	$24.95
Using Turbo Pascal	$29.95

For More Information, Call Toll Free!

1-800-428-5331

All prices and titles subject to change without notice. Non-U.S. prices may be higher. Printed in the U.S.A.

Word Processing Is Easy
When You're Using Que!

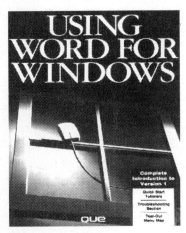

Using Word for Windows

Ron Person & Karen Rose

Complete coverage of program basics and advanced desktop publishing hints. Includes Quick Start lessons and a tear-out Menu Map.

Version 1.0

Order #886	$24.95 USA

0-88022-399-5, 500 pp., 7 3/8 x 9 1/4

Using LetterPerfect

Robert Beck

A comprehensive guide to this all-new condensed version of WordPerfect! Includes reference for error messages and formatting codes.

Version 1

Order #1277	$22.95 USA

0-88022-667-6, 500 pp., 7 3/8 x 9 1/4

Using Professional Write

Katherine Murray

Quick Start tutorials introduce word processing basics and help readers progress to advanced skills. Packed with easy-to-follow examples!

Through Version 2.1

Order #1027	$22.95 USA

0-88022-490-8, 343 pp., 7 3/8 x 9 1/4

More WordPerfect Titles From Que

Microsoft Word 5 Quick Reference

Que Development Group

Version 5.5

Order #976	$8.95 USA

0-88022-444-4, 160 pp., 4 3/4 x 8

Using Microsoft Word 5.5: IBM Version, 2nd Edition

Bryan Pfaffenberger

Through Version 5.5

Order #1252	$24.95 USA

0-88022-642-0, 500 pp., 7 3/8 x 9 1/4

Using DisplayWrite 4, 2nd Edition

David Busch

DisplayWrite 4 V2 & DisplayWrite 5 for OS/2

Order #975	$24.95 USA

0-88022-445-2, 438 pp., 7 3/8 x 9 1/4

Using MultiMate

Jim Meade

Version 4

Order #1093	$24.95 USA

0-88022-548-3, 450 pp., 7 3/8 x 9 1/4

Using WordStar, 3rd Edition

Steve Ditlea

Through Release 6.0

Order #1194	$27.95 USA

0-88022-606-4, 500 pp., 7 3/8 x 9 1/4

To Order, Call:
(800) 428-5331
OR (317) 573-2510

Complete Coverage From A To Z!

Que's Computer User's Dictionary

Que Development Group

This compact, practical reference contains hundreds of definitions, explanations, examples, and illustrations on topics from programming to desktop publishing. You can master the "language" of computers and learn how to make your personal computers more efficient and more powerful. Filled with tips and cautions, *Que's Computer User's Dictionary* is the perfect resource for anyone who uses a computer.

IBM, Macintosh, Apple, & Programming

Order #1086　　　　　　　**$9.95 USA**

0-88022-540-8, 500 pp., 4 3/4 x 8

The Ultimate Glossary Of Computer Terms— Over 200,000 In Print!

"Dictionary indeed. This whammer is a mini-encyclopedia...an absolute joy to use...a must for your computer library...."

Southwest Computer & Business Equipment Review

To Order, Call:
(800) 428-5331 OR (317) 573-2510

PROOFREADS FOR 25,000 GRAMMAR ERRORS
RightWriter 4.0 checks for:

- ✔ Subject-verb agreement
- ✔ Sentence fragments
- ✔ Run-on sentences
- ✔ Misused words
- ✔ Wrong verb forms
- ✔ Possessives
- ✔ Redundancy
- ✔ Capitalization
- ✔ Awkward sentences
- ✔ Long sentences and paragraphs
- ✔ Split infinitives
- ✔ Conjunctions
- ✔ Weak sentence structure
- ✔ Negative sentences
- ✔ Ambiguity
- ✔ Quotations
- ✔ Wordiness
- ✔ Missing punctuation
- ✔ Slang
- ✔ And more!

COMPATIBLE WITH ALL MAJOR WORD PROCESSING PROGRAMS

RightWriter works with Bank Street Writer®, Edix/Wordix®, Enable®, Home Word II®, IBM Writing Assistant®, Leading Edge® (LEWP), Microsoft® Word, Microsoft® Write, MultiMate®, MultiMate Advantage®, New Word®, Office Writer®, PC-Write®, Peachtext®, PFS®: First Choice , PFS®: Write , Professional Write®, Q&A®, Samna®, SideKick®, VolksWriter® (III, Deluxe, and plus), Word for Windows®, WordPerfect®, WordStar®, WordStar 2000®, XyWrite®, and all standard ASCII editors.

Detach and send this card to:

QUE *software*

Order Department
11711 N. College Ave.
Carmel, IN 46032